Tax Planning and Compliance for Tax-Exempt Organizations

Tax Planning and Compliance for Tax-Exempt Organizations: Forms, Checklists, Procedures
Second Edition

JODY BLAZEK
BLAZEK, ROGERS, AND VETTERLING

John Wiley & Sons

New York · Chichester · Brisbane · Toronto · Singapore

SUBSCRIPTION NOTICE

This Wiley product is updated on a periodic basis with supplements to reflect important changes in the subject matter. If you purchased this product directly from John Wiley & Sons, Inc., we have already recorded your subscription for this update service.

 If, however, you purchased this product from a bookstore and wish to receive (1) the current update at no additional charge, and (2) future updates and revised or related volumes billed separately with a 30-day examination review, please send your name, company name (if applicable), address, and the title of the product to:

Supplement Department
John Wiley & Sons, Inc.
One Wiley Drive,
Somerset, NJ 08875
1-800-225-5945

This text is printed on acid-free paper.

Copyright © 1990 and 1993 by John Wiley & Sons, Inc.

All rights reserved. Published simultaneously in Canada.

Reproduction or translation of any part of this work beyond that permitted by Section 107 or 108 of the 1976 United States Copyright Act without the permission of the copyright owner is unlawful. Requests for permission or further information should be addressed to the Permissions Department, John Wiley & Sons, Inc., 605 Third Avenue, New York, NY 10158-0012.

This publication is designed to provide accurate and authoritative information in regard to the subject matter covered. It is sold with the understanding that the publisher is not engaged in rendering legal, accounting, or other professional services. If legal advice or other expert assistance is required, the services of a competent professional person should be sought. *From a Declaration of Principles jointly adopted by a Committee of the American Bar Association and a Committee of Publishers.*

Library of Congress Cataloging in Publication Data:
Blazek, Jody.
 Tax planning and compliance for tax-exempt organizations: forms, checklists, procedures/Jody Blazek.—2nd ed.
  p. cm.—(Nonprofit law, finance, and management series)
 Rev. ed. of: Tax and financial planning for tax-exempt organizations. c1990.
 Includes bibliographical references and index.
 ISBN 0-471-58499-1 (cloth: acid-free paper)
 1. Nonprofit organizations—Taxation—Law and legislation—United States. 2. Taxation, Exemption from—United States. 3. Tax planning—United States. I. Blazek, Jody. Tax and financial planning for tax-exempt organizations. II. Title. III. Series.
KF6449.B58 1993
343.7305'2668—dc20
[347.30352668]
              92-35166
              CIP

Printed in the United States of America

10 9 8 7 6 5 4 3 2 1

ABOUT THE AUTHOR

Jody Blazek, CPA, is a partner in the accounting firm of Blazek, Rogers & Vetterling, which specializes in tax and financial planning for exempt organizations and the individuals who create, fund, and work for them. Her study of nonprofit organizations began in 1969, when KPMG Peat Marwick assigned her the task of studying and interpreting the Tax Reform Act of 1969 as it related to charitable organizations and the creation of private foundations.

Blazek is a founding director of the Texas Accountants and Lawyers for the Arts, a trustee of the Episcopal High School, and director of the Anchorage Foundations and the Planned Giving Council. She also serves on the planning committee for the University of Texas Nonprofit Institute and is a member of the Management Assistance Committee of the United Way of the Texas Gulf coast. She speaks annually at the Institute for Board Development and many other nonprofit symposia throughout Texas.

Blazek received her accounting degree from the University of Texas at Austin in 1964. From 1972 to 1981, she served as treasurer of the Menil Interests and worked with John and Dominique de Menil in planning for the Menil Collection and The Rothko Chapel.

This book was made possible through
the loving patience of my husband,
David Crossley,
and wonderful sons,
Austin and Jay Blazek Crossley,
to whom it is dedicated.

Preface

In 1969, when KPGM Peat, Marwick assigned me the task of studying, interpreting, and communicating the new private foundation rules to our Houston clients, I began a search for information to interpret the nonprofit organization tax laws and procedures and often found it lacking. This book represents a compendium of checklists, client memoranda, and materials developed over the years to provide guideposts for compliance and tax planning for exempt organizations.

My experience has been enriched by a myriad of wonderful people with ideas for improving the human condition. The wealth of altruism and kindness shared by benefactors and volunteers in the nonprofit community is an inspiration. From the vantage of the funder who wants to create a private foundation, the healer who senses the ability to cure a disease, and the artist who wants to paint a public mural, among many others, I have had the privilege of responding to a mandate to figure out the best financial and tax mode in which to establish an entity that can accomplish those goals. Five years as a KPGM Peat, Marwick tax specialist under the able tutelage of John Herzfeld and Lloyd Jard taught me that tax rules are not black and white—answers are complex and often gray. Achieving the best tax answer requires an exacting search, an ability to weigh alternatives, and the willingness to defend your choice.

As treasurer and chief financial officer of the Menil Foundation, The Rothko Chapel, and Menil Interests—the Houston based charitable ventures of Dominique and John de Menil—I had a unique hands-on opportunity to manage nonprofit organizations. Returning to public practice in 1982, I continued my commitment to nonprofit organizations and started an accounting firm that focuses on exempt organizations (EOs) and the people who work with and create them.

In the early eighties, a group of professionals started the Texas Accountants and Lawyers for the Arts. Our purpose was to improve the technical expertise and expand the body of law applicable to nonprofit organizations. With this goal in mind, seminars were organized and technical issues researched and reported. Since that time, the number of trained and willing volunteers has multiplied tenfold. This book is partly a result of all the questions asked during those seminars. It is a practical guide to establishing and maintaining tax-exempt status for nonprofit organizations.

The nonprofit segment, or so-called "Third Sector," of the United States economy is the fastest-growing sector according to the *Dallas Morning News*.[1]

---

[1]Article published March 29, 1992

PREFACE

The IRS 1991 annual report recorded that 50,664 applications for exemption were filed and 38,801 were approved. The total number of exempt organizations topped 1 million in 1988 and reached over 1.1 million by the end of 1991. This figure is based upon Forms 990 filed with the IRS and does not count the fairly large number of organizations not required to file, including an estimated 350,000 plus churches.

This book has been organized around five subjects essential to all nonprofits:

Part I: Qualifying for Exemption

Starting with Chapter 1, the characteristics of nonprofits are distinguished from for-profit organizations. Checklists designed to gauge the suitability of a project for tax-exempt status, along with other start-up tax and financial considerations, are provided. Types of organizations that *can* qualify and those that *cannot*—including charitable organizations, social clubs, business leagues, labor unions, civic leagues, and title-holding companies—are compared and contrasted in Chapters 2 through 10. The particular Internal Revenue Code (IRC) requirements for the six major §501(c) exemption categories are fleshed out.

How a charitable organization can qualify for and maintain status as a public charity is reviewed in Chapter 11. The distinctions between public and private organizations are discussed, along with a presentation comparing and contrasting the various types of public charities. You will discover how the IRS defines a "school," how a membership fee is classified, and the kinds of donations not counted as public support.

Part II: Private Foundations

Privately funded charities are subject to complex sanctions imposed by the Congress upon so-called "private foundations." Chapters 12 through 17 describe the special rules applicable to them. The dizzying labyrinth of excise taxes, definitions and applicability can be simplified using the material in these chapters. Despite the draconian tone of the sanctions, many exceptions apply. The types of investment income subject to and the types excluded from the annual excise tax are outlined.

Chapter 14 defines self-dealing and then explains its application and the exceptions by type of financial transactions—sales or leases of property, loans, compensation, payments on behalf of officers and directors, and nonmonetary payments. A private foundation must make "minimum distributions," or pay out a percentage of certain assets annually, and Chapter 15 discusses which assets are included in the formula and various methods of valuation. Restraints are placed on business ownership by a private foundation with the prohibition of "excess business holdings." Chapter 16 presents the permitted holdings and disposition periods for excesses received as gifts, along with a discussion of the types of speculative investments considered to be jeopardizing for a foundation.

Chapter 17 discusses the "taxable expenditure" rules that govern the manner in which a private foundation spends its money. This chapter also shows that a foundation's spending perimeters are actually very broad if enhanced documentation is maintained. As long as the purpose served is charitable, a private charity can conduct a breadth of activity similar to a public charity.

Part III: Internal Revenue Service Recognition

Chapter 18 provides a blueprint for seeking approval for exempt status from the Internal Revenue Service, including specific instructions for answering each question on Forms 1023 and 1024. Insights into the rationale behind the information requested by the IRS will enable the preparer to mold the prospective organization into an acceptable form. This chapter walks you through the steps involved in the approval process and provides practical advice on the alternatives available in contesting IRS determinations.

Part IV: Maintaining Exempt Status

After securing initial IRS approval, annual compliance measures assure ongoing exemption. Chapter 19 includes separate checklists for use by IRC §501(c)(3) and non (c)(3) organizations. We use these checklists annually to review our clients' local, state, and federal filing matters and to uncover any troublesome activity.

To qualify for exemption initially and on an ongoing basis, an exempt organization must operate to benefit its exempt constituency, not its creators, directors, or other self-interested persons. Chapter 20 defines impermissible private inurement or benefit, discusses the range of its application, and explains how the rules apply to different types of financial transactions. Yes, a salary can be paid to a member of the board of directors, but such compensation must be reasonable. Factors are presented for determining reasonableness in regards to salaries, loans, asset sales and purchases, conversion of a for-profit to a non-profit, joint ventures, and other financial arrangements.

As a source of funding, many exempt organizations charge for services they render or goods they produce. Most EOs are not necessarily prohibited from conducting an income-producing activity, particularly if it is related to the organization's exempt purposes. When an activity is unrelated, however, income tax may be due on the profits. The IRS now uses a "commerciality test" to decide when the level of income producing activity is so like a commercial business that the EO's underlying exempt status should be challenged. Chapter 21 covers the unrelated business income tax and its endless exceptions and modifications. The lack of clear guidance in the Internal Revenue Code and the number of conflicting decisions behoove organizations and their advisors to continually seek up-to-date information and to pay attention to potential new legislation on the subject of UBI.

The unrelated business income tax has been the subject of Congressional hearings for several years and proposals for its revision are reported in Section 21.21. In 1991, the Treasury Department recommended against making any changes because the task force proposals would not "significantly improve tax administration with respect to UBI" nor "command a broad base of support." Meanwhile, statistics have been gathered by the IRS since 1989 when the "Analysis of Income-Producing Activity" part was added to the Forms 990. Strategies for coping with the codes used to identify the EO's income for this report can be found in Section 27.9. Readers should be alert to the possibility of future changes.

Combinations of organizations, reorganizations, spin-offs, and joint ventures with business organizations are being considered and implemented by organizations as astute survival methods in today's difficult economic climate. This very important subject faces many tax-exempts as they seek enhanced efficiency and economies of scale. Forms 990 now request "Information Regarding Transfers, Transactions, and Relationships with Other Organizations" to enable the IRS to scrutinize such relationships. Chapter 22 addresses the issues involved when an EO forms a for-profit subsidiary corporation to conduct its business activity rather than carrying on the business itself. This chapter also considers the circumstances under which it is acceptable for an EO to form a partnership with investors, engage a manager under a profit-sharing arrangement, or have a relationship with another category of EO.

To accomplish their goals, many nonprofit organizations engage in lobbying or otherwise attempt to influence the making of laws. Participation in the election of the lawmakers, or political intervention, is also undertaken by certain types of EOs. The various constraints placed on EOs in regard to such activity—some of them absolute prohibitions—are discussed in Chapter 23 and should be carefully studied before an organization contemplates such actions. Charitable organizations engaging in lobbying must choose whether to elect to do so under IRC §501(h). This chapter presents the pros and cons of making the election and applying the regulations that were finalized in 1990 (after years of hearings and controversy). An organization whose purposes can only be accomplished through the passage of legislation cannot qualify as a charitable organization, as explained in Section 23.12 and Chapter 6.

Beginning in 1988, the IRS conducted an Exempt Organization Charitable Solicitations Compliance Improvement Program. Keep in mind that the tax deduction for a gift to charity must be reduced by the value of any goods and services received by the donor in connection with the donation. The format of the program was first to examine the charities to find fund-raising programs in which premiums, free admissions, dinners, raffles, and other benefits were used to entice donors. Once the list of such events was compiled from the charity's records, the IRS examined the donors to find out whether the tax deduction was overstated. The results were poor, but the checksheet designed for the program should still be used to evaluate an organization's potential exposure to the problem. The tax bill vetoed by then-President Bush in November, 1992, contained a requirement that charities report the deductible portion of contributions received. Future legislation on this matter can be expected. Chapter 24 discusses these rules in detail.

Prior to 1988, IRS exempt organization examiners did not review payroll tax matters. When they began to look, the results of their examinations caused concern; they found too many employees classified as independent contractors. EOs under examination face the possibility of payroll tax assessments for such workers. Chapter 25 outlines the issues and reporting requirements on this recently emphasized issue for EOs.

Bankruptcy is uncommon and certainly undesirable for a tax-exempt organization. Nevertheless, the unthinkable does happen. Chapter 26 reviews the tax consequences and filing requirements during a bankruptcy proceeding of an exempt organization.

Part V: Communicating with the IRS

The task of communicating successfully with the IRS once exempt status is granted hopefully will be made easier after consulting Chapters 27 and 28. Detailed suggestions for the completion of Form 990, 990T, 990PF, and 990EZ are presented. The reasons questions are asked and the import of the answers are shared. Where an item of income or expense may be reportable on more than one line, the choice is discussed and compared. Guidance for reporting expenses, with particular emphasis on cost allocations is provided.

When to report operational changes to the IRS voluntarily is sometimes a difficult question, and Section 28.2 considers the alternatives. Chapter 28 also includes suggestions on how to handle an IRS examination. In 1989, the IRS initiated a series of "Special Emphasis Programs," the first of which was the fund-raising scrutiny discussed in Chapter 24, in response to Congress' directive that the IRS improve the quality of its EO audit programs. The IRS EO Technical Division Director, Marcus Owen, announced a continuation of this program in 1992 with fewer but more extensive exams under a "large case initiative." Such exams are focused on conglomerate EOs with subsidiaries and for-profit/nonprofit related entities. Each key district was directed to examine two major hospitals and one large university in fiscal years 1992 and 1993. The team exams pooled income tax agents, lawyers, and other specialists with the EO technicians. The IRS hired additional tax law specialists and upgraded their positions to attract and retain the most qualified persons. The emphasis audits focused on several issues: reasonable compensation, particularly physician contract recruitment incentives; the employee versus independent contractor issues, including taxable fringe benefits; and overhead cost allocations in the UBI context. Undoubtedly, these issues will also be emphasized in all other EO exams. Corporate sponsorships, joint ventures with private investors, and tax-exempt bonds have also been top priority for IRS scrutiny. Lastly this book considers the consequences, both on the organization and its contributors, when an EO loses its exempt status.

To avoid confusion, I have consistently used the "§" symbol when referring to the Internal Revenue Code and the word "Section" when referring to specific parts of this book.

I am very pleased to present this *second edition*. The response to the first edition was positive and encouraging, and I welcomed the opportunity to add more materials and to consider many issues in more depth. The result is this greatly expanded second edition. Readers with technical inclinations will appreciate the inclusion of detailed tax citations. The original fifth chapter, "Fiscal Management of a Nonprofit Organization," has been reserved for expansion into a separate book to be published by Wiley in 1994.

I want to acknowledge the people who played an instrumental role in making this book possible. Bruce Hopkins, the series editor, and Jeffrey Brown, publisher at John Wiley & Sons, originally found merit in my materials and I thank them for their confidence. Marla Bobowick, my editor, pushed me to plan

PREFACE

this second edition and provided endless encouragement and invaluable assistance. Eric Pierson, the copy editor, asked great questions to clarify technical points, and Maggie Kennedy performed some miracles in overseeing the production. Elizabeth Costales combed through the maze of checklists, exhibits, and appendices, and greatly facilitated the process. Thanks to you all.

On a professional level, I am indebted to my colleagues at Blazek, Rogers & Vetterling, particularly my partner, Terri Rogers, for freeing my time to prepare this work. My clients ask me the questions that provide the fuel for materials I write and I thank them as well. Lastly I am forever indebted to my husband and sons for their patience and support while I devoted time to this project.

JODY BLAZEK

Houston, Texas
December 1992

Contents

CONTENTS

CONTENTS

PART IV: MAINTAINING EXEMPT STATUS

CONTENTS

Distinguishing Characteristics of Tax-Exempt Organizations

The world of exempt organizations includes a broad range of nonprofit institutions: charities, business leagues, political parties, schools, country clubs, united giving campaigns, and a wide variety of pursuits carried on to serve the public good. All exempt organizations share the common attribute of being organized for the advancement of a group of persons, rather than particular individuals or businesses. Most exempt organizations are afforded special tax and legal status precisely because of the unselfish motivation behind their formation.

The common thread running through the various types of exempt organizations is the lack of private ownership and profit motive. One definition of an exempt organization is a nonprofit organization operated without self-interest, none of the income or profit of which is distributable to its members, directors, or officers.

Federal and state governments view nonprofits as relieving their burdens and performing certain functions of government. Thus, many nonprofits are exempted from the levies that finance government, including income, sales, and ad valorem and other local property taxes. This special status recognizes the work they perform essentially on behalf of the government. In addition, for charitable nonprofits, labor unions, and certain business leagues, the deductibility of dues and donations given to such organizations further evidences the government's willingness to forego money in favor of such organizations. At the same time, of course, deductibility provides a major fund-raising tool for the exempt organizations. For complex reasons, some of which are not readily apparent, all nonprofits are not equal for tax deduction purposes, and not all "donations" are deductible, as discussed in Chapter 24.

On the federal level, Internal Revenue Code (IRC) §501 exempts twenty eight specific types of nonprofit organizations, plus pension plans (IRC §401), from income tax. Although exempt organizations are often perceived as charitable, there are many other kinds as well. States, cities, labor unions, cemeteries, employee benefit societies, social clubs, and many other types of organizations are listed in IRC §501. Exhibit 1–1 is the IRS master chart listing all categories of exempt organizations, and shows their total scope.

For purposes of federal tax exemption, each category has its own distinct set of criteria for qualification. Chapters 2 through 10 discuss the requirements for the most common types, compare the categories, explain the attributes that distinguish them from each other, and show instances in which they overlap. This introductory chapter presents the issues to be considered prior to establishing an exempt organization, along with checklists to serve as a guide. An enlightening and thorough treatise on exempt organizations, also part of the John Wiley & Sons Nonprofit Law, Finance, and Management Series, is *The Law of Tax-Exempt Organizations* by Bruce Hopkins, now in its sixth edition. It is an extremely valuable resource for in-depth historical context and explanation.

1.1 DIFFERENCES BETWEEN EXEMPT AND NONEXEMPT ORGANIZATIONS

An exempt organization (an EO or simply an "exempt") is distinguished from a nonexempt organization by its ownership structure, the motivation for its activities, and its sources of revenue to finance operations. Exempts are commonly called nonprofit organizations under state law, which leads to a certain amount of confusion. The term "nonprofit" certainly is a contradiction: To grow and be financially successful, an exempt can and often must generate profits, and must sometimes pay income tax on unrelated business income. Exempts are fascinating because they are full of paradoxes and surprises.

While businesses do not often give away food or housing to the poor, they do operate schools, hospitals, theaters, galleries, publishing companies, and other activities that are also carried on by exempts. The nature of the activity or business is often the same for both. One goal of this book is to provide the tools for understanding the differences between the two.

The requirements for nonprofit status vary from state to state, and few generalizations apply. Exempt charitable institutions are called "public benefit" corporations in some states. Business leagues and social clubs are sometimes called "mutual benefit" corporations. Rather than being organized to generate profits for owners or investors, exempts generate profits for their broadly-based public or membership constituents.

Exhibit 1–1
ORGANIZATION REFERENCE CHART

Section of 1986 Code	Description of organization	General nature of activities	Application Form No.	Annual return required to be filed	Contributions allowable
501(c)(1)	Corporations Organized Under Act of Congress (including Federal Credit Unions)	Instrumentalities of the United States	No Form	None	Yes, if made for exclusively public purposes
501(c)(2)	Title Holding Corporation For Exempt Organization	Holding title to property of an exempt organization	1024	990[1]	No[2]
501(c)(3)	Religious, Educational, Charitable, Scientific, Literary, Testing for Public Safety, to Foster National or International Amateur Sports Competition, or Prevention of Cruelty to Children or Animals Organizations	Activities of nature implied by description of class of organization	1023	990 or 990-PF[1]	Generally, Yes
501(c)(4)	Civic Leagues, Social Welfare Organizations, and Local Associations of Employees	Promotion of community welfare; charitable, educational or recreational	1024	990[1]	Generally, No[2,3]
501(c)(5)	Labor, Agricultural, and Horticultural Organizations	Educational or instructive, the purpose being to improve conditions of work, and to improve products and efficiency	1024	990[1]	No[2]
501(c)(6)	Business Leagues, Chambers of Commerce, Real Estate Boards, Etc.	Improvement of business conditions of one or more lines of business	1024	990[1]	No[2]
501(c)(7)	Social and Recreation Clubs	Pleasure, recreation, social activities	1024	990[1]	No[2]
501(c)(8)	Fraternal Beneficiary Societies and Associations	Lodge providing for payment of life, sickness, accident, or other benefits to members	1024	990[1]	Yes, if for certain Sec. 501(c)(3) purposes

[1] For exceptions to the filing requirement, see Chapter 2 and the Form instructions.

[2] An organization exempt under a Subsection of Code Sec. 501 other than (c)(3), may establish a charitable fund, contributions to which are deductible. Such a fund must itself meet the requirements of section 501(c)(3) and the related notice requirements of section 508(a).

[3] Contributions to volunteer fire companies and similar organizations are deductible, but only if made for exclusively public purposes.

[4] Deductible as a business expense to the extent allowed by Code section 192.

[5] Deductible as a business expense to the extent allowed by Code section 194A.

[6] Application is by letter to the key District Director. A copy of the organizing document should be attached and the letter should be signed by an officer.

[7] Contributions to these organizations are deductible only if 90% or more of the organization's members are war veterans.

Exhibit 1-1 (continued)

Section of 1986 Code	Description of organization	General nature of activities	Application Form No.	Annual return required to be filed	Contributions allowable
501(c)(9)	Voluntary Employees' Beneficiary Associations	Providing for payment of life, sickness, accident or other benefits to members	1024	990[1]	No[2]
501(c)(10)	Domestic Fraternal Societies and Associations	Lodge devoting its net earnings to charitable, fraternal, and other specified purposes. No life, sickness, or accident benefits to members	1024	990[1]	Yes, if for certain Sec. 501(c)(3) purposes
501(c)(11)	Teachers' Retirement Fund Associations	Teachers' association for payment of retirement benefits	No Form[6]	990[1]	No[2]
501(c)(12)	Benevolent Life Insurance Associations, Mutual Ditch or Irrigation Companies, Mutual or Cooperative Telephone Companies, Etc.	Activities of a mutually beneficial nature similar to those implied by the description of class of organization	1024	990[1]	No[2]
501(c)(13)	Cemetery Companies	Burials and incidental activities	1024	990[1]	Generally, Yes
501(c)(14)	State Chartered Credit Unions, Mutual Reserve Funds	Loans to members	No Form[6]	990[1]	No[2]
501(c)(15)	Mutual Insurance Companies or Associations	Providing insurance to members substantially at cost	1024	990[1]	No[2]
501(c)(16)	Cooperative Organizations to Finance Crop Operations	Financing crop operations in conjunction with activities of a marketing or purchasing association	No Form[6]	990[1]	No[2]
501(c)(17)	Supplemental Unemployment Benefit Trusts	Provides for payment of supplemental unemployment compensation benefits	1024	990[1]	No[2]

Section	Description	Application Form	Annual Return	Contributions Deductible
501(c)(18)	Employee Funded Pension Trust (created before June 25, 1959)	Payment of benefits under a pension plan funded by employees	No Form[6]	990[1]	No[2]
501(c)(19)	Post or Organization of Past or Present Members of the Armed Forces	Activities implied by nature of organization	1024	990[1]	Generally, No[7]
501(c)(21)	Black Lung Benefit Trusts	Funded by coal mine operators to satisfy their liability for disability or death due to black lung diseases	No Form[6]	990-BL	No[4]
501(c)(22)	Withdrawal Liability Payment Fund	To provide funds to meet the liability of employers withdrawing from a multi-employer pension fund	No Form[6]	990	No[5]
501(c)(23)	Veterans Organization (created before 1880)	To provide insurance and other benefits to veterans	No Form[6]	990	Generally, No[7]
501(d)	Religious and Apostolic Associations	Regular business activities. Communal religious community	No Form	1065	No[2]
501(e)	Cooperative Hospital Service Organizations	Performs cooperative services for hospitals	1023	990[1]	Yes
501(f)	Cooperative Service Organizations of Operating Educational Organizations	Performs collective investment services for educational organizations	1023	990[1]	Yes
501(k)	Child Care Organization	Provides care for children	1023	990	Yes
521(a)	Farmers' Cooperative Associations	Cooperative marketing and purchasing for agricultural producers	1028	990-C	No

[1] For exceptions to the filing requirement, see Chapter 2 and the Form instructions.

[2] An organization exempt under a Subsection of Code Sec. 501 other than (c)(3), may establish a charitable fund, contributions to which are deductible. Such a fund must itself meet the requirements of section 501(c)(3) and the related notice requirements of section 508(a).

[3] Contributions to volunteer fire companies and similar organizations are deductible, but only if made for exclusively public purposes.

[4] Deductible as a business expense to the extent allowed by Code section 192.

[5] Deductible as a business expense to the extent allowed by Code section 194A.

[6] Application is by letter to the key District Director. A copy of the organizing document should be attached and the letter should be signed by an officer.

[7] Contributions to these organizations are deductible only if 90% or more of the organization's members are war veterans.

■   7   ■

(a) Choosing a Category

Do not expect the distinctions among the categories to be clear or logical. The group of exempts has expanded considerably since the Tariff Act of 1894 established a single category of exempt organizations, which included charitable, religious, educational, fraternal, and certain building and loan, savings, and insurance organizations. Since that time, the number of categories has expanded to include at least twenty-eight distinct types.

As with all federal tax matters, the Internal Revenue Code expresses general concepts subject to endless interpretation. For example, only scholars of legislative history can explain why agricultural organizations and labor unions are coupled together. Why aren't agricultural groups considered business leagues? Why are agricultural auxiliaries classified as business leagues? Why was a separate category carved out for real estate title-holding companies with multiple parents, instead of placing them in the original §501(c)(2) for single parent organizations?

The choice of category is driven by a number of different factors that are compared and contrasted in Chapters 2 through 10. Sometimes the choice is influenced by the desire to receive tax deductible donations requiring a §501(c)(3) organization. However, the freedom to lobby is constrained under this category, so §501(c)(4) structure might instead be chosen.

(b) Profit Motive

Ironically, in order to succeed, a nonprofit must operate in a businesslike fashion, efficiently and often profitably. The distinguishing factor is the motivation for undertaking an activity and generating revenue. The fact that a nonprofit charges for the services it performs is not determinative. A hospital may pay all of its costs with patient charges. Whether such a hospital is exempt depends on whether it was created and operated to provide health care for the purpose of promoting the general public's health (see Chapter 4), or solely for the purpose of earning a profit.

An exempt organization can generate revenues in excess of its expenses and can accumulate a reasonable amount of working capital or fund balances. It can save money to purchase a building, to expand operations, or for any other valid reason serving its underlying exempt purposes. It can borrow venture capital to establish a new project. Basically, an exempt can operate without a profit motive and still produce a profit! It can pay salaries and employee benefits comparable to those of a nonexempt business. The one thing it cannot do with its net profit is distribute it as a return on capital to the persons who control the organization.

The focus and purpose of an EO's activity are outward, unselfish, directed at accomplishing a public purpose. One way to think of this characteristic is as a one-way street. Privately owned businesses, in contrast, operate on a two-way street. Their activity is directed at reaping something in return for their investment of funds. For-profit organizations generally receive funds from people who receive something in return. Exempt organizations' decisions are not always made with any return in mind. Much of the money received by exempts is primarily one-way money—donations made out of pure generosity, for which nothing is received or expected in return.

On a limited basis, an exempt is allowed to compute directly with nonexempt businesses. The Internal Revenue Code places such an exempt on the same footing as competing businesses, however, by imposing a regular income tax on such profits. If the unrelated business activity becomes too substantial, the EO can lose its exemption. Chapter 21 considers the question of when a business is "unrelated" and describes the level of business activity allowed.

1.2 NOMENCLATURE

The complexity of the subject is illustrated by the fact that the Internal Revenue Code does not contain the word nonprofit—it refers only to exempt organizations. The term nonprofit, or not-for-profit, describes the type of corporation created in most states, and is widely used to identify tax-exempt organizations. The terms are often used interchangeably, as they will be in this book.

Another factor coloring the distinctions is the language of the code. Tax rules are gray and not necessarily made clear by IRS rulings and decisions. In many cases, terms used do not necessarily possess their dictionary definitions. To obtain EO status, an organization applies for a *determination* by the EO branch of the Internal Revenue Service (IRS). Form 1023 or 1024 is submitted to allow the IRS to determine whether exempt status is appropriate. If the organization plans certain activities within an initial fiscal year of at least eight months, a *definitive determination* is granted. When the operation is prospective, a five-year *advance ruling* is granted, subject to a subsequent final determination.

An EO must be organized *exclusively* for exempt purposes within the specific terms described in the Code, and must operate *primarily* for such purposes. The primary test is applied by deciding whether *substantially all* of the activity is exempt. "Exclusively" does not mean 100 percent, and "primarily" can mean a little more than 50 percent. The *facts and circumstances* are examined in each case. The regulations provide a few specific numerical tests, which are indicated in the checklists when applicable. A numerical test is most often applied to gross revenues, but it can also be applied to net profits, direct costs, contributions in kind, and the like. In each case, the IRS examines the exact facts to determine whether exemption is in order. A glossary of tax and financial terms unique to exempts precedes the index.

1.3 OWNERSHIP AND CONTROL

As a general rule, directors or trustees may control and govern an exempt organization, but may not beneficially own it. Upon dissolution, a charitable exempt may not return any of its funds to its individual contributors or to controlling parties. Instead, its funds can only be paid to charitable organizations or other charitable beneficiaries. A business league, on the other hand, can rebate an accumulated surplus to its members, if building such a reserve is not a primary purpose of the league. A mutual insurance company continually reduces premiums by the profits earned on investments.

The code of conduct for directors of exempt organizations is most often found in state law defining fiduciary responsibility, and embodies the duties of care, loyalty, and obedience. Those who control an exempt are expected to manage the organization in the best interest of its exempt constituents, i.e., its charitable class or membership, not to benefit themselves or their families. The federal tax code and its regulations provide that no profits or assets can inure to the benefit of the officers and directors, but give very meager guidance regarding officer and director responsibility and constraints. For private foundations, specific prohibitions exist and violators are subject to excise taxes, as explained in Chapter 14. Special limitations concerning private inurement in insider transactions for public charities are outlined in Chapter 20.

A common question concerning exempts is whether paid staff members can serve on an exempt's board of directors. There is no clear answer. In Texas, a director may serve in a staff capacity for compensation as long as the pay is reasonable and not in violation of his or her fiduciary responsibility. Even private foundations can pay reasonable compensation to related parties for services rendered.

Paid directors cannot participate in votes approving their pay or in other financial transactions which affect them, to avoid conflicts of interest. However, there is no federal tax rule that prohibits a paid staff member from also serving as a board member. In California, on the other hand, no more than 49 percent of the board members may be staff members. This question should be investigated under the laws of the state in which the exempt conducts its activities.

1.4 THE ROLE OF THE INTERNAL REVENUE SERVICE

The IRS giveth and taketh away an organization's tax-exempt status. Only §501(c)(3) organizations need a determination by the IRS to qualify as exempt. A (c)(3) organization is not classified as exempt until it makes its request for such status by filing Form 1023. For all other kinds of exempts, being established and operated according to the characteristics described in the tax code is sufficient. However, most EOs seek IRS determination to secure proof of their status for local authorities, members, and in some cases, the IRS itself, and to insure against penalties and interest due on their income if they do not qualify. Chapter 18 explains the process by which application is made.

To qualify for exemption from inception, a prospective §501(c)(3) organization must file a determination application within 15 months of its creation. Later filing will result in a determination only from the date of filing, unless the IRS grants retroactive relief, which is unlikely. Careful timing in the formative stage is critical.

Annual information returns (Form 990 or 990PF) are filed by most EOs. Detailed balance sheets, income statements, lists of directors and officers and their compensation, and descriptions of activities must be submitted, along with any changes in the organization's form or purposes. The returns contain descriptions of the organization's exempt activity along with financial information, and are open to public inspection upon request. Chapter 27 contains examples and guidelines for completion of the forms.

A special division of the IRS handles exempt organization matters from nine key district offices located throughout the U.S. This division examines EO returns to ascertain that continued tax exemption is allowed and, subject to the statute of limitations, can propose revocation. Chapter 28 outlines matters that bring an organization into contact with the IRS, including changes in purpose, public status, accounting methods, fiscal year, and other situations. Chapter 28 also offers suggestions for successful communication with the IRS.

1.5 SUITABILITY AS AN EXEMPT ORGANIZATION

Before embarking on the creation of an exempt organization, some basic questions should be addressed, which may influence the decision to go forward. Although the rules are sometimes ambiguous, certain requirements are applied precisely. The IRS determination branch is highly skilled and thorough in its evaluation, and the taxpayer assisters in the key district determination offices are helpful people. The administrative burden and expense of the determination process and annual compliance are at least as great as for profit-motivated firms. Professional assistance from accountants and lawyers familiar with nonprofit matters will ease the process. If funds are limited, a qualified volunteer should be sought. In many states, pro bono assistance is available through Certified Public Accountant (CPA) societies and bar associations.

Four major questions should be asked to determine whether a proposed organization is suitable for qualification for tax-exempt status and ongoing operation as a nonprofit project.

Question 1 Is a new organization really necessary? Could the project be carried out under the auspices of an existing organization? Several factors can indicate that a new organization is not necessary. If it is a short-term or one-time project with no prospect for ongoing funding, it probably is not worth the trouble to set up an exempt to handle it. Maybe the project can operate as a branch of an existing exempt organization. If a local branch of an organization holding a group exemption is available through a national EO, starting a new exempt may not be a wise idea. If there would be a costly duplication of administrative effort, or if the cost of obtaining and maintaining independent exemption would be excessive in relation to the total budget, it makes sense to opt for another route.

Question 2 If the proposed organization passes the first test, it is time to choose the category of exemption best suited to the goals and purposes of the project. Because the §501(c)(3) exemption rules are so rigid and limiting, for certain activities other categories of exemption or creation of a for-profit company should be considered. These rules include a complete prohibition against involvement in political campaigns, and limitations on legislative and grassroots lobbying, as explained in Chapter 2. For such projects, a §501(c)(4) organization may be more suitable for the purposes of the founding group.

As explained in Chapters 6, 7, and 8, some projects can conceivably qualify for more than one category. There are garden clubs classified as charities under §501(c)(3), civic welfare societies under §501(c)(4), and social clubs under §501(c)(7). An association of business persons, such as the Rotary Club or the Lions Club, most often qualifies as a business league. If the activities of the group involve educational and/or charitable efforts, (c)(3) status, rather than (c)(6) status, might be sought. A breakfast group composed of representatives of many different types of businesses may not qualify under §501(c)(6), but might instead easily qualify under §501(c)(7). The tax deductibility of member dues and taxability of income influences the desired choice of category, as discussed later.

Question 3 Exempt organizations are traditionally supported by donations and member dues. Certain other sources of revenue are not suitable for exemption. Among them are sales of goods produced by members and income from services rendered in competition with nonexempt businesses (for example, insurance or legal services). Less than half of the EO's revenues may come from unrelated businesses, as discussed in Chapter 21. Self-dealing and certain other transactions are prohibited, and certain sources of support could result in the EO being designated a private foundation.

Question 4 Do the organization's creators desire economic benefits from the formation or ongoing operation of the organization? Will the organization be operated to serve the self-interested purposes of its creators? The "one-way street" characteristic of nonprofits is crucial to ongoing qualification for tax exemption. If the founders desire incentive compensation based on funds raised, or wish to gain from profits generated, an exempt organization may not be an appropriate solution. Reasonable compensation for services actually and genuinely rendered can be paid, as discussed in Chapter 20.

For a variety of reasons, it is sometimes desirable to convert a for-profit business into a nonprofit one. In the health and human service field, for example, funding is often available from both for-profit and nonprofit sources. An organization's direction may change or funds may become available only for tax-exempt organizations. When an exempt is created to take over the assets and operations of a for-profit entity, the buy-out terms will be carefully scrutinized. Too high a price, ongoing payments having the appearance of dividends, and assumptions of liability that take the creators off the hook are among the issues faced in this situation.

When a tax-exempt organization ceases to exist, its assets remaining upon dissolution must essentially be used for the same exempt purposes for which the organization was initially granted tax exemption. Charities exempt under §501(c)(3) can only distribute funds to another (c)(3) organization, and their charters must require this. Again, the "one-way street" concept is valuable. The creators must understand and intend from inception that they will gain no personal economic benefit from the organization's operations and benefits. Checklist 1–1 can be used to review the considerations in forming a new exempt organization.

1.5 SUITABILITY AS AN EXEMPT ORGANIZATION

Checklist 1–1

SUITABILITY FOR TAX-EXEMPT STATUS

1. Is a new organization necessary, or could the project be carried out as a branch of an existing organization?

   ☐ Life of the project is short.

   ☐ It is a one-time project with no prospect for ongoing funding.

   ☐ Project could operate under auspices of another EO.

   ☐ Duplication of administrative effort is too costly.

   ☐ Cost of obtaining and maintaining independent exemption is excessive in relation to total budget.

   ☐ Group exemption is available through a national EO.

2. Which §501(c) category of exemption is appropriate to the goals and purposes of the project?

   ☐ Absolutely no involvement in political campaigns for (c)(3)s. (Chapter 23.)

   ☐ Legislative and grassroots lobbying activity may be limited. (Chapters 6 and 23.)

   ☐ Private foundation strictures on activities may apply. (Chapters 12 through 17.)

   ☐ Compare the business versus social aspects of the future activities. (Chapters 8 and 9.)

3. Are the sources of revenue suitable for an exempt organization? (See Chapter 21.)

   ☐ Sales of goods produced by members.

   ☐ Services to be rendered in competition with nonexempt businesses, such as legal services or insurance.

   ☐ Over half of revenues to come from unrelated businesses operated in competition with for-profit companies.

   ☐ Support to come from a particular individual, family, or limited group of people that may require classification as a private foundation. (Chapter 11.)

■ 13 ■

Checklist 1–1 (*continued*)

SUITABILITY FOR TAX-EXEMPT STATUS

4. Do the creators desire economic benefits from the operation of the organization?

☐ What are the possibilities for private inurement? (Chapter 20.)

☐ Do the creators wish to be paid incentive compensation based upon funds raised or profitability of the organization?

☐ Are transactions with related parties anticipated?

☐ Is this an insider bailout? Are assets being purchased or debts being assumed?

☐ Will services or activities be available to a limited group of persons or members instead of a public class? (Chapter 2.)

☐ Who will use or benefit from the existence of the organization's physical facilities or other assets? (Chapter 2.)

☐ Upon dissolution of the organization, where will the assets go?

1.6 START-UP TAX AND FINANCIAL CONSIDERATIONS

Projects that meet the criteria in the previous section need to pass additional tests before an EO can be formed. People who are considering starting an EO must address issues of preliminary planning, financial management, and recordkeeping requirements. See Checklist 1–2 at the end of this section.

(a) Preliminary Planning

The next question to answer concerns the type of entity to be created. What type of organization should be formed—a corporation, trust, or association? Each structure has its benefits and drawbacks, as addressed in Section 1.7.

Future sources of funds for all categories of organizations should be projected in the planning stage, for reasons explained in the chapter pertaining to that particular type of organization. If the EO wishes to be classified as a charity, it is time to see whether the organization will qualify as a public charity or a private foundation. Expected donation levels must be quantified to measure public support, as described in Chapter 11. Social clubs are subject to strict numerical limits on the amount of non-member revenues they may receive. Business leagues and labor unions, like charities, cannot generate too much unrelated business income. The specific plans for the proposed organization should be tested at this point, using the basic rules for qualifying as a tax-exempt organization.

Whether or not the organization will operate as a membership group must be decided. The term "membership" is often misunderstood and misused. Some organizations use the term "member" to designate contributors who actually have no voting rights. Technically, a membership organization is one whose members elect the persons on the governing board. The democracy afforded by such a form of organization may or may not be desirable. A self-perpetuating board retaining control in the hands of a few persons may be appropriate.

The rules for governing the organization's future decision-making are normally outlined in the bylaws. Bylaws answer the following questions, among many others: How will officers be elected? When will meetings be held and who can call them? Who will serve as advisors? Who signs checks? What credentials will be required of board members, and what length of term will they serve? A skilled attorney can be very helpful in designing appropriate bylaws. The IRS and some states are not particularly interested in parliamentary procedures, in the author's experience. IRS Publication 557, *Tax-Exempt Status for Your Organization*, prescribes very particular provisions that must be contained in an organization's charter or exemption will not be granted. No sample bylaws are provided, however. For groups affiliated with a state or national group, model bylaws may be available. The minimal bylaws typically used in Texas are included in the sample Forms 1023 and 1024 in Chapter 18.

This is a good time to think about what name to bestow on the organization. A name that accurately presents the EO's purpose should be chosen. The name cannot repeat or conflict with names already in use. If there is already a Center for Genetic Research chartered in the state, a newly-created Center for Genetic Study may not be permitted. The availability of the chosen name can be investigated through the local and state authorities. In Texas, the office of the secretary of state can be called to reserve a name.

(b) Financial Management

In a nutshell, to be successful, a nonprofit organization should be financially managed just like a business. To be financially viable, an EO needs sufficient capitalization similar to a for-profit organization—and it cannot float a stock issue. The reliability of funding sources should be evaluated to assure sustainable spending levels. Before the final decision to establish a new organization is made, the exempt's future needs for capital and its ability to raise money must be projected.

The initial projections can be a starting point for ongoing planning that should improve the financial outlook for an exempt organization. Short-range budgets and long-range financial plans should be maintained and continually updated. Operating and capital budgets are recommended. Plans for maximizing yield on cash and other investment assets should be formulated. As much of the EO's money as possible should be kept in interest-bearing accounts, and professional investment managers can be sought once capital reserves exceed immediate needs.

An accounting system should be established to record, report, and internally control the financial resources in accordance with generally accepted accounting principles. This system should also maximize cash flow by billing customers and collecting from contributors as quickly as possible, while at the same time delaying payment of the organization's own bills for as long as is feasible.

Checklist 1–2

BASIC TAX AND FINANCIAL CONSIDERATIONS
IN STARTING A NEW ORGANIZATION

Before you Start

☐ Suitability for exempt organization status. (See Checklist 1–1.)

☐ Form of organization—corporation, trust, or association.

    ☐ Membership or not.

    ☐ Provisions of bylaws.

    ☐ Board composition and terms for advisors.

☐ Reserve name and check availability.

☐ Federal tax considerations.

    ☐ Private vs. public charity.

    ☐ Qualification for tax exemptions.

    ☐ Amount of business activity planned.

    ☐ Transactions with creators, directors and officers.

Financial Considerations

☐ Capitalization needs.

    ☐ Future need for capital and ability to raise funds.

    ☐ Reliability of funding sources.

☐ Financial planning systems.

    ☐ Long and short-range financial plans (budgets).

    ☐ Maximizing cash flow and investment income.

    ☐ Billing, collection, and bill paying policies.

☐ Internal control systems.

Checklist 1–2 (*continued*)

BASIC TAX AND FINANCIAL CONSIDERATIONS IN STARTING A NEW ORGANIZATION

Recordkeeping Requirements

☐ Primary accounting records (banking records, original invoices, and customer/patron/client billings).

☐ Secondary records (cash and general ledgers).

    ☐ Cash vs. accrual method.

    ☐ Computerized recordkeeping.

☐ Filing systems.

    ☐ Paid bills in alphabetical order.

    ☐ Permanent assets (individual files by objects or type).

    ☐ Establish "throwaway" date system.

    ☐ Exempt activity records (archives).

☐ Tax compliance systems. (Chapter 19.)

    ☐ Application for federal identification number and exemption.

    ☐ Complete federal tax compliance checklist.

    ☐ State and local registration, permits, and/or taxes.

☐ Employees vs. independent contractors. (Chapter 25.)

    ☐ Tax aspects: proper classification, withholding, and reporting requirements.

    ☐ Personnel policies: vacation, sick leave, written contracts, and job descriptions.

    ☐ Fringe benefits.

    ☐ Travel and expense documentation requirements.

1.7 CHOOSING THE BEST FORM OF ORGANIZATION

The choice of organizational form is influenced by the laws of the states in which the EO will operate. Certain categories of §501 organizations are limited in their choice of form. A title-holding company, for example, must be a corporation. Some §501 categories of exemption apply to clubs, associations, leagues, and posts, and may have unique organizational structures. The common choices are corporation, trust, or unincorporated association. An experienced attorney knowledgeable about nonprofit organizations can be extremely valuable in making this choice.

(a) Corporation

Corporate status is the most flexible and is the form of choice in most states. The American Bar Association, and more recently the Association of Attorneys General, have developed uniform exempt statutes that have been adopted by many states.

Creating a corporation as a separate entity creates a corporate "veil" that shields the individuals controlling the EO from liabilities incurred by the EO, unless they are negligent or otherwise remiss in their duties. Some states have adopted immunity laws augmenting protection against liability for directors and officers. In Texas, the Charitable Immunity and Liability Act of 1987 applies only to §501(c)(3) organizations. This statute shields a charity's officers, directors, and volunteers, regardless of the form of organization, thus obviating one of the advantages in establishing a corporation. In California, apparently only corporations are provided such immunity.

An exempt corporation can be formed without or without members. Unless the charter provides otherwise, members are presumed in some states. The primary role of members is to elect the board of directors, who in turn govern the organization. In a privately funded organization, the members may be family representatives whose job is to retain control. The founder of a charity can be named the only member. With most public benefit corporations, members serve to broaden the base of financial support and to involve the community in the EO's activities. In such cases, there may be hundreds or thousands of individual contributors who, as a group, control the organization because they elect the directors. Most mutual benefit societies, clubs, and the like are also controlled by their dues-paying members. The other choice is to allow the board of directors to govern the organization. Closer control can be maintained by a small, self-perpetuating board.

Caution must be used in drafting a charter. The federal requirements for some categories of exempt organizations are more extensive than the minimum requirements under most states' laws. See Chapters 2 and 18 for details of the federal requirements.

Bylaws must be adopted to provide rules of governance, such as the number of directors, duration of their terms, and procedures for removing them. Bylaws typically also address the frequency of meetings, notice procedures, type and duties of officers, delegation of authority to committees, and the extent of member responsibility. The manner in which the bylaws can be amended should also be covered in the bylaws. Indemnity to directors may be provided.

An advantage of the corporate form, as compared to a trust, is the ability to easily mold and change policies as the EO evolves. Usually, the currently-serving board has authority to make changes to both the bylaws and the charter.

(b) Trust

Individually- or family-funded charitable organizations are often organized in trust form, either by testamentary bequest under a will or by creating an inter vivos ("among the living") trust. Unlike a corporation, a trust can be totally inflexible, with no provisions for change in purpose or trustees. Thus, a donor with specific wishes may prefer this potentially unalterable form for a substantial testamentary bequest. Another advantage of a trust is that some states require no registration.

There is some argument that charitable trusts can violate the "rule against perpetuities." To get around this potential obstacle, a trust may contain a provision allowing the trustee(s) to convert the trust into an exempt corporation with identical purposes and organizational restraints if the trust form becomes disadvantageous.

Exempt organization immunity statutes do not apply to trusts in some states, and more stringent fiduciary standards are often imposed upon trustees than on corporate directors. As a rule, trustees are more exposed to potential liability for their actions than are corporate directors.

The tax rates on unrelated business income may be slightly lower for a trust than for a corporation.

(c) Unincorporated Association

The unincorporated association form is the easiest to establish. To qualify for exemption, an association must have organizing instruments outlining the same basic information found in a corporate charter or trust instrument. Rules of governance must be provided, and it must have regularly-chosen officers. Particularly for §501(c)(3) status, the IRS requires specific provisions in the documents prohibiting certain activities. The constitution or articles of association must be signed by at least two persons.[1] There are few established statutes or guidelines to follow. National, statewide, and area EOs with branches or chapters can facilitate orderly governance for their subordinates by furnishing a uniform structure document.

An unincorporated group faces substantial pitfalls. The primary concern is lack of protection from legal liability for officers and directors. Banks and creditors may be reluctant to establish business relationships without personal guarantees by the officers or directors.

---

[1] Form 1023, *Application for Recognition of Exemption*, p. 3.

Exhibit 1–2
COMPARISON OF REQUIREMENTS AND TAX ATTRIBUTES
FOR IRC §§501(c)(2), (3), (4), (5), (6), and (7)

	(c)(2)	(c)(3)	(c)(4)	(c)(5)	(c)(6)	(c)(7)
Exemption application required.	Y	Y	N	N	N	N
Time limit for filing IRS application for exemption (15 months)	N	Y	N	N	N	N
Form 1023 filed.	N	Y	N	N	N	N
Form 1024 filed.	Y	N	Y	Y	Y	Y
REGARDING CHARTER/INSTRUMENT:						
Purpose clause limiting.	Y	Y	N	N	N	N
Dissolution clause required.	N	Y	N	N	N	N
Activity limitations required.	Y	Y	N	N	N	N
REGARDING PAYMENTS TO EO:						
Receive tax deductible contributions	N	Y	N	N	N	N
Receive tax deductible business dues.	N	N	N/Y	Y/N	Y/N	Y/N
REGARDING REVENUES:						
Annual support test for private foundation class.	N	Y	N	N	N	N
Membership primary income source.	N	N/Y	Y/N	Y	Y	Y
Amount of nonmember income limited.	N	N	N	N	N	Y
REGARDING UBIT:*						
Investment income exempt from UBIT unless investment indebted.	Y	Y	Y	Y	Y	N
Volunteer and donated property exceptions available for UBIT.	Y	Y	Y	Y	Y	Y
Convenience exception.	N	Y	N	N	N	N
Amount of UBI† must be limited.	N	Y	Y	N	N	Y
REGARDING ACTIVITIES:						
Can engage in political campaigns.	N	N	N/Y	Y	Y	Y
Can engage in lobbying.	N	N/Y	Y	Y	Y	Y
Lobbying activity limited.	Y	Y	N	N	N	N
Broad purposes can be pursued.	N	Y	Y	N	N	N
Private inurement/benefit prohibited.	Y	Y	Y	Y	Y	Y
Operations must primarily be exempt	Y	Y	Y	Y	Y	Y
Can carry out active projects.	N	Y	Y	Y	Y	Y

*Unrelated business income tax.
†Unrelated business income.

1.7 CHOOSING THE BEST FORM OF ORGANIZATION

Once a decision has been made that a tax-exempt entity will be suitable and the necessary organizational requirements can be satisfied, the specific category of exemption can be chosen. Exhibit 1–1 lists the more than 25 types of organizations included in the Internal Revenue Code. Chapters 2 through 10 discuss the particulars of the first seven types. Exhibit 1–2 is a chart comparing the filing requirements and primary characteristics of categories (c)(2) through (c)(7).

Qualifying Under IRC §501(c)(3)

2.1 Organizational Test	**2.2 Operational Test**
(a) Charter, Constitution, or Instrument	(a) Charitable Class
(b) Registering with State	(b) Amount of Charitable Expenditures
(c) Dissolution Clause	(c) Income Accumulations
(d) Inurement Clause	(d) Commensurate Test
(e) Purpose Clause	(e) Business Activity
(f) Political Activities	(f) Importance of Sources of Support
(g) Private Foundations	(g) Action Organization

Organizations that qualify for exemption under IRC §501(c)(3) include "Corporations, and any community chest, fund, or foundation, organized and operated exclusively for religious, charitable, scientific, testing for public safety, literary, or educational purposes, or to foster national or international amateur sports competition (but only if no part of its activities involves the provision of athletic facilities or equipment), or for the prevention of cruelty to children or animals:

- No part of the net earnings of which inures to the benefit of any private shareholder or individual,

- No substantial part of the activities of which is carrying on propaganda, or otherwise attempting to influence legislation (except as otherwise provided in subsection (h), and which

- Does not participate in, or intervene in (including the publishing or distributing of statements), any political campaign on behalf of (or in opposition to) any candidate for public office."

In order to be exempt, an organization must also be both "organized and operated" for one or more of the exempt purposes specified in the statute.[1]

IRC §501(c)(3) organizations as a group are commonly referred to as "charitable," partly because they qualify for deduction under IRC §§170, 2055, 2106, and 2522 (income, estate, and gift tax deductions). The title of IRC §170 is

---

[1]Reg. §1.501(c)(3)-1(a).

"Charitable, *etc.*, Contributions and Gifts." Note, however, that "charitable" is only one of the eight categories listed in IRC §501(c)(3).

Our concept of charity in the United States is very broad, including far more than benevolence or philanthropy, the European notion. Charity is an evolving concept that has changed over the years to meet societal needs and occasionally to advance public policy. Private schools are allowed exempt status only if they adopt a policy prohibiting discrimination, for example. The tax laws evidence an intention to encourage private sector initiatives in a broad range of social programs that are typically governmental responsibilities in the rest of the developed world.

This section details the requirements for qualifying under IRC §501(c)(3), along with criteria for the different categories of exemption thereunder. This classification contains both the most numerous categories and the most controversial. Each category is the subject of myriad rulings and case decisions. Hopkins' *Law of Tax-Exempt Organizations*, contains over 250 pages on charitable organizations and includes a wealth of information beyond the scope of this book.

While this discussion provides guideposts for determining qualification under IRC §501(c)(3), it offers few hard and fast rules because the rules are broad and often vague. By far the largest body of law and written material concerning exempt organizations deals with charities. The possibilities for qualification are endless, and success lies in a thorough review of the alternatives. In a deceptively simple fashion, there are only two tests for qualification: organizational and operational.

2.1 ORGANIZATIONAL TEST

The organizational test dictates the rules of governance of the organization and restricts its purposes and goals to those specifically listed in the statute. Provisions in the governing instruments empowering the organization to conduct activities (except insubstantial ones) beyond the specified purposes are not permitted.[2] Assets must be permanently dedicated to (c)(3) exempt purposes in the organizational rules pertaining to dissolution, inurement, purpose, and prohibited activities.

(a) Charter, Constitution, or Instrument

To receive IRS approval of exempt status, an organization must be created with properly executed documents filed and approved by appropriate state officials. A formless aggregation of individuals cannot be exempt, nor can a partnership.[3] The IRS determination procedures generally assume two types of organizational documents:

1. Articles of incorporation or association or a trust instrument, and

2. Rules of governance under which the exempt organization (EO) is operated, usually bylaws.

[2]Reg. 1.510(c)(3)-1(b).
[3]Exempt Organization Handbook (IRM 7751) §321.1.

For a corporation, bylaws alone are not an organizing document, but merely the internal rules and regulations of the organization. For trusts and associations, however, the charter or constitution and bylaws are combined into one document. The form of organization must be a "corporation, community chest, fund or foundation." Individuals, partnerships, and formless groups of individuals cannot qualify.[4] See Section 1.7 for consideration of the different forms of organization.

A model charter and bylaws exemplifying the provisions that minimally satisfy this test have been developed by the American Bar Association. IRS Publication 557, *Tax-Exempt Status for Your Organization*, also contains samples and should be consulted to assure that proper provisions are included.

A charter defect cannot be overcome in the bylaws. The IRS routinely requires revision of deficient articles prior to issuing a positive determination of 501(c)(3) exempt status. Although they allow for amendment of a charter or bylaw deemed deficient during the review process, qualification may only be permitted from the effective date of such an amendment, not retroactively to the deficient charter date. A defective charter is also not overcome merely because the organization's activities are actually charitable; likewise, an acceptable charter cannot overcome nonexempt activity.[5]

IRS policy is to require the dissolution, inurement, purpose, and political action clauses of a proposed (c)(3) exempt organization to contain the literal term "501(c)(3)." Descriptive language limiting the activity solely to charitable purposes (without specifically mentioning 501(c)(3)) may be acceptable, but other language may not be, as discussed in Section 2.1(e). In response to a recent request to the Key District to verify exempt status by a ten year old organization, the IRS asked the EO to revise its charter accordingly. Their original charter had been approved by the IRS upon initial determination.

The Tax Court disagreed with this policy in *Colorado State Chiropractic Society*.[6] A charitable organization, in the court's opinion, need not satisfy the organizational test solely by language in its corporate articles. Other factual evidence in addition to the charter, such as the bylaws, can be considered in determining passage of the test. As of October 1992, however, the Dallas EO technical staff has not changed its policy to comply with this case. They continue to require language specifically limiting the purposes to charitable ones, and preferably using the term "501(c)(3)."

(b) Registering with State

The IRS does not ordinarily question the validity of the corporate status of an organization that has satisfied the formal requirements for such status under the law governing its creation.[7] However, the minimum requirement for establishing a nonprofit organization in some states, including Texas, is deficient by federal standards. The range of activities permitted a "nonprofit corporation" is commonly broader, for example, and a charter granting all powers provided

---

[4] IRS Instructions to Form 1023, at 2.
[5] Exempt Organizations Handbook (IRM 7751) §320(2).
[6] *Colorado State Chiropractic Society v. Commissioner*, 93 T.C. 39 (1989).
[7] Exempt Organizations Handbook (IRM 7751) §321.2.

under a state's nonprofit corporation act may not qualify.[8] The charter must be approved or registered with the applicable state agency, usually the secretary of state, before submission to the IRS.

Since many nonprofit organizations have similar names, it is very useful to investigate name availability before the documents are submitted to the state. Unlike a business corporation, an EO may not necessarily be required to use the words "corporation," "company," or "incorporated." A trust instrument need not be registered in some states, but must contain appropriate language as discussed above.

(c) Dissolution Clause

Specific language in the nonprofit's charter must describe the manner in which its assets will be distributed in the event of dissolution. Assets may not be returned to contributors, directors, or any non-501(c)(3) organization or purposes.[9] It is not sufficient to say that the assets will be dedicated to "nonprofit purposes," since nonprofit purposes are not necessarily 501(c)(3) purposes. Remaining assets at the time of dissolution must be either expended for 501(c)(3) purposes or given to another 501(c)(3) organization. The IRC section should be specifically mentioned by number.

Some state statutes make these provisions automatic unless otherwise stated in the corporate charter. The IRS has a list identifying states whose dissolution clauses qualify.[10] Even so, specific mention in the charter is advisable to avert IRS challenges to the charter when the application exemption is filed.

(d) Inurement Clause

The inurement clause of the charter must forbid distribution of any part of the organization's net earnings to its directors, officers, trustees, or to any private individual.[11] Although the section may not technically apply, it is instructive to consider IRC §503, listing five prohibited transactions that will cause certain EOs to be denied exemption:

1. Lending any part of its income or corpus, without receipt of adequate security and reasonable rate of interest,

2. Paying any compensation, in excess of a reasonable allowance for salaries or other compensation for personal services actually rendered,

3. Making any part of its services available on a preferential basis,

4. Selling any substantial part of its securities or other property, for less than an adequate consideration in money or money's worth, or

---

[8]G.C.M. 39,633.
[9]Reg. §1.501(c)(3)-1(b)(4); *Church of Nature in Man v. Commissioner*, 49 T.C.M. 1393 (1985).
[10]Rev. Proc. 82-2, 1982-1 C.B. 367.
[11]Reg. §1.501(c)(3)-1(c)(2).

5. Engaging in any other transaction that results in a substantial diversion of its income or corpus to the EO's creator, substantial contributors, family members, or controlled corporations of such persons.

See Chapter 22 for more discussion of transactions and associations between one exempt organization and another, and between an exempt organization and private individuals or businesses.

In determining whether the organization can satisfy the prohibition against use of its assets or income for the benefit of its directors or other private individuals, ask whether the organization will serve a charitable class. Will the product of its exempt activity (teaching, health care, and so on) be made available to a broad enough group of beneficiaries on a nondiscriminatory basis? Within each of the exempt purposes described in Chapters 2 through 11, you will find a variety of specific criteria applied by the IRS in answering this question.

The answer is not always logical. For example, why would a neighborhood youth sports organization qualify for exemption when an adult health club may not? How can the advancement of a particular ethnic group, such as Italians or Asians, be considered charitable when a genealogical society to trace family roots is not?

A campaign management school organized to train individuals for professional careers in managing political races was denied exemption because it provided "private benefit" to the Republican Party. Most of the school graduates were associated with Republican candidates and committees supporting them. In its application for exemption, the American Campaign Academy revealed that it was an outgrowth of a National Republican Congressional Committee project, and that its funding was provided solely by the National Republican Congressional Trust. The Academy argued, nevertheless, that it met all the definitions of a school and did not discriminate on the basis of political preference, race, color, or national or ethnic origins in its admission polices. The Tax Court agreed with the IRS that the facts—actual curriculum and admission applications—showed narrow partisan interests. The court found that the size of the class and number of Republican party members did not per se transform the benefitted class into a charitable class.[12]

Nonpartisan voter registration drives do not constitute prohibited political activity if they are truly nonpartisan. An organization ostensibly formed to engage in nonpartisan analysis, study, and research and to conduct educational programs for voters had its exemption revoked by the IRS because of its overt partisan activity.[13]

The Michigan Educational Trust was also denied exemption because its "sole direct benefit inures only to the individuals purchasing contracts."[14] The Michigan legislature created the trust to assist parents in financing their children's college education through advance tuition payment contracts. Based

---

[12]*American Campaign Academy v. Commissioner*, 92 T.C. 66 (1989).
[13]Priv. Ltr. Rul. 9117001.
[14]State of *Michigan v. U.S.*, No. 92-2 USTC ¶50,424 (D.C.W. Michigan 1992) The trust alternatively argued, unsuccessfully, that it was not subject to tax because it was a branch of the State of Michigan and should be exempt due to governmental immunity.

upon actuarially-determined amounts needed to pay their child's tuition at a state-operated college or university, parents purchased the right for their child to attend college. The IRS successfully argued that the tuition-guaranteeing service constituted substantial private benefit and defeated the organization's contention that the trust provided a broader public benefit to society by assuring a well-educated populace. See Chapter 20 for more discussion about inurement, and Section 2.2(a) for information regarding charitable class.

(e) Purpose Clause

Organizational documents must limit the purposes of the EO to one or more of the eight specific 501(c)(3) purposes listed below. To qualify under 501(c)(3), an exempt organization must also operate exclusively for one of these purposes. The only permitted purposes are:

1. Religious,

2. Charitable,

3. Scientific,

4. Testing for public safety,

5. Literary,

6. Educational,

7. Fostering national or international amateur sports competition,

8. Preventing cruelty to children or animals.

Ideally, the charter will describe one or more of the eight, such as charitable, charitable and scientific, or scientific and educational, along with the qualifier, "as defined in §501(c)(3) of the Internal Revenue Code." Words having similar meaning to those listed above cannot be used. The term "eleemosynary" may mean charitable but is not acceptable." Civic welfare," although listed as a charitable pursuit in the regulations, does not, standing alone, qualify under (c)(3)—although such words are suitable under (c)(4). Also, combining permissible with impermissible purposes is not acceptable.[15] The IRS provides the following examples:

ACCEPTABLE: "XYZ Organization is created to receive contributions and pay them over to the organization which are described in §501(c)(3) and exempt from income taxation under §501(a)."[16] It is also acceptable "to grant scholarships to deserving junior college students residing in Gotham City."[17]

NOT ACCEPTABLE: "MD, Inc. will operate a hospital (with no stipulation that the operation be charitable.)"[18] Nor is it acceptable to state that "ABC will

[15] Rev. Rul. 69-279, 1969-1 C.B. 152; Rev. Rul. 69-256, 1969-1C.B. 151.
[16] Reg. §1.501(c)(3)-1(b)(1)(ii).
[17] Exempt Organizations Handbook (IRM 7751) §322.2.
[18] Id. §322.2.

conduct adult education classes," without also stating that the organization is formed for charitable purposes.[19]

Reciting detailed descriptions of the organization's purpose in its charter is not advisable. Such explanations belong in the bylaws or a mission statement. An organization's activities tend to evolve over the years, and it is best to avoid the need to make formal charter changes that require approval by the state. Bylaw changes can be approved by the organization's governing body.

(f) Political Activities

The bylaws must absolutely prohibit political campaign involvement with the following language: "The EO shall not participate in, or intervene in (including the publication or distribution of statements) on behalf of or in opposition to any candidate for public office."[20]

Legislative lobbying must be limited by the following language: "No substantial part of the activities of the EO shall be the carrying on of propaganda, or otherwise attempting to influence legislation."[21] Note the word "substantial." Only a limited amount of lobbying can be conducted by a charity (except private foundations). The permissible limits apply to both grassroots and direct lobbying efforts. These limitations are outlined in Chapter 23.

(g) Private Foundations

Additional requirements are placed on charities classified as private foundations by IRC §508(e). Their charters must specifically prohibit actions that would cause the imposition of excise taxes. State laws have been passed to automatically incorporate the required language into a private foundation's charter, and the IRS has issued a ruling approving the list.[22] To be cautious, some counsellors recommend inclusion of the prohibitions anyway. A private foundation generally is an EO that receives its funding from a limited number of people, usually a family or a particular individual, as more fully explained in Chapter 12.

2.2 OPERATIONAL TEST

To qualify under RC§501(c)(3), an organization must also meet the operational test: The (c)(3) EO must operate "exclusively" to accomplish one of the eight purposes listed at Section 2.1(e) and discussed in Chapters 3, 4, and 5. The term "exclusively" for this purpose does not mean 100 percent, and a limited amount of nonexempt activity is permitted. Evidence for the operational test is found not only in the nature of the activities but also in the sources of financial support, the constituency for whom the organization operates, and the nature of the expenditures.

[19] Reg. §1.501(C)(3)-1(b)(1)(ii). This regulation essentially says that conducting classes is not necessarily educational unless the articles specify that term or the term "charitable."
[20] Reg. §1.501(c)(3)-1(b)(3)(ii).
[21] Reg. §1.501(c)(3)-1(b)(3)(i).
[22] Rev. Rul. 75-38, 1975-1 C.B. 161.

(a) Charitable Class

To be exempt as a charitable organization under (c)(3), an organization must operate to benefit an indefinite class of persons—a charitable class—rather than an individual or a limited group of individuals. It may not be "organized or operated for the benefit of private interests such as designated individuals, the creator's family, shareholders of the organization or persons controlled, directly or indirectly, by such private interests."[23] A trust established to benefit an impoverished retired minister and his wife cannot qualify.[24] Likewise, a fund established to raise money to finance a medical operation, rebuild a house destroyed by fire, or provide food for a particular person does not benefit a charitable class. An organization formed by merchants to relocate homeless persons ("throw the bums out") from a downtown area was found to serve the merchant class and promote their interests, rather than those of the homeless or the citizens.[25]

A comparatively small group of individuals can be benefitted as long as the particular persons are not identified. Also, the class need not be indigent nor poor and distressed.[26] A scholarship found for a college fraternity that provided school tuition for deserving members was ruled (in 1956) to be an exempt foundation.[27] On the other hand, a trust formed to aid destitute or disabled members of a particular college class was deemed to benefit the individuals. The IRS General Counsel stated that the "general law of charity recognizes that a narrowly defined class of beneficiaries will not cause a charitable trust to fail unless the trust's purposes are so 'personal, private or selfish' as to lack the element of public usefulness."[28] This question is of particular interest in the health care field.

A genealogical society tracing the migrations to and within the United States of persons with a common name qualifies as a social club, not a charity. Although the IRS and the courts admitted there was educational merit in the historical information compiled, the private interest of the family group predominated.[29] If membership in the society is open to all and its focus is educational—presenting lectures, sponsoring exhibitions, publishing a geographic area's pioneer history—it may be classified as charitable.[30] In contrast, a society limiting its membership to one family and compiling research data for family members individually cannot qualify.[31]

---

[23] Reg. §1.501(c)(3)-1(d)(1)(ii).
[24] *Carrie A. Maxwell Trust, Pasadena Methodist Foundation v. Commissioner*, 2 T.C.M. 905 (1943).
[25] *Westward Ho v. Commissioner*, T.C. Mem. 1992-192.
[26] *Consumer Credit Counseling Service of Alabama, Inc. v. U.S.*, 78-2 USTC ¶9468 (D.C. 1979), but see *El Paso del Aquila Elderly*, T.C. Memo, 1992.441. Making burial insurance available at cost for the elderly is a charitable activity only if distress is relieved (by allowing indigents to participate) and the community as a whole benefits.
[27] Rev. Rul. 56-403, 1956-2 C.B. 307.
[28] G.C.M. 39876 (July 29, 1992).
[29] *The Callaway Family Association, Inc. v. Commissioner*, 71 T.C. 340 (1978); Rev. Rul. 67-8, 1967-1 C.B. 142.
[30] Rev. Rul 80-301, 1980-2 C.B. 180.
[31] Rev. Rul. 80-302, 1980-2 C.B. 182.

Serving both charity and an individual is not permitted. A split interest trust that pays a fixed annual percentage of its income to its creator and pays the balance to a named charity is not exempt.[32] Nor is a trust paying a fixed annual sum for perpetual care of the creator's cemetery lot, with the balance paid to charities.[33]

(b) Amount of Charitable Expenditures

The Internal Revenue Code contains no rule requiring a specific amount of annual expenditures by a public charity except for the commensurate test Section 2.2(d). Presumably, it is left to the contributors and supporters of an organization to require that their money be spent for worthy causes and to monitor the manner in which funds are expended. Some states have rules governing spending by nonprofit organizations, which monitor particularly the level of administrative and fund-raising costs in relation to program costs.

A private foundation, partly because it is not scrutinized by public contributors, is subject to a "minimum distribution" requirement. At least five percent of the average annual value of its investment assets must be expended annually to make charitable grants, conduct programs, or purchase assets used in charitable activities. These rules are explained in Chapter 15. Nevertheless, private foundations and public charities can generate profit.

(c) Income Accumulations

One criterion for measuring whether an EO operates "exclusively" for charitable purposes is the portion of its revenues actually expended on charitable projects. Is the EO saving its income instead of spending it for charitable purposes? If the organization is squirreling away funds, why? Some profit, or excess of revenues over expenditures, can be accumulated. As a general rule, the purpose for which funds can be accumulated must be to better advance the charitable interests of the EO over a period of time. Acceptable reasons why funds might be saved include:

- To maintain sufficient working capital to assure ongoing, continuous provision of charitable services. Working capital can be saved to protect against years when income declines due to loss of grants, lower donations, reduced investment income, and other uncontrollable outside forces. The standards concerning for-profit corporation earnings accumulations can be applied. A minimum of one year's operating budget should be a minimum reasonable amount for a working capital fund.

- To replace obsolete equipment, acquire a new building, or acquire other capital assets dedicated to charitable purposes. The savings is prudent because the EO does not want to incur excessive indebtedness. In other instances, a sinking fund might be established to pay off a debt.

---

[32] Rev. Rul. 69-279, 1969-1 C.B. 152.
[33] Rev. Rul. 69-256, 1969-1 C.B. 151.

- To establish new programs or expand services for charitable constituents when the funds required exceed current available resources. Savings to self-finance expansion can be accumulated.

(d) Commensurate Test

Another criteria applied by the IRS is called the "commensurate test." Are the expenditures commensurate in scope to the financial resources of the EO? The theory was first espoused in 1964 in looking at what portion of the EO's assets could be invested in unrelated business activities.[34] In addition to operating exclusively for charitable purposes, a charity's primary purpose must also be charitable. The distinction between the two tests is minimal and no exact mathematical test is provided. It is sufficient to say that both should be satisfied to assure maintenance of exempt status.

Beginning in 1990, revenue agents examined fund-raising organizations with its special emphasis checklist found in Appendix 24–2. The tests measured whether professional fund-raisers receive an excessive portion of the funds they raise for charity. State charitable regulators are also concerned and may have specific limitations on such payments.

The commensurate test was used to revoke the exempt status of United Cancer Council, Inc. (UCC), a bogus charity which solicited funds by mail. Out of over $7 million raised during 1986, UCC spent less than $300,000 on patient services and research and paid the balance to its fund-raising counsel, Watson & Hughey. Needless to say, the commensurate test was failed. Bingo operations paying excessive operating costs and salaries, with little or no profits left for charity, also fail the test.[35] In the published determination letter of Temple City High School Bingo, the IRS applied at fifteen percent of gross receipts guideline to evaluate whether a commensurate amount of the receipts actually were paid to the high school the organization was formed to raise funds for.[36]

(e) Business Activity

The receipt of unrelated business income can jeopardize the organization's exemption. An organization that conducts a trade or business as a substantial part of its activities can be exempt, but only if the operation of the business furthers its exempt purpose. Its primary purpose must not be to carry on an unrelated trade or business.[37] What is meant by "substantial" is not numerically expressed and is measured after taking all of the facts and circumstances of the organization's operations into account. The size and extent of the trade or business in relation to the organization's exempt activity is determinative. A customary measure of "primariness" is the portion of the EO's overall budget produced by the business.

[34] Rev. Rul. 64-182, 1964 (Part 1) C.B. 186.
[35] Priv. Ltr. Rul. 9132005, May 3, 1991. For a good history of the commensurate issue, read G.C.M. 32689 published in 1963, G.C.M. 34682 in 1971, and G.C.M. 38742 in 1982.
[36] IRS Exemption Letter July 6, 1992.
[37] Reg. §1.501(c)(3)-1(e); Rev. Rul. 64-182. n 34.

It is "likely exempt status of an organization will be revoked where it regularly derives over one-half of its annual revenue from unrelated activities."[38] The regulations provide no specific numerical percentage level. The Second Circuit Court of Appeals thought one-third was excessive.[39] Another court indicated that a safe level of unrelated income would be under 20 to 25 percent of the EO's overall revenues.[40]

Proving that a business is related, rather than unrelated, may be necessary for an organization to achieve or maintain exempt status. In evaluating the relatedness of a business enterprise, the purpose toward which the activity is directed, rather than the nature of the activity itself, determines whether the activity serves an exempt purpose.[41] In other words, if a resale shop run with handicapped workers provides a livelihood for workers not otherwise able to support themselves, the fact that the shop is in business competing with commercial resale shops does not prevent relatedness.

The operation of a trade or business that furthers, or is related to, an organization's exempt purposes is clearly permitted. Consider Goodwill Industries: As a part of a job training program, handicapped workers repair and refurbish furniture and other items for resale. The primary motivation is to provide training and livelihood for the disadvantaged workers (a charitable purpose), not to operate the stores. An unlimited amount of such related business is permitted.

The profit from business activity that is unrelated to the organization's exempt purpose is subject to income tax. See Chapter 21 for a discussion of "unrelated" business activity methods of calculating the tax, and the evolving "commerciality" test.

(f) Importance of Sources of Support

The classic (c)(3) organization receives its financial support from voluntary contributions and from investment income produced from contributions it retains in an endowment or working capital fund. Its charitable nature is evidenced by its ability to attract such donations (one-way street gifts) in support of its activities.

The IRS applies support ratio tests in its determinations and examinations. Support coming from a limited group of donors may dictate or result in private foundation status. An absence of or limited amount of donations may imply noncharitable status.

The level of public support normally differs according to the type of organization. For example, a grant-making United Fund would receive the bulk of its revenues from donations; a university would receive a sizable part of its revenues from student tuition (exempt function income). See Chapter 11 for detailed definitions of various categories of public charities and requirements for obtaining public status.

[38] G.C.M. 39108.
[39] *Orange County Agricultural Society, Inc. v. Commissioner*, 893 F.2d 647 (2d Cir. 1990), *aff'g* 55 T.C.M. 1602 (1988).
[40] *Manning Association v. Commissioner*, 93 T.C.M. 596, 603-604 (1989).
[41] *Junaluska Assembly Housing, Inc. v. Commissioner*, 86 T.C.M. 1114, 1121 (1986).

(g) Action Organization

An organization whose purposes can only be accomplished through the passage of legislation—changing local, state or federal laws—is called an "action organization" and cannot qualify for exemption as a charity under (c)(3).[42] When a substantial part of the organization's activity is attempting to influence legislation by propaganda or otherwise, it is considered an action organization. Attempting to influence legislation means:

- Contracting, or urging the public to contact members of a legislative body (the Congress, any state legislature, local council or similar governing body or the public in a referendum) for the purpose of proposing, supporting, or opposing legislation, or

- Advocating the adoption or rejection of legislation.

Another kind of action organization is one that participates or intervenes, directly or indirectly, in any political campaign on behalf of or in opposition to any candidate for public office. Chapter 23 discusses these rules in detail, including when to consider the formation of a (c)(4) organization.

[42]Reg. §1.501(c)(3)-1(b)(3).

Religious Organizations

The first type of (c)(3) organization listed in the statute is "religious." An organization whose primary purpose is to conduct religious activities qualifies for exemption. However, the regulations do not define "religious" purposes, presumably to maintain the separation of church and state, and the IRS says that the term cannot be defined precisely.[1]

3.1 TYPES OF RELIGIOUS ORGANIZATIONS

A religious organization is basically one that concerns itself with a person's relationship to divine or superhuman powers, either to worship them through ritual or to study human manifestations of their teachings. The major American religions—Catholic, Baptist, Jewish and so on—clearly qualify as religious organizations and furthermore as churches. However, there are many non-churches that qualify for exemption as religious organizations. Churches have a special set of qualifications as discussed in Section 3.2.

(a) Ideology or Dogma Not Essential

Religion is not confined to a particular sect or ritual. A court has noted that the symbols of one religion may be anathema to another.[2] Another stated that judgments about the validity or truth of the organization's beliefs must be avoided by the courts: "It is not the province of government officials or courts to determine religious orthodoxy."[3] Religions that do not believe in a supreme being in the Judeo-Christian sense, such as Taoism, Buddhism, and secular

---

[1] Exempt Organizations Handbook (IRM 7751) §344.2.
[2] *Unity School of Christianity*, 4 B.T.A. 61 (1962), *acq.* VI-1C.B. 6 (1927).
[3] *Teterud v. Burns*, 522 F. 2d 357 (8th Cir. 1975).

humanism, are eligible for exemption.[4] It is unnecessary to inquire into the nature of the beliefs of an organization. A religion with thousands of adherents based upon supernatural revelations to its founder was found to operate for religious purposes, despite its total control by the founder and lucrative publication sales.[5]

(b) Examples of Qualifying Organizations

While religious orders and churches unquestionably qualify as religious organization, a vast array of organizations conducting related activities also qualify under the religious category. To illustrate the concepts, the following list compares qualifying organizations to other organizations with a similar focus that do not qualify for exemption.

- Weekend retreat center, open to individuals of diverse Christian denominations, where organized religious programs are presented and recreational time is limited, can qualify.[6] In contrast, an organization sponsoring religious cruises including extensive social and recreational activities was not permitted exemption.[7] Nor was a retreat center that held unscheduled and nonrequired religious activity available for its visitors, to encourage individual meditation and prayer. (It looked too much like a spa or vacation place).[8]

- Kosher food preparation and inspection of commercial products for compliance with religious belief advances religion and can be exempt.[9] However, a Seventh-Day Adventist Church affiliate was denied exemption for its vegetarian restaurant and food store that provided food stuffs in accordance with church doctrines. Although not so stated, perhaps the fatal flaw was the fact that the stores were open to the general public, evidencing a commercial purpose beyond that of ministering to the spiritual needs of the church members.[10]

- A religious publishing house that disseminates literature to promote its own beliefs can qualify for exemption.[11] Also, publication of a nondenominational newsletter is an exempt activity.[12] If, instead, the publish-

---

[4]*U.S. v. Seeger*, 380 U.S. 163 (1965).
[5]*Saint Germain Foundation*, 26 T.C. 648 (1956), acq., 1956-2 C.B. 8.
[6]Rev. Rul. 77-430, 1977-2 C.B. 1914.
[7]Rev. Rul, 77-366, 1977-2 C.B. 192.
[8]*The Schoger Foundation v. Commissioner*, 76 T.C. 380 (1981).
[9]Rev. Rul. 74-575, 1974-2 C.B. 161.
[10]*Living Faith, Inc. v. Commissioner*, T.C.M. Dec. ¶46,860, 60 T.C.M. 710, 1990-484.
[11]*Presbyterian and Reformed Publishing Co. v. Commissioner*, 743 F. 2d 148 (3rd Cir. 1984); *St. Germain Foundation, supra note 5; Unity School of Christianity, supra note 2; Pulpit Resource v. Commissioner*, 70 T.C. 594 (1978).
[12]Rev. Rul. 68-306, 1968-1 C.B. 257.

ing house sells a wide variety of religious publications and supplies in a profitable commercial manner, it looks to the IRS and the courts like a business venture and cannot qualify for exemption.[13]

- Communal living groups that practice religious functions also provide food, shelter, and other basic human needs that give individual benefit to the commune members. Newly-formed "new age" communes were found not qualify as exempt religious organizations in the late 1970s.[14] Later, the IRS recanted its seeming discrimination against alternative religions. When the living quarters and provisions are minimal and "do not exceed those strictly necessary," and few of the members work outside the community, and the group has a religious focus, the IRS may rule favorably.[15] Groups of monks, nuns, and other clerics traditionally have been allowed to qualify as religious organizations, and are often exempt as an integrated auxiliary of a church.[16] Special rules for religious orders and apostolic associations are discussed in Sections 3.3 and 3.4.

(c) Peripheral Religious Activity

Other types of organizations conducting activities associated with religious matters include:

- A religious burial service provided by an exempt organization, the purpose of which was to support and maintain basic tenets and beliefs of a religion regarding burial of its members.[17]

- A coffee house for college students to meet with church leaders, educators, and business leaders for discussion and counseling on religion, current events, social and vocational problems is exempt.[18]

- Radio and television broadcasts of religious materials and worship services is an exempt religious activity, and an organization presenting such broadcasts can qualify even when the station holds a commercial license, as long the amount of broadcasting devoted to advertisements is insignificant.[19]

---

[13]*Scripture Press Foundation v. U.S.*, 285 F. 2d 800 (1961), *cert. den* 368 U.S. 985, *Fides Publishers Association v. U.S.*, 263 F. Supp. 924 (1967); *Incorporated Trustees of the Gospel Workers Society v. U.S.*, 520 F. Supp. 924 (D.D.C. 1981).
[14]*Martinsville Ministries, Inc. v. U.S.*, 80-2 USTC ¶9710 (D.C. 1980); *Canada v. Commissioner*, 82 T.C. 973 (1984); *Beth El Ministries, Inc. v. U.S.*, 79-2 USTC ¶9412 (D.C. 1979).
[15]G.C.M. 38827 (1981).
[16]Priv. Ltr. Rul. 7838028–7838036.
[17]Rev. Rul. 79-359, 1979-2 C.B. 226.
[18]Rev. Rul. 68-72, 1968-1 C.B. 250.
[19]Rev. Rul. 68-563, 1968-2 C.B. 212, *amplified by* Rev. Rul. 78-385, 1978-2 C.B. 174, which added the comments about advertisements.

(d) Secular Groups

Spirituality, rather than secular or worldly issues, should be the focus of a religious organization. An organization practicing its doctrine of "ethical egoism" by holding dinner meetings and publishing a newsletter is not religious.[20] A nationwide broadcast ministry that engages in substantial legislative activity is also denied exemption.[21] In the absence of "any solid evidence of a belief in a supreme being, a religious discipline, a ritual, or tenets to guide one's daily existence," the Neo-American Church, whose beliefs focused on psychedelic substances, was denied exemption.[22]

An organization teaching "Gay Imperative" was denied exemption because it was a secular group.[23] The organization was dedicated to "religious explorations and a secular lifestyle for men and women who won't worship a god who oppresses Gays." Although the court accepted the sincerity of their belief, it found that the group's beliefs were not religious. The basis of the decision was threefold:

1. Religious beliefs must address fundamental and ultimate questions concerning the human condition—issues of right and wrong, life and death, good and evil. Focusing singularly on sexual preference and lifestyle was found not to be a religious question.

2. The beliefs must be comprehensive in nature and constitute an entire system of belief, instead of merely an isolated teaching. The court found no outward characteristics analogous to those of other religions. There is no published literature explaining its tradition, no formal written documentation of beliefs, such as the Bible or Koran, nor an oral literature reflecting its beliefs or history.

3. The beliefs must be manifested in external form. This group held no regular ceremonies or services.

(e) Pseudo-Religious Groups

Partly because of the lack of specific definitions, pseudo-religious groups formed to take advantage of favorable tax status have proliferated over the years. The primary reason for denying such groups exemption is that they provide private benefits to their members, who are often their founders. The classic example is the mail-order or personal church. For a few hundred dollars, anyone can buy a church—a charter, ordination papers, or other ministerial credentials—through the mail. In the typical scenario, the buyer takes a "vow of poverty" and gives all of his or her property to the church. Afterwards, the church pays all of the person's living expenses in a purportedly nontaxable manner. It has been easy

---

[20] *First Libertarian Church v. Commissioner*, 74 T.C. 396 (1980).
[21] *Christian Echoes National Ministry, Inc. v. U.S.*, 470 F. 2d 849 (10th Cir., 1972), *cert. den.*, 414 U.S. 864 (1972).
[22] *U.S. v. Kuch*, 288 F. Supp. 439, 443-444 (D.C. 1968).
[23] *Church of the Chosen People (North American Panarchate) v. U.S.*, 1982-2 USTC ¶9646 (Minn. 1982).

for the IRS and the courts to find that these organizations serve the private interests of their creators and cannot qualify for exemption.[24]

3.2 CHURCHES

Churches are an important subset of the religious exemption category, but there is no definition of church in the regulations under §501(c)(3). A brief definition of churches is found in the regulations on contributions and unrelated business income: the term "church" includes a religious order or organization if such entity (1) is an integral part of a church, and (2) is engaged in carrying out the functions of a church. What constitutes proper church conduct is to be determined by the tenets and practices of a particular religious body constituting a church. The functions of a church include only two activities:

1. Ministration of sacerdotal functions (communion, marriages, and so on), and

2. Conduct of religious worship.[25]

(a) Special Aspects of a Church

Apparently for reasons of respecting the separation of church and state, churches benefit from several special rules:

- A church and its integrated auxiliaries are automatically exempt from tax and need not seek recognition of exemption.

- No annual filing of Form 990 is required, and a high degree of abuse must be present for the IRS to seek to examine a church.[26]

- Parsonage allowances are exempt from income tax, and ministers have special employment tax rules (see Chapter 25).

- A church qualifies under IRC §170(b)(1)(a)(i) as a public charity without regard to its sources of support.

(b) Definition of Church

The IRS has developed a very specific set of characteristics that a church must possess to gain such favorable tax status. The fourteen attributes are:

1. Distinct legal existence.

2. Recognized form of worship and creed.

---

[24] *Basic Bible Church v. Commissioner*, 74 T.C. 846 (1980); Rev. Rul. 81-94, 1981-1 C.B. 330; *Church of the Transfiguring Spirit, Inc. v. Commissioner*, 76 T.C. 1 (1981); *Bubbling Well Church of Universal Love, Inc. v. Commissioner*, 74 T.C. 531 (1980); *American Guidance Foundation, Inc. v. U.S.*, 80-1 USTC ¶9452 (D.C. 1980); *Unitary Mission Church of Long Island v. Commissioner*, 74 T.C. 36 (1980); *Tony and Susan Alamo Foundation v. Commissioner*, T.C. Memo 199-155, Dec.48.078.

[25] Reg. §1.170-2(b)(2) and §1.511-2(a)(3)(ii).

[26] IRC §7611.

3. Definite and distinct ecclesiastical government.

4. Distinct religious history.

5. Formal code of doctrine and discipline.

6. Membership not associated with any other church or denomination.

7. Organization of ordained ministers.

8. Ordained ministers selected after completing prescribed courses of study.

9. Literature of its own.

10. Places of worship.

11. Regular congregations.

12. Regular religious services.

13. Sunday schools for religious instruction for youths.

14. Schools for preparation of its ministers.[27]

Items 5, 7, 11, 12, and 13 were cited as the most significant attributes in a presentation at an IRS annual training seminar for EO agents.[28] "At a minimum, a church includes a body of believers or communicants that assembles regularly in order to worship. Unless the organization is reasonably available to the public in its conduct of worship, its educational instruction and its promulgation of doctrine, it cannot fulfill this associational role," according to the IRS Exempt Organizations Handbook.

This fourteen-point test for qualifying as a church was applied by the Eighth Circuit Court of Appeals in 1991.[29] The church in question was founded for the stated purpose of spreading "God's love and hope throughout the world." It conducted bimonthly programs with prayers and gospel music in an amphitheater. It built a small chapel for unsupervised meditational activities and individual prayer, but did not conduct religious services in the chapel. Although the society argued that the test discriminated against new, rural, and poor religious organizations, the court agreed that the IRS's standard for qualification as a church was appropriate. The failure to meet three particular criteria influenced the court:

1. The society did not have a regular congregation and its attendees did not consider it their church.

2. It did not ordain ministers but held services conducted by guest ministers.

3. It did not conduct school for religious instruction of the young.

[27] Exempt Organizations Handbook (IRM 7751) §321.3; Rev. Rul. 59-129, 1959-1 C.B. 58.
[28] Exempt Organizations Continuing Education Technical Instruction Program for 1981, Training 3177-20 (1-18), TPDS 87196 at 44.
[29] *Spiritual Outreach Society v. Commissioner*, 91-1 USTC ¶50,111 (8th Cir. 1991).

A "television ministry" known as the Foundation for Human Understanding had its status as a church challenged by the IRS because about one-half of its budget went to pay for the broadcasts to its 30,000 regular listeners. Its estimated total audience was 2 million persons. There was no question that television broadcasts alone do not qualify an organization as a church. This entity, however, conducted regular services at two locations for 50 to 350 persons under the guidance of an ordained minister. Religious instruction was provided and it had a "distinct, although short, religious history."[30] Therefore the court felt it possessed most of the criteria to some degree, the critical factors were satisfied, and church status was permitted.

(c) Conventions and Auxiliaries

Conventions or associations of churches also qualify as churches.[31] Such organizations customarily undertake cooperative activities for churches of the same denomination, and, for some groups such as the United States Catholic Conference, represent a governing body. An interdenominational cooperative association of churches may also qualify as a church, as long as it otherwise qualifies as a religious organization.[32]

An integrated auxiliary of a church is afforded the same benefits as a church. Church schools, missionary groups, youth organizations, theological seminaries, and women's and men's fellowship associations are listed in the regulations as examples of qualifying auxiliary organizations. Hospitals, retirement homes, orphanages, and some schools do not perform religious functions and so are not auxiliaries. To qualify as an integrated auxiliary of a church, the organization must be:

- An exempt organization that operates exclusively for religious purposes, and

- Controlled by a church or an association of churches.[33]

(d) IRS Examination Protection

The IRS has limited information and power to review the tax exempt status of a church. As discussed in Chapters 18 and 27, churches are not required to file an application for recognition of exemption on Form 1023, nor annual information return on Form 990. The IRS must be able to prove an extraordinary abuse of the tax law to request to examine the records of a church. A church may only be audited by the IRS if the principal internal revenue officer for the IRS region in which the church is located or the Secretary of the Treasury reasonably believes on the basis of written facts and circumstances that the church is not exempted or may be carrying on an unrelated trade or business.[34]

---

[30]*Foundation for Human Understanding v. Commissioner*, 88 T.C. 1341 (1987).
[31]IRC §170(b)(1)(a)(i).
[32]Rev. Rul. 74-224, 1974-1 C.B. 61.
[33]Reg. §1.6033-2(g)(5).
[34]IRC §7611(a).

The Church of Scientology and some of its branches have won significant court battles with the IRS about the application of these rules. These decisions may influence the manner in which the IRS considers exemption of religious organizations and examination of churches. The Church won a limitation of the IRS's right to request information under the IRC §7611(b)(1)(A) summons provisions when the court found that the records were not necessary, rather than merely relevant, to determining the church's tax liability.[35] In similar battles in Florida and California, the government was more successful.[36] The Church in Los Angeles sued the IRS under the Freedom of Information Act for details of a "tax shelter litigation project" designating the Church and its parishioners.

3.3 RELIGIOUS ORDERS

The IRS has a list of criteria for qualifying as a religious order. The characteristics below will be considered by the IRS. Only the first factor must necessarily be present:

- The order is an organization otherwise qualifying for exemption under IRC §501(c)(3).

- The order is, directly or indirectly, under the control and supervision of a church or convention or association of churches.

- The members of the order vow to live under set rules of moral and spiritual self-sacrifice of their material well-being, and to dedicate themselves to the goals of the organization.

- Members make a long-term commitment, normally more than two years, to the organization after successful completion of the training and probationary period.

- The organization's members ordinarily live together in a community and are held to a significantly stricter level of moral and religious discipline than that required of lay church members.

- Members work or serve full-time on behalf of the religious, educational, or charitable goals of the organization.

- Members regularly participate in public or private prayer, religious study, teaching, care of the aging, missionary work, or church reform or renewal.[37]

---

[35] U.S. v. Church of Scientology of Boston, Inc., 90-2 USTC ¶50,349 (D.C. Mass).

[36] In U.S. v. Church of Scientology Flag Service Org., Inc., 90-1 USTC ¶50,019 (M.D. Fla. Dec. 1989) the church essentially lost when the case was referred to a magistrate to decide which requested items were necessary. Also, in U.S. v. Church of Scientology Western United States and U.S. v. Church of Scientology International, et al., CV 90-2690-HLH (Central D. Cal. Feb. 11, 1991) the court ordered the organizations to produce documents that the court found necessary to the IRS determinations.

[37] Rev. Proc. 91-20, 1991-10 IRB 26.

Status as a religious order is significant for group whose members wish to claim exemption from participation in the Social Security system under IRC §1402(c)(4).

3.4 RELIGIOUS AND APOSTOLIC ASSOCIATIONS

Religious and apostolic organizations that cannot qualify for exemption under IRC §501(c)(3) because they engage in business for the common good of their members may instead be classified as exempt from income tax under IRC §501(d). Such organizations are not eligible to receive tax deductible donations,[38] but need not pay income tax on annual profits, if any, that the organization itself generates. The members of such organizations, however, do pay income tax.

The spirit of this exemption is to prevent what Congress perceived in 1936 to be an unfair double tax on both the apostolic organizations and their members.[39] Since the rules of apostolic organizations, such as the House of David and the Shakers, prevent members from being holders of property in an individual capacity, the "undistributed profits tax" should not be imposed on their corporations. The organization must possess the following attributes.

- A common or community treasury must be maintained. Each member is not required to make a vow of poverty nor contribute private property to the organization.[40] It is the organization's property and earnings that are shared, placed in a common fund and used for the maintenance and support of the members.

- Each member reports as dividends his or her pro rata share of income (distributed or undistributed) from business conducted for the common benefit of the members.[41]

The earnings of such organizations are reported annually on Form 1065, U.S. Partnership Return of Income. Each member is treated as a partner and is taxed on his or her proportionate share of the organization's profits.[42] The income is not subject to self-employment tax.[43] No form is provided for making application for exemption under this section. Instead, a letter containing the information specified in Rev. Proc. 72-5 is submitted.[44]

[38]Rev. Rul. 57-574, 1957-2 C.B. 161.
[39]80 *Congressional Record* 9074 (1936).
[40]*Twin Oaks Community, Inc. v. Commissioner*, 87 T.C. 1233 (1986).
[41]Reg. §1.501(d)–(1)(a).
[42]Reg. §1.6033-1(a)(5); Reg. §1.501(d)(1)(b).
[43]Priv. Ltr. Rul. 7740009.
[44]Rev. Proc. 72-5, 1972-1 C.B. 709.

CHAPTER FOUR

Charitable Organizations

The second type of activity qualified for exemption under IRS §501(c)(3) is "charitable", which is expansively defined "in its generally accepted legal sense," meaning much more than relief of the poor.[1] Charity is an evolving concept, fashioned over the years by societal need and perceived abuses. The definition has changed depending on the policies of the administration currently in the White House: A shelter to house Vietnamese refugees qualified for exemption in 1978; but in 1987, the application for exemption for a similar shelter for Central American refugees was denied because the activity was "against government policy."

Charity connotes broad public benefit that is accomplished either by giving direct financial support to individuals or by operating projects that benefit the community at large. The courts have reminded the IRS that community benefit is not limited to housing the homeless or feeding the poor.[2] The education, culture, and health of the public are also charitable concerns. Although the IRS does not always agree, an organization that charges for its services and excludes those that cannot pay *may* qualify as a charitable one. Particularly in the health care arena, the requirement that the poor be served to achieve charitable classification has been for years the subject of a seesaw battle which continues today. The questions in proving exempt status are whether a

---

[1] Reg. §1.501(c)(3)-1(d)(2).

[2] *Consumer Credit Counseling Service of Alabama, Inc. v. U.S.*, 78-2 ¶9660 (D.C. 1978).

broad enough charitable class benefits, and whether the services convey a public benefit rather than an individual or private benefit.[3]

For example, a civic performing arts hall supported by the sale of $30–$50 tickets per performance is considered a charitable facility because it advances culture and educates the people in its community. Yet a community center located in a subdivision in a poor neighborhood where the residents own their own homes may not be classified as charitable, because it benefits them as individual owners. Such an entity would more likely be considered as a homeowners' association under §528. (see Section 6.6). Under each category outlined below, the evolving policy of the IRS regarding charitable class and charging for services is discussed in detail.

Charitable purposes are specifically listed in the regulations and include only the following:

- Relief for the poor and distress of the underprivileged,

- Advancement of religion,

- Advancement of education or science,

- Erection or maintenance of public buildings, monuments, or works,

- Lessening of the burdens of government, and

- Promotion of social welfare by organizations designed to accomplish one of the above listed purposes, or

- To lessen neighborhood tensions,

- To eliminate prejudice and discrimination,

- To defend human and civil rights secured by law, or

- To combat community deterioration and juvenile delinquency.[4]

This regulation specifies that "the fact that an organization, in carrying out its primary purpose, advocates social or civic changes or presents opinions on controversial issues with the intention of molding public opinion or creating public sentiment or an acceptance of its views does not preclude such organization from qualifying under IRC §501(c)(3) as long as it is not an *action* organization of any one of the types described" later in the Regulation (see Section 2.2(g)). It also provides that the receipt of voluntary contributions from the indigent persons whom the organization is operated to benefit will not necessarily prevent the organization from being exempt as charitable. This comment can be interpreted to permit an organization to charge for the services it renders—a policy which many exempt organizations adopt, including from schools, hospitals, health centers, and many other types of service-providing organizations.

[3]Rev. Rul. 75-74, 1975-1 C.B. 152.
[4]Reg. §1.501(c)(3)-1(d)(2).

4.1 RELIEF OF THE POOR

"Relief of the poor and distressed" can include a vast array of programs. Some organizations that qualify are those that provide:

- Promotion of rights and welfare for public housing occupants,[5]
- Vocational training,[6]
- Low-cost housing,[7]
- Legal aid,[8] (see also Section 23.10)
- Transportation for the handicapped and elderly,[9]
- Counseling for senior citizens,[10]
- Money management advice,[11]
- Assistance to widow(er)s and orphans of police officers,[12]
- Prisoner rehabilitation,[13]
- Disaster relief,[14]
- Day care for needy parents,[15] and
- Marketing of products made by the blind in programs designed to provide employment (including distribution of modest profits to the handicapped individuals).[16]

An organization seeking qualification because it "relieves the poor and distressed" is not precluded from exemption because it proposes to charge its charitable constituents. When services are to be provided for a fee, the issue in determining charitable status is how the proposed EO is distinguishable from a commercial business. The customary evidence of charity is to provide free, sliding scale, at cost, or reduced-price services to (in the context of this exemption category) the poor and indigent.

To clarify this distinction, consider two projects which the IRS ruled did not qualify as charitable. An employee benefit program for needy retired

[5]Rev. Rul. 75-283, 1975-2 C.B. 201.
[6]Rev. Rul. 73-128, 1973-1 C.B. 222; Priv. Ltr. Rul. 9150052.
[7]Rev. Rul. 70-585, 1970-2 C.B. 115.
[8]Rev. Rul. 78-428, 1978-2 C.B. 177; Rev. Rul. 76-22, 1976-1 C.B. 148.
[9]Rev. Rul. 77-246, 1977-2 C.B. 190.
[10]Rev. Rul. 75-198, 1975-1 C.B. 157.
[11]Rev. Rul. 69-441, 1969-2 C.B. 115.
[12]Rev. Rul. 55-406, 1955-1 C.B. 73.
[13]Rev. Rul. 70-583, 1970-2 C.B. 114; Rev. Rul. 67-150, 1967-1 C.B. 133; Rev. Rul. 76-21, 1976-1 C.B. 147.
[14]Rev. Rul. 69-174, 1969-1 C.B. 149.
[15]Rev. Rul. 70-533, 1970-2 C.B. 112.
[16]*Industrial Aid for the Blind v. Commissioner*, 73 T.C. 96 (1979), *acq.* C.B. 1980-2, 1.

workers of a particular business[17] was not exempt perhaps for the unexpressed reason that the organization relieved the burden in the company. Also, a discount pharmaceutical service for senior citizens[18] could not qualify because it made no provision for free or reduced-price drugs for the poor, and was therefore indistinguishable from a commercial business.

4.2 PROMOTION OF SOCIAL WELFARE

"Promotion of social welfare" is another mission considered legitimate for charitable organizations. One of the vaguest categories, it includes working to:

- Eliminate discrimination and prejudice in the workplace,[19] neighborhoods,[20] housing,[21] and against women;[22]

- Defend human and civil rights,[23] including the right to work;[24]

- Combat community deterioration,[25] lessen neighborhood tensions and combat juvenile delinquency;[26]

- Improve the economic climate in a depressed area;[27]

- Encourage building of low-cost housing[28] and monitor zoning regulations;[29]

- Acquire, restore, and maintain historic properties;[30]

- Preserve and protect the environment,[31] including instituting litigation as a party plaintiff to enforce environmental protection laws,[32] and conducting legal research to settle international environmental disputes through mediation;[33]

[17]Rev. Rul. 56-138, 1956-1 C.B. 202.
[18]*Federation Pharmacy Service, Inc. v. U.S.*, 625 F.2d 804 (8th Cir. 1980), *aff'g* 72 T.C. 687 (1979).
[19]Rev. Rul. 68-70, 1968-1, C.B. 248; Rev. Rul. 75-285, 1975-2 C.B. 203.
[20]Rev. Rul. 68-655, 1968-2 C.B. 613.
[21]Rev. Rul. 68-438, 1968-2 C.B. 609; Rev. Rul. 67-250, 1967-2 C.B. 182.
[22]Rev. Rul. 72-228, 1972-1 C.B. 148.
[23]Rev. Rul. 73-285, 1973-2 C.B. 174.
[24]*National Right to Work Legal Defense and Education Foundation, Inc. v. U.S.*, 487 F. Supp. 801 (E.D. N.Car. 1979).
[25]Rev. Rul. 76-147, 1976-1 C.B. 151.
[26]Rev. Rul. 68-15, 1968-1 C.B. 244.
[27]Rev. Rul. 76-419, 1976-2 C.B. 146; Rev. Rul. 77-111, 1977-1 C.B. 144.
[28]Rev. Rul. 67-138, 1967-1 C.B. 129.
[29]Rev. Rul. 68-15, *supra*, n. 26.
[30]Rev. Rul. 86-49, 1986-1 C.B. 243
[31]Rev. Rul. 67-292, 1967-2 C.B. 184; Rev. Rul. 76-204, 1976-1 C.B. 152.
[32]Rev. Rul. 80-278, 1980-2 C.B. 175.
[33]Rev. Rul. 80-279, 1980-2 C.B. 176.

- Promote of world peace, except through illegal protests;[34] and

- Maintain and set aside public parks and wildlife areas.[35]

Organizations qualifying in this category operate to benefit the community, which may be a town, the state, or the world. Under the social welfare umbrella, legislative initiative is one of the tools used to accomplish the organization's goals. If the social welfare can only be promoted through passage of legislation, the action organization rules may prevent charitable status. See the §501(c)(4) discussion and Chapters 6 and 23 concerning lobbying.

4.3   LESSENING THE BURDENS OF GOVERNMENT

"Lessening the burdens of government" overlaps social welfare and may include providing services usually rendered by a governmental agency, i.e., those facilities and services ordinarily furnished at taxpayer expense. Some disparate examples of projects qualifying as charitable under this category are:

- Erecting or maintenance of public buildings, monuments, or works;[36]

- Combating drug traffic;[37]

- Public transportation extension to an isolated community[38] or making grants to a city transit authority;[39]

- Maintaining a professional standards review committee to oversee Medicare or Medicaid programs;[40]

- Volunteer fire departments,[41] police performance award programs,[42] and

- Assisting police and fire departments during disasters.[43]

To test a proposed organization for qualification under this section, ask whether individual citizens normally provide the services for themselves. In some cities, the municipality provides garbage pickup for individuals, but not for businesses. Thus, an organization picking up commercial organizations' garbage would not lessen governmental burdens. It could, however, possibly qualify under the promotion of health category, if proper disposal of garbage can be tied to public health.

[34] Rev. Rul. 75-384, 1975-2 C.B. 204.
[35] Rev. Rul. 70-186, 1970-1 C.B. 128; Rev. Rul. 75-85, 1978-1 C.B. 150.
[36] Reg. §1.501(c)(3)-1(d)(2).
[37] Rev. Rul. 85-1, 1985-1 C.B. 177.
[38] Rev. Rul. 78-68, 1978-1 C.B. 149.
[39] Rev. Rul. 71-29, 1971-1 C.B. 150.
[40] Rev. Rul. 81-276, 1981-2 C.B. 128.
[41] Rev. Rul. 74-361, 1974-2 C.B. 159.
[42] Rev. Rul. 74-246, 1974-1 C.B. 130.
[43] Rev. Rul. 71-99, 1971-1 C.B. 151.

Whether or not an organization lessens the burdens of government is a matter of what the government "objectively manifests" its burdens to be. The degree of cooperation and involvement with the governmental body whose burdens are lessened is also relevant.[44]

During 1991, applications for exemption under this category were "national office" cases, meaning that they could be approved only by the Washington office, not by the key district offices. The import of this policy is that it is up to the government to decide whether its burdens need relieving. Without either written delegation of such responsibility or enabling legislation providing the framework, such exemptions are difficult to obtain. A two-part test is applied:

1. Are the activities the EO engages in ones which a governmental unit considers to be its burden, and does the governmental unit recognize that the EO as acting on its behalf?

2. Does the EO's performance of the activities actually lessen the burden of government?

The strictness with which the IRS determination branch applies this test caused Prison Industries, Inc. to fail to achieve exempt status. While federal and some state statutes encourage productivity of prisoners and programs providing for their rehabilitation, the rules specifically prohibit sales to the public in competition with private enterprise—the program which Prison Industries, Inc. planned. Thus, exempt status was denied.[45]

Proving that the EO will lessen the burden of government requires also that there be agreement on what those burdens are and whether or not it is the responsibility of the government to relieve them, which sometimes becomes a political philosophy question. Particularly when the government is not shouldering its burden, it may be difficult to qualify for this exemption.

In the case of a business consulting service, the "mere fact that [the EO's] activities might improve the general economic well-being of the nation or a state or reduce any adverse impact from the failure of government to carry out such activities is not enough" to prove that an EO is relieving the burden of government.[46] In other words, the fact that the government is not conducting the program may indicate that it is not the burden of government. Similarly, an EO operating a state motor vehicle registration office was not merely performing a service for the government for a fee is relieving the burdens of government.[47] Such a project might have more success applying to qualify as charitable under another category. Conversely, in private ruling 9243008, an entity that maintains databases of information, including vehicle registration, electronic tax filings, legal research, and state and federal court opinions and dockets, was determined to lessen the burden of government. This EO was created as a result of a state commission's recommendation. It was granted state

[44] Rev. Rul. 85-2, 1985-1 C.B. 178.
[45] *Prison Industries, Inc. v. Commissioner*, T.C.M. Dec. 47, 104(M), January 8, 1991.
[46] *B.S.W. Group, Inc. v. Commissioner*, 70 T.C. 352, 359 (1978); 838 F.2d 465 (4th Cir. 1988), *aff'g* 88 T.C. 1, 21 (1987).
[47] Tech. Adv. Memo. 9208002.

funds to purchase it original equipment. State agencies would have to perform its functions if it did not. Only 43 percent of the EO's customers paid for the information, with its remaining support coming from state and Federal government grants.

Note that this category applies to organizations operating independently of government, not as a branch, division, or agency of a governmental body. Instrumentalities of states and cities are technically not exempt under §501(c)(3), but rather under a concept of governmental immunity. Interestingly, governmental organizations do qualify to receive charitable contributions under IRC §170. See Section 11.2 for a discussion of the definition of a governmental unit.

4.4   ADVANCEMENT OF RELIGION

"Advancement of religion" is included under charitable purposes in the Regulations, and includes peripheral religious activities outside the real of sacerdotal functions. This category might include a religious publishing house or broadcast radio or TV station, a retreat center, or a burial group. These groups are discussed in Section 3.1(b) and (c).

4.5   ADVANCEMENT OF EDUCATION AND SCIENCE

"Advancement of education and science" reiterates two purposes specifically named in §501(c)(3). Perhaps it was added to clarify that auxiliary activities carried on separately from established educational or scientific institutions are exempt. Organizations qualifying under this category include those sponsoring:

- Scholarship programs,[48] even for members of a particular fraternity,[49] but not for contestants who had to participate in the Miss America Beauty Pageant to qualify;[50]

- Low-interest college loans[51] and student food and housing programs;[52]

- Vocational training for unemployed workers,[53] but not operation of a grocery store's training program;[54]

- National honor societies;[55]

- Foreign exchange programs;[56]

- Film series and bookstores;[57]

[48]Rev. Rul. 69-257, 1969-1 C.B. 151; Rev. Rul. 66-103, 1866-1 C.B. 134.
[49]Rev. Rul. 56-403, 1956-2 C.B. 307.
[50]*Miss Georgia Scholarship Fund, Inc. v. Commissioner*, 72 T.C. 267 (1979).
[51]Rev. Rul. 63-220, 1963-2 C.B. 208; Rev. Rul. 61-87, 1961-1 C.B. 191.
[52]Rev. Rul. 67-217, 1967-2 C.B. 181.
[53]Rev. Rul. 73-128, 1973-1 C.B. 222.
[54]Rev. Rul. 73-129, 1973-1 C.B. 221.
[55]Rev. Rul. 71-97, 1971-1 C.B. 150.
[56]Rev. Rul. 80-286, 1980-2 C.B. 179.
[57]*Squire v. Students Book Corp.*, 191 F.2d 1018 (9th Cir. 1951).

- Maintenance of library collections and bibliographic computer information networks;[58]

- Research journals[59] and law reviews;[60] and

- Medical seminars to provide postgraduate education to physicians.[61]

4.6 PROMOTION OF HEALTH

"Promotion of health" as a charitable pursuit is conspicuously absent from the Regulations. However, it took a court to remind the IRS that promotion of health is a charitable purpose under the law of charitable trusts.[62] Hospitals, clinics, homes for the aged, hospices, medical research organizations, mental health facilities, blood banks, home health agencies, organ donor retrieval centers, and many other entities perform health care.

The criteria for exemption under this category have been developed to distinguish charitable entities from privately owned businesses that provide identical health services. The issues involve charity care, private inurement, homes for the aged, health maintenance organizations (HMOs), medical centers, and hospital holding companies. The rules are constantly evolving, so any organization seeking qualification under this category must check the latest developments. The specific questions asked by the IRS on Schedule C of Form 1023 (Appendix 18-1) are very instructive. As the cost of medical care accelerated in the 1980s and the number of persons to whom such care was unavailable rose, pressure mounted on Congress to change the rules.

(a) Charity Care

The IRS's initial opinion on this subject was that a charity hospital "must be operated to the extent of its financial ability for those not able to pay for the services rendered and not exclusively for those who are able and expected to pay."[63] In 1969, the IRS eased this policy and recognized that the charitable purpose of promoting health is served even if the cost is borne by patients and insurance companies.[64] Later, the IRS refined its position: "[T]o be exempt a hospital must promote the health of a class of persons broad enough to benefit the community and must be operated to serve a public rather than a private interest."[65] Management style and financial facts which distinguish an exempt hospital from a for-profit one provide the evidence of public purpose. Non-

---

[58] Rev. Rul. 81-29, 1981-1 C.B. 329.
[59] Rev. Rul. 67-4, 1967-1 C.B. 121.
[60] Rev. Rul. 63-235, 1963-2 C.B. 210.
[61] Rev. Rul. 65-298, 1965-2 C.B. 163.
[62] *Eastern Kentucky Welfare Rights Organization v. Simon*, 506 F.2d 1278, 1287 (D.C. Cir. 1974).
[63] Rev. Rul. 56-185, 1956-1 C.B. 202.
[64] Rev. Rul. 69-545, 1969-2 C.B. 117.
[65] Exempt Organizations Handbook (IRM 7751) §343.5(2); Rev. Rul. 83-157, 1983-2 C.B. 94.

profit or community benefit standards or indicators include:

- Control by a community-based board of directors with no financial interest in the hospital;

- Open medical staff with privileges available to all qualified physicians;

- Emergency room open to all (unless this duplicates services provided by another institution in the area);

- Provision of public health programs and extensive research and medical training;

- No unreasonable accumulation of surplus funds;

- Limited funds invested in for-profit subsidiaries; and

- A high level of receivables from uncollected billings.

(b) Evolving Rules

In June 1990, the House Select Committee on Aging held hearings on hospital clientele and tax-exempt status. As of October 1992, no new legislation has passed, but the reader should be on the alert for it. The effective date of the Donnelly bill discussed below is immediate, so hospitals must be vigilant in monitoring the latest congressional and IRS developments.

The focus of the testimony was on charity care: Do tax-exempt hospitals provide enough care for those that cannot pay, and how much should they provide? The Government Accounting Office (GAO) released a study entitled *Nonprofit Hospitals: Better Standards Needed for Tax Exemption.* The study quantified the relationship between charity care and the value of federal and state exemptions. In 57 percent of the hospitals studied, the value of the charity care (not counting bad debt) was less than the tax benefits received by the organization, and the GAO concluded that a disproportionate share of charity care is provided by major urban teaching hospitals. The GAO recommended that criteria for tax exemption be revised to require certain levels of care to Medicaid patients, free care to the poor, or emphasis on improving the health of underserved portions of the community in which the hospital is located.

The IRS Assistant Chief Counsel for Employee Benefits and Exempt Organizations, James McGovern, reviewed the history of the tax law of health care organizations. At the hearing, he commented that the IRS would continue to follow its existing "community benefit" standard outlined above, which contains no specific numerical levels of charity care. At the minimum, he said, the IRS would expect all hospitals to meet the Medicare standards which require emergency facilities to be open to all regardless of ability to pay. He announced that the IRS would conduct joint audits with the Department of Health and Human Services, using teams of experts including exempt organization specialists, income tax agents, lawyers, and computer auditors, all with expertise in the health care field.

Representative Edward R. Roybal, chairman of the House Select Committee on Aging, has more specific proposals that he calls the Charity Care Act. As drafted, this proposal contains two specific requirements for exempt hospitals:

1. Serve a reasonable number, proportionate to the hospital's size, of Medicaid patients in a nondiscriminatory manner and provide documentation to that effect, and

2. Provide charity health care in a nondiscriminatory manner that at least equals the value of the hospital's tax benefits (calculated on a value of charges basis), unless the hospital can demonstrate financial inability.

Representative Brian Donnelly has introduced another legislative proposal under which a tax-exempt hospital would have to meet one of the following criteria:

1. The hospital is a sole community hospital for Medicare purposes, i.e., the hospital is located more than 35 miles from any other hospital;

2. The hospital serves a disproportionate share of low-income individuals and receives additional Medicare or Medicaid payments for such patients;

3. The hospital's percentage of indigent patients is within one standard deviation of the mean of all hospitals within the geographic area used to calculate Medicare wage adjustments;

4. Five percent or more of the hospital's gross revenue is devoted to the provision of charity care (not including bad debts); and

5. At least 10 percent of the hospital's gross revenue is used to provide "qualified services and benefits" in its community, including a community health center located in a medically underserved area offering primary health care, a drug addiction or substance abuse clinic, or other services to be outlined in the regulations.

In its 1990 *Audit Guide for Providers of Health Care Services*, the American Institute of Certified Public Accountants (AICPA) requires financial statement disclosure of charity care policies and the dollar amount of the hospital's charity care. The definition of "sufficient qualified charity care" is also under review.

The loss of tax-exempt status has expensive consequences for hospitals. These include loss of deductibility for donors, liability for income tax on any profits, loss of state and local property tax exemptions, and inability to issue private activity bonds. Thus, the hospital is deprived of its normal source of low-cost building capital, which presumably is fully available only if its bonds are tax-exempt to the purchasers (see Appendix 28–1).

(c) Private Inurement

To achieve and maintain tax exemption, a health care organization must operate to benefit the public, not its medical staff. The IRS closely scrutinizes contractual relationships with physicians. Factors that work against exemption include:

- Favorable rental rates and exclusive use of facilities to a limited group of doctors;[66]

- Profitable services (e.g., a lab) operated by private owners;[67]

- A newly-established EO paying a high price to purchase a proprietary hospital;[68]

- Excessive compensation to medical staff (Chapter 20) and joint ventures (Chapter 22).

(d) Care for the Aged

Until 1972,[69] homes for senior citizens were required to provide free or low-cost services. Today, a charitable home must provide for the primary needs of the aging—housing, health care, and financial security. In seeking approval for exemption, a home must furnish detailed information about its proposed or actual operation on Schedule F of Form 1023 (Appendix 18-1) The questions address the following specific tests that a home must meet to qualify as charitable:[70]

1. Have a commitment to maintain in the residence any person who becomes unable to pay his or her regular charges, or do all that is possible to make other suitable arrangements for their care.

2. Provide its services at the lowest feasile cost, taking the facts and circumstances of the home into account (for example, cost of facility or wages in the area).

3. The fees charged must be affordable by a significant segment of the elderly population so as to evidence benefit to the community in which it is located.

4. Because the homes cannot expel aged residents who become unable to pay, the home may adopt policies to protect itself financially. The home may require its applicants to surrend their assets, or at least sufficient assets to secure their care. The IRS approved the policy of a home which actuarially calculated the amount of assets that had to be deposited upon admission.[71] A home might also permit residents to establish trusts, the income of which is payable to the home during the

---

[66]*Harding Hospital, Inc. v. U.S.*, 505 F.2d 1068 (6th Cir. 1974); *Sonora Community Hospital v. Commissioner*, 46-T.C. 519 (1966), *aff'd*, 397 F.2d 814 (9th Cir. 1968).
[67]Rev. Rul. 69-383, 1969-2 C.B. 113.
[68]*State v. Wilmar Hospital*, 2 N.W. 2d 564 (Sup. Ct. Minn. 1942).
[69]Rev. Rul. 72-124, 1972-1 C.B. 145.
[70]Rev. Rul. 79-18, 1979-1 C.B. 152.
[71]Priv. Ltr. Rul. 9225041.

resident's life. Income from trusts is exempt function income to the home.[72]

A pharmacy organized to furnish discount drugs to senior citizens was denied exemption because it operated for commercial purposes and had no charitable attributes such as low-cost or free drugs to the indigent.[73]

(e) Health Maintenance Organizations (HMOs)

Health maintenance organizations providing prepaid medical care to members can be exempt if a large enough charitable class is benefited. HMOs providing "commercial-type" insurance as a substantial part of their activities are not, however, tax exempt under §501(m), which was enacted as a part of the Tax Reform Act of 1986. Insubstantial insurance activity that does not prevent exemption is subject to unrelated business income tax.

In September 1990, the IRS issued a memo setting forth the criteria it would follow for issuing exemptions to HMOs.[74] The standards are designed to assure that HMOs operate to benefit the community, and are similar to those applied for exemption of hospitals. The criteria are as follows:

- Health care services and facilities are provided;

- Emergency treatment is available without regard to ability to pay and this fact is communicated to the public;

- Membership organizations must make efforts to expand the number of members to spread the cost among more persons, seek individual members, have no age or eligibility barriers, and charge individuals rates similar to those charged groups;

- Nonmembers are served on a fee-for-service basis;

- Medicare, Medicaid, and other publicly assisted patients are accepted, and care is provided at reduced rates for indigents;

- Health education and research programs are provided;

- Health care providers are paid fixed compensation (no incentive pay);

- Operating surpluses are dedicated to improving facilities and health care programs; and

- The community is broadly represented on the governing body.

(f) Other Care Providers

Medical Centers. Tax-exempt status for medical center holding companies is not necessarily assured. Recently, such organizations containing both for-profit and

---

[72]Rev. Rul. 81-61, 1981-1 C.B. 355.
[73]*Federation Pharmacy Service, Inc. v. U.S., supra,* n. 18. Likewise an organization formed to help senior citizens with funeral expenses could not be exempt unless it allowed indigents to participate. *El Paso Del Aquila Elderly,* T.C. Memo, 1992, 441.
[74]G.C.M. 39828.

nonprofit components have come under scrutiny from two sources. The IRS withheld private letter rulings in this area for several years and has examined a major hospital in each key district. If one looks to the states for guidance, the Supreme Court of Utah held that such a 21-hospital complex was indistinguishable from a for-profit enterprise and subjected the complex to property taxes.[75]

Health/Fitness Centers. Operation of a health and fitness center providing access to handicapped persons and offering reduced daily rates for persons of limited financial means serves a health care organization's exempt purposes.[76] As a part of a new medical complex, a sports and physical medicine facility was designed to serve patients referred by the center's hospitals and physicians, as well as the general public. What primarily distinguishes this center as a charitable facility is its provision of services to patients and employees of the medical center. Its availability to the general public is provided in a noncommercial manner and contributes to the center's exempt purpose of providing health care to the community in which it is located. It was therefore granted exemption.

A similar conclusion was reached regarding a wellness center created as a joint venture of an acute care hospital, its parent, and an orthopedic hospital. The facilities provide physical rehabilitation services to patients and to the general public. Because the membership fee structure permits access to the general public and the facility serves the creators' exempt health care purposes, the center was considered exempt.[77]

Physician Clinics. A clinic providing private medical care to individuals is normally owned by the doctors and operated for their profit-making purposes, and cannot qualify for tax exemption even though it operates for the exempt purpose of promoting health. However, when a clinic has no private ownership, provides a reasonable level of free or reduced charge care to members of a charitable class, and otherwise distinguishes itself as a charitable organization, exemption can be sought.

Clinics operated in conjunction with charity hospitals and medical schools, so-called "faculty practice plans," have traditionally been granted exemption, but there are few clear precedents in the area. In one case approving exemption for such a clinic, the physicians were staff members of a teaching hospital and full-time medical school faculty members.[78] About 25 percent of the patients were indigent or students, and medical research was conducted, evidencing a significant element of charitable purpose in addition to the promotion of health.

Professional Standards Review Organizations. Under Social Security legislation in 1972, Congress authorized the creation of Professional Standards Review Organizations (PSROs). PSROs monitor and establish cost and quality controls for

---

[75]*County Board of Utilization of Utah County v. Intermountain Health Care, Inc.,* 709 P.2d 265 (Utah 1986).

[76]Priv. Ltr. Rul. 8935061.

[77]Priv. Ltr. Rul. 9226055.

[78]*University of Maryland Physicians, P.A. v. Commissioner,* 41 T.C.M. 732 (1981); See also *University of Massachusetts Medical School Group Practice v. Commissioner,* 74 T.C. 1299 (1980).

hospitals in their area with the intention of reducing overutilization of government-financed health programs. PSRO members must be licensed physicians. The exemption issue is whether the PSRO serves the public or the individual doctor members and the medical profession. A PSRO must possess the following attributes to qualify for exemption as a charity—otherwise, it may qualify as a business league:[79]

- It must operate to assure quality and care utilization for Medicare and Medicaid patients;

- Membership is open to all physicians without charge;

- The governing body cannot be controlled by or tied to a medical society; and

- The PSRO is authorized to act under the federal statutes.

4.7 COOPERATIVE HOSPITAL SERVICE ORGANIZATIONS

IRC §501(e) provides that a cooperative hospital service organization is a charitable organization. Two or more hospitals, either one of which meets the qualifications of IRC §170(b)(1)(A)(iii) or is operated by a governmental unit, may organize and operate under the following rules:

- It must perform, on a centralized basis, the following functions: data processing, purchasing (including insurance, warehousing, billing and collections, food, clinical, industrial engineering, laboratory, printing, communications, record center, and personnel (including selection, testing, training, and education);

- The cooperative cannot accumulate profits, but must distribute all net earnings to its patrons on the basis of services preformed for them; and

- Any stock issued by the cooperative must be owned by its patrons.

Note that the list does not include laundry—Congress deliberately omitted laundry services. The courts have agreed that only the specified services listed in the code may be performed on a cooperative basis.[80] A group providing laundry service may be treated as a cooperative under IRC §1388.

[79]Rev. Rul. 81-276, 1981-2 C.B. 128.
[80]*HCSC-Laundry v. U.S.*, 450 U.S. 1 (1981).

Educational, Scientific, and Literary Purposes and Prevention of Cruelty to Children and Animals

5.1 EDUCATIONAL PURPOSES

Educational purposes include "instruction or training of individuals to improve or develop their capabilities; or instruction of the public on subjects useful to the individual and beneficial to the community."[1] The regulation gives the following four examples of educational organizations:

- Primary or secondary school, colleges, or professional or trade schools.

- Public discussion groups, forums, panels, lectures, or similar programs. Such programs can be on radio or television.

[1]Reg. §1.501(c)(3)-1(d)(3).

- Organizations that presents courses of instruction by means of correspondence or through the utilization of television or radio.

- Museums, zoos, planetariums, symphony orchestras, and other similar organizations.

(a) Schools

Schools are granted public status regardless of their sources of support and are narrowly defined to include formal institutions with the following characteristics:[2]

- Regular faculty;

- Regularly scheduled curriculum;

- Regularly enrolled body of students in attendance at the location where the educational activities take place.

The following educational organizations have also been ruled to be schools:

- Early childhood education centers;[3]

- Boards of education which employ all the teachers in a school system and which supervise all the schools in a district.[4]

(b) Race Discrimination

Schools must also adopt and practice policies prohibiting racial discrimination and announce the policy by publishing it in a newspaper. A private school that adopted a nondiscrimination policy in connection with seeking application for recognition of its exemption as an educational organization was denied exemption when the facts revealed that it in fact did discriminate—it failed the "good faith" test. The Tax Court denied tax exemption for Calhoun Academy because the "clear and convincing evidence" indicated that the school operated in a discriminatory fashion. The school was established concurrently with court-ordered desegregation plans. Although the community in which it was located was 50 percent black, no black student had ever been admitted. The school argued, unsuccessfully, that none had applied. Although the school had been in existence for 15 years, the nondiscrimination policy was only implemented in connection with the exemption application. The Court noted that a school could qualify for tax-exempt status without establishing that it took the specific affirmative acts set forth in the IRS procedures, if in fact it operates in a racially nondiscriminatory manner.[5] See Form 5578, Appendix 27–4.

---

[2]*Id.*, n.1.
[3]*Michigan Early Childhood Center, Inc. v. Commissioner*, 37 T.C.M. 808 (1978); *San Francisco Infant School, Inc. v. Commissioner*, 69 T.C. 957 (1978); Rev. Rul. 70-533, 1970-2 C.B. 112.
[4]*Estate of Ethel P. Green v. Commissioner*, 82 T.C. 843 (1984).
[5]*Calhoun Academy v. Commissioner*, 94 T.C. 17 (1990).

(c) Day Care Centers

IRC §501(k) states that "providing care of children away from their homes" is an educational and therefore exempt purpose if:

- Substantially all of the care (at least 85 percent) is provided to enable individuals to be gainfully employed (including employees, self-employed, enrolled students or vocational trainees, and individuals who are actively seeking employment);[6] and

- The day care is available to the general public. Limitations based upon a geographic or political boundary are permissible. Restricting enrollment to children of employees of a particular employer, however, is not.[7]

Providing day care referrals and assistance information to the general public, however, is a service which the IRS says is ordinarily a commercial activity. Counseling parents and caregivers about day care was found not to be per se an educational or charitable activity. In an entity where 98 percent of its revenues came from charges for its services, the IRS refused to grant exempt status under IRC §501(c)(3).[8]

(d) Cooperative Educational Service Organizations

IRC §501(f) was added to the Code to sanction pooled investing by educational institutions. To qualify, the organization must be:

- Organized and operated to hold, commingle, and collectively invest and reinvest in stocks and securities, the moneys contributed by its members and to collect the income therefrom, and pay over the entire amount, less expenses, to the members;

- Organized and controlled by its members;

- Composed solely of organizations qualifying as schools under IRC §170(b)(1)(A)(ii) or IRC §115(a) (state schools).

(e) Informal Education

Organizations that present instructional materials or training on a less formal basis than a school can qualify as educational if they operate to benefit the general public. Discussion groups, retreat centers, apprentice training programs, and the many other types of educational programs listed below are exempt if

---

[6]Exempt Organization Handbook (IRM 7751) §345(11)2.
[7]G.C.M. 39613 and G.C.M. 39347.
[8]G.C.M. 39872, modifying G.C.M. 39622.

they can prove they provide the requisite instruction for the benefit of individuals:

- Training programs for bankers,[9] physicians,[10] artists,[11] credit union managers,[12] and dancers;[13]

- Travel study tours led by professionals which provide genuine cultural and educational programs, with no or limited recreational aspects;[14]

- On-the-job training of unemployed and underemployed workers, even if the toys they manufacture are sold;[15]

- Trade skill training for American Indians;[16]

- Counseling and educational instruction through publications concerning homosexuals[17] and voluntary sterilization methods;[18]

- Student and cultural exchange programs;[19]

- Studying and publishing reports on Civil War battles[20] or career planning and vocational counseling;[21]

- Computer users' groups are not exempt if their membership is limited to persons using a particular type of computer,[22] but they may qualify as business leagues (see Chapter 8).

(f) Performing Arts

Performing arts organizations presenting music, drama, poetry, film, and dance are classified as cultural, and thus, as educational organizations. Symphony orchestras, theaters, public television and radio, and other performing groups easily gain exempt status if they meet the basic organizational and operational tests. The few rulings on the subject follow:

- Repertory theater established to develop the public's interest in dramatic arts, and a foundation funding local community theaters;[23]

- Jazz music appreciation society presenting festivals and concerts;[24]

[9]Rev. Rul. 68-504, 1968-2 C.B. 211.
[10]Rev. Rul. 65-298, 1965-2 C.B. 163.
[11]Rev. Rul. 67-392, 1967-2 C.B. 191.
[12]Rev. Rul. 74-16, 1974-1 C.B. 126.
[13]Rev. Rul. 65-270, 1965-2 C.B. 160.
[14]Rev. Rul.70-534, 1970-2 C.B. 113.
[15]Rev. Rul. 73-128, 1973-1 C.B. 222.
[16]Rev. Rul. 77-272, 1977-2 C.B. 191.
[17]Rev. Rul. 78-305, 1978-2 C.B. 172.
[18]Rev. Rul. 74-595, 1974-2 C.B. 164.
[19]Rev. Rul. 80-286, 1980-2 C.B. 179; Rev. Rul. 68-165, 1968-1 C.B. 253.
[20]Rev. Rul. 67-148, 1967-1 C.B. 132.
[21]Rev. Rul. 79-71, 1968-1 C.B. 249.
[22]Rev. Rul. 74-116, 1974-1 C.B. 127.
[23]Rev. Rul. 64-175, 1964-1 (Part 1) C.B. 185; Rev. Rul. 64-174, 1964-1 (Part 1) C.B. 183.
[24]Rev. Rul. 65-271, 1965-2 C.B. 161.

- Weekly workshops, public concerts, and booking agency for young musicians;[25]

- Sponsor of annual film festival and symposium promoting unknown independent filmmakers;[26]

- Producer of cultural, educational, and public interest films that distributes them through public educational channels[27] or makes equipment available to the public to produce programs;[28]

Co-production of performances with commercial businesses can present challenges to an organization. See Section 22.3 for a discussion of permissible joint venture activities.

(g) Museums, Libraries, and Zoos

Organizations that collect and exhibit objects of a literary, artistic, historic, biological or other educational nature for the general public qualify as exempt educational organizations. There are few rulings on this subject, but the IRS has ruled that the following activities are educational:

- Acquiring, restoring, preserving, and opening to the public homes, churches, and public buildings having historic significance;[29]

- Operating a wild bird and animal sanctuary;[30]

- Operating a sports museum;[31]

- Operating the library of a bar association;[32]

- Organizing an international exposition;[33] and

- Promoting unknown but promising artists through exhibitions of their work[34] but cooperative art sales galleries are not exempt.[35]

(h) Sale of Art Objects

An art gallery that sells the works of art it exhibits must overcome a presumption that it is operating a business, rather than serving a purely educational purpose which would entitle it to exemption. The question is whether taking home the object enhances the customer's educational experience and thereby

[25] Rev. Rul. 67-392, 1967-2 C.B. 191.
[26] Rev. Rul. 75-471, 1975-2 C.B. 207.
[27] Rev. Rul. 76-4, 1976-1 C.B. 145.
[28] Rev. Rul. 76-443, 1976-2 C.B. 149.
[29] Rev. Rul. 75-470, 1975-2 C.B. 207.
[30] Rev. Rul. 67-292, 1967-2 C.B. 184.
[31] Rev. Rul. 68-372, 1968-2 C.B. 205.
[32] Rev. Rul. 75-196, 1975-1 C.B. 155.
[33] Rev. Rul. 71-545, 1971-2 C.B. 235.
[34] Rev. Rul. 66-178, 1966-1 C.B. 138.
[35] Rev. Rul. 71-395, 1971-2 C.B. 228.

produces "related" income. The answer depends upon whether the object is an original work of craft, an original work of fine art, a reproduction or replica of an object, or a handicraft item. An organization whose unrelated business activity is more than insubstantial (commonly thought to equal 15 percent) may not qualify for exemption. (See Section 21.19 for more details about art sales.)

(i) Publishing

Publishing projects have been a subject of controversy with the IRS. It is not sufficient that the subject matter of the published work be religious, cultural, scientific, or educational. An exempt publishing company must distinguish itself from a commercial one in the following ways:[36]

- The content of the publication must be educational;

- Preparation of the materials follows methods generally accepted as educational;

- Distribution of the materials is necessary or valuable in achieving the organization's educational and scientific purposes; and

- The manner in which the distribution is accomplished is distinguishable from ordinary commercial publishing practices.

Organizations distributing educational materials free[37] or at a nominal price[38] indisputably operate in a noncommercial manner. However, publishing a foreign language magazine on a subscription basis at a price and through channels used by commercial publishers is not exempt.[39] (See Section 21.20.)

(j) Political and Controversial Materials

Controversial information on issues of public interest is not necessarily educational in the eyes of the IRS. To be educational, information must be useful to the individual and beneficial to the community. Presentation of a sufficiently full and fair exposition of the pertinent facts about a subject, rather than an unsupported opinion, can be educational.

For example, the IRS denied the exemption application of Big Mama Rag, a lesbian newspaper, for failing the "full and fair" test. Upon appeal, the court found the Regulation's definition of education to be unconstitutional due to its vagueness. The court felt that it allowed the IRS too much administrative discretion in granting exemptions.[40]

However, the IRS continues to apply this vague "standard" without revision. Particularly in the case of issues that may be the subject of legislation

---

[36] Exempt Organization Handbook (IRM 7751) §345.(10)2; Rev. Rul. 67-4, 1967-1 C.B. 121.
[37] Rev. Rul. 66-147, 1966-1 C.B. 137.
[38] Rev. Rul. 68-307, 1968-1 C.B. 258.
[39] Rev. Rul. 77-4, 1977-1 C.B. 141.
[40] Big Mama Rag, Inc. v. U.S., 631 F. 2d 1030 (D.C. Cir. 1980).

or political debate, such as war or abortion, the question is not only whether the material is educational. A parallel, but different, issue is advocacy. Espousing a particular viewpoint with sufficient presentation of facts does not necessarily preclude exemption if the organization's goals can be accomplished without legislation. Classification as an action, or lobbying, organization, however, can. See Chapter 23 for further discussion.

5.2 LITERARY PURPOSES

In this category, the regulations are silent and contain no definition or criteria for qualification. Since literature is both educational and cultural, a literary organization can be exempt under one or both of those categories.

The most troublesome issue would involve private inurement. An organization established to encourage "emerging" writers by publishing their works in the small press market must prove that it does not primarily benefit the individual writers, but instead promotes literature or culture in a global sense. See the discussion of publishing in Sections 5.1(i) and 21.20.

Examples of literary pursuits include publishing of literature, including poetry, essays, fiction, nonfiction, and all other forms of written compositions. Other examples include a sponsor of poetry readings, a literary workshop to teach writing skills, a critical journal of reviews, a committee to aware a prize for excellence in literature (such as the Pulitzer Prize), and a preservation society for rare books.

5.3 SCIENTIFIC PURPOSES

The IRS admitted in 1966 that the term "scientific" is not one definable with precision.[41] The Regulations provide only that "scientific" includes the carrying on of scientific research in the public interest. Furthermore, the Regulations say, Research when taken alone is a word with many meanings; it is not synonymous with scientific and the nature of particular research depends upon the purpose which it serves. The determination as to whether research is "scientific" does not depend on whether such research is classified as "fundamental" or basic as contrasted with "applied" or practical.[42]

This apparent ambiguity is addressed by the Regulations' very exact and specific standards for judging whether scientific research is conducted in the private interest:

1. Results of the research, including patents, copyrights, processes, or formulas, must be made available to the public on a nondiscriminatory basis.

2. Research is performed for a federal, state, or local government.

---

[41]Rev. Rul. 66-147, 1966-1 C.B. 137.
[42]Reg. §1.501(c)(3)-1(d)(5).

3. Work is directed toward benefiting the public, pursuant to the following reasons given in the Regulations:

- To aid in scientific education of college students;

- To obtain information toward a treatise, thesis, or trade publication, or in any form available to the general public;

- To discover a cure for disease; or

- To aid a community or geographic area in attracting development of new industries.

4. Scientific research does *not* include activities of a type ordinarily carried on as an incident to commercial or industrial operations, as, for example, the ordinary testing or inspection of materials or products, or the designing or construction of equipment, buildings, etc.[43] (See Section 5.4, Testing for Public Safety.)

5. Retaining ownership or control of more than an insubstantial portion of the patents, copyrights, processes, or formulae resulting from an organization's research and not making them available to the public disqualifies it from exempt status.[44] If granting an exclusive right is the only practical manner in which the patent can be utilized to benefit the public for research conducted for the government or for the purposes listed under the third standard above, the information can be withheld.[45]

6. An exempt organization that performs research only for its non-501(c)(3) creators cannot be classified as a 501(c)(3) organization.[46]

A combined educational and scientific purpose may also qualify an organization for exemption, as the following examples illustrate:

- Surveying scientific and medical literature and abstracting and publishing it free of charge is an exempt activity.[47]

- Developing treatment for human diseases and disseminating the results through physicians' seminars, is also an exempt activity.[48]

- Manufacturing cast reproductions of anthropological specimens for sale to scholars and educational institutions was found to support a charitable research purpose.[49]

[43] Rev. Rul. 65-1, 1965-1 C.B. 226; Rev. Rul. 68-373, 1968-2 C.B. 206.
[44] Rev. Rul. 76-296, 1976-2 C.B. 141 discusses the timing of the release of public information under two different scenarios. Publication as a general rule can be withheld until the patent is issued, but may not delayed to protect the sponsor's business interests.
[45] Reg. §1.501(c)(3)-1(d)(5)(iv)(b).
[46] Rev. Rul. 69-526, 1969-2 C.B. 115.
[47] Rev. Rul. 66-147, *supra* n. 41.
[48] Rev. Rul. 65-298, 1965-2 C.B. 163.
[49] Rev. Rul. 70-129, 1970-1 C.B. 128.

- Conducting seed technology research, approving certification of crop seeds within a state, and providing instruction in cooperation with a university are scientific activities, and are therefore exempt.[50]

5.4 TESTING FOR PUBLIC SAFETY

The Regulations give only one example of an organization qualifying because it tests for public safety, and this is an organization which tests consumer products, such as electrical products, to determine whether they are safe for use by the general public.[51] Other exempt programs might include testing for structural building strength against violent weather, such as hurricanes and tornadoes, or earthquakes. Testing boat equipment and establishing standards for pleasure craft was also ruled to be an exempt activity.[52]

Similar to the scientific research constraints, testing must be performed to serve a public benefit, rather than the interests of private owners, such as drug manufacturers. This distinction is not always clear. In a published ruling, the IRS found that testing, research, and other work toward developing methods and safety certifications for shipping containers benefited the shipping industry and advanced international commerce and, therefore, was not an exempt organization, despite the fact that the stevedores working with shipping containers constitute a charitable class whose safety is significant and worthy of testing.[53] Similarly, a drug company's testing program prior to approval by the Food and Drug Administration was ruled to serve the manufacturer's private interest.[54]

Perhaps because their funds are raised through the provision of services, these organizations do not qualify as charitable organizations eligible to receive deductible contributions under IRC §170(c), even though they do qualify as exempt under §501(c)(3). They are excepted from private foundation classification under IRC §509(a)(4) presumably because they are not funded with private donations.

5.5 FOSTERING NATIONAL OR INTERNATIONAL AMATEUR SPORTS COMPETITION (but only if no part of its activities involve the provision of athletic facilities or equipment)

The parenthetical qualification to this exemption category was added in 1976 to prevent athletic or social clubs from qualifying under IRC §501(c)(3), while allowing charitable status to the Olympic and Pan-American Games. In a seemingly redundant provision, Congress in 1982 stipulated in §501(j) that

---

[50]*Indiana Crop Improvement Association, Inc. v.*, 76 T.C. 394 400 (1981).
[51]Reg. §1.501(c)(3)-1(d)(4).
[52]Rev. Rul. 65-61, 1965-1 C.B. 234.
[53]Rev. Rul. 78-426, 1978-2 C.B. 175.
[54]Rev. Rul. 68-373, 1968-2 C.B. 206.

so-called "qualified" organizations are not subject to the restriction in the parentheses. Curiously, the definition of such organizations is identical to the §501(c)(3) definition just noted. The Regulations concerning the 1976 changes were withdrawn in 1984.

The only reported case in this area involved the International E22 Class Association.[55] The organization was established to formulate and enforce measurements of a particular type of racing sailboat used in international competition. In addition to setting the standard, the association sold tools to measure compliance during construction of the boats and during races. The IRS argued that such devices were athletic equipment and refused to grant the organization an exemption. The Tax Court disagreed, saying that the measurement tools were not facilities, as clubhouses, swimming pools, and gymnasiums are. Equipment means property used directly in athletic endeavors. The court was not aware of any athletic exercise, game, competition, or other endeavor in which the tools could be used.

A national high school athletic association does not qualify as an amateur sports organization under this section, but qualifies instead as a charitable and educational entity exempt under IRC §501(c)(3). The organization coordinates the efforts of state high school associations by sponsoring meetings and conferences, setting activity rules, publishing educational materials, and serving as the national governing body.[56]

Local amateur athletic groups—YWCAs, YMCAs, Little Leagues, etc.—need not qualify under this category because they can instead qualify under the charitable category. Such organizations have traditionally served youths and have thereby relieved the burdens of government and served the poor and disadvantaged.

5.6 PREVENTION OF CRUELTY TO CHILDREN OR ANIMALS

This is another exemption category without explanation in the IRS Regulations. Thankfully, a few published rulings provide guidelines, as the following examples of exempt activities show:

- Animal protection accomplished by accreditation of animal care facilities that supply, keep, and care for animals used by medical and scientific researchers;[57]

- Preventing birth of unwanted animals by providing low-cost spaying and neutering operations;[58]

- Monitoring of hazardous occupations for violations of state laws and unfavorable work conditions, in order to protect child workers.[59]

---

[55] *International E22 Class Association v. Commissioner*, 78 T.C. 93 (1982).
[56] Tech. Adv. Memo. 9211004.
[57] Rev. Rul. 66-359, 1966-2 C.B. 219.
[58] Rev. Rul. 74-194, 1974-1 C.B. 129.
[59] Rev. Rul. 67-151, 1967-1 C.B. 134.

A troublesome case might be the provision of veterinary services to individual pet owners. While it could be argued that such services prevent cruelty, there is an additional burden to prove the public usefulness of the effort. Certain treatments probably deserve and could gain charitable status, such as rabies control, but the absence of individual benefit ultimately has to be proved in order to obtain exemption.

Civic Leagues and Local Associations of Employees: §501(c)(4)

It is well-established that "[a]n organization may be created to carry out its purposes through the development and implementation of programs designed to have an impact on community, state or national policymaking."[1] Environmental protection, housing, civil rights, aid to the poor, world peace, or other public concerns may be involved. The pursuit of such subjects is the focus of both 501(c)(3) and 501(c)(4) organizations. The term "social welfare" appears in the Regulations defining "charitable" for 501(c)(3) purposes. The questions are what distinguishes a 501(c)(3) from a 501(c)(4) organization, and which category is most appropriate for any particular organization.

The Regulations for IRC §501(c)(4) were adopted in 1959 and cover only half a page. They list two basic types of organization that fall into this category:

Type 1. A civic league or organization that is not organized or operated for profit and is operated exclusively for promotion of social welfare. "To promote social welfare means to promote in some way the common good and general welfare of the people of the community."[2] The concept includes bringing about civic betterments and social improvements. The Regulations state that a social welfare organization will qualify for exemption as a charitable organization unless it is an "action" organization (see Section 2.2(g). As will be seen below,

---

[1]Hopkins, *The Law of Tax-Exempt Organizations, Sixth Edition,* p. 549.
[2]Reg. §1.501(c)(4)-1(a)(1)(2)(i).

the phrase "exclusively operated for civic welfare" does not prohibit an organization from earning some unrelated business income.

Type 2. A local association of employees whose membership is limited to the employees of a designated person or persons in a particular municipality and whose net earnings are devoted exclusively to charitable educational or recreational purposes.[3]

6.1 DIFFERENCES FROM 501(c)(3) ORGANIZATIONS

Four criteria distinguish a §501(c)(4) organization from a §501(c)(3) organization:

1. A §501(c)(4) organization can engage in extensive "action" or lobbying efforts to influence legislation by propaganda and other means.

2. A §501(c)(4) organization is not required to have a specific dissolution clause in its charter; its only organizational test is that it not be for profit.

3. Participation in political campaigns cannot be the primary purpose of a §501(c)(4) organization, but there is no absolute prohibition. Participation in political campaigns is not the promotion of social welfare, and the IRS has ruled that §527 taxes the organization to the extent of its political expenditures.[4]

4. Donations to §501(c)(4) organizations are not deductible as charitable gifts under IRC §170.

6.2 SIMILARITIES TO 501(c)(3) ORGANIZATIONS

§501(c)(4) organizations have several elements in common with 501(c)(3) groups. For example, they conduct similar social welfare activities—lessening neighborhood tensions, eliminating prejudice and discrimination, defending human and civil rights secured by law, and combating community deterioration and juvenile delinquency. Other parallels include:

- Neither type of organization may be organized or operated for profit;

- Both must benefit the "community," defined as a charitable class (for example, a poor group, a minority group, or the population of an entire city, country, or the world);

- Membership in both types of organization must be open, and cannot be restricted to a limited or select group of individuals or businesses; and

- No private inurement or benefit to a select group of insiders is permitted.

[3]Reg. §1.501(c)(4)-1(b).
[4]Rev. Rul. 81.95, 1981-1 C.B. 332.

6.3 CHOOSING TO APPLY UNDER §501(c)(3) VERSUS §501(c)(4)

It is possible for some organizations to qualify for exemption under both §501(c)(3) and §501(c)(4), so an important choice must be made when the organization applies for its exempt status. Most often, (c)(4) status is sought by organizations that plan "action" and expect to engage in extensive lobbying beyond the limits permitted under (c)(3). There are very few circumstances when (c)(4) would be chosen in preference to (c)(3), particularly when tax deductible contributions can be sought. Most commonly, (c)(4)s are established to operate in tandem with charitable organizations.

The right choice is critical. A (c)(3) organization that loses its exemption because it engages in excessive lobbying cannot then convert to the (c)(4) class, but instead loses its exempt status and becomes a taxable entity.[5] Intentional avoidance of this rule was anticipated by Congress. A transfer of assets by a (c)(3) to create a separate (c)(4) organization may result in loss of its exempt status. The excessive activity is attributed to a (c)(3) spinning off assets to carry on the lobbying in the following circumstances:[6]

- Over 30 percent of the net fair market value of the (c)(3)'s (other than a church) assets or 50 percent of the recipient organization's assets are transferred to a controlled non-(c)(3) entity which then conducts excessive lobbying;

- The transfer is within two years of the discovery of excessive lobbying; and

- Upon transfer or at any time within ten years following such a transfer, the transferee is controlled by the same persons who control the transferor. "Control" means that the persons in authority can, by using their voting power, require or prevent the transferee's spending of funds.[7]

6.4 CONVERSION TO §501(c)(3) STATUS

To explore the issues involved in converting a (c)(4) organization to a (c)(3), consider two examples:

Example 1. Representing the population of a planned community of 100,000 residents qualifies for §501(c)(4) status, not (c)(3), in the opinion of the Tax Court.[8] Columbia Park and Recreation Association (CPRA) was a non-profit organization formed to build and operate "facilities and services for the common good and social welfare of the people" of Columbia, Maryland; to represent property owners and residents with respect to owner assessment and collection of fees for such services; and to enforce property covenants.

---

[5]IRC § 504.
[6]Reg. §1.504-2(e) and (f).
[7]Reg. §53.4942(a)-3(a)(3).
[8]*Columbia Park and Recreation Association, Inc. v. Commissioner*, 88 T.C. 1 (1987).

CPRA built the public utility and transportation systems, parks, pools, neighborhood and community centers, and recreational facilities such as tennis courts, golf courses, a zoo, an ice rink, boat docks, and athletic clubs for the community. CPRA essentially functions like a municipality, but is not a political subdivision of the country in which it is located. CPRA was formed by the private developers of Columbia. Columbia has "villages" that have formed separate civic associations.

For the first 12 years of CPRA's existence, it was classified as a §501(c)(4) organization. To qualify for tax-favored bond financing, CPRA sought reclassification as a §501(c)(3) organization in 1982. The IRS denied the (c)(3) exemption based upon failure of both the operational and organizational test, as follows:

Private benefit and control. Regardless of the size of the group benefited (there was no argument that Columbia resembles a city that would qualify), CRPA is owned and controlled by the homeowners and residents, and serves their private interests. Every property owner possesses an ownership right in CPRA's facilities and services. The facilities open to the public represented less than two percent of the total, and out of 110,000 families, only 190 received reduced fees.

Funding source. Another factor distinguishing CPRA from a §501(c)(3) organization was its source of funds: no voluntary contributions were solicited from the public, and the sole source of financing was property owner fees, which are nondeductible for §170 purposes.

No charitable purpose. CRPA did not lessen the burdens of government. There was no proof that the State of Maryland or Howard County accepted such responsibilities and based upon documents regarding the public transportation system, Columbia was expected to bear the cost.

Dissolution clause. There are three possible recipients of CRPA's assets upon dissolution: Howard County, an agency or instrumentality of the county, or one of the village associations. The first two qualify as §501(c)(3) recipients, but the last does not because village associations are (c)(4) organizations. Thus, the assets are not dedicated permanently to §501(c)(3) purposes.

Example 2. A civic welfare organization operated to meet the financial and emotional needs of individuals employed in an industry worldwide was allowed to merge itself into its subsidiary §501(c)(3) organization, since it possessed the requisite charitable characteristics, as follows:[9]

Contributions. Over one third of the organization's support is received from contributions from the general public i.e., non-industry members.

Charitable services. Gerontology, social services (legal and emotional counseling), job placement for the unemployed, and scholarships were considered charitable services.

Charitable class. Because of its size (over 10,000 members), its dedication to members of a particular industry was ruled not to negate its charitable purposes.

In both examples, note that the organizational activities benefit a limited class of individuals. What distinguishes the two is (1) the character of the activities and (2) the sources of support. Relieving suffering in distress situations is generally considered charitable, as is promotion of health and educa-

[9]Priv. Ltr. Rul. 9019046.

tion. Recreation, preservation of property values, and commuting to work are not generally classified as charitable activities. See Section 22.2 on relationships between §501(c)(3) and §501(c)(4) organizations.

6.5 EXAMPLES OF QUALIFYING CIVIC ORGANIZATIONS

The primary characteristic of a qualifying civic league is that it operates to benefit the members of a community as a whole, be it the world or a small town, as opposed to operating a social club for the benefit, pleasure, or recreation of particular individuals. Social events sponsored by civic leagues are permitted, if they are incidental to the group's primary function.[10] One court stated that "the organization must be a community movement designed to acomplish community ends."[11] Another said, "In short, social welfare is the well-being of persons as a community."[12] The following projects have been determined to be qualifying activities for civic leagues:

- Tenants' legal rights defense groups.[13]

- Renewal projects in blighted areas of cities.

- Unemployment relief efforts organized to provide loans to purchase and develop land and facilities to create jobs,[14] and a credit counseling service to prevent bankruptcy in the community.[15]

- Amateur baseball league[16] and a sports organization promoting the interest of youths by giving them free tickets to sporting events, thereby providing wholesome entertainment for the welfare of the community's youths.[17]

- Bus line providing transportation from a suburb to major employment centers in a metropolitan area.[18] However, a bus operation for the convenience of employees of a particular corporation would not qualify.[19]

- Junior chambers of commerce customarily qualify.[20]

- Anti-abortion league formed to educate the public, promote the rights of the unborn, and lobby for legislation to restrict women's access to abortions.[21]

---

[10] Rev. Rul. 74-361, 1974-2 C.B. 159; Rev. Rul. 66-179, 1966-1 C.B. 139.
[11] *Erie Endowment v. U.S.*, 361 F.2d 151 (3rd Cir. 1963).
[12] *Commissioner v. Lake Forest, Inc.*, 305 F.2d 814 (4th Cir. 1962).
[13] Rev. Rul. 80-206, 1980-2 C.B. 185.
[14] Rev. Rul. 64-187, 1964-1 C.B. (Part 1) 354; Rev. Rul. 67-294, 1967-2 C.B. 193.
[15] Rev. Rul. 65-299, 1965-2 C.B. 165.
[16] Rev. Rul. 69-384, 1969-2 C.B. 112.
[17] Rev. Rul. 68-118, 1968-1 C.B. 261.
[18] Rev. Rul. 78-69, 1978-1 C.B. 156.
[19] Rev. Rul. 55-311, 1955-1 C.B. 72.
[20] Rev. Rul. 65-195, 1965-2 C.B. 164.
[21] Rev. Rul. 76-81, 1976-1 C.B. 156.

- Society presenting an annual festival to preserve ethnic culture.[22]

- Parks or gardens for beautification of a city, including a group formed to maintain the public areas of a particular block.[23]

- County recreation facilities.

- Garden club to bring civic betterment and social improvement.[24]

- Bridge club providing recreational activity for a nominal fee to a community.[25]

(a) Nonqualifying Groups

A civic organization which benefit private individuals or operates for profit cannot qualify as a (c)(4) organization. The following groups have failed to receive exemption:

- Tenants' association for a particular apartment complex, and condominium management[26] or residential real estate management associations (see IRC §528);

- Individual practice association of local doctors benefited the member physicians, not a community;[27]

- Pirate ship replica operation and staging of annual mock invasion and parade was for the benefit of its members;[28]

- An ethnic group, whose members live in an area and receive sickness and death benefits, operates for its members;[29]

- Television antenna group organized on a cooperative basis to improve reception for a remote area on a fee basis to members does not qualify,[30] but a group with the same purpose supported by voluntary contributions and available to all that live in the area can qualify;[31]

- An educational camp society, formed to provide a rural retreat for a school's faculty and students, does not benefit the community.[32] Also, a vacation home established and controlled by a corporation for its female employees would not be approved today by the IRS, despite the

[22]Rev. Rul. 68-224, 1968-1 C.B. 222.
[23]Rev. Rul. 68-14, 1968-1 C.B. 243, *as distinguished by* Rev. Rul. 75-286, 1975-2 C.B. 210.
[24]Rev. Rul. 66-179, 1966-1 C.B. 139.
[25]Tech. Adv. Memo. 9220010.
[26]Rev. Rul. 74-17, 1974-1 C.B. 130.
[27]Rev. Rul. 86-98, 1986-2 C.B. 74.
[28]*Ye Krewe of Gasparilla*, 80 T.C. 755, Dec. 40,052.
[29]Rev. Rul. 75-159, 1975-1 C.B. 48.
[30]Rev. Rul. 54-394, 1954-2 C.B. 131.
[31]Rev. Rul. 62-167, 1962-2 C.B. 142.
[32]*The People's Educational Camp Society, Inc. v. Commissioner*, 331 F.2d 923 (2d Cir. 1964), *aff'g* 39 T.C. 756 (1963), *cert. den.*, 379 U.S. 839 (1964).

facts that it was open for public use and the general public used it 20 percent of the time.[33]

- An antiwar protest group that encourages people to commit illegal acts during demonstrations operates against public policy and is not exempt.[34]

6.6 NEIGHBORHOOD AND HOMEOWNER ASSOCIATIONS

To qualify under §501(c)(4), an organization must serve a constituency that constitutes a community rather than a limited group of individuals. The homeowner association exemplifies this distinction, and the IRS has issued a series of contradictory revenue rulings over the years.

A definition of "community" that is sometimes helpful was provided in one ruling: "The term has traditionally been construed as having reference to a geographic unit bearing a reasonably recognizable relationship to an area ordinarily identified as a governmental subdivision or a unit or district thereof."[35] This is a difficult question for which no hard and fast rules are available; the facts and circumstances of each case are determinative.[36] Taken as a whole, the rulings indicate that to prove that an organization operates for the benefit of the community as opposed to individual residents, the following factors must be present:[37]

1. The association does not maintain private residences, either exterior or interior. Such services are prima facie evidence that an organization is operated for private benefit.[38]

2. Common areas, including streets, sidewalks, and parks, are open to the general public for their use and enjoyment without controlled access restricted to members. Subdivisions may form a separate social club to operate a swimming pool or other recreational facility from which they want to exclude the public.

3. Association is not limited to a particular commercial development unless it conducts only those activities customarily reserved to a municipality. This is sometimes a difficult question, as the *Columbia Park* case[39] discussed in Section 6.4 indicates.

4. The organization must not have as its sole purpose providing basic services to residents (such as garbage pickup and security patrol).

---

[33]Rev. Rul. 80-205, 1980-1 C.B. 184, issued by the IRS to say that it will not follow *Eden Hall Farm v. U.S.*, 389 F. Supp. 858 (W.D. Penn. 1975), which held that a farm did qualify because the group of working women it served represented a community.
[34]Rev. Rul. 75-384, 1975-2 C.B. 204.
[35]Rev. Rul. 74-99, 1974-1 C.B. 131.
[36]Rev. Rul. 80-63, 1980-1 C.B. 116.
[37]Rev. Rul. 67-6, 1967-1 C.B. 135; Rev. Rul. 72-102, 1972-1 C.B. 149, mod. by Rev. Rul. 76-147, 1976-1 C.B. 151;
[38]Rev. Rul. 74-99, supra n. 34.
[39]*Columbia Park and Recreation Association, Inc. v. Commissioner*, supra n. 7.

5. Enforcing covenants for architectural appearance and limitations on commercial or multi-tenant occupancy with the intention of preserving the community provides a public benefit, despite the fact that it may serve also to maintain property values of the individual owners.[40]

6. Revenue for a civic league comes from a variety of usage fees, governmental grants, and voluntary donations, as distinguished from a homeowner association which normally finances all of its costs from member assessments.

(a) Characteristics of Homeowner Associations

Although it may have some activities that benefit the community, the typical homeowner association will not qualify for §501(c)(4) exemption if its primary focus is to benefit individual owners—items 1 and 4 above. To stop some of the controversy, clarify the rules, and allow tax relief for such associations, Congress in 1976 enacted IRC §528, which provides a special exemption section for homeowner associations. Two types of associations qualify—condominium management associations and residential real estate management associations.[41] The basic requirements for qualifying include:

- An annual election to be so taxed is made and filed by the due date of the return, including extensions.[42]

- It must be organized and operated to acquire, construct, manage, maintain, and care for association property, whether held in common for the owners, held privately by the owners, or held by a governmental unit for use by the owners.[43]

- 60 percent or more of its gross income must be "exempt function income," i.e., membership dues, fees, or assessments from member owners of residential units. A settlement for past underassessments of dues paid by a real estate developer is exempt function income.[44]

- 90 percent or more of its expenditures in a tax year must be for "exempt function purposes." These purposes include capital expenditures for property improvements or replacement costs, salaries of managers, clerical, maintenance, and security personnel, gardening, paving, street signs, property taxes, repairs to association property, and all other disbursements to acquire, construct, manage, and maintain the property.

[40]Rev. Rul. 72-102, supra n. 36.
[41]Reg. §1.528-2.
[42]IRS Instructions to Form 1120-H at 2. This election cannot be revoked retroactively to take advantage of a net operating loss. However, permission was granted by the IRS for revocation when an association had relied on inadequate tax advice provided by a professional tax advisor. Rev. Rul. 83-74, 1983-1 C.B. 112.
[43]Reg. §1.528-3.
[44]Rev. Rul. 88-56 1988-2 C.B. 126.

- 85 percent or more of the condominium, subdivision, development, or similar area related to the association must be used by individuals as residences. Vacant units are included if they were residences before they became unoccupied.[45]

- No part of its net earnings can inure to the benefit of any private shareholder or individual.

(b) Calculating the Tax

The tax relief is only partial. While all of a qualifying civic league's income is exempt from income tax, a homeowner association can elect to pay *either* a flat 30 percent tax on its nonexempt function income (basically, its investment in common area facilities, passive investment income, and any unrelated business income less deductions), *or* the normal corporate tax payable on all of its income. Exempt function revenues are those received from the member property owners as dues or assessments unless such fees or assessments represent payments for services rendered to the members.

Taxable revenues[46] for §528 purposes include:

- Interest earned on deposits and investments held in a sinking fund for improvements or repairs, including tax exempt interest;

- Member assessments for mortgage principal, interest, and real estate taxes on association property;

- Amounts received for work performed on privately owned property;

- Assessments for maintenance, trash collection, or snow removal;

- Nonmember usage fees, as well as member fees for special services;

Deductions from the above income items include expenses directly connected with producing the nonexempt function income, and there is a $100 exemption. No deduction for net operating loss or dividends received is allowed.

6.7 ANNUAL ELECTION

Note that an association has an annual choice of electing to pay as a normal corporation, and may possibly benefit from a lesser tax rate. For an association whose income is modest and taxable at the 15 percent corporate rate, the election to pay the 30 percent tax may not be suitable. The decision turns on factors that should be quantified in each case to make the correct choice. The tax rate is one factor and is influenced by both the amount of the income (nonelecting associations pay 15 percent tax on the first $50,000 of income and higher rates above that level) and by the kind of income that is taxable. The part of an association's net income which is considered exempt function income is

---

[45] Reg. §1.528-4.
[46] Reg. §1.528-9.

not taxed if the election is made, but it is taxed if the association elects to be taxed as a normal corporation.

A nonelecting homeowner association is subject to a deduction limitation rule under IRC §227, which allows deduction of expenses attributable to owner activities only to the extent of owner income. It is extremely important, therefore, to understand the interplay of IRC §277 and IRC §528, which contains the exclusions from income. In other words, even though the association's financial statements show no net profit, it may have taxable income.

Once the election is made or not made, the association may seek permission from the IRS to revoke or elect pursuant to the relief provision of IRC §9001. When the wrong decision was made based upon the recommendation of a professional advisor, revocation has been allowed.[47]

Form 1120H filers need not pay quarterly estimated tax. The balance of tax is due by the fifteenth day of the third month following the end of the taxable year. For further details, see IRS Publication 588, *Tax Information for Homeowners Associations*.

[47]Priv. Ltr. Rul. 9233025; Rev. Rul. 83-74, 1983-1 C.B. 112.

Labor, Agricultural, and Horticultural Organizations: §501(c)(5)

IRC §501(c)(5) encompasses three specific kinds of organizations: labor unions, agricultural groups, and horticultural groups. An organization qualifying under this section may have no net earnings inuring to the benefit of any member. These worker-oriented groups may only serve the three purposes provided in Regulations which have not been revised since 1958:

1. Betterment of conditions of those engaged in such pursuit.

2. Improvement of the grade of their products.

3. Development of a high degree of efficiency in their respective occupations.[1]

7.1 LABOR UNIONS

The IRS defines a labor organization as an "association of workers who have combined to protect or promote the interests of the members by bargaining collectively with their employers to secure better working conditions, wages and similar benefits." The term includes labor unions, councils, and committees.[2] However, it is not mandatory that the membership be exclusively employees. It is the purpose for which the organization is formed that determines exempt status.

[1]Reg. §1.501(c)(5)-1(a)(2).
[2]Exempt Organizations Handbook (IRM 7751) §521.

(a) Organizational Structure and Documents

The Internal Revenue Code and Regulations impose no requirements regarding organizational structure. Form 1024 (see Appendix 18–2), however, makes a very clear requirement: "If the organization does not have an organizing instrument, it will not qualify for exempt status. The bylaws of an organization alone are not an organizing instrument. They are merely the internal rules and regulations of the organization." IRS Publication 557, *Tax Exempt Status for your Organization*, makes the following suggestion to enable a proposed union to achieve recognition of its exempt status:

"To show that your organization has the purpose of a labor organization, you should include in the articles of organization or accompanying statement (submitted with your exemption application) information establishing that the organization is organized to carry out the betterment of the conditions of workers, the improvement of the grade of their products, and the development of a higher degree of efficiency in their respective occupations."

(b) Scope of Activities

Promoting and protecting the interests of workers can be accomplished in a variety of ways. Labor unions whose activities are limited to representing employee members are automatically granted exemption. Some peripheral activities have been allowed to qualify under the labor organization classification. Examples of permissible activities include:

- Improvement of professional abilities of members through seminars, courses and participation in conventions; securing better salaries and working conditions for workers through collective bargaining and processing grievance procedures.[3]

- Worker dispatch systems to provide equitable allocation of available work and to adjudicate and settle grievances.[4]

- Provision of strike benefits[5] and mutual death, sickness, accident, and similar benefits for union members only (from member-contributed funds),[6] but not accounting and tax services.[7]

- Apprenticeship committees with union and employer representatives to establish standards of employment and qualification in skilled crafts, and to arbitrate in apprentice-employer disputes.[8]

- A nurses' association established to bargain collectively with health institutions.[9]

[3]Rev. Rul. 76-31, 1976-1 C.B. 157.
[4]Rev. Rul. 75-473, 1975-2 C.B. 213.
[5]Rev. Rul. 67-7, 1967-1 C.B. 137.
[6]Rev. Rul. 62-17, 1962-1 C.B. 87.
[7]Rev. Rul. 62-191, 1962-2 C.B. 146.
[8]Rev. Rul. 59-6, 1959-1 C.B. 121.
[9]Rev. Rul. 77-154, 1977-1 C.B. 148.

- Seminars and training programs, newspapers,[10] conventions, and legal defense and litigation activities[11] by individual unions or associations of labor organizations and unions.

- Labor "temples" or centers containing offices, meeting and recreation halls, and a barbershop, and otherwise providing a home to 162 unions, and which are owned by the unions.[12]

(c) Non-(c)(5) Activities

Activities outside the historical role of unions may not be conducted as a primary purpose of a (c)(5) organization. Whether the union itself, a directly affiliated organization, or a totally separate group undertakes the activity can be determinative. The IRS has generally allowed unions to have concerns other than wages, working hours, and working conditions, but only when they are mutually beneficial to union members. Among the activities that have resulted in denial of union status are:

- Savings plans for individual members established under a collective bargaining agreement to collect money and disburse them annually to members, and unrelated to strikes or wage levels.[13]

- Businesses formed to provide employment for members.[14] The fact that the profits from such a business go to a union does not help.

- An association formed to collect and pay over federal and state employment taxes on behalf of a group of manufacturers.[15]

- An organization formed by individuals (not by a union) to pay weekly income to workers in the event of a strike called by the members' union, but not to represent the workers in employment matters, does not qualify.[16] But a labor union's provision of financial assistance to its members during a strike is an exempt activity.[17]

- "Unions" of individual business owners.[18]

A labor organization which primarily conducts exempt functions may also have a limited amount of unrelated business activity without necessarily losing its exempt status. See Chapter 21 for rules regarding unrelated activity.

---

[10]Rev. Rul. 68-534, 1968-2 C.B. 217.
[11]Rev. Rul. 74-596, 1974-2 C.B. 167; Rev. Rul. 75-288, 1975-2 C.B. 212.
[12]*Portland Co-operative Labor Temple Ass'n v. Commissioner*, 39 B.T.A. 450(1939), *acq.* 1939-1 C.B. 29.
[13]Rev. Rul. 77-46, 1977-1 C.B. 147.
[14]Rev. Rul. 69-386, 1969-2 C.B. 123.
[15]Rev. Rul. 66-354, 1966-2 C.B. 207.
[16]Rev. Rul. 76-420, 1976-2 C.B. 153.
[17]Rev. Rul. 67-7, supra. n. 5.
[18]Rev. Rul. 78-288, 1978-2 C.B. 179.

(d) Political Activities

Political action is permissible on a limited basis.[19] Lobbying and other attempts to influence legislation relating to labor union concerns can be a major activity of a union. Whether lobbying could be the primary activity (representing more than half the annual expenditures) is questionable.

Campaigning on behalf of candidates for public office is not specifically prohibited, as it is for organizations exempt under §501(c)(3).[20] However, campaigning cannot be a primary purpose. Funds expended, to the extent of the organization's investment income, are taxable under IRC §527. A segregated fund could be created to clearly delineate the activity and its income from the union's other sources of funds.

(e) Membership

Membership in a labor organization can include both employees, employers, and others. The presence of nonemployee members, however, raises additional questions. Do the revenues received from different categories of membership have varying tax characteristics? Do fees related to member services create related income for employee members and unrelated income for associate members?

Employees only. A nurses' association[21] and a plumbers' group[22] composed mostly of employees were allowed to qualify even though a limited number of their members were independent contractors working in the field. If, instead, most of the members are independent contractors, exemption must be sought under IRC §501(c)(6) as a business league.[23]

Associate memberships. Different types of members are permissible, but can be troublesome. Two cases involving insurance plans administered by the Office of Personnel Management through the Federal Employee Health Benefits Act (FEHBA) provide some insight into this issue.

The first case involved the American Postal Workers Union (APWU).[24] The IRS took the position that a portion of the associate (nonpostal worker) member dues was attributable to the group health insurance plan and thereby produced unrelated business income, essentially saying that associate member concerns were unrelated to the basic purpose of serving postal worker members. Thus, the IRS assessed unrelated business income tax on the profits from the associate member group insurance.

After reviewing the charter and bylaws of the union, the district court found that the APWU was organized to serve not only postal workers but any classified federal employee, and was not limited to those employed by the U.S. Postal Service. This broad scope of coverage of all federal employees is permissible under the §501(c)(5) regulations pertaining to labor unions, which say, "a

---

[19] Exempt Organizations Handbook (IRM 7751) §544.
[20] *Marker v. Schultz*, 485 F.2d 1003 (D.C. Cir. 1973).
[21] Rev. Rul. 77-154, supra, n. 9.
[22] Rev. Rul. 74-167, 1974-1 C.B. 134.
[23] Rev. Rul. 78-288, supra, n. 18.
[24] *American Postal Workers Union, AFL-CIO v. U.S.*, 925 F.2d 480 (D.C. Cir. 1991), **rev'g** 90-1 USTC ¶50,013 (D.C. 1989).

labor union is a voluntary association of workers which is organized to pursue common economic and social interests." Any union is free to define its constituents. Furthermore, the court found that there were "no requirements in the Internal Revenue Code that a union member receive any particular quantum of benefit in order to be considered a bona fide member." Likewise, the court found that the IRS position that members had to have the right to vote was wholly without authority.

The court decided that the APWU's sponsorship of a group insurance plan served an exempt purpose as a mutual benefit organization. The court also found that the insurance program was not undertaken to make a profit, and that "providing economic benefits to members in return for dues is not a trade or business," citing the 1921 Congressional Record.

The circuit court of Appeals, however, disagreed and found that the provision of insurance to nonpostal workers was not related to the union's stated focus on the interests of postal employees. The judge admitted that the case was difficult because nothing in the regulations or any other authoritative source defines the exempt purposes of a labor union. However, based upon a review of the organization's constitution, the court found that privileges of membership were granted only to active members, and that provision of insurance benefits to nonmembers could not be substantially related to the union's exempt purpose. The court was also swayed by the substantial profit generated by nonmember fees.

In a somewhat similar case, the Court of Claims decided that the National Association of Postal Supervisors (NAPS) was taxable on its health insurance activity, because this was an unrelated trade or business operated to produce a profit and was in competition with taxable insurance providers.[25]

The NAPS case facts were distinguishable from APWU in one important respect: The NAPS court decided that the associate members were not members. The nonpostal employee members were called "limited members." Their dues were calculated to produce a profit, they did not participate in other union programs, and their memberships were dropped if they failed to continue coverage in the health plan. Although it was not stated, perhaps the deciding factor in the NAPS case was the fact that within five years of starting the insurance program, the limited benefit members made up 71 percent of the total members in the plan. Thus, the facts supported the IRS's position that the insurance program's purpose was primarily to produce profit, not to serve members.

7.2 AGRICULTURAL GROUPS

Agricultural associations are subject to the same basic requirements and constraints outlined above for labor groups. Again, the Code, Regulations, and IRS Handbook are silent about the form of organization. In practice and for purposes of filing Form 1024, organizational documents must be adopted to establish governance rules and prohibit private inurement. The purpose must reflect that the organization is devoted to techniques of production, betterment

---

[25] *National Association of Postal Supervisors v. U.S.*, 90-2 USTC ¶50,445 (Ct.Cl. 1990).

of conditions to those engaged in agriculture or horticulture, development of efficiency, or improvement of the grade of products.

(a) Types of Crops

The IRS Exempt Organizations Handbook separately defines agriculture on the land and the sea because, until 1976, aquaculture was excluded. The Handbook first defines "agriculture" to include "the art and science of cultivating the ground, especially in fields or large quantities, including the preparation of the soil, planting of seeds, raising and harvesting of crops, and rearing, feeding and management of livestock, that is tillage, husbandry and farming."[26]

Next, it explains that IRC §501(g), added in 1976, includes the "harvesting of aquatic resources" and says that Congress now intends "agriculture" to include fishing and related pursuits such as the taking of lobsters and shrimp. Both freshwater and saltwater occupations are to qualify, along with the cultivation of underwater vegetation, such as edible sea plants. Finally, the Handbook says that agriculture includes the "cultivation of any edible organism." In addition to cattle, crops, and fish, fur-bearing animals and their pelts[27] have also been ruled to be agricultural products. An association formed to guard the purity of the Welsh pony breed also qualified.[28]

Agricultural products and pursuits do not include the following:

- Mineral resources, such as limestone. (But what about minerals used in vitamin supplements for human consumption?)
- Dogs not used as farm animals.[29]
- Horse racing, despite the fact that the horses are raised on a farm (unless the racing is a part of an agricultural fair and stock show).[30]

(b) Qualifying Activities

A broad range of activities associated with and supportive of agriculture may qualify under this category. The organization itself need not be directly involved in cultivation. Examples of agricultural groups which the IRS views as exempt include:

- State and county farm bureaus;[31]
- Promoters of artificial insemination of cattle;[32]
- A group to study aquatic harvesting of seaweed or organic gardening;
- A crop seed certification, seed technology research group;[33]

[26] Exempt Organizations Handbook (IRM 7751) §531.
[27] Rev. Rul. 56-245, 1956-1 C.B. 204.
[28] Rev. Rul. 55-230, 1955-1 C.B. 71.
[29] Rev. Rul. 73-520, 1973-2 C.B. 180.
[30] *Forest City Livestock and Fair Co. v. Commissioner*, B.T.A. Memo, 32, 215 (1932).
[31] Exempt Organizations Handbook (IRM 7751) §532.1(1)(a).
[32] *East Tennessee Artificial Breeders Ass'n v. U.S.* 63-2 USTC ¶9748 (E.D. Tenn 1963)
[33] *Indiana Crop Investment Association, Inc. v. Commissioner* 76 T.C. 394, (1981).

- A rodeo sponsor;[34]

- An association of farm women;[35]

- A producers association formed to negotiate crop prices (but not to market the crops as a sales agent).[36]

(c) Services to Members

Providing a direct business service for the economic benefit of members cannot be the primary purpose of an agricultural group. The rules generally place more constraints on agricultural groups than on unions. Activities which the IRS has deemed to convey such benefits, rather than advancing the "betterment of conditions of those engaged in agriculture," and which are therefore not appropriate activities for an exempt agricultural association, include:

- Management, grazing and sale of members' cattle;[37]

- A housing and labor pool for transient workers;[38]

- Cooperative marketing of products (as opposed to monitoring or controlling pricing);[39]

- Leasing a facility to weigh, sort, grade, and ship livestock;[40]

- A butter and cheese manufacturers institute (because butter is an agricultural by-product—milk is the agricultural product);[41] and

- Provision of welfare aid and financial assistance to members.[42]

To better illustrate the distinction between service to members and advancement of the industry, compare a producers group formed to process production data for its members' use in improving their herds' milk production[43] with a nationwide organization that gathers milk production statistics for the U.S. Department of Agriculture.[44] The former group was not granted exemption because it relieved the individual farmers to work they would have had to perform themselves, and did not necessarily improve the conditions of the milk industry.

---

[34]*Campbell v. Big Spring Cowboy Reunion*, 54-1 USTC ¶9232 (5th Cir. 1954).
[35]Rev. Rul. 74-118, 1974-1 C.B. 134.
[36]Rev. Rul. 76-399, 1976-2 C.B. 147.
[37]Rev. Rul. 74-195, 1974-1 C.B. 135.
[38]Rev. Rul. 72-391, 1972-2 C.B. 249.
[39]Rev. Rul. 66-105, 1966-1 C.B. 145.
[40]Rev. Rul. 77-153, 1977-1 C.B. 147.
[41]Rev. Rul. 67-252, 1967-2 C.B. 195.
[42]Rev. Rul. 67-251, 1967-2 C.B. 196.
[43]Rev. Rul. 70-372, 1970-2 C.B. 118.
[44]Rev. Rul. 74-518, 1974-2 C.B. 166.

7.3 HORTICULTURAL GROUPS

According to the IRS, horticulture is the cultivation of a garden or orchard, and the science or art of growing fruits, vegetables, and flowers or ornamental plants. Under the IRS guidelines, horticulture is a division of agriculture and is subject to the same rules. No specific guidance or rules are provided exclusively for horticulture. See Section 8.9 for discussion of the dilemma presented by rose growers, which conceivably can qualify both under IRC §501(c)(5) and (c)(6). Garden clubs also can qualify under IRC §501(c)(3) or (c)(4).

Business Leagues: §501(c)(6)

IRC §501(c)(6) provides exemption for business and professional associations not organized for profit and no part of the earnings of which inure to the benefit of private individuals or shareholders, and specifically names:

- Business leagues,

- Chambers of commerce,

- Real estate boards,

- Boards of trade, and

- Professional football leagues.

8.1 BASIC CHARACTERISTICS

To qualify under §501(c)(6), a business league must have the following attributes:[1]

---

[1] Reg. 1.501(c)(6)-1.

- It is an association of persons having some common business interest;

- Its organizational purpose is to promote such common interest and to improve conditions of one or more "lines of business;"

- It does not engage in a regular business of a kind ordinarily carried on for profit;

- It does not perform services for individuals or organizations as a primary activity; and

- It is not organized for profit, and no private inurement accrues to individuals.

8.2 MEANING OF "COMMON BUSINESS INTEREST"

To qualify as a business league, the members of the league must have a "common business interest." This essentially means that they form the league to advance a mutual goal of improving the industry, not their individual parts of the whole. Their purpose in joining together is to improve the overall economic condition of their field. Each member of the league typically conducts a profitable business operation in competition with the other members, some of whom can be involved a variety of occupations operating in the business. Examples include:

Physicians, lawyers and accountants. Professional groups such as the American Medical Association, the American Bar Association, and the American Society of Certified Public Accountants are classic examples of groups formed to advance their professions. The activities of such organizations unquestionably advance the interests of the industry. Standards are established to control and monitor admission into the profession, educational programs are conducted to maintain the technical performance of the members and to advance the body of knowledge about the field, and numerous other programs designed to promote the reputation and quality of work performed by the members are conducted.

Many business leagues also possess educational and charitable characteristics. Presenting public lectures, conducting research, maintaining libraries, and disseminating useful information can qualify as educational activity.[2] An organization conducting professional certification programs provides information to protect and benefit the general public, as well as the particular profession and its members, and may arguably qualify as both a 501(c)(3) and 501(c)(6) organization. However, in G.C.M. 39721, the IRS unequivocally took the position that certification programs are "directed in whole or in part to the support and promotion of the economic interests" of the members, not the public, and therefore could not qualify the organization for (c)(3) status. See Section 8.12 for discussion concerning formation of a separate charitable organization.

American Automobile Association. The AAA illustrated a lack of common business interest when it failed IRS and judicial scrutiny of its attempt to be classified as a business league. The interest of its members is not common, since it is open to individual motorists for their personal needs without regard to their trade or business association.[3]

---

[2]Rev. Rul. 71-504 and 71-504, 1971-2 C.B. 231, 232.
[3]*American Automobile Association*, 19 T.C. 1146 (1953).

Women's leagues. An organization formed to promote the acceptance and advancement of women in business and professions can qualify due to the shared business interest of its members.[4]

Dogs and horses. The American Kennel Club lost its fight to qualify as a business league because its member clubs were held to have a common sporting rather than a business interest.[5] On the other hand, the Jockey Club's members, breeders and owners of thoroughbred horses, are considered to have "some common business interest."[6]

Investors and stock exchanges. The IRS regulations specifically state that an association engaged in furnishing information to prospective investors to enable them to make sound investments is not serving a common business interest, nor does a stock or commodity exchange (§1.501(c)(6)-1).

Future Business Interests. A group of students pursuing a single profession formed a qualifying business league even though they were not yet engaged in the profession. The organization promoted their common business purpose as future members of the profession.[7]

8.3   LINE OF BUSINESS

Understanding what constitutes a "line of business" is the key to identifying groups which qualify as business leagues because they share a common business interest. According to the IRS, a "line of business" is a trade or occupation, entry into which is not restricted by a patent, trademark, or similar device that would allow private parties to restrict the right to engage in the business.[8]

The term "business" is construed broadly to include almost any enterprise or activity conducted for remuneration. The term encompasses professions as well as mercantile and trading businesses.[9] To qualify, a league's line of business must be broad; it must encompass the common business interest of an entire industry or one of its components, or an industry within a particular geographic area.

(a) User Groups

The computer industry provides good examples both of organizations deemed to serve a common business interest and nonexempt private groups. In a 1974 ruling, the IRS decided that an organization qualified as a business league because it was formed to stimulate the development a free exchange of information about computer systems and programming. The membership was diverse, including businesses that owned, rented, or leased computers of a variety of manufacturers. The organization sponsored semiannual conferences, open to

[4]Rev. Rul. 76-401, 1976-2 C.B. 175.
[5]*American Kennel Club v. Hoey*, 148 F.2d 290 (2d Cir. 1945).
[6]*The Jockey Club v. United States*, 137 F.Supp. 419 (Ct.Cl. 1956), *cert. denied*, 352 U.S. 834 (1957).
[7]Rev. Rul. 77-112, 1977-1 CB 149.
[8]IRS Exempt Organization Handbook (IRM 7751) §652(1).
[9]Rev. Rul. 70-641, 1970-2 CB 119.

the public, to discuss technical and operational issues. Conversely, organizations formed for the same purposes by users of particular manufacturers' computers are denied business league status by the IRS, and the courts have affirmed.[10] The user groups are deemed to promote the particular computer vendors, rather than to benefit the entire industry or all components of an industry within an area. The Guide International Corporation, limited in membership to IBM mainframe computer users, was denied exemption because it benefited IBM, a large but nonetheless a particular segment of the computer business, not the computer business in general.

(b) Dealer Associations

Associations of dealers and manufacturers of particular brands have been determined not to qualify for exemption as business leagues, because they failed to represent a "line of business:"

An association of Midas Muffler dealers formed to represent the dealers in negotiations with the manufacturer failed to convince the Supreme Court that it constituted a "line of business." It was deemed unfair to allow exemption to a group, the purpose of which is to compete with another group within an industry.[11] In an interesting earlier case, the Pepsi-Cola Bottlers Association was allowed an exemption, a decision which the IRS promptly announced that it would not follow.[12]

An association of licensed dealers of a patented product (held by the association) was deemed to be engaged in furthering the business interest of its member-dealers and not benefiting competing manufacturers of products of the same type covered by the patent.[13]

A shopping center merchants' association promotes too narrow an interest when its sole activity is to place advertisements to attract customers to the center and its membership is restricted to merchants in the one-owner shopping center.[14] If, instead, membership is open to all merchants within the neighborhood and if the association is not concerned with landlord-tenant matters relating to the shopping center, exemption is allowed.[15]

Dealers selling a particular type of car do not promote the automobile industry.[16] Franchisees of a particular chain, such as McDonald's restaurants, would similarly be precluded from forming an exempt group, but a league of franchise holders open to all types of merchants or food establishments would qualify.

---

[10] Rev. Rul. 83-164, 1983-2 CB 95; *National Prime Users Group Inc. v. United States*, 667 F.Supp. 250 (D.Md. 1987); *Guide International Corporation v. United States*, 90-1 USTC 50,304 (N.D. Ill. 1990).

[11] *Pepsi-Cola Bottlers' Association v. United States*, 369 F.2d 250 (7th Cir. 1966). The IRS announced its disagreement with this case in Rev. Rul. 68-182, 1968-1 CB 263.

[12] *National Muffler Dealers Association v. United States*, 440 U.S. 472, 477-479 (1979).

[13] Rev. Rul. 58-294, 1958-1 CB 244.

[14] Rev. Rul. 73-411, 1973-2 CB 180.

[15] Rev. Rul. 78-225, 1978-1 C.B. 159.

[16] Rev. Rul. 67-77, 1967-1 CB 138.

(c) Hobby or Recreational Groups

Hobby groups do not qualify as business leagues because a hobby is not a business.[17] To be characterized as a business, the activity must be entered into with the intention of producing a profit. For income tax purposes, an activity is presumed to be a hobby if it loses money for more than two years in a five year period.[18]

Gardeners, pet owners, card players, and collectors of antiques, baseball cards, fine art, and so on, form groups for purposes similar to those of typical business leagues. However, unless the members are pursuing their hobby interests for personal profit, and therefore for individual business purposes, exemption is not available for the group under §501(c)(6). Such a group may, however, qualify in other categories of exemption, such as social club, civic welfare organization, or (rarely) charitable, depending upon its purposes.

8.4 RENDERING SERVICES FOR MEMBERS

A qualifying business league must devote its efforts primarily to promoting the industry. A §501(c)(6) organization may not, as a significant activity, engage in a regular business of a kind ordinarily carried on for profit.[19] Services rendered for members aimed at improving the industry or maintaining its standards are classified as nonbusiness, or related, income and the rendering of such services will not jeopardize the exemption. Business income benefiting the individual members, however, is considered unrelated business income (UBI), and too much is not permitted. Examples of the types of services that have been held to be "related" or to serve the industry as a whole, rather than the individual members, follow.

(a) Services Benefiting the Industry

- Industry-wide advertising to encourage use of products.[20]
- Testing for quality control.[21]
- Examination and certification of professionals, peer review, and ethics audits.[22]
- Mediation service to settle disputes within the industry.[23]
- Research and publication of technical information,[24] but only if the information is available to the industry as a whole, rather than being available only to paying members.[25]

[17]Rev. Rul. 66-179, 1966-1 CB 139.
[18]IRC §183.
[19]*Supra*, n. 1.
[20]*Washington State Apples, Inc. v. Commissioner*, 46 B.T.A. 64 (1942).
[21]Rev. Rul. 81-127, 1981-1 C.B. 357; Rev. Rul. 70-187 1970-1 C.B. 131.
[22]Rev. Rul. 73-567, 1973-2 C.B. 178; Rev. Rul. 74-553, 1974-2 C.B. 168.
[23]*American Fisherman's Tuna Boat Association v. Rogan*, 51 F.Supp. 933 (S.D. Cal. 1943).
[24]Rev. Rul. 70-187, 1970-1 C.B. 131.
[25]Rev. Rul. 69-106, 1969-1 C.B. 153 and *Glass Container Industry Research Corp.*, 70-1 USTC ¶9214.

- Referral services available to the general public, if there is evidence of benefit to the public rather than to individual service providers.[26]

- A bid registry established and operated to encourage fair bidding practices with the industry.[27]

- Insurance associations that serve their industry without charge and essentially do not sell insurance. See Section 8.4 for discussion of nonqualifying insurance groups.

- Lobbying groups presenting information, trade statistics, and group opinions to government agencies and bureaus.[28]

(b) Disqualifying Services to Individual Members

Services giving benefit to the members as individuals rather than to the industry as a whole may disqualify a business league as an exempt league, if such services constitute a substantial and major activity of the organization. Services rendered for members for the purpose of improving the industry or maintaining its standards are classified as nonbusiness, or related, income, and the rendering of such services will not jeopardize the exemption. Individual benefit services potentially disqualify the organization for exemption, and are taxed as unrelated business income.

The distinction is often vague, but several factors evidence the difference. Of primary importance is the manner in which persons are charged for receiving the services, and whether the services are available to the general public. When the services are rendered in return for a specific charge or the services are only available to members, individual benefit is generally found. Activities for which individual members are not expected to pay are evidence of intangible industry-wide benefit. Making services available to all also reflects cooperative effort. By contrast, when members buy and the association sells services for member convenience or cost savings, individual benefit ensues. Examples of services that have been considered as providing individual benefit follow:

- Publication of catalogs containing advertisements for products manufactured by members[29] or a tourism promotion yearbook made up of advertisements from the association's members.[30] Compare these to ads promoting the entire industry, Section 8.4(a).

- Group insurance plans provided for members.[31]

---

[26]Rev. Rul. 80-287, 1980-2 C.B. 185. Also see *Kentucky Bar Foundation, Inc. v. Commissioner*, 49 T.C. 921, 930 (1982).
[27]Rev. Rul. 66-223, 1966-2 C.B. 224.
[28]Rev. Rul. 61-177, 1961-2 C.B. 117.
[29]Rev. Rul. 56-84, 1956-1 C.B. 201.
[30]Rev. Rul. 65-14, 1965-1 C.B. 236.
[31]*Oklahoma Cattlemen's Association v. U.S.*, 310 F.Supp. 320 (W.D. Okla. 1969); Rev. Rul. 70-95, 1970-1 C.B. 137; Rev. Rul. 67-176, 1967-1 C.B. 140.

- Real estate multiple listing services.[32]

- Employment placement services.[33]

- Credit rating or information services.[34]

- Collective bargaining agreement records.

- A luncheon or social meeting hall for members without a program for professional improvement did not qualify;[35] contrast this with a luncheon group devoted to discussion, review, and consideration of problems in a particular industry directed to the improvement of business conditions, which can qualify.[36]

- Trade shows organized primarily to allow members to sell merchandise individually, rather than to educate the audience, do not constitute qualifying business league activity.[37] Shows organized instead to attract persons to an industry by educating the public represent exempt activity.[38] See §513(d)(3) for a discussion of "Qualified Convention and Trade Show Activities," which provides the parameters for shows that are excluded from the unrelated business income tax.

- Sale of standardized forms for use by the profession and the public is a debatable type of service. The IRS has ruled that such activity is an unrelated trade or business.[39] The courts, however, felt that the San Antonio Bar Association improved relations between the bar, bench, and the public with its forms. Similarly, the Texas Apartment Association's lease forms and landlord manuals prevented controversy and maintained fairness in the industry.[40]

- Insurance company associations are presently a gray area. When the association provides its services or information to insurance companies without charge and is not selling the insurance itself, the requisite industry benefit is present. An organization created to carry out state-mandated rules concerning uninsured parties[41] and an association of

---

[32] Rev. Rul. 59-234, 1959-2 C.B. 149 and *Evanston-North Shore Board of Realtors*, 63-2 USTC ¶9604, 320 F.2d 375 (Ct. Cl. 1963), cent denied, 376 US 931 (1964).

[33] Rev. Rul. 61-170, 1961-2 C.B. 112.

[34] Rev. Rul. 68-265, 1968-1 C.B. 265 and Rev. Rul. 70-591, 1970-2 C.B. 118 and *Oklahoma City Retailers Ass'n*, 64-1 USTC ¶9467, 331 F.2d 328 (10th Cir. 1964).

[35] *The Engineers Club of San Francisco v. United States*, 609 F.Supp. 519 (N.D. Cal. 1985).

[36] Rev. Rul. 67-295, 1967-2 C.B. 197.

[37] Rev. Rul. 58-224, 1958-1 C.B. 242; *Men's and Boys' Apparel Club of Florida*, 64-2 USTC ¶9840; *Indiana Hardware Ass'n, Inc.*, 66-2 USTC ¶9691, 366 F.2d 998 (Ct.Cla. 1966).

[38] *American Woodworking Machinery and Equipment Show, Inc.*, 66-1 USTC ¶9219, 249 F.Supp. 393 (D.C. N.C. 1966).

[39] Rev. Rul. 78-51, 1978-1 C.B. 165.

[40] *San Antonio Bar Association v. United States*, 80-2 U.S.T.C. ¶9594 (W.D. Texas 1980); *Texas Apartment Association v. United States*, 869 F.2d 884 (5th Cir. 1989).

[41] Rev. Rul. 76-410, 1976-2 C.B. 155.

casualty companies settling claims against insolvent companies[42] were ruled exempt. In both cases, all companies within a state were required to be members and the expenses of the association were paid from member dues. On the other hand, an association of insurance companies that maintained a data bank and exchange for confidential life insurance underwriting information, made available for a fee to its members (who wrote 98 percent of the legal reserve life insurance in force in the United States), was determined to serve the individual interests of the members and not to qualify for exemption.[43] Likewise, an association furnishing medical malpractice insurance to health care providers was not exempt.[44] A thorough reading of the rulings and cases is warranted prior to forming such an organization.[45]

8.5 SOURCES OF REVENUE

The portion of total support received from members is a factor in determining qualification. The IRS expects "meaningful membership support," although the Code and Regulations contain no specific numerical support requirement. A safe rule of thumb is that more than 50 percent of the league's support should come from member dues and exempt function charges.

Revenue received in rendering services to individuals that do not benefit the industry as a whole cannot provide a major portion of the league's budget. As is true for other categories of exempt organizations, the statute and regulations contain no prohibition against a league earning such income as long as the amounts are insubstantial, but there is no exact numerical test. When a league's income from providing such services is excessive, its exempt status is jeopardized and the income is taxable. Decisions that illustrate the IRS's view on revenue sources follow:

- City contract revenue received by a tourism promotion organization was deemed to be related income and therefore member income. The ruling noted a high degree of member involvement, and opined that the organization should not lose its exemption "merely because a significant portion of its income was derived from other than traditional member sources."[46]

- "Incidental" television advertising activity and provision of laboratories for testing quality control on a fee basis was not enough to cause revocation of a league's exemption.[47]

[42] Rev. Rul. 73-452, 1973-2 C.B. 183.
[43] *MIB, Inc.*, 84-1 USTC ¶9476, 734 F.2d 71 (1st. Cir. 1984).
[44] Rev. Rul. 81-175, 1981-1 C.B. 337, distinguishing Rev. Rul. 71-155, 1971-1 C.B. 152.
[45] *North Carolina Association of Insurance Agents, Inc.* 84-2 USTC ¶9668, 739 F.2d 949 (4th. Cir. 1984); Priv. Ltr. Rul. 8841003, June 24, 1988.
[46] Priv. Ltr. Rul. 9032005, March 22, 1989.
[47] *American Plywood Ass'n*, 67-2 USTC ¶9568, 267 F.Supp. 830 (1967).

8.6   MEMBERSHIP CATEGORIES

An exempt business league may have different classes of members, as long as the purpose is to advance the interests of the profession and all members share the same common business interest. Junior, senior, retired, associate, student, supporters and other types of categories are common, in recognition of age, stature, or active versus peripheral involvement in the business. Varying level of dues can also be charged to different types of members, presumably based upon their ability to pay or their involvement in league activities. Those members required to have continuing education might pay more than inactive or student members who are not required to participate in classes, for example.

The charging of substantially greater dues to associate members may, however, evidence private inurement benefiting the active members. The IRS agrees that higher dues are permissible when the revenues benefit the entire industry by allowing more extensive programs.[48] The excess payments likewise did not constitute UBI, because the administration of associate member records under a graduated dues structure is not the performance of a service or sale of a good.

Tax-exempt organizations may also be members of a qualifying league, despite the fact that the regulations define a business league as an association of persons. A labor union and a business league have been permitted to form a qualifying league.[49]

Member dues and assessments are deductible as a business expenses for members who are actively engaged in a trade or business, except for the amount of the dues allocable to political activity or grassroots lobbying.

8.7   MEMBER INUREMENT

The league may not provide individual member inurement or operate primarily to benefit its members. The league may not, as its primarily activity, provide direct services of benefit to individual members, but it can provide a whole host of services designed to benefit their common interests. The IRS[50] and the courts have provided some additional guidance as to when inurement results, as follows:

- A charter provision that permits distributions of remaining assets to members upon dissolution of the league will not in and of itself preclude exemption.[51] However, regular distributions of income or accumulated surplus would constitute inurement.[52]

[48]Priv. Ltr. Rul. 9128002, August 17, 1990.
[49]Rev. Rul. 70-31, 1970-1 C.B. 130. *See also* Rev. Rul. 82-138, 1982-2 C.B. 106.
[50]Exempt Organizations Handbook §640.
[51]*Crooks v. Kansas City Hay Dealers Association*, 37 F.2d 83 1929.
[52]Exempt Organization Handbook §630.

- A league cannot be organized as a stockholding company with members holding the shares.[53]

- Newsletters and member "informational materials" do not provide impermissible benefit.

- Preferential pricing for members results in private inurement *unless* it is shown that the league supports the activity from member dues and the pricing reflects that revenue.[54]

- Refunds of dues paid proportionately to all classes of members is permitted.[55]

- A partial rebate of trade show advance deposits to exhibitors is permitted if all participants receive a share.[56] Rebates paid to members only out of income-producing activity represents inurement.[57]

- Financial aid and welfare services provided to members represents benefit to the individual members, in the eyes of the IRS.[58]

- Payment of malpractice defense costs and paying judgments rendered in such suits creates individual inurement.[59]

- Payment of excessive compensation or purchase price for property or services to a member, particularly to persons controlling the league, results in inurement of earnings. See Chapter 20 for more information.

8.8 CHAMBERS OF COMMERCE AND BOARDS OF TRADE

A chamber of commerce or board of trade is distinguishable from a business league because it serves the general economic welfare of a community. Their membership is typically open to all lines of business within a geographic area. Their activities must be directed at the promotion of the area's business and usually include the promotion of tourism, publishing directories of resources available in the area, developing programs to promote the business climate, conducting studies, and similar projects. The following activities have been ruled to be suitable for a chamber of commerce:

- Development of an industrial park to attract new businesses to an area, including the offering of below-cost rents and other subsidies.[60]

---

[53] Northwest Jobbers Credit Bureau v. Commissioner, 37 F.2d 880 (1930) Ct. D. 206, C.B. IX-2, 228.
[54] Exempt Organizations Annual Technical Review Institutes for 1979, page 354.
[55] Rev. Rul. 81-60, 1981-1 C.B. 335.
[56] Rev. Rul. 77-206, 1977-1 C.B. 149.
[57] *Michigan Mobile Home and Recreational Vehicle Institute*, 66 T.C. 770 (1976).
[58] Rev. Rul. 67-251, 1967-2 C.B. 196.
[59] *National Chiropractor Association v. Birmingham*, 96 F.Supp. 824 (D.C. Iowa 1951).
[60] Rev. Rul. 70-81, 1970-1 C.B. 131; Rev. Rul. 81-138, 1981-1 C.B. 358.

- Encouraging national organizations to hold their conventions in a city.[61]

- A "neighborhood community association" whose membership is open to all and whose purpose is to improve the business conditions of a neighborhood, as opposed to a particular subdivision or shopping area, can qualify.[62]

8.9   COMPARISON TO §501(c)(5)

The basic difference between §501(c)(5) and §501(c)(6) is sometimes gray, due both to industry type and to congressional logic. While (c)(5) is narrow and applies only to agricultural groups and labor unions, (c)(6) is broad and includes almost any business enterprise or activity.[63]

To contrast the two categories of §501(c) classification, consider a rose growers' association. Except for the roses, such an association would qualify as a business league under §501(c)(6). Nevertheless, the organization will be classified under §501(c)(5) as horticultural if its members are all directly involved in the cultivation of roses with the purpose of bettering the conditions of persons growing roses, improving the grade of roses, and developing growing systems. However, if group membership includes nongrowers such as shippers, pesticide suppliers, and florists, it will not qualify under §501(c)(5) and will instead have to meet the tests for §501(c)(6).

In many ways, the two categories are identical. For both, unrelated business income is taxed and must not be a substantial revenue source or activity. For both categories, economic benefits and services cannot generally be rendered to individual members. However, labor unions can provide mutually funded benefits for life, health, and accident insurance.

Neither political activity nor lobbying is prohibited under either §501(c)(5) or §501(c)(6). Advocacy of legislation beneficial to the common business interest could apparently be the group's primary purpose, if the activity is undertaken to improve working conditions, production, or efficiencies.[64] Whether an activity is "primary" is generally measured by dollars expended on that function in relation to the league's total budget.

8.10   FILING FOR RECOGNITION OF EXEMPTION

(a) Federal Recognition

File Form 1024 to achieve recognition of exemption. Statutorily, a league essentially qualifies if it meets the §501(c)(6) definitions and need not seek IRS approval to qualify. As a practical matter, however, the IRS requires filing of Form 1024 to avoid subjecting the league's income to tax. The information

[61]Rev. Rul. 76-207, 1976-1 C.B. 1578.
[62]Rev. Rul. 78-225, 1978-1 C.B. 159.
[63]Rev. Rul. 70-641, 1970-2 C.B. 119.
[64]Rev. Rul. 61-177, 1961-2 C.B. 117.

return, Form 990 or 990EZ, is filed annually to report activity and allow the IRS to review continued qualification. See Chapter 27.

(b) Organizational Requirements

The non-(c)(3) categories of tax-exempt organizations are not subject to a specific organizational requirement, as discussed in Section 7.1(a) concerning labor unions. The instructions to Form 1024, however, say that exemption will not be approved unless organizing documents are attached. They go on to say that bylaws are internal rules and are not, by themselves, organizational documents.

8.11 STATE EXEMPTIONS

A business league may be qualified for state and local tax exemptions. In Texas, for example, an automatic exemption from the corporate franchise tax is granted for organizations furnishing their IRS determination letter evidencing their qualification as a §501(c)(6) organization. The sales tax exemption is only granted to "a chamber of commerce or a convention and tourist promotional agency representing a Texas city or county," and then only if the entity is not organized for profit and no part of its earnings inure to a private shareholder or other individual. Most business leagues are subject to the sales tax on items they buy, lease, or consume.

8.12 FORMATION OF A RELATED CHARITABLE ORGANIZATION

Business, trade, and professional associations described in §501(c)(6) often form §501(c)(3) organizations to pursue their educational, cultural, scientific, health care-related, or other charitable interests. The motivation is usually fundraising —to seek money that would not otherwise be available without forming an organization whose supporters are entitled to charitable deductions for their payments. Consider an association that wishes to create a library of educational materials. Rather than raising the organization's dues overall, members capable of paying more can be asked to voluntarily contribute to the library. Gifts to the league itself for its use in establishing the library would not be deductible as contributions, but a gift to the league's separate charity for the same purpose would be.[65] Grants from foundations and corporations and testamentary bequests from members can also be sought.

The charitable organization cannot, of course, operate to benefit the business league, and care must be taken to insure that no interlocking personnel or other sharing arrangements result in such benefit. The charity can be controlled by the association as long as it meets the standards applied to such relationships discussed in Chapter 22. The controlled charity must also meet the standards for qualification as a charity under §501(c)(3).

[65]Rev. Rul. 58-293, 1958-1 CB 146 and Rev. Rul. 66-79, 1966-1 CB 48.

8.13   AVOIDING THE EXPLOITATION RULE

A business league which finances its activities by earning unrelated business income faces limitations on its deduction. In calculating the tax on unrelated business income, the "exploitation rule" disallows the deduction of expenses attributable to the league's member or exempt function activities.[66] In other words, member losses cannot be deducted against business income. Despite the economic fact that the league has a loss overall, it may have to pay tax. See Chapter 21 for more details.

To avoid this situation, one might think that the league should abandon its exempt status and file as a normal corporation showing no profit, but I.R.C. §277 is designed to prevent this tactic. Membership expenses are only deductible to the extent of membership income, and cannot be deducted against business income for a nonexempt taxpayer.

[66] Reg. §1.512(a)-1(d)(1).

Social Clubs: §501(c)(7)

Social clubs are defined in IRC §501(c)(7) as "clubs organized for pleasure, recreation, and other nonprofitable purposes, substantially all of the activity of which are for such purposes and no part of the net earnings of which inures to the benefit of any private shareholder." The tax exemption is based on the logic of allowing members to pool their funds for recreational purposes, and is fundamentally very different from other types of exemptions. A club is not exempt because it provides public benefit, but rather because it serves to benefit individuals. It is designed to allow individuals to join together on a mutual basis for personal reasons without tax consequences.[1] The types of organizations that typically qualify as social clubs include:

- Country clubs;

- Amateur hunting, fishing, tennis, swimming and other sport clubs;

- Variety clubs;

- Local women's or men's clubs;

- Hobby clubs; and

---

[1] Exempt Organizations Handbook (IRM 7751) §710.

- College fraternities operating chapter houses for students.

The most significant tax attributes of social clubs are that:

- Members are bound together with a common social goal;

- The club has specific criteria or standards for membership;

- Passive income from dividends, interest, and other investments is taxed, unlike most other types of exempt organizations; and

- Limited revenues come from nonmembers subject to a specific numerical tests.

9.1 ORGANIZATIONAL REQUIREMENTS

(a) Purpose Clause and Activities

The charter and bylaws of a social club should provide that the club is organized for pleasure, recreation, or other nonprofitable purposes of its members, *and* that it may not provide for discrimination on the basis of race, color, or religion. A club operating under a defective charter will qualify for exemption from the date it commenced operation if it has not conducted any of the proscribed activities permitted by the charter.[2] If impermissible activities have been conducted, exemption is only allowed beginning with the year of the revision.

Substantially all of the club's activities must be in pursuit of its recreational and social purposes. The charter should not expressly authorize the club to conduct activities beyond this (c)(7) scope, except that there can be provision for charitable, educational, and other (c)(3) purposes. See Section 9.5(g) regarding the charitable deduction against unrelated business income.

The activities of a social club must encourage and permit members to join together, i.e., the opportunity for social mingling and fellowship on a mutual basis must be present in club functions. Commingling by members must play a material part in the life of the organization.[3] Lack of personal contact may be an indication that the basic purpose of the organization is only to provide personal goods and services in a manner similar to commercial counterparts.[4]

(b) Examples of Qualifying Clubs

- A pet club,[5] a dog club,[6] a bowling tournament club,[7] a family historical society,[8] a garden club,[9] and a mineralogical and lapidary club[10] have been ruled to be exempt social clubs.

[2] Exempt Organizations Handbook (IRM 7751) §722(4).
[3] Rev. Rul. 58-589, 1958-2 C.B. 266.
[4] Rev. Rul. 69-635, 1969-2 C.B. 126.
[5] Rev. Rul. 73-520, 1973-2 C.B. 180.
[6] Rev. Rul. 71-421, 1971-2, C.B. 229; Rev. Rul. 73-520, 1973-2 C.B. 180.
[7] Rev. Rul. 74-148, 1974-1 C.B. 138.
[8] Rev. Rul. 67-8, 1967-1 C.B. 142.
[9] Rev. Rul. 66-179, 1966-1 C.B. 139.
[10] Rev. Rul. 67-139, 1967-1 C.B. 129.

- Owning a building and operating the social facilities in it for a tax-exempt lodge,[11] for a fraternity chapter house,[12] and for a veterans organization[13] also is considered to be qualifying activity for a social club. On the other hand, an organization whose primary activity was leasing building lots to members with peripheral recreational activity is not exempt.[14] The organization must itself be social or recreational in nature. If social activity predominates, rental activities restricted to members will usually be compatable with exemption as a social club. A fraternity can rent for rooms to its members for their private use, for example.[15]

- Gambling, even though illegal under local law, was ruled to be a permissible social club focus, when it was conducted only for members and their guests.[16] Similarly, a calcutta wagering pool conducted by a club in connection with its annual golf tournament was deemed exempt.[17]

- Two different flying clubs illustrate the rule. A hobby flying group which held informal meetings for members and owned an airplane that the members maintained, repaired, and flew together in small groups, qualified as a social club.[18] In contrast, a group which only provided "economical" facilities for members' plane storage, but held no meetings or other commingling activity for them, did not qualify as a social group.[19] Lack of a physical facility for regular gatherings implies lack of social purpose.

(c) Examples of Nonqualifying Groups

- A breakfast club established to assist its members working in business through study and discussion of problems at weekly meetings is not classified as a social club, but may qualify as a business league.[20]

- A television antenna service group formed to share the costs, but with no member mingling activities, is not a social group.[21]

- A community association operating a swimming pool that serves a social function for residents cannot qualify if it also maintains the streets, collects the trash, and pays the police and fire departments.[22]

[11] Rev. Rul. 56-305, 1956-2 C.B. 307.
[12] Rev. Rul. 64-118, 1964-1 (Part I) C.B. 182.
[13] Rev. Rul. 66-150, 1966-1 C.B. 147.
[14] Rev. Rul. 68-168, 1968-1 C.B. 269.
[15] Exempt Organizations Handbook (IRM 7751) §742.
[16] Rev. Rul. 69-68, 1969-1 C.B. 153.
[17] Rev. Rul. 74-425, 1974-2 C.B. 373.
[18] Rev. Rul. 74-30, 1974-1 C.B. 137.
[19] Rev. Rul. 70-32, 1970-1 C.B. 140.
[20] Rev. Rul. 69-527, 1969-2 C.B. 125.
[21] Rev. Rul. 83-170, 1983-2 C.B. 97; G.C.M. 39063.
[22] Rev. Rul. 75-494, 1975-2 C.B. 214.

- A club with mixed purposes—both a social club and provider of benevolent life insurance to members—cannot qualify (although two independent organizations separately conducting the same activities can independently qualify).[23]

- An automobile club providing lower cost services to its members, but no social activities in which its members mingle cannot qualify.[24]

- A club owning a multistory urban building in which it conducted a number of "nontraditional business activities" is not a qualifying club in the IRS's eyes. Operation of a parking garage, gas station, barber shop, flower shop, and liquor store, despite the fact that they were open only to members and their guests, does not serve a social purpose, but instead is the rendering of commercial services. Long term rental of at least 10 percent of the rooms for members' principal residences is also a nonexempt activity.[25]

- Sale of take-out food for members' consumption off club premises is not a social function.[26]

9.2 MEMBER INUREMENT PROHIBITED

The charter or organizational document establishing the club should provide that no private benefit can inure to any individual member of the club.[27] Chapter 20 defines and explores inurement concepts. Under two different circumstances, the governing rules can provide distributions to members that do not result in private benefit to the individual members:

1. Upon dissolution or termination of the club, payment of liquidation distributions to club members is acceptable.[28]

2. Upon an individual member's withdrawal from the club, the member's shares can be redeemed at their book value. A payment equal to the member's proportionate share of the underlying value of the club's assets is permitted. Essentially, members can be reimbursed their original membership cost, plus their share of increases in the value of club property and accumulated surpluses.[29] Dissolution payments can differ by membership category if they parallel and are attributable to differing levels of initiation fees or type of members. The IRS is suspicious of lower rates for a voting class of membership at the expense of higher-

[23]*Allgemeiner Arbeit Verein v. Commissioner*, 24 T.C. 371 (1955), *aff'd*, 237 F.2d 604 (1956) 3rd Cir.; Rev. Rul. 63-190, 1963-2 C.B. 212.
[24]*Keystone Auto Club v. Commissioner*, 181 F.2d 420 (3rd Cir. 1950), *aff'g* 12 T.C. 1038 (1949); Rev. Rul. 69-635, 1969-2 C.B. 126.
[25]G.C.M. 39115 (January 12, 1984).
[26]Tech. Adv. Memo. 9212002.
[27]*West Side Tennis Club v. Commissioner*, 111 F.2d 6 (2nd Circ. 1940).
[28]Rev. Rul. 58-501, 1958-2 C.B. 262.
[29]Rev. Rul. 68-639, 1968-2 C.B. 220.

paying nonvoting members.[30] Such a dues structure may reflect inurement, as does the lowering or reduction of member charges or dues with profits earned from nonmember activities. When there is some other reason for the difference, such as enhanced privileges, benefits may not inure.[31]

(a) Inurement from Nonmember Revenues

Reductions in member dues, facilities fees, and enhancement of club facilities, when financed by nonmember revenues, constitute member inurement.[32]

Distribution of proceeds from sale of club land or property to members may be viewed as providing impermissible private inurement, if the sale is profit-motivated. When club land is sold to take advantage of a land price boom with the profits distributed to the members, private benefit is found and the club's exemption revoked.[33] If, on the other hand, the club property is taken by a condemnation proceeding,[34] or is sold by a club because of encroaching urbanization and trespasses,[35] distribution of the proceeds to the members (with or without dissolution) has not been deemed to produce unallowed benefit.

(b) Direct Inurement to Members

Direct services rendered to members beyond the social purposes of the club may result in inurement. Examples of services that have been found to provide direct inurement, rather than to serve the social purposes of the club, include:

- Sale of packaged liquor to members for off-premises consumption;[36]

- Sickness and death benefit payments to members;[37] and

- Leasing building lots to members on a long term basis.[38]

9.3 MEMBERSHIP REQUIREMENTS

(a) Discrimination

Racial, color, and religious discrimination by social clubs is strictly prohibited.[39] The charter, bylaws, or other governing instrument or written policy statement may contain no provision providing for discrimination against any person based upon race, color, or religion. Note that the Code does not contain the

---

[30] Rev. Rul. 70-48, 1970-1 C.B. 133.

[31] *Pittsburgh Press Club v. U.S.*, 536 F.2d 572 (3rd Cir. 1976).

[32] Rev. Rul. 58-589, 1958-2 C.B. 266.

[33] *Juniper Hunting Club v. Commissioner*, 28 B.T.A. 525 (1933).

[34] Rev. Rul. 65-64, 1965-1 C.B. 241.

[35] Rev. Rul. 58-501, 1958-2 C.B. 262.

[36] Rev. Rul. 68-535, 1968-2 C.B. 219.

[37] Rev. Rul. 63-190, *supra*, n. 23.

[38] Rev. Rul. 68-168, 1968-1 C.B. 269.

[39] §501(i) was added to the Code in 1976.

word "sex." A written policy against discrimination is not absolutely necessary as long as the club obeys the spirit of the prohibition. It is actual discrimination that will cause revocation of exemption.

Two specific types of religious organizations are permitted to discriminate based upon religion, and are relieved from this sweeping requirement:

1. A fraternal beneficiary society, order, or association limiting its members to a particular religious group.

2. A club which in good faith limits it membership to the members of a particular religion in order to further the teachings or principles of that religion, and not to exclude individuals of a particular race or color.[40]

In a private ruling, the IRS stated its policy not to permit exemption for religious groups falling outside those specified above, and certainly not for ethnic groups.[41]

It is very important to note that sexual discrimination is not prohibited by the Code, and exemption of clubs that discriminate against one sex may not be challenged. Only under the broader civil rights legislation may such clubs be challenged. Princeton's last two "male only" social clubs were ordered to admit women by the Supreme Court of New Jersey in July, 1990. On the other hand, the Massachusetts Commission Against Discrimination refused in March, 1990 to require the Harvard Fly Club to admit women.

(b) Classes of Membership

The shared interest of social club members is evidenced by the limitations and prerequisites of its membership structure.[42] Membership requirements cannot be broad or vague, but should serve to limit membership to a clearly defined constituency. Different classes of members, however, are permitted. Membership distinctions based on amount of dues paid, age, residency, and facilities used do not, in and of themselves, indicate lack of social purpose. Different voting rights and different dissolution rights for different classes of membership are also permissible. A health club with 25 active members and 25,000 nonvoting associate members, however, "clearly was not of an exempt character."[43]

For social clubs that are geographically broad-based, mingling of members within each local chapter will suffice to meet IRS requirements.[44]

(c) Company Memberships

A social club must be a nonprofit membership organization of individuals. If corporate memberships are offered, individual representatives of the corporation must be subject to approval by the membership committee and must be granted the same privileges as other individual members.[45] The company can

---

[40] IRC §501(i)(1) and (2).
[41] Priv. Ltr. Rul. 8317004.
[42] *Arner v. Rogan*, 40-2 USTC ¶9567 (D.C. 1940).
[43] Rev. Rul. 58-588, 1958-2 C.B. 265.
[44] Rev. Rul. 67-248, 1967-2 C.B. 204.
[45] Rev. Rul. 74-168, 1974-1 C.B. 139.

pay the bill as long as the charges are for member use.[46] If, instead, the club allows member corporations to designate their representatives, the club cannot qualify for exemption.[47]

(d) "Subterfuge" Clubs

Clubs actually doing business with the public under the guise of a social club cannot qualify for exemption. Clubs created to "circumvent liquor laws, zoning ordinances, or laws enforcing civil rights" are among those considered as subterfuges by the IRS. The following factors evidence nonqualifying clubs:[48]

- The membership requirements are broad or vaguely stated;

- Initiation charges or dues are so low that one-time transient use of the facilities by the general public is encouraged;

- Management conducts vigorous public solicitations to expand club membership; and

- The club is closely associated with a for-profit hotel, restaurant, or health facility which also provides the management, the food services, and so on.

9.4 REVENUE TESTS

IRC §501(c)(7) was revised in 1976 to establish a specific member test by requiring that "substantially all" of a social club's activities involve its members. Based upon the committee reports, a so-called gross receipts test is used to measure compliance and would permit a limited amount of nonmember revenues. Prior to 1976, clubs had to operate "exclusively" for nonprofit purposes, and the regulations[49] provided that a club which engaged in business was not exempt, but no precise numerical test existed. Note that this regulation, proposed in 1956 and adopted in 1958, has not been revised since.

(a) "35/15" Test

The revenue test is two-pronged. First, an overall test requires that nonmember receipts, including investment income, cannot equal more than 35 percent of the club's "traditional, normal and usual activity." Extraordinary and nonrecurring income, such as gain on the clubhouse sale or member initiation and capital assessment fees, are excluded from the denominator and numerator for this test. Irregularly held events (but probably not annual events) are not counted. The revenues from a golf tournament held every twenty years were not counted in the test, but was subject to the tax on unrelated business

---

[46]Rev. Rul. 71-17, 1971-1 C.B. 683.
[47]Rev. Rul. 74-489, 1974-2 C.B. 169.
[48]Exempt Organization Handbook (IRM 7751) §727.
[49]Reg. §1.501(c)(7)-1(b).

income.[50] Capital gains from investment activity and unrelated business income (including that set aside for charity) are also included in gross receipts.[51]

The second prong of the test regards nonmember revenue only. The IRS provides the following guidelines for measuring nonmember usage and revenue:[52]

- Gross receipts from the general public (nonmember) facility and service charges may not exceed 15 percent of total receipts.

- The revenue generated from guest charges are attributed to members for bonafide guests—but only when the members pays.

- For auditing purposes, the IRS has provided that groups of eight or fewer persons which include one member are counted as a member receipt. For larger parties, guests may be treated as members if 75 percent or more of the group using club facilities are members. Typical business luncheon clubs hosting the Rotary Club, tax study forums, and similar groups have a hard time meeting this test.

- Reciprocal membership arrangements do not turn a visitor into a member.[53]

(b) Failing the Test

Failure of the 35/15 test in one year does not necessarily cause immediate revocation of exemption. The facts and circumstances of each case can be considered individually when the club makes its case for continued exemption. The IRS is more likely to be sympathetic if an organization fails the test because of an unusual or occasional special event, as opposed to receiving regular, perhaps daily, funds from nonmembers.[54] If the club experiences a one-year failure out of a number of years, as opposed to a small but recurring annual failure, continued qualification is more likely. The purpose for which facilities are made available to nonmembers will also be considered.

Accounting records are essential to document nonmember use and proper categories of gross receipts. The IRS procedures[55] contain detailed criteria which clubs serving nonmembers must study carefully to distinguish between member and nonmember income. The total income of a club failing to keep the required details is subject to the unrelated business income tax. The records must reflect:

- Date;

- Number in each party, indicating members and nonmembers;

[50] Priv. Ltr. Rul. 7838018.
[51] Senate Report 94-1318, 2nd Session, 1976-2 C.B. 597, 599.
[52] Rev. Proc. 71-17, 1971-1 C.B. 683.
[53] GCM 39343; Rev. Proc. 71-17.
[54] Exempt Organization Handbook (IRM 7751) §733(1).
[55] Rev. Proc. 71-17, *supra*, n. 46.

- Total charges attributable to members and nonmembers; and

- Charges paid by nonmembers (based upon signed statements regarding reimbursements, including those of employers).

9.5 UNRELATED BUSINESS INCOME TAX

Social clubs are significantly different from other tax-exempt entities in one important respect: the definition of their unrelated business income subject to regular income tax. IRC §512(a)(3)(A) provides a special definition for social clubs, as well as voluntary employee benefit associations (VEBAs), group legal services plans, and supplemental unemployment funds. Taxable income includes all gross income except exempt function income, rather than only gross income from an unrelated trade or business. Exempt function income is "gross income from dues, fees, charges, or similar amounts paid by members of the organization as consideration for providing such members or their dependents or guest goods, facilities, or services constituting the basis for exemption."

This definition subjects all other social club income to regular income tax, including nonmember revenues, special events, golf tournaments, royalties, rents, dividends, interest, all other investment income, and unrelated business income. Permissible deductions are discussed below. The dividend deduction is not allowed.[56] An unlimited charitable deduction is permitted as discussed in Section 9.5(g).

(a) Rationale for Different UBI Treatment

In extending the unrelated business income tax to social clubs in 1969, Congress reiterated its intention to allow individuals to join together to provide recreational or social facilities or other benefits on a mutual basis without tax consequences. However, it made clear that tax exemption is proper applied only to sources of income received from the membership. When the club receives income from sources outside the membership, such as interest income on its savings or charges to outsiders for use of its facilities, it is taxed. Exempting such income from tax would allow club members to use tax-free dollars to pay for recreational and pleasure pursuits.

Note that all types of nonexempt function income are subject to the tax without the "trade or business' standard applied to other types of exempt organizations. The sale of timber from a wildlife preserve necessary to maintain its usefulness, in the IRS's opinion, was not a business activity because the club's exempt purposes were furthered. Nonetheless, the sale generated UBI because it was not a direct exempt function.[57]

(b) Sales of Real Estate

A gain from sale of real estate used in regular club activity to perform its exempt function is not classed as UBI, to the extent that the proceeds are

[56] IRC §512(a)(3)(A).
[57] G.C.M. 39688 (December 18, 1987).

reinvested one year before or three years after the date of the sale.[58] Note the phrase "used in regular club activities." Property contiguous to the club, held for possible future expansion or simply to protect the club from the suburbs, is not used directly, according to the IRS. In its opinion, which has been sustained in court,[59] only property in actual, direct, continuous, and regular use for social and recreational purposes qualifies. A steep buffer tract heavily wooded with thick undergrowth, was found not to be used directly in exempt functions. Even though it served to isolate the club from the surrounding developed area and roads, its physical condition indicated that it was not devoted to exempt activity. Proceeds from granting a permanent easement for passage and use produced UBI.[60]

Because social clubs, particularly country clubs and old-line city clubs, often own valuable real estate, this exception can be valuable. When the property is considered to be used for a nonexempt function, the club must treat the revenue as nonmember revenue, and faces the possibility of failing the 35/15 test discussed in Section 9.4. Before that test was provided in 1976, a number of interesting cases used a slightly different, but instructive, standard for evaluating the relatedness of a piece of real estate. Continued exemption for the club was the issue. A Florida club sold a portion of its property to participate in a land price boom and distributed the proceeds to the members. The court noted that the sale was a "violent departure" from the club's normal behavior and not merely incidental to the regular functions of the club. Since financial gain was the aim, the court revoked the club's exemption.[61]

(c) Classification of Nonmember Losses

For years, the IRS and social clubs have been fighting in the courts about the offset of losses from nonmember activities against investment income. The battle has been fought on two different fronts: (1) how to calculate the loss (i.e., what portion of the club's fixed, or indirect, expenses are deductible), and (2) the deductibility of the loss itself.

IRC §512(a)(3)(A) allows deduction of expenses that are directly connected with the production of gross income otherwise allowed by the Code (i.e., ordinary and necessary business expenses allowed to for-profit businesses under §162). However, since 1981, the IRS has taken the position that a profit motive must be present for these expenses to qualify as allowable trade or business expenses.[62] The IRS has also argued that different activities are not to be aggregated.

In a 1985 memorandum decision, the Tax Court took the narrower position that The Brook's nonmember activity expenses were not "connected with the production of" income at all. In 1986, the Second Circuit Court of Appeals overruled the decision and held that all ordinary and necessary expenses of

---

[58] IRC §512(a)(3)(D).

[59] *Cleveland Athletic Club v. Commissioner*, T.C. Memo 1991-83 (1991); *Framingham Country Club v. U.S.*, 659 F. Supp. 650 (D. Mass. 1987).

[60] Tech. Adv. Memo. 9225001.

[61] *Juniper Hunting Club v. Commissioner*, *supra* n. 33.

[62] Rev. Rul. 81-69, 1981-1 C.B. 351.

producing nonmember income, including investment income, were deductions only so long as they were incurred for the purpose of producing a profit.[63] For a thorough history, see North Ridge Country Club[64] (in which the Ninth Circuit ruled against the club) and Cleveland Athletic Club[65] (in which the Sixth Circuit allowed losses).

(d) Direct and Indirect Costs

The issue of deductible expenses is even more complicated, because there are two types of expenses involved in calculating the profit or loss from any activity of the club:

1. *Fixed or indirect expenses,* such as club facility costs, insurance, mortgage interest, depreciation, utilities, managers, and other overhead, which the club incurs to serve its basic membership and sustains whether or not nonmembers are served ("but for expenses"); and

2. *Variable or direct expenses,* such as food, waiters, golf caddies, and other expenses incurred in direct relationship to number of persons served, including members and nonmembers.

The confusion starts from the fact that terms normally used in cost accounting texts—fixed and variable, direct and indirect—are absent from the Code. The regulations only add a stipulation that the expenses must have a proximate and primary relationship to the income, and provides for allocation of expenses attributable to both related and unrelated income.

In June, 1990, the Supreme Court unanimously decided that Portland Golf Club's nonmember activity losses were not deductible against investment income, because the activity was neither profitable nor profit-motivated. To calculate the loss for both purposes, direct and indirect costs had to be taken into account.[66] The Supreme Court agreed with the IRS's long-standing position that fixed and indirect expenses, which the club incurs whether or not it serves nonmembers, are not deductible to the extent they exceed nonmember income. Essentially, a social club cannot deduct an allocable portion of its basic member fixed expenses against its investment income, unless the nonmember activity is profit-motivated. The Court looked to the hobby loss standards of IRC §183 to test the profit motivation, particularly because the Portland Golf Club incurred losses in every year from 1975 through 1984.

(e) How to Measure Profit Motive

A secondary, but important, aspect of the *Portland Golf Club* case was an argument about how to measure profit motive. Are both direct and indirect

---

[63]*The Brook, Inc. v. Commissioner,* 86-2 U.S.T.C. §9646 (2nd Cir. 1989), *rev'g* 50 T.C.M. 959, 51 TCM 133 (1985).

[64]*North Ridge Country Club v. Commissioner,* 89-1 U.S.T.C. §9363 (9th Cir. 1989), *rev'g* 89 T.C. 563 (1987).

[65]*Cleveland Athletic Club, Inc. v. U.S.,* 86-1 U.S.T.C. §9116 (6th Cir. 1986).

[66]*Portland Golf Club v. Commissioner,* 90-1 U.S.T.C. §50,332 (110 S. Ct. 2780) 1990).

costs taken into account? Or is the fact that the nonmember direct income covers nonmember direct expenses (without any reduction for allocable indirect expense) sufficient evidence of profit motive? The Portland Golf Club argued that since its nonmember income exceeded its nonmember direct expenses, it had a profit motive. The Court disagreed, and unless Congress acts to change the tax laws, profit motive for this purpose is calculated by deducting both direct and indirect costs associated with nonmember income.

Another issue to consider is whether one cost allocation method can be used to measure profit motive while another method is used to calculate taxable income. This issue was not settled in *Portland Golf Club*, although most justices thought that only one method can be used for both purposes. The question then becomes which method to use. Any method reasonably calculated to arrive at a fair allocation, and consistently applied, can be used. The regulations under IRC §512 provide that allocations must be made on a reasonable basis. The two basic methods used in the social club field are:

1. *Gross-to-gross method.* Actual gross revenues from members and non-members are used to allocate the costs.

2. *Actual use method.* Square footage occupied and hours of actual use are tabulated to calculate fixed cost allocations. Here, the numerator of the equation is important. In a case involving a football stadium, the IRS and taxpayers have argued whether the proper divisor is the total number of hours in the year or the total number of hours the stadium was used. Sections 21.14 and 27.14 for further discussion of cost allocations.

(f) Aggregating Nonmember Activities

The last issue is whether all nonmember activities can be aggregated to evaluate profit motive and allocable costs. As of October, 1992, the Tax Court has sided with the Atlanta Athletic Club to allow aggregation. Losses from nonmember food and beverage sales and facility fees (e.g., golf greens, tennis, pool) were deductible against profits from two professional golf tournaments. The club argued that there was a common business purpose for promoting its nonmember undertakings, but the IRS said that each activity had to be considered separately, and any profitable activities taxed. The club's victory was only partial. The overall loss from nonmember activity was not deductible against other investment income because the court found the requisite profit motive lacking, following the *Portland* rationale.[67]

(g) Charitable Set-Aside

A charitable deduction is allowed to a social club for any income paid directly for charitable purposes or as a grant to a charitable organization. Funds that are earmarked or set aside for future charitable purposes may be deductible.[68]

---

[67]*Atlanta Athletic Club v. Commissioner*, T.C. Memo 1991-83 (1991).
[68]IRC Section §512(a)(3)(b)(i); *Phi Delta Theta Fraternity v. Commissioner*, 887 F.2d 1302 (6th Cir. 1989), *aff'g* 90 T.C.B. 1033 (1988).

Set-asides must meet the requirement of IRC §170(c)(4) that the contribution or gift be used only for specified charitable purposes. The IRS position was confirmed when a court ruled that the Phi Delta Theta fraternity magazine was not educational, but rather served the recreational purposes of the members. Endowment income used to support the publication did not qualify for the charitable set-aside donation.

9.6 FILING REQUIREMENTS

Social clubs file Form 1024 for recognition of exemption and file Form 990 or 990EZ annually to report financial activity to the IRS. See Chapter 18. Form 990T is filed to report unrelated business income. See Section 27.14.

A nonexempt membership club (or one whose exemption has been revoked) files Form 1120 as a regular corporation, subject to IRC §277, which allows deduction of expenses attributable to membership activities only to the extent of membership income, and taxes all other income. The primary difference is taxation of member operating profits.

Social clubs that claimed deductions subsequently disallowed by the *Portland Golf Club* case (discussed in Section 9.5) were expected to file amended returns to reflect the decision. In 1990, the IRS reopened cases held in suspense pending the decision.[69] Field offices have been instructed to monitor "filing patterns" of social clubs to see that amended Forms 990-T are filed.

[69] IRS Announcement 90-138, IRB 1990-51, November 29, 1990.

Instrumentalities of the Government: §501(c)(1), Title-Holding Corporations: §501(c)(2) and §501(c)(25)

10.1 QUALIFYING AS AN INSTRUMENTALITY OF THE UNITED STATES UNDER AN ACT OF CONGRESS: §501(c)(1)

IRC §501(c)(1) exempts "instrumentalities" of the United States organized specifically under an act of Congress. Among these instrumentalities are the following:

Federal Deposit Insurance Corporation (FDIC)
Federal Home Loan Banks
Federal Land Banks
Federal Intermediate Credit Banks
Federal National Mortgage Association (FNMA)
Federal Reserve Bank
Federal Crop Insurance Corporation
United States Housing Authority
Pennsylvania Avenue Development Corporation
Federal Credit Unions
Pension Benefit Guaranty Corporation

These creations of Congress are considered exempt because they are wholly owned by the United States government. They are not required to file annual information returns, nor to apply for exemption from income tax.

States and their municipalities, interestingly, are not exempted by this section nor by any other part of §501(c). They are presumed to be exempt because they can meet the definition of §501(c)(3).

10.2 QUALIFYING AS A TITLE-HOLDING CORPORATION: §501(c)(2)

According to IRC §501(c)(2), "Corporations organized for the exclusive purpose of holding title to property, collecting income therefrom, and turning over the entire amount thereof, less expenses, to an organization that itself is exempt" under IRC §501 are title-holding companies (THCs). After some years of confusion and hesitation, IRC §501(c)(25) was added in 1986 to permit THCs with multiple parents, as described below.

Essentially, a title-holding corporation is a passive entity whose tax exemption stems from its subservient relationship to another exempt organization. The full range of §501 organizations discussed in this part, including pension plans, are permissible beneficiaries. A THC is most often created to limit the exposure to liability for its creator(s) for owning the property transferred to or purchased by the THC. A separate property-owning arm may also be useful for administrative or management reasons, or to permit joint ownership under §501(c)(25).

10.3 ORGANIZATIONAL REQUIREMENTS UNDER §501(c)(2)

An IRC §501(c)(2) title-holding corporation, as its name implies, cannot be a trust, joint venture, or other unincorporated form of organization. It must be a corporation or an association classified as a corporation under IRC §7701(a)(3).

The "exclusive purpose" clause of the statute is strictly applied. The THC's purpose is reflected by its charter, its activities, and the facts and circumstances under which it was created. All of these factors are taken into account by the IRS in evaluating evidence that a THC's purposes are strictly limited to those provided in the statute. A THC will not be granted exemption if it engages in any business other than that of holding title to property and collecting income therefrom.[1] A charter containing language that empowers the organization to engage in broader activities is not acceptable.[2] When the charter language contains the appropriate constraints but the organization's proposed or actual activity goes beyond the limits, exemption may be denied. The (c)(25) THC must also comply with the specific requirements explained below.

(a) Connection to Beneficiary Organization

The amount of control and the relationship that must exist between the title-holding corporation and the exempt organization it benefits are not speci-

---

[1]Reg. §1501(c)(2)-1; Senate Report No. 2375, 81st Congress, 2d Session (1950), 1950-2 C.B. 483, 504.
[2]Rev. Rul. 58-455, 1958-2 C.B. 261.

fied in the statute or in the regulation (which is only two paragraphs long). However, the IRS *Exempt Organizations Handbook* provides some guidelines.

A parent-subsidiary relationship is the most common form for a THC. As a rule, the THC must be controlled by and be responsive to the exempt organization for which it holds property, despite the lack of specific requirements in the statute or regulations. In the IRS's view, the elements of control necessary include owning the voting stock of the THC, possessing the power to select nominees to hold the voting stock, or having the ability to appoint the directors.[3] A group of philanthropists was not allowed to establish a THC that would have essentially circumvented the private foundation rules.

A single controlling beneficiary organization is ostensibly required for §501(c)(2) entities. The long-standing policy of the IRS has been to consider multiple parents as evidence of asset pooling, not mere holding of title.[4] However, for some years the IRS debated the possibility that "conceivably a title-holding company might hold title for more than one kind of exempt."[5] Fortunately, in 1986 Congress created §501(c)25, allowing pooled ownership in real estate by a group of EOs.

The method of a title-holding company's formation may be controlled by state or local rules. In one example, a title-holding company was approved despite being controlled by a broad individual base of members (a college fraternity), when the stock conferred no rights to dividends or distributions to members. All of the income from the property was payable to the §501(c)(7) organization.[6]

A THC controlled by and created to benefit a private foundation may face additional constraints. See Chapters 12 through 17.

(b) Restrictions on Activity

The operating powers of a THC must be limited to those required to hold title to, conserve, keep up the property, and remit income to the beneficiary organization. Under §501(c)(2), "property" can include real and personal property, investments, and exempt function assets.[7] A (c)(25) THC, on the other hand, can only hold real estate. Traditionally, the title-holding corporation holds assets that need protection from exposure to operational liability, or holds property that would expose the benefited organization to unacceptable risks. There is no express reason why operational or exempt function assets cannot be kept in a holding company along with real estate. Actively operating exempt functions by the THC within the facility, however, is not permissible because it goes beyond "title-holding." A subsidiary of a veterans organization that held title to a building *and* operated the social facilities located in the building was not permitted THC status.[8]

---

[3] Rev. Rul. 71-544, 1971-2 C.B. 227.
[4] IRS General Counsel Memoranda 39341 and 37551.
[5] IRS Exempt Organizations Handbook (IRM 7751) §281.
[6] Rev. Rul. 68-222, 1968-1 C.B. 243.
[7] Rev. Rul. 76-335, 1976-2 C.B. 141.
[8] Rev. Rul. 66-150, 1966-1 C.B. 147.

An activity that generates unrelated business income (UBI) is generally not appropriate to be carried on by a THC, although certain types of UBI associated with real estate operations can be earned. Such income includes debt-financed income under IRC §514, net profits-based rental transactions, personal property rentals (alongside real property), and investment income earned by a title-holding entity taxed because it benefits a social club or voluntary employee benefits association (VEBA).[9] See Chapter 21 for a more detailed definition of UBI.

Passive investments suitable as THC holdings include stocks and bonds, rental real estate, and oil and gas royalties or production payments. Equipment related alongside real estate is also acceptable, and is common among universities and hospitals.

Operating a merchandise store, managing a hotel, providing investment management services,[10] holding a working interest in an oil well, and other active business pursuits are not permitted.[11] When business activity is anticipated, the property should instead be spun off or transferred to a taxable "feeder" subsidiary as provided in IRC §502.

IRC §511(c) provides that, for UBI purposes, the THC is to be treated as being organized for the same purposes for which its parent is organized, if it meets two requirements:

1. It turns over all of the net income to the parent; and

2. It files a consolidated return with the parent.

10.4 "TURNING OVER" THE INCOME

Accumulation of surplus income by a title-holding corporation generally is contrary to the statutory theme of "turning over" the income. As a rule, all net income must be paid over to the beneficiary organization. Deductions for depreciation[12] and reserves or sinking funds to make current or future mortgage payments[13] are allowed to be withheld from turnover. A reasonable provision for maintenance or restoration of the property can also be deducted from distributable income. Rents can also be used to repay an interest-free construction loan through an organization also controlled by the THC's parent.[14] Regarding the timing for distribution of funds, there is no specific requirement, but a delay with no justification, as evidenced by a substantial surplus, should be expected to bring IRS scrutiny.

Payment to the beneficiary is customarily made in the form of cash dividends, or grants in the case of a nonstock company. When the THC owns the building occupied by the parent and no rent is paid, there may be no

[9]Reg. 1.501(c)(2)-1(a).
[10]Rev. Rul. 69-528, 1969-2 C.B. 127.
[11]Rev. Rul. 66-295, 1966-2 C.B. 207.
[12]Rev. Rul. 66-102, 1966-1 C.B. 133.
[13]Rev. Rul. 77-429, 1977-2 C.B. 189.
[14]Priv. Ltr. Rul. 9213027.

income generated and available to be paid. In such cases, the rent-free use of the building fulfills the statutory scheme.

10.5 WHY FORM A TITLE-HOLDING CORPORATION?

A number of factors must be considered before deciding to form a title-holding corporation. Among the advantages of a THC are the opportunity it provides to shelter some assets from operating fund liabilities, and the fact that it increases the beneficiary organization's borrowing power. Setting up a THC also facilitates separate management and administration of a corporation's physical plant. Another advantage of a THC is that it creates a nonmember form of real estate ownership for a member-controlled organization.

There is, of course, a down side to the formation of a title-holding corporation. First, it increases paperwork burdens: Form 1024 must be filed in order for the IRS to recognize the exemption, and Form 990 must be filed annually if gross receipts normally exceed $25,000. Some relief of the compliance burden may be gained by filing a consolidated tax return, which is permitted by IRC §1504(e).

On the other hand, there are situations in which the formation of a THC is ill-advised. The tax exemption of the THC is dependent upon the continued qualification of its beneficiary. If the parent company loses its exemption, the THC automatically loses its §501(c)(2) status.[15] Also, the THC cannot be used as a fundraising vehicle, because donations to a THC generally do not qualify as charitable contributions under IRC §170. In a private ruling, the IRS has held that gifts dedicated expressly to a charitable project conducted by a THC are deductible.[16]

10.6 REQUIREMENTS FOR §501(c)(25) TITLE-HOLDING CORPORATIONS

The IRC §501(c)(25) THC serves a very narrow but significant purpose: to facilitate pooled purchasing and holding of real estate. It can hold no other type of asset and is only available to four specified types of organizations. Multiple unrelated exempt organizations may form a THC so long as it possesses the following characteristics:

1. It must be a corporation or a trust;

2. It must have no more than 35 shareholders or beneficiaries;

3. It must have only one class of stock or beneficial interest;

4. It must be organized for the exclusive purposes of acquiring real property, holding title to and collecting the income from such property, and remitting the income (net of expenses) to one or more qualifying shareholders or beneficiaries; and

---

[15]Rev. Rul. 68-371, 1968-2 C.B. 204.
[16]Priv. Ltr. Rul. 8705041.

5. Its shareholders must be one of the following types of organizations:

- §501(c)(3) organization,

- §401(a) qualified employee plan,

- §414(d) government plan, or

- Federal, state, or local government agency or instrumentality.

Since this type of exempt organization was created in 1986, the IRS has issued two Notices providing detailed guidance for their establishment, which must be carefully studied by anyone contemplating the creation of a (c)(25) THC. There still are no regulations as of October 1992, and exemption applications for this type of THC are reviewed and determinations are issued only by the national office. The expanded criteria for qualification as fleshed out by the IRS include:

1. The articles of incorporation, bylaws, or trust document must contain language that clearly demonstrates that the entity satisfies the five statutory requirements listed above;

2. Removal of the investment advisor must be permitted by a majority vote of the beneficial owners; and

3. Termination of a beneficiary's interest must be allowed in one of two ways:

   - By selling or exchanging its stock or interest to another qualifying (c)(25) organization (provided that the total number of shareholders remains below 35), or

   - Upon 90 days notice, by having its shares or beneficial interest redeemed.[17]

[17] Notice 87-18, 1987-1 C.B. 455; Notice 88-121, 1988-2 C.B. 457.

CHAPTER ELEVEN

Public Charities

The significance of "public charity" status for organizations tax exempt under IRC §501(c)(3) is multifaceted, and is of utmost importance to both private and public exempt organizations. Knowing the meaning of the four parts of IRC §509 is the key to understanding public charities. *All* §501(c)(3) organizations, other than those listed in §509(a)(1), (2), (3), and (4) are private foundations, and are subject to the operational constraints outlined in Chapters 12 through 17. The specific requirements of each of the §509 categories are described below. Briefly, the four categories of public charities are:

§509(a)(1)—Organizations engaging in inherently public activity and those supported by the general public.

§509(a)(2)—Organizations supported by charges for services.

§509(a)(3)—Supporting organizations.

§509(a)(4)—Organizations that test for public safety.

11.1 DISTINCTIONS BETWEEN PUBLIC AND PRIVATE

Private foundations must comply with a variety of special rules and sanctions, so it is useful, when possible, to obtain and maintain public status. The important attributes of private foundations (PFs), compared to public charities (in parentheses) include:

- The percentage limitation on deductions for contributions by individuals under IRC §170 is only 30 percent of adjusted gross income for cash gifts, and 20 percent for appreciated property gifts. (Up to 50 percent of one's AGI can be deducted for cash gifts to public charity, and 30 percent for gifts of appreciated property.) To illustrate, assume that a generous taxpayer with an income of $1 million wants to annually give $500,000 in cash for charitable pursuits. Only $300,000 of the annual gift would be deductible if it is given to a private foundation. The full $500,000 is deductible if it is given to a public charity.

- Appreciated property, other than corporate stock for which a quotation is readily available on an established securities market, is not fully deductible when given to a PF—only the basis of real estate, closely held company stock, or other types of property is deductible.[1] (A full deduction is potentially available for a gift of such property to a public charity.)

- An excise tax of two percent must be paid on a PF's investment income, as outlined in Chapter 13. (There is no tax on investment income for a public charity.)

- A PF cannot buy or sell property, nor enter into most "self-dealing" transactions with its directors, officers, contributors, or their family members, under any circumstances. (Public charities can have business dealings with their insiders, within limits. See Chapter 20 for a discussion of private inurement and Chapter 14 regarding self-dealing.)

- Annual returns must be filed by PFs regardless of support levels and value of assets. (No return is required for certain public organizations, and an EZ form is available for many others. See Chapter 27.)

- Fundraising between PFs is constrained by "expenditure responsibility" requirements which prohibit one private foundation from giving to another without contractual agreements and follow-up procedures. See Chapter 17. (No such policing of grant moneys is required for public charities.)

- Absolutely no lobbying activity by PFs is permitted. (See Chapter 23 for lobbying activity allowed by public charities.) Absolutely no *political* activity is permitted either for public or private charities.

- A PF's annual spending for grants to other organizations and charitable projects must meet the "minimum distribution" requirement described in Section 15.3 (A public charity has no specific spending requirement.)

---

[1] IRC §170(e)(1)(B) and (e)(5).

Exhibit 11–1

DIFFERENCES BETWEEN PUBLIC AND PRIVATE CHARITABLE ORGANIZATIONS

	Charitable Deduction	Excise Tax	Activities	Minimum Distribution Requirements	Annual Filings
Private Foundations	• limited to 30% of AGI* for cash and qualified appreciated stock gifts; • other property is limited to 20% and basis	• 2% of investment income • 5–15% of amount of disqualified transactions	• grants to other organizations • no lobbying • limits on grants to other PFs • self-initiated projects	• 5% of fair market value for investment assets	• all must file Form 990PF • newspaper notice
Private Operating Foundations	• limited to 30% for appreciated property, 50% for cash	• same as for PFs	• carries out self-initiated projects • no lobbying	• $3\frac{1}{3}$% fair market value investment assets	• same as for private
Public Charities	• same as for POFs	• No tax on income (except UBI) • Excise tax on excess lobbying	• can lobby • grant-making or carry out own projects	• none • no excess accumulation of surplus	• file if gross revenue over $25,000. Form 990 or 990EZ.

*Adjusted gross income.

- Holding more than 20 percent of a business enterprise, including shares owned by board members and contributors, is prohibited for PFs as are "jeopardizing investments," as discussed in Chapter 16. (No such limits are placed on public charities.)

Exhibit 11–1 summarizes these differences.

11.2 "INHERENTLY PUBLIC ACTIVITY" AND BROAD PUBLIC SUPPORT: §509(a)(1)

A wide variety of organizations qualify as public charities under IRC §509(a)(1). The (a)(1) category includes all those organizations described in IRC §170(b)(1)(A)(i)–(vi), which defines organizations eligible to receive deductible charitable contributions. The definition is complicated and rather unwieldy because it includes six distinct types of exempt entities. Because of the Code's design, the categories are labeled with numerical letters.

The first five categories include those organizations that perform what the IRS calls "inherently public activity."[2] The first three achieve public status because of the nature of their activities without regard to sources of funds with which they pay their bills—even if they are privately supported. The fourth and fifth are closely connected with governmental support and activities. Last but certainly not least, because it includes a wide variety of charities, the sixth category includes those organizations balancing their budgets with donations from a sizable group of supporters, such as the United Way or American Red Cross. They must meet a mathematically-measured contribution base formula.

(a) Churches

The first category includes a "church, convention, or association of churches." Churches are narrowly defined and not all religious organizations are regarded as churches. Chapter 3 is devoted to these distinctions. Perhaps due to the need to separate church and state, neither the Internal Revenue Code nor the IRS regulations define a church.

(b) Schools

Although the title does not say "school," the second category basically includes formal schools. To qualify as a school, the Code says that this type of public organization must be an "educational organization that normally maintains a regular faculty and curriculum and normally has a regularly enrolled body of pupils or students in attendance at the place where its educational activities are regularly carried on." Note that the world of educational organizations for purposes of IRC §501(c)(3) is much broader, as discussed in Chapter 5. For this reason, the term "school" is used in this discussion.

---

[2] 1992 Exempt Organizations Continuing Professional Education Technical Instruction Program, p. 216.

The presentation of formal instruction must be a primary function of a school. The term includes primary, secondary, preparatory, and high schools, and colleges and universities. Schools publicly supported by federal, state, and local governments qualify for this category, and in some cases also qualify as governmental units under (e), discussed below.[3]

What the regulations call "noneducational" activities must be incidental. A recognized university can operate a museum or sponsor concerts and remain a school. A museum's art school, however, does not make the museum a school.[4]

All four elements must be present to achieve recognition as a school: regular faculty, students, curriculum, and facility. A home-tutoring entity providing private tutoring was held not to be an educational organization for this purpose.[5] Likewise, a correspondence school was not approved under this section because it lacked a physical site where classes were conducted.[6]

The word "curriculum" was loosely construed in a ruling which permitted an elementary school to qualify despite the fact that it had no "formal course program" and espoused an open learning concept.[7] However, leisure learning classes, in the eyes of the IRS, do not present a sufficiently formal course of instruction to qualify as a school. Lectures and short courses on a variety of general subjects not leading to a degree or accreditation do not constitute a curriculum.[8] Also, invited authorities and personalities recognized in the field are not considered to be members of a regular faculty.[9]

The duration of the courses has not been considered a barrier by the IRS. An outdoor survival school whose classes lasted only 26 days, but were conducted with regular teachers, students, and course study, was classified as a school, despite the fact that part of the facilities it used were wide open spaces.[10]

(c) Hospitals

This class of public charity includes hospitals, the principal purpose or function of which is providing medical or hospital care, medical education, or medical research. An organization directly engaged in continuous, active medical research in conjunction with a hospital may also qualify if, during the year in which the contribution is made, the funds are committed to be spent within five years.

Medical care includes the treatment of any physical or mental disability or condition, on an inpatient or outpatient basis. A rehabilitation institution, outpatient clinic, or community mental health or drug treatment center may qualify. Convalescent homes, homes for children or the aged, handicapped vocational training centers, and medical schools are not considered to be

[3]Reg. §1.170A-9(b).
[4]Rev. Rul. 76-167, 1976-1 C.B. 329.
[5]Rev. Rul. 76-384, 1976-2 C.B. 57.
[6]Rev. Rul. 75-492, 1975-2 C.B. 80.
[7]Rev. Rul. 72-430, 1972-2 C.B. 105.
[8]Rev. Rul. 62-23, 1962-1 C.B. 200.
[9]Rev. Rul. 78-82, 1978-1 C.B. 70.
[10]Rev. Rul. 73-434, 1973-2 C.B. 71.

hospitals.[11] An animal clinic was also found not to be a hospital.[12] The issues involved in qualifying for exemption as a hospital are evolving, and close attention must be paid to the latest information. These issues are discussed in Section 4.6 and Appendix 28–1.

Medical research is the conduct of investigations, experiments, and studies to discover, develop, or verify knowledge relating to the causes, diagnosis, treatment, prevention, or control of physical or mental diseases and impairments of man. "Appropriate equipment and qualified personnel necessary to carry out its principal function must be regularly used." The disciplines spanning the biological, social, and behavioral sciences, such as chemistry, psychiatry, biomedical engineering, virology, immunology, biophysics, and associated medical fields must be studied.[13] Such organizations must conduct research directly. Granting funds to other organizations, while possible, may not be a primary purpose.[14] The rules governing a research organization's expenditure of funds and its endowment levels are complicated, and the regulations must be studied to understand this type of public organization.

(d) College and University Support Organizations

An entity operating to receive, hold, invest, and administer property and to make expenditures to or for the benefit of a college or university qualifying under 170(b)(1)(A)(ii) are public charities. Such entities must normally receive a substantial part of their support from governmental grants and contributions from the general public, other than exempt function revenue.

(e) Governmental Units

The United States, District of Columbia, states, possessions of the United States, and their political subdivisions are classified as governmental units. Importantly, such a unit qualifies as a public charity without regard to its sources of support, partly because, by its nature, it is responsive to all citizens. The regulations contain no additional definition or explanation of the meaning of the term, but two cases shed some light.

An unincorporated intergovernmental cooperative organization established by an act of the Texas legislature on behalf of a consortium of eleven Texas public school districts was found to be a private foundation, not a governmental unit, for two reasons:[15]

1. Its source of support was a particular private foundation which granted it the money to undertake its curriculum research and development. .

2. It was not a governmental unit. Although the cooperative arguably was an instrumentality of the state, it had no sovereign powers, such as the

[11] Reg. §1.170A-9(c)(1).
[12] Rev. Rul. 74-572, 1974-2 C.B. 82.
[13] Reg. §1.170A-9(c)(2)(iii).
[14] Reg. §1.170A-9(c)(2)(v)(c).
[15] *Texas Learning Technology Group v. Commissioner*, 96 T.C. 28 (April 30, 1991).

right of eminent domain, the power to assess and collect taxes, or police powers. The fact that it was an integral part of a group of governmental units—the public schools by which it was established—did not make it a governmental unit.

The Michigan Education Trust likewise was not classified as a governmental unit.[16] Although it was created by the legislature, its directors were appointed by the governor, its investments were managed by employees of the state Department of Treasury, and its assets were payable to the state upon dissolution, it was not an integral part of the state. Its assets were not available to state creditors, and the advance tuition contracts issued by the trust were not secured by state funds.

(f) Publicly Supported Organizations

Public charities under this category are those organizations which normally receive at least 33 1/3 percent of their annual support from donations from members of the general public (not including fees and charges for performing exempt functions).[17] "Normally" means based on an aggregation of the four years preceding the year in question: for 1993, the revenue for 1989 through 1992 is used.[18] As Exhibits 11–2 and 11–3 illustrate, the numerical test for this category is similar to the (a)(2) test shown in Exhibits 11–4 and 11–5. The exhibits reflect two different approaches to the calculation. The IRS chart adds the qualifying types of income. The author's chart starts with total gross and deducts support not counted. In either case, the result should be the same. Many of the concepts and definitions overlap and are defined and compared below in Section 11.4(a). To arrive at includable donations for this type of public charity, one particular concept is vital.

Two Percent Gifts. There is a two percent ceiling for donations included as public support. Only a minimal amount of a particular contributor's annual gift is counted in public donations, whether that contributor is an individual, corporation, trust, private foundation, or other type of entity (and related parties).

Take, for example, an organization receiving total support during the four year test period of $1 million. In such a case, all contributions of up to $20,000 could be counted as public donations. If one person gave a total of $80,000, or $20,000 each year, only $20,000 is counted. The $1 million organization must receive at least $333,333 in public donations of $20,000 or less each. It could receive $666,666 from one source and $10,000 from 33 sources or $20,000 from 17 sources, for example.

A public donation = Up to and no more than 2% of total support
$20,000 = 2% of $1 million.

---

[16]*Michigan v. U.S.,* 92-2 U.S.T.C. §50, 424 (D.C. W. Mich 1992).
[17]Reg. §1.170A-9(e)(2).
[18]Reg. §1.170A-9(e)(4).

PUBLIC CHARITIES

Exhibit 11-2
IRC §509(a)(1) TEST FOR PUBLIC SUPPORT
Under IRC §170(b)(1)(A)(vi)

Preceding Years	1st	2nd	3rd	4th	Total
SUPPORT Gross revenues less:					
1. Exempt function revenue					
2. Capital gains or losses					
3. Unusual grants					
4. Tax on UBI					
5. Expenses of UBI acquired before June 30, 1975					
6. In-kind services or facilities not furnished by governmental unit					
TOTAL SUPPORT:					
PUBLIC SUPPORT					
1. Grants from governmental units					
2. Grants from other §107(b)(1)(A)(vi) organizations					
3. All other contributions, excluding the amount by which any donor's (and related persons) total gifts exceed for the four years exceed two percent of total support					
TOTAL PUBLIC SUPPORT:					

ONE-THIRD SUPPORT TEST

$$\frac{\text{Total Public Support}}{\text{Total Support}} = \quad \%*$$

* Percentage must be at least 33 1/3 to qualify automatically as "public" under IRC §170(b)(1)(A)(vi). If it is between 10 and 33 1/3, the organization may qualify as "public" if it meets the facts and circumstances test.

Exhibit 11–3
INTERNAL REVENUE SERVICE TRAINING FORM

---

4. Making the Calculation

a. A Support Test Worksheet for IRC 509(a)(1)/ 170(b)(1)(A)(vi) Organizations

Preceding Years ▶	(a) 1st	(b) 2nd	(c) 3rd	(d) 4th	(e) Total
1 Gifts,grants and contributions received (Do not include unusual grants)					
2. Membership fees received.................					
3 Gross income from interest, dividends, amounts received from payments on securities loans (IRC 512(a)(55), rents, royalties and unrelated business tax-able income (less IRC 511 taxes) from business acquired by the organization after June 30, 1975					
4 Net income from unrelated business activities not included in line 3					
5 Tax revenues levied for the organization's benefit and either paid to it or expended on its behalf					
6 The value of services of facilities fur-nished by a governmental unit without charge.Do not include the value of services or facilities generally furnished to the public without charge.					
7 Other income. Do not include gain (or loss) from sale of capital assets					
8 Total of lines 1 through 7..................					

9 Enter 2% of line 8(e).. _____

10 Add lines 1(e), 2(e), 5(e), and 6(e) .... _____

11 Less: Contributions of individual donors in excess of 2% of aggregate total support (line 9).... _____

12 Total public support (numerator) .... _____

13 Aggregate total support from line 8(e) (denominator) .... _____

14 Public support percentage (line 12 divided by line 13).. _____

If line 14 is 33⅓% or more, the organization qualifies under IRC 509(a)(1)/170(b)(1)(A)(vi). If line 14 is less than 33⅓%, consider the facts and circumstances 10% test.

1992 Exempt Organizations Continuing Professional Education Technical Instruction Program, p. 223.

PUBLIC CHARITIES

Exhibit 11–4
IRC §509(a)(2) TEST FOR PUBLIC SUPPORT

Preceding Years	1st	2nd	3rd	4th	Total
SUPPORT Gross revenues less:					
1. Capital gains or losses					
2. Unusual grants					
3. Tax on UBI					
4. Expenses of UBI acquired before June 30, 1975					
5. In-kind services or facilities not furnished by governmental unit					
TOTAL SUPPORT:					
PUBLIC SUPPORT					
1. All contributions except amounts from disqualified persons					
2. Membership dues (under the greater of $5000 or one percent of support each)					
3. Exempt function revenue, except amounts in excess of $5000 (or one percent of total support if greater) from any one person or grantor					
TOTAL PUBLIC SUPPORT:					

ONE-THIRD SUPPORT TEST

$$\frac{\text{Total Public Support}}{\text{Total Support}} = \quad \%*$$

* Percentage must be at least 33 1/3 to qualify automatically as "public" under IRC §170(b)(1)(A)(vi). If it is between 10 and 33 1/3, the organization may qualify as "public" if it meets the facts and circumstances test.

INVESTMENT INCOME TEST

$$\frac{\text{Gross Dividends, Interest, Rent, Royalties, and UBI less UBIT}}{\text{Total Support}}$$

*The percentage for support should be 33 1/3 or more, and the percentage for investment income should be 33 1/3 or less, for the organization to qualify automatically as "public" under IRC §509(a)(2).

Exhibit 11–5

INTERNAL REVENUE SERVICE TRAINING FORM

E. A Support Test Worksheet for IRC 509(a)(2) Organizations

Preceding Years	(a) 1st	(b) 2nd	(c) 3rd	(d) 4th	(e) Total
1 Gifts, grants and contributions received (Do not include unusual grants)					
2 Membership fees received					
3 Gross receipts from admissions, merchandise sold or services performed or furnishing of facilities in any activity that is not a business unrelated to the organization's charitable, etc., purposes					
4 Gross income from interest, dividends, amounts received from payment on securities loans (IRC 512(a)(5)), rents, royalties, and unrelated business taxable income (less IRC 511 taxes) from businesses acquired by the organization after June 30, 1975					
5 Net income from unrelated business activities not included in line 4					
6 Tax revenues levied for the organization's benefit and either paid to it or expended on its behalf					
7 The value of services or facilities furnished by a governmental unit without charge. Do not include the value of services or facilities generally furnished to the public without charge					
8 Other income. Do not include gain (or loss) from sale of capital assets					
9 Total of lines 1 through 8					
10 Enter 1% of line 9					

11 Add lines 1(e), 2(e), 3(e), 6(e) and 7(e) .... _____

12 Deduct: Income from disqualified persons.. _____

Exempt function income exceeding $5,000/1% limit.. _____

13 Line 11 less line 12 = public support (numerator) .... _____

14 Total support from line 9(e) (denominator) .... _____

15 Public support percentage (line 13 divided by line 14) .... _____

> *If line 15 is 33⅓% or more, the public support test is met. Go on to gross investment test. If line 15 is less than 33⅓%, the organization will not qualify under IRC 509(a)(2).*

16 Investment income from line 4(e)..

17 Unrelated business income on line 5(e) less tax paid on that income ....

18 Total of lines 16 and 17 (numerator) ....

19 Total support from line 9(e) (denominator) ....

20 Gross investment percentage (line 18 divided by line 19) ....

> *If line 20 is less than 33⅓%, the gross investment test is met. If line 20 is 33⅓% or more, the organization will not qualify under IRC 509(a)(2).*

1992 Exempt Organizations Continuing Professional Education Technical Instruction Program, p. 231.

Public Charity Grants. Gifts received from another public charity or from a governmental unit are counted fully as donations from the general public,[19] unless the gift was passed through as a donor-designated grant as discussed in Section 11.4(c).

Facts and Circumstances Test. The history of the organization's fundraising efforts and other factors can be considered as an alternative method to the strict mathematical formula for qualifying for public support under (a)(1). This test is not available under (a)(2). IRS approval must be sought for this status. Several factors must be present to meet this test:[20]

- Public support must be at least 10 percent of the total support, and the higher the better.

- The organization must have an active "continuous and bona fide" fundraising program designed to attract new and additional public and governmental support. Consideration will be given to the fact than, in its early years of existence, the EO may limit the scope of its solicitations to those persons deemed most likely to provide seed money in an amount sufficient to enable it to commence its charitable activities and to expand its solicitation program.

- Other favorable factors must be present, such as

  (a) The composition of the board is representative of broad public interests;

  (b) Support comes from governmental and other sources representative of the general public;

  (c) Facilities and programs are made available to the general public, such as a museum or symphony society; and

  (d) Programs appeal to a broadly-based public.

Community Foundations. Another potential (a)(1) entity is a community foundation or trust. Such organizations are designed to attract capital and endowment gifts for the benefit of a particular community or area by pooling donations from benevolent citizens. The requirements, qualifications, and constraints on operation of community foundations are a mixture of the rules governing both private and public charities, and are quite complicated in their application.[21]

A community foundation serves as a convenient vehicle for givers who do not wish to create their own private foundations, but who wish to make bequests, endowments, or other permanent charitable gifts. Donors may designate the purpose for which their gift is to be used, subject to ultimate control by

---

[19] Reg. §1.170A-9(e)(6)(i).
[20] Reg. §1.170A-9(e)(3).
[21] Reg. §1.170A-9(e)(10)–(13).

the foundation's board of directors. "Component parts" can be established by the foundation to hold contributors gifts for restricted purposes.

11.3 SERVICE-PROVIDING ORGANIZATIONS: §509(a)(2)

Like organizations conducting "inherently public" activities, the second major category of public charity is measured by sources of revenue, but there are significant differences. Public support for (a)(2) purposes includes "exempt function income" as shown in Exhibits 11–4 and 11.5. Thus, this category usually includes organizations receiving a major portion of their support from fees and charges for activity participation, such as day care centers, animal shelters, theaters, and educational publishers.

A two-part support test must be met to qualify under this category:

1. Investment income cannot exceed 1/3 of the total support. (Total support basically means the organization's gross revenue except for capital gains.)

2. Over 1/3 of the total support must be received from exempt function sources made up of a combination of the following:

   ■ Gifts, grants, contributions, and membership dues received from non-disqualified persons.

   ■ Admissions to exempt function facilities or performances, such as theater or ballet performance tickets, museum or historic site admission fees, movie or video tickets, seminar or lecture fees, and athletic event charges.

   ■ Fees for performance of services, such as school tuition, day care fees, hospital room and laboratory charges, psychiatric counseling, testing, scientific laboratory fees, library fines, animal neutering charges, athletic facility fees, and so on.

   ■ Merchandise sales of goods related to the organization's activities, including books and educational literature, pharmaceuticals and medical devices, handicrafts, reproductions and copies of original works of art, byproducts of a blood bank, and goods produced by handicapped workers.

Exempt function revenues received from one source are not counted if they exceed $5,000 or one percent of the EO's support, whichever is higher.

Investment income. Dividends, interest, payments with respect to security loans, rents, royalties, and net unrelated business income (less the unrelated business income tax (UBIT)) are treated as investment income for this purpose.[22] Program-related investments, such as low-income housing loans, do not produce investment income but rather exempt function gross receipts.[23]

---

[22] IRC §509(e).

[23] Reg. §1.509(a)-3(m). For discussion of program-related investments, see Chapter 16.2(d).

11.4 DIFFERENCE BETWEEN §509(a)(1) and §509(a)(2)

Some organizations, including typical churches, schools, and hospitals, can qualify for public status under both §509(a)(1) and (a)(2). In such cases, an (a)(1) class will be assigned by the IRS in making a determination of public status.

For purposes of annual reporting, unrelated business, limits on deductions for donors, and most other tax purposes, the two categories are virtually the same, with one important exception: To receive a terminating distribution from a private foundation upon its dissolution, the charity must be an (a)(1) organization.[24]

(a) Definition of Support

The items of gross income included in the requisite "support" is different for each category, and does not equal total revenue under either class. "Support" forms the basis of public status for both categories, and the calculations are made on a four-year moving average basis using the cash method of accounting.[25]

For (a)(1) purposes, certain revenues are not counted as support and are not included in the numerator or the denominator:[26]

- Exempt function revenue, or that amount earned through charges for the exercise or perfomrance of exempt activities, such as admission tickets, patient fees, etc.;

- Capital gains or losses; and

- Unusual grants.

For (a)(2) purposes, total revenue less capital gains or losses and unusual grants equals total support.

(b) Major gifts

Contributions received are counted as public support differently for each category. For planning purposes, these rules are extremely important to consider. Under the (a)(1) category, a particular giver's donations are counted only up to an amount equal to two percent of the total "support" for the four-year period, as discussed under Section 11.2(f). Gifts from other public charities and governmental entities are not subject to this two percent floor.

For (a)(2) purposes, all gifts, grants, and contributions are counted as public support, except those received from disqualified persons.[27] Such a person may be a substantial contributor, or one who gives over $5,000 if such amount is more than two percent of the organization's aggregate contributions

---

[24] IRC §507(b)(1)(A). Also see Section 12.6 regarding termination of private foundations.
[25] Gen. Coun. Memo 39109 and Reg. §1.509(a)-3(k).
[26] Reg. §1.170A-9(e)(7).
[27] "Disqualified persons" are defined in IRC §4946 and discussed in Chapter 12.

for its life, or a relative of such a person.[28] For (a)(2) purposes, gifts from these insiders are not counted at all. Subject to the two percent ceiling, their gifts are counted for (a)(1) purposes.

(c) Types of Support

Not all revenue is counted as support. The basic definition of "support" excludes capital gains from the sale or exchange of capital assets. Some types of gross revenue are counted differently under differing circumstances.

Membership fees for both classes may represent donations or charges for services rendered. In some cases a combined gift and payment for services may be present. The facts in each circumstance must be examined to properly classify the revenue. A membership fee is a donation if it is paid by a person to support the goals and interests they have in comon with organization rather than to purchase admission, merchandise, services, or the use of facilities. The regulations say that when services are provided to members as a part of overall activity, the payment may still be classed as member dues.[29] Under the enhanced scrutiny of the IRS's Special Emphasis Program[30] on deductibility of charitable gifts, some organizations are realizing that their members are not necessarily making contributions. Particularly for (a)(1) purposes, this distinction is very important, because exempt function fees are not included in the public support calculations.

Grants for services to be rendered for the granting organization, such as a state government's funding for home health care, are treated under both categories as exempt function income, not donations or grants.[31] A grant is normally made to encourage the grantee organization to carry on certain programs or activities in furtherance of its own exempt purposes; no economic or physical benefit accrues to the grant-maker.[32] "Gross receipts," however, result whenever the recipient organization performs a service or provides a facility or product to serve the needs of the grantor.

Under both categories, this distinction is important to determine amounts qualifying as contributions. For (a)(2) status, the distinction has yet another dimension. Only the first $5,000 of fees for such services received from a particular person or organization is includable in public support.[33] Moneys received from a third party payor, such as Medicare or Medicaid patient receipts[34] or blood bank charges collected by a hospital as agent for a blood bank,[35] are attributed to gross receipts from the individual patients.

[28]See Section 12.4 for definitions of these terms.
[29]Reg. §509(a)-3(h).
[30]See Chapter 24.
[31]Rev. Rul. 83-153, 1983-2 C.B. 48 provides similar treatment for state agency payments to a youth care facility.
[32]Reg. §1.509(a)-3(g).
[33]IRC §509(a)(2)28(ii).
[34]Rev. Rul. 83-153, 1938-2 C.B. 48 says that these payments are gross receipts from an exempt function, not a government grant, because individuals choose their own health care providers.
[35]Rev. Rul. 75-387, 1975-2 C.B. 216.

Pass-through grants received from another public charity are totally counted towards public support unless the gift represents an indirect grant expressly or implicitly earmarked by a donor to be paid to a sub-grantee organization. In that case, the donor is the individual.[36] *Donor-designated* grants therefore require careful scrutiny. The basic question is whether the intermediary organization received the gift as an agent or whether it can freely choose to regrant the funds. Donations received under a donor designation and donor-advised funds should qualify as public support to the initial recipient organization (and again to the ultimate recipient) because it retains ultimate authority to approve the regrants.[37]

Unusual grants are excluded from gross revenue in calculating total support for (a)(1) and (a)(2) purposes. When inclusion of such a gift causes loss of public status, the exception is very important. A grant is unusual if it is an unexpected and substantial gift attracted by the public nature of the organization *and* received from a disinterested party. A number of factors are taken into account and no single factor is determinative. The positive factors are shown below, along with their opposites in parentheses:[38]

1. The contribution is received from a party with no connection to the organization. (The gift is received from a person who is a substantial contributor, board member, manager, or related to one.)

2. The gift is in the form of cash, marketable securities, or property that furthers the organization's exempt purposes. (The property is illiquid, difficult to dispose of, and not pertinent to the organization's activities —useless, in other words.) A gift of a painting to a museum, or a gift of wetlands to a nature preservation society would be useful and appropriate property.[39]

3. No material restrictions are placed on the gift. (Strings are attached.)

4. The organization attracts a significant amount of support to pay its operating expenses on a regular basis, and the gift adds to an endowment or pays for capital items. (The gift pays for operating expenses for several years and is not added to an endowment.)

5. The gift is a bequest. (The gift is an inter vivos transfer.)

6. An active fundraising program exists and attracts significant public support. (Fund solicitation programs are unsuccessful.)

7. A representative and broadly-based governing body controls the organization. (Related parties control the organization.)

---

[36] Reg. §1.509(a)-3(j).

[37] Gen. Coun. Memo 39748 was issued in 1988 to clarify this subject, and was later withdrawn with Gen. Coun. Memo 39875.

[38] Reg. §1.509(a)-3(c)(4).

[39] See Rev. Rul. 76-440, 1976-2 C.B. 58 concerning gift of large tract to be used in perpetuity to preserve the natural resources of a town.

8. Prior to the receipt of the unusual grant, the organization qualified as publicly supported. (The unusal grant exclusion was relied upon in the past to satisfy the test.)

If the grant is payable over a period of years, it can be excluded each year, but any income earned on the sums would be included.[40] The IRS has provided a set of "safe harbor" reliance factors to identify unusual grants. If the first four factors listed above are present, unusual grant status can automatically be claimed and relied upon. As to item 4, the terms of the grant cannot provide for more than one year's operating expense.[41]

Supporting organization grants and split-interest trust gifts to (a)(2) entities may retain their character as investment income for purposes of limiting the amount of investment income an (a)(2) organization is allowed to receive.[42]

Change of category from (a)(1) to (a)(2) or vice versa is discussed in Chapter 27. If a material change in the organization's sources of support does not qualify as an unusual grant, a five year testing period may apply.[43] Special rules also apply for new organizations.[44] Until a change of status is announced in the Internal Revenue Bulletin, contributors are entitled to rely upon the latest IRS letter. A donor who is responsible for or otherwise aware of the changes is not entitled to such reliance.[45]

11.5 SUPPORTING ORGANIZATIONS: §509(a)(3)

The third category of organizations that escape the stringent requirements placed upon private foundations is the so-called supporting organization (SO). If such organizations are sufficiently responsive to and controlled or supervised by one or more public charities, they are classified as public charities themselves, even if they are privately funded.

Basically, supporting organizations dedicate all of their assets to one or more public charities but may be separately controlled (except that they may not be controlled by disqualified persons). Beneficiary organization(s) must be specified, but can be changed under certain conditions. This flexibility makes this type of foundation popular with benefactors who want neither to create a private foundation nor to make an outright gift to an established charity. The rules are not entirely logical and the regulations are quite detailed and extensive, but anyone considering the creation of an SO must read and try to understand them. The questions that must be answered on Form 1023, Schedule D (Appendix 18–1) for organizations seeking this classification are also instructive. An SO must meet three unique organizational and operational tests.

[40] Reg. §1. 170A-9(e)(6)(ii)(c).
[41] Rev. Rul. 81-7, 1981-1 C.B. 621.
[42] Reg. §1.509(a)-5(a)(1); Priv. Ltr. Rul. 9203040.
[43] Reg. §1.509(a)-3(c)(1)(ii).
[44] Reg. §1.509(a)-3(c)(1)(iv).
[45] Reg. §1.509(a)-3(c)(1)(iii).

It must be:

1. Organized, and at all times thereafter, be operated exclusively for the benefit of, to perform the functions of, or to carry out the purposes of one or more specified public charities (purpose);

2. Operated, supervised, or controlled by or in connection with one or more public charities (organizational test); and

3. Not controlled, directly or indirectly, by one or more disqualified persons.[46]

The following IRS chart provides an excellent overview of the complex tests that have to be satisfied for an organization to gain the SO classification.[47]

The three different types of relationship will be described in the following materials as Type A, B, and C as defined in Exhibit 11–6.[48]

(a) Purpose Clause

SOs must be organized, and at all times thereafter be operated exclusively:

- For the benefit of,

- To perform the functions of, or

- To carry out the purposes of one or more specified IRC §509(a)(1) or (2) organizations, a "public charity."[49]

The articles of organization must limit the purposes to those listed above, in addition to the regular constraints on operations outlined in Chapter 2.[50] The categories of purpose—whether charitable, religious, or educational—may be very broad. Classic examples of suitable SO purposes would be to raise money for the publicly supported hospitals in an urban medical center, to fund the medical library of the center, or to build and maintain a chapel for the center.

(b) Specified Public Charities

Most commonly, an SO operates to benefit one or more specified public charities. Although the Code and Regulations specifically require the supported organization(s) be named in the articles, under a complex labyrinth of terms, nondesignation can occur. When the Type A relationship exists ("operated, supervised or controlled by"), a class of organizations dedicated to a specific purpose can be named.[51]

[46] IRC §509(a)(3)(A).
[47] 1992 Exempt Organizations Continuing Professional Education Technical Instruction Program, page 233.
[48] IRC §509(a)(3)(A), (B), and (C).
[49] IRC §509(a)(3)(A).
[50] Reg. §1.509(a)-4(c)(1).
[51] Reg. §1.509(a)-4(d).

11.5 SUPPORTING ORGANIZATIONS: §509(a)(3)

Exhibit 11-6
BASIC STEPS IN MAKING AN IRC §509(a)(3) DETERMINATION

Of the tests set forth in the statute, the relationship test of IRC §509(a)(3)(B) is the most important. Therefore, whether there is a proper relationship between the organizations should be determined first. The order to proceed in making a determination under IRC §509(a)(e) is as follows:

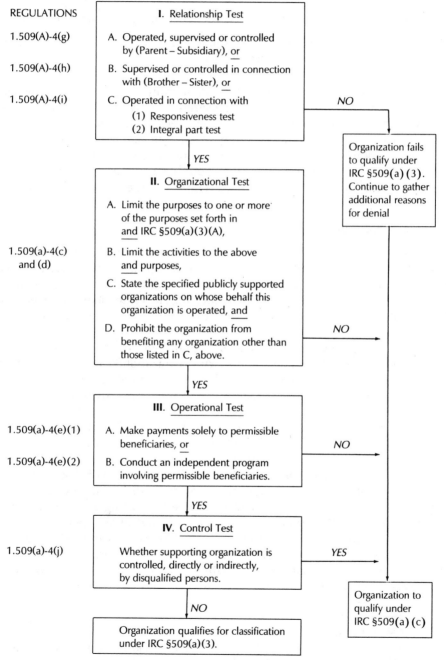

REGULATIONS

I. Relationship Test

1.509(A)-4(g)
A. Operated, supervised or controlled by (Parent – Subsidiary), or

1.509(A)-4(h)
B. Supervised or controlled in connection with (Brother – Sister), or

1.509(A)-4(i)
C. Operated in connection with
   (1) Responsiveness test
   (2) Integral part test

NO

YES

Organization fails to qualify under IRC §509(a)(3). Continue to gather additional reasons for denial

II. Organizational Test

A. Limit the purposes to one or more of the purposes set forth in and IRC §509(a)(3)(A),

1.509(a)-4(c) and (d)
B. Limit the activities to the above and purposes,

C. State the specified publicly supported organizations on whose behalf this organization is operated, and

D. Prohibit the organization from benefiting any organization other than those listed in C, above.

NO

YES

III. Operational Test

1.509(a)-4(e)(1)
A. Make payments solely to permissible beneficiaries, or

1.509(a)-4(e)(2)
B. Conduct an independent program involving permissible beneficiaries.

NO

YES

IV. Control Test

1.509(a)-4(j)
Whether supporting organization is controlled, directly or indirectly, by disqualified persons.

YES

NO

Organization qualifies for classification under IRC §509(a)(3).

Organization to qualify under IRC §509(a)(c)

Source: Chart prepared by Jeanne S. Gessay, Chief of Exempt Organization Rulings Branch II, IRS National Office, Washington, DC.

A class of beneficiary organizations, such as "Catholic churches in Milwaukee" or "institutions of higher learning in California" may be named (rather than naming individual churches or schools), if the public charities are in control. The SO's charter can have the following latitude:[52]

- It may permit the substitution of public charities;

- It may permit new or additional beneficiaries of the same class; and

- It may permit the SO to vary the amount of support among different public organizations within the class.

Slightly different rules exist for Type B, or entities "operated in connection with." First and foremost, specific beneficiaries must be named in the charter. However, the articles may permit certain changes.[53] Particularly when one of the benefited organizations loses its tax exemption, fails, or abandons operations, substitution is permitted. However, it is not permissible to retain the right to change when the supported organization becomes "unnecessary, undesirable, impractical, impossible, or no longer adapted to the needs of the public."[54]

(c) Operational Control

The supporting organization must have one of three special types of relationship with its supported public charities, as shown below. Simply turning over all of the SO's income to a specifically-named charity in accordance with the SO's articles of incorporation is not sufficient. An entity may not meet this operational test even though it satisfies the §501(c)(3) operational tests. The three types are:[55]

Type A: Operated, Supervised, or Controlled By. An SO is operated, supervised, or controlled by its beneficiary organization(s) when it essentially functions in a parent-subsidiary relationship. A substantial degree of direction is exercised by the parent over programs, policies, and activities. The SO, or subsidiary, is accountable and responsible to the parent, or supported organization. This type is found when a majority of the controlling officials of the SO are appointed by the supportees, although any one of a group of beneficiaries need not control if all are represented.

Type B: Supervised or Controlled in Connection With. This type of relationship exists when the same persons control both the supporting and the supported organization, or in other words, there supporting and the supported organization, or in other words, there is common control or supervision.

Type C: Operated in Connection With. This type is the most independent, as it may have a totally independent board with specific named beneficiary organization(s). Because of its relative freedom, it must meet two additional tests to qualify: the responsiveness and the integral part tests.

[52] Reg. §1.509(a)-4(d)(3).
[53] Reg. §1.509(a)-4(d)(4).
[54] *William F., Mable E., and Margaret K. Quarrie Charitable Fund v. Commissioner*, 70 T.C. 182, 187 (1978), *aff'd*, 603 F. 2d 1274 (7th Cir. 1979).
[55] Reg. §1.509(a)-4(f).

Responsiveness. To meet the responsiveness test, the supported organization must have a significant voice in the SO's governance.[56] This voice is gained when one or more officers or directors of the SO are appointed or elected by the supported organization's board or officers. In the case of a charitable trust, responsiveness is present when the supportee is named, and the named supportee has the power to enforce the trust and to compel an accounting under state law.

Integral Part. The integral part test essentially determines whether the supportee is dependent upon the SO.[57] The SO must maintain a significant involvement in the public organization's activities. The SO may meet this test one of two ways. The SO may carry out a function or activity which the public organization itself would normally carry out. Another way the SO can meet this test is to use substantially all of its annual income for the purposes of the supportee, either through direct expenditures for or grants to the supportee. "Income" is not defined under the Regulations, although an early ruling prescribes that 85 percent of the income is the minimum amount to be distributed. (This is the same rule as for private operating foundations).[58] In calculating the annual income, neither long- not short-term capital gains are considered as income required to be distributed annually for this test.[59]

Attentiveness. A subset of the income test portion of the integral part test, entitled "attentiveness," requires SO support to be sufficient in amount to assure that the public organization will be attentive to the operation of the SO.[60] All of the income need not be paid over in the year in which it is earned, and a reasonable accumulation is permitted.[61] In other words, the money paid must be important enough to the charity. The Regulations suggest that the test is passed when it can be shown that the funds are needed to avoid an interruption of the supported organization's particular functions or activities. "Actual attentiveness" in the form of required reporting, investment oversight, or scope of accomplishments can be taken into consideration. For a good example of a "circumstances" application, see *Cockerline Memorial Fund*.[62] For an example of an organization that did not meet the "in connection with" relationship test, see *Roe Foundation Charitable Trust*.[63]

(d) Control by Disqualified Persons

An SO cannot be controlled by disqualified persons other than their own managers or the public charities that they benefit.[64] The control can be neither direct nor indirect. For example, a funder's employees cannot substitute for the funder. The Regulations provide that an organization will be considered con-

[56] Reg. §1.509(a)-4(i)(2).
[57] Reg. §1.509(a)-4(i)(3).
[58] Rev. Rul. 76-298, 1976-1 C.B. 161.
[59] Priv. Ltr. Rul. 9021060.
[60] Reg. §1.509(a)-4(i)(3)(iii)(d).
[61] Gen. Coun. Memo 36523.
[62] *Cockerline Memorial Fund v. Commissioner*, 86 T.C. 53 (1986).
[63] *Roe Foundation Charitable Trust v. Commissioner*, T.C. M. 1989-566 (1989).
[64] IRC §509(a)(3)(C); Reg. §1.509(a)-4(j).

trolled by disqualified persons if, by aggregating their votes or positions of authority in the organization, they can require the organization to perform any act that significantly affects its operations. Lack of control is evidenced when the disqualified persons have under 50 percent of the voting power or lack the right to veto actions of the board.

(e) Permissible Activities

In operating to benefit particular organization(s), the SO need not necessarily pay over all of its income, although that is common. The SO may conduct its own active programs to accomplish the purposes of the beneficiaries, or it may provide and maintain facilities or equipment, as well as make direct grants of funds to its named supportees.[65] The SO may conduct fund-raising programs and unrelated businesses (on limited scale) to raise funds in support of its publicly supported organization.

(f) Conversion to Private Foundation

If the circumstances of the benefited organization or the funders change, it is possible for an SO to cease to operate solely to benefit the current public charity(ies), and convert itself into a private foundation (or a public foundation, for that matter). Two important questions arise in such a conversion:

1. The SO should agree to its ceasing to be supported. As a practical matter, since the supported organization normally controls the SO, this factor is almost always present. There may be a price for agreement. In a conversion sanctioned by a private ruling,[66] the retiring public charity supportee was given about half of the foundation's assets upon termination of the SO status.

2. The conversion must not be part of a plan arranged when the SO was created, to enable the creators or donors to circumvent some tax limitation or private foundation sanction.

For example, it is common for SOs to be created when the property to be given is closely held corporate stock. A private foundation cannot hold more than two percent of the shares of a company owned more than 20 percent by the persons who control or create the foundation, and such "excess business holdings" must be sold by the PF within five years of their receipt. Thus, in the case of conversion of an eight-year-old SO to a private foundation in the same year that its stock holdings were purchased in a public offering, it might well be asked if such a conversion was originally intended.

Without question, a conversion within a few years of original creation would be suspect, when the SO's public status afforded the donors a contribution carryover or higher percentage limitation on deductions than that allowed to a private foundation.

---

[65] Reg. §1.509(a)-4(e)(2).
[66] Priv. Ltr. Rul. 9052055.

(g) Noncharitable Beneficiaries

Business leagues, chambers of commerce, civic leagues, social welfare organizations, labor unions, and agricultural and horticulture organizations are themselves normally publicly supported, and can meet the IRC §509(a)(2) support tests. For that reason, they may also be a beneficiary organization of an SO. Since the SO qualifies for receipt of deductible contributions, an SO formed with such a beneficiary must, of course, meet the organizational and operational tests of §501(c)(3).[67] In other words, an organization performing the charitable or other IRC §170(c)(2) purpose activities for an IRC §501(c)(4), (5), or (6) organization *and* meeting the IRC §509(a)(3)(B) control tests may qualify as a supporting organization.

11.6 TESTING FOR PUBLIC SAFETY: §509(a)(4)

An organization that is organized and operated exclusively for testing for public safety is also treated as a public charity. This category is of limited use, however, because IRC §170 does not provide for deductibility of donations to such organizations. Thus, organizations seeking this status must also satisfy the requirements for a research organization in order to qualify to receive donations.[68]

[67]See Chapter 2.
[68]See Chapter 5.

PART TWO

Private Foundations

CHAPTER TWELVE

Private Foundations—General Concepts

Private foundations were segregated by Congress in 1969 from "public charities," which are organizations that traditionally receive their contributions from a wide range of supporters, rather than from particular individuals. In the exempt organization community and throughout this book, private foundations are referred to as PFs. The persons who create, contribute to, and manage PFs are "disqualified persons" and are referred to as DPs.

12.1 HOW AND WHY PRIVATE FOUNDATIONS ARE SPECIAL

Private foundations are a viable and valuable type of nonprofit organization, despite the fact that they warrant six chapters in this book. A PF is often the best tool to accomplish an individual's philanthropic goals. Unfortunately, some professional advisors discourage the formation of PFs because of the sanctions outlined in Section 12.3. Granted, the rules are a bit more complicated than those for publicly supported charities, but they can be mastered, and become easy once their logic is understood. Some prefer them to the often vague rules applicable to public charities, and it has been suggested that all charities should be subject to similar rules.

Private foundations are a perfect vehicle for funders who do not want a public board. A charitable trust or corporation whose sole trustee/director is also the creator can qualify for exemption. Commonly, the donor and his or her children make up the board of a private foundation. Although financial transactions with the creators, and certain other activities, are strictly constrained by the PF rules, nothing prevents absolute control of the organization by founders and their families.

Funders who wish to be flexible in their grant-making programs may prefer a privately controlled foundation for a similar reason. A modest grant payout requirement, annually equal to 5 percent of the PF's investment assets (as more fully explained in Section 15.3) must be maintained. There is considerable latitude in designing charitable programs. The private operating foundation (discussed in Section 15.5) is a perfect example of this latitude. The funder can establish a PF, hire a staff, and work to further his or her own charitable purposes, as long as genuine public interest programs are undertaken and the rules are followed.

Another possible advantage is the fact that family members or other disqualified persons (defined in Section 12.4) can be compensated with a director or trustee fees for their work in serving on the organization's board. Disqualified person can also be paid salaries for services genuinely rendered in a staff capacity. Those who learn the rules and plan well to adhere to them need not allow sanctions to discourage creation of a private foundation.

Finally, a private foundation can serve as a perfect income and estate tax planning tool for taxpayers with charitable interests. The classic example is a philanthropist who is ready to realize a large capital gain on the sale of a corporation. A PF could be created in the year of sale, gifting the shares or proceeds of the sale to the foundation. (The alternative minimum tax rules could limit the benefit of gifting appreciated shares.) As much as 50 percent of the philanthropists's income could be given to an operating foundation (compared to 30 percent to a normal PF) to substantially reduce his or her income tax burden. The best part is that the money given to create the foundation need not be given away immediately. The foundation must essentially spend only the income produced by the capital gift for its charitable purposes.

Philanthropists who make charitable bequests under their wills can create private foundations to receive bequests while they are still living, and thereby obtain a double deduction. Current gifts to the PF are deductible and increase the estate by reducing income tax. The property gifted to the PF and the undistributed income accumulating in the PF are not subject to estate tax. The foundation can also serve as the beneficiary of a charitable remainder trust created during one's lifetime. Such plans usually result in more after-tax money for the charity and for other beneficiaries. There are many possibilities for the charitably-minded taxpayer, and a detailed discussion of the giving rules is beyond the scope of this book. *Charitable Giving* by Sue Stern Stewart is a good resource for planning ideas.

12.2 DEFINITION OF PRIVATE FOUNDATION

Private foundations are defined negatively by what they are not. All domestic and foreign charities qualifying for exemption under IRC §501(c)(3) are presumed to be private foundation *unless* they fit into one of the following categories:[1]

- Churches;

- Schools;

- Hospitals;

- Medical research organizations;

- "Publicly supported charities" (defined in Chapter 11);

- "Supporting organizations" established to benefit specific public charities (also defined in Chapter 11); and

- Organizations that test for public safety.

PFs are most often supported by a particular individual, family group, corporation, or endowment, and do not restrict their activities. They accomplish their charitable purposes by making grants to other public organizations of the types listed above and, less frequently, by spending money directly for charitable projects. It is interesting to note, however, that the first four categories of public organizations listed are public, even if they are privately supported, because of the nature of their activities. Bruce Hopkins' book, *The Law of Tax-Exempt Organization*, 6th edition, provides more details and a historical perspective on private foundations, which are beyond the scope of this book.

Throughout the following five chapters, note the importance of public charities to PFs, both as the usual recipients of their annual gift-giving bounty and as potential recipients of "terminating distributions." Exhibit 11–1 charts some of the distinctions between public and private charitable organizations, and may make it easier to recall the differences.

The burden of proving non-PF status rests with each exempt organization. A charitable exempt organization is presumed to be a private foundation until proper notice is filed with the IRS on Form 1023 (see Appendix 18–1).[2] If the EO fails to file its notice for determination on time, it must be careful to avoid being subject to PF excise taxes and sanctions. The IRS does not count support received during the delinquency period in determining qualification as a public charity, and only an advance ruling can be obtained.

Unless state law effectively does so automatically, the charter or instrument creating a PF must contain language that prohibits violation of the private foundation sanctions. Every state except Arizona and New Mexico has passed

[1] IRC §509(a).
[2] IRC §508(b).

such a statute.[3] Without proper organizational restraints, the PF cannot be exempt, nor is it eligible to receive charitable contributions.

If circumstances change or if its creators, for whatever reason, wish it, a PF can terminate its status. For example, its public support might have increased to the point that it can qualify as a public charity. It can distribute all of its assets to a public charity, or to another private foundation, and go out of business. It can split itself into two or more parts. Voluntary and involuntary termination of PF status are discussed in Section 12.6.

12.3 PRIVATE FOUNDATION SANCTIONS

When Congress segregated privately funded charities and gave them special status, the following sections were added to the Internal Revenue Code. These sections have operational constraints to govern the conduct of private foundations and impose excise taxes for failures to adhere to the rules.

- IRC §4940 Excise Tax Based on Investment Income.

- IRC §4941 Taxes on Self-Dealing.

- IRC §4942 Taxes on Failure to Distribute Income.

- IRC §4943 Taxes on Excess Business Holdings.

- IRC §4944 Taxes on Investments That Jeopardize Charitable Purpose.

- IRC §4945 Taxes on Taxable Expenditures.

- IRC §4946 Definitions and Special Rules.

- IRC §4947 Application of Taxes to Certain Nonexempt Trusts.

- IRC §4948 Foreign Private Foundations.

Sanctions for failure to comply with PF rules potentially include a tax (called the Chapter 42 tax) on both the PF and its disqualified persons, loss of exemption, and repayment of all tax benefits accrued during the life of the PF. Exhibit 12–1 tabulates the tax rates and persons subject to the tax. Form 4720, *Return of Certain Excise Taxes on Charities and Other Persons under Chapters 41 and 42 of the IRC*, (Appendix 27–6) is filed to report the incidents and calculate any taxes due. Under circumstances explained in Chapters 14–17, certain of the taxes can be abated if the violation was due to reasonable cause, rather than for willful and intentional reasons,[4] and if the violation is corrected.

[3]Rev. Rul. 75-38, 1975-1 C.B. 161.
[4]Reg. §53.4941(a)-1(b)(4).

12.4 DEFINITIONS AND SPECIAL RULES

(a) Disqualified Persons

To determine who is in control of a private foundation and thereby subject to restraints against self-dealing and other sanctions, persons and entities in certain relationships to PFs are treated as disqualified persons (DPs).[5] Individuals, corporations, trusts, partnerships, estates, and other foundations can be DPs. The list of DPs encompasses substantial contributors to the foundation, foundation managers, entities that own more than 20 percent of a "substantially contributing" business, family members, and corporations, truss, or estates that are more than 35 percent owned by disqualified persons.

(b) Substantial Contributors

Using the cumulative total of all contributions and bequests received during the PF's existence, a substantial contributor (SC) is one who has given more than $5,000 or two percent of the total aggregate contributions the organization has ever received, whichever is greater. A creator of a trust is also a substantial contributor, regardless of support level.

With one exception, once one becomes an SC, one remains an SC, regardless of changing PF support levels or death. The exception is this: If, for ten years, an SC has made no contribution to the PF, is not a manager, and his, her, or its aggregate contributions are insignificant, that person ceases to be treated as an SC.[6]

One becomes a substantial contributor the moment after the transaction in which he or she (or it) makes the substantial gift, as result of the transaction.[7] Thus, self-dealing does not occur with respect to the transaction in which one becomes an SC. A testamentary bequest causes the testator to become an SC, so her or his children become disqualified persons upon the testator's death.

(c) Foundation Managers

A private foundation's officers, directors, and trustees, and individuals having similar powers or responsibilities, are its managers.[8] If an employee has actual or effective responsibility or authority for the foundation's action or failure to act, he or she is a manager. A person is considered to be an officer is he or she is specifically so designated under the certificate of incorporation, by-laws, or other constitutive documents of the PF, or if he or she regularly exercises general authority to make administrative or policy decisions on behalf of the PF. Advisers, engaged as independent contractors with no direct legal authority, are not managers. However, employees of a bank that serves as a PF trust

---

[5] IRC §4946(a).

[6] IRC §507(d)(2)(c). Note: a disqualified person for reasons of being a manager or stockholder ceases to be a DP the day that status changes. See Priv. Ltr. Rul 9210029 for example of use of this rule to avoid self dealing.

[7] Reg. §1.507-6(b).

[8] IRC §4946(b); Reg. §53.4946-1(f).

Exhibit 12 –1
PRIVATE FOUNDATION EXCISE TAXES

Sanction	Tax Imposed On		Initial Tax		Additional Tax	
	Private Foundation	Managers	1st Tier Rate	Imposed	2nd Tier Rate	Assessed:
Section 4940 Investment Income Tax	X		2%	of investment income imposed annually when Form 990-PF filed.	N / A	not applicable
	X		1%	Tax reduced by one percent for PFs increasing grants annually.		
Section 4941 Self-Dealing		On self-dealer X	5%	of "amount involved" for each year transaction outstanding.	200%	if self-dealing not "corrected."
		On manager X	$2\frac{1}{2}\%$	of "amount involved" for each year transaction outstanding. Participating managers jointly and severally liable; can agree to allocate among themselves; maximum for managers $10,000.	50%	if manager refuses to agree to part or all of correction. Maximum additional tax $10,000.

Section			Initial Rate	Basis	Additional Rate	Basis
Section 4942 Undistributed	X		15%	of "undistributed income" for each year undistributed.	100%	for each year income remains undistributed.
Section 4943 Excess Business Holdings	X		5%	on fair market value of excess holdings each year.	200%	of excess holdings at end of "taxable period."
Section 4944 Jeopardizing Investments	X		5%	on amount so invested for each year of "taxable period."	25%	of amount not removed from jeopardy.
		X	5%	on amount so invested for each year of investment. Participating managers jointly and severally liable for maximum tax of $5,000 per investment.	5%	of amount on managers who refused to agree to part or all of removal from jeopardy; maximum for management $10,000.
Section 4945 Taxable Expenditures	X		10%	of each taxable expenditure.	100%	of uncorrected expenditure at end of "taxable period."
		X	$2\frac{1}{2}\%$	of each taxable expenditures for any manager who knew of and agreed to the expenditure. Maximum for all managers $5,000.	50%	of expenditure manager who refuses to correct all or part of taxable amount; maximum amount $10,000.

officer—although employees of the bank, not the PF—are treated as PF managers for accounts over which "they are free, on a day-to-day basis, to administer the trust and distribute the funds according to their best judgment.[9]

(d) "20 Percent Plus" Owners

An owner of over 20 percent of a substantially contributing business is a DP. Ownership is measured differently for different businesses.[10]

- For a corporation, it means ownership of over 20 percent of the "combined voting power."

- For a partnership, it means ownership of the net profits.

- For an unincorporated business, the distributive share of profits determines ownership. If there is no fixed agreement, the right to receive assets upon dissolution determines.

- For a trust, ownership is actuarially calculated.

(e) Family Members

A "family member" of any person listed here so far is a DP. The term "family member" includes:[11]

- Spouse;

- Ancestors;

- Children, grandchildren, and great-grandchildren;

- Spouses of children, grandchildren, and great-grandchildren; and

- Legally adopted children.

- *Not* defined as family members for this purpose are siblings, cousins, aunts, uncles, nieces, nephews, and any more distant relatives.

(f) "35 Percent Plus" Businesses

A corporation of which more than 35 percent of the total combined voting power is owned by one or more disqualified persons is disqualified itself, as is a partnership of which more than 35 percent of the profit interest is owned by a DP. If a disqualified person owns more than 35 percent of the beneficial interest of a trust or estate, then the trust or estate is also considered a DP.[12]

---

[9] Rev. Rul. 74-287, 1974-1 C.B. 327.
[10] Reg. §53.4946-1(a)(3).
[11] IRC §4946(d).
[12] IRC §4946(a)(1)(E), (F) and (G).

(g) Other Disqualified Persons

For two limited purposes, other private foundations and government officials are treated as disqualified persons.

Related Private Foundations. For the sole purpose of calculating excess business holdings (explained in Chapter 16), another private foundation that is effectively controlled, either directly or indirectly, by the PF in question is treated as a DP. The related PF's stock ownership is therefore attributed to the other PF. A PF that, for its entire existence, has received at least 85 percent of contributions from the same persons contributing to another PF is also related for this purpose.[13]

Government Officials. For self-dealing purposes only, a government official is a DP with whom financial transactions are generally prohibited. A person who, at the time of the act of self-dealing, holds one of the following offices is a governmental official:[14]

1. An elective public office in the executive or legislative branch of the government of the United States.

2. An office in the executive or judicial branch of the United States government that is appointed by the president.

3. A position in the executive, legislative, or judicial branch of the government of the United States which is listed in schedule C of rule VI of the Civil Service Rules, or the compensation for which is equal to or greater than the lowest rate of compensation prescribed for GS-16 of the General Schedule under IRC §5332 of Title 5 of the United States Code.

4. A position under the House of Representatives or the Senate of the United States held by an individual receiving gross compensation at an annual rate of $15,000 or more.

5. An elective or appointive public office in the executive, legislative, or judicial branch of the government of a state, possession of the United States, or political subdivision or other area of any of the foregoing, or of the District of Columbia, held by an individual receiving gross compensation at an annual rate of $20,000 or more.

6. A position as personal or executive assistant or secretary to any of the foregoing.

12.5 APPLICATION OF TAXES TO CERTAIN NONEXEMPT TRUSTS

To prevent the creation of trusts to avoid the PF rules, a wholly charitable trust is treated as a PF despite the fact that it does not have formal recognition as an exempt charitable organization.[15] To be so treated, "all of the unexpired

[13] Reg. §4946-1(b).
[14] IRC §4946(a)(c); Reg. §53.4946-1(g).
[15] IRC §4947(a)(1); Reg. §53.4947-1(b).

interests of the trust" must be devoted to charitable purposes[16] and income, estate, or gift tax deductions must have been allowed for gifts made to the trust. The tax on investment income and all the other PF sanctions are imposed on a wholly charitable trust. Form 990PF is filed annually and Form 1041 is also filed if the trust has any taxable income.

Split-interest trusts, or those holding property devoted to both charitable and noncharitable beneficiaries, are subject to some of the PF rules.[17] For example, such a trust might have a remainder interest payable to a named charity with the current income payable to the creator's son. These trusts are not formally exempt because of their unexpired noncharitable interests, but a deduction has been allowable for the value of the charitable interests placed in them. The sanctions against self-dealing (Chapter 14) and excess business holdings and jeopardizing investments (Chapter 16) apply to them as if they were private foundations. Either Form 1041, accompanied by 1041-A, or Form 5227 is filed annually.

12.6 TERMINATION OF PRIVATE FOUNDATION STATUS

A private foundation may wish to voluntarily terminate its existence for a number of reasons, or the IRS may cause it to be involuntarily terminated. In either case, the PF must carefully follow the rules for ceasing to exist, as some of them are serious and costly.

(a) Involuntary Termination

The ultimate penalty for failure to play by the excise tax rules designed by Congress to curtail PF operations is involuntary termination, sometimes called the "third tier tax." When a PF has willfully repeated a flagrant act or failure to act giving rise to the imposition of the sanctions set out in IRC §§4941 through 4945, the IRS will notify the PF that it is liable for a termination tax.[18] The termination tax equals the lower of the aggregate tax benefit resulting from §501(c)(3) status or the PF's net assets.

Aggregate Tax Benefit. The sum of the tax benefits resulting from the PF's exempt charitable status is potentially due to be paid—all of the income, estate, and gift taxes saved by the PF's substantial contributors. The amount equals the total tax that would have been payable if deductions for all contributions made after February 28, 1913 had been disallowed.

Repeated Acts. At least two acts or failures to act, which are voluntary, conscious, and intentional, must be committed.[19] The offense must appear to a reasonable person to be a gross violation of the sanctions, and the managers must have "known" that they were violating the rules. The "knowing" rules are discussed in Section 16.2(b).

---

[16]According to IRC §170(c)(2)(B) per Reg. §53.4947-1(b)(2)(i).
[17]IRC §4947(a)(2).
[18]IRC §507(a).
[19]Reg. §1.507-1(c)(1).

(b) Voluntary Termination

When the directors or trustees decide for whatever reason that they cannot continue to operate a private foundation, they can avoid the termination tax by giving all the assets away to a public charity, converting the PF into a public charity, or transferring the assets to another private foundation, and notifying the IRS of their intent to terminate and requesting abatement from the termination tax.[20]

(c) Transfer of Assets to a Public Charity

A PF that wishes to terminate can transfer or donate all of its assets to one or more public charities qualified under IRC §509(a)(1). The terminating PF must not have had any flagrant or willful acts or failure to acts giving rise to the penalty taxes.

Qualifying Recipients. The recipient organization must have been in existence for at least 60 continuous months.[21] Only churches, schools, hospitals, and charities supported with public donations qualify as recipients. Organizations classified as public under IRC §509(a)(2) and §509(a)(3), i.e., organizations supported primarily by their exempt function revenues (symphony societies, theaters, and scientific research organizations for examples) do not qualify.[22]

Filing Requirements. Advance notice to or approval by the IRS prior to termination in this fashion is not necessary. Complete details should be included in Form 990-PF for the year of the termination, as described in Chapter 27.[23] Proof of public status must be maintained in the files of the terminating PF.

Restrictions and Conditions. "All right, title, and interest in and to all of the net assets" must be transferred. No material restrictions or conditions can be imposed preventing free and effective use of the assets by the public charity. The following questions are used to find restrictions:[24]

- Is the public charity owner in fee of the assets?

- Are the assets used by the public charity for its exempt purposes? Are the assets subject to liabilities, leases, or other obligations limiting their usefulness?

- Does the public charity's governing body have ultimate authority and control over the assets?

- Is the public charity operated separately and independently of the PF?

- Were members of the public charity board chosen by the PF?

---

[20] IRC §507(g).
[21] IRC §507(b)(1)(A); Reg. §1.507-2(a)(2).
[22] Reg. §1.507-2(1)(3).
[23] Reg. §1.507-2(a)(6); IRC 6043(b).
[24] Reg. §1.507(a)(8).

It is permissible for the public charity to name a fund to hold the assets after the terminating PF or its founders. The charitable purpose for which the transferred funds are to be used can be designated. Finally, the transferor can require that the property be retained and not sold when it is important to the charitable purpose, such as a nature preserve or historic property.

(d) Conversion of a Private Foundation to a Public Charity

A private foundation can change its method of operation or sources of support and become a public charity.[25] Basically, the PF adopts plans to qualify under IRC §509(a)(1), (2), or (3) and submits an application for approval to the key district office. The information outlined in the regulations[26] must be submitted. Beware, as timing here is very important. The termination notice must be filed in advance of the year in which it is effective.

60-Month Termination. This type is called a 60-month termination because the requirements are to be met throughout and by the end of the continuous period of 60 months. The statute of limitations is extended during the 60 months to impose excise taxes for any year in which the reformed PF fails to qualify as publicly supported. Actually, the converted PF could revert from public status if its plans fail in the sixth, sixteenth (or whatever) year beyond sixty months.

Why Convert? A variety of circumstances could arise to make conversion to a public charity desirable. For example, because of a delay in start-up of operations and attendant fund-raising programs, an organization classified as public during its advance ruling period might mathematically fail to receive over one-third of its support from the general public. The current year support levels might qualify it as public, but the cumulative totals for the first five years do not. In a timely fashion, this organization might be able to continue its public status by adopting a sixty month termination.

Another example would be a privately endowed operating foundation, say a museum, that plans to undertake a major public campaign to expand its operations. It is privately funded in the early years, but converts as soon as possible to public status. Sometimes a private foundation ceases grant-making and converts its operations to a type that qualifies for public status, such as a hospital or school.

(e) Transfer Assets to Another PF

A PF desiring to terminate can also transfer all of its assets to one or more existing or newly created PFs.[27] This transfer is simple because the old foundation is deemed not to terminate. Assets transferred to the recipient PF carry transferee liability and retain characteristics possessed by the transferring PF. Any previously undistributed income, for example, must be distributed by the recipient PF; likewise, prior excess distributions can be carried over. The transferring PF must exercise expenditure responsibility over the transferred

---

[25] IRC §507(b)(1)(B).
[26] Reg. §1.507-2(b) and (d).
[27] IRC §507(a)(2).

assets unless it distributes all of its assets. Most significantly, the recipient bears any burden for a termination tax, in the unlikely event that one is assessed.

IRS Private Letter Rulings 9033054 and 9033044 make it clear that the division of all assets of one PF to two other PFs, to enable the trustees to pursue their divergent charitable interests, does not terminate the transferor's PF status or result in §507(c) termination tax. The IRS's conclusion was based upon two facts: The transferor had not given notice of intent to terminate, and there was no evidence that the original PF had violated any of the PF sanctions so as to cause the IRS to terminate it involuntarily.

The treatment of the old and new organizations in a private foundation split-up was further clarified in a 1991 ruling.[28] According to the IRS, neither the old nor the newly created organization are treated as newly created, (a seemingly impossible situation). The attributes of the old organization are attributed proportionately to each of the "new-old" PFs.

Examples. The private letter rulings offer many examples of split-ups that have been blessed by the IRS. A sampling from 1991 included:

- A merger of two private operating foundations to manage a recreational complex.[29]

- Three new organizations—one public to receive half of the assets and two private foundations each to receive one-fourth of the assets—formed from one private foundation.[30]

- A private foundation's legal structure converted to a nonprofit corporation from its original form as a charitable trust.[31]

- One private foundation split into three.[32]

- A combination of three commonly controlled foundations into one,[33] or two into one.[34]

Foreign Private Foundations. The termination tax does not apply to termination of a foreign private foundation which has received substantially all of its support, other than gross investment income, from sources outside the U.S.[35]

(f) Conversion to a Taxable Entity

Listed first in the statute, but the least likely choice for termination, is a voluntary termination by conversion to a taxable entity.[36] A PF can notify the

---

[28] Priv. Ltr. Rul. 9121036.
[29] Priv. Ltr. Rul. 9052025.
[30] Priv. Ltr. Rul. 9101020.
[31] Priv. Ltr. Rul. 9103035.
[32] Priv. Ltr. Rul. 9204016.
[33] Priv. Ltr. Rul. 9132052.
[34] Priv. Ltr. Rul. 9115057.
[35] IRC §4948.
[36] IRC §507(a)(1).

IRS of its intent to terminate and request abatement or pay tax, which, of course, it will probably have to pay.

In most cases, the assets remain dedicated to charitable purposes under charter provisions or a trust instrument, and thereby, under state law. Once notice is given, the PF is treated as a newly created organization. If, for some unlikely reason, it wanted to resecure tax-exempt status, it would have to refile Form 1023 to be recognized as exempt.[37]

[37] Reg. §1.507-1(b)(3).

CHAPTER THIRTEEN

Excise Tax Based on Investment Income: IRC §4940

To pay the cost of "extensive and vigorous" enforcement sanctions imposed upon privately funded charities, Congress in 1969 adopted a tax on private foundation investment income. Congress felt that foundations should continue to be exempt from income tax, so the tax was enacted as an excise tax rather than the normal income tax imposed by IRC §1.

13.1 RATE OF TAX

The private foundation (PF) tax was described by the Congress as a "charge or audit fee" and was initially set at four percent of the foundation's investment income. When the tax being collected was revealed to actually be much more than the cost of examining PFs, the tax was cut to two percent in 1978.

(a) Reducing Rate to One Percent

In 1984 the tax was reduced again, but only for foundations which essentially pay our part of the tax in the form of charitable grants and projects. If the foundation pays out the penny to charity, it need not pay it to the government

—it only pays a one percent tax.[1] Basically, to qualify for the reduced tax, the foundation simply increases its level of giving by one percent. The average of the foundation's annual *qualifying distributions* as a portion of its average investment assets each year is calculated. For example, a foundation has $1 million of assets and it makes grants totaling $60,000 each year. Its distribution payout ratio is six percent of its assets. Taking into account the payout percentage for the five year period preceding the current year, an average payout ratio is determined. If the current year's distributions equal the average plus one percent of the current year investment income, only a one percent excise tax is due. See the sample completed Form 990PF in Appendix 27–5 for an illustration.

(b) Non-Exempt Foundations

To discourage foundations from purposefully losing exempt status to avoid this excise tax, IRC §4940(b) provides that a taxable foundation must still pay the two percent excise tax *plus* the unrelated business income tax, unless the ordinary income tax on its overall income is higher.

13.2 FORMULA FOR TAXABLE INCOME

The excise tax is imposed on NET INVESTMENT INCOME FOR EACH TAX-ABLE YEAR, which equals:

$$
\begin{array}{c}
\text{Gross} \\
\text{investment} \\
\text{income}
\end{array}
+
\begin{array}{c}
\text{Net} \\
\text{capital} \\
\text{gain}
\end{array}
-
\text{Deductions}
=
\begin{array}{c}
\text{Net} \\
\text{investment} \\
\text{income}
\end{array}
$$

(a) Gross Investment Income

Only five specifically named types of income are included in gross investment income: interest, dividends, rents, payments with respect to securities loans (as defined in IRC §512(a)(5)), and royalties from all sources. Any such income subject to the unrelated business income tax (UBIT) of IRC §511 is not taxed twice, but is excluded from this excise tax.[2] The income is reportable using the method of accounting normally used by the foundation for financial statement purposes, with certain exceptions discussed below.[3] Income of the five types listed above that is produced by both investment and exempt function assets is taxed.[4]

[1] IRC §4940(e).
[2] IRC §4940(c)(2) and Reg. §53.4940-1(d).
[3] Reg. §53.4940-1(c).
[4] Reg. §53.4940-1(d)(1).

(b) Interest

Interest income is taxed if it is earned on the following types of obligations and investments:

- Bank savings or money market accounts, certificates of deposit, commercial paper, and other temporary cash investment accounts;

- Commercial paper, U.S. Treasury bills, notes, bonds and other interest-bearing government obligations, and corporate bonds; and

- Interest on student loans receivable,[5] on mortgage loans to purchasers in low income housing projects, and loans to minority business owners as a program-related investment.

Series E bond interest, not previously reported by a decedent or by the estate, is taxed to the foundation.[6] Municipal bond interest paid by state and local government is excluded and is not taxed.

(c) Dividends

Dividends that are taxable include the following:

- Dividends paid on all types of securities, whether listed and marketable or privately held and unmarketable;

- Mutual fund dividends, not including the capital gain portion;

- For-profit subsidiary dividends;

- Corporate liquidating distributions classified as dividends under IRC §302(b)(1), but not including payments on complete redemption of shares that are classified as capital gains;[7] and

- Payments on collateral security loans as defined in IRC §512(a)(5).

(d) Rentals

Amounts paid in return for the use of real or personal property, commonly called rent, are taxable—whether the rental is related or unrelated to the private foundation's exempt activities.[8] The portion of rental from debt financed real estate includible in UBIT is excluded.[9]

---

[5] Reg. §53.4940-1(d)(1).
[6] Rev. Rul. 80-118, 1980-1 C.B. 254.
[7] Priv. Ltr. Rul. 8512090, 8326125, 8043112, 8001046.
[8] Instructions to Form 990PF, Part I, column (b), at p. 6.
[9] IRC §514(a)(1) and 4940(1)(2).

(e) Royalties

Payments received in return for assignments of mineral interests owned by the foundation, including overriding royalities, are taxed. Only cost, not percentage, depletion is permitted as an offset. Royalty payments received in return for use of a PF's intangible property, such as the foundation's name or a publication containing a literary work commissioned by the foundation, are also taxable.

(f) Estate or Trust Distributions

Payments to the foundation from an estate or trust do not generally "retain their character in the hands" of the foundation. In other words, such payments do not pass through to the foundation as taxable income.[10] Part of the reason for this rule lies in the fact that the wholly charitable trust pays its own two percent investment income tax, and its distributions are not taxed again to the foundation upon their receipt. Income earned during administration of an estate and set aside for the foundation is not taxable to either the estate or the foundation (unless administration is unreasonably continued).[11]

However, payments from a split-interest trust created after May 26, 1969 do pass through to the foundation and are taxed if they are attributable to trust income from interest, dividends, or the other specific types of taxable investment income.

13.3 CAPITAL GAINS

Net short- and long-term capital gains from the sale of property used for the production of the specific types of income subject to the investment income tax —interest, dividends, royalties, rents, and security loan payments—are also taxed.[12] Gains or losses from sales of assets used directly by the PF in conducting its exempt activities are not taxed, nor is the gain from property used in an unrelated trade or business if it subject to the UBI tax. Mutual fund capital gain dividends, both short- and long-term, are classified as capital gain.[13]

(a) Basis

The basis for calculating gain or loss is equal to the amount paid by the PF for the assets it purchases or constructs, less any allowable depreciation or depletion. Assets acquired by gift, on the other hand, retain the donor's, or a so-called carryover, basis. To follow accounting principles, the PF may record the donation at its value on the date the property is given. For tax purposes, however, it may not "step-up" the tax basis to such value. Essentially, the PF pays the tax unpaid by the donor (even when the alternative minimum tax applies). The

[10] Reg. §53.4940-1(d)(2).
[11] Priv. Ltr. Rul. 8909066.
[12] IRC §4940(c)(4)(A).
[13] Rev. Rul. 73-320, 1973-2 C.B. 385.

basis of inherited property is equal to its Form 706 value, which ordinarily is its value on the date of the decedent's death. The normal income tax rules under IRC §1015 are used to measure the carryover basis.[14]

For property held by a PF on December 31, 1969—the date when the tax became effective—special rules apply. The tax basis for any property held on that date is equal to its December 31, 1969 valuation, unless a loss is realized on the sale using such a value.[15] The IRS *Private Foundation Handbook* still contains 25 pages of stock quotations from that date for reference.[16] Property held in a trust or in an estate created before 1969 may also use the 1969 basis.[17] A trust created in 1935, subject to a life estate expiring in 1970, was ruled to be "constructively received" in 1935 and therefore to be owned by the PF in 1969. The basis of the shares received upon the life tenant's death was stepped-up to the 1969 value, rather than retaining the 1935 basis.[18]

(b) Questionable Types of Gain

Gain from sale of property capable of producing the specific types of income listed above (interest, dividends, rent security loans, and royalties) are taxed even if the property is disposed of immediately after the foundation receives it. Since the statute applies to "property used for the production" of the specified income, clever PFs in the early days escaped tax on highly-appreciated property gifts by selling them as soon as the property was given.[19] The PFs argued that they never held the property to produce the specified types of income, so therefore the tax shouldn't apply.

Effective December 31, 1972, the IRS provided by regulation that the tax applies even if the property was immediately disposed on upon its receipt, *if* "the property was of a type which generally produces interest, dividends, rents royalties or capital gain through appreciation, such as rental real estate, stocks, bonds, mineral interests, mortgages, and securities. The courts have agreed with the IRS.[20]

A case involving a sale of timber land further clarified the application of the tax. Even though it was conceivable that the real estate in question could have been used to produce rental income, it was not. Instead, it was "economically prudent and reasonable" for the Zemurray Foundation to grow and cut the timber. Since the foundation did not use the land to produce a type of income specified in the statute, gain on its sale was not subject to the tax. The court held that only property that "can be reasonably expected to generate one or more of the four types of income" is subject to the tax.[21] Other assets that

[14]Reg. §53.4940-1(f)(2).
[15]IRC §4940(c)(4)(B); Rev. Rul. 74-403, 1974-2 C.B. 381.
[16]IR Manual 7752, Exhibit (12)00-1.
[17]Rev. Rul. 76-424, 1976-2 C.B. 367.
[18]Priv. Ltr. Rul. 8539001 and 8150002.
[19]Rev. Rul. 74-404, 1974-2 C.B. 382.
[20]*Ruth E. and Ralph Friedman Foundation, Inc. v. Commissioner*, 71 T.C. 40 (1978); *Greenacre Foundation v. U.S.*, 762 F.2d 965 (Fed. Cir. 1985, aff'g 84-2 U.S.T.C. ¶9789 (Ct. Cl. 1984): and *Balso Foundation v. U.S.*, 573 F. Supp. 191 (D. Conn. 1983).
[21]*Zemurray Foundation v. U.S.*, 84-1 U.S.T.C. ¶9246 (E.D. La. 1983).

should fall into this nontaxable category include collectibles such as art works, gold, and antiques, and undeveloped raw land. Non-dividend-paying common stock is, in the opinion of the IRS *capable* of producing dividends. The appreciation, therefore, is subject to the tax.

(c) Nontaxed Gains

Certain capital gains are not taxed:

- Gain from sale of exempt function assets, including program-related investments. Such property producing "incidental" income is fully excluded from the tax. Property used both for exempt and income-producing purposes, such as an office building partly used for administrative offices and partly rented to paying tenants, however, will produce *pro rata* nontaxable and taxable gain or loss.[22]

- Distribution of property for charitable purposes is not considered a sale or other disposition for purposes of this tax. Thus, the gain inherent in appreciated property distributed as a grant to another charity is not taxed.[23]

- Gain from disposition of "excess business holdings" held on December 31, 1969 (or received as a bequest under a trust irrevocable on May 26, 1969) and sold to or redeemed by a disqualified person to reduce the holdings pursuant to IRC §4943.[24]

- Gain realized in a merger or corporate reorganization ruled to be tax free under IRC §368 or other section of IRC Subchapter C.[25]

- Appreciation on warrants or options to purchase securities.[26]

13.4 REDUCTIONS TO GROSS INVESTMENT INCOME

Gross investment income is reduced by "all the ordinary and necessary expenses paid or incurred for the production or collection of property held for the production of gross investment income or for the management, conservation, or maintenance of property held for the production of such income." Most foundations' operating expenses must be allocated between those attributable to investment activity and to exempt functions, as described in the regulations:

"A private foundation's operating expenses include compensation of officers, other salaries and wages of employees, outside professional fees, interest, and rents and taxes upon property used in the founda-

---

[22] Reg. §53.4940-1(f)(1); Priv. Ltr. Rul. 8425114.
[23] Reg. §53.4940-1(f)(1).
[24] Reg. §53.4940-1(d)(3); Priv. Ltr. Rul. 8214023.
[25] Priv. Ltr. Ruls. 8906013 and 8730061.
[26] Priv. Ltr. Ruls. 8852001, 8846005, 8752033 and 8650049.

tion's operations. Where a private foundation's officers or employees engage in activities on behalf of the foundation for both investment purposes and for exempt purposes, compensation and salaries paid to such officers and employees must be allocated."[27]

(a) Deductions Allowed

The following deductions are permitted:

- Depreciation using a straight line method, but no accelerated systems are allowed.[28] Basis for calculating depreciation for purchased or constructed assets is equal to their cost. Donated property retains the donor's or so-called carryover basis. The normal income tax rules under IRC §1015 are used to measure this basis. Special rules apply to assets held by a foundation before 1969 when it began to claim depreciation for the first time in 1970.

- Cost, but not percentage, depletion.[29]

- Investment management or counselling fees, except the portion allocable to tax-exempt interest under IRC §265.

- Legal and accounting fees allocable to investment income activity. Private foundations have been known to ask their advisors to render billings specifically identifying such an allocation based upon time actually spent.[30]

- Taxes, insurance, maintenance, and other direct and specifically identifiable costs paid for property producing rental income, and an allocable part of such costs for administrative offices. Space rental would be similarly treated.

- A proportionate part of operating expenses, including officer and staff salaries and associated costs, occupancy costs, office and clerical costs, professional fees, and bank trustee fees.

- An allocable portion of expenses paid or incurred incident to a charitable program that produces investment income is deductible to the extent of the income earned.[31]

- Bond premium amortization deductible under IRC §171.[32]

(b) Deductions Not Allowed

As a general rule, no deduction is permitted for costs associated with a foundation's grant-making and other charitable or exempt function projects.

[27] Reg. §53.4940-1(e)(1)(i).
[28] IRC §4940(c)(3)(B)(i).
[29] IRC §4940(c)(3)(B)(ii).
[30] Rev. Rul. 75-410, 1975-2 C.B. 446.
[31] Reg. §53.4940-1(e)(2)(iv) and Priv. Ltr. Rul. 8047007.
[32] Rev. Rul. 76-248, 1976-1 C.B. 353.

When a project or asset produces or is operated to produce some income, the deductions with the activity are allocated between the exempt and investment uses.[33] With such joint purpose activities, however, the primary motivation for undertaking the project (investment or gratuitous) must be determined. When the expenses are incurred in connection with an exempt function project, the regulations provide that allocable expenses are deductible only to the extent of the gross investment income from the project.[34] An investment project conceivably could result in a deductible loss. Clearly, few historic building restorations are untaken to produce net income. Since admission charges for visiting such buildings are normally incidental to the overall cost of the project, it would be hard to prove that the building loss is deductible.

No expense allocation method is prescribed, so the foundation is free to use any reasonable method consistently (from year to year). When personnel costs need to be allocated, the preferred method is for the employees involved to maintain actual records of their time devoted to investment and exempt activities. The concepts and rules applicable to deductible expenses for unrelated business income tax purposes can be used as a guideline. Documentation should be maintained as evidence of the manner in which the allocations are made. See Section 21.15(b) for more discussion. The following items are examples of nondeductible expenses for investment income purposes:

- Charitable distributions and administrative expenses associated with grant-making program costs are not deductible.[35] No charitable deduction similar to IRC §170 or §642(c) is permitted. Similarly, expenses of programs directly conducted by the foundation are not deductible.

- Purchase of exempt function assets, depreciation of their cost, and cost of their maintenance, repair or conservation are not deductible.[36]

- Capital losses in excess of capital gains are not deductible, nor is a carryover permitted to the succeeding year.[37] This is a potentially costly rule to a PF that does not properly time its asset dispositions.

- Operating losses incurred in a preceding year do not carry forward from year to year.[38]

- The allocable portion of expenses of exempt function income-producing property or activity in excess of the income produced therefrom and reportable as investment income.[39]

- Expenses allocable to taxable unrelated business income. (The income is also not includible.)[40]

[33] Reg. §53.4940-1(e)(1)(ii).
[34] Supra, n. 31.
[35] Julia R. and Estelle L. Foundation, Inc., 79-1 U.S.T.C. ¶9363 (2d Cir., 1979), aff'g 70 T.C. 1, Dec. 35,086.
[36] Historic House Museum Corp., 70 T.C. 12, Dec. 35,087.
[37] Reg. §53.4940-1(f)(3).
[38] Reg. §53.4940-1(e)(1)(iii).
[39] Supra, n. 31.
[40] Reg. §53.4940-1(e)(1)(i).

- Interest paid on borrowing to acquire exempt function assets is not deductible. For example, interest paid on a bond issue floated to finance building a retirement community is not paid on behalf of an investment.[41] If the financial building is rental property, however, the interest and other property maintenance and operational expenses should be deductible.[42] See notes above regarding possible limits on loss deductions.

- Interest paid on borrowing funds which a foundation relends to another charitable organization (presumably interest-free) has been ruled not deductible.[43] Such interest expense should be deductible only to the extent of any interest income collected from the relending.

- A trust termination fee paid by the sole beneficiary private foundation was not paid for the production of income, nor were the unused deductions from the final trust return (customarily deductible to a noncharitable beneficiary under §642(h)(2)) deductible to the PF.[44]

- The special corporation deductions including the dividends received deduction are not allowed.[45]

13.5 FOREIGN FOUNDATIONS

As a general rule, foreign private foundations are taxed at a rate of four percent on their U.S. source (IRC §861) investment income calculated under the IRC §4940(c)(2) rules discussed above.[46] Tax treaties with some foreign countries, including Canada, provide an exemption from the tax.[47]

13.6 TIMELY PAYMENT OF EXCISE TAX

The balance of any excise tax shown due on Form 990PF is payable by the return due date, or 4 1/2 months after the year end (May 15 for a calendar year PF). Under IRC §6651, any unpaid tax is subject to an underpayment penalty of 1/2 of one percent per month for each month payment is late. Interest at the current prevailing rate is also charged, pursuant to IRC §6621. Additionally, an IRC §6655 excise tax may be due, as discussed below.

Effective for 1987 tax years, an excise tax is payable in advance under the corporate estimated tax system when a foundation's tax liability is $500 or more. The tax for each year is estimated or projected, and is to be paid quarterly on or before the fifteenth day of the fourth, sixth, ninth, and twelfth months of the

---

[41]Priv. Ltr. Rul. 8802008; Rev. Rul. 74-579, 1974-2 C.B. 383.

[42]*Indiana University Retirement Community, Inc.*, 92 T.C. 891, Dec. 45, 674 (Acq.).

[43]Rev. Rul. 74-579, 1974-2 C.B. 383.

[44]*L.P. Whitehead Foundation, Inc. v. U.S.*, 79-2 U.S.T.C. ¶9706 (5th Cir. 1979).

[45]IRC §4940(c)(3) and Reg. §53.4940-1(e)(1)(iii).

[46]IRC §4948(a).

[47]Rev. Rul. 74-183, 1974-1 C.B. 328.

tax year.[48] Form 990-W can be used to calculate the quarterly liability. As in the corporate system, many foundations can make "safe" payments based upon the immediately preceding tax year. As long as 100 percent of the prior tax year's liability is paid quarterly, or 90 percent of the tax actually due for the year is paid, no penalty is imposed on any balance of tax due at year end. Form 2220 is attached to Form 990PF to calculate any penalty.

Large foundations whose annual income was $1 million or more in any one of its three preceding years can base only the first quarterly payment on the prior year tax.[49] For the second, third, and fourth installment, the tax must be projected based upon actual income and deductions earned through the end of the month before the payment is due. At the other end of the scale, a foundation whose tax is $500 or less is excused from paying the excise tax in advance.

Any excise tax due must be deposited with an authorized federal depository bank using preprinted depository receipts (Form 8109, the same form used for payroll and income taxes). The forms are customarily sent to a new foundation when it is issued an employer identification number. A foundation should contact the local IRS by telephone to obtain the receipts, as only forms preprinted with the foundation's identifying number can be used.

13.7 EXEMPT OPERATING FOUNDATIONS

No excise tax is due from a special category of private foundation known as an exempt operating foundation, created in 1984 by Congress.[50] To be exempt, a PF must meet the following qualifications:

- It must have been a private operating foundation as of January 1, 1983;

- It must have been publicly supported for at least 10 years;

- At least 75 percent its board members cannot be disqualified persons;

- Its board members must be broadly representative of the general public, and

- No officer can be a disqualified person at any time during the taxable year.

---

[48] IRC §6655.
[49] Since Form 990PF is not due until the fifteenth day of the fifth month following the close of the foundation's fiscal year, this exception is convenient.
[50] IRC §4940(d).

CHAPTER FOURTEEN

Self-Dealing: IRC §4941

IRC §4941 prevents the use of privately controlled charitable organizations as a source of funds by the persons who create, fund, and manage them. Among the practices Congress found troublesome in 1969 were loans and stock bailouts between certain privately funded organizations and their creators and creator's families. Former IRC §503 (now repealed) permitted such transactions as long as a reasonable rate of interest was charged and the fair market value (hereafter referred to as FMV) was paid. Nevertheless, Congress felt that private foundations were being used as extra pocketbooks for funds not necessarily available from other sources, so it set out to completely eliminate self-interested financial activity between a private charity and its insiders.

14.1 DEFINITION OF SELF-DEALING

As a basic concept, all direct and indirect financial transactions are prohibited between a private foundation (PF) and its disqualified persons (DPs)—those persons who control and fund the foundation. There are exceptions, but most of the rules are draconian. In the IRS's opinion, "It is immaterial whether the transaction results in a benefit or a detriment to the PF."[1] Even if only $1 is paid by the PF for a DP's $1,000,000 building, such a bargain sale is absolutely prohibited, regardless of the gain to the charity. Such a sale can occur between the PF and a person who at the time of the sale is not a disqualified person, even though the transaction causes the person to become a substantial contributor and consequently a DP. Also drawn into the web are "indirect acts," those between the DPs and organizations controlled by the PF, or vice versa. This chapter addresses the complex subject of self-dealing from several different perspectives by presenting:

- The six absolute rules as found in the Internal Revenue Code;

- Exceptions found both in the statute and in the regulations;

- Examples of acceptable and unacceptable self-dealing transactions;

- Suggestions for documenting associations that could conceivably produce self-dealing; and

- Procedures and rules to follow if self-dealing occurs.

(a) Statutory Language

Six specific acts of prohibited self-dealing between a private foundation and a disqualified person are listed in the statute.[2] The specified transactions cannot occur directly between the PF and its insiders, nor indirectly through an entity controlled by such DPs or by the PF. These transactions are:

1. Sale, exchange, or leasing, of property;

2. Lending of money or other extension of credit;

3. Furnishing of goods, services, or facilities;

4. Payment of compensation (or payment or reimbursement of expenses);

5. Transfer to, or use by or for the benefit of, a DP of any income or assets of the PF; and

6. Agreement to pay a government official.

(b) Statutory Exceptions

What the statute calls "Special Rules" provide both clarification and certain exceptions, remove some of the absoluteness of the "six sins," and bring some

---

[1]Reg. §53.4940(d)-1(a).
[2]IRC §4941(d)(1).

reasonableness to the rules. The basic concept underlying these exceptions is to permit certain transactions that actually provide benefit to the PF without producing gain to any DPs. The following transactions are permitted:[3]

1. Transfer of indebted real or personal property is considered a sale to the PF, if the foundation assumes a mortgage or similar debt, or if it takes the property subject to a debt placed on the property by the DP within a 10 year period ending on the date of gift.

2. A DP can make a loan that is without interest or other charge to the PF if the funds are used exclusively for §501(c)(3) or charitable purposes.

3. Offering a no-rent lease or furnishing free use of a DP's goods, services, or facilities to the PF is permissible, as long as they are used exclusively for exempt purposes.

4. Furnishing a DP with exempt-function goods, facilities, or services which the private foundation regularly provides to the general public is not self-dealing, if conditions and charges for the transaction are the same as for the public.

5. Reasonable compensation, payment of expenses, and reimbursement of expenses for a DP can be paid by the PF to a DP, if the amounts are reasonable and necessary to carry out the PF's exempt purposes. (See Chapter 20 regarding private inurement, including criteria for reasonable salaries.) The definition of reasonable compensation relied upon by the IRS national office is found in Reg. §1.165-7(b)(3): "such amount as would be ordinarily be paid for like services by like enterprises under like circumstances.[4]

6. Proceeds of a corporate liquidation, merger, redemption, recapitalization, or other corporate adjustment, organization, or reorganization, can be received by a PF if "all securities of the same class as that held by the PF are subject to the same terms and such terms provide for receipt by the PF of no less than FMV."

7. Certain scholarship, travel, and pension payments to elected or appointed federal and state government officials are not considered self-dealing, as discussed below in Section 14.6.

8. Leasing by a DP to a PF of space in a building with other unrelated tenants is acceptable if:

   - The lease was binding on October 9, 1969, or pursuant to renewals of such lease;

   - Execution of the lease was not a prohibited transaction under former IRC §503, now repealed.

   - The lease terms and its renewals reflect an arm's-length transaction.

---

[3]IRC §4941(d)(2).

[4]Tech. Adv. Memo 9008001. A September 8, 1992 article in *The Chronicle of Philanthropy* reported that the typical foundation chief earns $75,000. The same article reported the names of 37 PF chief executives whose annual compensation exceeds $200,000.

(c) Exceptions Provided in Regulations

Additional exceptions to the (at first glance) absolute rules are found in the regulations, which provide that the following types of "indirect" transactions also do not constitute self-dealing:[5]

- Certain business transactions between an organization controlled by the PF and its DPs. Control, for purposes of these exceptions, means that the PF or its managers, acting in their capacity as such, can cause the transaction to take place.

- A grant to an uncontrolled intermediary organization that plans to use the funds to make payments to governmental officials is not self-dealing, as long as the intermediary is in fact in control of the selection process and makes its decision independently.

- Transactions during administration of an estate or revocable trust in which the PF has an interest or expectancy, if the specific requirements of are satisfied (see Section 14.10).

- Transactions totaling up to $5,000 a year and arising in the "normal course" of a retail business are permitted between a DP and a controlled business, as long as the prices are the same as for other customers.

- Stocks owned on May 26, 1969 and required to be distributed to avoid the IRC §4943 tax on excess business holdings can be sold, exchanged, or otherwise disposed of to a DP.[6]

14.2 SALE, EXCHANGE, OR LEASE OF PROPERTY

Sales and exchanges of property between a PF and its DPs are absolutely prohibited. Interestingly, the rules regarding purchases and sales of tangible objects are much stricter than those regarding compensation. Even the "sale of incidental supplies" is self-dealing.[7] A PF's purchase of a mortgage held by its bank trustee (a DP) was found to be self-dealing, even though the rate was much more favorable than would otherwise have been available. The self-dealing occurred because the bank was selling its own property, not simply handling the purchase of an investment instrument from an independent source.[8]

The sale to an unrelated party of an option to buy shares in a corporation that is a disqualified person is not self-dealing, even though the exercise of the option by the PF would be.[9]

---

[5] Reg. §53.4941(d)-1(b).
[6] Reg. §53,4941(d)-4(b)(1); Rev. Rul. 75-25, 1975-1 C.B. 359.
[7] Reg. §53.4941(d)-2(a).
[8] Rev. Rul. 77-259, 1977-2 C.B. 387.
[9] Priv. Ltr. Rul. 8502040.

(a) Transactions through Agents

A sale handled by an outside agent will not circumvent the rules, but can be attributed to the PF. In a case involving an art object consigned to a commercial art auction house, the purchase of the object by a DP constituted self-dealing.[10] On the other hand, even though the same banking institution served as trustee for both parties, a sale to a PF by a testamentary trust (which is not a DP of the purchasing PF) is not self-dealing.[11] However, a sale to the bank itself by either party would be self-dealing, because the bank is a DP of both parties, but neither is to the other.

The leasing of property to a DP by a management company resulted in self-dealing when the PF controlled the manager's actions through a retained veto power.[12]

(b) Exchanges

A transfer of shares of stock in payment of an interest-free loan is "tantamount to a sale or exchange."[13] Similarly, a transfer of real estate equal to the amount of the DP's loan (in an effort to correct self-dealing) was ruled to be a second act of self-dealing.[14] On the other hand, a transfer of real estate in satisfaction of a pledge to pay cash or readily marketable securities was held not to be a "sale or exchange" because the pledge was not legally enforceable and because a pledge is not considered a debt (See Section 14.7). Thus, no self-dealing resulted from the transfer because it was essentially a gift.[15]

An exchange of a PF's securities in a reorganization or merger of a corporation that is a DP is not necessarily an act of self-dealing. All of the securities of the same class as those held by the foundation (prior to the transaction) must be subject to the same, or uniform, terms. The foundation must also receive the full FMV for its securities.[16]

(c) Use of Property

Property can be provided to a private foundation for rent-free use, but the foundation cannot permit a DP to use its property unless there is some exempt purpose. No rent can be charged, either by the PF nor by the DP, for use of property. Permissible payments include those for janitorial services, utilities, and other maintenance costs, as long as payments are not made directly or indirectly to the DP.[17] There are circumstances in which property can be used.

Assume that a private foundation borrows an art object from its creator at no cost to display in its museum. The PF pays the maintenance and insurance to independent parties. The IRS has ruled that this "use of property" is not

---

[10] Rev. Rul. 76-18, 1976-1 C.B. 355.
[11] Rev. Rul. 78-77, 1978-1 C.B. 378.
[12] Priv. Ltrl. Rul. 9047001.
[13] Rev. Rul. 77-379, 1977-2 C.B. 387.
[14] Rev. Rul. 81-40, 1981-1 C.B. 508.
[15] Priv. Ltr. Rul. 8723001.
[16] Reg. §53-4941(d)-3(d)(1).
[17] Reg. §53.4941(d)-2(b)(2).

self-dealing, and has provided some interesting facts. First, the PF is allowed to pay the DP's costs of owning the art object, which, in these days of high auction prices, represents a substantial benefit. It is important to note that the PF did not reimburse the DP; it paid the costs directly to unrelated parties. The reason for permitting this arrangement is that the public benefits: art that would not otherwise be available can now be seen. On the other hand, placement of PF art in the DP's private home, away from public view, is clearly not allowed.[18] Displaying art on the DP's property that is open to the public has been permitted, but only because the PF's collection was displayed throughout the city, primarily on public lands, as a part of a comprehensive "Outdoor Museum" program.[19]

Furnishing living quarters in a historic district to a substantial contributor (who worked 25 to 35 hours a week overseeing the complex and managing the foundation's financial affairs) was also found not to be self-dealing, as long as the fair value of the space is treated as compensation (whether or not it is actually taxable under IRC §119), and as long as the total compensation is reasonable.[20]

A PF's rental of a charter aircraft from a charter aircraft company that is itself a disqualified person, is an act of self-dealing.[21] Donating use of the plane to the PF however, would be allowed. If the charter company officials travel on bona fide foundation business, the foundation could directly pay for their direct out-of-pocket expenses, such as fuel or hanger rental in the city visited, as long as the goods and services were purchased from an independent party. See Section 14.8 for more discussion.

14.3 LOANS

The lending of money or extension of credit is a self-dealing act. Even if a circuitous route is followed, with the foundation not being the first lender, indebtedness payable to or from the foundation is prohibited. If a PF sells property in return for a mortgage to a third party who later resells the property to a DP in relation to the PF, self-dealing occurs with the second sale.[22]

A loan without interest from a DP to a PF is permitted[23] if the proceeds of the loan are used exclusively in carrying out the foundation's exempt activities. Repayment of such a loan with property other than cash will be an act of self-dealing.[24]

A gift of a whole life insurance policy subject to a cash surrender loan is also an act of self-dealing, unless the loan was placed on the policy more than

---

[18]Rev. Rul. 74-600, 1974-2 C.B. 385.

[19]Tech. Adv. Memo. 9221002. But see Priv. Ltr. Rul. 8824001 for the opposite result when, due to the fact that the sculptures were placed on the DP's private residential grounds not physically open to the public but only available for viewing from the street, self-dealing occurred.

[20]Priv. Ltr. Rul. 8948034.

[21]Rev. Rul. 73-363, 1973-2 C.B. 383.

[22]Reg. §53.4941(d)-2(c)(1).

[23]Reg. §53.4941(d)-2(c)(2).

[24]Rev. Rul. 77-379, 1977-2 C.B. 387.

ten years before the gift. Even though the insurer does not demand repayment of the loan and failure to repay simply reduces the death benefits, the loan is valid indebtedness that causes self-dealing.[25] The date on which the loan is made, not when the loan or line of credit was approved, is the date from which the ten year exception is measured. It is normally the date a lien is actually placed on the property for purposes of the exception discussed in Section 14.1(b)(1).[26]

A gift of stock in a rental property holding company that was indebted to the substantial contributor was ruled not to result in self-dealing. The loan was made for business reasons prior to the transfer of the shares.[27]

A future obligation to pay expenses to maintain gifted property is not indebtedness for this purpose. A loan by the PF to a DP/trustee's client is self-dealing because the transaction confers benefit on the trustee by providing service to the trustee's client.

14.4 COMPENSATION

An extremely important and frequently used exception to self-dealing is the provision allowing payment of compensation for personal services. If the amount is reasonable (i.e., not excessive) and the services paid for are actually rendered in carrying foundation affairs, a foundation can pay a disqualified person for personal services and can reimburse expenses borne in doing the job. The services can be rendered by an individual, a partnership, or other form of service provider. "Personal services" includes the services of a broker acting as agent for the foundation, legal services, investment advice, and commercial banking services.[28]

(a) Definition of Reasonable

The factors for evaluating whether private inurement has occurred (outlined in Chapter 20) are relevant in determining whether PF compensation is reasonable. The IRS also directs the PF to consult the IRC §162 regulations to tell if pay is excessive.[29] To prove that compensation is reasonable, a PF must show that the pay is equal to "such amount as would ordinarily be paid for like services by like enterprises under like circumstances." Annual compensation 75 percent higher than the average for a private foundation of comparable size listed in the Council on Foundations' *1986 Foundation Management Report* which also represented 35 percent of the foundation's grant expense, was found to be excessive and an act of self-dealing.[30]

---

[25] Rev. Rul. 80-132, 1980-1 C.B. 255.
[26] Rev. Rul. 78-395, 1978-2 C.B. 270.
[27] Priv. Ltr. Rul. 8409039.
[28] Reg. §53.4941(d)-3(c)(1).
[29] Reg. §1.162-7.
[30] Priv. Ltr. Rul. 9008001.

(b) Commissions

Commissions paid to a DP/art dealer were ruled not to be self-dealing when the terms of the commissions were based upon a customary scale prevailing in the work's normal market (i.e., the amount was reasonable). Advice was sought by a private foundation created by an artist. After the artist's death, the art work was to be sold by the same dealer who had represented the artist while living, to fund the foundation's programs.[31] The most useful aspect of this ruling is an outline of what the IRS calls "comparability factors," which the foundation is to use to determine whether compensation is reasonable. The factors are:

1. Commissions charged by non-disqualified persons for selling the (same) artist's work;

2. Commissions paid by the artist during his or her lifetime to persons who are now disqualified persons and to others;

3. Commissions that agents charge to sell art of the same school as the artist; and

4. Commissions that are received by agents who sell art generally from the foundation's geographic area.

Brokerage commissions can be paid to an investment manager that is a related party as long as the amount is customary and normal for the industry. Total compensation that included the normal transactions fees plus 50 percent of the account's annual equity value increases in excess of 15 percent, was deemed reasonable, because it was consistent with practices in the industry.[32]

(c) Advances

Advances that are "reasonable in relation to the duties and expense requirements of a foundation manager" are permitted.[33] Cash advances should not ordinarily exceed $500, according to the regulations. If the advance is to cover anticipated out-of-pocket current expenses for a reasonable period (such as a month), self-dealing will not occur:

- When the PF makes an advance;

- When the PF replenishes the funds upon receipt of supporting vouchers from the manager; or

- If the PF temporarily adds to the advance to cover extraordinary expenses anticipated to be incurred in fulfillment of a special assignment, such as long distance travel.

[31] Priv. Ltr. Rul. 9011050.
[32] Priv. Ltr. Rul. 9237035.
[33] Reg. §53.4941(d)-3(c)(1).

(d) Insurance Premiums

Several types of insurance coverage can be provided by the foundation to its managers, if the premiums are treated as part of the manager's compensation. The PF can furnish health, disability, life, and other personal insurance coverage that, although it is considered part of compensation for determining whether pay is excessive, is tax free under §106 or under a §125 cafeteria plan for employees (even if they are DPs). Liability insurance to reimburse the foundation for costs associated with indemnifying its DPs can also be paid on the DPs' behalf.[34]

After some years of confusion, the IRS issued proposed regulations in December, 1991, to treat "bona fide volunteers who perform services for exempt organizations" as employees eligible for the working condition fringe benefit tax exclusion. Insurance, transportation, meals, and other expenses paid by all exempt organizations would not be taxable to volunteer directors, including disqualified persons.[35] The total insurance premiums paid are combined with all other types of compensation to determine if the total compensation is excessive.[36]

(e) Bank Fees

Banks and trust companies often serve as trustees for PFs, and in this role often face self-dealing possibilities. Certain banking functions which the bank performs for all of its customers can be performed for its PFs.[37] Taking into account a fair interest rate for the use of the funds by the bank, reasonable compensation can be paid. The "general banking services" permitted are:

- Checking accounts, as long as the bank does not charge interest on any overdrafts. Payment of overdraft charges not exceeding the bank's cost of processing the overdraft have been ruled to be acceptable;[38]

- Savings accounts, as long as the foundation may withdraw its funds on no more than 30 days' notice without subjecting itself to a loss of interest on its money for the time during which the money was on deposit; and

- Safekeeping activities.

Transactions outside the scope of these three relationships may be troublesome. When a PF left funds earning no interest in a DP's bank, self-dealing was found.[39] The bank's purchase of securities owned by independent parties for a PF's account is not self-dealing, but purchase of the bank's own mortgage loans

---

[34]Rev. Rul. 82-223, 1982-2 C.B. 301.

[35]Reg. §1.132-5(m) was not finalized as of October, 1992. See Priv. Ltr. Rul. 8708029 and 8503098 and Rev. Rul. 82-223 for detailed discussion of this issue.

[36]Reg. §53.4941(d)-2(f)(3).

[37]Reg. §53.4941(d)-2(c)(4).

[38]Rev. Rul. 73-546, 1973-2 C.B. 384.

[39]Rev. Rul. 73-595, 1973-2 C.B. 384.

would be.[40] The purchase of certificates of deposit by a PF is unacceptable if the certificates provide for a reduced rate of interest if they are not held to the full maturity date.[41]

14.5 PAYMENTS ON BEHALF OF DISQUALIFIED PERSONS

Certain payments, aside from compensation for personal services, cannot be paid by a private foundation on behalf of its officers, directors, major contributors, or other disqualified persons.

(a) Indemnification of Disqualified Persons

Indemnification of foundation managers is permitted with respect to their defense in judicial or administrative proceedings. In a private letter ruling, the IRS stipulated that the indemnification exception applies to all civil matters.[42] Indemnity for all expenses (other than taxes, penalties, or expenses of correction) in connection with the IRC Chapter 42 excise taxes (and local laws relating to mismanagement of funds of charitable organizations and fiduciary responsibilities of managers) is not an act of self-dealing *if*:[43]

- Such expenses are reasonably incurred by the manager in connection with the proceedings; and

- The manager is successful in the defense, or the proceedings are terminated by settlement; and

- The manager has not acted willfully and without reasonable cause with respect to the act or failure to act which led to liability for tax under IRC Chapter 42.

An unsuccessful defense would evidence wrongdoing, and payment of costs in a lost cause would be self-dealing. The PF's payment of any amount in settlement of a claim results in self-dealing if the amount is a personal liability of the DP.[44] The regulations consider payment of insurance premiums on behalf of DPs to fund the indemnification, including payment of settlement amount, is not self-dealing. The premiums paid on behalf of the DPs, however, must be treated as part of their compensation.

A PF's payment of legal defense fees awarded by a court on behalf of a director, who brought suit against the other directors to require them to carry on the foundation's charitable program, was held not to constitute an act of self-dealing.[45]

[40] Rev. Rul. 77-259, 1977-2 C.B. 387.
[41] Rev. Rul. 77-288, 1977-2 C.B. 388.
[42] Priv. Ltr. Rul. 8202082.
[43] Reg. §53.4941(d)-2(f)(3).
[44] Rev. Rul. 82-223, 1982-2 C.B. 301.
[45] Rev. Rul. 73-613, 1973-2 C.B. 385.

Guarantee of a disqualified person's loan by a PF is considered self-dealing as is indemnification of the lender.[46] A student loan guarantee program funded by a PF through a public charity resulted in self-dealing for the DP's children.[47]

(b) Excise Taxes

A PF cannot pay the excise taxes imposed upon disqualified persons for their participation in a violation of any of the private foundation sanctions. The payment is considered a transfer of PF property for the benefit of the DP, and is self-dealing.[48]

(c) Memberships

Payment of church membership dues for a DP was found to be self-dealing because the membership provided a direct economic benefit to the individual.[49] It is common for grant recipient organizations to identify their contributors as members eligible for special privileges. When the PF makes such a gift, the individual trustees or other PF representatives are customarily provided such member benefits. The question in such a situation is whether the individual can accept such benefits as a representative of the PF. Also, ask whether there is some personal obligation in the matter which the PF is satisfying on the DP's behalf. Some PFs have adopted a policy of disclaiming membership "perks", others have their DPs pay for their own individual memberships to avoid the issue.

(d) Benefit Tickets

Self-dealing was found when a joint purchase of benefit tickets was made by sharing the ticket cost. The PF paid the deductible or charitable contribution portion of the ticket; the DP paid that part of the ticket price allocable to the FMV of the dinner, entertainment, and other benefits provided to contributors in connection with a charity fund raiser.[50]

Because IRC §4941 provides that "self-dealing" means any direct or indirect transfer to, or use by or for the benefit of, a DP of income or assets of a PF, the IRS found self-dealing in this case. The DPs reaped benefit to the extent that the PF paid expenses which the DPs would otherwise have been expected or required to pay. Thus, the partial purchase of ticket by the PF constituted direct economic benefit to the DPs, and resulted in self-dealing. Some foundations argue that it is appropriate for their DPs to attend fund-raising events as representatives of the foundation, and that private benefit does not result.

---

[46] Reg. §53.4941(d)-2(f)(1).
[47] Rev. Rul. 77-331, 1977-2 C.B. 388.
[48] Id.
[49] Rev. Rul. 77-160, 1970-1 C.B. 351.
[50] Priv. Ltr. Rul. 9021066.

14.6 PAYMENTS TO GOVERNMENT OFFICIALS

The basic statutory provision absolutely prohibits payments to government officials, but there are a number of exceptions. Self-dealing results if a private foundation enters into an agreement to make payments of money or other property to a government official (see Chapter 12 for definition), *other than* an agreement to employ the person, unless the official's government service is terminating within 90 days of the date of the offer.[51]

Certain de minimus payments to government officials are permitted, as follows:[52]

- A prize or award which is not includible in gross income under IRC §74(b), if the government official receiving the prize is selected from the general public. (The prize must be paid over to a charitable institution.)

- A scholarship or fellowship grant which is excludable from gross income under IRC §117(a) and which is to be utilized for study at an IRC §151(e)(4) educational institution (but only for tuition, fees, and books).

- Certain types of pension plans and annuity payments.

- Contributions, gifts, services, or facilities provided to or made available to a government official totaling no more than $25 in any one year.

- Government employee training program payments.

- Reimbursement of the actual cost of travel within the United States for attendance at a charitable function, not to exceed 125% of the prevailing per diem rate.

14.7 NONMONETARY DEALINGS

Certain transactions between a private foundation and its supporters involve intangible and nonquantifiable matters, and for the most part do not result in self-dealing.

(a) Charitable Pledges

If a PF satisfies a charitable pledge made by one of its individual DPs and thereby relieves the DP of an individual debt, self-dealing may occur.[53] Payment of church membership dues for a DP was found to be self-dealing when the membership provided a personal benefit to the individual.[54] A foundation created by a group of corporations committed an act of self-dealing when it

---

[51] IRC §4941(d)(1)(F).
[52] IRC §4941(d)(2)((G); Reg. §53.4941(d)-3(e).
[53] Reg. §53.4941(d)-2(f)(1) and Rev. Rul. 77-160, 1977-1 C.B. 351.
[54] Rev. Rul. 77-160, 1970-1 C.B. 351.

paid pledges entered into by and legally binding on the corporations before the PF was established.[55]

However, pledges obligating a DP to make a gift to the PF itself may not create self-dealing. The regulations say:

> "The making of a promise, pledge or similar arrangement to a PF by a DP, whether evidenced by an oral or written agreement, a promissory note, or other instrument of indebtedness, to the extent motivated by charitable intent and unsupported by consideration, is not an extension of credit before the date of maturity.[56]"

Modification of a DP's charitable pledge to a foundation prior to its maturity is acceptable. The IRS looked at the case of a PF that operated both with current contributions from its substantial contributor and with loans made by a bank against pledges made periodically by the DP. When the DP reduced his current promised payments before their maturity, but pledged a larger amount later, self-dealing was held not to occur.[57]

Return of a conditional gift by the PF to a contributor who stipulated that it be returned if his donation were disallowed was found not to be self-dealing.[58]

(b) Name Recognition

What the regulations call "incidental or tenuous benefit" can be bestowed upon a disqualified person without adverse consequence.[59] Any public recognition or prestige which a person may receive, arising from the charitable activities of a PF to which that person is a substantial contributor, does not, in itself, result in self-dealing.[60]

A PF grant to a public charity made on the condition that the charity change its name to that of the PF's substantial contributor (and that it not change it again for 100 years) did not result in self-dealing.[61] Grants by a PF to charity, private or public, with interlocking board members are permitted.[62] The fact that the board members are recognized for causing the grants to be awarded does not amount to self-dealing.

The goodwill generated by a company foundation scholarship program is also treated as incidental. As long as the program meets the "objective and nondiscriminatory" requirements discussed in Chapter 17, the awarding of grants to children of the corporation's employees is not self-dealing.

Similarly, the fact that a corporation plans to recruit and hire graduates of a university engineering program results only in an incidental benefit. The

---

[55] Priv. Ltr. Rul. 8128072.

[56] Reg. §53.4941(d)-3(c).

[57] Tech. Adv. Memo. 8723001.

[58] *G. M. Underwood, Jr. v. U.S.*, 78-2 USTC ¶9831 (N.D. Tex. 1978).

[59] Reg. §53.4941(d)-2(f)(2).

[60] Rev. Rul. 77-331, 1977-2 C.B. 388.

[61] Rev. Rul. 73-407, 1973-2 C.B. 383.

[62] Rev. Rul. 80-310, 1980-2 C.B. 319; Rev. Rul. 82-136, 1982-2 C.B. 300, clarifying Rev. Rul. 75-42, 1975-1 C.B. 359.

company's foundation can fund the program without self-dealing unless the corporation is given preferential treatment in access to the graduates.[63]

14.8 SHARING SPACE, PEOPLE, AND EXPENSES

As a practical matter, many private foundations are operated alongside of their creators, whether these are corporations or family groups. At least until the foundation achieves a certain volume of assets with consequential grant activity (and maybe thereafter), rental of a separate office and engagement of staff is beyond the PF's reasonable economic capability, particularly when such expenditures take funds away from grant-making activity.

(a) What Can the Private Foundation Pay?

When can a PF pay for its portion of the expenses in such a sharing situation? The Internal Revenue Code specifically prohibits the "furnishing of goods, services or facilities" between (to or from) a PF and a DP. The types of property which the IRS intends to cover by this rule include office space, automobiles, auditoriums, secretarial help, meals, libraries, publications, laboratories, and parking lots.[64]

When Congress imposed these strict rules in 1969, it provided a transitional period until 1980, during which existing and contractual sharing arrangements could be phased out.[65] As time passed and the costs of the absolute rule became unreasonable in certain circumstances, the IRS in private letter rulings relaxed what looked like an impenetrable barrier to any arrangements in which a PF and DPs share space, people, or other expenses.

A PF was allowed to rent contiguous space with a common reception area, but with separate offices from its DP. Separate leases were entered into and the DPs received no benefit in the form of reduced rent because of the PF's rental in the related space.[66] In another ruling, a PF and DP together bought a duplicating machine and hired a shared employee. Time records were kept to determine each entity's share of the cost of the machine and the allocable time of the employee. Because "nothing was paid directly or indirectly to the DP" and there was "independent use" by the PF that was measurable and specifically paid for to outside parties, no self-dealing resulted from what certainly appears to have been a "sharing arrangement," supposedly phased out and consequentially prohibited by IRC §4941.[67]

Similarly, a "time-sharing arrangement" of a DP management company's employees was condoned by the IRS. The basis for the favorable ruling was the fact that, in the first place, a PF is permitted to pay reasonable compensation to a disqualified person for the performance of personal services necessary to carry out its exempt purposes. Perhaps more importantly, the IRS found that the

[63] Rev. Rul. 80-310, 1980-2 C.B. 319.
[64] Reg. §53.4941(d)-2(d)(1).
[65] Reg. §53.4941(d)-4(d).
[66] Priv. Ltr. Rul. 8331082.
[67] Tech. Adv. Memo 7734022, see also Priv. Ltr. Rul. 8824010.

Exhibit 14–1

EXPENDITURE DOCUMENTATION POLICY
Sample Foundation

Introduction

As a private foundation (PF), Sample Foundation (Sample) is responsible for proving that all of its expenditures are made for charitable purposes, and that it makes no expenditures on behalf of nor has any financial transactions with its "disqualified persons" (DPs), meaning major contributors and managers. Sample will establish its headquarters and laboratory in the office building owned by its president and contributor, XYZ, who is a DP in relation to Sample. Therefore, Sample wishes to adopt procedures to meet its responsibility. Specifically, the "self-dealing" provisions of the Internal Revenue Code prohibit the following:

- Sale, exchange, or lease of property between the PF and DP, except at no charge;

- Lending of money or extension of credit between PF and DP;

- Furnishing of goods, services, or facilities between a PF and DP, unless the DP furnishes them to the PF without charge; and

- Payment of compensation or reimbursement of expenses from the PF to the DP, unless such payments are reasonable and necessary to carrying out the exempt purposes of the PF.

Policy

To insure adherence to these requirements, Sample adopts the following rules:

Office Space. Sample is entering into a lease agreement with XYZ stipulating that the space is furnished to Sample at no charge. Maintenance, repair, and utilities attributable to the space occupied by Sample will be paid by Sample directly. For example, the space leased to Sample represents _____ percent of the total square footage of the building. Therefore, _____ percent of the utility bill will be paid by Sample. Any expenses not directly attributable to Sample space will be paid by XYZ.

Personnel. Sample will hire a project manager, and possibly other personnel, to work exclusively on foundation projects. Because Sample is small and is just getting started, it does not need a full-time secretary or accountant. Therefore, it will hire the current employees of XYZ on a part-time basis. It is estimated that the receptionist and business manager will devote approximately half of their time to Sample's business. Therefore, half of their salaries, employee benefits, and taxes will be paid by Sample. Each person will maintain a record of his or her actual time and the ratio will be evaluated periodically.

Office Furnishings and Equipment. XYZ owns a telephone system, copy machine, computers, and other equipment that Sample is allowed to use

Exhibit 14–1 *(continued)*

EXPENDITURE DOCUMENTATION POLICY

rent-free. To the extent that Sample incurs direct costs in connection with such equipment, it will pay the bills directly. For example, long distance phone calls, photocopy paper, and other expendable supplies directly related to foundation activities will be paid by Sample.

Automobile. XYZ is furnishing Sample with a vehicle for its use in connection with foundation projects. Sample will pay the expenses attributable to its actual use of the vehicle. A mileage log will be maintained to evidence the usage.

Asset Purchases and Sales and Debt Payments. Sample hereby adopts a policy that it will not engage in any financial transactions with XYZ or with any other DP that would cause it to "self-deal" as that term is defined in Chapter 42 of the Internal Revenue Code.

---

benefit to the management company in being relieved from paying a percentage of the salaries of its employees was incidental and tenuous.[68]

Group insurance policies present similar situations. Corporate and other conglomerate groups funding private foundations have been allowed to include their private foundation employees in a common health insurance policy. The foundation pays directly for the premiums allocable to its employees, or reimburses the company. (Direct payment is strongly preferred, but if it is impossible, the IRS may allow reimbursement.) The rationale is found in the "Special Rules" of IRC §4941(d)(2)(B), which provides that the lending of money by a disqualified person to a private foundation shall not be an act of self-dealing if the loan is without interest or other charge and if the proceeds of the loan are used exclusively for purposes specified in §501(c)(3).

See Exhibit 14–1 for an example of an expenditure documentation agreement between a DP and a PF, for a PF occupying office space donated by a DP. The PF maintains records to document and pay for its "independent use" of the equipment, staff, and other systems in the office.

(b) Public Facilities

A private foundation that operates a museum, maintains a wildlife preserve, or produces an educational journal is faced with a decree that it must not furnish goods, services, or facilities to its DPs. Taken literally, the rule prevents DPs from visiting the sites or purchasing the journal. A PF's furnishing of goods, services, or facilities normally open to the general public to a DP, however,

---

[68]Priv. Ltr. Rul. 9226067.

comes within another of the useful exceptions to the general rules. Such activity is not self-dealing *if*:[69]

- The property involved is "functionally related to the exercise or performance by the PF of its charitable, educational, or other purpose or function forming the basis for its exemption;
- The number of persons (other than the DPs) who use the facility is substantial enough to indicate that the general public is genuinely the primary user; and
- The terms for DP usage are not more favorable than the terms under which the general public acquires or uses the property.

If a PF's library meeting room is regularly used by the community at large for exempt function-related affairs, the use of the room by a government official who is also a disqualified person was permitted.[70] Similarly, the use of a public thoroughfare situated on the foundation's property was permitted for access to the headquarters and manufacturing plant of its corporate disqualified person.[71] The road apparently provided access to both the PF's museum and to the company facility, and the company paid for the road's upkeep. Whether an allocation of cost would be permitted is unknown.

14.9   INDIRECT DEALS

Transactions between a disqualified person and an organization controlled by a PF (controlled organization or CO) may be classified as an indirect act of self-dealing as to the foundation itself, even though the funds never touch the PF. For example, a private foundation owns a 70 percent interest in a real estate rental partnership and two of the PF's directors own a construction company. The partnership, because it is controlled by the PF, cannot hire the construction company owned by its DPs to repair its apartment buildings.

The regulations define an indirect transaction by describing circumstances in which a business transaction will not be considered as self-dealing. The regulations provide that indirect self-dealing does not occur in these situations:[72]

- Transactions in place prior to the creation of the control relationship which caused the self-dealing are allowed.
- Transactions at least as favorable to the CO as an arm's length transaction with an unrelated party would have been allowed, but only if (1) the CO could have engaged in the transaction with someone other than the DP only at a severe economic hardship to the CO, or (2) because of the unique nature of the product or services provided by the

---

[69] Reg. §53.4941(d)-3(b).
[70] Rev. Rul. 76-10, 1976-1 C.B. 355.
[71] Rev. Rul. 76-459, 1976-2 C.B. 369.
[72] Reg. §53.4941(d)-1(b)(1).

CO, the DP could not have engaged in the transaction with anyone else.

- De minimus transactions with a CO engaged in a retail business with the general public, such as office supplies, are not indirect self-dealing if the transactions' total amount in one year does not exceed $5,000.

A private foundation was found guilty of indirect self-dealing when space in a building owned by the PF was leased to a company controlled by one of its DPs. The entire building was subleased to an independent management company which, in turn, subleased the spaces, so that the foundation was not a party to the building subleases. However, the master lease granted the PF, as landlord, the power of approval over the form and content of any long-term leases entered into by the management company. Thus, the PF essentially controlled the management company and, for self-dealing purposes, became a party to the lease with the DP.[73]

14.10 PROPERTY HELD BY FIDUCIARIES

Estate executors may find that property bequeathed to a private foundation (PF) (for example, undivided interests in property) is not suitable to be held by a PF. At times, the best solution to the situation is a self-dealing transaction, either direct or indirect. Because the property has not yet become the property of the foundation, the regulations grant a fair degree of leeway to the estate or revocable trust officials in allocating or selling assets among beneficiaries. Transactions during administration regarding the PF's interest or expectancy in property held by the estate (regardless of when title vests under local law) are not self-dealing, if all five of the following conditions are met:[74]

1. The executor, administrator, or trustee has authority to either sell the property or reallocate it to another beneficiary, or is required to sell the property by its the terms of the trust or will.

2. A probate court having jurisdiction over the estate approves the transaction. It is unclear whether this approval must be granted specifically for the transaction, or whether the court's acceptance by of the final estate accounting and its release of the parties is sufficient.

3. The transaction occurs before the estate or trust is terminated.

4. The estate or trust receives FMV for the PF's portion of the property.[75]

5. The PF receives an interest at least as liquid as the one given up for an exempt function asset, or receives an amount of money equal to that required under an option binding upon the estate.

[73] Priv. Ltr. Rul. 9047001.
[74] Reg. §53.4941(d)-1(b)(3).
[75] See also *Rockefeller v. U.S.*, 572 F. Supp. 9 (E.D. Ark. 1982), *aff'd*, 718 F.2d 290 (8th Cir. 1983), *cert. den.*, 466 U.S. 962 (1984), in which it was found that the full FMV was not paid for the estate's shares and, consequently, indirect self-dealing occurred. See also Priv. Ltr. Rul 9210040.

14.11 UNIQUE TRANSACTIONS WITH DISQUALIFIED PERSONS

The contribution of substantially appreciated antique automobiles to a nonoperating private foundation (that, according to the facts in the ruling, intends to sell them) is not self-dealing. The "unavoidable use by the contributor collector (DP) to "drive the antique automobiles from time to time and to travel with them on behalf of the foundation to maintain and show them" is also not self-dealing. The foundation in this case bears all expense of refurbishment, shipment, and travel for the autos. Because the cars are not capable of producing the types of income specifically listed in IRC §4940, such as rentals or dividends, any gain realized by the foundation upon sale of the cars is not subject to the investment income excise tax, nor does it produce UBI. Particularly since the foundation is not an operating one, it would have been helpful if the ruling had explained how the cars were related to the foundation's exempt purposes.[76]

Formation of a partnership between a private foundation and its three benefactor §4947(a)(2) split-interest charitable lead trusts did not result in self-dealing.[77]

14.12 ISSUES ONCE SELF-DEALING OCCURS

Once it has been determined that self-dealing has occurred, the self-dealing must be corrected and an excise tax return must be filed on Form 4720. The steps involved in repairing the damage include "undoing" the deal, assigning an "amount" attributable to the self-dealing, deciding who has to pay an excise tax, and advancing any reasonable cause to reduce or avoid the tax.

(a) Undoing the Transaction

To undo self-dealing, the deal must be corrected and rescinded (i.e., the property returned) if possible. The financial position of the private foundation after the correction must be no worse than it would have been if the original transaction had not occurred.[78] Very specific rules govern sales by or to the PF, uses of property, and compensation deals.

Sales by the Foundation. If the purchaser still holds the property, the sale must be rescinded and the PF must take back the property.[79] The PF is to repay the purchaser the sales price or the current FMV of the property at the time of the correction, whichever is less. Any income earned by the DP buyer from the property in excess of the PF's earnings on the money (from investment of the sales proceeds) during the self-dealing period should be restored to the foundation, essentially reducing the repayment of the purchase price by the foundation. If the property has been resold, the foundation is to receive the greater of

[76]Priv. Ltr. Rul. 9119009.
[77]Priv. Ltr. Rul. 9015070.
[78]Reg. §53.4941(e)-1(c)(1).
[79]Reg. §53.4941(e)-1(c)(2).

the original proceeds which it received or what the DP received upon the resale.

Sales to the Foundation. Again, rescission of the sale is required. Fair market value and resale considerations similar to those above are taken into account, to assure that the foundation is restored to the financial position it would have been in, had it not purchased the property. For example, a PF sold 100 shares of stock to a DP for $4000 in 1992, at a time when the FMV was $3,500. The DP sells the shares in 1993 for $6,000 although the shares had been quoted at $6,700 at one point during the year. The PF must be paid $6,700 to cure the transaction. The first-tier tax will be charged based upon the $5,000. If the self-dealing is not corrected and the second-tier tax applies, the tax is calculated based upon $6,700.[80]

Uses of Property by a DP. The use must be stopped. If the rent paid exceeded the FMV, an imputed rent factor based upon fair market differentials, if any, must be repaid to the foundation. Different corrections are specified in the regulations, depending on whether the PF or the DP rented the property.[81]

Uses of Property by the PF. Again, the lease must be terminated and the FMV differential repaid.[82]

Unreasonable Compensation. When excessive or unreasonable salaries have been paid to a DP, the excess must be repaid to the foundation. However, termination of the employment or independent contractor arrangement is not required.[83]

(b) Amount Involved

The penalties for entering into a self-dealing transaction are based upon what the statute calls "Amount Involved," which is defined as follows:

> "The greater of the amount of money and the fair market value of the other property given or the amount of money and the fair market value of the other property received."[84]

If a PF leases office space from a DP for $30,000, but the FMV of the space is $25,000, the "amount" is $30,000. If a PF loans a DP money at a below-market interest rate, the "amount" equals the principal of the loan plus the interest that would have been charged at the prevailing market rate at the time the loan is made.[85] In certain cases, the full FMV is not used:

Compensation. In the case of compensation paid for personal services to persons other than government officials, the "amount involved" is the portion of the total compensation in excess of the amount that would have been reasonable.

[80] Reg. §53.4941(e)-1(b)(4), Example 4.
[81] Reg. §53.4941(e)-1(c)(4).
[82] Reg. §53.4941(e)-1(c)(5).
[83] Reg. §53.4941(e)-1(c)(6).
[84] Reg. §53.4941(e)(2); Reg. §53.4941(e)-1(b)(2).
[85] Reg. §53.4941(e)-1(b)(4).

Stock Redemptions and Other Permitted Dealings. Sometimes a transaction that is permitted by the statutory exceptions listed in Section 14.1(b) goes amiss, and a tax is imposed. This occurs particularly often under exceptions 6 and 8, in which the value is determinative. In such cases, the "amount involved" is only the amount by which the redemption price is deficient (i.e., the amount by which the property was undervalued) or the taxable self-dealing. Two conditions must be present to show that the parties made a good faith effort to determine the FMV:

1. The appraiser who arrived at the value must be competent to make the valuation, must not be a DP, and must not be in a position, whether by stock ownership or otherwise, to derive an economic benefit from the value utilized; and

2. The method utilized in making the valuation must be a generally accepted method for valuing comparable property, stock, or securities for purposes of arm's length business transactions in which valuation is a significant factor.

For example, a corporation that is a DP as to a PF redeems the PF's stock for $200,000. Assume that the correct valuation is later determined to be $250,000. Self-dealing has occurred in the amount of $50,000.

(c) Date of Valuation

To calculate the so-called "first-tier" tax initially imposed upon a sale, exchange, or lease of property, the amount involved is determined as of the date on which the self-dealing occurred. If the self-dealing goes uncorrected and the additional or "second-tier" tax is calculated, the valuation is equal to the highest value during the period of time the self-dealing continued uncorrected. For an entertaining saga of one foundation's attempts to cure a self-dealing transaction, see the Dupont case.[86]

(d) How Much Tax is Due?

The basic tax of five percent of the amount involved in each year in the taxable period is payable by the self-dealer. A two and a half percent tax is also imposed on any persons who approved the transaction.[87] The "taxable period" begins with the date on which the transaction occurred and ends on the earliest of the date of mailing of the notice of deficiency with respect to the initial tax, the date on which the initial tax is assessed, or the date on which correction of the transaction is completed.[88]

The "first tier" tax may be abated if the act was due to reasonable causes and not to willful neglect, and if it is corrected.[89]

[86] *Dupont v. Commissioner,* 74 T.C. 498 (1980).
[87] IRC §4941(a)(2).
[88] IRC §4941(e)(1).
[89] IRC §4962.

An additional tax of 200 percent of the amount involved is imposed on the self-dealer if the correction is not made. A foundation manager who refuses to agree to the correction faces a penalty of 50 percent of the amount involved.[90]

The so-called "third tier" tax, the IRC §507 termination tax, will be charged if the transactions are never cured. A foundation that conducts repeated and willful violations of the IRC Chapter 42 sanctions is liable to be terminated, with all tax benefits it and its contributors have ever received being repaid to the government—very likely, all of the assets held in the PF.

See Exhibit 12–1 for a list of the rates of tax and the parties upon whom the tax is imposed.

(e) Who Pays the Tax?

The tax is imposed on the individual(s) or corporate self-dealer(s) participating in the prohibited transaction, but not on the PF itself. The self-dealer is taxed even if he or she was unaware that a rule was being violated. Foundation managers who condoned the action are also taxed, but only if they knowingly and willfully participated in the self-dealing. Basic fiduciary responsibility rules apply, and a PF manager is expected to be aware of the PF sanctions and to remain sufficiently informed of the PF's affairs to prevent any violations of the sanctions.[91] The managers are jointly and severally liable for the tax imposed upon them, up to a maximum of $10,000.[92]

Advice of Counsel. Tax is not imposed upon a PF manager if a full disclosure of the facts was made to counsel, a "reasoned legal opinion" was issued, and the manager relied upon that opinion in deciding that no sanctions were violated.[93]

---

[90] IRC §4941(b).
[91] Reg. §53.4941(a)-1(b)(3).
[92] IRC §4941(c).
[93] Reg. §53.4941(a)-1(b)(6).

Minimum Distribution Requirements: IRC §4942

Before 1970, all IRC §501(c)(3) exempt organizations were subject to a vague and unenforceable prohibition against accumulating income unreasonably. Assets could be invested in a no- or low-income producing manner, with very little money being given to charity. A family could take tax deductions, in some years offsetting as much as 90 percent of its income, for placing shares of the family business in a foundation. The company could pay out no dividends to the shareholders and instead pay whatever money as salaries the family needed to live on. The only persons benefitting from such arrangements were the family members, not the intended beneficiaries of charitable organizations.

To stem such abuses, Congress enacted IRC §4942, which requires private foundations (PFs) to satisfy a strict numerical test for making annual expenditures for charitable projects and grants. A PF must annually make "qualifying distributions," or charitable grants or project expenditures, equal to its prior year's minimum investment return (MIR). The MIR is approximately five percent of the value of the PF's investment assets.

Before 1982, PFs were required to distribute the higher of MIR or actual net investment income. When interest rates were over 20 percent, the actual income was often a much higher amount. PFs convinced Congress that they needed to reserve some of their income against future inflation.

15.1 ASSETS USED TO CALCULATE MINIMUM INVESTMENT RETURN

Stated most simply, a private foundation annually is required to spend or pay out for charitable and administrative purposes at least five percent of the average fair market value (FMV) of its investment assets for the preceding year, less the amount of any debt incurred to acquire the property. See Chapter 21 for discussion of acquisition indebtedness.

$$(\text{PF Investment Assets} - \text{Debt}) \times 5\% = \text{MIR}$$

Successful calculation of MIR depends upon distinguishing investment assets from exempt function assets. This concept of exempt function versus investment is an important key to understanding MIR. If the foundation holds an asset as an investment, five percent of its value is payable annually for charitable purposes, even if it is not producing any current income. This scheme is very different from that of IRC §4940, under which income from certain types of assets is excluded and not taxed.

(a) What are Investment Assets?

The statute applies the percentage to "the aggregate fair market value of all assets other than those which are used (or held for use) directly in carrying out the foundation's exempt purposes, over [i.e., less] the acquisition indebtedness with respect to such assets."[1]

The typical PF investment portfolio of stocks, bonds, certificates of deposit, and rental properties forms the basis for calculating the distributable amount. Funds of all sorts—current, deferred grants, capital, endowment, and similar types of reserves—are all includible in the formula.

(b) Future Interests or Expectancies

Certain assets provide beneficial support to the PF in an indirect fashion. Assets over which the PF has no control and in which it essentially holds no present interest are not included in the MIR formula. These assets most often are not

---

[1]IRC §4941(f)(1)(A); Reg. §53.4942(a)-2(c)(1).

actually in the possession or under the control of the PF, nor are they customarily included in the financial records or statements of the foundation. These include:[2]

- Charitable remainders and other future interests in property created by someone other than the PF itself, until the intervening interests expire or are otherwise set apart for the PF. If the foundation is able to take possession of the property at its will or to acquire it readily upon giving notice, the property is included. The rules of "constructive receipt" for determining when a cash basis taxpayer receives an item of income are relevant.

- Present interests in a trust, usually called a "charitable lead trust." However, income from any such trusts created after May 26, 1969 is includible in the adjusted net income and can effect a private operating foundation.[3]

- Pledges of money or other property to the PF, whether or not the pledges are legally enforceable.

- Property bequeathed to the PF is excluded while it is held by the decedent's estate. If and when the IRS treats the estate as terminated because the period of administration is prolonged,[4] the assets are treated as PF assets from the time of such IRS determination.

- Options to sell property are excluded, (unless they are readily marketable and have an ascertainable value, such as listed options on common stocks).

(c) Exempt Function Assets

Income need not be imputed to property held by and actually used by the foundation in conducting its charitable programs. Such assets are called *exempt function assets*, and are not usually held for the production of income (although they do in some cases). Included are "assets used (or held for use) directly in carrying out the foundation's exempt purpose" only if the assets are actually used by the foundation in the carrying out of the charitable, educational, or other similar purpose which gives rise to the exempt status of the foundation. The most common type of assets excluded from the MIR formula follow.[5]

Administrative offices, furnishings, equipment, and supplies used by employees and consultants in working on the foundation's charitable projects are not counted. However, the same property, if used by persons who manage the investment properties or endowments, is treated as investment property.

---

[2] Reg. §53.4942(a)-2(c)(2).

[3] *The Ann Jackson Family Foundation v. Commissioner*, 97 TC 4, No. 35.

[4] See Reg. §1.1641(b)-3 for circumstances under which administration of an estate is considered to be unreasonably prolonged.

[5] Reg. §53.4942(a)-2(c)(3)(ii).

Buildings, equipment and facilities used directly in projects are clearly not counted as investment property. Examples include:

- Historic buildings, libraries, and the furnishings in such buildings;

- Collections of objects on educational display, such as works of art or scientific specimens, including art works loaned to other organizations;[6]

- Research facilities and laboratories, including a limited access island held vacant to preserve its natural ecosystem, history, and archaeology;[7]

- Print shops, and educational classrooms; and

- Property used for a nominal or reduced rent by another charity. No figures are furnished in the regulations. The asset test for private operating foundations, however, defines a rental property leased to carry out an exempt purpose. The property is considered to be exempt property if the rent is less than the amount which would be required to be charged in order to recover the cost of property purchase and maintenance.[8]

Reasonable cash balances are considered to be necessary to carry out exempt functions. One and one-half percent of the included investment assets is presumed to be a reasonable cash balance, even if a smaller cash balance is actually maintained.[9] An amount of money that the PF "needs to have around to cover expenses and disbursements" is allowable. When one and one-half percent is insufficient, the PF can apply to the IRS to permit a higher amount.[10] Money needed for asset acquisitions would not be included for this purpose.

Future use property is not investment property if it is acquired for prospective exempt use and temporarily leased for a "reasonable period" of a year or so while it is being readied for exempt use.

Program-related investments under IRC §4944 are not considered as investment assets. Examples include a low rent indigent housing project, a student loan fund, and a functionally related business operated within a larger aggregate of charitable endeavors. A restaurant and hotel complex operated by a separate taxable corporation within a historic village, and advertising sold for an otherwise educational journal are given as examples in the regulations.[11] Such properties are not included in investment assets even if they are unrelated businesses subject to income tax under IRC §512.

(d) Dual-Use Property

In many cases, a PF owns and uses property for managing or conducting both its investments and its charitable projects. In such situations, an allocation

---

[6]Rev. Rul. 74-498, 1974-2 C.B. 387.
[7]Rev. Rul. 75-207, 1975-1 C.B. 361.
[8]Reg. §53.4942(b)-2(a)(2).
[9]Rev. Rul. 75-392, 1975-2 C.B. 447.
[10]Reg. §53.4942(a)-2(c)(3)(iv).
[11]Reg. §53.4942(a)-2(c)(3)(iii).

between these two uses must be made. For assets used 95 percent or more for one purpose, the remaining five percent is ignored. An office building housing the foundation would be allocated based upon the functions performed by the persons occupying the spaces. Consider the following example:

Investment department	1,125 square feet	25%
Program offices	3,375 square feet	75%
	4,500	100%

In such a case, 25 percent of the building's value would be treated as an investment asset. In a very large foundation, the formula may be more complicated. A third category, administration, may need to be included in the formula when the staff is sophisticated and separate personnel, accounting, and central supply departments serve the investment and program groups.

For property that is partly used by the foundation and partly rented to others, the IRS has ruled that an allocation based upon the fair rental value of the respective spaces, rather than the square feet, is appropriate.[12]

(e) Assets Held for Future Use

Sometimes it takes a number of years to piece together a project using hard assets like land, buildings, and equipment. When a PF has future plans for use of property and "establishes to the satisfaction of the Commissioner" (i.e., obtains IRS approval) that its immediate use of the property is impractical, an asset held for future use is excluded. Definite plans must exist to commence use within a reasonable period of time, and all of the facts and circumstances must prove the intention to devote the property to such use.[13] See the discussion of "set asides" at Section 15.4(c) for more details.

Property acquired to be devoted to exempt purposes may be treated as exempt function property from the time it is acquired, even if it is temporarily rented.[14] Its acquisition is also treated as a qualifying distribution, as discussed in Section 15.4. The rental status must be for a reasonable and limited period of time and only while the property is being made ready for its intended use, such as during remodeling or acquisition of adjacent pieces of property. IRS approval is not necessary if the property conversion takes only one year. However, if the property is rented for more than a year, it is treated as investment property during the second year and thereafter until it is devoted to exempt purposes. This change is also reflected for qualifying distribution purposes. Property reclassified as investment property would be treated as a negative distribution. See Section 15.3.

---

[12] Rev. Rul. 82-137, 1982-2 C.B. 303.
[13] Reg. §53.4942(a)-2(c)(3)(i).
[14] Id.

15.2 MEASURING FAIR MARKET VALUE

The minimum investment return is based on a percentage of the average fair market value (FMV) of the includible investment assets. Different methods and revaluation times and frequencies are provided for various types of investment assets that a private foundation might need to value.

(a) Valuation Methods

Any "commonly acceptable method of valuation" may be used, as long as it is reasonable and consistently used. Valuations made in accordance with the methods prescribed for estate tax valuation under the IRC §2031 regulations are acceptable.[15] Presumably, the rules governing valuation of charitable gifts (IRS Publication 561) would also be acceptable.

Outside appraisals are only required for real estate. For all other assets, the PF itself can establish a consistent method for making a good faith determination of the value of most of its assets.

(b) Date of Valuation

Different valuation dates are prescribed for different kinds of assets:

Cash	Monthly
Marketable securities	Monthly
Real estate	Every five years
All other assets	Annually

Assets valued annually can be valued on any date, as long as the same date is used each year.[16] Likewise, real estate valuation should be done on approximately the same date every fifth year.

The average value of an asset held by the foundation for part of a year is calculated by using the number of days in the year that the asset was held as the numerator, and 365 is the denominator. The includible value is thereby reduced to equate to the partial year holding period. For example, for a $100,000 piece of real estate acquired on July 1, the includible amount would be

$$\$100{,}000 \times 182/365 \text{ or } \$50{,}000.$$

(c) Readily Marketable Securities

Securities for which a market quotation is readily available must be valued monthly, using any reasonable and consistent method.[17] Securities include (but

[15] Reg. §53.4942(a)-2(c)(4)(i)(*b*) and (iv)(*c*).
[16] Reg. §53.4942(a)-2(c)(4)(vi).
[17] Reg. §53.4942(a)-2(c)(4)(i)(*a*).

are not limited to) common and preferred stocks, bonds, and mutual fund shares.[18] The monthly security valuation method applies to:

- Stocks listed on the New York Stock Exchange, the American Stock Exchange, or any city or regional exchange in which quotations appear on a daily basis, including foreign securities listed on a recognized foreign national or regional exchange;

- Stocks regularly traded in a national or regional over-the-counter market, for which published quotations are available; and

- Locally traded stocks for which quotations can readily be obtained from established brokerage firms.

The quotation system can be one of a variety of methods, again as long as a consistent pattern is followed. The following examples are given in the regulations:[19]

- The classic method averages the high and low quoted price on a particular day each month, which could be the 1st, 5th, last, or any other day.

- A formula averaging the first, middle, and last day closing prices for each month.

- The average of the bid and asked price for over-the-counter stocks or funds on a consistent day, using the nearest day if no quote was available on the regular day.

Portfolio reports generated by a computer pricing system and prepared monthly for securities held in trust by a bank or other financial institution may be acceptable. The bank's or investment advisor's system must be accepted as a valid method for valuing securities for federal estate tax purposes. The foundation has a responsibility to inquire of the bank as to its method of valuation, and to obtain evidence that its system is approved. Banks commonly have certification from bank examiners, and investment advisory firms have their license renewals from the Securities and Exchange Commission. If these systems conform to the quotation system outlined above, in the author's experience, the IRS does not require proof that the bank's system has specific IRS approval, even though the regulations require it.

Blockage discounts of no more than 10 percent are permitted to reduce the valuation of securities when a foundation can "show that the quoted market prices do not reflect FMV"[20] for one or more of the following reasons:

- The block of securities is so large in relation to the volume of actual sales on the existing market that it could not be liquidated in a reasonable time without depressing the market.

---

[18] Reg. §53.4942(a)-2(c)(4)(v).
[19] Reg. §53.4942(a)-2(c)(4)(e).
[20] Reg. §53.4942(a)-2(c)(4)(i)(*c*).

- Sales of the securities are few or sporadic in nature, and the shares are in a closely held corporation.

- The sale of the securities would result in a forced or distress sale because the securities cannot be offered to the public without first being registered with the Securities and Exchange Commission.

Essentially, a foundation is permitted to use the price at which the securities could be sold by an underwriter outside the normal market. The discount is limited to 10 percent for unrestricted listed securities, and is unlimited otherwise.[21]

(d) Cash

Cold hard dollars are valued by taking the average of the cash on hand at the beginning and end of each month. Thus, a PF cannot easily manipulate its cash balance.

(e) Common Trust Funds

Foundation funds invested in a common trust fund qualifying under IRC §584 can use the fund's valuation reports. Fund participants typically receive periodic valuations of their interests from the fund manager throughout the year, and can calculate the average of these valuation reports. If the fund issues valuations quarterly, the simple average of the four reported valuations is the FMV reportable as an investment asset.

(f) Real Estate

"Certified, independent appraisals made in writing by a qualified person who is not a disqualified person with respect to, or an employee of, the foundation" are required to be made every five years for investment real estate held by a PF.[22] An appraisal is considered "certified" only if it includes a statement that, in the opinion of the appraiser, the values placed on the land appraised were determined in accordance with valuation principles regularly employed in making appraisals of such property using all reasonable valuation methods.

More frequent valuations can be made when circumstances dictate, as for example, when real estate has declined substantially in value. The IRS "will not disturb" a valuation properly made during the five year period even when the valuation has increased materially.[23]

(g) Other Types of Assets

All other assets are valued on an annual basis using a reasonable and consistent method.

[21] IRC §4942(e)(2).
[22] Reg. §53.4942(a)-2(c)((4)(iv)(b).
[23] Id.

Mineral interests valuations are based on reserve studies conducted by independent petroleum evaluation engineers. These studies are customarily updated every five years, like real estate, although there is no mention of oil properties in the IRS literature on the subject.

A *closely held business* can be valued on any day of the year (but consistently from year to year). Estate tax valuation methods apply.

Valuations of *computers, office equipment, and other tangible assets used in managing the investment activity* can be obtained from the local newspaper's classified advertisements for used equipment, or by obtaining a quotation from a used office furniture dealer.

The value of a *whole life insurance policy* is its cash surrender value.

Notes and accounts receivable are included at their net realizable value, or their face value discounted for any uncollectible portion.

Collectibles such as gold, paintings, and gems are valued under estate tax valuation rules.

15.3 AMOUNT ACTUALLY DISTRIBUTABLE

To arrive at what the Internal Revenue Code calls the "distributable amount" (DA), or the amount required to be paid out annually, the PF follows this formula:

$$A + B - C = DA$$

A = Minimum investment return (MIR) as defined in Section 15.1.

B = Any amounts previously included as qualifying distributions, but now not qualifying, such as:

- Grants repaid or returned to the PF for any reason. See IRC §4945 for grant agreements and expenditure responsibility grants.

- An asset which ceases to be an exempt function asset, whose purchase or conversion was previously included as a qualifying distribution. The sale proceeds or FMV at the time of conversion of the asset is the amount added back.

- Unused set-aside funds which are no longer earmarked for a charitable project or which are ineligible because of excessive time lapse.

C = The IRC §4940 tax imposed for the year.

Controversial addition. Until 1982, a private foundation distributed the higher of its "adjusted net income" or its MIR. Adjusted net income (defined by IRC §4942(f) and still relevant for private operating foundations, as discussed in Section 15.5) includes distributions received from an IRC §4947(a)(2) split interest trust attributable to amounts placed in trust after May 26, 1969. (The guaranteed annuity amount payable to the PF by such a trust is includible, even if the amount is not paid).[24] The regulation defining the "distributable amount" still adds the trust income to the MIR, despite the fact that IRC §4942(d) does not. The Ann Jackson Family Foundation challenged the IRS and convinced the Tax Court that the regulation was an "unwarranted extension of the statutory provision."[25]

Form 990PF (Part XI, Distributable Amount), the instructions to the form, and IRS Publication 578, *Tax Information for Private Foundations and Foundation Managers* (revised in January 1989), each provide that split interest trust distributions are to be added to the distributable amount. Despite the clarity of the statute, cautious PFs have continued to count trust distributions in calculating required distributions until the controversy is settled.

15.4 QUALIFYING DISTRIBUTIONS

Not all contributions or disbursements "qualify" or count when a PF tallies up its expenses to see if it meets the minimum distribution requirements. There are two sets of tests to meet: Of primary importance is that the expenditure must be in pursuit of a charitable purpose under IRC §170(c)(1) or (c)(2)(B). Second, the foundation must actually let go of the funds, i.e., it cannot retain control over the use of the funds nor earmark them for its own restricted purposes. The rules are designed to assure that the "distributable amount" is used to serve broad charitable purposes each year.

(a) Direct Grants

Charitable grants paid directly to publicly supported §501(c)(3) organizations, for general support or for a wide range of specific charitable purposes, comprise by far the bulk of qualifying distributions made by private foundations. Grants to any type of exempt or nonexempt organization anywhere throughout the world can qualify, if the proper procedures are followed. See Chapter 17 for a discussion of grant-making requirements.

Certain grants, however, do not qualify. A private foundation is not prevented from making such grants, but the disbursements do not count toward meeting the distribution requirement. Payments to two particular types of organization do not qualify to offset the DA:

1. Another private foundation, unless the PF is an operating foundation or the receiving PF "redistributes" the funds, as discussed below. A grant to an unrelated private operating foundation *does* count.

2. A "controlled" organization, either private or public, again, unless the funds are properly redistributed.

The recipient organization (or donee, in the language of the regulations) is controlled by the PF or by one or more of its disqualified persons if any of such

[24]Reg. §53.4942(a)-2(a)(2).
[25]*Ann Jackson Family Foundation v. Commissioner*, 97 T.C. No. 35 (1991).

persons can, by aggregating their votes or positions of authority, require the recipient organization to make an expenditure, or prevent it from making an expenditure, regardless of the method by which control is exercised or exercisable.[26]

Redistribution by the controlled organization or unrelated PF is accomplished if "not later than the close of the first taxable year after the donee organization's taxable year in which such contribution is received, such donee organization makes a distribution equal to the full amount of such contribution." Also, the donee may not count the distribution toward satisfying its own requirement, but instead must treat its regranting of the money as a payment out of corpus. The donor PF must obtain proof that the redistribution was accomplished in the form of a donee statement containing very specific information, as described in the regulation.[27]

Earmarked grants can be troublesome. It is acceptable for the PF to direct the purpose for which the funds are used by a grant recipient. The creation of a separate fund or special budgetary controls can be required. However, there must be no "material restriction" on their use. The recipient must be free to use the grant for its own exempt purposes.[28] Funds cannot be earmarked for lobbying, a specific individual grant, or any other expenditures the PF itself would not be permitted to make.

In-kind gifts not paid in cash, such as rent-free use of space, are not counted.[29] To avoid any questions about whether an amount is "paid," it is advisable for cash to change hands, even though the economic result is essentially the same. For example, instead of a no-rent lease; rent the space and make a grant to the lessor.

Pledges to make a gift in the future, likewise, do not qualify as an actual distribution. The word "paid" in IRC §4942(g)(1) means that a distribution is counted in the year in which it is actually paid, not the year in which a donation is approved or promised.[30] Thus, a PF that pledged a gift to a public charity to help build a museum could not count the gift until the funds were actually paid. Holding the funds to earn interest for the three year period before construction began so that the PF could earn interest precludes treating the funds as distributed.[31] See the "set-aside" discussion below.

Noncash Grants. A qualifying grant can be paid in either cash or property. When a building used by the PF in its own exempt activities was subsequently donated to another charity, the IRS considered the gift to be a qualifying distribution. Because the PF had previously considered the purchase of the building as a distribution, only the current FMV in excess of the cost was counted.[32]

---

[26] Reg. §53.4942(a)-3(a)(3).

[27] Reg. §53.4942(a)-3(c).

[28] Reg. §53.4942(a)-3(a)(3) refers back to §1.507-2(a)(8) to define materials restriction.

[29] Priv. Ltr. Rul. 8719004.

[30] Priv. Ltr. Rul. 8839003; see also Priv. Ltr. Rul. 8750006 concerning the proper reporting for deferred grant awards.

[31] Rev. Rul. 79-319, 1979-2 C.B. 388; but see Rev. Rul. 77-7, 1977-1 C.b. 354.

[32] Rev. Rul. 79-375, 1979-2 C.B. 389.

(b) Direct Charitable Expenditures

Any amount paid to accomplish a charitable purpose is eligible to be treated as a qualifying distribution, unless it is disqualified for some other reason.

Exempt function assets (as defined in Section 15.1(c)) purchases facilitate a PF's conduct of its projects and are treated as charitable disbursements. The full purchase price of the asset if counted even if part or all of the purchase price is borrowed. Depreciation does *not* count.[33]

Conversion of a previously nonexempt purpose asset to a new use as an exempt function asset is counted. For example, a building rented to commercial tenants might be converted to rent-free use by a public charity. The distribution amount is equal to the FMV on the date of conversion. The data on which the foundation approves the plan for conversion, rather than the date the conversion is completed, is the effective date of change.[34]

Grant administrative expenses are fully includible as qualifying distributions. For years beginning after 1984 and before 1991, a limitation was placed on the amount of administrative expense added to qualifying distributions. No more than 0.65 percent of the PF's net investment assets over a three-year period could be claimed.

Organizational administrative costs not directly related to grants, such as fund-raising expenses, preparation of Form 990-PF and annual reports, and technical assistance to grantees or governments also qualify. Furthermore, legal fees paid in a suit involving an exempt charitable trust seeking to clarify its beneficiaries were treated as a qualifying distribution.[35]

Self-sponsored charitable program expenses paid directly by the PF count. Examples are endless, and include operating a museum or library, running a summer camp for children, conducting research and publishing books, and preserving historic houses. Charitable projects can be carried out in any location. There is no constraint against a private foundation conducting activities outside the United States.

Individual grants count as qualifying distributions if they are paid under a program meeting the requirements of IRC §4945. Academic grants are considered to be fully counted when the recipients can expend a portion of the funds granted on child care, as long as such spending enables the grantees to continue research and are not made in accordance with individuals' personal or family needs.[36]

Program-related investments that meet the requirements of both IRC §4944 and §4945, including interest-free or low-interest loans to other exempt organizations or individuals, also are counted as qualifying distributions.

(c) Set-Asides

Money set-aside or saved for specific future charitable projects rather than being paid out currently, can be considered to be qualifying distributions in the

---

[33] Rev. Rul. 74-560, 1974-2 C.B. 389.
[34] Rev. Rul. 78.102, 1978-1 C.B. 379.
[35] Rev. Rul. 75-495, 1975-2 C.B. 449.
[36] Priv. Ltr. Rul. 9116032.

year saved.[37] Such funds, of course, are not counted again when they are actually paid out in a subsequent year.

The PF must have plans to use the money within 60 months after its set-aside for a specific project. In one type of set-aside, prior IRS approval is required before reserved funds can be claimed as a qualifying distribution. In a second type, a newly-created organization must satisfy a mathematical test. The two types of set-asides can be viewed as tests, as follows.

Suitability Test. The PF must convince the IRS that a project is worthy and that it can be better accomplished with several years of income (but not more than five, initially) which it plans to save rather than pay out. Approval must be sought before the end of the year of set-aside. To be approved, the project should include "situations where relatively long-term grants or expenditures must be made to assure the continuity of particular charitable projects or program-related investments, or where grants are made as part of a matching grant program."[38] Examples include:

- A plan to erect a museum building to house the PF's art collection, even though the exact location and architectural plans have not been finalized;

- Purchase of an art collection offered for sale as a unit at a price in excess of one year's income;

- A plan to fund a specific research program of such magnitude as to require an accumulation of funds before beginning the research, even though not all of the details of the program have been finalized;[39]

- The set-aside period can be extended if good reasons are submitted to the IRS.[40] An extension was granted because a local building moratorium caused a delay in acquiring the necessary property;[41] however,

- Setting aside all three years of the pledged amount of fixed-sum research grants and renewable scholarships did not qualify.[42]

To obtain approval, a PF must write to the IRS National Office in Washington. Details of the information to be submitted are outlined in IRS Publication 578, *Tax Information for Private Foundations and Foundation Managers.*

Cash Distribution Test. For a new organization, reduced distributions may be possible. Particularly for a PF planning major asset acquisitions or planning a project that will require more funds than can reasonably be allocated to the project in its first few years, this lower distribution requirement is useful. This set-aside may also allow a new PF to build up its asset base.

Essentially, DA is equal to the sum of only 20% of DA in the first year, 40% in the second, 60% in the third, 80% in the fourth *as long as the PF fully meets the*

[37] Reg. §53.4942(a)-3(b).

[38] Rev. Rul. 77-7, 1977-1 C.B. 540.

[39] Reg. §53.4942(a)-3(b)(2).

[40] Reg. §53.4942(a)-3(b)(1).

[41] Priv. Ltr. Rul. 78221141.

[42] Rev. Rul. 75-511, 1975-2 C.B. 450.

distribution requirements in year five and thereafter. Distributions in excess of the minimum amounts can also be carried forward to offset future DA. Details of how a PF plans to meet these requirements must be attached to the Form 990PF. The rules are very specific, so it is important to study the regulations and instructions to Form 990PF in detail before claiming a set-aside.[43]

15.5 PRIVATE OPERATING FOUNDATIONS

IRC §4942(j)(3) creates a special type of foundation that is essentially a cross between a private foundation and a public organization. A private operating foundation (POF) is a charity that "does its own thing," or, in the language of the statute,

> "actively conducts activities constituting the purpose or function for which it is organized and operated."

In other words, it sponsors its own charitable projects rather than making grants to other organizations. (See note at end of Section 15.5(b), grants can be made.) Typically, a POF is a privately funded entity started by a person of means who has strong ideas about charitable objectives he or she wants to accomplish through self-initiated projects.

(a) Direct Charitable Projects

The most significant attribute of a POF is sometimes the most difficult step towards qualifying as one. The private operating foundation must be "significantly involved" in its projects in a continuing and sustainable fashion. Examples include operating a museum, conducting scientific research, or publishing monographs, lectures, and exhibitions about historic properties. Optimally, a POF is identified in the public eye with and by its projects. The IRS regulations give a number of useful examples.[44]

Ghetto improvement project: An organization was created to improve conditions in an urban ghetto. Ten percent of the POF's income is spend to conduct surveys of the ghetto's problems. The remaining 90 percent is used to make grants to other nonprofit organizations doing work in the ghetto. Since only 10 percent of the EO's funds are directly expended, it cannot qualify as a POF. If, instead, it spent all of the money directly to analyze the results, develop recommendations, publish the conclusions of its studies, and hire community advisors to assist business developers and other organizations working in the area, it might qualify.

Teacher training program. An entity is formed to train teachers for institutions of higher education. Fellowships are awarded to students for graduate study leading towards advanced degrees in college teaching. Pamphlets encouraging prospective college teachers and describing the POF's activity are

---

[43]Reg. §53.4942(a)-3(b)(3) and (4).
[44]Reg. §53.4942(b)-1(d).

widely circulated. Seminars, attended by fellowship recipients, POF staff and consultants, and other interested parties, are held each summer and papers from the conference are published. Despite the fact that a majority of the organization's money is spent for fellowship payments, the program is comprehensive and suitable to qualify as an active project.

Medical research organization (MRO). An MRO is created to study heart disease. Physicians and scientists apply to conduct research at the MRO's center. Its professional staff evaluates the projects, reviews progress reports, supervises the projects, and publishes the resulting findings.

Historical reference library. A library organization is established to hold and care for manuscripts and reference material relating to the history of the region in which it is located. Additionally, it makes a limited number of annual grants to enable post-doctoral scholars and doctoral candidates to use its library. Sometimes, but not always, the POF can obtain the rights to publish the scholar's work.

Set-asides of funds for a specific future project are permitted for POFs. The requirements discussed in Section 15.4(c) must be met for the amounts set aside to be counted as qualifying distributions.

(b) Grants to Other Organizations

While one or more other charities may be involved in some manner, the POF must expend a prescribed amount of its funds directly. POFs usually maintain professional staffs to manage projects, although the staff can be volunteer and can include contributors, if their work involvement is genuine. Acquisition and maintenance of assets, and payment of administrative costs, project expenses, travel, and supplies used directly by the staff and volunteers is also appropriate. The regulations provide that qualifying distributions are not made by a foundation

> "directly for the active conduct... unless such distributions are used by the foundation itself, rather than by or through one or more grantee organizations."[45]

A grant to another organization is presumed to be indirect conduct of exempt activity, even if the activity of the grantee organization helps the POF accomplish its goals. However, there are a few situations in which a grant to another organization may qualify as direct involvement on the POF's part. The IRS allowed a charitable trust to be classified as an operating foundation even though it granted all of its adjusted net income to a conduit organization. The intervening organization was set up for liability reasons and served in a fiduciary capacity on behalf of the charitable trust. Although the corporation actually operated the cultural center, its activities were attributed to the POF.[46]

Note: Grants to other organizations can be made; they simply do not count towards satisfying the POF's distribution requirements.

[45]Reg. §53.4942(b)-1(b).
[46]Rev. Rul. 78-315, 1978-2 C.B. 271; see also Priv. Ltr. Rul. 9203004.

(c) Individual Grant Programs

Payments to individuals under a scholarship program, a student loan fund, a minority business enterprise capital support project, or similar charitable effort, can qualify as appropriate activity for a POF.[47] The facts and circumstances surrounding the project must indicate that the POF is "significantly involved." Merely selecting, screening, and investigating applicants for grant or scholarships is insufficient. When the recipients perform their work or studies alone or exclusively under the direction of some other organization, the individual grants are not considered to be direct qualifying payments. The administrative costs of such screening and investigation, as opposed to the individual grants themselves, may be treated as direct activity disbursements.

"Significant involvement" of the POF and its staff exists when the individual grants are a part of a comprehensive program. The regulations give two examples of such programs. In one, the POF's purpose is to relieve poverty and human distress, and its exempt activities are designed to ameliorate conditions among the poor, particularly during national disasters. The POF provides food and clothing to such indigents, without the assistance of an intervening organization or agency, under the direction of the POF's salaried or voluntary staff of administrators, researchers, or other personnel who supervise and direct the activity.

In the second example, a POF develops a specialized skill or expertise in scientific or medical research, social work, education, or the social sciences. A salaried staff of administrators, researchers, and other personnel supervise and conduct the work in its particular area of interest. As a part of the program, the POF awards grants, scholarships, or other payments to individuals to encourage independent study and scientific research projects, and to otherwise further their involvement in the POF's field of interest. The POF sponsors seminars, conducts classes, and provides direction and supervision for the grant recipients. Based upon these facts, the individual grants are treated as active and thus qualify under the POF distribution test.

(d) Tests to Qualify as a Private Operating Foundation

To qualify as a private operating foundation, the private foundation must meet two IRC §4942(j) tests:

(1) An income test,[48] and

(2) An asset, endowment, or support test.[49]

Income Test. The first test measures the annual expenditures on the POF's active projects under the rules discussed in Section 15.4. It must spend substantially all (85 percent) of the lesser of its adjusted net income or its minimum investment return.

---

[47] Reg. §53.4942(b)-(1)(b)(2).
[48] Reg. §53.4942(b)-1(a)(1).
[49] Reg. §53.4942(b)-2.

Asset Test. At least 65 percent of assets must be devoted to the active conduct of the POF's charitable activities, a functionally related business, or stock of a controlled corporation, substantially all of the assets of which are so devoted. The concepts of exempt function and dual-use assets discussed in Section 15.1(c) are followed to identify assets qualifying for this test.

Endowment Test. The POF's annual distributions must equal at least two-thirds of its minimum investment return (MIR). This test is designed to prevent a private foundation from seeking POF status to take advantage of the income test that requires distribution of income or MIR, which is lower. For example, a PF holds marketable securities that pay no dividends. The income test, taken alone, would require no current charitable spending. The POF's portfolio can remain in noncurrent income producing property, but part of the organization's principal or contributions received would be distributable to meet this test.[50]

Support Test. Support (not including investment income) must be received from the general public and from five or more noncontrolled §501(c)(3) organizations, with none giving more than 25 percent of the POF's support. An organization wishing to meet this test must carefully study the regulations.[51]

(e) Adjusted Net Income

Before 1982, all private foundations were required to distribute their adjusted net income or their minimum investment return (MIR), whichever was higher. Effective for years beginning in 1982, only MIR need be paid out, and adjusted net income is not relevant. POFs, however, distribute their MIR or the adjusted net income whichever is *lower*.

Adjusted gross income is calculated using the following formula:[52]

$$A - B - C - D = \text{Adjusted Net Income}$$

A = Gross income for the year, including unrelated income and tax exempt interest.

B = Long term capital gains.

C = Contributions received.

D = Ordinary and necessary expenses paid or incurred for the production or collection of gross income or for the management, conservation, or maintenance of property held for the production of such income.[53]

---

[50] Reg. §53.4942(b)-2(b)(1).
[51] Reg. §53.4942(b)-2(c).
[52] Reg. §53.4942(a)-2(d)(1); IRS Form 990PF Instructions, p. 8.
[53] Reg. §53.4942(a)-2(d)(4).

Over the years, a few rulings have been published to clarify the amounts includible in adjusted net income. A brief summary follows:

- Bond premium amortization is permitted, following the rules of IRC §171.[54]

- Annuity, IRA, and other employee benefit plan payments are includible to the extent that the amount exceeds the value of the right to receive the payment on the decedent's date of death.[55]

- Capital gain dividends paid or credited for reinvestment by a mutual fund are *not* included, because they are considered as long term by IRC §852(b)(3)(B).[56]

(f) Compliance Period

The income test and the asset, endowment, or support tests are applied each year for a four year period that includes the current and past three years. The POF has a choice of methods to calculate its compliance with the tests:

(1) All four years can be aggregated, i.e., the distributions for four years are added together. The POF must use only one of the asset, endowment, or support tests for all four years.

(2) For three of the four years, the POF meets the income test *and* any one of the asset, endowment, or support tests.

If the POF fails to qualify for a particular year, it is treated as an ordinary private foundation for that year. It can return to POF classification as soon as it again qualifies under both the income test and the assets, endowment, or support test.

New organizations generally must meet the test in their first year. If application for exemption is made prior to the completion of the proposed POF's first fiscal year, the IRS will accept the organization's assertion, based upon a good faith determination, that it plans to qualify.[57] Form 1023 and its instructions contain a workpaper for submitting the appropriate information. Failure in the first year can be remedied if the POF does in fact qualify in its second, third, and fourth years.

An IRS advance ruling is not technically required for a PF to convert to operation as a POF. The foundation is qualified if it meets the tests by changing its method of operation or mix of assets. However, most trustees seek the comfort of an IRS determination to sanction the conversion. The question arises because the transition takes four years and the one-year time lag for making charitable distributions is lost.

---

[54] Rev. Rul. 76-248, 1976-1 C.B. 353.
[55] Rev. Rul. 75-442, 1975-2 C.B. 448.
[56] Rev. Rul. 73-320, 1973-2 C.B. 385.
[57] Reg. §53.4942(b)-3.

(g) Advantages and Disadvantages of Private Operating Foundations

Private operating foundations have several special advantages.

Contribution deduction limits are better. The percentage limits for charitable deductions are higher for POFs than for private foundations. They are the same as the deductions permitted for public charities. A full 50 percent of an individual's income can be sheltered by contributions to a POF, but only 30 percent of one's income can be deducted for gifts to a normal PF. The reduction for gain on appreciated property donations is not required, and appreciated gifts need not be redistributed.

Distributable amount may be lower. The minimum distribution requirement for a POF may be lower than for normal private foundations. In some cases, given a sufficient return on investment, a POF can better build an endowment over the years. It must only distribute its actual net income when it is lower than MIR, and only need to pay out two thirds of its MIR.

The primary *disadvantage* is that the one-year delay afforded to PFs to meet the minimum distribution requirement is lost. The POF must distribute either its adjusted net income for the year in question or its MIR.

15.6 EXCISE TAX FOR FAILURE TO DISTRIBUTE

If a private foundation fails to pay out its DA and has "undistributed income," the deficiency must be made up and a tax is likely to apply. Failure to correct a deficiency and repeated deficiencies can result in loss of exemption. The deficiency equals:

Current year DA (defined in Section 15.3)

less

Qualifying distributions (defined in Section 15.4) that are not applied either to offset prior deficits or to corpus.

An initial tax of 15 percent is imposed for each year that the deficit goes uncorrected.[58] Correcting the deficiency is accomplished by making grants that are "qualifying distributions."

(a) Timing of Distributions

To identify a deficiency in the DA and to correct it, one must understand how payments are applied. The PF's charitable expenditures that are considered "qualifying distributions" are totalled for each year in which they are paid, but they are not necessarily applied in that year. The terminology is confusing here because the current year DA is based upon the prior year's MIR. Nevertheless,

---

[58] IRC §4942(a)(1).

Exhibit 15-1
DISTRIBUTION APPLICATION AND CARRYOVERS

Corpus		1990	1991	1992	1993	1994	1995
Distributable Amount		100	100	100	100	100	100
Qualifying Distributions			250	70	140	80	130
Apply annual amount			−100	−70	−100	−80	−100
Apply '91 excess +50		+100	−150				
Cover '92 deficit −30				−30			
Apply '93 excess +40					−40		
Cover '94 Deficit −20						−20	
Apply '95 excess +30							−30
Balance	+70	0	0	0	0	0	0

qualifying distributions are applied as follows:

- First, to make up any prior year's deficiency of DA (for a year in which the PF has undistributed income subject to the excise tax).

- Next, the remaining qualifying distributions are applied to the current year's DA (essentially, the prior year's adjusted MIR).

- Finally, any remaining distributions are taken out of corpus.[59] Remember, the redistribution of a grant received by one PF from another PF must be charged against corpus and cannot reduce the donee PF's own DA. See Section 15.4(a). Also, a gift from a contributor who wishes to receive a higher percentage contribution deduction limitation must be paid from corpus.[60]

Distributions in excess of the DA applied to corpus are carried forward for five years and can offset the future DA. See Exhibit 15–1 for an example. IRS Chief Counsel has issued a memorandum entitled *Adjustments of Excess Distribution Carryovers From Closed Years*, taking the position that adjustments to years closed by the statute of limitations is permissible.[61] The memorandum recognizes the fact that in any one year, a nonoperating PF has excessive or deficient distributions and, therefore, a carryover of excess distributions is an accumulation of all post-1969 years. It is an unusual foundation that pays out the exact minimum distribution amount.

A single error in calculating the qualifying distributions or the amount required to be distributed in any one year causes all years to be wrong. Thus,

[59] Reg. §53.4942(a)-3(d).
[60] IRC §170(b)(1)(E).
[61] Gen. Coun. Memo. 39808.

the IRS takes the position, as yet unchallenged in court, that the years from 1970 forward are open years for purposes of distribution carryovers.[62]

Note that the excess applied to corpus is available to be carried forward for five years. The excesses are applied in the order in which they occur so that by 1994, no 1991 excess remains because it offset the 1990 and 1993 deficits. (Note also that a penalty tax would have been due on 1990.) The 1993 excess of $40 can be carried to 1998 and the 1995 excess of $30 can be carried to 2000.

(b) Calculating the Tax

A foundation that fails to make the required charitable expenditures in a timely manner is subject to an excise tax of 15 percent on the undistributed amount. The tax is charged for each year or partial year that the deficiency remains "uncorrected." Essentially, the tax calculation starts on the first late day and continues until a notice of the deficiency is issued by the IRS (but in whole year increments). This so-called "taxable period" also closes on the date of voluntary payment of the tax.[63]

Assume that a calendar year PF fails to distribute $50,000 of its 1991 DA by December 31, 1991. If the amount is distributed within the first year after the deadline (by December 31, 1992), a 15 percent tax is due. If the correction takes two years, or is not fixed until the second year after it was due (on or before January 1, 1994), another 15 percent is due, or a total of 30 percent. The additional 15 percent would be due even if the payment was made on January 2, 1993.

An additional 100 percent tax is triggered if the PF fails to make up the deficient distributions within 90 days of receiving IRS notification of the problem. The "allowable correction period" is 90 days after the date of mailing of the deficiency notice.[64]

(c) When Notices are Mailed

The notice date is critical to calculating the tax. If the deficiency is self-admitted on the face of Form 990PF, Part XIII or XI, an accompanying Form 4720 is due to be filed to calculate the tax due. If the deficiency is not self-admitted, the IRS computers should recognize the problem and generate a notice within a few months beyond the return filing date.

In the more common situation, the underdistribution is found by the IRS upon examination, and the notice is mailed when the examination is completed. The PF has 90 days from the date of the notice to correct the problem by making grants. If it does not, the 100 percent additional penalty tax is imposed.

(d) Valuation Errors

If the failure to distribute is due solely to an incorrect valuation of assets, the tax may be excused.[65] In the interest of being fair, the Code provides that the tax

---

[62] Priv. Ltr. Rul. 9116032.
[63] Reg. §53.4942(a)-1(c)(1)(ii).
[64] IRC §4942(j)(2).
[65] IRC §4942(a)(2).

does not apply if:

- The failure to value the assets properly was not willful and was due to reasonable cause;

- Such amount is in fact distributed within the "allowable distribution period;"

- The foundation notifies the IRS of such distribution; and

- The qualifying distributions for the year involved are recalculated to treat the amount as being distributed in that year.

(e) Abatement of the Tax

IRC §4962 gives the IRS discretion to abate the first-tier tax, or 15 percent penalty, in certain cases, but not including self-dealing offenses. This exception applies if:

(1) The taxable event was due to reasonable cause and not to willful neglect; and

(2) The event was corrected within the correction period for such event.

The second-tier taxes may also be abated under circumstances described in IRC §4961.

CHAPTER SIXTEEN

Excess Business Holdings and Jeopardizing Investments: IRCs §4943 and 4944

16.1 EXCESS BUSINESS HOLDINGS

A private foundation's level of ownership in an operating business, which is not conducted as a charitable activity, is limited by IRC §4943, entitled "Excess Business Holdings." Specific time periods are prescribed for disposition of such holdings received by the PF through donation or inheritance. The basic rule is that the combined ownership of the private foundation and its insiders in a business enterprise of any legal form—a corporation, partnership, joint venture, or other unincorporated company—must not exceed 20 percent.

(a) Definition of Business Enterprise

The regulations define "business enterprise" broadly:

"A business enterprise includes the active conduct of a trade or business, including any activity which is regularly carried on for the production of income from the sale of goods or the performance of services and which constitutes an unrelated trade or business under IRC §513."[1]

The ownership limits apply whether or not the business produces a profit. A bond or other form of indebtedness is treated as a business holding if it is essentially a disguised equity holding. A leasehold interest in real estate, the rent from which is based upon profits, is customarily not considered to be a business interest.

IRC §4943(d)(b) only provides a negative definition by saying what a "business enterprise" is not. The two enterprises that can be owned without limitation include a functionally related business and a business 95 percent of whose income is from passive sources.

Functionally related business. A business conducted to accomplish program-related purposes is not treated as a business enterprise.[2] Such businesses include those that are excused from the unrelated business income tax as being basically unbusinesslike (as described in Chapter 21), and include:

- A business the conduct of which is substantially related (aside from the mere provision of funds for the exempt purpose) to the exercise or performance by the private foundation of its charitable, educational, or other purpose or function constituting the basis for its exemption. A music publishing company that concentrates on classical or serious music was considered related to the purposes of a PF promoting music education and the choice of music as a career;[3]

- A business in which substantially all of the work is performed for the foundation without compensation;

- A business carried on by the foundation primarily for the convenience of its members, students, patients, officers, visitors, or employees, such as a cafeteria operated by a hospital or museum;

- A business that consists of selling merchandise, substantially all of which has been received by the foundation as gifts or contributions; and

- An activity carried on within a larger combination of similar activities that are related to the exempt purposes of the foundation.

Passive holding company. A company that obtains at least 95 percent of its gross income from the passive sources listed in IRC §512(b)(1), (2), (3), and (5) is not considered a business. The word "passive" was provided in this Code section in 1969, well before the Tax Reform Act of 1986 gave it a different meaning. For purposes of excess holdings, passive income is classified as

---

[1] Reg. §53.4943-10(a).
[2] IRS Publication 578, *Tax Information for Private Foundations and Foundation Managers*, Chapter X, p. 32.
[3] Priv. Ltr. Rul. 8927031.

investment income, and includes the following:[4]

- Dividends, interest, and annuities;

- Royalties, including overriding royalties, whether measured by production or by gross or taxable income from the property. Working interests in mineral properties are active businesses;[5]

- Rental income from real property and from personal property leased alongside real property, if the rent is incidental (less than 50 percent of the total rent);

- Gains or losses from sales, exchanges, or other dispositions of property other than stock in trade held for regular sale to customers; and

- Income from the sale of goods if the seller does not manufacture, produce, physically receive or deliver, negotiate sales of, or keep inventories in the goods.

(b) Corporate Holdings

Permitted holdings of business enterprises by a PF vary according to the form of ownership, type of entity, and other variables. A private foundation may hold 20 percent of the voting stock in an incorporated business enterprise, reduced by the percentage of voting stock owned by all disqualified persons.[6] In other words, the PF and its contributors and managers and their families cannot together control more than 20 percent of a corporation.

Nonvoting stock. If all of the DPs together own no more than 20 percent of the corporation's voting stock, the foundation can own any amount of nonvoting stock.[7] Stock carrying contingent voting rights is treated as nonvoting until the event triggering the right to vote occurs. An example is preferred stock that can be voted only if dividends are not paid; such shares are considered nonvoting until the voting power is exercisable. This exception only applies to an incorporated entity, not to a partnership or other form.[8]

Thirty-five percent. Up to 35 percent ownership in a business can be held aggregately by the PF and its DPs, when the foundation establishes to the satisfaction of the IRS that the enterprise is controlled by a "third person" (i.e., an unrelated person). Control for this purpose means possession, directly or indirectly, of the power to direct or cause the direction of the management and policies of the enterprise, whether through ownership of voting stock, the use of voting trusts, contractual arrangements, or otherwise. It is the reality of control which is decisive, not its form or the means by which it is exercisable.[9] The IRS requires actual proof of outside party control.[10]

---

[4]Reg. §53.4942-10(c)(2).
[5]Priv. Ltr. Rul. 8407095.
[6]IRC §4943(c)(2); Reg. §53.4943-3(b)(1).
[7]IRC §4943(c)(2).
[8]Reg. §53.4943-3(c)(4)(i).
[9]Reg. §53.4943-3(b)(3).
[10]Rev. Rul. 81-811, 1981-1 C.B. 509.

Two percent. The PF can own up to two percent of voting stock and up to two percent in value of all outstanding shares of all classes of stock, called a de minimus amount, regardless of DP holdings.[11] Any commonly-controlled PFs' holdings are combined with the PF's for this purpose.

(c) Partnerships, Trusts, and Proprietorships

The permitted holdings in partnerships and other forms of ownership are essentially the same in concept as those allowed in corporations. Only the terms identifying the ownership change. In a general or limited partnership or a joint venture, "profit interest" and "capital interest" are substituted for "voting stock" and "nonvoting stock" in the IRC §4943(c)(2) rule for corporations.[12]

The interest of a PF and its DPs in a partnership is determined using the distributive share concepts of IRC §704(b). Absent a formal partnership agreement, the PF's ownership is measured by the portion of assets which the PF is entitled to receive upon withdrawal or dissolution, whichever is greater.

For trusts, the term "beneficial interest" is used to measure ownership, and the permitted holdings are limited to 20 percent.

No interest in a proprietorship is allowed.[13] However, the gift or bequest (but not the purchase) of a proprietorship is permitted, and the PF has five years to dispose of such a business.

(d) Constructive Ownership

The stock or other interest owned, directly or indirectly, by or for a corporation, partnership, estate, or trust is considered as being owned proportionately by or for its shareholders, partners, or beneficiaries.[14] Corporations engaged in active business are exempt from this attribution rule.[15]

Powers of appointment. Any interest in a business enterprise over which the PF or a disqualified person has a power of appointment exercisable in favor of the PF or the DP is also treated as owned by the PF or person holding the power of appointment.

Material restrictions. If the PF disposes of any interest in a business with any material restrictions or conditions that prevent free use of or prevent disposition of the transferred shares, then the PF is treated as owning the interest until the restrictions or conditions are eliminated.

(e) Disposition Periods

Five-year period. A private foundation is given five years to dispose of excess business holdings acquired by gift or bequest. During the disposition

---

[11] IRC §4943(c)(2)(C); Reg. §53.4943-3(b)(4).
[12] Reg. §53.4943-3(c)(2).
[13] IRC §4943(c)(3)(B); Reg. §53.4943-3(c)(3).
[14] Reg. §53.4943-8.
[15] Reg. §53.4943-8(c).

period, the PF is not treated as owning the shares. The statute says:

> "If there is a change in the holdings in a business enterprise (other than by purchase by the private foundation or by a disqualified person) which causes the PF to have excess holdings, the interest of the PF shall be treated as held by a disqualified person during the 5-year period beginning on the date of such change in holdings."[16]

For shares received under a will or from a trust, the 5-year period begins at the time of actual distribution from the fiduciary.[17] If the foundation already holds excess shares of the business at the time it is given additional shares, special rules apply.[18]

Extension of time. A foundation that is attempting to sell its excess business holdings within the permissible time period (ending on or after November 1, 1983) but is unable to do so can request an additional five-year extension of the time under IRC §4943(c)(7). To obtain permission, the foundation must demonstrate that:

- The gift is an unusually large gift or bequest of diverse business holdings or holdings with complex corporate structures;

- It has made diligent efforts to dispose of the holdings within the initial five-year period;

- Disposition of the holdings was not possible during the first five years because of the size and complexity or diversity of the holdings, except at a price substantially below fair market value. Congressional hearing testimony considered five percent below FMV to be substantial; and

- Before the close of the first five years, the foundation submits a disposition plan to the IRS and seeks approval of its state attorney general (or similar responsible authority).

Private letter rulings show a favorable pattern of granting extensions for PFs which have "made diligent effort."[19] A plan developed by an independent financial consultant to assist the foundation to sell its holdings, in conjunction with the substantial contributor's family members who also owned the same holdings, was approved by the IRS.[20]

Ninety-day period. When a purchase by a disqualified person creates excess business holdings, the PF has 90 days from the date it knows, or has reason to

---

[16] IRC 4943(c)(5).
[17] Reg. §53.4943-6(b)(1).
[18] Reg. §53.4943-6(a)(i)(*iii*).
[19] Priv. Ltr. Rul. 8514098, 8508114, 8737085, and 9029067. In the 1990 ruling, the IRS found that the PF had not been diligent and denied an extension.
[20] Priv. Ltr. Rul. 9115061.

know, of the event which caused it to have such excess holdings.[21] The excise tax is not applied if the holdings are properly reduced within the 90 day period. The period can be extended to include any period during which a foundation is prevented by federal or state securities law from disposing of the excess holdings.

No period. An interest purchased by the PF itself that causes the combined ownership to exceed the limits must be disposed immediately, and the foundation is subject to tax. If the foundation had no knowledge, nor any reason to know, that its holdings had become excessive, the 90 day period is applied and the tax is excused.

Twenty, fifteen, and ten years. Interests held on May 26, 1969 (when these rules were added to the Code) are called "present interests." Any excess ownership held at that time was disposable over 10, 15, or 20 years, depending on the amount of combined ownership. An interest received from a trust irrevocable on May 26, 1969, or from a will in effect and never revised since that date, is still subject to these longer time periods.[22] The selling off of excess business holdings by many PFs during the 1970s and 1980s was a major undertaking. The regulations contain 30 pages of instructions, exceptions, downward ratchet rules, and complicated procedures that must be carefully studied by any PF in order to avail itself of the long disposition periods.

(f) Business Readjustments

Any increases in a PF's holdings due to a "readjustment" are treated as if they were not acquired by purchase. This means that the PF either has 90 days or five years to dispose of them, as a general rule.[23] A "readjustment" may be a merger or consolidation, a recapitalization, an acquisition of stock or assets, a transfer of assets, a change in identity, form or place of organization, a redemption, or a liquidating distribution.[24]

If the readjustment results in the PF owning a larger percentage than owned prior to the change, a taxable event may occur, and the rules need to be carefully studied.

(g) Tax on Excess Holdings

If the excess holdings are not disposed of within the time periods described above, an initial tax is due. The tax is imposed on the private foundation and is equal to five percent of the highest value of the excessive amount of the shares during each year. The tax is payable for each tax year during what is called the "taxable period." Form 4720 is filed to calculate and report the tax due. The valuation is determined under the estate tax rules.[25]

---

[21] Reg. §53.4943-2(a)(1)(ii).
[22] IRC §4943(c)(4); Reg. §53.4943-4 and 5.
[23] Reg. §53.4943-6(d).
[24] Reg. §53.4943-7(d)(1).
[25] IRC §4943(a); Reg. §53.4943-2(a).

Taxable period. The taxable period begins with the first day that excess business holdings exist, and ends on the earlier of the following dates:

- The date on which the IRS mails a deficiency notice under §6212;

- The date on which the excess is eliminated; or

- The date on which the tax is assessed.
  If the deficiency is self-admitted by filing Form 4720, the period ends when the return is filed. An underdistribution found by the IRS upon examination results in the IRS issuing the assessment.

Additional Tax. If excess holdings exists at the end of the taxable period, an additional 200 percent tax is imposed on the value of the excess still held.[26]

Tax Abatement. The IRC §4962 tax abatement rules discussed in Chapter 15 may also apply, if the excess holdings were due to reasonable causes.

16.2 JEOPARDIZING INVESTMENTS

A private foundation has a fiduciary responsibility as a nonprofit and charitable organization under most state laws to safeguard the assets on behalf of the organization's charitable constituency. In a similar spirit, Congress has provided that PFs may not

> "invest any amount in such a manner as to jeopardize the carrying out of any of its exempt purposes."[27]

(a) Managers' Responsibility

The Internal Revenue Code requires PF managers to use a high degree of fiduciary responsibility in investing foundation funds. The purpose is to shield private foundation assets from risk, so as to maximize both capital and income available for charity. A manager fails to exercise the appropriate level of responsibility if he or she fail to exercise

> "[o]rdinary business care and prudence, under the facts and circumstances prevailing at the time the investment is made, in providing for the long and short term needs of the PF to carry out its exempt purposes."[28]

[26] IRC §4943(b); Reg. §53.4943-2.
[27] IRC §4944(a)(1).
[28] Reg. §53.4944-1(a)(2).

Factors which PF managers consider in exercising the requisite standard of care and prudence include:

- Expected return, including both income and appreciation of capital;

- Risk of rising and falling price levels; and

- Need for diversification in the portfolio with respect to type of security, type of industry, maturity of company, degree of risk, and potential for return.

(b) Tax on Managers

The jeopardy tax is charged both to the foundation and to certain of its managers for any investment that jeopardizes carrying out the private foundation's charitable purposes. PF managers who participate in making a decision, knowing that it is a jeopardizing one, pay a tax, unless their participation is not willful and is due to reasonable cause.[29] A manager is treated as "knowing" only if three factors are present:

- She or he has actual knowledge of sufficient facts so that, based solely upon such facts, such investment would be a jeopardizing one;

- She or he is aware that such an investment under such circumstances may violate IRC §4944; and

- She or he negligently fails to make reasonable attempts to ascertain whether the investment is a jeopardizing investment, or she or he is in fact aware that it is such an investment.

Knowledge. "Knowing" does *not* mean "having reason to know." The question is whether the manager actually did know. The actual facts and circumstances are examined to find out why the manager did not know. To be excused, the manager has to be essentially ignorant of the facts. Assume that a foundation's board has ten members, with a three member finance committee. The written investment policy of the PF provides that the board approves investment actions proposed by the finance committee, based upon the advice of independent counselors. Non-finance committee board members should not be expected to be aware of details discussed in finance committee meetings.

Willfulness. A manager's participation must be willful to subject him or her to tax. Voluntary, conscious, and intentional ignorance of the facts pointing to jeopardy is willful participation.

Reasonableness. The manager must have a good reason for not knowing. To show reasonable cause for not knowing, the manager must prove that good business judgment was exercised with ordinary business care and prudence.

Participation. Any manifestation of approval of the investment in question is considered to be participation in the decision to make the investment. Clearly, a vote as a board member to approve a purchase is participation. Board members who do not attend meetings but sanction investment decisions may

---

[29] Reg. §53.4944-1(b)(2).

be derelict in their fiduciary responsibility, but their inability to participate in the decision and resulting lack of knowledge may shield them from the tax. If they receive a board information packet revealing the questionable investment, they have knowledge, but the tax only applies if they participate in the approval.

Advice of Counsel. A manager who relies upon outside advisors will not be treated as "knowingly" and "willfully" participating in a jeopardizing investment, and may be excused from the tax. The factual situation must be fully disclosed to the outside advisor. The types of reliance permitted may be different for different types of investments:

- For *program-related investments*, a manager may rely upon a reasoned written legal opinion that a particular investment would not jeopardize the carrying out of any of the foundation's exempt purposes. The opinion must state that, as a matter of law, the investment is a program-related one not classified as a jeopardizing investment under the Internal Revenue Code.

- For *financial investments* from which the PF derives its operating income, qualified investment counselors are appropriate to rely upon. Again, all facts must be disclosed to the advisor. Advisors must render advice "in a manner consistent with generally accepted practices" of persons in their business. The written advice must recommend investments that provide for the PF's long- and short-term financial needs.

The fact that a manager failed to seek advice is one of the factors pointing to willful participation.[30] It is very important to note that managers found to be guilty are jointly and severally liable for the tax.[31] On a positive note, the maximum tax in the case of the first tier of five percent is $10,000, and in the second tier of 25 percent, the maximum is $10,000.

(c) Identifying Jeopardy

The existence of jeopardy is made on an investment-by-investment basis, in each case taking into account the foundation's portfolio as a whole. The identification of jeopardy is to be made as of the time that the foundation makes the investment, not subsequently on the basis of hindsight. Once it is ascertained that an investment is prudent and not jeopardizing, the investment, according to the regulations, can never be considered to be a jeopardizing one, even though the PF loses money as a result. On the other hand, a change in the form of terms of an investment will be considered to be a new investment as of the date of the change, and a new determination is to be made at that time.[32]

Certain types of investments are typically risky and will be closely scrutinized. After granting that no category of investment will be treated as per se

---

[30] Reg. §53.4944-1(b)(2)(v).
[31] IRC §4944(d).
[32] Reg. §53.4944-1(a)(2)(iii).

jeopardizing, the IRS identifies the following types of investment as risky:

- Trading in securities purchased on margin;

- Trading in commodity futures;

- Working interests in oil and gas;

- Puts, calls, and straddles;

- Purchases of warrants; and

- Selling short.

More latitude is permissible in the sophisticated financial markets of the 1990s, which were not anticipated when the regulations were written in 1970. In 1992, the American Law Institute revised its *Restatement of the Law, Trusts—Prudent Investor Rule*,[33] containing the basic rules governing the invest-ment of trust assets. This update is a useful guide that reflects modern invest-ment concepts and practices. The "prudent investor rule" recognizes that return on investment is related to risk, that risk includes the risk of deteriora-tion of real return owing to inflation, and that the risk/return relationship must be taken into account in managing trust assets.

Under the prudent investor rule, a PF which maintained all of its funds in certificates of deposit during 1991 and 1992, when rates of return fell from eight to three percent, could be accused of making jeopardizing investments. There are precious few rulings on this subject. The only published ruling as of October, 1992 concerns a whole life insurance policy. The PF received a gift of a indebted policy covering an insured with a ten year life expectancy. Based upon the expected death benefit, the PF could expect to pay more in premiums and loan interest than it would receive. Each payment on the policy was found to be a jeopardizing investment.[34]

The purchase of gold stocks to protect a portfolio as a hedge against inflation was not treated as jeopardizing, despite a net loss of $7,000 on a $14,500 investment. The PF bought the shares over three years, and made money on one block and lost on two others. The ruling noted that the PF had realized $31,000 in gains and $23,000 in dividends during the same period on its whole portfolio. The portfolio performance as a whole was found to enable the PF to carry out its purposes, and the investments were found not to be jeopardizing.[35] Note that selling options against the foundation's portfolio in a "covered option trading" program is considered to be a prudent way to enhance yield without risk. Conceivably, failure to conduct such a program could be considered to create jeopardy.

A "managed commodity trading program" was found to give diversity to a PF's marketable security portfolio and not to be a jeopardizing investment. Since commodity futures have little or no correlation to the stock market, the

[33]American Law Institute Publishers, St. Paul, Minnesota.
[34]Rev. Rul. 80-133, 1980-1 C.B. 258.
[35]Priv. Ltr. Rul. 8718006.

added diversity may provide less risk for the PF's overall investment. The foundation proposed to invested 10% of its portfolio.[36]

(d) Safe Assets

The following investments are not considered to be jeopardizing:

- Program-related investments, e.g., investments the primary purpose of which is to accomplish one or more charitable purposes. Production of income or appreciation is not a significant motivation for making the investment.

- Property received as gifts or by gratuitous transfers are not jeopardizing, unless the PF pays some consideration in connection with the gift, such as a bargain sale.

- Stock received in a corporate reorganization within the meaning of IRC §368 is not jeopardizing.

Program related investments are best described by the criteria used by the IRS to define them:

1. The primary purpose of the investment is to accomplish an exempt charitable purpose.

2. No significant purpose of the investment is the production of income or the appreciation of property.

The following IRS examples illustrate the concept:[37]

- A small business enterprise, X, is located in a deteriorated urban area and is owned by members of an economically-disadvantaged minority group. Conventional sources of funds are unwilling or unable to provide funds to the enterprise. A PF makes a below-market interest rate loan to encourage economic development.

- The PF described above allows an extension of X's loan in order to permit X to achieve greater financial stability before it is required to repay the loan. Since the change is not motivated by attempts to enhance yield, but by an effort to encourage success of an exempt project, the altered loan is also considered to be program-related.

- Assume instead that a commercial bank will loan X money if it increases the amount of its equity capital. PF's purchase of X's common stock, to accomplish the same purposes as the loan described above, is a program-related investment.

- Assume instead that substantial citizens own X, but continued operation of X is important for the economic well-being of the low-income

---

[36] Priv. Ltr. Rul. 9237035.
[37] Reg. §53.4944-1(b).

■   227   ■

persons in the area. To save X, PF loans X money at below-market rates to pay for specific projects benefiting the community. The loan is program-related.

- PF wants to encourage the building of a plant to provide jobs in a low-income neighborhood. PF loans the building funds at below-market rates to SS, a successful commercial company that is unwilling to build the plant without such inducement. Again, the loan is program-related.

- A loan program established to make low interest rate loans to blind persons unable to obtain funds through commercial sources constitutes a program-related investment.[38]

- Land purchased for land conservation, wildlife preservation, and the protection of open and scenic spaces is program-related.[39]

(e) Double Jeopardy

The PF excise taxes are not applied exclusively, so an investment could conceivably cause three taxes to occur simultaneously.[40] If the PF bought a disqualified person's 40 percent share of an indebted computer software development company, self-dealing occurs (because the purchase takes place between the PF and a DP), there is an excess business holding (because the combined ownership exceeds 20 percent), and a jeopardizing investment has been made (assuming the PF is not focused on scientific or scholarly development of software and the company is not a functionally related business). The unrelated business income tax might also apply to the income from such a business investment.

(f) Additional tax

When an investment is found to jeopardize the PF's financial status, the initial tax of five percent of the value of the investment is imposed. If the jeopardy is not removed within the so-called "taxable period," an additional 25 percent tax is due. See Section 16.1(g) for an explanation of the correction period. Removal of jeopardy occurs when the asset is sold, the terms of repayments are altered, or other steps are taken to improve the financial position of the PF. Correction may be difficult or impossible if the asset is not marketable. An effort to maximize available funds from the investment may help to avoid the additional tax.

[38]Rev. Rul. 78-90, 1978-1 C.B. 380.
[39]Priv. Ltr. Rul. 8832074.
[40]Reg. §53.4944-1(a)(2)(iv).

Taxable Expenditures: IRC §4945

In response to abuses uncovered by the Filer Commission and by Congressional committee hearings, a sanction was added to the Internal Revenue Code to limit the manner in which a private foundation (PF) can spend its money to accomplish its exempt purpose. While other types of exempt organizations can engage in some amount of nonexempt activity without losing their exempt status, PFs have no such leeway and pay a tax on any violations.

The PF must first meet the organizational and operational tests of IRC §501(c)(3) as described in Chapter 2, which require that it operate "exclusively" for exempt purposes, but "exclusively" does not mean 100 percent. IRC §4945, however, adds the absolute. A PF must operate under a higher standard within the constraints outlined in this chapter and can conduct absolutely no nonexempt activity such as lobbying. Potential PF creators and managers need not be discouraged by this fact, however. The rules are actually broader than many realize. Once the rules are understood and procedures are in place to review compliance, a PF has a fairly high degree of latitude in developing its grant and activity programs. Efforts directed at improving matters of broad social and economic impact, such as health care or the environment, have needlessly been foregone by some PFs. As discussed in Section 17.1, educational and scientific efforts involving such subjects are not necessarily legislative efforts, even if the problems are of a type that government would be ultimately expected to deal with.[1]

Essentially, IRC §4945 prohibits transactions called "taxable expenditures." The private foundation and its disqualified persons will incur an excise tax, and possibly lose the PF's exemption, if any amount is paid or incurred for the following purposes:[2]

1. To carry on propaganda or otherwise to attempt to influence legislation (see Chapter 23).

2. To influence the outcome of any specific election, or to carry on any voter registration drive (except efforts of at least five states in scope, as described below).

3. As a grant to an individual for travel, study, or other similar purpose, unless it meets the conditions listed below.

4. As a grant to an organization unless:

   - it is a publicly supported §501(c)(3) organization as defined in IRC §509(a)(1), (2), or (3); or

   - it is an exempt operating foundation,[3] a special type of PF controlled by a public board (see Section 13.7); or

   - the PF making the grant exercises "expenditure responsibility."

5. For any purpose not specified in IRC §170(c)(2)(B), i.e., religious, charitable, scientific, literary, educational, to foster national or international amateur sports competition, or to prevent cruelty to children or animals.

17.1 LOBBYING

A private foundation is strictly prohibited from carrying out propaganda or otherwise attempting to influence legislation—defined as "any attempt to influence any legislation" through:

- An attempt to affect the opinion of the general public or any segment thereof (called "grassroots lobbying"); or

- An attempt to influence legislation through communication with any member or employee of a legislative body, or with any other govern-

---

[1] Reg. §53.4945-2(d)(4).
[2] IRC §4945(d).
[3] IRC §4940(d)(2).

ment official or employee who may participate in the formulation of the legislation (except technical advice or assistance provided to a governmental body or to a committee or other subdivision thereof in response to a written request by such body or subdivision, as the case may be), other than through making available the results of nonpartisan analysis, study, or research.[4]

The definition of lobbying for PF purposes is now fortunately cross-referenced to the regulations applicable to those public charities that elect to lobby.[5] While there was some uncertainty before the regulations were finalized, PFs can now enjoy an expanded range of activity involving public issues that may be the subject of legislation. See Chapter 23 for more information.

(a) Germane Lobbying

A PF can spend its money to make an appearance before, or communicate to, any legislative body with respect to a possible decision of such body which might affect the existence of the PF, its powers and duties, its tax-exempt status, or the deduction of contributions to it.

The existence of the organization is not affected, in the IRS's view, by a possible loss of economic support.[6] Lobbying in favor of an appropriations bill funding a program from which the PF has received grants in the past is not self-defense. Thus, a PF that provides care for the elderly is lobbying when its executive director appears before the state legislature to oppose a bill authorizing the state to provide nursing care for the aged. Likewise, a PF conducting contract research for the government is lobbying when it testifies about the advisability of continuing the program. It is the economic condition and the resulting scope of the PF's operation, not its underlying existence, that is at issue in these examples.

On the other hand, an effort to influence a state's reformation of its charitable corporation statutes to include provisions not now present in a PF's charter would be self-defense and therefore permissible legislative activity.

(b) Broad Social, Economic, and Similar Problems

Sponsoring discussions or conferences, conducting research, and publishing educational materials about matters of broad social and economic subjects, such as human rights or war and peace, are appropriate and permissible activities for a PF. Such topics are often the subject matter of legislation, involve public controversy, and raise the possibility of the PF being treated as conducting prohibited legislative activity. However, a PF is safe in sponsoring such discussions and examining such issues, as long as three important factors are *not* present. The PF's written communications, either directly with members of the

---

[4]IRC §4945(e).
[5]Reg. §53.4945-2(a)(1).
[6]Reg. §53.4945-2(d)(3)(ii), Examples 3 & 4.

general public or with the legislators themselves, may not:

- Mention or refer in any way to specific legislation;

- Take a position on any legislation; or

- Recommend that the reader take any steps to contact legislators, employees of legislators, or government officials or employees involved in legislation, or contain a so-called "call to action."[7]

(c) Nonpartisan Analysis, Study, or Research

A PF can conduct an independent and objective exposition or study of particular subject matters, and can make the information or results of its work available to the general public and to governmental bodies, officials, or employees. When a communiqué distributing the results presents a particular viewpoint or position—for example, that oil tankers should have double hulls to lessen the possibility of oil spills—the materials must be educational in content. Mere opinion, unsupported by pertinent facts enabling individuals to form their own opinions, is not nonpartisan. The regulations contain twelve examples that can be studied for more examples.[8] See also Chapter 23 regarding advocacy.

A broadcast or publication series must meet the same standards on an overall basis. One of the presentations can contain biased information if another part of the series (broadcast within six months of the initial viewing) contains contrary information or the other side of the argument. If the PF selects the time for presentation of information to coincide with a specific legislative proposal, the expenses of preparing and distributing that part of the study will be a taxable expenditure.[9]

(d) Grants to Public Charities that Lobby

As a general rule, a PF can make a grant to a public charity that conducts legislative lobbying, whether or not it has made the §501(h) election. The PF's money cannot be earmarked for lobbying. There must be no agreement, oral or written, that the granting PF can direct the manner in which the funds are expended.[10] Also, the PF's grant cannot be more than the amount needed to fund the recipient organization's budget for non-lobbying projects. If, after a grant satisfying these rules is paid, the grant recipient loses its exempt status due to excessive lobbying, the money paid is not a taxable expenditures if:

- The grant was not earmarked for lobbying;

- The recipient has a valid determination of its public status;

---

[7]Supra, note 1 , 4945-2(d)(4).
[8]Reg. §53.4945-2(d)(1)(vii).
[9]Reg. §53.4945-2(d)(1)(ii).
[10]Reg. §53.4945-2(a)(5) and (6).

- Notice of the revocation was not published when the grant was made; and

- The PF does not control the public charity.[11]

(e) Summary of Permissible Activity

A PF and its managers can engage in a number of efforts that involve the legislative process that do not constitute legislative intervention. Those activities include:

- Self-defense (or "germane") lobbying.

- Technical assistance or expert testimony upon request.

- Grants (not earmarked) to public charities that lobby.

- Nonpartisan analysis, study, or research.

- Programs involving topics that are the subject of legislation.

- Direct communication with government officials, including legislators, and also with the general public, without reference to and not in support of specific legislation.

- Efforts to influence regulations or other administrative rules clarifying and interpreting existing laws.

- Lobbying efforts of managers acting on their own behalf.

17.2 VOTER REGISTRATION DRIVES

All charitable §501(c)(3) organizations, including PFs, are prohibited from participating in elections of public officials and influencing elections. However, as discussed in Chapter 23, certain educational efforts in connection with the political process may be permitted. What a PF is specifically forbidden to do is "[t]o attempt to influence the outcome of any specific public election, or to carry on, directly or indirectly, any voter registration drive."[12] In the South during the early 1960s, certain foundations financed voter drives aimed specifically at registering blacks to vote, in connection with the foundations' effort to eliminate discrimination. Partly as a result, very specific rules govern a PF's participation in such efforts. A PF is permitted to make a grant to another organization, including a PF, that itself conducts a voter registration drive if the recipient organization meets the following requirements:

- The organization is a charitable one exempt under IRC §501(c)(3);

- Activities of the organization are nonpartisan, are not confined to one specific election period, and are carried on in five or more states;

[11] Reg. §53.4945-2(a)(7).
[12] IRC §4945(d)(2).

■ 233 ■

- At least 85 percent of the EO's income is spent directly on the active conduct of its charitable purposes;

- At least 85 percent of its support (other than gross investment income as defined in IRC §509(e)) comes from other EOs, the general public, and governmental units, and not more than 25 percent comes from a single EO; and

- Contributions to the EO for voter registration drives cannot be earmarked for particular states or political subdivisions.[13]

17.3   GRANTS TO INDIVIDUALS

A PF may make grants to individuals for travel, study, or other similar purposes, but to do so it must first obtain written permission from the District Director of Internal Revenue.[14] A taxable expenditure results if some (but not all) individual grants are paid without approval. The grants also cannot be earmarked to be used for political, legislative, or other noncharitable activities.[15] Travel, study, or similar purpose grants must also be one of the following:

- A grant constituting a scholarship or fellowship grant which would be subject to the provision of IRC §117(a) (as it was in effect prior to the Tax Reform Act of 1986) to be used at an educational institution described in IRC §170(b)(1)(A)(ii).

- A prize or award subject to the provision of IRC §74(b), if the recipient of such prize or award is selected from the general public.

- A grant to achieve a specific objective, produce a report or other similar product, or improve or enhance a literary, artistic, musical, scientific, teaching, or other similar capacity, skill, or talent of the grantee.[16]

(a)   Meaning of "Travel, Study or Other Purposes"

Only grants paid to individuals for the above three specified purposes are subject to the prior plan approval rules. The IRS provided a good illustration of the concepts in a ruling containing three scenarios.[17] In the first, the grant is not subject to IRS approval but in the second and third, approval is required.

Scenario 1. A PF organized to promote the art of journalism makes awards to persons whose work represent the best example of investigative reporting on matters concerning the government. Potential recipients are nominated; they do not apply for the award (thus, the IRC §74 exclusion will not apply). The awards are granted in recognition of past achievement and are not intended to finance any specific activities of the recipients nor to impose any conditions on

[13] Reg. §53.4945-3(b)(1).
[14] Reg. §53.4945-4(a)(5).
[15] IRC §4945(d)(3).
[16] IRC §4945(g).
[17] Rev. Rul. 77-380, 1977-2 C.B. 419.

the manner in which the award is expended by the recipient. Therefore, since the payments are not to finance study, travel, or a similar purpose, the awards project was not subject to prior approval.

Scenario 2. Assume instead that the annual award recipients are required to take a three-month summer tour to study government at educational institutions. These awards are subject to prior approval because the payment is required to be used for study and travel.

Scenario 3. The facts are the same as in Scenario 1, except that the award must be used to pursue study at an educational institution and qualifies as a scholarship under IRC §117(a). Again, prior approval is required.

A similar conclusion was reached in a ruling concerning grants to science fair winners that required them to use the prizes for their education. The program was a scholarship plan requiring approval.[18]

Other purposes. The meaning of grants for "other similar purposes" is elusive. The regulations say that student loans and program-related investments constitute such grants.[19] If the payment is given with the expectation or requirement that the recipient perform specific activities not directly of benefit to the PF, a grant occurs. Research grants, and payments to allow recipients to compose music or to choreograph a ballet, are all examples of awards for "similar purposes" when the recipient must perform to earn the award.

No strings attached. Grants given with no strings attached are not subject to the rules. A payment to an indigent individual for the purchase of food or clothing is not paid for travel, study, or other purpose, and is not subject to these rules.[20] Awards paid to winners of a craft school competition on an unconditional and unrestricted basis were also deemed not to be grants for this purpose.[21] Grants in recognition of literary achievement not given to finance future activity and not imposing any future condition on the recipient were ruled not to be grants.[22]

(b) Compensatory Payments

Grants do not include payments for personal services, such as salaries, consultant fees, and reimbursement of travel and other expenses incurred on behalf of the foundation, if paid to persons working on the PF's own project. The PF can freely hire persons to assist it in planning, evaluating, or developing projects and program activity by consulting, advising, or participating in conferences organized by the foundation.[23] Persons hired to develop model curricula and educational materials were not grant recipients.[24]

In 1986, Congress gutted the tax-free treatment of scholarships, fellowships, and prizes. As a result, all payments to grant recipients are taxable, other than those paid for tuition, books, and fees. Nevertheless, certain scholarships

[18]Rev. Rul. 76-461, 1976-2 C.B. 371.
[19]Reg. §53.4945-4(a)(2).
[20]Reg. §53.4945-4(a)(3)(i).
[21]Rev. Rul. 76-460, 1976-2 C.B. 371.
[22]Rev. Rul. 75-393, 1975-2 C.B. 451 and Priv. Ltr. Rul. 9151040.
[23]Reg. §53.4945-4(a)(2).
[24]Rev. Rul. 74-125, 1974-1 C.B. 327.

and particularly fellowships are taxable for another reason—the fact that the recipient is expected to render services in return for receiving the grant. Where there is quid pro quo, the grant is made primarily for the benefit of the grantor PF, and the approval rules do not apply. A PF formed to aid worthy college students who plan to teach in a particular state's public schools makes scholarship grants. As a condition of the grant, recipients must indicate they are willing to teach for two years in state public schools after receiving their degrees. Even though the obligation carries no financial guarantee and is only a moral obligation of the student, the IRS found that such scholarships were not described in IRC §177(a) and, therefore, that prior approval was not required.[25]

Alternatives. After the 1986 Tax Reform Act, almost all grant payments are taxable to the recipients, so the old award systems have lost part of their appeal. Rather than fund research under a grant program, some PFs have avoided the approval process by establishing internal research projects. Other methods of avoiding the process include awarding non-performance, non-study grants in recognition of achievement. Still, such awards should not be made on a discriminatory basis to assure they are awarded to members of a charitable class.

(c) Selection Process

Once a PF chooses to make grants subject to the approval process, it must adopt a suitable plan. The primary criterion for approval of a plan for making individual grants is that the grants must be awarded on an "objective and nondiscriminatory basis." The plan must contain the following provisions:

1. An "objective and nondiscriminatory" method of choice, consistent with the PF's exempt status and the purpose of the grant, is used.

2. The group from which grantees are selected is sufficiently broad so as to constitute a charitable class (defined in Chapter 2). The size of the group may be small if the purpose of the grant so warrants, such as research fellows in a specialized field.

3. Criteria used in selecting the recipients include academic performance, recommendations from instructors, financial need, and/or motivation and personal character.

4. Selection committee members are not in a position to derive a private benefit, directly or indirectly, if one person or another is chosen.

5. Grants are awarded for study at an academic institution, fellowships, prizes or awards, or study or research involving a literary, artistic, musical, scientific, or teaching purpose.

6. Plans to obtain reports are provided for scholarships, fellowships, and research or study grants.[26]

---

[25] Rev. Rul. 77-44, 1977-1, C.B. 118.
[26] IRC §4945(g); Reg. §53.4945-4(b) and (c).

Class of potential grantees. Item 2 on the previous page requires the group from which the grantees are chosen to be sufficiently broad. A group including all students in a city or all valedictorians in a state clearly qualifies. The regulations sanction a plan to grant 20 annual scholarships to members of a certain ethnic minority living within a state.[27] However, a group of girls and boys with at least 1/4 Finnish blood living in two particular towns was found to be a discriminatory group and not sufficiently broad.[28] Likewise, a plan that gave priority to family members and relatives of the trust's creator, if their qualifications were substantially the same as an unrelated party, was found to be discriminatory.[29]

Scholarships and fellowships. A report of the grantee's courses taken and grades earned in each academic period is to be collected at least once annually and verified by the educational institution. For grantees whose work does not involve classes but only the preparation of research papers or projects, such as a doctoral thesis, the foundation should receive an annual report approved by the faculty members supervising the grantee or other school official. Upon completion of a grantee's study, a final report must also be obtained.

Research or study grants. At least annually, a report of progress and use of funds is due. A final report describing the grantee's accomplishments and funds expended with respect to the grant must also be made.

Investigation of diversions. Procedures must be established to investigate when no reports are filed, or when reports indicate that funds are being diverted. The PF will not be treated as making a taxable expenditure if the recipient has not previously misused funds and if the PF takes the following steps during its investigation:

- During the investigation, the PF must withhold additional payments until it receives the grantee's assurances that future diversions will not occur, and must require the grantee to take extraordinary precautions to prevent future diversions from occurring.

- The PF must take reasonable steps to recover the funds.

- If a grantee was reprieved after an initial investigation and the PF reinstituted the grant only to have the funds diverted for a second time, a taxable expenditure will not occur if the same steps are repeated and the diverted funds are recovered.[30]

(d) Recordkeeping

The PF must maintain and keep available for IRS examination documentation that the grant recipients are chosen in a nondiscriminatory manner and that

---

[27] Reg. §53.4945-4(b)(5), Example 2.
[28] Priv. Ltr. Rul. 7851096.
[29] Rev. Rul. 85-175, 1985-2 C.B. 276.
[30] Reg. §53.4945-4(c)(5)(ii).

proper follow-up is accomplished. The following records must be kept:

- Information used to evaluate the qualification of potential grantees;

- Reports of any grantee/director relationships;

- Specification of amount and purpose of each grant; and

- Grade reports and diversion investigation reports.

(e) Company Scholarship Plans

The regulations and countless rulings have approved scholarship plans established by a company's PF for children of the company's employees.[31] The issue with such plans is whether they discriminate in favor of the corporate executives or shareholders and thus represent a means of paying additional compensation. Specific guidelines exist and should be carefully studied prior to application for approval of such a plan.[32] Similar rules apply to a company PF educational loan program.[33] The primary criteria are:

(1) The scholarship plan must not be used by the employer, the PF, or the organizer thereof, to recruit employees or to induce continued employment;

(2) The selection committee must be wholly made up of totally independent persons, not including former employees, and preferably including persons knowledgeable about education.

(3) Identifiable minimum requirements for grant eligibility must be established. Eligibility should not depend on employment-related performance, although up to three years of service for the parent can be required;

(4) Selection criteria must be based upon substantial objective standards such prior academic performance, tests, recommendations, financial need, and personal interviews;

(5) A grant may not be terminated because the recipient or parent terminates employment;

(6) The courses of study for which grants are available must not be limited to those of particular benefit to the employer;

(7) The terms of the grant and course of study must serve to allow recipients to obtain an education in their individual capacities solely for their personal benefit and must not include any commitments, understandings, or obligations of future employment; and

---

[31]Reg. §53.4945-4((b)(5), example 1; Priv. Ltr. Rul. 9115061.
[32]Rev. Rul. 76-47, 1976-2 C.B. 670, clarified by Rev. Proc. 81-65, 1981-2 C.B. 690, and amplified by Rev. Proc. 77-32, 1977-2 C.B. 541; see also Rev. Proc. 85-51, 1985-2 C.B. 717.
[33]Rev. Proc. 80-39, 1980-2 C.B. 772.

(8) No more than 10 percent of the eligible persons and no more than 25 percent of the eligible persons who submitted applications and were considered by the selection committee, can be awarded grants.

Due to the self-dealing rules, no grants can be paid to children of disqualified persons. The plan must avoid a disproportionate amount of grants to executives' children. Application for approval is the same as for other scholarship plans, although satisfaction of the eight tests listed above must be outlined.

(f) Seeking Approval

Application for approval of a scholarship plan is an IRS ruling request, and is submitted to the IRS Key District Office.[34] The approval process is intended to review the PF's standards, procedures, and follow-up designed to meet the Code's requirements for all of the PF's individual grant programs.[35] The PF submits its proposed procedures for awarding grants, including the methods of meeting the six selection process requirements listed in Section 17.3(c), and shown in Exhibit 17–1. Written approval is not sent by the IRS to successful

[34] The procedures for issuing rulings for exempt organizations are outlined by the IRS in a revenue procedure issued each spring. The ruling effective as of publication date was Rev. Proc. 92-4, 1992-1 C.B. 66.
[35] Reg. §53.4945-4(d)(1).

Exhibit 17–1

SAMPLE REQUEST FOR IRS APPROVAL OF INDIVIDUAL GRANT

Internal Revenue Service
CSB:1200:DAL:SUPPORT TWO
Key District Office in Area
1100 Commerce Street
Dallas, TX 75242

> RE: Sample Foundation
> ID #70-0000000
> Request for Approval
> of Scholarships

Dear IRS,

From 1900 to 19XX, the Sample Foundation operated a medical research facility and was classified as a public charity pursuant to Internal Revenue Code (IRC) §509(a)(1). During that time a scholarship fund was established in the memory of Dr. XYZ, one of the founders of Sample. For the past 20 years, scholarship grants have been paid annually. As of MMMM, 19XX, Sample discontinued the research facility and was reclassified as a private foundation. Your approval for the scholarship program is hereby sought.

Exhibit 17–1 (*continued*)

SAMPLE REQUEST FOR IRS APPROVAL OF INDIVIDUAL GRANT

The XYZ Scholarship will further Sample's educational purposes by enabling deserving men and women to complete a medical-related education in the graduate schools of their choice, so that they will be able to serve honorably and effectively in their chosen medical field.

The scholarship will be a "grant" within the meaning of IRC §4945(d)(3) and will satisfy the requirements of IRC §4945(g) in all respects.

The grant will be awarded on an objective and nondiscriminatory basis. The grant will be excluded from gross income under IRC §117(a), to the extent that it is used for tuition, books, and equipment required for educational courses. The purpose of the grant is to promote medical-related education for graduate degree candidates, and the recipient of the grant will be selected from the population of graduate school medical students.

As provided by Internal Revenue Service Publication 578, Chapter VI, the grant-making procedures will be as follows:

Grantee class. Any graduate college student seeking a degree in medical-related education may be considered for the scholarship.

Selection criteria. The selection criteria for the scholarship will include, but not be limited to, the student's demonstrated academic ability and desire, character, good citizenship, and economic necessity. A recipient cannot be related to a member of the committee or to any "disqualified persons" in relation to Sample.

Selection committee. The selection committee shall be composed of members of the board of directors of Sample. Members of the selection committee will not be in a position to receive private benefit, directly or indirectly, if certain potential grantees are selected over others.

Progress reports. The scholarships will be about $2,500 per semester and can be renewed annually for a maximum of three years, provided that the student is not on academic or disciplinary probation and is making satisfactory progress toward completion of a medical-related degree. A student need not have an "A" average, but should be of a caliber to indicate an ability to profit from and be intellectually equal to work on a graduate level. Progress reports will be obtained and verified with the educational institution each semester. Upon completion of the grantee's study, a final report will be collected from the grantee.

Report follow-up. If no report is filed by the student, or if reports indicate that the funds are not being used in furtherance of the scholarship purpose, a member of the board of directors will investigate the grant. While conducting this investigation, Sample will withhold further payments from the grantee and will take reasonable steps to recover grant funds until

Exhibit 17–1 (*continued*)

SAMPLE REQUEST FOR IRS APPROVAL OF INDIVIDUAL GRANT

it has determined that the funds are being used for their intended exempt purpose.

Recordkeeping. The foundation will retain all records submitted by the grantees and their educational institutions. Sample will obtain and maintain in its file evidence that no recipient is related to the foundation or to any members of the selection committee.

Sample trusts that the above criteria and purpose for its educational scholarship satisfy the requirements of IRC §4945 and respectfully requests your approval of its procedures.

Under penalties of perjury, I declare that I have examined this request, including accompanying documents, and to the best of my knowledge and belief, the facts presented in support of the request are true, correct, and complete.

_____   _____

Date   Sample Officer

---

applicants; instead, silence signifies approval. If within 45 days after submission of the plan, no notification is received that the procedures are unacceptable, the PF can consider the plan approved.

The user fee for making application for approval of an individual grant program is $1,250 ($400 for organizations with annual gross receipts less than $150,000), effective March 31, 1990.[36] Newly-created foundations, however, can seek approval for their plans in connection with filing Form 1023 and need not make a separate application.

(g) Individual Grant Intermediaries

For organizations wishing to avoid the administrative burden and cost of applying for approval and disbursing scholarships directly, an alternative is to fund a grant program at an independent public charity. As long as the PF has no control over the choice of recipients, the PF is not considered to have made the grants directly to the individuals.[37] There must be no agreement, oral or written, that the PF can cause the selection of particular individuals. In other words, no earmarking is permitted.

The PF can stipulate the parameters of the grant, such as choosing the discipline for study—medicine or law, for example—or recommending qualifications, such as grades or civic achievement. Suggesting the class of grantees,

---

[36] Rev. Proc. 90-17, 1990-1 C.B. 479.
[37] Reg. §53.4945-4(a)(4).

however, is risky. The IRS has ruled that a grant to fund scholarships for children of employees results in individual grants by the company PF itself, not by the college administering the plan.[38] Actually suggesting the individual grantee is permitted, as long as there is an objective manifestation of the public charity's control over the selection process. Maintaining the right to veto a potential recipient is "de facto control."[39] Likewise, a research grant disbursed by a college was found to be a direct PF grant, when the funding was contingent upon supervision by the professor designated by the PF, the PF reserved rights to patents, inventions, and publication arising from the research, and the PF retained authority to approve the professor's project and any of his scientific work.[40] The regulations contain useful examples for further study.[41]

17.4 GRANTS TO PUBLIC CHARITIES

Most private foundations make "safe" grants to public charities, or those specifically excluded from the taxable expenditures list in IRC §4945(d)(4)(A). This is true partly because so much charitable work is performed by those organizations. Private foundations have traditionally used their endowments to fund such public charitable institutions.

It is extremely important, however, to note that a PF is permitted to make a grant to any type of organization, exempt or nonexempt, if it properly documents its purposes in making the grant and insures the transaction with "expenditure responsibility" agreements. Grants to public charities are often preferred simply because they require less documentation. Public charities often serve a broad constituency that monitors their responsiveness to public needs and assures that their funds are used for charitable purposes. The purpose of these rules is to see that PF funds are used for such purposes, not for the private interests of their creators.

(a) Definition of Public Charity

A PF can make a grant to a public charity without exercising expenditure responsibility. Such charities qualify first as exempt organizations under IRC §501(c)(3) (see Chapter 2) and are further classified as public by IRC §509(a)(1), (2), and (3). The definition is a bit convoluted because the bulk of organizations so qualifying are those defined in IRC §170(b)(1)(A). The list includes churches, schools, hospitals, medical research organizations, branches of the government, states, cities and municipalities, and organizations receiving their support from the general public, such as the United Way, a community foundation, or the American Red Cross. See Chapter 11 for more details about public status.

---

[38]Rev. Rul. 81-217, 1981-2 C.B. 217.
[39]Priv. Ltr. Rul. 8542004.
[40]Rev. Rul. 73-564, 1973-2 C.B. 28.
[41]Reg. §53.4945-4(a)(4)(iv).

Exempt operating foundations are treated as public for this purpose.[42] A grant to an instrumentality of a foreign government is also considered to be a grant to a public charity, as long as it is made for charitable purposes;[43] likewise, an instrumentality of a U.S. political subdivision is treated as a public charity.[44]

(b) Proof of Public Status

Since 1969, PFs have funded public charities for another reason: simplicity. Exercising expenditure responsibility takes more effort and increases the chance of mistake. Even though grants to public charities have preferred status, the PF still has the burden of proving that the grantees are indeed so classified *and* that the grants will be used for charitable purposes. Successful completion of Checklist 17–1 and Exhibit 17–2 or 17–3 should assist the PF to avoid its public charity grants being treated as taxable expenditures.

[42] IRC §4940(d)(2).
[43] Reg. §53.4945-5(a)(4).
[44] Rev. Rul. 81-125, 1981-1 C.B. 515.

Checklist 17–1

GRANTS CHECKLIST

The following documentation should be obtained by a private foundation before it issues a check for a grant.

☐ 1. Obtain the grant proposal indicating the exempt purpose of the grant. If you are unilaterally giving a grant to an established charity for an exempt project, a transmittal letter stating that it is for general support will suffice, if a grant agreement is received and this checklist is completed.

☐ 2. Read the proposal to assure that the grant will not be expended for:

   ☐ a political campaign or influencing voters.

   ☐ influencing legislation at the national, state, or local level.

   ☐ individual grants (unless the recipient's choice is totally under the control of the recipient organization).

   ☐ a grant to another private foundation, unless there is an "expenditure responsibility" contract.

   ☐ a commercial venture (except for related projects and unless there is an expenditure responsibility agreement).

☐ 3. Obtain a determination letter stating that the recipient is exempt under IRC §501(c)(3) and is publicly supported under IRC §509(a)(1), (2), or (3), or that it is an exempt operating foundation.

☐ 4. Verify the recipient's public status in IRS Publication 78, *Cumulative List of Organizations Described in IRC §170* and check additions and deletions announced in the Internal Revenue Bulletin since its latest update.

☐ 5. Ascertain the possibility that this grant will cause the recipient to lose public status (see Rev. Proc. 89-23).

☐ 6. Request a grant agreement from the recipient if there is any question about its status or the exempt nature of its project. See Exhibit 17–1 or 17–2.

Exhibit 17–2

GRANT AGREEMENT

This letter requests tax status information before a grant is paid.

(Version 1)

GRANTEE ORGANIZATION
ADDRESS

DEAR GRANT RECIPIENT:

As a private foundation, Sample Foundation must ascertain that your organization is exempt from income tax under Internal Revenue Code §501(c)(3) and is classified as a publicly supported organization under IRC §509(a)(1), (2), or (3).

According to the information that was furnished to us with the proposal, your organization is so qualified. Please inform us only if there has been a change in your tax status since then.

In addition, we must be assured that our grant will be expended for an educational, scientific, literary, or other charitable purpose. We ask that you use our funds exclusively to carry out the project described in the application. Also, we ask you not to use any of our funds to influence legislation, to influence the outcome of any election, or to carry on any voter registration drive.

Finally, we ask that any funds not expended for the purposes for which the grant is being made be returned to us.

Please signify your agreement with these conditions by returning a signed copy of this letter to us.

Thank you.

_____

for Sample Foundation

Acknowledged by: _____
Date: _____

Exhibit 17–3

GRANT PAYMENT TRANSMITTAL

This letter conveys the grant payment check for repeating grant recipients.

(Version 2)

GRANT RECIPIENT
ADDRESS

DEAR GRANT RECIPIENT:

We are happy to enclose our check for $____ in payment of a grant for [name] project as described in your request dated [date].

As a private foundation, we must document that our grant is expended for a charitable or educational purpose. We must ask that you use our funds exclusively to carry out the project described in your request. You must not use any of our funds to influence legislation, to influence the outcome of any election, or to carry on any voter registration drive.

We must have proof that your organization continues to be exempt under Internal Revenue Code §501(c)(3) and is still classified as a publicly supported organization pursuant to IRC §509(a)(1), (2), or (3). Kindly send us a copy of your most recent Internal Revenue Service tax determination letter, your financial statements, Form 990, and any annual report for the year in which our grant funds are expended.

Finally, we must ask that any funds not expended for the purposes for which the grant is being made be returned to us. Please indicate your agreement with these conditions by returning a signed copy of this letter.

Thank you.

_____
for Sample Foundation

Acknowledged by_____
Date_____

(c) The Reliance Problem

A PF can rely upon its grantee organization's proof, or its determination letter stating that it is a public charity, until a notice of its revocation is published in the weekly Internal Revenue Bulletin or is otherwise made public.[45] A prudent PF would obtain copies of this list. The IRS also updates its Publication 78 three times a year to provide a master list of charitable organizations, along with their public or private status. If the grantee organization is not controlled by the PF (i.e., the PF cannot cause it to act or prevent its acts), the PF need not investigate the effect of its grant on the recipient.[46]

When the PF has a relationship with the grantee organization, and certainly if the PF controls it, the PF also has a responsibility to determine whether its grant will cause the recipient organization to lose its public status. When a public entity undergoes a "substantial and material change," the PF has three choices if it chooses to make a grant:

1. The PF can satisfy itself that it was not responsible for the change by reviewing financial information from the grantee's officers. The grantor is not responsible if its gift in a year is less than 25 percent of the recipient's total gifts for the immediately preceding four years.

2. The PF can ascertain that the grant is an unusual one that will not cause the grantee to lose public status.

3. The PF can exercise expenditure responsibility.[47]

(d) Controlled Grantees

A PF grant to an intermediary organization may be treated as a grant by the PF to the ultimate grantee.[48] The rules are identical to the individual grantee rules discussed in Section 17.3(g). The "look-through" applies when the PF earmarks its grant in an oral or written manner. If the regrant is to another public charity, there is no problem. If the regrant is to another PF or for some other purpose described in IRC §4945, a taxable expenditure may occur.

(e) Foreign Organizations

A foreign government and any agency or instrumentality thereof is treated as a public organization for this purpose. Certain international organizations also qualify as public charities, such as the World Health Organization, the United Nations, the International Bank for Reconstruction and Development, the International Monetary Fund, and others designated by the president.[49]

[45] Reg. §§1.170A-9(e)(4(v)(b) and 1.509(a)-3(c)(1)(iii)(a).
[46] Rev. Proc. 89-23, 1989-1 C.B. 844.
[47] Priv. Ltr. Rul. 8542004; Rev. Proc. 81-6, 1981-1 C.B. 620.
[48] Reg. §53.4945-5(a)(5).
[49] Reg. §53.4945-5(a)(4)(iii). The international organizations are designated by executive order under 22 U.S.C. §288.

A foreign charitable organization that does not have an IRS determination letter, but that is equivalent to and would in fact qualify as a public charity if it sought approval, may also be treated as a public entity. The PF is allowed to make a good faith determination of the foreign organization's status. An affidavit from the foreign entity or an opinion of counsel should be obtained, and sufficient facts concerning the operations and support of the grantee should be revealed in a manner that would allow the IRS to determine whether the organization would qualify as a public charity.[50]

The equivalency method of proving public status does not necessarily apply to a foreign organization that receives over 15 percent of its support from US. sources. IRC §508(a) notice is required from such organizations to prove their public status.

Documentation. Seeking the appropriate information from a foreign organization is often difficult due to language, currency, and legal differences. Due to these difficulties, PFs sometimes find it more comfortable to treat such foreign grants as expenditure responsibility grants to avoid unexpected results. The paperwork is similar and the possibility for a taxable expenditure is less.[51]

Charitable deduction connection. Among the reasons why a private foundation would involve itself in foreign projects is the IRC §170 rule that disallows income deductions for gifts to foreign charities. When the US. charity's board (private or public) has control and discretion as to the use of the funds raised, the fact that the funds are raised for projects outside the United States does not render contributions to the U.S. foundation nondeductible.

In a ruling concerning deductibility of gifts to a charity with foreign projects, the IRS allowed deductions and by reference sanctioned the exempt status for a pair of organizations established to build a basketball stadium in the foreign country and to sponsor and operate the games in the foreign country. Interestingly, only one organization was designed to qualify for US. charitable deductions. Organization #1 raised funds to regrant to organization #2 and to build and own the stadium in which organization #2 would operate. The ruling continues the tax policy regarding charity which recognizes the exempt nature of the activity, regardless of its location.[52]

17.5 EXPENDITURE RESPONSIBILITY GRANTS

To assure accountability for grants and program-related investments by private foundations, recordkeeping requirements are more stringent when a grant is made to:

- Another PF or POF;

- An organization exempt under some other §501(c) category; or

---

[50] Reg. §53.4945-5(a)(5); see Rev. Proc. 92-94, 1992-46 I.R.B. 34 for contents of a "currently qualified" affadavit from the grantee.

[51] Priv. Ltr. Rul. 8030104 and 8515070 indicate the extent to which some PFs go in assuring that their grants to foreign organizations meet the expenditure responsibility test.

[52] Priv. Ltr. Rul. 9129040.

- A nonexempt business. (The regulations require that the grant itself constitute a direct charitable act or a program-related investment.[53])

Such grants are *not* prohibited. The regulations say that the private foundation is not the "insurer of the activities of grantee."[54] The PF can make the grant "as long as it exerts all reasonable efforts and establishes adequate procedures" to:

- See that the grant is spent solely for the purpose for which it is made; and

- Obtain full and complete reports with respect to the expenditures to the Commissioner (IRS).

Grants to 501(c)(7) organizations. As an example of the latitude available, a PF may make a grant to a social club if the grant is suitably dedicated for charitable purposes. A PF made a grant to a social fraternity's §501(c)(2) title-holding organization to build a study room in the chapter house. The facility will contain exclusively educational equipment and furniture, along with computers linked to the university's mainframe. The university sanctioned the grant by certifying in writing that the room benefits the school by supplementing its resources, alleviating overcrowding in its library and study areas, and providing additional computer terminals. The fraternity agreed to return any grant funds not used for construction of the study space. There was no time period stipulated for this guarantee, but the foundation required that it be able to inspect the room annually.[55]

The steps to be taken to fulfill the PF's responsibility are outlined in Exhibit 17–4, and include the following:

1. Conduct a "pre-grant inquiry."

2. Establish proper terms for the grant or program-related investment.

3. Enter into a written agreement requiring the terms to be followed and establishing a reporting system for the grantee.

4. Follow up by receiving and reviewing grantee reports.

5. Investigate any diversions of funds.

6. Annually disclose proper information on Form 990PF evidencing compliance with the steps.

7. Keep documentation of these steps for IRS inspection.

---

[53] Reg. §53.4945-6(c).
[54] Reg. §53.4945-5(b)(1).
[55] Priv. Ltr. Ruls. 9050030 and 9219033.

Exhibit 17–4

PRE-GRANT INQUIRY
Sample Foundation

Name of Proposed Grantee: _____

Tax status? 501(c)(3)_____ 501(c)(4)_____ Other_____

506(a)(1)_____ 509(a)(2)_____ 509(a)(3)_____

Copy of IRS determination letter obtained: ____yes ____no

Written request with full details: ____yes ____get one

Complete financial information submitted: ____yes ____no

Other sources of support: _____

_____

Contacts: Name   Date of meeting/call

                  _____   _____

                  _____   _____

References: _____

_____

Prior grants: _____ Date_____

_____ Date_____

Reports on time: ____yes____no and why

Reasons grantee
  is qualified: _____

_____

_____

_____

Is project achievable? _____

_____

Supplemental information (not required, but helpful):

Organizational history   Publications/reports of projects

List of board members   Projects of grantee

Letters of reference   Annual report

Organization budgets   Needs analysis

(a) Pre-Grant Inquiry

The first step to take is to investigate the grantee organization and its proposed project. A pre-grant inquiry is a limited inquiry directed at obtaining enough information to "give a reasonable man assurance that the grantee will use the grant for the proper purposes."[56] The inquiry should concern itself with matters such as:

- The identity, prior history, and experience (if any) of the grantee organization and its managers. Is the other PF or organization capable of accomplishing the grant purposes?

- Information about the management, activities, and practices of the grantee organization, obtained either through the PF's prior experience and association with the grantee or from other readily available sources.

The scope of the inquiry is expected to be tailored to the particular grantee's situation, the period over which the grant is to be paid, the nature of the project, and the PF's prior experience with the grantee. The regulation examples present the following profiles of successful inquiries:[57]

- A PF is considering a grant to a newly-created drug rehabilitation center located in a neighborhood clinic and classified as a §501(c)(4) organization because it is an "action" organization. One of its directors, they are informed, is an ex-convict. The PF determines that he is fully rehabilitated and that the board as a whole is well-qualified to conduct the program, since they are members of the community and more likely to be trusted by drug offenders.

- A grant recipient provides medical research fellowships. It has conducted the program for years and receives a large number of other PF grants. Another PF which supports this recipient informs the PF that it is satisfied that its grants have been used for the purposes for which they were made.

If the grantee has received prior expenditure responsibility grants from the PF and has satisfied all of the reporting requirements, a pre-grant inquiry is not necessary. Likewise for a grant to a split-interest trust which is required by its instrument to make payments to a specified public charity, a less extensive inquiry would be necessary.[58]

Checklist 17–2 can be used to monitor the information gathered and form the basis for the grant decision as a result of the pre-grant inquiry.

[56] Reg. §53.4945-5(b)(2).
[57] Reg. §53.4945-5(b)(2)(ii).
[58] *Id.*

Checklist 17–2

EXPENDITURE RESPONSIBILITY CONTROL CHECKLIST

Sample Organization

Do Not Proceed to Next Step Until Answers Are Yes!

	Date	Initial
Step 1. Pre-grant inquiry completed.		
Step 2. Expenditure responsibility contract signed.	_____	_____
Step 3. Grant timetable prepared.	_____	_____
Step 4. Form 990-PF attachment prepared (Regulation 53.4945-5(d)).	_____	_____
Step 5. Delinquent reports or diversions investigated.	_____	_____
Step 6. Withhold payments.	_____	_____
Step 7. Segregate documents in a manner to assure that they are saved for four years.	_____	_____

By:_____

(b) Grant Terms

An officer, director, or trustee of the grant recipient must sign a written commitment that, in addition to stating the charitable purposes to be accomplished, obligates the grantee to do the following. (See Exhibits 17–5 and 17–6.)

(1) Repay any portion of the amount granted which is not used for the purposes of the grant;

(2) Submit full and complete annual reports on the manner in which the funds are spent and the progress made in accomplishing the purposes of the grant;

(3) Maintain records of the receipts and expenditures, and make its records available to the grantor at reasonable times; and

(4) Not to use any of the funds for electioneering, lobbying, or other purposes that result in taxable expenditures according to IRC §4945(d).[59]

[59] Reg. §53.4945-5(b)(3)(i), (ii), (iii), and (iv).

Exhibit 17–5

EXPENDITURE RESPONSIBILITY AGREEMENT

Sample Organization

(Version 1)

Name of Grantee Organization
Address

Dear _____,

_____ (Name of Grantor) is pleased to inform you that its Board of Directors has approved a grant of $_____ to the _____ (Name of Grantee) pursuant to the grant application dated _____.

Since your organization and ours are private foundations, we must again enter into an expenditure responsibility agreement.

Use of Funds

Our grant must be expended for charitable, scientific, literary, or educational purposes as defined under Internal Revenue Code §501(c)(3), and more specifically for _____ (Description of purpose of grant, title if any) or general support of the grantee. ANY FUNDS NOT SO EXPENDED MUST BE RETURNED TO _____ (Grantor). Funds may not be used to influence legislation or the outcome of any election, to carry on a voter registration drive, or to make grants to individuals for travel or study.

Annual Report

_____ (Grantee) will provide a narrative and financial report to us by _____ (Date). The narrative portion should include a copy of publications, catalogs, and other materials describing the accomplishments of the program or project. The financial report must be attested to by an outside accountant and must contain details of expenditures, such as salaries, travel, supplies, and the like.

Although grant funds need not be physically separated, records of receipts and expenditures under the grant, as well as copies of the report furnished to us, should be kept available for our inspection until _____ (four years from grant).

Exhibit 17–5 (*continued*)

EXPENDITURE RESPONSIBILITY AGREEMENT

Payment Terms

Payments under the grant will be made on the following dates, after receipt of a signed copy of this agreement:

_____   _____

_____   _____

(Date)   (Amount)

Sign and Return

If this agreement meets with your approval, kindly sign it and return one copy to us. On behalf of _____ (Grantor), I extend every good wish for the success of this endeavor.

Acknowledged by:

_____   _____

For Sample Foundation   For Grantee Organization

_____   _____

Date   Date

Exhibit 17–6

EXPENDITURE RESPONSIBILITY AGREEMENT

(Version 2)

Grantee: _____

Amount of Grant	Grant Payment Dates
$ _____	— —
_____	— —
_____	— —
_____	— —

Total Grant Awarded $ _____

Grant Term in Years: _____

Purpose of Grant: _____

_____

_____

_____

_____

and as further described in your grant request dated _____.

Terms of Grant:

A.   Funds granted will be expended only for the purposes for which the grant is being made. You will notify us if there are any changes in your plans. ANY FUNDS NOT SO USED MUST BE RETURNED TO SAMPLE FOUNDATION.

B.   A financial report attested to by an independent accountant must be furnished annually by _____ (date), along with a narrative report of accomplishments and any reports, publications, or other materials prepared in connection with the project.

C.   Financial records pertaining to the grant must be maintained in accordance with generally accepted accounting principles. Receipts and other documentation in connection with the grant will be maintained for at least four years and be open to our inspection at any time during that period.

D.   No funds may be used to:

   1. carry on propaganda, or otherwise attempt to influence legislation (as defined by IRC §4945);

Exhibit 17–6 (*continued*)

EXPENDITURE RESPONSIBILITY AGREEMENT

2. influence the outcome of any specific public election, or carry on, directly or indirectly, any voter registrative drive (as defined in IRC §4945);

3. make an individual grant or regrant funds to another organization unless the requirements of IRC §4945 are met; or

4. advance any purpose other than one specified in IRC §170(c)(2)(B).

E. If Sample Foundation becomes aware that the funds are not being used for the purposes described above, we reserve the right to be reimbursed for the amounts so diverted, and will withhold any future grant payments.

Acknowledged by:

_____   _____
For Sample Foundation   For Grantee Organization

_____   _____
Date   Date

Program-related investments. In addition to the information required above, the recipient of program-related investment funds must also agree to:

- Repay the funds not invested in accordance with the agreement, but only to the extent permitted by applicable law concerning distributions to holders of equity interests;

- Submit financial reports of a type ordinarily required by commercial investors under similar circumstances, and a statement that it has complied with the terms of the investment; and

- Maintain books and records of a type normally required by commercial investors.[60]

Foreign grants. The agreement should phrase the restrictions in appropriate terms under foreign law or custom. While not specifically required, an affidavit or opinion of counsel stating that the agreement is valid under the foreign laws is "sufficient."[61]

[60]Reg. §53.4945-5(b)(4).
[61]Reg. §53.4945-5(b)(5).

(c) Grantee Reports

Each year, the grantor PF must receive a report on the use of the funds, such as salaries, travel, and supplies, compliance with the terms of the grant, and the progress made by the grantee toward achieving the purposes for which the grant was made. The reports are to be made at the end of the grantee's fiscal year for each year the grant is outstanding, and should be received within a reasonable time after the close of the year. For multiyear grants, a final report summarizing all expenditures, should be submitted.[62]

Endowment grants. A grant of endowment funds to another PF for the purchase of capital equipment or other capital purposes is monitored for the year of the grant and for the two following years. The use of the principal and income (if any) from the grant funds is to be reported.[63] Such grants are outstanding for 990PF purposes for three years.

Private foundation successor organizations. A private foundation that distributes part of its assets to another private foundation in a termination distribution, as explained in Chapter 12, also has a duty to exercise expenditures responsibility indefinitely.[64]

Grantee accounting records. The recipient grantee need not maintain separate bank accounts or books for the grant unless the PF requires it. However, records of the manner in which the funds are expended must be maintained for at least four years after completion of the use of the funds. The grantor PF is entitled to rely on information submitted by its grantees.

(d) Reporting to the IRS

Each year, a foundation must provide information about each "outstanding" expenditure responsibility grant as an attachment to Form 990PF. No special form is provided. Under the regulations, the following data is to be submitted:

- Name and address of grantee;
- Date and amount of the grant;
- Purpose of the grant;
- Amounts expended by grantee based upon the most recent report;
- Whether (to the knowledge of the grantor) the grantee has diverted any portion of the funds, or income therefrom in the case of an endowment, from the intended purpose;
- Dates of any reports received from the grantee; and
- Dates and results of any verification of grantee reports undertaken because the PF doubted their accuracy or reliability.[65]

[62] Reg. §53.4945-5(c)(1).
[63] Reg. §53.4945-5(c)(2).
[64] Reg. §§53.4945-5(b)(7) and 1.507-3(a)(7) and (8).
[65] Reg. §53.4945-5(d)(2).

Strict enforcement. The IRS strictly enforces the expenditure responsibility reporting requirement. Reporting the information on an amended return does not correct the taxable expenditure,[66] but if a PF relied upon professional advice or has some other reasonable cause for its failure to report, it might attempt to seek relief from the IRS.[67]

Stiff penalties were upheld against a group of three commonly controlled organizations in *Hans S. Mannheimer Charitable Trust*.[68] Their Form 990PF contained no report. The foundation argued unsuccessfully that all of its internal documents, meeting transcriptions, and actual observations of the activities amounted to the exercise of expenditure responsibility. Despite the facts and the foundation's argument that its failure to report was due to an oversight, the penalty assessment was upheld.

Meaning of "outstanding" grants. Each year, details must be provided for each grant upon which "any amount or any report is outstanding at any time during the taxable year." Endowment and capital grants to other PFs are considered outstanding for three years, as described above. The Charles Stewart Mott Foundation found out the hard way that program-related investments must be reported for the life of the loan or as long as the investment is held (in its case, 12 years).[69] Mott had relied upon the three-year endowment reporting requirement.

(e) Grant Diversions

Rules similar to those governing scholarship fund diversions apply to grant fund diversions. The grant is not considered to be a taxable expenditure even though the grantor PF finds that any or all of the funds were used for improper purposes, if the grantor PF:

- Takes all reasonable and appropriate steps either to get the funds back or to cause the grantee to use other funds to satisfy the grant terms; and

- Withholds, as soon as it discovers the problem, any further payments to the grantee until it receives the grantee's assurance that future diversions will not occur, and requires the grantee to take extraordinary precautions to prevent future diversion from occurring.[70]

If a grantee fails to make reports, a taxable expenditure will result unless the PF:

- Originally made the grant following the appropriate steps (which are listed at the beginning of Section 17.5);

- Complied with all reporting requirements;

[66]Rev. Rul. 77-213, 1977-1 C.B. 357.
[67]Temp. Reg. §301.9100-1.
[68]*Hans S. Mannheimer Charitable Trust v. Commissioner*, 93 T.C. 5 (1989).
[69]*Charles Stewart Mott Foundation v. U.S.*, 91-2 USTC ¶50,340 (6th Cir. 1991).
[70]Reg. §53.4945-5(e)(1)(iii).

- Makes a reasonable effort to obtain the required report; and

- Withholds any future payments on the specific grant and on any other grants to the same grantee.[71]

17.6 NONCHARITABLE EXPENDITURES

The last category of expenses that result in taxable expenditure are those not expended for the charitable purposes for which the PF is exempt.[72] The IRS has provided a list of expenditures that will not be classified as noncharitable, even though they are neither grants nor project expenditures. The list includes:

- Payments to acquire investments entered into for the purpose of obtaining income or funds to be used in furtherance of charitable pursuits;

- Payment of taxes;

- Expenses deductible against unrelated business income;

- Payments constituting a qualifying distribution under IRC §4942 or a deduction against investment income under IRC §4940;

- Reasonable expenses to evaluate, acquire, notify, and dispose of a program-related investment; and

- Business expenses by the recipient of a program-related investment.[73] Conversely, the following expenses are taxable expenditures:

- Unreasonable administrative costs, including consulting fees;

- Payment of unreasonable compensation;[74]

- Return of contingent contributions;[75]

- Payment of legal costs and settlement amounts to defend officers and directors in an unsuccessful state mismanagement action.[76]

Payments to a cemetery company eligible to receive charitable contributions under IRC §170(c)(5)[77] (because they are not technically a public charity under IRC §509(a)(1).

[71]Reg. §53.4945-5(e)(2).
[72]IRC §4945(d)(5).
[73]Reg. §53.4945-6(b).
[74]*Kermit Fisher Foundation v. Commissioner*, T.C. Memo 1990-300.
[75]*Underwood v. U.S.*, 461 F. Supp. 1382 (N.D. Tex. 1978).
[76]Rev. Rul. 82-223, 1982-2 C.B. 301.
[77]Rev. Rul. 80-97, 1980-1 C.B. 257.

17.7 EXCISE TAXES PAYABLE

A tax of 10 percent of the amount of any taxable expenditure is imposed on the private foundation making the expenditure. A two and a half percent tax is payable by any foundation manager who willfully agreed to the expenditure knowing that it was such an expenditure, up to a maximum of $5,000. The rules for excusing the managers and the possible abatement of the tax are the same as those outlined in Section 15.6(d).

If the taxable expenditure is not "corrected" before the date of mailing a notice of deficiency or the date on which the initial tax is assessed, known as the "taxable period," an additional tax of 100 percent of the expenditure is imposed upon the foundation.[78] The knowing managers are jointly and severally liable for an additional tax of 50 percent, up to a maximum of $10,000.

Correcting the taxable expenditure is accomplished when the PF takes whatever corrective steps the IRS recommends, including the following:[79]

- Requiring that any unpaid funds due the grantee be withheld;
- Requiring that no further grants be made to the grantee;
- Requiring additional, possibly quarterly, reports to be made;
- Improving methods of exercising expenditure responsibility; and
- Improving methods of selecting recipients of individual grants.

If the taxable expenditure was caused by inadequate reporting by grantees, receipt of the appropriate reports is a correction. For failure to obtain advance approval for a scholarship or fellowship grant program, obtaining such advance approval for grant-making procedures is a correction.

[78] IRC §4945(i)(2).
[79] Reg. §53.4945-1(d).

IRS Recognition

Chapter Eighteen
Obtaining Recognition of Exempt Status

Obtaining Recognition of Exempt Status

IRS approval, called recognition, of an organization's exempt status is secured by submitting Form 1023 or 1024 to one of nine Key District Offices. The desired result is a determination letter describing the category of exemption granted (Exhibit 18–3).

The process of completing these forms is actually a healthy exercise for a new organization's creators. All aspects of the organization's structure, purposes, finances, and relationships are explored in the process of answering the questions. Proposed activities and grant programs are to be described, along with information about where the money will come from and how much will be spent. Fund raising plans are to be fleshed out and solicitation letters submitted. The gathering of the necessary information provides a good opportunity for long-range planning, and allows the organizers to focus on realizable goals and discard any ill-conceived or potentially nonexempt projects.

The terms used to define organizations qualifying for exemption connote different meanings to different people. What is religious to one may be sacrilegious to another. The Key District Office specialist responsible for approving or denying an application construes the meaning of a proposed organization's exempt purpose within the context of his or her understanding of the rules. The girth of Chapters 2 through 10 indicates the vaguaries of the rules and suggests the care with which applications must be prepared. While the IRS specialists are knowledgeable and cooperative, they may not perceive a proposed organization in the same light as its creators. Therefore it is useful to review the lists of qualifying and nonqualifying organizations found in those chapters while preparing the application.

18.1 INITIAL QUESTIONS

Before plunging into the time-consuming process of preparing and submitting the application, the following questions, distilled from the suitability and new organization checklists in Chapter 1, should be reviewed.

- Is there a need to create a new organization, rather than carry out the project through an existing organization?

- What is the best form of organization: nonprofit corporation, trust, or unincorporated association?

- Which category of exemption is appropriate to the goals and purposes of the organization: IRC §501(c)(3) or §§501(c)(4)–(25)?

- Can the organizational and operational tests be met?

- Might a profit-making organization be preferable? Are the creators or managers willing to forego potential profits? Will business activity be substantial? Are prospects for raising venture capital better than for getting grants?

- Should more than one exempt organization be created in view of differing purposes or funding sources? A supporting organization? A lobbying branch qualified under IRC §501(c)(4)? A for-profit subsidiary?

- Is a broadly based governing board appropriate? Should the organization be controlled by its membership?

- Will any of the following advantages prove useful to the proposed organization?

  - Exemption from federal income tax, except on unrelated business income. Exemption from other taxes, such as the federal unemployment tax and state and local taxes.

  - Eligibility to receive tax deductible charitable contributions for income, estate, and gift tax purposes.

  - Qualification for grant funding from foundations and government entities.

  - Potential for other benefits, such as tax-deferred annuities and postal rate privileges.

18.2   FORM 1023: EXEMPTION UNDER IRC §501(c)(3)

This chapter contains strategies for obtaining IRS recognition of exempt status. It will take you step by step through Form 1023, Application for Recognition of Exemption Under Section 501(c)(3) of the Internal Revenue Code (Appendix 18–1). It discusses the statutory requirements for exemption, and explains how to complete the form, including important deadlines and group exemptions. Strategies for solving problems, such as denial of the application or late filing, are then presented.

The IRS now makes a copy of favorable determination letters available for 30 days beyond their issuance in its Washington Freedom of Information Reading Room.[1]

(a) Statutory Requirements for Exemption

In order to qualify for exemption under IRC §501(c)(3), an organization must be a corporation, community chest, fund, or foundation, organized and operated exclusively for one of the following specific purposes:

1. Religious;

2. Charitable;

3. Scientific;

4. Testing for public safety;

5. Literary;

6. Educational;

7. To foster national or international amateur sports competition (but only if no part of its activities involve the provision of athletic facilities or equipment); or

8. For the prevention of cruelty to children or animals;

---

[1]IRS Notice 92-28, 1992-25 I.R.B. 5.

Furthermore, the organization's documents must require that:

- No part of its net earnings shall inure to the benefit of any private shareholder or individual;

- No substantial part of its activities shall be the carrying on of propaganda, or otherwise attempting to influence legislation (except as otherwise provided in IRC §501(c)(h)); and

- The organization shall not participate in or intervene in (including publishing or distributing statements) any political campaign on behalf of (or in opposition to) any candidate for public office.

Note that one of the eight specified purposes must be the organization's focus. An entity established "to promote community benefits" and "to develop the art of dance" would not qualify, unless its charter also stated that its purposes were exclusively educational or charitable. See Chapter 2 for a detailed discussion of the organizational and operation tests for qualifying under IRC §501(c)(3). See Chapters 3, 4, and 5 for a review of the characteristics and special rules applicable to each category of qualifying organizations.

(b) No Charitable Status Until Filing

Even through a newly-formed organization meets all of the qualifications to be exempt under (c)(3), it is not eligible to receive tax deductible contributions until it properly notifies the IRS of its existence.[2] An exempt organization is also presumed to be a private foundation unless its properly completed Form 1023 furnishes information proving its public status.

To be recognized as exempt under IRC §501(c)(3), a new organization submits Form 1023 to the Employee Plans/Exempt Organizations Division of the Key District Office for the area where the organization's principal place of business is located.[3] Form 1023 contains the addresses of the Key District Offices, including the IRS mail codes that insure proper receipt.

Organizations that meet other §501(c) statutory definitions are exempt without filing such notice, although they usually file Form 1024 (see Appendix 18–2) to obtain proof of exemption.

(c) Proper Timing

An application for recognition of exemption is due to be filed 15 months after the end of the month the organization is "formed."[4] For example, an exempt organization (EO) organized on January 5, 1993, must submit Form 1023 by April 30, 1994. The exempt status is effective from the EO's date of organization

---

[2] IRC §508(d)(3)(B).

[3] IRC §508(a) provides that a new organization must give notice of its status in the manner prescribed by the Secretary of the Treasury, as delegated to the Internal Revenue Service. Instructions to Form 1023 outline the rules for providing the required notice.

[4] Form 1023, General Instructions, pg. 1.

if the application is timely filed and accepted by the IRS. Applications filed late (after 15 months) are effective only from the date of filing. In the previous example, if the application is filed on June 30, 1994, the (c)(3) exemption begins June 30, 1994. However, status as a (c)(4) organization can be requested from the date of formation to the filing date. Income taxes may be due on income the EO has received prior to the effective date of exemption, unless the (c)(4) status is permitted.

The postmark stamped on the envelope transmitting the application determines the date of filing. Absent such a pastmark, the date the application is stamped as received by the IRS is the receipt date.[5] If the application is simply dropped into a post box and is subsequently lost, the EO has no way to prove that it was sent. Certified mail, return receipt requested, is therefore recommended for submitting the application, to prove timely filing.

(d) Date Organization Formed

Timely filing is measured from the date the organization is "formed," or the date it becomes a legal entity.[6] For a corporation, this would be the date that the articles of incorporation are approved by the appropriate state official. For unincorporated organizations, it is the date the constitution or articles of association are adopted. The IRS has ruled that the date of formation is the date on which the organization comes into existence under applicable state law.[7]

(e) Extension of Filing Deadline

If the exempt organization runs out of time or is unable to secure all of the required information, the question arises: Should a hastily prepared and possibly incomplete application be filed, or is it possible to obtain an extension of time?

Extensions of time to file Form 1023 may be granted by the Key District Director if the EO files the request within a "reasonable time under the circumstances."[8] The request for extension is not absolutely required to be filed before the deadline, but the chances of receiving a favorable response are greatly enhanced if the request is filed before the 15 months are past. An exempt organization can take several steps to increase the likelihood of IRS approval:

- *Facts and circumstances.* The EO should document the reasons for the delinquency and be able to show "good cause." The IRS will consider all factors, and is generally very reasonable.

- *Due diligence.* What actions (if any) did the EO take to ascertain filing deadlines and requirements? Were knowledgeable accountants or lawyers consulted? Does the EO have a record of names and titles of

---

[5]Rev. Rul. 77-114, 1977-1 C.B. 153.
[6]Form 1023, Instructions to Part I, Line 5.
[7]Rev. Rul. 75-390, IRB 1975-29, 17.
[8]Rev. Proc. 79-63, 1979-3 C.B. 578, modified by Rev. Proc. 80-31, 1980-1 C.B. 646.

IRS personnel it contacted to ascertain its federal filing requirements, along with dates and substance of the information obtained?

- *Prompt action.* Is the EO making its request promptly after discovering that the deadline could not be (or had not been) met? How and when did the EO discover its filing needs?

- *Intent of EO officials.* Was the failure to file on time due to mere inadvertence or to significant intervening circumstances beyond the control of the EO's creators? Any information which the EO believes may establish good cause for not filing on time, or otherwise justifying the granting of an extension, should be submitted.

(f) Incomplete Applications

The regulations take a surprisingly lenient position regarding incomplete applications. "The failure to supply, within the required time, all of the information required to complete the form, is not alone sufficient to deny exemption from the date of organization to the date such complete information is submitted by the organization. If the organization supplies the necessary additional information at the request of the Commissioner within the additional time period allowed by him (her), the original notice will be considered timely."[9]

The instructions to Form 1023 provide that an incomplete return will be "sent back to you without taking any action on it." If the application is completed and returned within the deadline provided, it will be considered filed on time. What constitutes a complete return is described in the procedures for filing a declaratory judgment to appeal an adverse determination. These reveal a concept of a "substantially complete" application, which must contain the following elements:

1. Signature of an authorized individual;

2. Employer identification number or Form SS-4;

3. Information regarding previously-filed federal income tax and exempt organization information returns;

4. Statement of receipts and expenditures and balance sheet for the current and three preceding years (or all years of existence if less than four). For EOs that have not yet completed an accounting period, a two-year proposed budget and current balance sheet are adequate;

5. Statement of proposed activities and description of anticipated receipts and contemplated expenditures;

6. Conformed copy of organizing documents; and

7. Conformed copy of bylaws.[10]

---

[9]Reg. §1.508-1(a)(3)(ii).
[10]Rev. Proc. 84-46, 1984-1 C.B. 541 and Rev. Proc. 84-47, 1984-1 C.B. 545.

(g) Expeditious Handling

It normally takes from 90 to 120 days after filing a complete and unquestioned application to receive a determination letter. The timing depends upon the IRS's workload, which is usually heavier in the fall at year-end tax planning time, when many organizations are formed to receive deductible gifts from substantial contributors.

When 120 days is too long, an exempt organization can request a speedy determination or expeditious handling. Such a request may be granted when the EO can prove that it will lose a significant grant or source of funding without a determination of its exempt status. A good candidate for expeditious handling would be a newly-created EO with an offer for a major grant from a private foundation which wishes to satisfy its minimum distribution requirements before the determination can reasonably be expected, but which will not make the grant without an IRS determination. The specific steps to take in requesting expeditious handling include the following:

- Enclose a money order or cashier's check in payment of the filing fee, to eliminate check clearing delays. Application processing awaits the clearing of the check in payment of the fee, which may take up to two weeks.

- A cover letter requesting special handling and describing the reason why speed is necessary. Good reasons include the emergency nature of the project, such as disaster relief, or the possibility that a grant will not be received if approval is delayed.

- If possible, include independent documentation of reasons, such as a letter from a prospective funder denying funds if there is a delay.

Absent approval for special handling, careful preparation of the application can save considerable time in obtaining approval. In June, 1990, the General Accounting Office (GAO) released a helpful study of the process, entitled *Tax Administration: IRS Can Improve Its Process for Recognizing Tax-Exempt Organizations*.[11] Several issues are addressed: the determination process, advance ruling follow-ups, and case closing procedures. Of primary importance is a discussion of the IRS "expedited determination process." Beginning in 1987, the Key District Offices have been authorized to dispose of cases quickly. The process allows experienced personnel to make a final decision on qualification for exemption without referring the file to specialists. Certain types of organizations, such as schools and churches, which often cause controversy during the determination process because of their complexity, are not eligible for expedited determination. The GAO criticizes the IRS for failing to develop a list of exemption categories that could qualify.

The GAO found that the use of the process varies among Key District Offices, with the highest district reporting a 17 percent usage rate and the lowest using the process for only two percent of its cases. Lack of guidance from the IRS National Office was faulted by the GAO for low, sporadic, and

---

[11]GAO/GGD-90-55 (1990).

inconsistent usage of the abbreviated processing system. The GAO encourages use of the system and made two recommendations: (1) evaluate its usage with a goal to establish clear guidance on when the process is used, and (2) assess the possibility of increasing use of the expedited determination process and freeing IRS funds for examination. The GAO has created an opportunity for Form 1023 preparers.

A complete and clearly prepared application has the possibility of immediate approval, which is always the desired result. Contributors and volunteers are often waiting in the wings to move into action upon receipt of the IRS determination.

(h) National Office

Applications which present questions not specifically answered by stature, regulation, IRS ruling, or court decision are sent to Washington D.C. for determination by the National Office. From time to time, the EO branch reserves issues about which there is controversy, or when rules are in transition. In the past few years, the IRS has withheld rulings regarding hospital reorganizations, relieving the burdens of government, and sheltering Central American refugees, among other issues.

An EO that believes its case involves an issue on which there is no precedent or nonuniformity between the districts can ask the Key District to obtain technical advice from the IRS National Office.

(i) Organizations That Need Not File

Three types of organizations are not required to file Form 1023, so that exemption is automatic.[12] Despite their exception from the requirement, some new organizations find it desirable to file nonetheless, for a number of reasons. They may need written IRS approval of their exempt status to evidence eligibility to receive tax deductible donations. Exempt status in some states is dependent upon federal approval. Nonprofit mailing privileges and other benefits of exempt organizations are most readily obtained by organizations that can furnish a federal IRS determination letter.

Churches. The first type is churches, including local affiliates and integrated auxiliaries, and conventions or associations of churches. Even though filing is not required, IRS determination may be desirable to remove uncertainty in the case of an unrecognized sect or a branch of a church established outside the United States. The IRS has developed 14-point definition of a church, outlined in Section 3.2. Schedule A was added to the 1990 version of Form 1023 to submit information to satisfy this test. Churches are generally granted favorable status; for example, they need not file annual Form 990 and may receive more liberal local tax exemptions.

Modest organizations. The second type of organization that does not need to file is one whose gross revenue is normally under $5,000 and which is not a private foundation. The term "normally" means that the organization received $7,500 or less in gross receipts in its first taxable year, $12,000 or less during its

---

[12] IRC §508(c)(3).

first two tax years combined, and $15,000 or less total gross receipts for its first three tax years combined. If an organization has gross receipts in excess of the minimal amounts above during any year after its formation, it must file Form 1023 within 90 days after the close of that year.[13]

Subordinate EOs. The third type of organization that need not file Form 1023 is the subordinate organization covered by a group exemption, for which the parent annually submits the required information, as explained below.

(j) Group Exemptions

To reduce overall compliance efforts, an affiliated group of organizations centralized under the common control of a parent organization can obtain a "group exemption letter." Subordinate chapters, posts, or local units of a "central organization," such as the Girl Scouts of America or the National Parent-Teacher Association, need not file separate applications for exemption or annual Forms 990, if they are covered by the group letter. All of the subordinate EOs in the group must qualify for the same category of exemption (for example, §501(c)(3) for an educational group), although the parent can have a different category from its subordinates.

The parent organization files Form 1023 to obtain recognition of its own exemption. Then, it separately applies by letter to the IRS Key District for approval of its group.[14]

Information submitted. A letter requesting recognition of the parent's group is submitted, along with a $500 filing fee. The letter must contain the following information for subordinates, which the IRS will then include in a group exemption letter:

1. List of names, addresses, federal employer identification numbers (each subordinate must have a separate number), description of purpose, proposed activities, and financial projections. Any subordinate that already has a separate determination should be identified.

2. Sample copy of the uniform governing instruments to be adopted by subordinates, which assure that affiliated organizations are subject to the general supervision and control of the central EO.

3. Affirmative statement that all subordinates have given written authorization to be included in the group exemption, and are under the control of the central EO.

4. Statement that all subordinates qualify for exemption under the same paragraph of IRC §501(c) (though not necessarily the same paragraph under which the central organization is exempt).

5. Statement that every organization in the group agrees to have the same accounting fiscal year.

---

[13] Reg. §1.508(a)(3)(ii).
[14] IRS Publication 557, *Tax-Exempt Status for Your Organization* (Rev. Jan. 92), pg. 4.

6. For a (c)(3) group, two additional issues must be addressed. First, the effective date of organization of all entities must be furnished to ascertain timely filing (see Section 18.2(c)). If a member of the group has been in existence longer than 15 months, the group exemption will be issued only from the date of filing. Also, public charity status must be indicated, since no private foundations can be included with public charities.[15]

New group members. Subordinates created after issuance of the IRS group determination letter report only to the central EO, not to the IRS. The new group member executes organizing documents subjecting itself to central control (before the end of the fifteenth month of organization, for a (c)(3)).

Annual filings. Each member of the group is excused from filing for itself. Annually, within 90 days before the end of the accounting period, the central organization updates the master list of its subordinates at the Internal Revenue Service Center where it files its return. It informs the IRS of any changes in purpose, character, or method of operation of any subordinates included in the group exemption, and gives the names, addresses, and employer identification numbers of any subordinates whose addresses have changed during the year, any subordinates that are no longer members of the group, and new subordinates added during the year.

Withdrawal from group. For a variety of reasons, a subordinate organization covered by a group exemption may wish to withdraw from the group and operate independently. The question that arises is how such an organization can assure that is qualification as a tax-exempt organization is ongoing and uninterrupted. A new Form 1023 for the withdrawing member is due to be filed within fifteen months of the date of withdrawal.[16]

18.3 SUGGESTIONS FOR COMPLETING FORM 1023

A sample Form 1023 for a fictitious entity, the Campaign to Clean Up America, is included as Appendix 18–1 and can be used as a guide for filling out a Form 1023. The exhibit also includes a sample articles of incorporation, bylaws, a copy of a fund-raising letter, a detailed description of the EO's proposed activities, and a proposed budget. This section contains suggestions for completing each part of Form 1023, and the reader may find it helpful to have a blank copy of Form 1023 to follow along with the text.

Note in the upper left-hand corner of Appendix 18–1 that Form 1023 was revised in September, 1990. The IRS expects to issue a new version of Form 1023 in the summer of 1993 and had no draft available as of November, 1992. Only minimal changes are expected, but preparers should submit the most recent version of the form.

---

[15]Rev. Proc. 80-37, 1980-1 C.B. 677.
[16]G.C.M. 39833, released December 10, 1990.

18.3 SUGGESTIONS FOR COMPLETING FORM 1023

(a) Part I, Identification of Applicant

Line 1, Full name of organization. The name "exactly" as it appears on the organizational documents must be entered here. The determination will be issued in that name. If, for some reason, the EO will conduct its activities in some other name, the new name should be shown in parentheses. If the organization intends to operate under a name not on its organizing documents, registering a formal change of name with state authorities prior to application might be preferable. This may save considerable time explaining to donors why the determination letter has a different name.

Line 2, Employer identification number. For all federal tax filing purposes, starting with Form 1023, an exempt organization must secure and use a federal employer identification number (EIN). Form SS-4 is used to request the number. The IRS Center, not the Key District Office, assigns EINs, and no special category or type of identifying number is issued to an EO. Although the Form SS-4 may accompany Form 1023 if a number has not yet been obtained, it may slow the process. It is preferable to obtain the number separately. In some districts, the number can be obtained by phone. For filers with the Austin, Texas Service Center, a call to (512) 462-7843 with a completed Form SS-4 in hand results in an instant number.

Line 3, Person to contact. The name and telephone number of the person (or persons) to contact during business hours for additional information is requested. The instructions to the form suggest choosing a person familiar with the EO's activities, preferably an officer, director, or authorized representative. The best choice is someone qualified to answer any IRS telephone inquiry and to prepare written responses to questions, ideally, an accountant or attorney experienced in EO matters.

If representatives are used, Form 2848, *Power of Attorney and Declaration of Representative*, or Form 8821, *Tax Information Authorization*, must be completed and attached to the application, and the representative's name(s) are placed in Line 3.

Line 4, Accounting year. The choice of fiscal year is influenced by several factors, including the type of ruling being sought. A definitive ruling "cannot be issued before the close of an EO's first fiscal year having at least eight months,"[17] as discussed in Section 18.6. In many cases, an advance ruling is sought, so any fiscal year can be chosen to accommodate this requirement.

Another factor in choosing the fiscal year is the EO's programming period. Schools and performing arts organizations normally operate on a September 1 to August 31 year, for example. EOs funded by federal government grants often find it convenient to match the federal year that ends September 30. A summer or fall fiscal year end is sometimes chosen to accommodate accountants' workload.

Be sure that the application agrees with the organization's bylaws and Form SS-4. If an incorrect fiscal year was indicated on a separately filed Form SS-4, or if for any other reason the EO needs to change its fiscal year, see Section 28.4(a).

---

[17]Form 1023, Instructions to Part III, Line 10 at page 5. See Section 18.7 regarding definitive and advance rulings.

Line 5, Date incorporated or formed. See the discussion at Section 18.2(d).

Line 6, Activity code. The choice of activity code is sometimes tough, and the wrong choice can lead to closer scrutiny from the determination agent. The list printed on the back of Form 1023 includes all types of EOs and is identical to the Form 1024 list. Sprinkled among some 300 possibilities are many non-(c)(3) activities. For example, "Advocacy, attempts to influence public opinion" is included in a list of more than 30 issues such as gun control, birth control methods, and ecology. An EO that chooses any of these codes will be required to prove that it is not an "action" organization, as discussed in Section 2.2(g).

Many codes fall into more than one exemption category. For example, a "nurses' register" might be a (3) or (6); a community center or a voter education project might be classed as a (c)(3) or (4); a horticulture society might fall into (c)(3), (4), (5), (6), or (7). The codes are to be entered in order of their significance to the organization's overall activities. Only one or two codes may be appropriate.

Line 7, Miscellaneous categories. In addition to (c)(3)s, the following organizations also file Form 1023:

- IRC §501(e), cooperative hospital service organization (see Section 4.7);

- IRC §501(f), cooperative service organization of operating educational organization (see Section 5.1(d);

- IRC §501(k), organization providing child care (see Section 5.1(c).

Line 8, Other applications. The IRS wants to know if the applicant has previously applied for recognition of exemption, and if so, under what category. As discussed in Section 6. 4, a (c)(3) that loses its status because of excess lobbying cannot later qualify as a (c)(4). Conversely, the IRS wants to be alerted up front if a (c)(4) or any other type of EO is applying to convert to a (c)(3).

Line 9, Prior returns. To enable the IRS to verify compliance with annual filing requirements, the applicant is asked whether any prior returns have been filed—either an income tax return or an exempt information return. An organization in existence for over one year would have been responsible to file one of those returns.

Line 10, Organizational documents. The papers legally establishing the organization are attached as follows:

1. Articles of incorporation signed by the directors and "approved (certified, in most states) and dated by the Secretary of State or other appropriate state official," along with the adopted bylaws; or

2. Constitution or articles of association, including evidence that the organization was formed by two or more persons; or

3. Trust instrument.

The documents must be "conformed" copies, or ones that agree with the original and all amendments to them. A sworn statement (not necessarily notarized) signed by an officer or director, that reads: "I swear that the attached copies of the charter and bylaws (and amendments, if any) are true and correct copies of the originally executed documents," is sufficient.

These documents are used by the IRS to conclude that the EO meets the organizational test. Faulty limitations on activities and/or dissolution clauses will cause the IRS to return the application and deny exemption until the faults are cured. If the EO is relying upon state law to impose dissolution or other provisions, the statute should be cited and summarized.[18] Review Section 2.1 for more details on this extremely important subject.

(b)   Part II, Activities and Operational Information

This part fleshes out the candidate for exemption and paints a picture of the proposed organization. The IRS wants to know where the money to operate the exempt organization will come from, the manner in which it will be obtained, how it will be spent, who will decide, who gets to participate or receive benefits, why the EO was created, whether it evolved from a previous life, whether it will benefit a limited group of people (particularly those who control it), and other information to determine that it will qualify as a charitable organization.

Successful preparation of Form 1023 involves weighing the material facts that should be submitted against their potential for generating controversy with the IRS. While the facts must be accurate, there is room for judgment in the presentation of a potentially nonexempt activity. If there is a reasonable chance that a potentially unrelated activity might be approved and the EO is prepared to agree not to undertake the activity if it is not acceptable, inclusion is warranted.

Another important aspect to consider is that the EO will be somewhat constrained to operate in the manner presented in Form 1023. The organizers must look to the future and the possibilities must be exhaustively surveyed before the application is submitted. Any future "substantial change" in operations necessitates resubmission or communication with the IRS, as discussed in Chapter 28.

Finally, the application will be viewed by many persons in the future for a number of reasons. EO board and staff members should review the original Form 1023 annually to assure that everyone understands why the IRS considers the organization to be exempt, and to see if there has been a "material change" in its operations. The application must also be available for public inspection.

Line 1, Narrative description of activities. The essence of the applicant's charitable nature is reflected in the description of proposed activities. The space allotted may suffice in some cases, (and the IRS is suggesting by the limited amount of space that the description should be concise). However, there are no instructions to this part of the form, and a complete picture of the EO must be painted. Spare no words, but choose them carefully.

Information submitted in the narrative description must be coordinated with answers to other questions as well. If, for example, the description states that monetary assistance will be provided to needy families, the IRS technician

---

[18]Form 1033, Instructions to Part I, line 10, at pg. 3.

may want to know how the recipients will be chosen, and will look to line 11(b) for a description of the criteria.

As another example, assume that the description states that the organization is established for literary purposes and that it plans to encourage emerging writers. The IRS will want to know how those writers will be chosen, how their works will be published, and who will own the copyright to the works. This time, the answers at lines 11(a) and (b) are relevant. Most importantly, the answers will indicate to the IRS how the activity furthers the exempt interests of the general public while, as a byproduct of accomplishing its purpose, it also may provide some benefits to individual writers.

The proposed activities to be carried out in accomplishing the exempt purposes must be described in sufficient detail to permit the IRS to conclude that the EO clearly meets the particular requirements discussed in Chapters 2, 3, 4, and 5. The standards, criteria, procedures, or other means adopted or planned for choosing participants and recipients of the EO's activities must not only be explained but must meet IRS standards. For example, a public interest law firm is subject to specific rules outlined in Section 23.10.

A mere restatement of the organization's exempt purposes, with a statement that proposed activities will further such purposes, is *not* sufficient. The author prefers to answer Line 1 in outline form, highlighting categories of activities. A sample response is shown in Exhibit 18–1.

Line 2, Sources of financial support. The EO's anticipated revenue sources should be summarized briefly according to the categories in the financial data statement in Part IV. The proportions should agree with the financial information presented in the proposed budgets or actual financial results. This line alerts the technician to private foundation status and to possible unrelated business income issues. The form asks that sources be listed in order of size. It is useful to indicate size with percentages similar to these:

Individual membership dues	30%
Government grants	20
Private foundation grants	20
Contributions from disqualified persons	15
Exempt function revenues	10
Investment income	5
	100%

Line 3, Fund-raising program. A thorough description of both actual and planned fund-raising activities is crucial to a complete application. The instructions define solicitations for contributions, functionally related activities, and unrelated business activities as "fund raising." Issues raised by the answers include:

- Possible private inurement to fund-raisers through payments of unreasonable salaries or fees based upon a high percentage of the contributions collected. Private benefit to substantial contributors may also result through bailout of mortgaged property or property with high operating costs or limited marketability, as outlined in Section 20.6.

Exhibit 18–1

SAMPLE NARRATIVE DESCRIPTION OF ACTIVITIES

XYZ is a newly-formed organization located in an area of the city with a high degree of poverty. XYZ's primary purpose is to lessen the suffering of the poor (or XYZ is an outgrowth of a citizens committee formed by the STU Community Center informally assisting underprivileged members of the area). XYZ will conduct the following activities in space donated rent-free by the STU Community Center.

Educational Programs. XYZ will hold weekly public forums. Representatives of local, county, state, and national government agencies that provide assistance for the poor will be invited to speak to members of the community about services and financial assistance available to them. XYZ will publicize the forums by circulating fliers throughout the community. XYZ will hold tutorial classes for children after school to assist them in succeeding in their schoolwork and to keep them from dropping out of school.

Nutritional Counseling. XYZ will seek a volunteer nurse to conduct a class at STU Community Center to teach nutrition. Health education of children and pregnant women will be emphasized, as well as substance abuse information.

Credit and Debt Counseling. XYZ plans to establish a group of business volunteers to counsel and assist community members in debt. Free income tax assistance will be offered during tax time. XYZ will contact the Better Business Bureau and other agencies offering help to the poor in gathering information to structure the program.

Grocery Cooperative. XYZ will provide management assistance for members of the community to operate a food cooperative previously sponsored by the STU Community Center. The cooperative will be run with volunteers and will enable the poor to purchase more vegetables, grains, and high-protein foods to provide better nutrition for their families. The nutritional courses will be coordinated with foods purchased.

Future Programs. Although no definite plans are being made at this time because of funding constraints, funding for drug and job counseling programs will be sought. The state agencies providing such funding require that the organization be in existence for over two years before applying for funds.

- Businesslike taint of purported exempt revenues, such as research fees, advertising, sales of books or other publications, premiums from group insurance, or income from a restaurant. IRS specialists are also alert to other unrelated business activity disguised as a donation program—for example, premiums with a cost in excess of $6 offered in return for contributions, as discussed in Section 21.10(a).

- The proper distinctions between deductible and nondeductible portions of benefit dinners, auctions, and other events are scrutinized. Since issuing Publication 1391 in 1988, which asks (c)(3)s to voluntarily furnish donors with tax information, the IRS requests details regarding fund-raising activities in connection with the determination process. (See Chapter 24 for more details.)

- Satisfaction of the "commensurate test" is evaluated here. This test measures the net profit produced by fund-raising programs. If promoter fees and other expenses are excessive, the organization itself may be deemed to operate to benefit the fund-raisers rather than the required charitable constituency, as discussed in Section 2.2(d).

It is possible (but not necessarily desirable) to state that the fund-raising program has not yet been developed. If the projected sources of support consist primarily of grants from other exempt organizations, a lack of plans will probably not pose problems. If fund-raising events and exempt function revenues are to be the primary sources of support, the IRS will require detailed plans. At a minimum, the organizers must prepare sample letters requesting contributions for attachment.

The answers given for types of assets and charges for services rendered on lines 8 and 11 of Part II may signal the need to submit income-producing information. Conversely, answers about the fund-raising program should be reflected in those questions, especially in the financial data of Part IV.

Line 4, Governing body. The questions about board membership enable the IRS to determine whether unreasonable salaries will be paid, whether the board includes political officials or disqualified persons, and what types of financial transactions are planned with insiders.

Line 4a, Names and addresses. Fill in the names, addresses, and titles of officers, directors, trustees, or other governing officials. Although it is no longer requested, their expertise and occupations could be submitted. A factor useful in proving the "public" nature of a project could be the presence of a broadly based board of independent experts. Take, for example, an EO that is being formed in association with a commercial business. The occupations and expertise of outside directors might improve the EO's chances for approval.

Advisory board members who have no voting authority are not commonly included, nor are their names requested. If their statuture adds to the EO's credibility and shows responsiveness to the public, the information could be voluntarily submitted.

Line 4b, Compensation. A key question in evaluating an exempt organization's qualification for charitable status is the possibility of "inurement of earning" to members of the board by virtue of payment of unreasonable compensation to them.

Total annual compensation is to be reported, including salary, bonus, and other forms of payment to the individual for services while employed by the organization. There is no prohibition against such payments, but there is enhanced scrutiny, as discussed in Chapter 20. The instructions do not direct that pension or other fringe benefits be included.

Line 4c, Public officials. Persons who serve on the governing body by reason of being public officials or being appointed by public officials are to be named here. The self-dealing sanctions specifically govern a private foundation's relationship to officials (see Chapter 14). For public charities, the question is fishing for association with politicians who might try to use a charitable organization to collect political gifts.

The basis for their selection must be explained. Again, this answer can be useful in proving public scrutiny and responsiveness on the EO's part, particularly when the officials rotate as their terms expire. For example, a drug prevention program might benefit from participation by the director of the local health department. On the other hand, a voter education project might be denied exemption if representatives of only one political party are members.

Line 4d, Disqualified persons. For purposes of constraining their relationship with the EO, the Internal Revenue Code identifies certain insiders as disqualified persons (DPs). DPs can serve as members of the board and can be paid reasonable compensation for services they actually render, and stand in relationship to the organization just as any other person. They are simply "red flagged" for scrutiny. For purposes of this question, disqualified persons are defined by IRC §4946 to include:

- Substantial contributors (generally over $5,000);

- Creators of trusts regardless of contribution level;

- Foundation managers;

- Lineal members of family (children, parents, grandparents, or great-grandparents, but not siblings or aunts or uncles);

- Controlled corporations, partnerships, trusts, or estates (over 35 percent); and

- Another EO controlled by the EO itself or by the same persons.

This question asks the preparer to "explain" any members of governing body who are disqualified persons. Typically, their names and the relationship are reported, although it is unlcear if additional information should be included.

In the past, Form 1023 asked if assets would be assigned. Although it is not now required, anticipated donations by major contributors can be explained here, particularly if they involve the answers to other questions.

Gifts of cash or marketable securities need little or no explanation. Gifts of encumbered land, art works, patents, copyrights, or certain other types of personal or real property may raise issues with the IRS. If closely held corporate stock is to be given and a buy/sell or redemption agreement is planned, the agreement could be attached. Real estate gifts could be described by attaching the deed, if possible, and a report on the purpose for which the property will be used (for example, an office building to be held as an investment property or used for administrative offices).

Debt reported on line 14 of Part IV must be explained in detail. A gift of property subject to debt should be explained. The IRS will require proof that its fair market value exceeds the debt to which it is subject. An independent appraisal may be requested. Repayment terms and any other obligations the charity is assuming or taking the property subject to must also be reported.

Documents creating an income interest in property might be attached, and must evidence the donative intent and benefit to be received by the charity. Types of instruments that might be attached include a trust instrument creating a life estate or a royalty interest assignment.

Line 5, Control of / by another organization. The proposed exempt organization's relationship to another entity, either a predecessor or one controlled by the same persons, must be described. Control is not defined in the instructions, but they suggest examples of "special relationship," such as common officers and the sharing of office space or employees. The manner in which control is effected, whether with bylaw provisions, appointment of directors by the other EO, contractual terms, or otherwise, should be explained.

Control is not necessarily a negative factor; the question is whether the interests of the general public will be respected and advanced. The following situations warrant answers to this question:

- Creation and control of a charitable exempt organization by a business or civic league or a social club (also requires information on Line 6);

- Facilities and other costs shared with a related EO of another category such as a (c)(6), a substantial contributor, or even another (c)(3) organization, as discussed in Chapter 22;

- Successor to a nonexempt entity must complete Schedule I, Successors to "For Profit" Institutions, and can answer this question by referring to that schedule. The issue is whether the predecessor reaps any gain from the takeover. As with the problems anticipated in line 4d, if liabilities are being assumed, evidence that the new charity is ending up in a positive financial position must be attached;

- A new supporting organization reveals its relationship with its supported organization by referring to the answers on Schedule D.

Line 6, Transactions with non-(c)(3)s. The details of any transactions anticipated to occur between the applicant and a political or other non-(c)(3) nonprofit organization must be revealed. This question is asked again each year on Form 990, and seeks to assure that the charitable (c)(3) is not operated to benefit a (c)(4) or other non-(c)(3) nonprofit organization.

Line 7, Accountability to another EO. If the exempt organization is financially accountable to another organization, the terms, written agreements, reporting forms, or other requirements should be described here. Sometimes the question is whether to report potential requirements. For example, a newly-created EO hopes to become a United Way agency or to received substantial governmental funding. It could include a statement of the possibility and the fact that extensive annual reporting will be required if it is successful. If available, grant reporting forms might be attached.

A §509(a)(3) supporting organization should briefly describe any formal system it has developed for reporting to its supported organization. It would also refer to Schedule D.

Line 8, Exempt function assets. This question adds facts to complete the picture of the EO in a physical sense. No information concerning investment assets or endowments is requested (as was the case in the 1986 and prior versions of the form). Examples of possible answers include:

- XYZ will operate from a rent-free leasehold. Administrative assets, including computers, photocopiers, and office equipment, will be purchased. As funds become available, it is hoped that a vehicle for transporting neighborhood children, display cases for the food cooperative, and desks, speaker systems, and other assets to enhance the educational classes will be obtained.

- EO is a grant-making private foundation that will obtain administrative assets, such as computers, telephone systems, file cabinets, and other office equipment and furniture.

- EO will operate a hospital. As reflected on the attached capital budget projections, a building will be constructed and furnished with equipment necessary to operate the hospital, its laboratories, cafeteria, and other patient care facilities.

Line 9a, Facilities manager. The IRS is looking for the possibility of private inurement in this question.

- Do management arrangements in any way take unfair advantage of the charity?

- Is the fee reasonable for services to be rendered?

- How does it compare to prevailing rates charged other businesses? To the overall EO budget?

- Is the fee related to performance, e.g., a percentage of profits or other arrangement reflecting a business transaction?

- Are contracts entered into with related parties?

Except for a private foundation, there is no prohibition against a board member managing an exempt organization's property or engaging in other business transactions with the EO. But there is a need to verify the fairness of the transaction and the absence of private inurement.

Line 9b, Leases. The applicant must attach a copy of any leases it is a party to, along with an explanation of the relationship between the organization and the lessor. Arrangements for office space and equipment rentals are the most common examples. An arm's length agreement with an unrelated party needs no explanation beyond the lease itself. For a related party lease, evidence that the terms of the lease are fair should be submitted, along with other information described in Chapter 20.

Line 10, Membership organizations. The IRS suggests that the membership question be answered "Yes" only if three factors are present:

- Members share the common goal for which the organization was created;

- members actively participate in achieving the organization's purposes; and

- Members pay dues.

Some argue that an EO is a membership organization only if members have voting control pursuant to the charter. "Membership" created solely as a fund-raising device without governance powers may not convert the EO to a membership organization.

Line 10a, Membership requirements and dues. The purpose of this question is to determine whether the EO's membership aspect serves its exempt purposes exclusively, or whether members received private benefit. When members are contributors and receive no monetary benefits, there is no problem. Among membership requirements that suggest nonexempt characteristics are a high membership fee, with only members eligible to participate in exempt activities. Membership open only to a narrow group, such as those living in a particular subdivision or on a specific street, might also be suspect. Another example is an art appreciation society whose membership is limited to persons who own works of a particular living artist.

Line 10b, Efforts to Attract Members. Examples of membership solicitation brochures or flyers should be attached. If benefits are available to nonmembers, even for some charge, the limited membership may not cause a challenge to exemption. Estimate the number of members and nonmembers benefiting from services to reflect the EO's public nature.

Try to show a public benefit unrelated to direct participation. For example, a research organization may limit use of its laboratories to members but have a policy of publishing results and conducting seminars.

Line 10c, Benefits to Members. This question is a two-edged sword. Of most concern is the issue of whether the organization operates to benefit only its members rather than a charitable class of individuals. The discussions of inurement at Section 2.1(d) and charitable class at Section 2.2(a) are relevant.

Second, the IRS Special Emphasis Program on Fund-raising (discussed in Chapter 24) should be reviewed before this question is answered. Charities must quantify and report to members the value of the "benefits" provided to them. It behooves a membership EO to be sure that any brochure attached to Form 1023 complies with the disclosure requirements. Unrelated business issues may also be involved.

Line 11a, Charges for exempt services / products. If the exempt organization plans to charge for services it renders or products it sells, the method of determining the charges must be described. Services do not have to be provided for free to be charitable, and there is no prohibition against some amount of built-in profit, as the prices of private college tuition and hospital stays exemplify. This information, however, allows the IRS specialist to evaluate the possibility of unrelated business activity. (See Chapter 21.) Some possible answers follow:

- Classes, workshops, and educational materials will be priced according to their direct cost; overhead expenses will be covered by donations.

- Charges for hospital services will be determined in accordance with the guidelines for Medicare/Medicaid reimbursements and the currently prevailing rate for comparable services in the community. Charges will be waived for persons who prove that they are unable to pay.

- Donated clothing will be resold in a volunteer-run shop at prices similar to those of other nonprofit and for-profit resale shops in the city.

- Charges for legal services will be determined on a sliding scale according to the client's family income level. See attached client engagement letter and fee arrangement for details.

Line 11b, Limitation on service recipients. How the charitable class of beneficiaries is selected, if there is a limitation, is to be explained here. Restrictions can cause denial of exemption.

For example, schools must adopt a nondiscrimination policy and comply with requirements outlined in Schedule B. Hospitals may be denied exemption unless they provided free emergency care or can otherwise prove their charitable nature, as discussed in Section 4.6. An artists' cooperative that exhibited only work of its members has been found to serve its members, not the general public. It was therefore not exempt, despite the educational nature of the art.

Line 12, Lobbying. Publicly supported organizations may spend limited funds on attempts to influence legislation by contacting members of a legislative body directly or by advocating to the general public adoption or rejection of legislation. See Chapter 23 to evaluate limitations and the propriety of choosing the "election method" for measuring permissible lobbying. A private foundation must answer this question "No." For public charities, a "Yes" answer leads to two possibilities.

An electing exempt organization may (and preferably does) attach Form 5768, Election/Revocation of Election by an Eligible Section 501(c)(3) Organization to Make Expenditures to Influence Legislation, (Appendix 23–1). The form makes it easier to provide the correct information. A non-electing EO must attach details of planned lobbying efforts, including:

- Dollar amount to be expended annually and calculation of percentage of total budget;

- Amount of time to be expended by organization representatives (both paid and unpaid) on behalf of the EO, in connection within lobbying efforts;

- Description of issues involved and method proposed for carrying out lobbying activities; and

- Any written materials published or disseminated to the public or to government officials.

Line 13, Political campaigns. The answer to this question must be "No!" To receive a determination that it qualifies as a (c)(3) organization, the application cannot intervene in any way in a political campaign, and its organizational documents must prohibit such involvement.

(c) Part III, Technical Requirements

Lines 1—6, Timely filing. It is highly desirable that Line 1 be answered "Yes" and the remaining lines 2—6 not be relevant. If the application is being filed more than fifteen months beyond the end of the month when the EO was established, refer to Sections 18.2(c)—(e) to complete this page.

If §501(c)(3) status is not available because the application is late, question 6 provides the opportunity to be classified as a (c)(4) organization for the period between organization and filing. Although the contribution deduction is lost for any gifts the organization has received before the filing date, at least none of the income will be taxable. Sections 6.1 and 6.2 discuss the similarities between (c)(3)s and (c)(4)s, and indicate why this temporary classification is possible.

Line 7, Private foundation status. The new organization must state whether it is or is not a private foundation.

Line 8, Private operating foundations. A private foundation planning to conduct self-initiated projects may qualify as an operating foundation. If so, Schedule E is to be completed.

Line 9, Public charity classification. One of ten blanks must be checked by organizations claiming to qualify for public charity status. Organizations qualify as public for one of three reasons. Types (a), (b), (c), (d), and (f) are public by virtue of the activities they conduct. They may claim a definitive ruling from their inception, as long as they can satisfy the requirements for those classifications. Types (e) and (g) operate to benefit another type of public entity. Types (h) and (i) may qualify based upon their revenue sources.

(a) Churches complete Schedule A and must meet a strict fourteen-point test outlined in Section 3.2.

(b) Schools are discussed at Section 5.1(a) and must complete Schedule B.

(c) Hospitals and medical research groups are subject to some evolving rules outlined in Section 4.6, and must complete Schedule C.

(d) Governmental units furnish no special information. Section 11.2(e) explains this category.

(e) Supporting organizations check this blank and complete Schedule D. The requirements are presented in Section 11.5.

(f) Entities testing for public safety are discussed in Section 11.6.

(g) A supporting organization benefiting a college or university that is a governmental unit also need not furnish special information.

(h) Publicly supported organizations qualifying because their support comes from a broad segment of the public (also known as §509(a)(1) organizations) must meet the mechanical tests illustrated in Exhibit 11–2 and proceed to line 10.

(i) Service-providing organizations must satisfy the tests shown in Exhibit 11–3 and also proceed to line 10.

(j) Entities that are not sure which category they qualify under check this blank to request the IRS decide. There is little downside to this choice.

Line 10, Definitive ruling. As the name connotes, a definitive ruling is essentially a "permanent ruling" of public status, effective until the exempt organization's sources of support cause it to fail the public support tests mathematically. A calculation is made annually when Form 990, Schedule A is filed. The IRS has found that it can make up its mind about the public status of most EOs that have been in existence for a taxable year of at least eight months. A definitive ruling need not be chosen if, during the first year of activity, sufficient public support has not been received. Such an organization can request an advance ruling to avoid private foundation classification.

A newly-created organization with limited operational history receives an advance ruling that it will be treated as a publicly supported EO, subject to a redetermination at the end of five years. At the end of the advance ruling period, the organization must furnish a detailed report of its sources of support during the past five years to allow the IRS to make a final determination of public charity status.

An organization receiving an advance ruling must agree to extend the statute of limitations during the five years. Form 872-C, Consent Fixing Period of Limitation Upon Assessment of Tax under IRC §4940 of the Internal Revenue Code, must be signed and filed (in duplicate) to evidence agreement to pay the private foundation excise tax on investment income earned during the advance ruling period if public status is not achieved.

A report of support sources is to be filed five years later, within 90 days after the period ends. *Failure to file will result in reclassification as a private foundation.* Placing a tickler on a reliable person's or firm's calendar is very important.

Donors may rely upon the public status determination until the IRS publishes a notice of revocation, unless the donors are in a position to cause or be aware of the organization's failure to qualify. The significance of definitive versus advance rulings is discussed in Section 18.7.

Line 11, Unusual grants. To calculate an EO's qualification as a publicly supported organization under type (h) or (i), unusual grants are omitted. These are significant grants from unrelated parties having the characteristics described in Section 11.4(b).

Line 12, Under two percent donors. See Section 11.2(f) to understand the information requested on this line.

Line 13, $5,000 fees. See Sections 11.3 and 11.4 before answering this part.

Line 14. Carefully check the blanks on this line, because each "Yes" check requires an attached schedule.

(d) Part IV, Financial Data

A "Statement of Revenue and Expenses" is required for all organizations, both newly-formed ones presenting projected or proposed financial data and those having actual financial history. Financial information for the current year must end within 60 days of the application date. An exempt organization that has been in existence less than one year should include financial statements to date, plus projected budgets for the next two years. The IRS may request information for up to four years. Depending upon the organization's chosen fiscal year, an EO filing on November 1 might include four sets of numbers.

Example. An EO is chartered on January 1 and chooses a fiscal year ending in June. The following information is submitted:

Column (a) A six month statement as of June 30, the first tax year.

Column (b) Two month statement for July and August.

Column (c) Ten month projection ending June 30 of the second year.

Column (d) Additional year's projection.

The arrangement of the lines for reporting the financial information is different from Forms 990 and 990PF, but the contents are basically the same. Chapter 27 can be reviewed for the types of income and expenses reportable on each line.

Line 1, Gifts, grants and contributions received. Income reportable in Part I, line 1 of Forms 990, 990PF, and 990EZ are to be submitted on this line. No details of contributors are requested, and unusual grants are reported separately on line 12. For organizations seeking recognition of their public status based upon their sources of support, contributor and support data is furnished at Part III, lines 11–13.

Line 2, Membership fees. Amounts paid by members to support the organization are reported on this line. Charges for member services (such as admissions, merchandise, or use of facilities) are included on line 4 or 9, not here. Line 3 of Forms 990 and 990EZ contains the same revenue.

Line 3, Gross investment income. Dividends, interest, payments on security loans, rents, and royalties are the common forms of investment income. Interest received for program related investments, such as student loans, are reported on line 8. This amount comes from lines 4–7 on Form 990, lines 2–5 on Form 990PF, and line 4 of Form 990EZ.

Line 4, Unrelated business net income. Income from unrelated businesses that are regularly carried on in a businesslike manner and reportable on Form 990T are included on line 4. If such income is excepted from taxability because it is operated by volunteers, for member convenience, or some other exception, it is not included here but instead on line 8. See Chapter 21 for detailed rules. There is no comparable reporting on Forms 990.

Line 5, Beneficial tax levies. Amounts collected by local tax authorities from the general public and either paid to or spent on behalf of the EO are to be reported here. Schools and human service organizations receive this type of revenue, which is commonly reportable on line 1 of Forms 990 unless the amounts are paid in return for services the EO renders.

Line 6, Governmental unit "in kind" donations. Facilities and services donated to the EO from a governmental unit are reported on this line. No other types of in kind donations are reported in the financial data.

Line 7, Other income. In the author's experience, an amount is seldom reported on this line.

Line 9, Exempt function income. This line asks for gross receipts (meaning without reduction for related costs) paid to the organization by participants in charitable, educational, or other exempt activities. Student tuition, hospital charges, publication sales, and laboratory fees are good examples. Unlike on Forms 990, nontaxable unrelated business income is also included here. Fund-raising events and projects, raffles, bingo, thrift shop, and other revenue-producing activities are to be recorded here, except for the donation portion that is put on line 1. Although an explanation is not required, the application is more understandable if the details of this revenue are submitted and coordinated with the answer to Part II, line 11a. For example, the description for exempt function might say:

Tuition charges from students	$100,000
Sale of textbooks	8,000
Student activity fees	10,000
Laboratory usage fees	5,000

Line 11, Capital gains or losses. Property held by an EO as investment or exempt function property constitutes the EO's capital assets. A description of each asset sold, the name of the person to whom it was sold, and the amount received is to be reported in detail for capital transactions. For security sales through a brokerage company, the purchaser is not required. Sales of objects held for resale in both an exempt function and fund-raising context are reported on line 9.

Line 14, Fund-raising expenses. The IRS's concern for this subject is shown by its appearance as the first expense item. However, neither Form 990EZ nor 990PF reflect this item. On Form 990, page 2, the direct costs associated with fund-raising events and inventory sales are deducted against the gross revenue to arrive at total revenue on page 1. However, on Form 1023, it is not clear where such expenses are to be reported. The instructions to this line suggest that "total expenses incurred in soliciting contributions, gifts, grants, etc." be included and logically, cost of goods sold should be included. Some people suggest that such expense be reported on line 22.

Line 15, Grants paid. A schedule is to be attached, showing the name of each recipient, a brief description of the purposes or conditions of payment, and the amount paid. If the organization is new and has made no actual payments, the total amount projected to be paid with a reference back to Part II, line 1 (where the grant program is described) may be suitable. If scholarship grants are planned, this information should be coordinated with Schedule H. Similar information is submitted on Forms 990.

Line 16, Disbursements for members. A schedule should be submitted show-ing the name of each recipient, a brief description of the purposes or conditions of payment, and the amount paid. This category of expense is potentially a "red flag" area. Member benefits must serve a charitable purpose, such as a newslet-ter published for educational purposes. Review the discussions of charitable class at Section 2.2(a) and member benefits at Section 20.9(c).

Line 17, Officer, director and trustee compensation. This line calls for the name of each officer, his or her office or position, the average amount of time devoted to organization per week or month, and the amount of annual compensation. This information should agree with Part II, line 4b. Not for this purpose, but for Forms 990, fringe benefit and expense account information is to be furnished. The question the IRS is asking on this line is whether the compensation is so excessive as to result in private inurement, as discussed in Chapter 20.

Line 18, Employee salaries. All other compensation paid to persons treated as employees for whom income tax is withheld is to be reported on this line. Consultants, accountants, lawyers, and other independent contractors are re-ported on line 22, except for fund-raisers reported on line 14. Again, private benefit could be an issue if the amounts are high in relation to other expenses.

Line 19, Interest expense. Total interest expense, except that paid on a mortgage, is reported here. It is unusual for a new organization to have such expense, except for equipment purchases. If interest is being paid on a loan from a disqualified person, the organization should be prepared to explain how the loan serves its exempt purposes. Details of loans may be furnished as an attachment to the balance sheet, and this answer should be coordinated with line 14 or 15.

Line 20, Occupancy. The total cost of the physical space occupied by the EO for offices and exempt function activities is to be presented, including rent, mortgage interest, taxes, utilities, maintenance, and other costs of the facilities.

Line 21, Depreciation and depletion. Any depreciation and depletion calcu-lated by the organization for accounting purposes goes here. For a private foundation, this expense may raise a question because assets purchased for exempt purposes are treated totally as a charitable disbursement in the year acquired, as explained in Section 15.4(b). No detail is requested here, but line 8 of the balance sheet does ask for details.

Line 22, Other. All other "significant" expenses not listed on some other line are to be reported. The instructions suggest that a single total may be reported if the amount is not substantial. In the interest of avoiding questions that may delay the application process, detail is recommended unless the amount is under five percent of the total and is truly miscellaneous. Use page 2 of Form II, Statement of Functional Expenses on Form 990 (Appendix 27–1) as a guide to the suitable types of expense categories.

Line 24, Excess of revenue over expenses. This excess is not totaled because the amounts may include projections as well as actual results. When actual financial results are reported in columns (a)–(d), this bottom line 24 should tie to line 17, or the total fund balance on the balance sheet for the current tax year.

A balance sheet as of the end of the current tax year is requested. In the example at the beginning of this section, September 30 would be its date. The information is to be presented according to the generally accepted accounting principles used by the organization for maintaining its books and records, although the categories may be different than those reflected on the EO's independent auditor's report. It may also be useful to note that the balance sheet does not segregate assets of an unrelated business activity that are most often shown as investment assets for financial purposes.

Line 1, Cash. All cash assets, including checking, petty cash, savings, money market, and certificates of deposits and U.S. Treasury obligations due in less than one year are included on this line.

Line 2, Accounts receivable. Amounts due to be paid to the EO that arose from the sale of goods or performance of services (related and unrelated) are presented here. For example, a university might report tuition receivable, amounts due on a grant paid on a reimbursement basis, accounts receivable for its literary press, football season ticket holder balances, and insurance reimbursements due to the health center. Charitable gifts payable under a pledge system would be reported on line 10.

Line 3, Inventories. Materials, supplies, and goods purchased or manufactured by the EO and held to be sold or used in some future period are considered inventory. The university's bookstore, science lab, football team, fund-raising department, and property management office might all have inventory. Although items that produce both related and unrelated income are reported here, the proceeds of selling them is reportable either on line 4 or 9 of the Statement of Revenue and Expense.

Line 4–7, Investments. Organizations owning bonds, notes receivable, stocks, buildings, land, mineral interests, or any other investment assets report them on these lines. Details are requested and in the case of stocks, both the book and fair market value must be reported. The instructions should be consulted directly.

Line 8, Buildings and equipment. Real and tangible personal property not held for investment, but used instead for exempt purposes, is reported here. A detailed list of the assets should be attached, along with the depreciation information to coordinate with line 21 of the Expense Statement.

Line 9, Land. Land held for exempt purposes, not for investment, is presented here. Land purchased for exempt use in the future is included if it is not income producing; otherwise, it would be shown as an investment.

Line 12, Accounts payable. Amounts due to be paid to suppliers and others, such as salaries, accrued payroll taxes, and interest accrued on notes payable are reported here.

Line 13, Grants payable. Commitments for grants and contributions to other organizations and individuals due to be paid in the future and booked under the EO's method of accounting (accrual) are reportable as due to be paid.

Line 14, Mortgages and notes payable. Details including the lender, terms for repayment and interest, purpose of the loan, and the original amount, are called for. This line should be coordinated with line 19 on the Expense Statement.

Line 17, Fund balance or net assets. All of the EO's assets are reported in total on the balance sheet. If the organization uses fund accounting, all funds are combined. Likewise, all cash accounts are reported on line 1 and are not segregated by fund.

(e) Special Attachments

The following types of organizations must answer specific questions to enable IRS specialists to satisfy themselves that the organization can qualify for such a category of (c)(3) exemption.

Schedule A: Churches. To preserve the separation of church and state, churches are granted automatic exemption and actually need not file Form 1023. For groups not formed as a part of the established Judeo-Christian religions, proving that they are a church often requires such filing. This schedule's 19 questions are designed to ascertain whether the church meets the IRS's 14-part test discussed in Section 3.2. The questions probe for private benefit to the church's creators.

Schedule B: Schools, college and universities. The special nondiscriminatory requirements for schools are covered in the ten questions asked on this schedule.

Schedule C: Hospitals and medical research organizations. The rules governing the charitable status of hospitals began to evolve in the late 1980s and are still in a state of flux. The evolving rules are presented in Section 4.6. The concerns, as evidenced by the questions, are twofold: provision of health services to the nonpaying public, and private inurement to the physicians. Private benefit in the form of low rents, excessive salaries, or royalties from research patents paid to doctors can prevent exemption, as can profit motive evidenced by lack of indigent care, academic connections, or public interest research.

Schedule D: IRC §509(a)(3) supporting organizations. This part seeks information to prove that the requisite control and relationship exist between the newly-created organization and the public charity it is organized to support (PSO). The rules for qualification as a supporting organization are complex, as indicated by the Code designations, which allow three types:

- An EO operated, supervised, or controlled by the PSO;

- An EO supervised or controlled in connection with the PSO; or

- An EO operated in connection with the PSO.

While Form 1023 seeks information to prove the connection, it does not explain why the questions are asked. See Section 11.5 for a discussion of the distinctions and their implications.

Schedule E: Private operating foundation. A private operating foundation (POF) is a private foundation (PF) that dedicates its assets and its income to self-initiated projects. The typical PF only makes grants to other organizations. A POF may make direct grants, but only in addition to spending the minimally required amounts on its own activities. A POF endowed with $1 million must spend $33,333 annually on projects it institutes and conducts directly with its own staff and facilities.

Schedule E may be difficult to complete without an understanding of certain terms peculiar to PFs. Study Section 15.5 before attempting to calculate the answers. Very generally, a POF must first meet an income test requiring that it spend a minimal amount annually, three and one-third percent of its investment assets, on its direct charitable activities. Secondly, the POF must meet either the asset, endowment, or support test. In brief:

- Asset test: over 65 percent are exempt function assets.

- Endowment test: over three and one-third percent of the average value of investment assets is spent on direct charitable projects.

- Support test: more than 25 percent of support comes from the general public or from five or more other exempts.

Schedule F: Homes for the aged or handicapped. This schedule is largely self-explanatory. See Section 4.6(d) for citations to published rulings on the subject.

Schedule G: Child care organizations. Day care centers must generally answer questions 1, 4 and 5 "Yes," as explained in Section 5.1(c).

Schedule H: Organizations providing scholarship benefits, student aid, etc., to individuals. Private foundations must obtain advance IRS approval of their scholarships plans.[19] The purpose is to establish that individual grants will be made in an objective and nondiscriminatory manner. The form is designed to assure that no favoritism is given to certain individuals, particularly not to family members of founders, directors, trustees, or other interested parties. In addition, plans may not discriminate according to race, creed, or sex.

This schedule is used by new private foundations to seek approval. Although public charities are not required to receive advance permission, they may not make grants that convey private benefit. This form should be completed if IRS approval of a plan is desired.

Schedule I: Successors to "for profit" institutions. A nonprofit organization created to receive the assets and operations of a for-profit entity has the burden of proving that the transfer creates no unacceptable benefits to the for-profit at the expense of the new nonprofit. Private benefit may be indicated by the terms of the deal, the price being paid for the predecessor's assets, liabilities being assumed, excessive rental for privately owned facilities or equipment, and other benefits to insiders or controlling individuals. This schedule fishes for such factors. (See Section 20.9.)

18.4   FORM 8718: USER FEE

A user fee, or filing fee, is due to be paid and attached to Form 8718, User Fee for Exempt Organization Determination Letter Request, and must accompany Forms 1023 and 1024. The IRS will not process the application until the fee is paid, but will send the application back if it is omitted. Submission of a cashier's check payable to the IRS, rather than a bank check requiring clearing, may

---

[19] IRC §4945(g).

speed the process. The charges effective September 30, 1990 through October 1, 1995 are as follows:

- Organizations with gross receipts averaging not more than $10,000 annually = $150

- Gross annual receipts exceed $10,000 = $375

- Group Exemption = $500

- Final letter of termination of private foundation status = $200[20]

Note that the 1990 version of Form 1023 issued by the IRS does not contain Form 8718. (Appendix 18–1, page 326.)

18.5   FORM 1024: EXEMPTION UNDER IRC §501(a)

Form 1024 is filed to seek application for recognition of exemption for organizations exempt under IRC §501 (other than §501(c)(3)) and IRC §120. The instructions to the form and Part I are almost identical for both applications, and the discussion under Section 18.3(a) can be referred to. In Part II, questions 1–5 are basically the same as in Form 1023 except that question 3 is omitted. Section 18.3(b) explains the duplicated questions. Again, the reader should obtain a blank copy of the form to read along with this Section. The completed Form 1024 of a mock organization, the Disposable Bottle Action Committee, is provided as Appendix 18–2.

(a) Special Aspects of Form 1024.

In Part II, beginning with Question 6, there is a perceptible change in tone from Form 1023. The questions begin to probe for information regarding member benefits. Schedules A–M continue to solicit information necessary for qualification for each type of organization. The reasons why these questions are asked, and the rules that have been developed by the IRS and the courts in granting exempt status to some of these entities, are discussed in Chapters 6–10. The reader should also study the parts of IRS Publication 557, Tax-Exempt Status for your Organization, applicable to the particular type of EO the application is being prepared for.

    With Form 1024, it is important to paint a complete picture of the organization and its proposed activities. Membership solicitation materials, brochures, and newsletters are requested as evidence of how the organization presents itself to the public. Such materials can be prepared with a view toward depicting the proposed exempt organization comprehensively and accurately.

[20]Rev. Rul. 90-17, 1990-12, I.R. 9, modified by Rev. Proc. 91-44, 1991-31 I.R.B. 35.

The financial data is to be presented in a similar manner to that required for Form 1023. Consult Section 18.3(d) for suggestions on completion of this part.

(b) Timing

Exempt status for organizations filing Form 1024 does *not* depend upon when the form is filed. The critical need for (c)(3) organizations to file Form 1023 in a timely manner, explained in Section 18.3(c), is absent here, because qualification is a matter of law. If an exempt organization meets the requirements for any category, exempt status is automatically granted with no action on the EO's part. There is no deadline for filing Form 1024.

(c) Verification of Exemption

As a practical matter, even though exemption for non (c)(3)s is automatic without action on the EO's part, many exempt organizations choose to request a determination letter from the IRS to remove any uncertainty. Particularly when an EO plans to enter into unrelated business activity or projects that might be questioned by the IRS, it is prudent to settle the questions early in the life of the EO. Also, filing Form 990 triggers a request for an exemption application in some areas.

Some states also rely upon the federal determination letter to grant exemption for income, franchise, sales, or other tax purposes. Having the federal letter also makes U.S. Postal Service nonprofit bulk mailing permits easier to obtain.

18.6 GETTING A POSITIVE DETERMINATION

Once Form 1023 or 1024 is completed with the kinds of answers the IRS prefers, the next requirement is patience. It normally requires 80 to 120 days to receive a determination letter. If the examining specialist questions any of the facts or circumstances or denies the organization's eligibility for exemption, some methods of responding are more effective than others.

(a) Application Processing System

An IRS notice of receipt, Form 5548 (Exhibit 18–2), may be expected to arrive a month to six weeks from the date of original filing. A case number and contact person are assigned, and an estimated time the case will take to process is provided in the notice of receipt. Subsequent inquiries about the application should be referenced with the case number. Failure to receive such notice means that something is amiss and the Key District should be contacted, particularly if timely filing might be an issue.

At this point, the case has not been assigned to a particular technical specialist. The processing of an application for exemption submitted to a Key District Office is graphically portrayed in Exhibit 18–3, a chart prepared by Jeanne S. Gessay, Chief of Exempt Organizations Rulings Branch II of the IRS National Office in Washington, D.C.

Exhibit 18–2

> ### IRS LETTER FORM 5548: NOTICE OF RECEIPT
>
> ```
> INTERNAL REVENUE SERVICE          DEPARTMENT OF TREASURY
> DISTRICT DIRECTOR
> 1100 COMMERCE STREET
> DALLAS, TX  75242-0000
>                                   Date of this Notice:
>                                      AUG. 10, 1992
>                                   Person to Contact:
>                                      SHARI FLOWERS
>                                   Telephone Number:
>                                      (214) 767-3526
> TEXAS FOUNDATION FOR PSYCHIATRIC   Case Number:
> C/O JODY BLAZEK CPA AND TERRI ROGERS    752219045
> CPA                                File Folder Number
> 3101 RICHMOND AVENUE SUITE 220        750164848
> HOUSTON, TX  77098                 Days to Process:  80
>
>
>
> --
> ```
>
> Application for Recognition of Exemption from Federal Income Tax
>
> We have received your application for recognition of exemption from Federal income tax and have assigned it the case number listed above. You should refer to that number in any communication with us concerning your application.
>
> We will review your application and send you a reply as soon as possible. However, we must process applications in the order that we receive them.
>
> You may normally expect to hear from us within the above processing time. If you do not hear from us within that period and choose to write again, please include a copy of this letter with your correspondence. Also, please provide a telephone number and the most convenient time to call if we need to contact you.
>
> Thank you for your cooperation.
>
> Form 5548

Exhibit 18–3

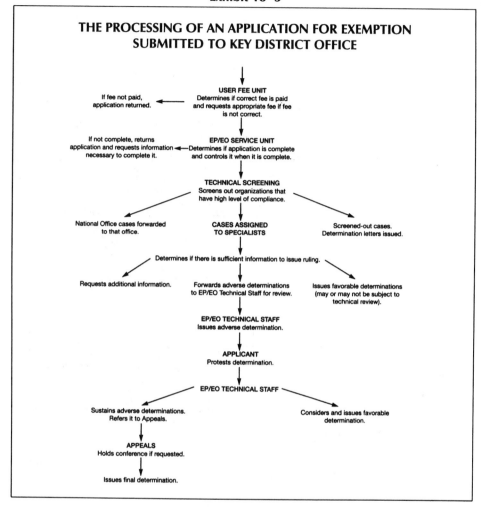

THE PROCESSING OF AN APPLICATION FOR EXEMPTION SUBMITTED TO KEY DISTRICT OFFICE

USER FEE UNIT
Determines if correct fee is paid and requests appropriate fee if fee is not correct.

If fee not paid, application returned.

EP/EO SERVICE UNIT
Determines if application is complete and controls it when it is complete.

If not complete, returns application and requests information necessary to complete it.

TECHNICAL SCREENING
Screens out organizations that have high level of compliance.

National Office cases forwarded to that office.

CASES ASSIGNED TO SPECIALISTS

Screened-out cases. Determination letters issued.

Determines if there is sufficient information to issue ruling.

Requests additional information.

Forwards adverse determinations to EP/EO Technical Staff for review.

Issues favorable determinations (may or may not be subject to technical review).

EP/EO TECHNICAL STAFF
Issues adverse determination.

APPLICANT
Protests determination.

EP/EO TECHNICAL STAFF

Sustains adverse determinations. Refers it to Appeals.

Considers and issues favorable determination.

APPEALS
Holds conference if requested.

Issues final determination.

(b) Best Case Scenario

In the best case scenario, a Determination Letter (Exhibit 18–4) is received within the processing time. This letter may be the single most important piece of paper an exempt organization possesses. It can be furnished to state and local authorities to obtain their tax exemptions. Without it, contributions for (c)(3)s from some sources such as private foundations, are impossible. Obtaining a replacement copy is a time-consuming process.

(c) When Questions are Asked

IRS examining specialists often seek additional information through standard letter 1312 (Exhibit 18–5). Nonsubstantive amendments are often made during this time, and do not alter the effective date of the application in most cases. For

Exhibit 18–4

IRS LETTER FORM 1045: DETERMINATION LETTER

INTERNAL REVENUE SERVICE
DISTRICT DIRECTOR
1100 COMMERCE STREET
DALLAS, TX 75242-0000

DATE: MAY 15, 1992

EARTH DWELLERS
C/O JODY BLAZEK AND TERRI ROGERS CPA
3103 RICHMOND SUITE 220
HOUSTON, TX 77098

DEPARTMENT OF THE TREASURY

Employer Identification Number:
  74-2626286
Contact Person:
  SHARI FLOWERS
Contact Telephone Number:
  (214) 767-3526
Accounting Period Ending:
  August 31
Foundation Status Classification:
  509(a)(1)
Advance Ruling Period Ends:
  November 27, 1991
Advance Ruling Period Ends:
  August 31, 1996
Addendum Applies:
  No

Dear Applicant:

Based on information you supplied, and assuming your operations will be as stated in your application for recognition of exemption, we have determined you are exempt from federal income tax under section 501(a) of the Internal Revenue Code as an organization described in section 501(c)(3).

Because you are a newly created organization, we are not now making a final determination of your foundation status under section 509(a) of the Code. However, we have determined that you can reasonably expect to be a publicly supported organization described in sections 509(a)(1) and 170(b)(1)(A)(vi).

Accordingly, during an advance ruling period you will be treated as a publicly supported organization, and not as a private foundation. This advance ruling period begins and ends on the dates shown above.

Within 90 days after the end of your advance ruling period, you must send us the information needed to determine whether you have met the requirements of the applicable support test during the advance ruling period. If you establish that you have been a publicly supported organization, we will classify you as a section 509(a)(1) or 509(a)(2) organization as long as you continue to meet the requirements of the applicable support test. If you do not meet the public support requirements during the advance ruling period, we will classify you as a private foundation for future periods. Also, if we classify you as a private foundation, we will treat you as a private foundation from your beginning date for purposes of section 507(d) and 4940.

Letter 1045(DO/CG)

Exhibit 18–4 (*continued*)

IRS LETTER FORM 1045: DETERMINATION LETTER

–2–

EARTH DWELLERS

Grantors and contributors may rely on our determination that you are not a private foundation until 90 days after the end of your advance ruling period. If you send us the required information within the 90 days, grantors and contributors may continue to rely on the advance determination until we make a final determination of your foundation status.

If we publish a notice in the Internal Revenue Bulletin stating that we will no longer treat you as a publicly supported organization, grantors and contributors may not rely on this determination after the date we publish the notice. In addition, if you lose your status as a publicly supported organization, and a grantor or contributor was responsible for, or was aware of, the act or failure to act, that resulted in your loss of such status, that person may not rely on this determination from the date of the act or failure to act. Also, if a grantor or contributor learned that we had given notice that you would be removed from classification as a publicly supported organization, then that person may not rely on this determination as of the date he or she acquired such knowledge.

If you change your sources of support, your purposes, character, or method of operation, please let us know so we can consider the effect of the change on your exempt status and foundation status. If you amend your organizational document or bylaws, please send us a copy of the amended document or bylaws. Also, let us know all changes in your name or address.

As of January 1, 1984, you are liable for social securities taxes under the Federal Insurance Contributions Act on amounts of $100 or more you pay to each of your employees during a calendar year. You are not liable for the tax imposed under the Federal Unemployment Tax Act (FUTA).

Organizations that are not private foundations are not subject to the private foundation excise taxes under Chapter 42 of the Internal Revenue Code. However, you are not automatically exempt from other federal excise taxes. If you have any questions about excise, employment, or other federal taxes, please let us know.

Donors may deduct contributions to you as provided in section 170 of the Internal Revenue Code. Bequests, legacies, devises, transfers, or gifts to you of for your use are deductible for Federal estate and gift tax purposes if they meet the applicable provisions of sections 2055, 2106, and 2522 of the Code.

Donors may deduct contributions to you only to the extent that their contributions are gifts, with no consideration received. Ticket purchases and similar payments in conjunction with fundraising events may not necessarily qualify as deductible contributions, depending on the circumstances. Revenue Ruling 67-246, published in Cumulative Bulletin 1967-2, on page 104, gives guidelines regarding when taxpayers may deduct payments for admission to, or other participation in, fundraising activities for charity.

Letter 1045(DO/CG)

Exhibit 18–4 *(continued)*

IRS LETTER FORM 1045: DETERMINATION LETTER

-3-

EARTH DWELLERS

You are not required to file Form 990, Return of Organization Exempt From Income Tax, if your gross receipts each year are normally $25,000 or less. If you receive a Form 990 package in the mail, simply attached the label provided, check the box in the heading to indicate that your annual gross receipts are normally $25,000 or less, and sign the return.

If you are required to file a return you must file it by the 15th day of the fifth month after the end of your annual accounting period. We charge a penalty of $10 a day when a return is filed late, unless there is reasonable cause for the delay. However, the maximum penalty we charge cannot exceed $5,000 or 5 percent of your gross receipts for the year, whichever is less. We may also charge this penalty if a return is not complete. So, please be sure your return is complete before you file it.

You are not required to file federal income tax returns unless you are subject to the tax on unrelated business income under section 511 of the Code. If you are subject to this tax, you must file an income tax return on Form 990-T, Exempt Organization Business Income Tax Return. In this letter we are not determining whether any of your present of proposed activities are unrelated trade or business as defined in section 513 of the Code.

You need an employer identification number even if you have no employees. If an employer identification number was not entered on your application, we will assign a number to you and advise you of it. Please use
that number on all returns you file in all correspondence with the Internal Revenue Service.

If we said in the heading of this letter that an addendum applies, the addendum enclosed is an integral part of this letter.

Because this letter could help us resolve any questions about your exempt status and foundation status, you should keep it in your permanent records.

We have sent a copy of this letter to your representative as indicated in your power of attorney.

If you have any questions, please contact the person whose name and telephone number are shown in the heading of this letter.

Sincerely yours,

Gary O. Booth
District Director

Enclosure(s):
Form 872-C

Letter 1045(DO/CG)

Exhibit 18–5

IRS LETTER FORM 1312: REQUEST FOR INFORMATION

```
INTERNAL REVENUE SERVICE          DEPARTMENT OF THE TREASURY
DISTRICT DIRECTOR
1100 COMMERCE STREET
DALLAS, TX  75242-0000

Date:
                                  Employer Identification
                                  Number:
JUSTICE AND PEACE ACTION FORUM        76-0233671
C/O JODY BLAZEK, CPA              Contact Person:
3101 RICHMOND STE 220                 RICHIE HEIDENREICH
HOUSTON, TX  77098                Contact Telephone Number:
                                      (214) 767-3501
                                  Response Due Date:
                                      September 30, 1992
```

Dear Applicant:

   Before we can determine whether your organization is exempt from Federal income tax, we must have enough information to show that you have met all legal requirements. You did not include the information needed to make that determination on your form 1023, Application for Recognition of Exemption Under Section 501(c)(3) of the Internal Revenue Code.

   To help us determine whether your organization is exempt from Federal income tax, please send us the requested information by the above date. We can then complete our review of your application.

   If we do not hear from you within that time, we will assume you do not want us to consider the matter further and will close your case. In that event, as required by Code section 6104(c), we will notify the appropriate state officials that, based on the information we have, we cannot recognize you as an organization of the kind described in Code section 501(c)(3). As a result, the Internal Revenue Service will treat your organization as a taxable entity. If we receive the information after the response due date, we may ask you to send us a new Form 1023.

   In addition, if you do not provide the requested information in a timely manner, we will consider that you have not taken all reasonable steps to secure the determination you requested. Under Code section 7428(b)(2), your not taking all reasonable steps in a timely manner to secure the determination may be considered as failure to exhaust administrative remedies available to you within the Service. Therefore, you may lose your rights to a declaratory judgment under Code section 7428.

                              Letter 1312(DO/CG)

Exhibit 18–5 (*continued*)

IRS LETTER FORM 1312: REQUEST FOR INFORMATION

-2-

JUSTICE AND PEACE ACTION FORUM

    All information should be furnished over the signature of a
principal officer or other person acting with proper
authorization.

Please mail the information requested in this letter to the
following address:

             Internal Revenue Service
             EP/EO Division - MC 4913 DAEA
             1100 Commerce Street
             Dallas, TX   75242

    If you have any questions, please contact the person whose
name and telephone number are shown in the heading of this
letter.

Thank you for your cooperation.

                      Sincerely yours,

                              Letter 1312(DO/CG)

Exhibit 18–5 *(continued)*

IRS LETTER FORM 1312: REQUEST FOR INFORMATION

-3-

JUSTICE AND PEACE ACTION FORUM

Code section 501(c)(3) precludes exemption for and organization which participates in or intervenes in (including the publishing or distributing of statements) any political campaign on behalf of or in opposition to any candidate for public office. This is frequently referred to as political activity. This is an absolute prohibition. There is no requirement that political activity be substantial.

You state that you never participate nor intervene in political campaigns, never endorse candidates in political campaigns, and never single out any specific legislator. However, in the July 1992 issue of "'Til Justice Reigns," your quote of the month is a derogatory statement about a vice presidential candidate, you congratulated Senator Bentsen on his sharp criticism of the Bush administration, and printed political cartoons.

You state that you conduct no grassroots lobbying; however, in monthly newsletters you select one or two piece of legislation and encourage your members to personally contact their congressional representatives.

It appears that you cannot qualify for exemption under Code section 501(c)(3). It is possible that you might qualify for exemption under Code section 501(c)(4).

If you continue to pursue exemption under Code section 501(c)(3) you must provide the following:

1. All organizations exempt from Federal income tax under Code section 501(c)(3) must meet and organizational test. To meet this test you must amend your Articles of Incorporation. Delete your Article I and replace it with Articles Third, Fifth and Sixth of the enclosed "Draft A." Submit a state approved copy of your amended Articles of Incorporation. If this requires more than 21 days, contact the person named in the heading of this letter.

2. Provide us with a copy of the pre-addressed postcard from Amnesty International which was enclosed in the July 1992 Issue of "'Til Justice Reigns" and in which you urged the reader to sign, date and mail to help in the struggle for human rights.

3. Provide a copy of "'Til Justice Reigns" for each month it has been published since October 15, 1987.

4. Provide schedules of all programs you have conducted or sponsored.

Letter 1312(DC/CG)

Exhibit 18–5 (*continued*)

IRS LETTER FORM 1312: REQUEST FOR INFORMATION

–4–

JUSTICE AND PEACE ACTION FORUM

5. You state that until the election "'Til Justice Reigns" will offer listing of some principles and issues which the USCC board believes are important in the national debate during 1992. Provide copies of all issues that have been published and drafts of those issues that will be published through November 1992.

6. You state that Houston Strategy meetings will be held for upcoming protests corresponding with the Republican Convention August 17-20. Explain your relationship with the sponsoring organization and exactly what your role was in these meetings and the resulting protests.

7. Provide a copy of the 6-11-92 letter to Sen. Bentsen congratulating him on his sharp criticism of the Bush administration's effort to address our nations foster care and child welfare problems.

8. You state that lobbying amounts to less than 8% of your newsletter, less that 5% of staff time and less than 1% of your annual budget, or a few hundred dollars per year. Provide detailed schedules to explain how you arrived at these figures.

9. Complete Form 872-C.

10. Provide copies of all letters sent to legislative bodies since August 1991.

11. If you wish to request consideration under Code section 501(c)(4) you must provide the following:
    a. Complete pages 1-4 of Form 1024.
    b. Answer all of the above questions except #1.
    c. Provide a statement requesting exemption under Code section 501(c)(4) and no further consideration under Code section 501(c)(3).

Letter 1312(DO/CG)

example, the agent might recommend one of the following tactics:

- Amend the charters dissolution or purpose clause to specifically name IRC §501(c)(3) in order to restrict distributions and activities to (c)(3) purposes. In some states, the standard nonprofit charter acceptable to the state does not contain this restriction distinction, which is necessary to meet the federal requirements. Review Section 2.1 concerning charter requirements.

- Change the public status category from §509(a)(2) to §509(a)(1), or vice versa. The IRS policy is to grant §509(a)(1) status in all cases when the EO qualifies for both types of public status. See Chapter 11 for the details of these categories.

- Reclassify sources of support to reflect the deductibility of fund-raising revenues. See Chapter 24.

- Change level of lobbying activity planned and propose classification as a (c)(4) rather than a (c)(3) organization. See Chapter 23.

(d) Eligibility for Exemption Questioned

What if the IRS questions your application? It is extremely important to request the "basis in law" for suggestions made by the IRS specialists. For example, ask why you must have independent outsiders (not staff) on your board. Why must your artists' press satisfy the requirements found in a revenue ruling on a spiritual press? Why does your discussion group have to meet the qualifications for a school? Why can't you criticize the president for sending troops?

Consider seeking the assistance of a knowledgeable professional if the exempt organization is unwilling to make a change or is skeptical about the need for the change. If funds are not available to hire a professional, a volunteer may be found through a public service agency. While most EO specialists are well-trained, helpful, and cooperative, the EO seeking exemption must remember that the rules are broad and vague. The specialists often apply published revenue rulings to judge your newly-established organization, even though it is unique and distinguishable. In these cases, the EO may find knowledgeable advisers particularly useful.

If the examiner suggests a negative answer, submit a well-reasoned brief indicating reasons and citing authority for your position that the EO should be exempt. Before an adverse determination is issued, the case will be reviewed. Your brief can make it easier for the specialist's superior to overturn the recommendation for denial.

The policies followed by the examiners are contained in IRS Manual 7751: *Exempt Organizations Handbook*, Manual 7752: *Private Foundations Handbook*, and the annual *Exempt Organizations Continuing Professional Educational Technical Instruction Program*.

Occasionally, the Key District specialist is unable to consider an application and will refer it to the National Office for determination. Such a referral is made automatically for any type of organization whose exempt status is pending in litigation or is under consideration within the IRS. In the past, hospital reorganizations, publications with advertising, mail-order churches, and other controversial exemptions have been sent to Washington.

(e) Disputed Cases

When the IRS specialist cannot make a favorable determination, there are a number of steps an organization can take. The choice of alternatives is guided primarily by the strength of the case. If the EO clearly qualifies for exemption, but the facts and circumstances are apparently being misunderstood by the examining agent, an appeal may be indicated.

Appeal. Allow the examiner to issue an adverse report denying exemption and follow the appeal procedure. A protest of the determination may be filed within 30 days from the date of the adverse letter. Request a conference in the Appeals Office. See IRS Publication 557, page 3, for more information, and seek competent counsel. Proper appeal procedures must be followed to be able later, if desired, to file an appeal in court.

Amend. If the reasons for denial are curable and negotiations remain amicable, the EO can request (or the IRS may offer) the opportunity to amend the application, altering planned projects or fund-raising activities to eliminate the ones not considered appropriate for an exempt organization. Usually, the EO examiner gives the organization 60 to 90 days to reform itself and essentially resubmit the application. When the EO has already commenced operations and the changes are substantive, the exemption may be granted only prospectively, from the effective date of the changes in operations.

Withdraw. An application can be withdrawn at any time before issuance or denial of a determination letter. The effects of withdrawing an application are outlined by the IRS under three different scenarios. As a rule, the withdrawal cancels previous notice, the time period prior to withdrawal is lost, and a resubmitted application is treated as a new filing, so that exemption will be effective prospectively from the date of resubmission.[21] The IRS considered the following possibilities:

Scenario 1. Form 1023 seeking §501(3)(3) status is timely filed, but is withdrawn. Two years later, the application is resubmitted, asserting that the organization had operated as exempt from "day one" and, therefore, that exemption should be allowed from the original date of filing.

Scenario 2. Same facts as Scenario 1, except that upon withdrawal of the original application, the organization requests treatment as a §501(c)(4) organization.

Scenario 3. A subordinate member of a group exemption withdraws from the group and, within fifteen months of withdrawal, submits an independent application.

In the first two scenarios, exemption is effective only from the date of resubmission. In the third, exemption is effective from the original inclusion in a group continuing on with new timely filing when such notice was required.

Withdrawal may be indicated when an EO has failed to file income tax or other returns that were required of it as a nonexempt organization. Upon withdrawal, no notification is made to the Internal Revenue Service Center.

[21]Rev. Rul. 90-100, 1990-2 C.B. 156.

Upon denial, however, the Center is notified. Procedurally, it is desirable to voluntarily file delinquent returns and to request relief from any penalties for failure to file, rather than being notified of the need to file.

A principal officer or representative with a power of attorney must make a written withdrawal request. No information submitted to the IRS will be returned but it can be used by the IRS in any subsequent examination of the organization's returns or requests.

(f) Declaratory Judgment

When all administrative remedies have been exhausted in negotiating a positive determination of exempt status and the IRS persists in denying exemption, a declaratory judgment may be requested. See IRS Publication 556 for appeals to the courts. It is important to remember that the correct steps must be taken first, and court is the last resort.

18.7 ADVANCE VS. DEFINITIVE RULINGS

In response to Form 1023 or 1024 application, the IRS determines whether the organizational and operational plans of the EO entitle it to be classified as an exempt organization. For Form 1023 filers, a determination is also made as to whether the EO is a public charity, rather than a private foundation. This determination is based either upon the organization's sources of support and revenue, or upon its activities. Churches, schools, hospitals, and certain types of charities listed in Part III, line 9 of Form 1023 qualify as public due to their activities without regard to their support sources. For public status due to sources of support, the determination is either definitive or advance.

(a) Definitive Ruling

A definitive, or final, determination as to public status is issued if two factors are present:

1. Completion of at least an eight month tax year.

2. Suitable support and activity.

Most importantly, the organization must have completed a tax year that includes eight months.[22] Therefore, the choice of fiscal year is important for an EO seeking this type of determination. For example, an entity incorporated in May which adopts a year ending prior to December 31 cannot file timely (within fifteen months after the date of its incorporation) and seek a definitive ruling. Choosing a year ending between December and April would be neces-

[22] Instruction to Form 1023, Part III, line 10, at pg. 5.

sary. The EO can subsequently change its tax year if necessary, according to the rules set out in Chapter 28.

Second, the EO's sources of support and revenue and activities must be clearly and unquestionably suitable for public status. If the ratios are too close or if fund-raising plans are insufficient, the IRS may prefer to make the tentative, or advance, ruling described below.

A final determination is effective until the exempt organization notifies the IRS of a major change in the operations, support, or purposes that reuqires a change in status or until the IRS, upon examination, revokes or changes the status. Contributors can rely upon the final ruling as described in Section 18.8.

(b) Advance Determination

An advance determination is a final determination as to operations and struc- ture, but is tentative as to public vs. private foundation status. An advance ruling is effective for the exempt organization's first five tax years.[23] For all purposes, the exempt organization is considered a public charity during the advance period. Contributors who were not in a position to know that the EO would not qualify for public status are entitled to calculate their income tax deductions based on public status.[24]

Eligibility for advance determination is indicated by two factors.

1. First tax year is less than eight months.

2. Contributions and activities during start-up phase.

The information furnished to the IRS for the newly-created organization must indicate that the organization can reasonably be expected to meet the public support tests. The "pertinent facts and circumstances taken into account by the IRS" include:

Composition of governing body. Is the board made up of persons represent- ing a broad segment of the community in which the charity is organized? Does it include persons having specialized knowledge relevant to the EO's activities? Is the entity a membership organization anticipating a broad base of individual members? A small board made up of major donors indicates private status.

Initial funding. Will the EO's initial funding come from a few contributors or from many? Are the anticipated projects the type that will attract a broad base of support, or are they attractive only to a few contributors? Initial funding from only a few contributors must be offset with anticipated public appeal.

Fund-raising plans. Are concrete solicitation programs implemented or anticipated to reach a broad group of contributors? Are there firm funding commitments from or working relationships established with civic, religious, charitable, or similar community groups?

---

[23]Reg. §1.509(a)-3(d). The regulation provides for a two year advance period because it was adopted prior to passage of the Deficit Reduction Act of 1984, by which Congress extended the period to five years.

[24]Reg. §1.509(a)(3)(e)(2).

Government or public grants. Will part of the revenue be received from governmental agencies or public charities in support of its community services, such as slum clearance and employment opportunity programs?

Membership dues. Will the EO enroll a substantial number of persons in a community, area, profession, or field of special interest as contributing members?

Exempt function revenues. Does the EO plan to conduct exempt activities for which it will charge, such as theater performances, job counseling, or educational classes?[25]

(c) Reporting Back to the IRS

It is important to emphasize the temporary nature of an advance determination, because failure to report at the end of the advance period results in reclassification as a private foundation. An EO holding an advance recognition as a public charity must report back to the Key District Office at the end of its first five years of operation. Under current rules, the EO is to report within 90 days of an advance determination's ending date. Since this step is critical to ongoing public status, the most recent filing deadline should be verified.

Adequate information must be submitted to show whether it has gained the requisite base of public support to receive a final determination of its non-PF status. If the amounts of contributions or exempt function revenues are sufficient, the IRS issues a definitive or permanent ruling. See Chapter 11 for details of revenues qualifying as public support.

In a report entitled *Tax Administration: IRS Can Improve Its Process of Recognizing Tax-Exempt Organizations*, the General Accounting Office (GAO) suggested that the IRS expand its advance ruling follow-ups to include consideration of activities.[26] The GAO report criticizes the IRS for making no effort to look at the manner in which the charities use their support, and recommends that the advance ruling process be expanded to include a review of activities. The GAO observed that "the expenditures data as well as revenue data could provide IRS insight into whether the organization is fulfilling its exempt purpose and whether there are other potential issues, such as private inurement or unreported unrelated business income."

(d) Failure to Meet Support Tests

If the exempt organization fails to meet the public support tests and is reclassified as a private foundation after its advance period, it must pay the excise tax on investment income, plus interest, for income earned during the advance ruling period. Even if the EO receives sufficient public support, failure to report back to the Key District causes the organization to be reclassified as a private foundation. In such a circumstance, the public entity would have to apply to terminate its private foundation status, according to the procedures discussed in Section 12.6.

---

[25] Reg. §1.509(a)-3(d)(3).
[26] GAO/GGD-90-55 (1990).

18.8 RELIANCE ON DETERMINATION LETTER

After a positive determination letter is issued, the exempt organization can rely upon the IRS's approval of its exempt status as long as there are no substantial changes in its purposes, operations, or character. Absent such changes, the IRS can only revoke exemption due to changes in the law or other good causes, and usually can do so only prospectively. Thus, it is very important that Form 1023 accurately portray the proposed operations.

Contributors, however, cannot necessarily rely upon the IRS's original determination of overall exempt status and qualification for public charity status. A critical question for givers and grant makers to publicly supported §501(c)(3)s, particularly private foundations, is whether an organization's status is the same as originally stated in its determination letter. Has a publicly supported organization become a private foundation?

(a) Checking Current Status

Current status must be checked in two different IRS publications. The first place to check on the status of a (c)(3) organization is the IRS master list of exempt organizations, Publication 78, *Cumulative List of Organizations Described in IRC §170(c) of the Internal Revenue Code of 1986*. This publication lists all organizations currently qualifying under IRC §501(c)(3) and indicates their public or private status. The list is issued annually with a semiannual updates and includes organizations qualifying according to the IRS master file.

The second place to check is the Internal Revenue Bulletin. Revocation of exemption and removal from the list is reported to the general public in the weekly Internal Revenue Bulletin in a "deletions list." Until the IRS communicates a deletion, contributors are entitled to rely upon Publication 78 unless the contributor was responsible for or aware of the EO's loss of such status.[27] When the IRS failed to publish notice in the Bulletin when it revoked a school's exemption, the Tax Court ruled that more omission of the school's name from Publication 78 was sufficient notice.[28]

It is important to remember that the reliance cushion is different for insiders or donors who are in a position to be aware of organizational changes. For them, the change in status is effective retroactively to the time the change occurred. A private foundation making a grant to another organization whose revocation has not been announced can rely upon the determination letter, unless the public charity is controlled by the PF.[29]

(b) Names Missing from Publication 78

Absence from the list does not necessarily mean that the entity has lost is exempt status. The IRS automatically excludes organizations that have not filed annual Form 990 (for two years). This policy omits a significant group of charities, including churches and their affiliates, state colleges and universities,

---

[27] Rev. Proc. 82-39, 1982-17 I.R.B. 18; Reg. §1.170A-9(e)(5).
[28] *Estate of Sally H. Clopton*, 93 T.C. 25 (1989).
[29] Rev. Proc. 89-23, 1989-1 C.B. 844.

and those not technically required to file Form 990 because their annual gross revenue is under $25,000. The United States Catholic Conference and some state universities, among others, have specifically sought group exemptions, despite the fact that filing is not required to assure their inclusion in Publication 78.

Individuals and organizations must complete a thorough investigation of a proposed grant recipient's tax status and cannot rely totally upon inclusion in or exclusion from Publication 78. The IRS has reinforced its policy that omission from Publication 78 is sufficient notice of loss of exemption. The omission of nonfilers will continue and the burden to prove exemption on those organization's behalf remains.[30]

(d) Call the IRS

For determinations issued by the Dallas Key District Office, there is a simple way to find answers. By calling the taxpayer information line, (214)-767-3526, the current status of an organization (according to the IRS master file) can be verified over the phone. Presumably, all Key District Offices can furnish similar information. Also, an organization that has lost its determination letter can write to its Key District Office to receive a verification of its continued exempt status. See Chapter 28 for more information regarding communication with the IRS, when to report back to the IRS, and the consequences to donors and tax filing status of an organization that loses its exemption.

18.9 STATE TAX EXEMPTIONS

Many states allow exemption from their income, franchise, licensing fees, property, sales, or other taxes to religious, charitable, and educational organizations and other §501(c) organizations. The process for obtaining such exemptions varies with each state and locality. Each new exempt organization should obtain current information and forms directly from the appropriate state or local authorities.

In Texas, by way of example, the state filing schedule starts when a nonprofit charter is filed with the secretary of state. There is no filing or registration for trusts or unincorporated associations. A status report is next filed with the comptroller of public accounts, indicating which category of federal exemption is being sought. No formal application process is required for exemption. State exemption is automatically granted when the exempt organization furnishes a copy of its federal exemption to the comptroller's office. The EO may furnish a copy of its completed Form 1023 and a letter requesting state exemption, if it desires state recognition prior to receiving the federal approval. Sample letters to and from the comptroller follow as Exhibits 18–6 and 18–7.

The effective date of Texas sales and franchise tax exemption is the date of qualification for §501(c) exemption. If the federal exemption process is delayed one year, a franchise tax may be due to be filed. That tax is refundable once the exemption is approved.

---

[30]G.C.M. 39809.

Exhibit 18–6

SAMPLE LETTER TO THE COMPTROLLER

Blazek, Rogers & Vetterling
CERTIFIED PUBLIC ACCOUNTANTS

3101 Richmond Avenue, Suite 220
Houston, Texas 77098
(713) 523-5739
(FAX) 523-5758

November 23, 1992

Stephanie Medack
Comptroller of Public Accounts
P.O. Box 13528
Austin, Texas 78711

Re: Texas Foundation For Psychiatric Education And Research
    EIN: 74-2631823
    Status Classification :IRC §501(c)(3)

Dear Ms. Medack:

On behalf of our client, we are writing to inform you that Texas Foundation For Psychiatric Education And Research is organized and operated for charitable purposes and has received a determination of exemption from Federal Income Tax as an organization defined under Internal Revenue Code 501(c)(3) as of November 9, 1992. A copy of the Internal Revenue Service determination letter is enclosed for your reference.

We respectfully request that you issue Texas Foundation For Psychiatric Education And Research an exemption from the Texas sales, excise, and use tax pursuant to Section 151.310 of the Texas Tax Code and also that you recognize the organization as exempt from state franchise tax pursuant to Section 171.063 of the Texas Tax Code.

Thank you for your consideration. If we can furnish any additional information, please call on us.

Sincerely,

Terri G. Rogers, Partner

enclosures

Exhibit 18–7

SAMPLE LETTER FROM THE COMPTROLLER

JOHN SHARP
Comptroller

COMPTROLLER OF PUBLIC ACCOUNTS
STATE OF TEXAS
AUSTIN, 78774

June 4, 1992

Sharon Taylor
Blazek, Rogers & Vetterling
3101 Richmond Ave., Ste. 220
Houston, Texas 77098

Dear Ms. Taylor:

We have determined that Earth Dwellers, Taxpayer No. 3-01156-2057-4, qualifies for exemption from state franchise tax and state sales tax. In the event that we have reason to believe that it no longer qualifies for the exemptions, we will notify the registered agent that the exempt status is under review. The franchise tax exemption as a 501(c)(3) organization is effective November 27, 1991.

This corporation also qualifies for exemption from the state and local sales taxes effective the date of this letter as a 501(c)(3) organization. It may now issue an exemption certificate in lieu of the sales tax on taxable items if they relate to the purpose of the exempt organization and are not used for the personal benefit of a private stockholder or individual. The certificate does not require a number to be valid and may be reproduced in any quantity.

If the organization changes its name, Registered Agent or address, it is required to notify the Secretary of State.

If you have questions regarding this matter, please write or call the Exempt Organizations Section at 1-800-531-5441, extension 3-4142. For general tax information, call toll free at 1-800-252-5555. The regular number is 512/463-4600.

Sincerely,

Stefanie B. Medack

Stefanie B. Medack
Exempt Organizations

SBM/sm74

an equal opportunity employer

Two significant cases have considered eligibility for exemption from local sales taxes. The Supreme Court decided in *Jimmy Swaggart Ministries v. Board of Equalization of California*[31] that a sales tax could be imposed upon the sale of religious articles if it is equally imposed on other nonprofit organizations. The arguments focused primarily upon the First Amendment is protection of the free exercise of religion.

In *Texas Monthly, Inc. v. Bullock*, the Supreme Court held that state sales tax exemption for religious publications violates the establishment clause of the First Amendment when religious organizations are the only beneficiaries of the exemption.

Local property tax exemptions may also be available. Some (but not all) §501(c)(3) organizations qualify under the Texas Property Tax Code for exemption. YWCAs and YMCAs have faced challenges to their local property tax exemptions in California and in Oregon, with conflicting results. The primary issue has been the level of free services furnished to the needy. In Utah, a hospital system conglomerate's local property tax exemption was revoked.

Charitable solicitation registration is required in certain municipalities and states, as discussed in Chapter 24.

[31]January 17, 1990.

Appendix 18–1

FORM 1023

<table>
<tr>
<td>Form 1023
(Rev. September 1990)
Department of the Treasury
Internal Revenue Service</td>
<td colspan="2">Application for Recognition of Exemption
Under Section 501(c)(3) of the Internal Revenue Code</td>
<td>OMB No. 1545-0056
If exempt status is
approved, this application
will be open for public
inspection.</td>
</tr>
</table>

Read the instructions for each Part carefully.
A User Fee must be attached to this application.

If the required information and appropriate documents are not submitted along with Form 8718 (with payment of the appropriate user fee), the application may be returned to you.

Part I   Identification of Applicant

1a Full name of organization (as shown in organizing document)	**2** Employer identification number (If none, see instructions.)
CAMPAIGN TO CLEAN UP AMERICA	44 : 4444444

1b c/o Name (if applicable)	**3** Name and telephone number of person to be contacted if additional information is needed
	JODY BLAZEK, CPA

1c Address (number, street, and room or suite no.)	
1111 ANY STREET	(444) 444-4444

1d City or town, state, and ZIP code	**4** Month the annual accounting period ends
HOMETOWN, TX 77777	JUNE

5 Date incorporated or formed	**6** Activity codes (See instructions.)			**7** Check here if applying under section:
May 26, 1992	354	125	402	a ☐ 501(e) b ☐ 501(f) c ☐ 501(k)

8 Did the organization previously apply for recognition of exemption under this Code section or under any other section of the Code? . . . . ☐ Yes   ☒ No
If "Yes," attach an explanation.

9 Has the organization filed Federal income tax returns or exempt organization information returns? . . . . . ☒ Yes   ☐ No
If "Yes," state the form numbers, years filed, and Internal Revenue office where filed.

     990EZ for fiscal year ending June 30, 1992   Austin, Texas

10 Check the box for your type of organization. BE SURE TO ATTACH A COMPLETE COPY OF THE CORRESPONDING DOCUMENTS TO THE APPLICATION BEFORE MAILING.

  a ☒ Corporation— Attach a copy of your Articles of Incorporation, (including amendments and restatements) showing approval by the appropriate State official; also include a copy of your bylaws.   EXHIBIT 1

  b ☐ Trust— Attach a copy of your Trust Indenture or Agreement, including all appropriate signatures and dates.

  c ☐ Association— Attach a copy of your Articles of Association, Constitution, or other creating document, with a declaration (see instructions) or other evidence the organization was formed by adoption of the document by more than one person; also include a copy of your bylaws.

If you are a corporation or an unincorporated association that has not yet adopted bylaws, check here . . . . ▶ ☐

I declare under the penalties of perjury that I am authorized to sign this application on behalf of the above organization and that I have examined this application, including the accompanying schedules and attachments, and to the best of my knowledge it is true, correct, and complete.

Please
Sign   _John J. Environmentalist_ .... President .... April 7, 1993
Here   (Signature)   (Title or authority of signer)   (Date)

For Paperwork Reduction Act Notice, see page 1 of the instructions.

Complete the Procedural Checklist (page 7 of the instructions) prior to filing.

Appendix 18–1

FORM 1023 (*continued*)

Form 1023 (Rev. 9-90)   CAMPAIGN TO CLEAN UP AMERICA   44-4444444   Page **2**

Part II   **Activities and Operational Information**

1   Provide a detailed narrative description of all the activities of the organization—past, present, and planned. **Do not merely refer to or repeat the language in your organizational document.** Describe each activity separately in the order of importance. Each description should include, as a minimum, the following: **(a)** a detailed description of the activity including its purpose; **(b)** when the activity was or will be initiated; and **(c)** where and by whom the activity will be conducted.

Exhibit 2

2   What are or will be the organization's sources of financial support? List in order of size.

Contribution/disqualified person	5	%
Contributions/general public	52	%
Grants/corportion and private foundations	37	%
Exempt function revenues	5	%
Investment income	1 = 100%	

3   Describe the organization's fundraising program, both actual and planned, and explain to what extent it has been put into effect. Include details of fundraising activities such as selective mailings, formation of fundraising committees, use of volunteers or professional fundraisers, etc. Attach representative copies of solicitations for financial support.

The fundraising program will commence with selective mailings and other attempts to reach the general public with brochures, flyers, and news notices. The campaign will seek gifts of money and property, including charitable bequests; a capital fund drive is anticipated, but not yet formalized. A professional fundraising consultant will be hired, but no agreements have been reached (budgeted at $15,000/20,000).

A copy of a sample fundraising letter is attached at Exhibit 3.

Appendix 18–1

FORM 1023 *(continued)*

Form 1023 (Rev. 9-90)   CAMPAIGN TO CLEAN UP AMERICA   44-4444444   Page **3**

Part II **Activities and Operational Information** *(Continued)*

4 Give the following information about the organization's governing body:

a Names, addresses, and titles of officers, directors, trustees, etc.	b Annual Compensation
John J. Environmentalist, President 333 First Steet, Hometown, TX 77777	none
Jane D. Environmentalist, Secretary/Treasurer 333 First Street, Hometown, TX 77777	none
James F. Friend, Vice President 444 Second Street, Hometown, TX 77777	none

c Do any of the above persons serve as members of the governing body by reason of being public officials or being appointed by public officials?. . . . . ☐ **Yes** ☒ **No**
If "Yes," name those persons and explain the basis of their selection or appointment.

d Are any members of the organization's governing body "disqualified persons" with respect to the organization (other than by reason of being a member of the governing body) or do any of the members have either a business or family relationship with "disqualified persons"? (See the specific instructions for line 4d.) . . . . ☐ **Yes** ☒ **No**
If "Yes," explain.

5 Does the organization control or is it controlled by any other organization? . . . . ☐ **Yes** ☒ **No**
Is the organization the outgrowth of (or successor to) another organization, or does it have a special relationship with another organization by reason of interlocking directorates or other factors? . . . . ☐ **Yes** ☒ **No**
If either of these questions is answered "Yes," explain.

6 Does or will the organization directly or indirectly engage in any of the following transactions with any political organization or other exempt organization (other than 501(c)(3) organizations): (a) grants; (b) purchases or sales of assets; (c) rental of facilities or equipment; (d) loans or loan guarantees; (e) reimbursement arrangements; (f) performance of services, membership, or fundraising solicitations; or (g) sharing of facilities, equipment, mailing lists or other assets, or paid employees?. . . . . ☐ **Yes** ☒ **No**
If "Yes," explain fully and identify the other organizations involved.

7 Is the organization financially accountable to any other organization? . . . . ☐ **Yes** ☒ **No**
If "Yes," explain and identify the other organization. Include details concerning accountability or attach copies of reports if any have been submitted.

Appendix 18-1

FORM 1023 *(continued)*

Form 1023 (Rev. 9-90)   CAMPAIGN TO CLEAN UP AMERICA   44-4444444   Page **4**

Part II   **Activities and Operational Information** *(Continued)*

8 What assets does the organization have that are used in the performance of its exempt function? (Do not include property producing investment income.) If any assets are not fully operational, explain their status, what additional steps remain to be completed, and when such final steps will be taken. If "None," indicate "N/A."

The Campaign will acquire computers, desks, office furniture, trash cleaning tools, and other assets to carry out its exempt activities.

9a Will any of the organization's facilities or operations be managed by another organization or individual under a contractual agreement? . . . . ☐ Yes ☒ No

b Is the organization a party to any leases? . . . . ☒ Yes ☐ No

If either of these questions is answered "Yes," attach a copy of the contracts and explain the relationship between the applicant and the other parties. The Campaign will initially sublease office space in its President's office (building owned by unrelated party). A proportionate part of the current rent based upon space actually used by the Campaign will be paid. There is no written lease; the sublease is month-to-month; as funds are available new space will be sought. Considerable cost savings to the Campaign will be gained by this sublease.

10 Is the organization a membership organization? . . . . ☐ Yes ☒ No

If "Yes," complete the following:

a Describe the organization's membership requirements, and attach a schedule of membership fees and dues.

b Describe your present and proposed efforts to attract members, and attach a copy of any descriptive literature or promotional material used for this purpose.

c What benefits do (or will) your members receive in exchange for their payment of dues?

11a If the organization provides benefits, services or products, are the recipients required, or will they be required, to pay for them? . . . . ☐ N/A ☒ Yes & ☒ No

If "Yes," explain how the charges are determined, and attach a copy of your current fee schedule.

Most of the Campaign's educational materials will be distributed free of charge. A minimal charge designed to defray costs will be made for seminars and publications, as projected on line 9 of Part IV.

b Does or will the organization limit its benefits, services or products to specific individuals or classes of individuals? . . . . ☐ N/A ☐ Yes ☒ No

If "Yes," explain how the recipients or beneficiaries are or will be selected.

12 Does or will the organization attempt to influence legislation? . . . . ☒ Yes ☐ No

If "Yes," explain. Also, give an estimate of the percentage of the organization's time and funds which it devotes or plans to devote to this activity. The Campaign may spend up to one percent of its annual budget on legislative activity. See also response to Part II, item 1.

13 Does or will the organization intervene in any way in political campaigns, including the publication or distribution of statements? . . . . ☐ Yes ☒ No

If "Yes," explain fully.

Appendix 18–1

FORM 1023 (continued)

Form 1023 (Rev. 9-90) CAMPAIGN TO CLEAN UP AMERICA   44–4444444   Page 5

Part III   **Technical Requirements**

1 Are you filing Form 1023 within 15 months from the end of the month in which you were created or formed?   ☒ Yes   ☐ No
If you answer "Yes," do not answer questions 2 through 6.

2 If one of the exceptions to the 15-month filing requirement shown below applies, check the appropriate box and proceed to question 7.

Exceptions—You are not required to file an exemption application within 15 months if the organization:

   ☐ **(a)** Is a church, interchurch organization, local unit of a church, a convention or association of churches, or an integrated auxiliary of a church;

   ☐ **(b)** Is not a private foundation and normally has gross receipts of not more than $5,000 in each tax year; or,

   ☐ **(c)** Is a subordinate organization covered by a group exemption letter, but only if the parent or supervisory organization timely submitted a notice covering the subordinate.

3 If you do not meet any of the exceptions in question 2, do you wish to request relief from the 15-month filing requirement? . . . . ☐ Yes   ☐ No

4 If you answer "Yes" to question 3, please give your reasons for not filing this application within 15 months from the end of the month in which your organization was created or formed. (**See the Instructions before completing this item.**)

5 If you answer "No" to both questions 1 and 3 and do not meet any of the exceptions in question 2, your qualification as a section 501(c)(3) organization can be recognized only from the date this application is filed with your key District Director. Therefore, do you want us to consider your application as a request for recognition of exemption as a section 501(c)(3) organization from the date the application is received and not retroactively to the date you were formed? . . . . ☐ Yes   ☐ No

6 If you answer "Yes" to question 5 above and wish to request recognition of section 501(c)(4) status for the period beginning with the date you were formed and ending with the date your Form 1023 application was received (the effective date of your section 501(c)(3) status), check here ▶ ☐ and attach a completed page 1 of Form 1024 to this application.

Appendix 18-1

FORM 1023 *(continued)*

Form 1023 (Rev. 9-90) CAMPAIGN TO CLEAN UP AMERICA   44-4444444   Page **6**

Part III **Technical Requirements** *(Continued)*

7 Is the organization a private foundation?
☐ **Yes** (Answer question 8.)
☒ **No** (Answer question 9 and proceed as instructed.)

8 If you answer "Yes" to question 7, do you claim to be a private operating foundation?
☐ **Yes** (Complete Schedule E)
☐ **No**

After answering this question, go to Part IV.

9 If you answer "No" to question 7, indicate the public charity classification you are requesting by checking the box below that most appropriately applies:

THE ORGANIZATION IS NOT A PRIVATE FOUNDATION BECAUSE IT QUALIFIES:

(a) ☐ As a church or a convention or association of churches (CHURCHES MUST COMPLETE SCHEDULE A).	Sections 509(a)(1) and 170(b)(1)(A)(i)
(b) ☐ As a school (MUST COMPLETE SCHEDULE B).	Sections 509(a)(1) and 170(b)(1)(A)(ii)
(c) ☐ As a hospital or a cooperative hospital service organization, or a medical research organization operated in conjunction with a hospital (MUST COMPLETE SCHEDULE C).	Sections 509(a)(1) and 170(b)(1)(A)(iii)
(d) ☐ As a governmental unit described in section 170(c)(1).	Sections 509(a)(1) and 170(b)(1)(A)(v)
(e) ☐ As being operated solely for the benefit of, or in connection with, one or more of the organizations described in (a) through (d), (g), (h), or (i) (MUST COMPLETE SCHEDULE D).	Section 509(a)(3)
(f) ☐ As being organized and operated exclusively for testing for public safety.	Section 509(a)(4)
(g) ☐ As being operated for the benefit of a college or university that is owned or operated by a governmental unit.	Sections 509(a)(1) and 170(b)(1)(A)(iv)
(h) ☒ As receiving a substantial part of its support in the form of contributions from publicly supported organizations, from a governmental unit, or from the general public.	Sections 509(a)(1) and 170(b)(1)(A)(vi)
(i) ☐ As normally receiving not more than one-third of its support from gross investment income and more than one-third of its support from contributions, membership fees, and gross receipts from activities related to its exempt functions (subject to certain exceptions).	Section 509(a)(2)
(j) ☐ We are a publicly supported organization but are not sure whether we meet the public support test of block (h) or block (i). We would like the Internal Revenue Service to decide the proper classification.	Sections 509(a)(1) and 170(b)(1)(A)(vi) or Section 509(a)(2)

If you checked one of the boxes (a) through (f) in question 9, go to question 14.
If you checked box (g) in question 9, go to questions 11 and 12.
If you checked box (h), (i), or (j), go to question 10.

Appendix 18–1

FORM 1023   (*continued*)

Form 1023 (Rev. 9-90) CAMPAIGN TO CLEAN UP AMERICA	44-4444444	Page 7

Part III **Technical Requirements** *(Continued)*

---

10 If you checked box (h), (i), or (j) in question 9, have you completed a tax year of at least 8 months?

    ☒ Yes—Indicate whether you are requesting:

        ☐ A definitive ruling (Answer questions 11 through 14.)

        ☒ An advance ruling (Answer questions 11 and 14 and attach 2 Forms 872-C completed and signed.)

    ☐ No—You must request an advance ruling by completing and signing 2 Forms 872-C and attaching them to your application.

11 If the organization received any unusual grants during any of the tax years shown in Part IV-A, attach a list for each year showing the name of the contributor; the date and the amount of the grant; and a brief description of the nature of the grant.

---

12 If you are requesting a definitive ruling under section 170(b)(1)(A)(iv) or (vi), check here ▶ ☐ and:

a Enter 2% of line 8, column (e) of Part IV-A _____

b Attach a list showing the name and amount contributed by each person (other than a governmental unit or "publicly supported" organization) whose total gifts, grants, contributions, etc., were more than the amount you entered on line 12a above.

13 If you are requesting a definitive ruling under section 509(a)(2), check here ▶ ☐ and:

a For each of the years included on lines 1, 2, and 9 of Part IV-A, attach a list showing the name of and amount received from each "disqualified person."

b For each of the years included on line 9 of Part IV-A, attach a list showing the name of and amount received from each payer (other than a "disqualified person") whose payments to the organization were more than $5,000. For this purpose, "payer" includes, but is not limited to, any organization described in sections 170(b)(1)(A)(i) through (vi) and any governmental agency or bureau.

14 Indicate if your organization is one of the following. If so, complete the required schedule. (Submit only those schedules that apply to your organization. **Do not submit blank schedules.**)

	Yes	No	If "Yes," complete Schedule:
Is the organization a church?		X	A
Is the organization, or any part of it, a school?		X	B
Is the organization, or any part of it, a hospital or medical research organization?		X	C
Is the organization a section 509(a)(3) supporting organization?		X	D
Is the organization an operating foundation?		X	E
Is the organization, or any part of it, a home for the aged or handicapped?		X	F
Is the organization, or any part of it, a child care organization?		X	G
Does the organization provide or administer any scholarship benefits, student aid, etc.?		X	H
Has the organization taken over, or will it take over, the facilities of a "for profit" institution?		X	I

Appendix 18–1

FORM 1023 (*continued*)

Form 1023 (Rev. 9-90)   CAMPAIGN TO CLEAN UP AMERICA   44-4444444   Page **8**

Part IV   Financial Data

Complete the financial statements for the current year and for each of the 3 years immediately before it. If in existence less than 4 years, complete the statements for each year in existence. If in existence less than 1 year, also provide proposed budgets for the 2 years following the current year.

A.—Statement of Revenue and Expenses

		Current tax year	3 prior tax years or proposed budget for 2 years			
		(a) From 6/92 to 3/93	(b) 1993/94	(c) 1994/95	(d) 1995/96	(e) TOTAL
1	Gifts, grants, and contributions received (not including unusual grants—see instructions)Exh. 4	10,000	60,000	260,000	910,000	1,240,000
2	Membership fees received					
3	Gross investment income (see instructions for definition)	0	500	1,000	10,000	11,500
4	Net income from organization's unrelated business activities not included on line 3					
5	Tax revenues levied for and either paid to or spent on behalf of the organization					
6	Value of services or facilities furnished by a governmental unit to the organization without charge (not including the value of services or facilities generally furnished the public without charge)					
7	Other income (not including gain or loss from sale of capital assets) (attach schedule)					
8	**Total** (add lines 1 through 7)	10,000	60,500	261,000	920,000	1,251,500
9	Gross receipts from admissions, sales of merchandise or services, or furnishing of facilities in any activity that is not an unrelated business within the meaning of section 513		1,000	10,000	40,000	51,000
10	**Total** (add lines 8 and 9)	10,000	61,500	271,000	960,000	1,302,500
11	Gain or loss from sale of capital assets (attach schedule)					
12	Unusual grants					
13	**Total** revenue (add lines 10 through 12)	10,000	61,500	271,000	960,000	1,302,500
14	Fundraising expenses	1,000	10,000	25,000	50,000	
15	Contributions, gifts, grants, and similar amounts paid (attach schedule)					
16	Disbursements to or for benefit of members (attach schedule)					
17	Compensation of officers, directors, and trustees (attach schedule)					
18	Other salaries and wages	2,000	10,000	113,000	410,000	
19	Interest					
20	Occupancy (rent, utilities, etc.)	1,000	2,000	45,000	110,000	
21	Depreciation and depletion			2,000	5,000	
22	Other (attach schedule)Exh. 4	1,000	5,000	41,000	185,000	
23	**Total** expenses (add lines 14 through 22)	5,000	27,000	226,000	760,000	
24	Excess of revenue over expenses (line 13 minus line 23)	5,000	34,500	45,000	200,000	

Revenue — Expenses

Appendix 18–1

FORM 1023 *(continued)*

Form 1023 (Rev. 9-90)	CAMPAIGN TO CLEAN UP AMERICA	44–4444444	Page **9**

Part IV   **Financial Data** *(Continued)*

B.—Balance Sheet (at the end of the period shown)		Current tax year Date March 31, 1993
Assets		
1	Cash	1	5,000
2	Accounts receivable, net	2	
3	Inventories	3	
4	Bonds and notes receivable (attach schedule)	4	
5	Corporate stocks (attach schedule)	5	
6	Mortgage loans (attach schedule)	6	
7	Other investments (attach schedule)	7	
8	Depreciable and depletable assets (attach schedule)	8	
9	Land	9	
10	Other assets (attach schedule)	10	
11	**Total assets** (add lines 1 through 10)	11	5,000
Liabilities		
12	Accounts payable	12	
13	Contributions, gifts, grants, etc., payable	13	
14	Mortgages and notes payable (attach schedule)	14	
15	Other liabilities (attach schedule)	15	
16	**Total liabilities** (add lines 12 through 15)	16	–0–
Fund Balances or Net Assets		
17	Total fund balances or net assets	17	5,000
18	**Total liabilities and fund balances or net assets** (add line 16 and line 17)	18	5,000

If there has been any substantial change in any aspect of your financial activities since the end of the period shown above, check the box and attach a detailed explanation . . . . ▶ ☐

Appendix 18–1

FORM 1023 *(continued)*

Form **872-C** (Revised 9-90) Department of the Treasury Internal Revenue Service	**Consent Fixing Period of Limitation Upon Assessment of Tax Under Section 4940 of the Internal Revenue Code** (See instructions on reverse side.)	OMB No. 1545-0056 To be used with Form 1023. Submit in duplicate.

Under section 6501(c)(4) of the Internal Revenue Code, and as part of a request filed with Form 1023 that the organization named below be treated as a publicly supported organization under section 170(b)(1)(A)(vi) or section 509(a)(2) during an advance ruling period,

CAMPAIGN TO CLEAN UP AMERICA
(Exact legal name of organization as shown in organizing document)

1111 ANY STREET
HOMETOWN, TX 77777
(Number, street, city or town, state, and ZIP code)

} and the

District Director of Internal Revenue, or Assistant Commissioner (Employee Plans and Exempt Organizations)

Consent and agree that the period for assessing tax (imposed under section 4940 of the Code) for any of the 5 tax years in the advance ruling period will extend 8 years, 4 months, and 15 days beyond the end of the first tax year.

However, if a notice of deficiency in tax for any of these years is sent to the organization before the period expires, the time for making an assessment will be further extended by the number of days the assessment is prohibited, plus 60 days.

Ending date of first tax year .....June 30, 1992.................
(Month, day, and year)

Name of organization (as shown in organizing document) CAMPAIGN TO CLEAN UP AMERICA	Date April 7, 1993
Officer or trustee having authority to sign Signature ► *John J. Environment*	
For IRS use only	
District Director or Assistant Commissioner (Employee Plans and Exempt Organizations)	Date

By ►

For Paperwork Reduction Act Notice, see page 1 of the Form 1023 Instructions.

Appendix 18-1

FORM 1023 (*continued*)

You must complete this form and attach it to your application if you checked box (h), (i), or (j) of Part III, question 9, and you have not completed a tax year of at least 8 months.

> For example: If you incorporated May 15 and your year ends December 31, you have completed a tax year of only 7½ months. Therefore, Form 872-C must be completed.

(a) Enter the name of the organization. This must be entered exactly as it is written in the organizing document. Do not use abbreviations unless the organizing document does.

(b) Enter the current address.

(c) Enter ending date of first tax year.

>   For example:

>   (a) If you were formed on June 15 and you have chosen December 31, as your year end, enter December 31, 19 ....

>   (b) If you were formed June 15 and have chosen June 30 as your year end, enter June 30, 19 .... In this example your first tax year consists of only 15 days.

(d) The form must be signed by an authorized officer or trustee, generally the President or Treasurer.

(e) Enter the date that the form was signed.

DO NOT MAKE ANY OTHER ENTRIES.

FORM 1023 (*continued*)

Form **2848** (Rev. March 1991) Department of the Treasury Internal Revenue Service	**Power of Attorney and Declaration of Representative** ▶ For Paperwork Reduction and Privacy Act Notice, see the Instructions.	OMB No. 1545-0150 Expires 5-31-93

Part I Power of Attorney

1 Taxpayer Information

Taxpayer name(s) and address (Please type or print.) CAMPAIGN TO CLEAN UP AMERICA 1111 Any Street Hometown, TX 77777	Social security number(s) Daytime telephone number ( )	Employer identification number 44-4444444 Plan number (if applicable)

hereby appoint(s) the following representative(s) as attorney(s)-in-fact:

2 Representative(s) (Please type or print.)

Name and address	
Jody Blazek, CPA 3101 Richmond, Suite 220 Houston, TX 77098	CAF No. 7800-88888R Telephone No. (713) 523-5739 Fax No. (713) 523-5758 Check if new: Address ☐ Telephone No. ☐
Terri Grigsby Rogers, CPA 3101 Richmond, Suite 220 Houston, TX 77098	CAF No. 7800-66666R Telephone No. (713) 523-5798 Fax No. (713) 523-5758 Check if new: Address ☐ Telephone No. ☐
Name and address	CAF No. Telephone No. ( ) Fax No. ( ) Check if new: Address ☐ Telephone No. ☐

to represent the taxpayer(s) before the Internal Revenue Service for the following tax matters:

3 Tax Matters

Type of Tax (Income, Employment, Excise, etc.)	Tax Form Number (1040, 941, 720, etc.)	Year(s) or Period(s)
Exempt Organization under IRC 501(c)(3)	Form 1023 Form 990	1991-1995

4 Specific Use Not Recorded on Centralized Authorization File (CAF).—If the power of attorney is for a specific use not recorded on CAF, please check this box. (See the instructions for *Specific Use Not Recorded on CAF* on page 4.) . . . . ▶ ☐

5 Acts Authorized.—The representatives are authorized to receive and inspect confidential tax information and to perform any and all acts that I can perform with respect to the tax matters described in line 3, for example, the authority to sign any agreements, consents, or other documents. The authority does not include the power to receive refund checks or the power to sign certain returns. (See instructions.)
List any specific additions or deletions to the acts otherwise authorized in this power of attorney: ....

Note: *In general, an unenrolled preparer of tax returns cannot sign any document for a taxpayer. See Revenue Procedure 81-38, printed as Pub. 470, for more information.*

Note: *The tax matters partner/person of a partnership or S corporation is not permitted to authorize representatives to perform certain See the instructions for more information.*

6 Receipt of Refund Checks.—If you want to authorize a representative named in line 2 to receive, **BUT NOT TO ENDORSE OR CASH,** refund checks, initial here _____ and list the name of that representative below.

Name of representative to receive refund check(s) ▶

Cat. No. 11980J   Form **2848** (Rev. 3-91)

Appendix 18–1

FORM 1023 *(continued)*

CAMPAIGN TO CLEAN UP AMERICAN   EIN # 44-4444444

Form 2848 (Rev. 3-91)   Page **2**

7 Notices and Communications.—Notices and other written communications will be sent to the first representative listed in line 2.
  a If you want the second representative listed to receive such notices and communications, check this box . . . . ▶ ☐
  b If you do not want any notices or communications sent to your representative, check this box . . . . ▶ ☐
8 Retention/Revocation of Prior Power(s) of Attorney.—The filing of this power of attorney automatically revokes all earlier power(s) of attorney on file with the Internal Revenue Service for the same tax matters and years or periods covered by this document. If you do not want to revoke a prior power of attorney, check here . . . . ▶ ☐
    YOU MUST ATTACH A COPY OF ANY POWER OF ATTORNEY YOU WANT TO REMAIN IN EFFECT.
9 Signature of Taxpayer(s).—If a tax matter concerns a joint return, both husband and wife must sign if joint representation is requested, otherwise, see the instructions. If signed by a corporate officer, partner, guardian, tax matters partner/person, executor, receiver, administrator, or trustee on behalf of the taxpayer, I certify that I have the authority to execute this form on behalf of the taxpayer.
  ▶ **If this power of attorney is not signed, it will be returned.**

Signature	4.7.93 *Date*	President *Title (if applicable)*
Print Name		
Signature	*Date*	*Title (if applicable)*
Print Name		

Part II   Declaration of Representative

Under penalties of perjury, I declare that:

  • I am not currently under suspension or disbarment from practice before the Internal Revenue Service;
  • I am aware of regulations contained in Treasury Department Circular No. 230 (31 CFR, Part 10), as amended, concerning the practice of attorneys, certified public accountants, enrolled agents, enrolled actuaries, and others;
  • I am authorized to represent the taxpayer(s) identified in Part I for the tax matter(s) specified there; and
  • I am one of the following:
  a Attorney—a member in good standing of the bar of the highest court of the jurisdiction shown below.
  b Certified Public Accountant—duly qualified to practice as a certified public accountant in the jurisdiction shown below.
  c Enrolled Agent—enrolled as an agent under the requirements of Treasury Department Circular No. 230.
  d Officer—a bona fide officer of the taxpayer organization.
  e Full-Time Employee—a full-time employee of the taxpayer.
  f Family Member—a member of the taxpayer's immediate family (*i.e.*, spouse, parent, child, brother, or sister).
  g Enrolled Actuary—enrolled as an actuary by the Joint Board for the Enrollment of Actuaries under 29 U.S.C. 1242 (the authority to practice before the Service is limited by section 10.3(d)(1) of Treasury Department Circular No. 230).
  h Unenrolled Return Preparer—an unenrolled return preparer under section 10.7(a)(7) of Treasury Department Circular No. 230.
▶ **If this power of attorney is not signed, it will be returned.**

Designation —Insert above letter (a–h)	Jurisdiction (state) or Enrollment Card No.	Signature	Date
b	Texas		4.6.93
b	Texas		4.6.93

OBTAINING RECOGNITION OF EXEMPT STATUS

Appendix 18–1

FORM 1023 *(continued)*

| Form **8718**
(Rev. October 1990)
Department of the Treasury
Internal Revenue Service | **User Fee for Exempt Organization**
Determination Letter Request
▶ Attach this form to determination letter application.
(Form 8718 is NOT a determination letter application) | **For IRS Use Only**
Control number _____
Amount paid _____
User fee screener _____ |

1 Name of organization

CAMPAIGN TO CLEAN UP AMERICA   EIN # 44-4444444

2 Type of request (check only one box and include a check or money order made payable to Internal Revenue Service for the amount of the indicated fee): **Fee**

a ☐ Initial request for an exempt organization determination letter (do NOT use for a pension plan determination letter) by an organization whose annual gross receipts have not exceeded (or are not expected to exceed) $10,000, averaged over the preceding four taxable years, or new organizations which anticipate annual gross receipts averaging not more than $10,000 during their first four years. If you check this box you must complete the income certification below . . . . **$ 150**

Certification

I hereby certify that the annual gross receipts of .... have not
                                                    (enter name of organization)
exceeded (or are not expected to exceed) $10,000, averaged over the preceding four (or the first four) years of

operation.

Signature ▶ .... Title ....

b ☒ Initial request for an exempt organization determination letter (do NOT use for a pension plan determination letter) by an organization whose annual gross receipts have exceeded (or are expected to exceed) $10,000, averaged over the preceding four taxable years, or a new organization which anticipates annual gross receipts averaging more than $10,000 during their first four years . . . . **$ 375**

c ☐ Private foundation which has completed a section 507 termination and which seeks a determination letter that it is now a public charity . . . . **$ 200**

d ☐ Group exemption letters . . . . **$ 500**

Instructions

The Omnibus Budget Reconciliation Act of 1990 requires payment of a user fee for determination letter requests submitted to the Internal Revenue Service. The fee must accompany each request submitted to a key district office.

The fee for each type of request for an exempt organization determination letter is listed in item 2 of this form. Check the block that describes the type of request you are submitting, and attach this form to the front of your request form along with a check or money order for the amount indicated. Make the check or money order payable to the Internal Revenue Service.

Determination letter requests received with no payment or with an insufficient payment will be returned to the applicant for submission of the proper fee. To avoid delays in receiving a determination letter,

be sure that your application is sent to the applicable address shown below. These addresses supersede the addresses listed in Publication 557 and all application forms.

If entity is in this IRS District ▼	Send fee and request for determination letter to this address ▼
Albany, Augusta, Boston, Brooklyn, Buffalo, Burlington, Hartford, Manhattan, Portsmouth, Providence	Internal Revenue Service EP/EO Division P. O. Box 1680, GPO Brooklyn, NY 11202
Baltimore, District of Columbia, Pittsburgh, Richmond, Newark, Philadelphia, Wilmington, any U.S. possession or foreign country	Internal Revenue Service EP/EO Division P. O. Box 17010 Baltimore, MD 21203
Cincinnati, Cleveland, Detroit, Indianapolis, Louisville, Parkersburg	Internal Revenue Service EP/EO Division P. O. Box 3159 Cincinnati, OH 45201

Albuquerque, Austin, Cheyenne, Dallas, Denver, Houston, Oklahoma City, Phoenix, Salt Lake City, Wichita	Internal Revenue Service EP/EO Division Mail Code 4950 DAL 1100 Commerce Street Dallas, TX 75242
Atlanta, Birmingham, Columbia, Ft. Lauderdale, Greensboro, Jackson, Jacksonville, Little Rock, Nashville, New Orleans	Internal Revenue Service EP/EO Division P.O. Box 941 Atlanta, GA 30370
Anchorage, Boise, Las Vegas, Los Angeles, Honolulu, Portland, Laguna Niguel, San Jose, Seattle	Internal Revenue Service EP/EO Division Room 5127, P. O. Box 486 Los Angeles, CA 90053-0486
Sacramento, San Francisco	Internal Revenue Service EO Application Receiving Stop SF 4446 P. O. Box 36001 San Francisco, CA 94102
Aberdeen, Chicago, Des Moines, Fargo, Helena, Milwaukee, Omaha, St. Louis, St. Paul, Springfield	Internal Revenue Service EP/EO Division 230 S. Dearborn DPN 20-5 Chicago, IL 60604

Attach Check or Money Order Here

Attaching a money order, rather than a check, may speed up the processing time.

*U.S. Government Printing Office: 1991 — 618-198/40438   Form **8718** (Rev. 10-90)

Appendix 18–1

FORM 1023 *(continued)*

Letter of Conformance, Articles of Incorporation, and Bylaws

CAMPAIGN TO CLEAN UP AMERICA   EIN #44-4444444

I swear that the attached copies of the articles of incorporation and bylaws of the Campaign to Clean Up America are true and correct copies of the originally executed documents.

4.7.93
Date

Authorized officer

Exhibit 1, page 1

FORM 1023 (*continued*)

DJ –CH

The State of Texas
Secretary of State

CERTIFICATE OF INCORPORATION

OF

CAMPAIGN TO CLEAN UP AMERICA
CHARTER NUMBER 01233017

THE UNDERSIGNED, AS SECRETARY OF STATE OF THE STATE OF TEXAS, HEREBY CERTIFIES THAT THE ATTACHED ARTICLES OF INCORPORATION FOR THE ABOVE NAMED CORPORATION HAVE BEEN RECEIVED IN THIS OFFICE AND ARE FOUND TO CONFORM TO LAW.

ACCORDINGLY, THE UNDERSIGNED, AS SECRETARY OF STATE, AND BY VIRTUE OF THE AUTHORITY VESTED IN THE SECRETARY BY LAW, HEREBY ISSUES THIS CERTIFICATE OF INCORPORATION.

ISSUANCE OF THIS CERTIFICATE OF INCORPORATION DOES NOT AUTHORIZE THE USE OF A CORPORATE NAME IN THIS STATE IN VIOLATION OF THE RIGHTS OF ANOTHER UNDER THE FEDERAL TRADEMARK ACT OF 1946, THE TEXAS TRADEMARK LAW, THE ASSUMED BUSINESS OR PROFESSIONAL NAME ACT OR THE COMMON LAW.

DATED MAY 26, 1992

John Hannah Jr
Secretary of State

Exhibit 1, page 2

FORM 1023 *(continued)*

ARTICLES OF INCORPORATION
OF
CAMPAIGN TO CLEAN UP AMERICA

I,   the undersigned natural person of the age of eighteen
(18) years or more, acting as incorporator of a corporation
under the Texas Non-Profit Corporation Act, do hereby adopt the
following Articles of Incorporation for such Corporation.

ARTICLE ONE
Name

The name of the Corporation is CAMPAIGN TO CLEAN UP AMERICA.

ARTICLE TWO
Nonprofit Corporation

The Corporation is a nonprofit corporation.

ARTICLE THREE
Duration

The period of the Corporation's duration is perpetual.

ARTICLE FOUR
Purposes

Section 4.01. The Corporation is organized exclusively for
charitable, scientific and educational purposes as defined in
Section 501(c)(3) of the Internal Revenue Code. These activities
shall include but not be limited to acquiring by gifts and donations funds to be donated to other charitable entities as defined
in Section 501 (c)(3).

Section 4.02. Notwithstanding any other provision of these
Articles of Incorporation:

a. No part of the net earnings of the Corporation shall
inure to the benefit of any director of the Corporation,
officer of the Corporation, or any private individual
(except that reasonable compensation may be paid for services rendered to or for the Corporation affecting one or
more of its purposes); and no director, officer or any
private individual shall be entitled to share in the distribution of any of the corporate assets on dissolution of the
Corporation. No substantial part of the activities of the
Corporation shall be the carrying on of propaganda, or
otherwise attempting to influence legislation, and the
Corporation shall not participate in, or intervene in
(including the publication or distribution of statements)
any political campaign on behalf of any candidate for
public office.

Exhibit 1, page 3

1

FORM 1023 *(continued)*

b. The Corporation shall not conduct or carry on any activities not permitted to be conducted or carried on by an organization exempt from taxation under Section 501(c)(3) of the Internal Revenue Code and its Regulations as they now exist or as they may hereafter be amended, or by an organization, contributions to which are deductible under 170(c)(2) of the Internal Revenue Code and Regulations as they now exist or as they may hereafter be amended.

c. Upon dissolution of the Corporation or the winding up of its affairs, the assets of the Corporation shall be distributed exclusively to charitable organizations which would then qualify under the provisions of Section 501(c)(3) of the Internal Revenue Code and its Regulations as they now exist or as they may hereafter be amended.

d. The Corporation is organized pursuant to the Texas Non-Profit Corporation Act and does not contemplate pecuniary gain or profit and is organized for nonprofit purposes.

ARTICLE FIVE
Membership

The Corporation shall have no voting members.

ARTICLE SIX
Initial Registered Office and Agent

The street address of the initial registered office of the Corporation is CAMPAIGN TO CLEAN UP AMERICA and the name of its initial registered agent is John J. Environmentalist.

ARTICLE SEVEN
Directors

The number of Directors constituting the initial Board of Directors of the Corporation is three (3), and the names and addresses of those people who are to serve as the initial Directors are:

Name	Address
John J. Environmentalist	333 First Street Hometown, TX 77777
Jane D. Environmentalist	333 First Street Hometown, TX 77777
James F. Friend	444 Second Street Hometown, TX 77777

2

Exhibit 1, page 4

Appendix 18–1

FORM 1023 (*continued*)

ARTICLE EIGHT
Indemnification_of_Directors_and_Officers

Each Director and each officer or former Director or officer of the Corporation may be indemnified and may be advanced reasonable expenses by the Corporation against liabilities imposed upon him or her and expenses reasonably incurred by him or her in connection with any claim against him or her, or any action, suit or proceeding to which he or she may be a party by reason of his or her being, or having been, such Director or officer and against such sum as independent counsel selected by the Directors shall deem reasonable payment made in settlement of any such claim, action, suit or proceeding primarily with the view of avoiding expenses of litigation; provided, however, that no Director or officer shall be indemnified (a) with respect to matters as to which he or she shall be adjudged in such action, suit or proceeding to be liable for negligence or misconduct in performance of duty, (b) with respect to any matters which shall be settled by the payment of sums which independent counsel selected by the Directors shall not deem reasonable payment made primarily with a view to avoiding expense of litigation, or (c) with respect to matters for which such indemnification would be against public policy. Such rights of indemnification shall be in addition to any other rights to which Directors or officers may be entitled under any bylaw, agreement, corporate resolution, vote of Directors or otherwise. The Corporation shall have the power to purchase or maintain at its cost and expense insurance on behalf of such persons to the fullest extent permitted by this Article and applicable state law.

ARTICLE NINE
Limitation_on_Scope_of_Liability

No Director shall be liable to the Corporation for monetary damages for an act or omission in the Director's capacity as a Director of the Corporation, except and only for the following:

a. A breach of the Director's duty of loyalty to the Corporation;

b. An act or omission not in good faith by the Director or an act or omission that involves intentional misconduct or knowing violation of the law by the Director;

c. A transaction from which the Director gained any improper benefit whether or not such benefit resulted from an action taken within the scope of the Director's office; or

d. An act or omission by the Director for which liability is expressly provided by statute.

3

Exhibit 1, page 5

Appendix 18–1

FORM 1023 *(continued)*

```
                    ARTICLE  TEN
                    Incorporator
```

The name and street address of the incorporator is:

Name	Address
John J. Environmentalist	333 First Street Hometown, TX 77777

In witness whereof, I have hereunto set my hand, this _2/ 8+_ of May, 1992.

John J. Environmentalist ·

```
STATE OF TEXAS
COUNTY OF HARRIS
```

Before me, a Notary Public, on this _21ˢᵗ_ day of May, 1992 personally appeared John J.Environmentalist who being duly sworn by me first, declared that he is the person who signed the foregoing document as an incorporator, and that the statements therein contained are true and correct.

Sharon Joy Taylor
Notary Public in and for
Harris County,
State of Texas.

SHARON JOY TAYLOR
Notary Public, State of Texas
My Commission Expires
DECEMBER 20, 1995.

4

Exhibit 1, page 6

Appendix 18–1

FORM 1023 *(continued)*

EIN # 44-4444444

BYLAWS
OF

CAMPAIGN TO CLEAN UP AMERICA

ARTICLE I

<u>Name</u> of <u>Corporation</u>   A Texas nonprofit corporation named Campaign to Clean Up America (the "Campaign") has been established and its principal office is in Hometown, Texas.

ARTICLE II

<u>Purposes</u>   The Campaign is organized exclusively for charitable and educational purposes as defined in Internal Revenue Code §501(c)(3).

ARTICLE III

<u>Members</u>   The Campaign will have no voting members.

ARTICLE IV

<u>Board</u> of <u>Directors</u>   The Campaign's affairs shall be managed by its Board of Directors.

There shall be no less than three (3) nor more than nine (9) directors who will serve one year terms. Directors shall be self-perpetuating and shall elect new directors at the annual meeting. Any Director may resign by giving written notice to the other directors. The resignation shall be effective at the next regular meeting of the Board of Directors. A Director may be removed with or without cause by the other directors. Replacement directors will be named by the directors.

Exhibit 1, page 7

Appendix 18–1

FORM 1023 (*continued*)

CAMPAIGN TO CLEAN UP AMERICA   EIN #44-4444444

ARTICLE IV, continued

Directors shall not receive compensation for their services as directors but can receive reimbursement for expenses and can be engaged to perform other services for the Campaign as long as the compensation is not excessive as that term is used in IRC §4941(d)(2)(E).

ARTICLE V

Meetings of the Board   The Board of Directors shall have one annual meeting. Special meetings, as needed, may be called by the president. Notice of the meeting should be given ten days in advance either in writing or by telephone. Attendance at the meeting shall constitute waiver of notice except where a Director attends the meeting with the express purpose of objecting to the transaction of any business because the meeting is not lawfully called or convened.

A majority of the directors present at any meeting shall constitute the quorum for purposes of transacting any business of the Campaign. A Director may vote in person or by proxy executed in writing. A proxy shall be valid for three months from date of execution and is irrevocable.

ARTICLE VI

Officers   The officers of the Campaign shall consist of a President, a Vice President/Treasurer, and a Secretary. The officers of the Campaign shall be elected by the Board of Directors at the annual meeting. Any officer of the Corporation may be removed by a vote of the majority of the Board of Directors then in office.

President   The President shall supervise and conduct Campaign activities and operations. He or she shall preside at all meetings and shall keep the Board informed concerning the activities of the Campaign. He or she may sign, in the name of the Campaign, all contracts and documents authorized by the Board. He or she shall have the authority to establish committees and to appoint members to serve on such committees.

Exhibit 1, page 8

Appendix 18-1

FORM 1023 *(continued)*

CAMPAIGN TO CLEAN UP AMERICA   EIN #44-4444444

ARTICLE VI, continued.

    <u>Vice</u> <u>President</u>   The Vice President shall have such powers and duties delegated to him or her by the President. He or she will serve as president during the absence of the President.

    <u>Secretary.</u>   The Secretary shall act as Secretary of all meetings of the Board of Directors, and shall keep the minutes of all such meetings. He or she shall attend to the giving and serving of all notices of the Campaign. He or she shall perform all duties customarily incident to the office of Secretary.

    <u>Treasurer</u>   The Treasurer shall have custody of all funds and securities of the Campaign. He or she shall keep or cause to be kept full and accurate accounts of receipts and disbursements of the Campaign and shall deposit all moneys and other valuable effects of the Campaign in such banks or depositories as the Board of Directors may designate.

ARTICLE VII

<u>General</u> <u>Provisions</u>   <u>Contracts.</u>   The Board of Directors may authorize any officer or officers to enter into any contract on behalf of the Campaign; such authority must be in writing.

    <u>Checks,</u> <u>Drafts,</u> <u>etc.</u>   All checks, drafts and other orders for payment of money shall be signed by Board designated officers.

    <u>Gifts.</u>   The Board of Directors may accept on behalf of the Campaign any contribution, gift, bequest of devise for general purposes or for any special purpose of the Campaign.

    <u>Books.</u>   There shall be kept at the office of the Campaign correct books of account of the activities and transactions of the Campaign, including a minute book which shall contain a copy of the Articles of Incorporation, these bylaws and all minutes of the meetings of the Board of Directors.

Exhibit 1, page 9

Appendix 18–1

FORM 1023 *(continued)*

CAMPAIGN TO CLEAN UP AMERICA   EIN #44-4444444

ARTICLE VII, continued

Indemnification. The Directors shall be indemnified by the Campaign against liabilities imposed upon them and expenses reasonably incurred by them in connection with any claim against them, or any action, suit or proceeding to which they may be a party by reason of their being a director. No director is indemnified (a) with respect to matters for which they shall be adjudged in such action, suit or proceeding to be liable for negligence or misconduct in performance of duty, (b) with respect to any matters which shall be settled by the payment of sums which independent counsel selected by the member(s) shall not deem reasonable payment made primarily with a view to avoiding expense of litigation, or (c) with respect to matters for which such indemnification would be against public policy.

Fiscal Year. The year shall be from July 1 to June 30.

Amendments. The directors may amend the bylaws at any regular or special meeting prior to which proper notice was given.

CERTIFICATE

I HEREBY CERTIFY that the foregoing is a true, complete and correct copy of the Bylaws of Campaign to Clean Up America, a Texas nonprofit corporation, in effect on the date hereof.

IN WITNESS WHEREOF, I hereunto set my hand this 4 day of April, 1993.

Jane Environmentalist
Secretary

Exhibit 1, page 10

Appendix 18–1

FORM 1023 *(continued)*

Activity Description

CAMPAIGN TO CLEAN UP AMERICA   EIN #44-4444444
Attachment to Form 1023
PART II, Question 1

The purpose of the Campaign to Clean Up America ("Campaign") is to rid the cities, towns, suburbs, and other areas of the United States of trash, debris, and other litter, as the name of the organization indicates. It is the vision of those who have formed the organization that the beauty of the landscapes of this country should not be tarnished, or hidden, by accumulations of garbage and other trash.

It is the Campaign's belief that much of the solution to the nation's trash problem lies in individuals' attitudes and mindsets. An area that is clean is less likely to be trashed than one that is already littered. A community where its occupants are sensitized to the litter accumulation problem is less likely to be full of trash than the one where its occupants have subconsciously repressed the ugly sights. A community whose members are willing to rid the area of trash, and keep it that way, will be a far more beautiful place to live and work, and be proud of, than one that is constantly strewn with litter.

VOLUNTEER TEAMS: The Campaign will focus on the prevention of littering and the pick-up of litter where it is found. As to the latter, the Campaign will, on a community-by-community basis, organize teams of volunteers who will pick up trash so as to keep their community clean and scenic. It will supply these teams with the equipment necessary to achieve this end, including rakes, shovels, gloves, trash bags, and safety signs to alert traffic that Clean Up America teams are at work in their community. If funding permits, the Campaign will provide members of these teams with *CLEAN UP AMERICA* tee-shirts, to both stimulate spirit in their volunteer work and advertise the program of the Campaign.

The Campaign will provide these teams with information as to organizational techniques, safety matters, and ideas for coordinating their efforts with local governmental officials. This latter aspect will also be of importance in organizing means of trash disposal. The Campaign will also provide the teams with practical guidelines on matters such as trespassing, personal safety, and similar aspects that involve considerations of law.

Exhibit 2, page 1

Appendix 18–1

FORM 1023 *(continued)*

CAMPAIGN TO CLEAN UP AMERICA   EIN #44-4444444
Attachment to Form 1023
PART II, Question 1, continued

PUBLIC EDUCATION PROGRAM: The Campaign will endeavor to prevent littering from occurring in the first instance through public education programs. These will consist of the distribution of literature, media advertising, and community meetings. The public education aspect of the Campaign's program will be intertwined with its fundraising program. Essentially, the public education component of the Campaign's efforts will be directed to ways to sensitize individuals to the problems of litter accumulation, in the hope that they will not litter, be moved to dispose of litter caused by others, and join a Campaign volunteer team to make and keep their community trash-free.

It is the belief of the Campaign that a community that is physically attractive (litter-free) is a community that will have other desirable attributes that contribute to a better way of life of its citizens.

LEGISLATIVE ACTIVITY: The Campaign will undoubtedly engage in some attempts to influence legislation, mostly at the local level, such as laws to toughen the fines for littering and to force trucks to travel with their loads covered. However, any such activities will be insubstantial in relation to total activities and less than 1% of the budget would be devoted to lobbying.

UNRELATED BUSINESS ACTIVITY: The Campaign may engage in some activities that may constitute unrelated business. For example, the Campaign may sell trash bags (bearing its name and an anti-litter message) to the general public. Unrelated business activities, if any, will be insubstantial in relation to total activities.

Exhibit 2, page 2

Appendix 18–1

FORM 1023 *(continued)*

Fund-Raising Letter

ATTACHMENT TO FORM 1023   EIN #44-4444444
Part II, Question 3

CAMPAIGN TO CLEAN UP AMERICA
1111 Any Street
Hometown, Texas 77777

September 1, 19XX

Joe Goodman, President
XYZ FOUNDATION
Central National Bank Building
Norman, OK 33333

Dear Joe,

Our CAMPAIGN TO CLEAN UP AMERICA (Campaign) has been established to rid our cities, towns and countrysides of the trash, debris and other litter which defaces our land. It is our vision that the beauty of the landscapes of this country should not be tarnished, or hidden, by accumulations of garbage and other trash that can be reused..

Part of our strategy is to change people's attitudes towards trash. Our municipality's experience is that a clean area is less likely to be trashed than one that is already littered. A community whose occupants are sensitized to the litter accumulation problem is less likely to be full of trash than the one where its occupants have subconsciously repressed the ugly sights. A community whose members are willing to rid the area of trash, and keep it that way, will be a far more beautiful place to live and work, and be proud of, than one that is constantly strewn with litter.

We will initially target three towns in Texas and two in Oklahoma. We respectfully request that your foundation serve as our official Oklahoma sponsor. Your foundation's name would be featured on all of our educational materials and volunteer packets distributed in the State of Oklahoma for the first two years. We are asking you to grant us one-third of the estimated cost of our Oklahoma activities, or $50,000 a year for two years.

Exhibit 3, page 1

FORM 1023 *(continued)*

CAMPAIGN TO CLEAN UP AMERICA   EIN #44-4444444
Grant request to XYZ Foundation
September 1, 19xx

The campaign's efforts in the first two years will be focused upon:

PROJECT	ESTIMATED COST
VOLUNTEER TEAMS	$ 350,000
PUBLIC EDUCATION	150,000
PROGRAMS AND SEMINARS	70,000
GENERAL & ADMINISTRATIVE	100,000
FUND RAISING	30,000
	$ 700,000

      A detailed budget and description of the Campaign's projects are enclosed for your reference. We would be happy to meet with you at your convenience to answer any questions or furnish more details. We would welcome your help by way of introductions to folks in Oklahoma as well.

      Our long range plans for the Campaign, along with wiping out litter, include fostering nationwide recycling habits by elimination of disposable containers and toxic containers which pollute our air, land and waters.

      We trust our purposes are in line with those of the XYZ Foundation and hope you decide to work with us in eliminating the environmental problems of our nation.

With best regards,

Jane

Jane D. Environmentalist

enclosures

Exhibit 3, page 2

Appendix 18–1

FORM 1023 (*continued*)

Proposed Budgets

CAMPAIGN TO CLEAN UP AMERICA   #44-4444444

PROJECTED REVENUES AND EXPENSES

	19X0	19X1
REVENUES:		
Support:		
Contributions/disqualified persons	$ 50,000	$ 10,000
Contributions/general public	150,000	500,000
Grants/corporations	60,000	200,000
Grants/private foundations	0	200,000
Total support	$ 260,000	910,000
Exempt function charges:		
Seminars		20,000
Publications		20,000
Total exempt function revenue		40,000
Investment Income	1,000	10,000
TOTAL PROJECTED REVENUES	$ 260,000	$1000,000
EXPENSES:		
Personnel:		
Executive Director	$ 30,000	60,000
Senior staff (3)	40,000	120,000
Staff	25,000	160,000
Payroll costs and fringes	18,000	70,000
Total personnel	113,000	410,000
Occupancy	20,000	50,000
Telephone/fax	5,000	20,000
Printing public information	20,000	100,000
Meetings/travel/conferences	1,000	30,000
Professional fees	15,000	20,000
Administration	5,000	30,000
Lobbying	2,000	100,000
Fundraising mailings	25,000	60,000
Acquisition of office eqp/furnishings	20,000	40,000
TOTAL CASH EXPENSES	$ 226,000	$ 860,000
Working Capital Reserve	35,000	140,000
	$ 261,000	$1000,000

Exhibit 4

Appendix 18–1

FORM 1023 (*continued*)

Form 1023 (Rev. 9-90)　　CAMPAIGN TO CLEAN UP AMERICA　　　　　　44-4444444　　Page **11**

Schedule A.—Churches　　N/A

1　Provide a brief history of the development of the organization, including the reasons for its formation.

2　Does the organization have a written creed or statement of faith? . . . . . . ☐ **Yes**　☐ **No**
　If "Yes," attach a copy.

3　Does the organization require prospective members to renounce other religious beliefs or their membership in other churches or religious orders to become members? . . . . ☐ **Yes**　☐ **No**

4　Does the organization have a formal code of doctrine and discipline for its members? . . . . ☐ **Yes**　☐ **No**
　If "Yes," describe.

5　Describe your form of worship and attach a schedule of your worship services.

6　Are your services open to the public? . . . . ☐ **Yes**　☐ **No**
　If "Yes," describe how you publicize your services and explain your criteria for admittance.

7　Explain how you attract new members.

8　(a) How many active members are currently enrolled in your church?

　(b) What is the average attendance at your worship services?

9　In addition to your worship services, what other religious services (such as baptisms, weddings, funerals, etc.) do you conduct?

Appendix 18–1

FORM 1023 *(continued)*

Form 1023 (Rev. 9-90)	CAMPAIGN TO CLEAN UP AMERICA	44–4444444	Page 12

Schedule A.—Churches *(Continued)* N/A

10 Does the organization have a school for the religious instruction of the young? ☐ **Yes** ☐ **No**

11 Were your current deacons, minister, and pastor formally ordained after a prescribed course of study? . . . . ☐ **Yes** ☐ **No**

12 Describe your religious hierarchy or ecclesiastical government.

13 Does your organization have an established place of worship? . . . . ☐ **Yes** ☐ **No**

If "Yes," provide the name and address of the owner or lessor of the property and the address and a description of the facility.

If you have no regular place of worship, state where your services are held and how the site is selected.

14 Does (or will) the organization license or otherwise ordain ministers (or their equivalent) or issue church charters? . . . . ☐ **Yes** ☐ **No**

If "Yes," describe in detail the requirements and qualifications needed to be so licensed, ordained, or chartered.

15 Did the organization pay a fee for a church charter? . . . . ☐ **Yes** ☐ **No**

If "Yes," state the name and address of the organization to which the fee was paid, attach a copy of the charter, and describe the circumstances surrounding the chartering.

16 Show how many hours a week your minister/pastor and officers each devote to church work and the amount of compensation paid each of them. If your minister or pastor is otherwise employed, indicate by whom employed, the nature of the employment, and the hours devoted to that employment.

Appendix 18–1

FORM 1023 (*continued*)

Form 1023 (Rev. 9-90)	CAMPAIGN TO CLEAN UP AMERICA	44–4444444	Page **13**

Schedule A.—Churches *(Continued)*   N/A

17 Will any funds or property of your organization be used by any officer, director, employee, minister, or pastor for his or her personal needs or convenience? . . . . ☐ **Yes** ☐ **No**

If "Yes," describe the nature and circumstances of such use.

18 List any officers, directors, or trustees related by blood or marriage.

19 Give the name of anyone who has assigned income to you or made substantial contributions of money or other property. Specify the amounts involved.

Instructions

Although a church, its integrated auxiliaries, or a convention or association of churches is not required to file Form 1023 to be exempt from Federal income tax or to receive tax deductible contributions, such an organization may find it advantageous to obtain recognition of exemption. In this event, you should submit information showing that your organization is a church, synagogue, association or convention of churches, religious order or religious organization that is an integral part of a church, and that it is carrying out the functions of a church.

In determining whether an admittedly religious organization is also a church, the Internal Revenue Service does not accept any and every assertion that such an organization is a church. Because beliefs and practices vary so widely, there is no single definition of the word "church" for tax purposes. The Internal Revenue Service considers the facts and circumstances of each organization applying for church status.

The Internal Revenue Service maintains two basic guidelines in determining that an organization meets the religious purposes test:

(a) that the particular religious beliefs of the organization are truly and sincerely held, and

(b) that the practices and rituals associated with the organization's religious beliefs or creed are not illegal or contrary to clearly defined public policy.

In order for the Internal Revenue Service to properly evaluate your organization's activities and religious purposes, it is important that all questions in this Schedule are answered accurately.

The information submitted with this Schedule will be a determining factor in granting the "church" status requested by your organization. In completing the Schedule, the following points should be considered:

(a) The organization's activities in furtherance of its beliefs must be exclusively religious,

(b) An organization will not qualify for exemption if it has a substantial nonexempt purpose of serving the private interests of its founder or the founder's family.

Appendix 18–1

FORM 1023 (*continued*)

Form 1023 (Rev. 9-90)   CAMPAIGN TO CLEAN UP AMERICA   44–4444444   Page 15

Schedule B.—Schools, Colleges, and Universities   N/A

1 Does, or will, the organization normally have: **(a)** a regularly scheduled curriculum, **(b)** a regular faculty of qualified teachers, **(c)** a regularly enrolled body of students, and **(d)** facilities where its educational activities are regularly carried on? . . . . ☐ Yes   ☐ No
If "No," do not complete the rest of this Schedule.

2 Is the organization an instrumentality of a State or political subdivision of a State? . . . . ☐ Yes   ☐ No
If "Yes," document this in Part II and do not complete items 3 through 10 of this Schedule. (See instructions for Schedule B.)

3 Does or will the organization (or any department or division within it) discriminate in any way on the basis of race with respect to:

a Admissions? . . . . ☐ Yes   ☐ No
b Use of facilities or exercise of student privileges? . . . . ☐ Yes   ☐ No
c Faculty or administrative staff? . . . . ☐ Yes   ☐ No
d Scholarship or loan programs? . . . . ☐ Yes   ☐ No
If "Yes" for any of the above, explain.

4 Does the organization include a statement in its charter, bylaws, or other governing instrument, or in a resolution of its governing body, that it has a racially nondiscriminatory policy as to students? . . . . . . ☐ Yes   ☐ No
Attach whatever corporate resolutions or other official statements the organization has made on this subject.

5a Has the organization made its racially nondiscriminatory policies known in a manner that brings the policies to the attention of all segments of the general community that it serves? . . . . ☐ Yes   ☐ No
If "Yes," describe how these policies have been publicized and how often relevant notices or announcements have been made. If no newspaper or broadcast media notices have been used, explain.

b If applicable, attach clippings of any relevant newspaper notices or advertising, or copies of tapes or scripts used for media broadcasts. Also attach copies of brochures and catalogues dealing with student admissions, programs, and scholarships, as well as representative copies of all written advertising used as a means of informing prospective students of your programs.

6 Attach a numerical schedule showing the racial composition, as of the current academic year, and projected as far as may be feasible for the next academic year, of: **(a)** the student body, and **(b)** the faculty and administrative staff.

7 Attach a list showing the amount of any scholarship and loan funds awarded to students enrolled and the racial composition of the students who have received the awards.

8a Attach a list of the organization's incorporators, founders, board members, and donors of land or buildings, whether individuals or organizations.

b State whether any of the organizations listed in **8a** have as an objective the maintenance of segregated public or private school education, and, if so, whether any of the individuals listed in **8a** are officers or active members of such organizations.

9a Indicate the public school district and county in which the organization is located.

b Was the organization formed or substantially expanded at the time of public school desegregation in the above district or county? . . . . ☐ Yes   ☐ No

10 Has the organization ever been determined by a State or Federal administrative agency or judicial body to be racially discriminatory? . . . . ☐ Yes   ☐ No
If "Yes," attach a detailed explanation identifying the parties to the suit, the forum in which the case was heard, the cause of action, the holding in the case, and the citations (if any) for the case. Also describe in detail what changes in your operation, if any, have occurred since then.

For more information, see back of Schedule B.

FORM 1023 (*continued*)

Instructions

A "school" is an organization that has the primary function of presenting formal instruction, normally maintains a regular faculty and curriculum, normally has a regularly enrolled body of students, and has a place where its educational activities are carried on. The term generally corresponds to the definition of an "educational organization" in section 170(b)(1)(A)(ii). Thus, the term includes primary, secondary, preparatory and high schools, and colleges and universities. The term does not include organizations engaged in both educational and non-educational activities unless the latter are merely incidental to the educational activities. A school for handicapped children would be included within the term, but an organization merely providing handicapped children with custodial care would not.

For purposes of this Schedule, "Sunday schools" that are conducted by a church would not be included in the term "schools," but separately organized schools (such as parochial schools, universities, and similar institutions) would be included in the term.

A private school that otherwise meets the requirements of section 501(c)(3) as an educational institution will not qualify for exemption under section 501(a) unless it has a racially nondiscriminatory policy as to students. This policy means that the school admits students of any race to all the rights, privileges, programs, and activities generally accorded or made available to students at that school, and that the school does not discriminate on the basis of race in the administration of its educational policies, admissions policies, scholarship and loan programs, and athletic, or other school-administered programs. The Internal Revenue Service considers discrimination on the basis of race to include discrimination on the basis of color and national or ethnic origin. A policy of a school that favors racial minority groups in admissions, facilities, programs, and financial assistance will not constitute discrimination on the basis of race when the purpose and effect is to promote the establishment and maintenance of that school's racially nondiscriminatory policy as to students. See Rev. Proc. 75-50, 1975-2 C.B. 587, for guidelines and recordkeeping requirements for determining whether private schools that are applying for recognition of exemption have racially nondiscriminatory policies as to students.

Line 2.—An instrumentality of a State or political subdivision of a State may qualify under section 501(c)(3) if it is organized as a separate entity from the governmental unit that created it and if it otherwise meets the organizational and operational tests of section 501(c)(3). (See Rev. Rul. 60-384, 1960-2 C.B. 172.) Any such organization that is a school is not a private school and, therefore, is not subject to the provisions of Rev. Proc. 75-50.

Schools that incorrectly answer "Yes" to line 2 will be contacted to furnish the information called for by lines 3 through 10 in order to establish that they meet the requirements for exemption. To prevent delay in the processing of your application, be sure to answer line 2 correctly and complete lines 3 through 10 if applicable.

Appendix 18–1

FORM 1023 (*continued*)

Form 1023 (Rev. 9-90)   CAMPAIGN TO CLEAN UP AMERICA   44–4444444   Page **17**

Schedule C.—Hospitals and Medical Research Organizations N/A

☐   Check here if you are claiming to be a hospital; complete the questions in Section I of this Schedule; and write "N/A" in Section II.
☐   Check here if you are claiming to be a medical research organization operated in conjunction with a hospital; complete the questions in Section II of this Schedule; and write "N/A" in Section I.

Section I   **Hospitals**

1a   How many doctors are on the hospital's courtesy staff?   . . . . _____

   b   Are all the doctors in the community eligible for staff privileges? . . . . ☐ Yes   ☐ No
       If "No," give the reasons why and explain how the courtesy staff is selected.

2a   Does the hospital maintain a full-time emergency room?   . . . . ☐ Yes   ☐ No
   b   What is the hospital's policy on administering emergency services to persons without apparent means to pay?

   c   Does the hospital have any arrangements with police, fire, and voluntary ambulance services for the delivery
       or admission of emergency cases?   . . . . ☐ Yes   ☐ No
       Explain.

3a   Does or will the hospital require a deposit from persons covered by Medicare or Medicaid in its admission
       practices? . . . . ☐ Yes   ☐ No
       If "Yes," explain.

   b   Does the same deposit requirement apply to all other patients? . . . . ☐ Yes   ☐ No
       If "No," explain.

4   Does or will the hospital provide for a portion of its services and facilities to be used for charity patients? . . . ☐ Yes   ☐ No
       Explain your policy regarding charity cases. Include data on the hospital's past experience in admitting charity
       patients and arrangements it may have with municipal or government agencies for absorbing the cost of such
       care.

5   Does or will the hospital carry on a formal program of medical training and research? . . . . ☐ Yes   ☐ No
       If "Yes," describe.

6   Does the hospital provide office space to physicians carrying on a medical practice?   . . . . ☐ Yes   ☐ No
       If "Yes," attach a list setting forth the name of each physician, the amount of space provided, the annual rent,
       the expiration date of the current lease and whether the terms of the lease represent fair market value.

Section II   **Medical Research Organizations**

1   Name the hospitals with which you have a relationship and describe the relationship.

2   Attach a schedule describing your present and proposed (indicate which) medical research activities; show the nature of the
       activities, and the amount of money that has been or will be spent in carrying them out. (Making grants to other organizations is not
       direct conduct of medical research.)

3   Attach a statement of assets showing the fair market value of your assets and the portion of the assets directly devoted to medical
       research.

For more information, see back of Schedule C.

Appendix 18–1

FORM 1023 *(continued)*

Form 1023 (Rev. 9-90)   Page **18**

Additional Information

Hospitals.—To be entitled to status as a "hospital," an organization must have, as its principal purpose or function, the providing of medical or hospital care or medical education or research. "Medical care" includes the treatment of any physical or mental disability or condition, the cost of which may be taken as a deduction under section 213, whether the treatment is performed on an inpatient or outpatient basis. Thus, a rehabilitation institution, outpatient clinic, or community mental health or drug treatment center may be a hospital if its principal function is providing the above described services. On the other hand, a convalescent home or a home for children or the aged would not be a hospital. Similarly, an institution whose principal purpose or function is to train handicapped individuals to pursue some vocation would not be a hospital. Moreover, a medical education or medical research institution is not a hospital, unless it is also actively engaged in providing medical or hospital care to patients on its premises or in its facilities on an inpatient or outpatient basis.

Cooperative Hospital Service Organizations.— Cooperative hospital service organizations (section 501(e)) should not complete Schedule C.

Medical Research Organizations.—To qualify as a medical research organization, the principal function of the organization must be the direct, continuous and active conduct of medical research in conjunction with a hospital that is described in section 501(c)(3), a Federal hospital, or an instrumentality of a governmental unit referred to in section 170(c)(1). For purposes of section 170(b)(1)(A)(iii) only, the organization must be set up to use the funds it receives in the active conduct of medical research by January 1 of the fifth calendar year after receipt. The arrangement it has with donors to assure use of the funds within the five-year period must be legally enforceable. As used here, "medical research" means investigations, experiments and studies to discover, develop, or verify knowledge relating to the causes, diagnosis, treatment, prevention, or control of the physical or mental diseases and impairments of man. For further information, see Regulations section 1.170A-9(c)(2).

Appendix 18–1

FORM 1023 *(continued)*

Form 1023 (Rev. 9-90)   CAMPAIGN TO CLEAN UP AMERICA   44–4444444   Page **19**

Schedule D.—Section 509(a)(3) Supporting Organization N/A

1a Organizations supported by the applicant organization: Name and address of supported organization	**b** Has the supported organization received a ruling or determination letter that it is not a private foundation by reason of section 509(a)(1) or (2)?	
....	☐ **Yes**	☐ **No**
....	☐ **Yes**	☐ **No**
....	☐ **Yes**	☐ **No**
....	☐ **Yes**	☐ **No**
....	☐ **Yes**	☐ **No**

c If "No" for any of the organizations listed in 1a, explain.

2 Does the organization you support have tax-exempt status under section 501(c)(4), 501(c)(5), or 501(c)(6)?   ☐ **Yes**   ☐ **No**
If "Yes," attach: **(a)** a copy of its ruling or determination letter, and **(b)** an analysis of its revenue for the current year and the preceding three years. (Provide the financial data using the formats in Part IV-A (lines 1–13) and Part III (questions 11, 12, and 13).)

3 Does your governing document indicate that the majority of your governing board is elected or appointed by the supported organizations? .   .   .   . ☐ **Yes**   ☐ **No**
If "Yes," skip to question 9.
If "No," you must answer questions 4 through 9.

4 Does your governing document indicate the common supervision or control that you and the supported organizations share? .   .   .   . ☐ **Yes**   ☐ **No**
If "Yes," give the article and paragraph numbers. If "No," explain.

5 To what extent do the supported organizations have a significant voice in your investment policies, in the making and timing of grants, and in otherwise directing the use of your income or assets?

6 Does the mentioning of the supported organizations in your governing instrument make you a trust that the supported organizations can enforce under state law and compel to make an accounting? .   .   .   . ☐ **Yes**   ☐ **No**
If "Yes," explain.

7a What percentage of your income do you pay to each supported organization?

b What is the total annual income of each supported organization?

c How much do you contribute annually to each supported organization?

For more information, see back of Schedule D.

Appendix 18–1

FORM 1023 *(continued)*

CAMPAIGN TO CLEAN UP AMERICA 44-4444444

Schedule D.—Section 509(a)(3) Supporting Organization *(Continued)*

8 To what extent do you conduct activities that would otherwise be carried on by the supported organizations? Explain why these activities would otherwise be carried on by the supported organizations.

9 Is the applicant organization controlled directly or indirectly by one or more "disqualified persons" (other than one who is a disqualified person solely because he or she is a manager) or by an organization which is not described in section 509(a)(1) or (2)? . . . . ☐ **Yes** ☐ **No**

If "Yes," explain.

Instructions

For an explanation of the types of organizations defined in section 509(a)(3) as being excluded from the definition of a private foundation, see Publication 557, Chapter 3.

Line 1.—List each organization that is supported by your organization and indicate in item 1b if the supported organization has received a letter recognizing exempt status as a section 501(c)(3) public charity as defined in section 509(a)(1) or 509(a)(2).

If you answer "No" in 1b to any of the listed organizations, please explain in 1c.

Line 3.—Your governing document may be articles of incorporation, articles of association, constitution, trust indenture, or trust agreement.

Line 9.—For a definition of a "disqualified person," see specific instructions for Part II, line 4d, on page 3 of the application's instructions.

Appendix 18–1

FORM 1023 *(continued)*

Form 1023 (Rev. 9-90)   CAMPAIGN TO CLEAN UP AMERICA   44-4444444   Page **21**

Schedule E.—Private Operating Foundation   N/A

Income Test

			Most recent tax year
1a	Adjusted net income, as defined in Regulations section 53.4942(a)-2(d)	1a	
b	Minimum investment return, as defined in Regulations section 53.4942(a)-2(c)	1b	
2	Qualifying distributions:		
a	Amounts (including administrative expenses) paid directly for the active conduct of the activities for which organized and operated under section 501(c)(3) (attach schedule)	2a	
b	Amounts paid to acquire assets to be used (or held for use) directly in carrying out purposes described in section 170(c)(1) or 170(c)(2)(B) (attach schedule)	2b	
c	Amounts set aside for specific projects that are for purposes described in section 170(c)(1) or 170(c)(2)(B) (attach schedule)	2c	
d	**Total** qualifying distributions (add lines 2a, b, and c)	2d	
3	Percentages:		
a	Percentage of qualifying distributions to adjusted net income (divide line 2d by line 1a)	3a	%
b	Percentage of qualifying distributions to minimum investment return (divide line 2d by line 1b) . . . . . (Percentage must be at least 85% for 3a or 3b)	3b	%

Assets Test

4	Value of organization's assets used in activities that directly carry out the exempt purposes. Do not include assets held merely for investment or production of income (attach schedule)	4	
5	Value of any stock of a corporation that is controlled by applicant organization and carries out its exempt purposes (attach statement describing corporation)	5	
6	Value of all qualifying assets (add lines 4 and 5)	6	
7	Value of applicant organization's total assets	7	
8	Percentage of qualifying assets to total assets (divide line 6 by line 7—percentage must exceed 65%) . . .	8	%

Endowment Test

9	Value of assets not used (or held for use) directly in carrying out exempt purposes:		
a	Monthly average of investment securities at fair market value	9a	
b	Monthly average of cash balances	9b	
c	Fair market value of all other investment property (attach schedule)	9c	
d	**Total** (add lines 9a, b, and c)	9d	
10	Acquisition indebtedness related to line 9 items (attach schedule)	10	
11	Balance (subtract line 10 from line 9d)	11	
12	Multiply line 11 by 3⅓% (⅔ of the percentage for the minimum investment return computation under section 4942(e)). Line 2d above must equal or exceed the result of this computation	12	

Support Test

13	Applicant organization's support as defined in section 509(d)	13	
14	Gross investment income as defined in section 509(e)	14	
15	Support for purposes of section 4942(j)(3)(B)(iii) (subtract line 14 from line 13)	15	
16	Support received from the general public, 5 or more exempt organizations, or a combination of these sources (attach schedule)	16	
17	For persons (other than exempt organizations) contributing more than 1% of line 15, enter the total amounts that are more than 1% of line 15	17	
18	Subtract line 17 from line 16	18	
19	Percentage of total support (divide line 18 by line 15—must be at least 85%)	19	%
20	Does line 16 include support from an exempt organization that is more than 25% of the amount of line 15? . .	☐ Yes ☐ No	

21 Newly created organizations with less than one year's experience: Attach a statement explaining how the organization is planning to satisfy the requirements of section 4942(j)(3) for the income test and one of the supplemental tests during its first year's operation. Include a description of plans and arrangements, press clippings, public announcements, solicitations for funds, etc.

22 Does the amount entered on line 2a include any grants that you made? . . . . ☐ Yes   ☐ No
If "Yes," attach a statement explaining how those grants satisfy the criteria for "significant involvement" grants described in section 53.4942(b)-1(b)(2) of the regulations.

For more information, see back of Schedule E.

Appendix 18–1

FORM 1023 *(continued)*

Form 1023 (Rev. 9-90)   Page **22**

Instructions

If the organization claims to be an operating foundation described in section 4942(j)(3) and—

(a) bases its claim to private operating foundation status on normal and regular operations over a period of years; or

(b) is newly created, set up as a private operating foundation, and has at least one year's experience;

provide the information under the income test and under one of the three supplemental tests (assets, endowment, or support). If the organization does not have at least one year's experience, provide the information called for on line 21. If the organization's private operating foundation status depends on its normal and regular operations as described in (a) above, attach a schedule similar to the one shown on the front of this schedule showing the data in tabular form for the three years preceding the most recent tax year. (See Regulations section 53.4942(b)-1 for additional information before completing the "Income Test" section of this schedule.) Organizations claiming section 4942(j)(5) status must satisfy the income test and the endowment test.

A "private operating foundation" described in section 4942(j)(3) is a private foundation that spends substantially all of the lesser of its adjusted net income (as defined below) or its minimum investment return directly for the active conduct of the activities constituting the purpose or function for which it is organized and operated. The foundation must satisfy the income test under section 4942(j)(3)(A), as modified by Regulations section 53.4942(b)-1, and one of the following three supplemental tests: (1) the assets test under section 4942(j)(3)(B)(i); (2) the endowment test under section 4942(j)(3)(B)(ii); or (3) the support test under section 4942(j)(3)(B)(iii).

Certain long-term care facilities described in section 4942(j)(5) are treated as private operating foundations for purposes of section 4942 only.

"Adjusted net income" is the excess of gross income for the tax year over the sum of deductions determined with the modifications described below. Items of gross income from any unrelated trade or business and the deductions directly connected with the unrelated trade or business will be taken into account in computing the organization's adjusted net income:

Income modifications (adjustments to gross income).—

(1) Section 103 (relating to interest on certain governmental obligations) does not apply. Thus, interest that otherwise would have been excluded should be included in gross income.

(2) Except as provided in (3) below, capital gains and losses are taken into account only to the extent of the net short-term gain. Long-term gains and losses will be disregarded.

(3) The gross amount received from the sale or disposition of certain property should be included in gross income to the extent that the acquisition of the property constituted a qualifying distribution under section 4942(g)(1)(B).

(4) Repayments of prior qualifying distributions (as defined in section 4942(g)(1)(A)) will constitute items of gross income.

(5) Any amount set aside under section 4942(g)(2) that is "not necessary for the purposes for which it was set aside" will constitute an item of gross income.

Deduction modifications (adjustments to deductions).—

(1) Expenses for the general operation of the organization according to its charitable purposes (as contrasted with expenses for the production or collection of income and management, conservation, or maintenance of income producing property) should not be taken as deductions. If only a portion of the property is used for production of income subject to section 4942 and the remainder is used for general charitable purposes, the expenses connected with that property should be divided according to those purposes and only expenses related to the income producing portion will be allowed as a deduction.

(2) Charitable contributions, deductible under section 170 or 642(c), should not be taken into account as deductions for adjusted net income.

(3) The net operating loss deduction prescribed under section 172 should not be taken into account as a deduction for adjusted net income.

(4) The special deductions for corporations (such as the dividends-received deduction) allowed under sections 241 through 250 should not be taken into account as deductions for adjusted net income.

(5) Depreciation and depletion should be determined in the same manner as under section 4940(c)(3)(B).

Section 265 (relating to the expenses and interest connected with tax-exempt interest) should not be taken into account.

You may find it easier to figure adjusted net income by completing Column (c), Part 1, Form 990-PF, according to the instructions for that form.

An organization that has been held to be a private operating foundation will continue to be such an organization only if it meets the income test and either the assets, endowment, or support test in later years. See Regulations section 53.4942(b) for additional information. No additional request for ruling will be necessary or appropriate for an organization to maintain its status as a private operating foundation. However, data related to the above tests must be submitted with the organization's annual information return, Form 990-PF.

Appendix 18–1

FORM 1023 (*continued*)

CAMPAIGN TO CLEAN UP AMERICA   44-4444444

Schedule F.—Homes for the Aged or Handicapped   N/A

1   What are the requirements for admission to residency? Explain fully and attach promotional literature and application forms.

2   Does or will the home charge an entrance or founder's fee? . . . . ☐ **Yes**   ☐ **No**
     If "Yes," explain and specify the amount charged.

3   What periodic fees or maintenance charges are or will be required of its residents?

4a What established policy does the home have concerning residents who become unable to pay their regular charges?

b   What arrangements does the home have or will it make with local and Federal welfare units, sponsoring organizations, or others to absorb all or part of the cost of maintaining those residents?

5   What arrangements does or will the home have to provide for the health needs of its residents?

6   In what way are the home's residential facilities designed to meet some combination of the physical, emotional, recreational, social, religious, and similar needs of the aged or handicapped?

7   Provide a description of the home's facilities and specify both the residential capacity of the home and the current number of residents.

8   Attach a sample copy of the contract or agreement the organization makes with or requires of its residents.

For more information, see back of Schedule F.

Appendix 18–1

FORM 1023 (*continued*)

Instructions

Line 1.— Provide the criteria for admission to the home and submit brochures, pamphlets, or other printed material used to inform the public about the home's admissions policy.

Line 2.— Indicate whether the fee charged is an entrance fee or a monthly charge, etc. Also, if the fee is an entrance fee, is it payable in a lump sum or on an installment basis? If there is no fee, indicate "N/A."

Line 4.— Indicate the organization's policy regarding residents who are unable to pay. Also, indicate whether the organization is subsidized for all or part of the cost of maintaining those residents who are unable to pay.

Line 5.— Indicate whether the organization provides health care to the residents, either directly or indirectly, through some continuing arrangement with other organizations, facilities, or health personnel. If no health care is provided, indicate "N/A."

Appendix 18–1

FORM 1023 *(continued)*

Form 1023 (Rev. 9-90)	CAMPAIGN TO CLEAN UP AMERICA	44–4444444	Page **25**

Schedule G.—Child Care Organizations N/A

1 Is the organization's primary activity the providing of care for children away from their homes? . . . . ☐ **Yes** ☐ **No**

2 How many children is the organization authorized to care for by the State (or local governmental unit), and what was the average attendance during the past 6 months, or the number of months the organization has been in existence if less than 6 months?

3 How many children are currently cared for by the organization?

4 Is substantially all (at least 85%) of the care provided for the purpose of enabling parents to be gainfully employed or to seek employment? . . . . ☐ **Yes** ☐ **No**

5 Are the services provided available to the general public? . . . . ☐ **Yes** ☐ **No**
If "No," explain.

6 Indicate the category, or categories, of parents whose children are eligible for your child-care services (check as many as apply):

☐ low income parents

☐ any working parents (or parents looking for work)

☐ anyone with the ability to pay

☐ other (explain)

Instructions

Line 5.— If your services are not available to the general public, indicate the particular group or groups that may utilize your services.

REMINDER—If this organization claims to operate a school, then it must also fill out Schedule B.

Note: Page 26 is blank.

Appendix 18–1

FORM 1023 *(continued)*

Form 1023 (Rev. 9-90)　　CAMPAIGN TO CLEAN UP AMERICA　　　　　　44-4444444　　Page **27**

Schedule H.—Organizations Providing Scholarship Benefits, Student Aid, Etc., to Individuals N/A

1a Describe the nature and the amount of the scholarship benefit, student aid, etc., including the terms and conditions governing its use, whether a gift or a loan, and how the availability of the scholarship is publicized. If the organization has established or will establish several categories of scholarship benefits, identify each kind of benefit and explain how the organization determines the recipients for each category. Attach a sample copy of any application the organization requires individuals to complete to be considered for scholarship grants, loans, or similar benefits. (Private foundations that make grants for travel, study, or other similar purposes are required to obtain advance approval of scholarship procedures. See Regulations sections 53.4945-4(c) and (d).)

b If you want this application considered as a request for approval of grant procedures in the event we determine that you are a private foundation, check here . . . .▶ ☐

c If you checked the box in 1b above, indicate the sections for which you wish to be considered.

　☐ 4945(g)(1)　　　　　☐ 4945(g)(2)　　　　　☐ 4945(g)(3)

2 What limitations or restrictions are there on the class of individuals who are eligible recipients? Specifically explain whether there are, or will be, any restrictions or limitations in the selection procedures based upon race or the employment status of the prospective recipient or any relative of the prospective recipient. Also indicate the approximate number of eligible individuals.

3 Indicate the number of grants you anticipate making annually . . . . ▶

4 If you base your selections in any way on the employment status of the applicant or any relative of the applicant, indicate whether there is or has been any direct or indirect relationship between the members of the selection committee and the employer. Also indicate whether relatives of the members of the selection committee are possible recipients or have been recipients.

5 Describe any procedures you have for supervising grants (such as obtaining reports or transcripts) that you award, and any procedures you have for taking action if the terms of the grant are violated.

For more information, see back of Schedule H.

Appendix 18–1

FORM 1023 *(continued)*

Additional Information

Private foundations that make grants to individuals for travel, study, or other similar purposes are required to obtain advance approval of their grant procedures from the Internal Revenue Service. Such grants that are awarded under selection procedures that have not been approved by the Internal Revenue Service are subject to a 10% excise tax under section 4945. (See Regulations sections 53.4945-4(c) and (d).)

If you are requesting advance approval of your grant procedures, the following sections apply to line 1c:

4945(g)(1)— The grant constitutes a scholarship or fellowship grant that meets the provisions of section 117(a) prior to its amendment by the Tax Reform Act of 1986 and is to be used for study at an educational organization (school) described in section 170(b)(1)(A)(ii).

4945(g)(2)— The grant constitutes a prize or award that is subject to the provisions of section 74(b), if the recipient of such a prize or award is selected from the general public.

4945(g)(3)— The purpose of the grant is to achieve a specific objective, produce a report or other similar product, or improve or enhance a literary, artistic, musical, scientific, teaching, or other similar capacity, skill, or talent of the grantee.

Appendix 18–1

FORM 1023 *(continued)*

Form 1023 (Rev. 9-90)   CAMPAIGN TO CLEAN UP AMERICA   44-4444444   Page **29**

Schedule I.—Successors to "For Profit" Institutions   N/A

1   What was the name of the predecessor organization and the nature of its activities?

2   Who were the owners or principal stockholders of the predecessor organization? (If more space is needed, attach schedule.)

Name and address	Share or interest

3   Describe the business or family relationship between the owners or principal stockholders and principal employees of the predecessor organization and the officers, directors, and principal employees of the applicant organization.

4a   Attach a copy of the agreement of sale or other contract that sets forth the terms and conditions of sale of the predecessor organization or of its assets to the applicant organization.

  b   Attach an appraisal by an independent qualified expert showing the fair market value at the time of sale of the facilities or property interest sold.

5   Has any property or equipment formerly used by the predecessor organization been rented to the applicant organization or will any such property be rented? . . . . ☐ **Yes**   ☐ **No**
  If "Yes," explain and attach copies of all leases and contracts.

6   Is the organization leasing or will it lease or otherwise make available any space or equipment to the owners, principal stockholders, or principal employees of the predecessor organization? . . . . ☐ **Yes**   ☐ **No**
  If "Yes," explain and attach a list of these tenants and a copy of the lease for each such tenant.

7   Were any new operating policies initiated as a result of the transfer of assets from a profit-making organization to a nonprofit organization? . . . . ☐ **Yes**   ☐ **No**
  If "Yes," explain.

Additional Information

A "for profit" institution for purposes of this Schedule includes any organization in which a person may have a proprietary or partnership interest, hold corporate stock, or otherwise exercise an ownership interest. The institution need not have operated for the purpose of making a profit.

Appendix 18–2

FORM 1024

Form **1024** (Rev. December 1989) Department of the Treasury Internal Revenue Service	**Application for Recognition of Exemption** **Under Section 501(a)** **or for Determination Under Section 120**	OMB No. 1545-0057 If exempt status is approved, this application will be open for public inspection

Read the instructions for each Part carefully.
A User Fee must be attached to this application.
If the required information and appropriate documents are not submitted along with Form 8718 (with payment of the
appropriate user fee), the application may be returned to you.
Complete the Procedural Checklist on page 4 of the instructions.

Part I.—Identification of Applicant (Must be completed by all applicants; also complete appropriate Schedule.)

Check the appropriate box below to indicate the section under which you are applying:

a ☐ Section 501(c)(2)—Title holding corporations (Schedule A, page 6)
b ☒ Section 501(c)(4)—Civic leagues, social welfare organizations (including certain war veterans' organizations), or local
associations of employees (Schedule B, page 7)
c ☐ Section 501(c)(5)—Labor, agricultural, or horticultural organizations (Schedule C, page 8)
d ☐ Section 501(c)(6)—Business leagues, chambers of commerce, etc. (Schedule C, page 8)
e ☐ Section 501(c)(7)—Social clubs (Schedule D, page 9)
f ☐ Section 501(c)(8)—Fraternal beneficiary societies, etc., providing life, sick, accident, or other benefits to members (Schedule E, page 11)
g ☐ Section 501(c)(9)—Voluntary employees' beneficiary associations (Schedule F, page 12)
h ☐ Section 501(c)(10)—Domestic fraternal societies, orders, etc., not providing life, sick, accident or other benefits (Schedule E, page 11)
i ☐ Section 501(c)(12)—Benevolent life insurance associations, mutual ditch or irrigation companies, mutual or cooperative
telephone companies, or like organizations (Schedule G, page 13)
j ☐ Section 501(c)(13)—Cemeteries, crematoria, and like corporations (Schedule H, page 14)
k ☐ Section 501(c)(15)—Mutual insurance companies or associations, other than life or marine (Schedule I, page 15)
l ☐ Section 501(c)(17)—Trusts providing for the payment of supplemental unemployment compensation benefits (Schedule J, page 16)
m ☐ Section 501(c)(19)—A post, organization, auxiliary unit, etc., of past or present members of the Armed Forces of the United
States (Schedule K, page 17)
n ☐ Section 501(c)(20)—Trust/organization for prepaid group legal services (Parts I, II, and Schedule M, page 21)
o ☐ Section 501(c)(25)—Title holding corporations or trusts (Schedule A, page 6)
p ☐ Section 120—Qualified group legal services plans (Parts I, II, and Schedule L, page 19)

1a Full name of organization (as shown in organizing document)	2 Employer identification number (**If none,** **see Specific Instructions**)
DISPOSABLE BOTTLE ACTION COMMITTEE	42–2222222
1b c/o Name (if applicable)	

1c Address (number and street)	
1111 ANY STREET	

1d City or town, county, state, and ZIP code HOMETOWN, TX 77777	3 Name and telephone number (including area code) of person to be contacted during business hours if more information is needed Jody Blazek, CPA (444) 444-4444

4 Month the annual accounting period ends JUNE	5 Date incorporated or formed 1-1-xx	6 Activity codes (see back cover) 480 | 350 | 189

7 Did the organization apply for recognition of exemption under this Code section or under any other section of the Code? ☐ Yes ☒ No
If "Yes," attach an explanation.

8 Has the organization filed Federal income tax returns or exempt organization information returns? . . . . ☐ Yes ☒ No
If "Yes," state the form number(s), years filed, and Internal Revenue office where filed.

9 Check the box for your type of organization. BE SURE TO ATTACH A COMPLETE COPY OF THE CORRESPONDING DOCUMENTS TO
THE APPLICATION BEFORE MAILING.

a ☒ Corporation—Attach a copy of your Articles of Incorporation, (including amendments and restatements) showing approval by the
appropriate state official; also attach a copy of your bylaws.   EXHIBIT 1
b ☐ Trust—Attach a copy of your Trust Indenture or Agreement, including all appropriate signatures and dates.
c ☐ Association—Attach a copy of your Articles of Association, Constitution, or other creating document, with a declaration (see instructions) or
other evidence that the organization was formed by adoption of the document by more than one person. Include also a copy of your bylaws.
If you are a corporation or an unincorporated association that has not yet adopted bylaws, check here ▶ ☐

PLEASE SIGN HERE ▶	I declare under the penalties of perjury that I am authorized to sign this application on behalf of the above organization, and that I have examined this application including the accompanying schedules and attachments, and to the best of my knowledge it is true, correct, and complete.
	Linda Lockard (Signature) *Secretary* (Title or authority of signer) 4.4.93 (Date)

Appendix 18–2

FORM 1024 (*continued*)

Form 1024 (Rev. 12-89) DISPOSABLE BOTTLE ACTION COMMITTEE   42–2222222   Page **2**

Part II.—Activities and Operational Information (Must be completed by all applicants)

1 Provide a detailed narrative description of all the activities of the organization—past, present, and planned. Do not merely refer to or repeat the language in your organizational document. Describe each activity separately in the order of importance. Each description should include, as a minimum, the following: (a) a detailed description of the activity including its purpose; (b) when the activity was or will be initiated; and (c) where and by whom the activity will be conducted.

EXHIBIT 2

2 List the organization's present and future sources of financial support, beginning with the largest source first.

Membership dues   75%
Exempt function sales   25%

Appendix 18-2

FORM 1024 (*continued*)

Form 1024 (Rev. 12-89)   DISPOSABLE BOTTLE ACTION COMMITTEE   42-2222222   Page 3

Part II.—Activities and Operational Information (continued) **(Must be completed by all applicants)**

3 The membership of the organization's governing body is:

a Names, addresses, and titles of officers, directors, trustees, etc.	**b** Annual compensation
Gary G. Generous President 222 Fifth St., Hometown, TX 77777	None
Samantha Zealot Vice President 404 University Dr., Austin, TX 78777	None
Linda Lockard Sec/Treasurer 982 Pine Valley, Dallas, TX 75555	None
Jane D. Environmentalist Director 333 First Street, Hometown, TX 77777	None

4 If you are the outgrowth or continuation of any form of predecessor(s), state the name of each predecessor, the period during which it was in existence, and the reasons for its termination. Submit copies of all papers by which any transfer of assets was effected.

Not applicable

5 If you are now, or plan to be connected in any way with any other organization, describe the organization and explain the relationship (such as: financial support on a continuing basis; shared facilities or employees; same officers, directors, or trustees).

Disposable Bottle Action Committee (DBAC) is being formed by individuals who also serve as directors of a private foundation, Environmentalist Fund, and a publicly supported EO, Campaign to Clean up America. There will be no financial relationship between the organizations and the individuals will not control DBAC.

6 If you have capital stock issued and outstanding, state: (1) class or classes of the stock; (2) number and par value of the shares; (3) consideration for which they were issued; and (4) whether any dividends have been paid or whether your creating instrument authorizes dividend payments on any class of capital stock.

Not applicable

7 State the qualifications necessary for membership in the organization; the classes of membership (with the number of members in each class); and the voting rights and privileges received. If any group or class of persons is required to join, describe the requirement and explain the relationship between those members and members who join voluntarily. Submit copies of any membership solicitation material. Attach sample copies of all types of membership certificates issued.

Membership is open to all persons who can pay the basic dues of $10.

8 Explain how your assets will be distributed on dissolution.

Assets would be distributed to either the Campaign to Clean up America, a publicly supported 501(c)(3) organization, or the Environmentalist Fund, a private foundation, at the discretion of the board of directors.

OBTAINING RECOGNITION OF EXEMPT STATUS

Appendix 18–2

FORM 1024 (*continued*)

Form 1024 (Rev. 12-89) DISPOSABLE BOTTLE ACTION COMMITTEE   42-2222222   Page **4**

Part II.—Activities and Operational Information (continued) **(Must be completed by all applicants)**

9 Have you made or do you plan to make any distribution of your property or surplus funds to shareholders or members?   ☐ Yes ☒ No
If "Yes," state the full details, including: (1) amounts or value; (2) source of funds or property distributed or to be distributed· and (3) basis of, and authority for, distribution or planned distribution.

10 Does, or will, any part of your receipts represent payments for services performed or to be performed? . . ☐ Yes ☒ No
If "Yes," state in detail the amount received and the character of the services performed or to be performed

11 Have you made, or do you plan to make, any payments to members or shareholders for services performed or to be performed? . . . . ☐ Yes ☒ No
If "Yes," state in detail the amount paid, the character of the services, and to whom the payments have been, or will be made.

12 Do you have any arrangement to provide insurance for members, their dependents, or others (including provisions for the payment of sick or death benefits, pensions or annuities)? . . . . ☐ Yes ☒ No
If "Yes," describe and explain the arrangement's eligibility rules and attach a sample copy of each plan document and each type of policy issued.

13 Are you under the supervisory jurisdiction of any public regulatory body, such as a social welfare agency, etc.? . . ☐ Yes ☒ No
If "Yes," submit copies of all administrative opinions or court decisions regarding this supervision as well as copies of applications or requests for the opinions or decisions.

14 Do you now lease or do you plan to lease any property? . . . . ☒ Yes ☐ No
If "Yes," explain in detail. Include the amount of rent, a description of the property, and any relationship between your organization and the other party. Also, attach a copy of any rental or lease agreement.

DBAC will lease one room on a month to month basis at actual cost from a director. The sublease is unwritten and the building is owned by an unrelated party.

15 Have you spent or do you plan to spend any money attempting to influence the selection, nomination, election or appointment of any person to any Federal, state, or local public office or to an office in a political organization? . . . . ☐ Yes ☒ No
If "Yes," explain in detail and list the amounts spent or to be spent in each case.

16 Do you publish pamphlets, brochures, newsletters, journals, or similar printed material? . . . . . . ☐ Yes ☒ No
If "Yes," attach a recent copy of each.

Appendix 18-2

FORM 1024   (*continued*)

Form 1024 (Rev. 12-89)   DISPOSABLE BOTTLE ACTION COMMITTEE   42-2222222   Page **5**

Part III.—Financial Data (Must be completed by all applicants)

Complete the financial statements for the current year and for each of the 3 years immediately before it. If in existence less than 4 years, complete the statements for each year in existence. If in existence less than 1 year, also provide proposed budgets for the 2 years following the current year.

A—Statement of Revenue and Expenses

Revenue	(a) Current Tax Year	(b) 19	(c) 19	(d) 19	(e) Total
	From _____ To _____	3 Prior Tax Years or Proposed Budget for 2 Years			
1 Gross dues and assessments of members . . .	No				
2 Gross contributions, gifts, etc.	financial				
3 Gross amounts derived from activities related to the organization's exempt purpose (attach schedule) .	activity				
4 Gross amounts from unrelated business activities (attach schedule)	to date.	See projections at Exhibit 3.			
5 Gain from sale of assets, excluding inventory items (attach schedule)					
6 Investment income (see instructions)					
7 Other revenue (attach schedule)					
8 Total revenue (add lines 1 through 7)					
Expenses					
9 Expenses attributable to activities related to the organization's exempt purposes					
10 Expenses attributable to unrelated business activities					
11 Contributions, gifts, grants, and similar amounts paid (attach schedule)					
12 Disbursements to or for the benefit of members (attach schedule)					
13 Compensation of officers, directors, and trustees (attach schedule)					
14 Other salaries and wages					
15 Interest					
16 Occupancy					
17 Depreciation and depletion					
18 Other expenses (attach schedule)					
19 Total expenses					
20 Excess of revenue over expenses (line 8 minus line 19)					

B—Balance Sheet (at the end of the period shown)

Assets		Current Tax Year as of ....
1 Cash	1	No
2 Accounts receivable, net	2	assets.
3 Inventories	3	
4 Bonds and notes receivable (attach schedule)	4	
5 Corporate stocks	5	
6 Mortgage loans (attach schedule)	6	
7 Other investments (attach schedule)	7	
8 Depreciable and depletable assets (attach schedule)	8	
9 Land	9	
10 Other assets (attach schedule)	10	
11 **Total assets**	11	0
Liabilities		
12 Accounts payable	12	
13 Contributions, gifts, grants, etc., payable	13	
14 Mortgages and notes payable (attach schedule)	14	
15 Other liabilities (attach schedule)	15	
16 **Total liabilities**	16	
Fund Balances or Net Assets		
17 Total fund balances or net assets	17	
18 **Total liabilities and fund balances or net assets** (add line 16 and line 17)	18	0

If there has been any substantial change in any aspect of your financial activities since the end of the period shown above, check the box and attach a detailed explanation . . . . ▶ ☐

Appendix 18–2

FORM 1024 (*continued*)

NOTE Schedule B was attached to DBAC's application. Choose and attach the schedule attributable to the category of exemption being sought.

Form 1024 (Rev. 12-89)   Page **6**

Schedule A **Organizations described in section 501(c)(2) or 501(c)(25) (Title holding corporations or trusts)**

1   State the complete name, address and employer identification number of each organization for which title to property is held and the number and class(es) of shares of your stock held by each organization.

2   State whether the annual excess of revenue over expenses is or will be turned over to the organization for which title to property is held and, if not, the purpose for which the excess (income) is or will be held.

3a   In the case of a corporation described in section 501(c)(2), state the purpose(s) of each organization for which title to property is held (as shown in its governing instrument) and the Code section(s) under which each is classified as exempt from income tax.

3b   In the case of a corporation or trust described in section 501(c)(25), state the basis whereby each shareholder is described in section 501(c)(25)(C).

INSTRUCTIONS

Line 1.—Provide the requested information on each organization for which your organization holds title to property. Also indicate the number and type(s) of shares of your organization's stock that are held by each.

Line 2.—For purposes of this question, "excess of revenue over expenses" is all of the organization's income for a particular tax year less operating expenses.

Line 3a.—Give the exempt purpose of each organization which is the basis for its exempt status and the Internal Revenue Code section that describes the organization (as shown in its IRS determination letter).

Line 3b.—Indicate if the shareholder is one of the following:

(1) a qualified pension, profit-sharing, or stock bonus plan that meets the requirements of the Code;

(2) a government plan;

(3) an organization described in section 501(c)(3); or

(4) an organization described in section 501(c)(25).

Appendix 18–2

FORM 1024 (*continued*)

Form 1024 (Rev. 12-89) DISPOSABLE BOTTLE ACTION COMMITTEE   EIN # 42-2222222   Page **7**

| Schedule B | Organizations described in section 501(c)(4) (Civic leagues, social welfare organizations (including posts, councils, etc., of veterans' organizations not qualifying or applying for exemption under section 501(c)(19)) or local associations of employees.) |

1 Has the Internal Revenue Service previously issued a ruling or determination letter recognizing you (or any predecessor organization listed in item 4 of Part II) to be exempt under section 501(c)(3) and later revoked that recognition of exemption on the basis that you (or your predecessor) were carrying on propaganda or otherwise attempting to influence legislation or on the basis that you engaged in political activity? . . . . ☐ Yes ☒ No

If "Yes," indicate the earliest tax year for which recognition of exemption under section 501(c)(3) was revoked and the IRS district office that issued the revocation.

2 Do you perform or plan to perform (for members, shareholders, or others) services, such as maintaining the common areas of a condominium; buying food or other items on a cooperative basis; or providing recreational facilities or transportation services, job placement, or other similar undertakings? . . . . ☐ Yes ☒ No

If "Yes," explain the activities in detail, including income realized and expenses incurred. Also, explain in detail the nature of the benefits to the general public from these activities. (If the answer to this question is explained in Part II (pages 2, 3, and 4), enter the page and item number here.)

3 If you are claiming exemption as a homeowners' association, is access to any property or facilities you own or maintain restricted in any way?. . . . . N/A ☐ Yes ☐ No

If "Yes," explain.

4 If you are claiming exemption as a local association of employees, state the name and address of each employer whose employees are eligible for membership in the association. If employees of more than one plant or office of the same employer are eligible for membership, give the address of each plant or office.

Appendix 18–2

FORM 1024 *(continued)*

Form 1024 (Rev. 12-89)   Page **8**

Schedule C | **Organizations described in section 501(c)(5) (Labor, agricultural, including fishermen's organizations, or horticultural organizations) or section 501(c)(6) (business leagues, chambers of commerce, etc.)**

1   Describe any services you perform for members or others. (If the description of the services is contained in Part II, enter the page and item number here.)

2   Fishermen's organizations only.—What kinds of aquatic resources (not including mineral) are cultivated or harvested by those eligible for membership in your organization?

3   Labor organizations only.—Are you organized under the terms of a collective bargaining agreement? . . . . . □ **Yes** □ **No**

If "Yes," attach a copy of the latest agreement.

Appendix 18-2

FORM 1024 *(continued)*

Form 1024 (Rev. 12-89)   Page **9**

Schedule D **Organizations described in section 501(c)(7) (Social clubs)**

1 Have you entered or do you plan to enter into any contract or agreement for the management or operation of your property and/or activities, such as restaurants, pro shops, lodges, etc.? . . . . □ **Yes** □ **No**

If "Yes," attach a copy of the contract or agreement. If one has not yet been drawn up, please explain your plans.

2 Do you seek or plan to seek public patronage of your facilities or activities by advertisement or otherwise? . . . . □ **Yes** □ **No**

If "Yes," attach sample copies of the advertisements or other requests.

If you plan to seek public patronage, please explain your plans.

3a Are nonmembers, other than guests of members, permitted or will they be permitted to use the club facilities or participate in or attend any functions or activities conducted by the organization? . . . . □ **Yes** □ **No**

If "Yes," describe the functions or activities in which there has been or will be nonmember participation or admittance. (Submit a copy of your house rules, if any.)

b State the amount of nonmember income included in Part III, lines 3 and 4, column (a) . . . .

c Enter the percent of gross receipts from nonmembers for the use of club facilities . . . . %

d Enter the percent of gross receipts received from investment income and nonmember use of the club's facilities . . . . %

4a Does your charter, bylaws, other governing instrument, or any written policy statement of your organization contain any provision which provides for discrimination against any person on the basis of race, color, or religion? . . . . □ **Yes** □ **No**

b If "Yes," state whether or not its provision will be kept.

c If you have such a provision which will be repealed, deleted, or otherwise stricken from your requirements, state when this will be done . . . . _____

d If you formerly had such a requirement and it no longer applies, give the date it ceased to apply . . . . . . _____

e If the organization restricts its membership to members of a particular religion, check here and attach the explanation specified in the instructions . . . . □

See reverse side for instructions

Appendix 18–2

FORM 1024 (*continued*)

Instructions

Line 1.—Answer "Yes," if any of the organization's property or activities will be managed by another organization or company.

Lines 3b, c, and d.—Enter the figures for the current year. On an attached schedule, furnish the same information for each of the prior tax years for which you completed Part III of the application.

Line 4e.—If the organization restricts its membership to members of a particular religion, the organization must be:

(1) an auxiliary of a fraternal beneficiary society that:

(a) is described in section 501(c)(8) and exempt from tax under section 501(a), and

(b) limits its membership to members of a particular religion; or

(2) a club which, in good faith, limits its membership to the members of a particular religion in order to further the teachings or principles of that religion and not to exclude individuals of a particular race or color.

If you checked 4e, your explanation must show how you meet one of these two requirements.

Appendix 18–2

FORM 1024 (*continued*)

Form 1024 (Rev. 12-89)   Page 11

| Schedule E | Organizations described in section 501(c)(8) or 501(c)(10) (Fraternal societies, orders, or associations) |

1 Are you a college fraternity or sorority, or chapter of a college fraternity or sorority? . . . . ☐ Yes ☐ No
If "Yes," read the instructions for Line 1 before completing this schedule.

2 Does or will your organization operate under the lodge system? . . . . ☐ Yes ☐ No
If "No," does or will it operate for the exclusive benefit of the members of an organization operating under the lodge system? . . . . ☐ Yes ☐ No

3 Are you a subordinate or local lodge, etc.? . . . . ☐ Yes ☐ No
If "Yes," attach a certificate signed by the secretary of the parent organization, under the seal of the organization, certifying that the subordinate lodge is a duly constituted body operating under the jurisdiction of the parent body.

4 Are you a parent or grand lodge? . . . . ☐ Yes ☐ No
If "Yes," attach a schedule for each subordinate lodge in active operation showing: (a) its name and address; (b) the number of members in it; and (c) how often it holds periodic meetings.

Instructions

Line 1.—To the extent that they qualify for exemption from Federal income tax, college fraternities and sororities generally qualify as organizations described in section 501(c)(7). Therefore, if you are a college fraternity or sorority, please refer to the discussion of section 501(c)(7) organizations in Publication 557. If section 501(c)(7) appears to apply to you, complete Schedule D instead of this schedule.

Line 2.—Operating under the lodge system means carrying on activities under a form of organization that is comprised of local branches, chartered by a parent organization, largely self-governing, and called lodges, chapters, or the like.

Appendix 18–2

FORM 1024 (*continued*)

Form 1024 (Rev. 12-89) Page **12**

Schedule F Organizations described in section 501(c)(9) (Voluntary employees' beneficiary associations)

1 Describe the benefits available to members. Include copies of any plan documents that describe such benefits and the terms and conditions of eligibility for each benefit.

2 Are any employees or classes of employees entitled to benefits to which other employees or classes of employees are not entitled? . . . . ☐ **Yes** ☐ **No**

If "Yes," explain.

3 Give the following information as of the first day of the first plan year for which you are filing this application and enter that date here . . . . _____

a Total number of persons covered by the plan who are highly compensated individuals (See instructions.) . . . _____
b Number of other employees covered by the plan . . . . _____
c Number of employees not covered by the plan . . . . _____
d Total number employed* . . . . _____

  * Should equal the total of **a, b,** and **c**—if not, explain any difference. Describe the eligibility requirements that prevent those employees not covered by the plan from participating.

4 State the number of persons, if any, other than employees and their dependents (for example, the proprietor of a business whose employees are members of the association) who are entitled to receive benefits . . . . ▶

Instructions

Line 3a.—The definition of "highly compensated individual" varies depending on the tax year. For tax years beginning after December 31, 1984, and beginning before January 1, 1988, it is defined as any individual who is:

  (a) one of the five highest paid officers of the employer;

  (b) a shareholder who owns more than 10% of the value of the stock of the employer; or

  (c) among the 10% of the highest paid employees of the employer.

For tax years beginning after December 31, 1987, "highly compensated individuals" are employees who at any time during the year (or preceding year):

  (a) owned a 5% or larger interest in the employer;

  (b) had compensation from the employer in excess of $81,720;*

  (c) were in the top 20% of employees in compensation and had compensation in excess of $54,480;* or

  (d) were officers of the employer and received compensation in excess of $45,000.*

*At some point in the future, these figures may change because of an inflation factor built into the Internal Revenue Code.

Appendix 18–2

FORM 1024 *(continued)*

Form 1024 (Rev. 12-89)   Page **13**

Schedule G	Organizations described in section 501(c)(12) (Benevolent life insurance associations, mutual ditch or irrigation companies, mutual or cooperative telephone companies, or like organizations)

1   Attach a schedule in columnar form for each tax year for which you are claiming exempt status. On each schedule:

a   Show the total gross income received from members or shareholders.

b   List, by source, the total amounts of gross income received from other sources.

---

2   If you are claiming exemption as a local benevolent insurance association, state:

a   The counties from which members are accepted or will be accepted.

b   Whether stipulated premiums are or will be charged in advance, or whether losses are or will be paid solely through assessments.

---

3   If you are claiming exemption as a "like organization," explain how you are similar to a mutual ditch or irrigation company, or a mutual or cooperative telephone company.

---

4   Are the rights and interests of members in your annual savings determined in proportion to their business with you?   ☐ **Yes**   ☐ **No**

If "Yes," do you keep the records necessary to determine at any time each member's rights and interests in such savings, including assets acquired with the savings? . . . . ☐ **Yes**   ☐ **No**

---

5   If you are a mutual or cooperative telephone company and have contracts with other systems for long-distance telephone services, attach copies of the contracts.

Instructions

Mutual or cooperative electric or telephone companies should show income received from qualified pole rentals separately. Mutual or cooperative telephone companies should also show separately: the gross amount of income received from nonmember telephone companies for performing services that involve their members and the gross amount of income received from the sale of display advertising in a directory furnished to their members.

Do not net amounts due, or paid to, other sources against amounts due, or received from those sources.

Appendix 18–2

FORM 1024   (*continued*)

Form 1024 (Rev. 12-89)   Page **14**

| Schedule H | Organizations described in section 501(c)(13) (Cemeteries, crematoria, and like corporations) |

1   Attach the following documents:

a   Complete copy of sales contracts or other documents, including any "debt" certificates, involved in acquiring cemetery or crematorium property.

b   Complete copy of any contract you have that designates an agent to sell your cemetery lots.

c   A copy of the appraisal (obtained from a disinterested and qualified party) of the cemetery property as of the date acquired.

2   Do you have, or do you plan to have, a perpetual care fund? . . . . ☐ **Yes** ☐ **No**
If "Yes," attach a copy of the fund agreement and explain the nature of the fund (cash, securities, unsold land, etc.)

3   If you are claiming exemption as a perpetual care fund for an organization described in section 501(c)(13), has the cemetery organization, for which funds are held, established exemption under that section?. . . . . . ☐ **Yes** ☐ **No**
If "No," explain.

Appendix 18–2

FORM 1024 (*continued*)

Form 1024 (Rev. 12-89)   Page **15**

Schedule I	Organizations described in section 501(c)(15) (Small insurance companies or associations)

Note: *Section 501(c)(15) was amended in 1986 to provide new requirements for qualifying under that section. Therefore, complete lines 2 through 5 below only for years beginning after December 31, 1986, for which the organization claims to qualify under section 501(c)(15).*

1 Is the organization a member of a controlled group of corporations as defined in section 831(b)(2)(B)(ii)? (Disregard section 1563(b)(2)(B) in determining whether the organization is a member of a controlled group.) . . ☐ **Yes** ☐ **No**

If "Yes," include on lines 2 through 5 the total amount received by the organization and all other members of the controlled group.

If "No," include on lines 2 through 5 only the amounts that relate to the applicant organization.

	(a) Current Year	3 Prior Tax Years		
	From _____ To	(b) 19....	(c) 19....	(d) 19....
2 Direct written premiums				
3 Reinsurance assumed				
4 Reinsurance ceded				
5 Net written premiums (line 2; plus line 3; minus line 4) . . .				

6 If you entered an amount on line 3 or line 4, attach a copy of the reinsurance agreements you have entered into.

Instructions

Line 1.—Answer "Yes," if the organization would be considered a member of a controlled group of corporations if it were not exempt from tax under section 501(a). In applying section 1563(a), use a "more than 50%" stock ownership test to determine whether the applicant or any other corporation is a member of a controlled group.

Line 2.—In addition to other direct written premiums, include on line 2 the full amount of any prepaid or advance premium in the year the prepayment is received. For example, if a $5,000 premium for a 3-year policy was received in the current year, include the full $5,000 amount in the Current Year column.

Appendix 18–2

FORM 1024   (*continued*)

Form 1024 (Rev. 12-89)   Page **16**

Schedule J Organizations described in section 501(c)(17) (Trusts providing for the payment of supplemental unemployment compensation benefits)

1   If benefits are provided for individual proprietors, partners, or self-employed persons under the plan, explain in detail.

2   If the plan provides other benefits in addition to the supplemental unemployment compensation benefits, explain in detail and state whether the other benefits are subordinate to the unemployment benefits.

3   Give the following information as of the first day of the first plan year for which you are filing this application and enter that date here . . . . _____

a   Total number of employees covered by the plan who are shareholders, officers, self-employed persons, or highly compensated (see instructions for line 3a of Schedule F) . . . . _____

b   Number of other employees covered by the plan . . . . _____

c   Number of employees not covered by the plan . . . . _____

d   Total number employed* . . . . _____

*Should equal the total of **a**, **b**, and **c**—if not, explain the difference. Describe the eligibility requirements that prevent those employees not covered by the plan from participating.

4   At any time after December 31, 1959, did the trust engage in any of the transactions listed below with any of the following: the creator of the trust or a contributor to the trust; a brother or sister (whole or half blood), a spouse, an ancestor, or a lineal descendant of such a creator or contributor; or a corporation controlled directly or indirectly by such a creator or contributor?

Note: *If you know that you will be, or are considering being, a party to any of the transactions (or activities) listed below, check the "Planned" box. Give a detailed explanation of any "Yes" or "Planned" answer in the space below.*

a   Borrow any part of your income or corpus? . . . . ☐ Yes ☐ No ☐ Planned
b   Receive any compensation for personal services? . . . . ☐ Yes ☐ No ☐ Planned
c   Obtain any part of your services? . . . . ☐ Yes ☐ No ☐ Planned
d   Purchase any securities or other properties from you? . . . . ☐ Yes ☐ No ☐ Planned
e   Sell any securities or other property to you? . . . . ☐ Yes ☐ No ☐ Planned
f   Receive any of your income or corpus in any other transaction? . . . . ☐ Yes ☐ No ☐ Planned

5   Attach a copy of the Supplemental Unemployment Benefit Plan and related agreements.

Appendix 18-2

FORM 1024 *(continued)*

Form 1024 (Rev. 12-89)   Page **17**

Schedule K	Organizations described in section 501(c)(19)—A post or organization of past or present members of the Armed Forces of the United States, auxiliary units or societies for such a post or organization, and trusts or foundations formed for the benefit of such posts or organizations.

1   *To be completed by a post or organization of past or present members of the Armed Forces of the United States.*

a   Total membership of your post or organization . . . .

b   Number of your members who are present or former members of the U.S. Armed Forces . . . .

c   Number of members who are cadets (include students in college or university ROTC programs or at armed services academies only), or spouses, widows, or widowers, of cadets or past or present members of the U.S. Armed Forces

d   Do you have a membership category other than the ones set out above? . . . . ☐ **Yes**   ☐ **No**

     If "Yes," please explain in full. Enter number of members in this category . . . . _____

e   If you wish to apply for a determination that contributions to you are deductible by donors, enter the number of your members from line 1b who are war veterans, as defined below . . . . _____

     A war veteran is a person who served in the Armed Forces of the United States during the following periods of war: April 21, 1898, through July 4, 1902; April 6, 1917, through November 11, 1918; December 7, 1941, through December 31, 1946; June 27, 1950, through January 31, 1955; and August 5, 1964, through May 7, 1975.

2   *To be completed by an auxiliary unit or society of a post or organization of past or present members of the Armed Forces of the United States.*

a   Are you affiliated with and organized according to the bylaws and regulations formulated by such an exempt post or organization? . . . . ☐ **Yes**   ☐ **No**

     If "Yes," submit a copy of such bylaws or regulations.

b   How many members do you have? . . . .

c   How many are past or present members of the Armed Forces of the United States themselves, their spouses, or persons related to them within two degrees of blood relationship? (Grandparents, brothers, sisters, and grandchildren are the most distant relationships allowable.) . . . .

d   Are all of the members themselves members of a post or organization, past or present members of the Armed Forces of the United States, or spouses of members of such a post or organization, or are related to members of such a post or organization within two degrees of blood relationship? . . . . ☐ **Yes**   ☐ **No**

3   *To be completed by a trust or foundation organized for the benefit of an exempt post or organization of past or present members of the Armed Forces of the United States.*

a   Will the corpus or income be used solely for the funding of such an exempt organization (including necessary related expenses)? . . . . ☐ **Yes**   ☐ **No**

     If "No," please explain.

b   If the trust or foundation is formed for charitable purposes, does the organizational document contain a proper dissolution provision as described in section 1.501(c)(3)-1(b)(4) of the Income Tax Regulations? . . . . ☐ **Yes**   ☐ **No**

FORM 1024 *(continued)*

Note There is no page 18 in Form 1024.

Schedule L   Qualified Group Legal Services Plans (Section 120)

1a Name of plan ▶ _____

b Plan number (See instructions.) . . . . ▶ _____

c Date the plan year ends . . . . ▶ _____

2 A qualification determination or ruling is requested for:

a ☐ Initial qualification—date the plan was adopted . . . . _____

b ☐ Amendment—date adopted . . . . _____

If you check "a," submit a copy of the documents establishing the plan, including a copy of the plan and any related trust instrument. If the plan was subject to collective bargaining, include a copy of the collective bargaining agreement pertaining to it. If you check "b," submit a copy of the amendment.

3 Describe the legal services covered by the plan, if they are not described in the plan or collective bargaining agreement.

4 Give the following information as of the first day of the first plan year for which you are filing this application and enter that date here . . . . ___/___/___ _____

a Total number of employees covered by the plan who are shareholders, officers, self-employed persons, or highly compensated (see instructions for line 3a of Schedule F) . . . . _____

b Number of other employees covered by the plan . . . . _____

c Number of employees not covered by the plan . . . . _____

d Total number employed* . . . . _____

*Should equal the total of **a, b,** and **c**—if not, explain the difference. Describe the eligibility requirements that prevent those employees not covered by the plan from participating.

5 If all eligible employees are NOT entitled to the same benefits, explain the differences.

6 Manner of funding the plan (Check the appropriate box(es).)

a ☐ Payments to insurance companies

b ☐ Payments to organizations described in section 501(c)(20)

c ☐ Payments to organizations described in section 501(c), which are to pay or credit your payments to other organizations described in section 501(c)(20)

d ☐ Prepayments to providers of legal services

See reverse side for instructions.

Appendix 18–2

FORM 1024 *(continued)*

Instructions

If you are filing separate applications under sections 120 and 501(c)(20) at the same time, please indicate this in each application.

Applicants for plan approval under section 120 should read all instructions for Schedules L and M before filling in the application because the same rules do not apply in every situation. Unless you are aware of all the exceptions, you may spend time giving unnecessary information or omit some necessary information. Either could delay getting the plan approved.

(a) In general, all applicants under section 120 should complete Part I and Schedule L. When completing Schedule L, each applicant should supply information regarding its own employees only, not all employees covered by the plan.

(b) Usually, when two or more employers contribute to the same plan, only one applicant must submit a completed application as indicated in (a). Any other or subsequent applicant under the same plan only has to supply enough information to identify the employer and the plan, plus information on Schedule L relating to its own employees.

(c) Except as noted in (d), if an application is filed for a plan to which more than one employer contributes, and the plan is maintained pursuant to a collective bargaining agreement, then only one application, as outlined in (a), is required.

(d) When more than one employer contributes to a plan pursuant to a collective bargaining agreement, and all the employers are corporations that are members of a controlled group, the filing requirements in (b) apply.

(e) If an employer has employees covered by multiple collective bargaining agreements, and one or more of such agreements includes a group legal services plan, which excludes employees under any of the other agreements from participating, then explain such arrangements. The explanation should include a list of the agreements; show the employees included; and explain why.

Line 1a.—Enter the name you chose for your plan.

Line 1b.—Enter the plan number. You must assign a 3-digit number to each adopted plan to identify it. All plan number sequences begin at "501." If you have more than one plan, number them 501, 502, etc. Once you have assigned a plan number, it cannot be changed or used for another plan.

Appendix 18–2

FORM 1024 (*continued*)

Form 1024 (Rev. 12-89)   Page **21**

| Schedule M | Trust or organization set up under section 501(c)(20) |

1a Was this trust or organization created or organized in the United States? . . . . ☐ Yes ☐ No

b If "Yes," was it created or organized to form part of a group legal services plan or plans qualified under section 120? ☐ Yes ☐ No
If "Yes," enter name of plan: _____

c Has the plan (or plans) qualified under section 120? . . . . ☐ Yes ☐ No
If "Yes," submit a copy of the ruling or determination letter(s). If "No," attach an explanation.

2 If the trust or organization provides legal services or indemnification against the cost of legal services unassociated with a qualified group legal services plan, describe the nature and extent of these services.

Attach copies of all plan documents.

Instructions

Complete this schedule if you are applying for exempt status as a trust or other organization organized as part of one or more qualified group legal services plans under section 120. An exemption under 501(c)(20) cannot be recognized unless you are part of a section 120 plan.

If you are filing separate applications under section 120 and 501(c)(20) at the same time, please indicate this in each application.

Line 1c.—If you answered "No" to 1c, but have requested a determination letter, please attach an explanation giving the plan name; the IRS office to which the request was submitted; and the date submitted. All other "No" answers for Schedule M also must be explained.

Appendix 18–2

FORM 1024   (*continued*)

Letter of Conformance

DISPOSABLE BOTTLE ACTION COMMITTEE   EIN #42-2222222

Attachment to Form 1024

I swear that the attached copies of the charter and bylaws of the Disposable Bottle Action Committee are true and correct copies of the originals.

4.4.93
date

Jane Environmental
authorized official

Exhibit 1

NOTE   Forms 2848 and 8717 illustrated with
        Form 1023 would also be attached.

Appendix 18–2

FORM 1024 (*continued*)

EIN # 42-2222222

ARTICLES OF INCORPORATION

OF

DISPOSABLE BOTTLE ACTION COMMITTEE

We, the undersigned natural persons of the age of eighteen (18) years or more, acting as incorporators of a corporation under the Texas Non-Profit Corporation Act, do hereby adopt the following Articles of Incorporation for such corporation.

ARTICLE ONE
Name

The name of the Corporation is DISPOSABLE BOTTLE ACTION COMMITTEE.

ARTICLE TWO
Nonprofit Corporation

The corporation is a nonprofit corporation.

ARTICLE THREE
Duration

The period of the Corporation's duration is perpetual.

ARTICLE FOUR
Purposes

Section 4.01. The Corporation is organized exclusively for promotion of civic welfare purposes as defined in Section 501(c)(4) of the Internal Revenue Code of 1986.

Exhibit 1, page 2

Appendix 18–2

FORM 1024 *(continued)*

DISPOSABLE BOTTLE ACTION COMMITTEE   EIN # 42-2222222

Section 4.02. Notwithstanding any other provisions of these Articles of Incorporation:

    a. No part of the net earnings of the Corporation shall inure to the benefit of any director or officer of the Corporation or any private individual (except that reasonable compensation may be paid for services rendered to or for the Corporation affecting one or more of its purposes); and no director, officer, or any private individual shall be entitled to share in the distribution of any of the corporate assets on dissolution of the Corporation.

    b. The Corporation shall not conduct or carry on any activities not permitted to be conducted or carried on by an organization exempt from taxation under Section 501(c)(4) of the Internal Revenue Code of 1986 and its Regulation as they now exist or as they may hereafter be amended.

    c. Upon dissolution of the Corporation or the winding up of its affairs, the assets of the Corporation shall be distributed to the CAMPAIGN TO CLEAN UP AMERICA, or if it is not in existence, to another nonprofit organization operating to advance civic welfare.

    d. The corporation is organized pursuant to the Texas Non-Profit Corporation Act and does not contemplate gain or profit and is organized for non-profit purposes.

ARTICLE FIVE
Membership

The Corporation shall have no voting members.

Exhibit 1, page 3

Appendix 18–2

FORM 1024 (*continued*)

DISPOSABLE BOTTLE ACTION COMMITTEE   EIN # 42-2222222

ARTICLE SIX
Initial Registered Office and Agent

The street address of the initial registered office of the Corporation is 1111 Any Street, Hometown, TX 77777, and the name of its initial registered agent is Jane D. Environmentalist.

ARTICLE SEVEN
Board of Directors

The number of Directors constituting the initial Board of Directors of the Corporation is three (3), and the names and addresses of those people to serve as the initial Directors are:

Name	Address
Gary G. Generous	222 Fifth Street Hometown, TX 77777
Samantha Zealot	404 University Dr. Austin, TX 78777
Jane D. Environmentalist	333 First Street Hometown, TX 77777

ARTICLE EIGHT
Incorporators

The names and street addresses of the incorporator is:

Name	Address
Jane D. Environmentalist	333 First Street Hometown, TX 77777

Exhibit 1, page 4

Appendix 18–2

FORM 1024 (*continued*)

DISPOSABLE BOTTLE ACTION COMMITTEE   EIN # 42-2222222

ARTICLE NINE
Indemnification

The Corporation shall indemnify every director or officer or former director or officer of the Corporation against all judgments, penalties (including excise and similar taxes), fines, amounts paid in settlement with the view of avoiding the expense of litigation and reasonable expenses actually incurred in connection with any proceeding in which he or she was, is, or is threatened to be named defendant or respondent, or in which he or she was or is a witness without being named a defendant or respondent, by reason, in whole or in part, or his or her serving or having served in the capacity of a director or officer, or having been nominated or designated to serve if it is determined that he or she has conducted himself or herself in good faith, reasonably believed that his or her conduct was in the Corporation's best interest and in the case of a criminal proceeding, had no reasonable cause to believe that his or her conduct was unlawful, provided, however, no director or officer shall be indemnified (a) with respect to matters as to which he or she shall be adjudged in such action, suit, or proceeding or be liable to the corporation, (b) with respect to matters as to which he or she shall be adjudged in such action, suit or proceeding to be liable for negligence or intentional misconduct in performance of duty, (c) with respect to any matters which shall be settled by the payment of sums which independent counsel selected by the directors shall not deem reasonable payment, made primarily with a view to avoiding expense of litigation, (d) with respect to any matters in which he or she is found liable on the basis that personal benefit was improperly received by him or her, or (e) with respect to matters for which such indemnifications would be against public policy. A determination of indemnification shall be made by either a majority vote of a quorum consisting of directors who at the time of the vote are not named defendants or respondents in the proceeding or by an independent legal counsel selected by the board of directors. Such rights of directors or officers may be entitled under any bylaw, agreement, corporate resolution, vote of directors or otherwise. The Corporation shall have the power to purchase or maintain at its cost and expense insurance on behalf of such persons to the fullest extent permitted by this Article and applicable state law.

Exhibit 1, page 5

Appendix 18–2

FORM 1024 *(continued)*

DISPOSABLE BOTTLE ACTION COMMITTEE   EIN # 42-2222222

ARTICLE TEN
Limitation of Liability

No director shall be liable to the Corporation for monetary damages for an act or omission in the director's capacity as a director of the corporation, except and only for the following:

      (a)   A breach of the director's duty or loyalty to the Corporation;

      (b)   An act or omission not in good faith by the director or an act or omission that involves intentional misconduct or knowing violation of the law by the director;

      (c)   A transaction from which the director gained any improper benefit whether or not such benefit resulted from an action taken within the scope of the director's office; or

      (d)   An act or omission by the director for which liability is expressly provided for by statute.

      IN WITNESS WHEREOF, the undersigned incorporator does hereby affix her signature.

3.10.93   *Jane Environmentalist*

Appendix 18–2

FORM 1024   (*continued*)

EIN # 42-2222222

BYLAWS

OF

DISPOSABLE ACTION BOTTLE COMMITTEE

ARTICLE I
Name of Corporation

A Texas non-profit corporation named DISPOSABLE ACTION BOTTLE COMMITTEE (the "Committee") has been established and its principal office is in HOMETOWN, TEXAS.

ARTICLE II
Purposes

The Committee is organized exclusively for the promotion of social welfare as defined in Internal Revenue Code §501(c)(4).

ARTICLE III
Members

The Committee shall have no members.

ARTICLE IV
Board of Directors

Committee affairs shall be managed by its Board of Directors.

There shall be no less than three (3) nor more than nine (9) directors who will serve one year terms. Directors shall be appointed by the member(s). Any Director may resign by giving written notice to the member(s). The resignation shall be effective at the next regular meeting of the Board of Directors. A Director may be removed with or without cause by the member(s). Replacement directors will be named by the member(s).

Exhibit 1, page 7

Appendix 18–2

FORM 1024 (*continued*)

EIN # 42-2222222

DISPOSABLE ACTION BOTTLE COMMITTEE   BYLAWS, page 2

Directors shall not receive compensation for their services as Directors but can receive reimbursement for expenses and can be engaged to perform other services for the Committee as long as the compensation is not excessive as that term is used in Section 4941(d)(2)(E) of the Internal Revenue Code.

ARTICLE V
Meetings of the Board

The Board of Directors shall have one annual meeting. Special meetings, as needed, may be called by the president. Meeting notice should be given five days in advance either in writing or by telephone. Attendance at the meeting shall constitute waiver of notice except where a Director attends the meeting with the express purpose of objecting to the transaction of any business because the meeting is not lawfully called or convened.

A majority of the Directors present at any meeting shall constitute the quorum for purposes of transacting any business of the Committee.

A director may vote in person or by proxy executed in writing. A proxy shall be valid for three months from date of execution and is irrevocable.

ARTICLE VI
Officers

The officers of the Committee shall consist of a President, a Vice President/Treasurer, and a Secretary.

The officers of the Committee shall be elected by the Board of Directors at the annual meeting. Any officer of the Corporation may be removed by a vote of the majority of the Board of Directors then in office.

Exhibit 1, page 8

Appendix 18–2

FORM 1024 (*continued*)

EIN # 42-2222222

DISPOSABLE ACTION BOTTLE COMMITTEE   BYLAWS, page 3

President. The President shall supervise and conduct Committee activities and operations. He or she shall preside at all meetings and shall keep the Board informed concerning the activities of the Committee. He or she may sign, in the name of the Committee, all contracts and documents authorized by the Board. He or she shall have the authority to establish committees and to appoint members to serve on such committees.

Vice President. The Vice President shall have such powers and duties delegated to him or her by the President. He will serve as president during the absence of the President.

Secretary. The Secretary shall act as Secretary of all meetings of the Board of Directors, and shall keep the minutes of all such meetings. He or she shall attend to the giving and serving of all notices of the Committee. He or she shall perform all duties customarily incident to the office of Secretary.

Treasurer. The Treasurer shall have custody of all funds and securities of the Committee. He or she shall keep or cause to be kept full and accurate accounts of receipts and disbursements of the Committee and shall deposit all moneys and other valuable effects of the Committee in such banks or depositories as the Board of Directors may designate.

ARTICLE VII
General Provisions

Contracts. The Board of Directors may authorize any officer or officers to enter into any contract on behalf of the Committee; such authority must be in writing.

Checks, Drafts, etc. All checks, drafts and other orders for payment of money shall be signed by Board designated officers.

Gifts. The Board of Directors may accept on behalf of the Committee any contribution, gift, bequest of devise for general purposes or for any special purpose of the Committee.

Exhibit 1, page 9

FORM 1024 *(continued)*

EIN # 42-2222222

DISPOSABLE ACTION BOTTLE COMMITTEE   BYLAWS, page 4

ARTICLE VII, continued.

<u>Books.</u> There shall be kept at the office of the Committee correct books of account of the activities and transactions of the Committee, including a minute book which shall contain a copy of the Articles of Incorporation, these bylaws and all minutes of the meetings of the Board of Directors.

<u>Indemnification.</u> The Directors shall be indemnified by the Committee against liabilities imposed upon them and expenses reasonably incurred by them in connection with any claim against them, or any action, suit or proceeding to which they may be a party by reason of their being a director. No director is indemnified (a) with respect to matters for which they shall be adjudged in such action, suit or proceeding to be liable for negligence or misconduct in performance of duty, (b) with respect to any matters which shall be settled by the payment of sums which independent counsel selected by the member(s) shall not deem reasonable payment made primarily with a view to avoiding expense of litigation, or (c) with respect to matters for which such indemnification would be against public policy.

<u>Fiscal Year.</u> The year shall be from July 1 to June 30.

<u>Amendments.</u> The member(s) may amend the bylaws at any regular or special meeting prior to which proper notice was given.

CERTIFICATE

I HEREBY CERTIFY that the foregoing is a true, complete and correct copy of the Bylaws of DISPOSABLE BOTTLE ACTION COMMITTEE, a Texas nonprofit corporation, in effect on the date hereof.

IN WITNESS WHEREOF, I hereunto set my hand this 2 day of *April* 19 93.

Linda Lockard
Secretary

Exhibit 1, page 10

Appendix 18–2

FORM 1024 (*continued*)

Disposable Bottle Action Committee   EIN #42-2222222

Attachment to Form 1024, Part II, item 1.

Disposable Bottle Action Committee (DBAC) was formed to initiate a nationwide campaign to propose and pass legislation to eliminate disposable containers and reward recycling efforts. By reducing trash, encouraging the conservation of resources, and curtailing pollutants to our land, water, and air, DBAC's goal is to advance the community welfare.

LEGISLATION--DBAC plans to be an action organization, whose purposes are accomplished through passage of legislation. Model legislation will be drafted (based upon the California and Washington state models) for passage of a comprehensive waste management law based upon eventual elimination of disposable containers and other toxic wastes. Committees will be formed in as many states as possible to conduct petition campaigns to lobby congress people to support the legislation.

RESEARCH--The Ecology Department of Michigan State University and Northwestern University were contacted and have agreed to cosponsor a year long research project to evaluate the economic and ecological consequences of disposable containers. While DBAC will not contribute financially to the efforts, the results of the studies will be available for use in the legislative efforts. It is hoped that the University of California at Berkeley or a similar West Coast institution will be convinced to study the consequences of their existing beverage container laws.

FUND RAISING and PUBLIC EDUCATION--Committees will be formed in key states to raise funds to finance the campaign and raise the consciousness about the issue of wastes and the need for reducing garbage through recycling and elimination of disposable containers. Funds will be raised through outright gifts, dinners, and sale of bumper stickers, buttons, and other campaign materials.

Exhibit 2

Appendix 18–2

FORM 1024 (*continued*)

Disposable Bottle Action Committee   EIN #42-2222222

Proposed Budgets

DISPOSABLE BOTTLE ACTION COMMITTEE
REVENUES AND EXPENSES

	19X0	19XI
Membership dues	$ 25,000	$ 50,000
Exempt function sales:		
Bumper stickers	5,000	10,000
Posters	2,000	5,000
Buttons	2,000	5,000
Model legislation	2,000	5,000
TOTAL REVENUES	36,000	75,000
Campaign coordinator*	$ 10,000	30,000
Telephone	5,000	12,000
Mailing	5,000	12,000
Printing	5,000	12,000
Cost of stickers, posters,		
buttons	2,000	6,000
Occupancy**	2,000	3,000
TOTAL EXPENDITURES	29,000	75,000
Working capital reserve	7,000	0
	$ 36,000	$ 75,000

*The Campaign coordinator is an independent contractor who serves as consultant to nonprofit organizations conducting lobbying campaigns. Compensation is based upon actual time expended at the rate of $15 per hour plus reimbursement of direct out-of-pocket expenses.

**DBAC will sublease one room in an office building owned by an unrelated party from a director, Jane D. Environmentalist. The lease will be at cost on a month-to-month basis.

Exhibit 3

Maintaining Exempt Status

CHAPTER NINETEEN

Maintaining Exempt
Status

Once an organization's tax-exempt status is recognized by the Internal Revenue Service, applicable states, and other authorities, the task is to maintain such status. This chapter contains checklists that outline compliance requirements and areas of primary concern. The checklists are designed to remind an exempt organization (EO), its managers, and professionals who assist EOs of areas of concern deserving annual review. The objective is to assure an organization's ongoing qualification for exemption.

The sheer number of items on the lists is evidence of the complexity and scope of issues involved in maintaining exempt status. As you first read the opening checklist, do not expect to understand all the terms if you are not a nonprofit organization specialist. Many of the issues are considered in depth in other chapters, and they will hopefully become clear as the materials are studied.

The Annual Tax Compliance Checklist for 501(c)(3)s (Checklist 19–1) can be used yearly to test compliance with a variety of requirements, including the organizational test, the operational test, identification of unrelated business income, payroll tax compliance, public support tests, private foundation sanctions, filing requirements, excise and estimated tax requirements, property contributions, fund-raising event disclosures, public inspection requirements, and group exemption filing requirements.

The Annual Tax Compliance Checklist for Exempt Organizations other than 501(c)(3)s (Checklist 19–2) asks similar questions. It is completed for exempt organizations qualifying in categories 501(c)(2), (4), (5), (6), (7), and so on.

The Short Form Exempt Organization Annual Tax Compliance Checklist 19–3 provides an abbreviated checklist for use with all types of organizations.

ANNUAL TAX COMPLIANCE FOR 501(c)(3) ORGANIZATIONS

Organizational Test

☐ 1. Have all exemptions been applied for in a timely manner? (See Chapter 18.)

a. Federal exemption (Form 1023).

i. Newly created organization: Has Form 1023 been filed within 15 months after organization began to do business? ____

ii. Young organization (one to five years old): When does the advance ruling period expire? Has an IRS report been filed within 90 days of that date? ____

iii. All organizations: Review Form 1023 and determination letter for exempt purposes originally represented to the IRS and to verify the category of exemption. Satisfy yourself that current activities are in keeping with that purpose. ____

b. State franchise and sales tax.

i. Obtain a copy of Secretary of State's exemption letter or prepare application for exemption Exhibit 18 – 7. ____

ii. Does the organization use the proper form to claim exemption? ____

iii. Is the organization subject to sales tax on its sales activity? Does it have a permit? Are quarterly returns filed? ____

c. Local property taxes.

i. Does the organization pay real or personal property tax? ____

ii. Does it qualify for exemption? ____

iii. Does it rent or make other commercial use of property for which exemption was previously granted? ____

☐ 2. Charter and bylaws. (See Chapter 2.)

a. Were there any changes to the charter or bylaws during the year? ____

b. Review the minutes of directors' meetings. Do they reflect the exempt purpose of the organization's activities? ____

c. Were there any substantial changes in structure or purpose that require reporting to the IRS? (See Chapter 28.) ____

i. Change reported on Form 990? ____

ii. New Form 1023 required? ____

Checklist 19–1 (*continued*)

ANNUAL TAX COMPLIANCE FOR 501(c)(3) ORGANIZATIONS

Operational Test

☐ 1. Is there private inurement? (See Chapter 20.) ___

    a. Does the organization do business with directors or substantial contributors? ___

    b. Is the amount of compensation paid to officers, directors, and staff reasonable? ___

    c. Does the organization benefit a limited number of persons? ___

    d. Are loans made to officers or directors? ___

    e. Does the organization sell services or goods produced by its staff or members? ___

    f. Does the EO operate to benefit a related organization? (See Chapter 22.) ___

☐ 2. Exempt activities. (See Chapters 2–5.)

    a. Do activities further the purposes for which the organization was exempt (as stipulated in Form 1023)? Has it started new projects or discontinued old ones? ___

    b. Are files maintained to document the nature of activities? (For example, copy of exhibition invitations, class schedules, grants paid.) ___

    c. Does the organization lobby? If so, has it filed Form 5768? Does it meet the limitations? (See Chapter 23.) ___

    d. Has the organization participated in any political campaigns? Review newsletters for endorsements of candidates. ___

    e. Does the organization have unrelated business income? If so, complete Form 990-T (see Chapter 27) and the UBI portion of this checklist. ___

    f. Does the organization comply with payroll withholding and reporting requirements? (Complete employees and payroll taxes checklist and see Chapter 25.) ___

    g. Has the IRS ever examined the organization? Review reports for compliance with any changes. (See Chapter 28.) ___

☐ 3. Complete the "publicly supported" or "private foundation" checklist.

Checklist 19–1   (*continued*)

ANNUAL TAX COMPLIANCE FOR 501(c)(3) ORGANIZATIONS

Unrelated Business Income

☐ 1. Does the organization sell goods or services in an activity that does not relate to or further its exempt purposes? (See Chapter 21.)

☐ 2. Is the business activity substantial (as measured by gross revenue or staff time devoted to it) in relation to the organization's exempt activity?

☐ 3. Has Form 990-T been filed in prior years?

☐ 4. Does the gross income exceed $1,000? Even if losses are realized, Form 990-T is required and desirable to establish net operating loss carryover or carryback.

☐ 5. Do the accounting records allow for allocation for all applicable expenses?

    a. Time records for staff.   ____

    b. Square footage of spaces used.   ____

    c. Allocation of membership dues to publications.   ____

☐ 6. Does the organization do any of the following?

    a. Sell advertisements in its publications? (Complete worksheet (Exhibit 21–2) on calculation of taxable income.)   ____

    b. Rent personal or real property?   ____

    c. Earn any income from indebted property, margin accounts, or loans?   ____

    d. Sell its mailing list?   ____

    e. Operate a bookstore, restaurant, or parking lot? (Does the fragmentation rule apply to classify a portion of sales from bookstore or shop as unrelated, even though most items are related?)   ____

    f. Furnish or sell services?   ____

    g. Carry out any of the above activities through a separate but controlled business corporation or partnership?   ____

ANNUAL TAX COMPLIANCE FOR 501(c)(3) ORGANIZATIONS

☐ 7. Do the following exceptions apply? ___

   a. The activity is not carried on regularly. ___

   b. Substantially all (85 percent) of the work in carrying out the trade or business is performed by volunteers. ___

   c. The facility is operated for the convenience of persons participating in the organization's activities. ___

   d. The items sold are either donated, educational, or directly related to the exempt function. ___

   e. Items are "low-cost" premiums sold for significantly more than their value. (See Section 21.10(a).) ___

   f. The income is of a passive nature (e.g., dividends, interest, or royalties). ___

Employees and Payroll Taxes (Complete Checklist 25–2.)

☐ 1. Does the organization have a policy for distinguishing between employees and independent contractors? ___

☐ 2. Verify timely filing of the following federal forms:

☐ 3. Verify timely deposit of employment taxes.

☐ 4. Does the organization meet all the requirements of its state employment commission?

Publicly Supported Organizations

☐ 1. Can the organization meet its public support tests under either IRC §509(a)(1) or §509(a)(2)? Complete the support test worksheet in Chapter 11 on a cash basis.

☐ 2. If the organization claims to be a supporting organization, can satisfaction of the "responsiveness" or "control and supervision" tests be documented?

☐ 3. Are deadlines for filing a report scheduled before the 60-month termination date?

☐ 4. Is fund-raising conducted in a state that requires reports? Does a state charitable solicitation act apply?

Checklist 19–1 (*continued*)

ANNUAL TAX COMPLIANCE FOR 501(c)(3) ORGANIZATIONS

☐ 5. Has the organization complied with an IRS request for fair market value information regarding donated property, pursuant to publication 1391? (See Chapter 24.)

☐ 6. Are there sales of donated property (other than listed securities) to be reported?

☐ 7. Have expense allocations and shared expenses with related §501(c)(4), (c)(5), or (c)(6) organizations been calculated accurately?

☐ 8. If the EO is a school, has notice of its nondiscrimination policy been published in newspaper of general circulation in the area? (See Exhibit 27–4.)

☐ 9. Compile, review, or audit the checklist to insure proper financial reporting and adherence to accounting principles.

Private Foundation Considerations

☐ 1. Should the foundation consider conversion to a public charity or private operating foundation? (See Section 12.6.)

☐ 2. Should the foundation choose to make qualifying distributions to reduce its excise tax? (Section 13.1.)

☐ 3. Does the foundation have substantially appreciated property it could distribute to grantees to reduce excise taxes on sale of the property?

☐ 4. Has the foundation maintained records to support allocation of its expenses among investment, administrative, and exempt activities? Is the allocation consistent with those for prior years? (Section 13.4.)

☐ 5. Is the tax basis of assets maintained separately from the book basis?

☐ 6. Must adjustments be made to "qualifying distributions" for the following? (Section 15.3.)

    a. Sale of exempt assets previously classified as distribution. ____

    b. Amounts not redistributed in a timely manner by another private foundation or controlled organization. ____

    c. Set-asides not used for an approved purpose. ____

Checklist 19–1 *(continued)*

ANNUAL TAX COMPLIANCE FOR 501(c)(3) ORGANIZATIONS

☐ 7. Use the Form 990-PF questions (Appendix 27–6) and checklist to verify the following:

   a. No self-dealing. (See Chapter 14.)   ___

   b. No failure to meet minimum distribution requirements. (See Chapter 15.)   ___

   c. No jeopardizing investments. (See Chapter 16.)   ___

   d. No excess business holdings. (See Chapter 16.)   ___

   e. No taxable expenditures. (See Chapter 17.)   ___

☐ 8. Have expenditure responsibility reporting and monitoring systems been reviewed and information submitted on Form 990PF?

☐ 9. Must sales of donated property (other than listed securities) be reported?

☐ 10. Has a compilation, review, or audit checklist been completed to insure proper financial reporting and adherence to accounting principles?

Filing Requirements (See Chapter 27.)

☐ 1. Form 990-PF must be filed for all private foundations, regardless of support levels (including a PF on 60-month termination).

☐ 2. Form 990 and Form 990, Schedule A, must be filed for publicly supported §501(c)(3) organizations whose total annual gross *receipts* exceed $25,000, except:

   a. One-year-old EO whose receipts are $37,500 or less.   ___

   b. Two- or three-year-old EO whose receipts average $30,000 or less.   ___

☐ 3. Form 990EZ must be filed for EOs with between $25,000 and $100,000 of gross receipts and under $250,000 of assets.

☐ 4. A preprinted Form 990 received by an EO not required to file should be filed with the IRS, after checking the box (now H) on page one indicating receipts under $25,000.

ANNUAL TAX COMPLIANCE FOR 501(c)(3) ORGANIZATIONS

☐ 5. Churches, church affiliates, §501(c)(1) organizations, state or municipal institutions (IRC §115 income), and religious orders (Form 1065 filed for income-producing activities, if any) are not required to file regardless of receipt levels.

☐ 6. Exempt organizations whose *net* gross revenue is under $25,000 (shown on line 12 of page 1) need not report expenses on Part B by functions and can omit balance sheet details.

☐ 7. Extension of time to file can be requested using:

    a. Form 2758 for Forms 990 and 990-PF.   ____

    b. Form 7005 for Form 990-T.   ____

☐ 8. The penalty for failure to file is $10 a day up to $5,000 or 5 percent of gross receipts if that amount is less than $5,000.

    a. Managers can also be penalized individually if the return is still not filed after the IRS makes a written demand.   ____

    b. Notice mailed to an organization's last known address is valid.   ____

Excise Taxes

☐ 1. Is Form 4720 required? (Exhibit 12–2.)

    a. Private foundation violating IRC §4941 or §4945 sanctions.   ____

    b. Public charity with excess lobbying (IRC §4911).   ____

    c. Disqualifying lobbying expenditures made (IRC §4912).   ____

    d. Political expenditures made (IRC §4955).   ____

☐ 2. Is the private foundation subject to IRC §4945 tax on political activities?

☐ 3. Reconsider the need to elect IRC §501(h) for lobbying activities, in view of IRC §4912.

Estimated Taxes

☐ 1. Are quarterly payments of tax due with Forms 990-T or 990-PF?

☐ 2. Are federal tax deposit coupons (Form 8109) available?

Checklist 19–1 *(continued)*

ANNUAL TAX COMPLIANCE FOR 501(c)(3) ORGANIZATIONS

Property Contribution Requirements

☐ 1. Has the organization received gifts of property for which Form 8283 is required?

☐ 2. Must Form 8282 be filed to report sales of any donated property (valued over $5,000) within two years from date of gift? (The form might trigger a reduction in the donor's deduction.)

Fund-Raising Events and Sales Deductibility

☐ 1. Do contribution solicitations reveal the fair market value of goods or services or other consideration given to donors? (See Rev. Rul. 67-246, 1967-2 C.B. 104; IRS Publication 1391; and Chapter 24.)

☐ 2. Is a reasonable effort made to measure fair market value and document the deductible amount for donors?

☐ 3. Are records maintained for possible IRS scrutiny?

Public Inspection Requirements (See Section 27.2.)

☐ 1. Information is subject to the public inspection requirements of IRC §6104.

    a. Form 990 (but not 990-T) must be made available to the general public upon request for three years from its filing date. (Form 990-PF for 180 days.) ____

    b. Complete copies, with all schedules and attachments except contributor lists, must be shown. ____

    c. Form 1023 — with IRS letters, documents issued, legal briefs, and correspondence concerning the application — must also be made available. An EO that applied before July 15, 1987 is excused from this requirement if it had no copy on July 15, 1987. ____

☐ 2. The penalty for noncompliance is $10 for each day inspection is not allowed, up to a maximum of $5,000 for each return. (There is no maximum for failure to supply Form 1023.)

Checklist 19–1 (*continued*)

ANNUAL TAX COMPLIANCE FOR 501(c)(3) ORGANIZATIONS

Group Exemptions (See Section 18.1.)

☐ 1. If the exempt organization is part of a group, will it be included in a consolidated return filed for subordinates?

  a. If so, has financial information been furnished to the parent organization? ___

  b. If not, must the EO file a separate Form 990? ___

☐ 2. The parent must file its own return, excluding subsidiaries, if its receipts exceed $25,000. ___

☐ 3. For parent: At least 90 days before close of social year, file annual report of subsidiary changes.

☐ 4. For subsidiaries: In time to allow the parent to timely file annually, furnish parent changes.

Checklist 19–2

ANNUAL TAX COMPLIANCE FOR NON-501(c)(3) ORGANIZATIONS

Organizational Test

☐ 1. Have all exemptions been applied for in a timely manner? (See Section 18.5.)

    a. Federal exemption (Form 1024).

        i. Newly created organizations: Should Form 1024 be filed to obtain assurance that the proposed operations qualify for exemption?   ____

        ii. All organizations: Review Form 1024 and determination letter for exempt purposes originally represented to the IRS and to verify the category of exemption. Satisfy yourself that current activities are in keeping with that purpose.   ____

    b. State franchise, sales, or income taxes.

        i. Ascertain whether the exempt organization qualifies for any tax exemptions.   ____

        ii. Does the organization use the proper form to claim exemption?   ____

        iii. Is the organization subject to sales tax on its sales activity? Does it have a permit? Are quarterly returns filed?   ____

    c. Local property taxes.

        i. Does the organization pay real or personal property tax?   ____

        ii. Does it qualify for exemption?   ____

        iii. Does it rent or make other commercial use of property for which exemption was previously granted?   ____

☐ 2. Charter and bylaws.

    a. Were there any changes to the charter or bylaws during the year?   ____

    b. Review the minutes of directors' meetings. Do they reflect the exempt purpose of the organization's activities?   ____

    c. Were there any substantial changes in structure or purpose that require reporting to the IRS? (See Chapter 28.)   ____

        i. Change reported on Form 990?   ____

        ii. New Form 1024 required?   ____

Checklist 19–2 *(continued)*

ANNUAL TAX COMPLIANCE FOR NON-501(c)(3) ORGANIZATIONS

Operational Test

☐ 1. Is there private inurement? (See Chapter 20.)

    a. Does the organization do business with directors or substantial contributors? ____

    b. Is the amount of compensation paid to officers, directors, and staff reasonable? ____

    c. Does the organization benefit a limited number of persons? ____

    d. Are loans made to officers or directors? ____

    e. Does the organization sell services or goods produced by its staff or members? ____

    f. Does the EO operate to benefit a related organization? (See Chapter 22.) ____

☐ 2. Exempt activities. (See Chapters 6 – 9.)

    a. Do activities further the purposes for which the organization was exempt (as stipulated in Form 1024)? Has it started new projects or discontinued old ones? ____

    b. Are files maintained to document the nature of activities? (For example, conferences, peer reviews, club meetings.) ____

    c. Does the organization lobby? Is the lobbying germane to exempt purposes? If not, is it excessive? (See Chapter 23.) ____

    d. Has the organization participated in any political campaigns? Does involvement serve an exempt purpose? ____

    e. Does the organization have unrelated business income? If so, complete Form 990-T and the UBI portion of this checklist. ____

    f. Does the organization comply with payroll withholding and reporting requirements? (Complete employees and payroll taxes checklist and see Chapter 25.) ____

    g. Has the IRS ever examined the organization? Review reports for compliance with any changes. (See Chapter 28.) ____

☐ 3. Has a compilation, review, or audit checklist been completed to insure proper financial reporting and adherence to accounting principles?

Checklist 19–2 *(continued)*

ANNUAL TAX COMPLIANCE FOR NON-501(c)(3) ORGANIZATIONS

Unrelated Business Income (See Chapter 21.)

☐ 1. Does the organization sell goods or services in an activity that does not relate to or further its exempt purposes?

☐ 2. Is the business activity substantial (as measured by gross revenue or staff time devoted to it) in relation to the organization's exempt activity?

☐ 3. Has Form 990-T been filed in prior years?

☐ 4. Does the gross income exceed $1,000? Even if losses are realized, Form 990-T is required and desirable to establish net operating loss carryover or carryback.

☐ 5. Do the accounting records allow for allocation for all applicable expenses?

    a. Time records for staff.   ____

    b. Square footage of spaces used.   ____

    c. Allocation of membership dues to publications.   ____

☐ 6. Does the organization do any of the following?

    a. Sell advertisements in its publications? (Complete worksheet in Exhibit 21 – 2 on calculation of taxable income.)   ____

    b. Rent personal or real property?   ____

    c. Earn any income from indebted property, margin accounts, or loans?   ____

    d. Sell its mailing list? Insurance? Forms?   ____

    e. Operate a bookstore, restaurant, or parking lot? (Does the fragmentation rule apply to classify portion of sales from bookstore or shop as unrelated, even though most of items are related?)   ____

    f. Furnish or sell services?   ____

    g. Carry out any of the above activities through a separate but controlled business corporation or partnership?   ____

Checklist 19–2   (*continued*)

ANNUAL TAX COMPLIANCE FOR NON-501(c)(3) ORGANIZATIONS

Employees and Payroll Taxes (See Chapter 25.)

☐ 1. Does the organization have a policy for distinguishing between employees and independent contractors?

    a. Verify satisfaction of the tests for employee versus independent contractor status.   ____

    b. Does the organization have contracts with independent contractors?   ____

    c. Are vendor invoices issued by independent contractors?   ____

    d. Are signed Forms W-9 on file for contractors, showing their social security numbers and withholding exemptions? (Exhibit 25–2.)   ____

☐ 2. Are meals, cars, tuition, or housing allowances furnished to employees? Determine whether they are reportable compensation.

☐ 3. Is Form 5500, 5500C, or 5500R required for a pension plan?

☐ 4. Are ERISA rules complied with for pension plans?

☐ 5. Is there proper documentation of nonqualified deferred compensation arrangements?

☐ 6. Verify timely filing of the following federal forms:

    a. Form 941, employer's quarterly federal tax return.   ____

    b. Forms W-2 to all employees.   ____

    c. Forms W-2P for pension recipients.   ____

    d. Forms W-2G for prizes and awards.   ____

    e. Form W-3 to IRS with copies of Forms W-2.   ____

    f. Form 940 to report unemployment taxes.   ____

    g. Forms 1096 and 1099 for all independent contractors.   ____

    h. Form W-4 placed in each employee's file.   ____

☐ 7. Verify timely deposit of employment taxes.

Checklist 19–2 (*continued*)

ANNUAL TAX COMPLIANCE FOR NON-501(c)(3) ORGANIZATIONS

☐ 8. Does the organization meet all the requirements of its state employment commission?

    a. Has the organization obtained an account number by filing with the state employment commission for recognition of status?   ____

    b. Are reports filed quarterly?   ____

    c. Were timely deposits of taxes made?   ____

Filing Requirements (See Chapter 27.)

☐ 1. Form 990 must be filed annually for all exempt organizations whose total gross *receipts* exceed $25,000, except:

    a. One-year-old EO whose receipts are $37,500 or less.   ____

    b. Two- or three-year-old EO whose receipts average $30,000 or less.   ____

☐ 2. Form 990EZ must be filed by an EO with between $25,000 and $100,000 of gross receipts and under $250,000 of assets.

☐ 3. A preprinted Form 990 received by an EO not required to file should be filed with the IRS, after checking the box on page one indicating receipts under $25,000.

☐ 4. Exempt organizations whose *net* gross revenue is under $25,000 (shown on line 12 of page 1) need not report expenses on Part B by functions and can omit balance sheet details.

☐ 5. Extension of time to file can be requested:

    a. Form 2758 for Forms 990 and 990-PF (two months).   ____

    b. Form 7005 for Form 990-T (six months).   ____

☐ 6. The penalty for failure to file is $10 a day up to $5,000, or 5 percent of gross receipts if the result is less than $5,000.

    a. Managers can also be penalized individually if the return is still not filed after the IRS makes a written demand.   ____

    b. Notice mailed to an organization's last known address is valid.   ____

Checklist 19–2 (*continued*)

ANNUAL TAX COMPLIANCE FOR NON-501(c)(3) ORGANIZATIONS

Estimated Taxes

☐ 1. Are quarterly payments of income tax due with Form 990-T?

☐ 2. Are federal tax deposit coupons (Form 8109) available?

Tax on Political Activity

☐ 1. Is Form 1120-POL required to be filed?

☐ 2. Are expense allocations and expenses shared with related §501(c)(3), (4), (5), or (6) organizations accurately calculated?

Notice of Nondeductibility

☐ 1. Any fund-raising solicitations must "conspicuously" disclose on the request for funds that contributions will not qualify for deduction as charitable gifts.

    a. Exempt organizations whose receipts normally do not exceed $100,000 are exempt.   ____

    b. The type size used to print the notice must be at least as large as other type on the solicitation.   ____

☐ 2. The penalty for noncompliance is $1,000 for each day of failure, up to a maximum of $10,000.

Public Inspection Requirements

☐ 1. Information is subject to the public inspection requirements of IRC §6104.

    a. Form 990 (but not 990-T or 1120-POL) must be made available to the general public upon request for three years from its filing date.   ____

    b. Complete copies, with all schedules and attachments, must be shown.   ____

    c. The public reviewer must be allowed to take notes.   ____

    d. Copies to take away need not be provided, but the EO is expected to make copying possible. If it is agreeable to both, the reviewer can be allowed to take copies and be charged up to one dollar for the first page and 25 cents for each page thereafter.   ____

Checklist 19–2 *(continued)*

ANNUAL TAX COMPLIANCE FOR NON-501(c)(3) ORGANIZATIONS

    e. Form 1024 — with IRS letters, documents issued, legal briefs, and correspondence concerning the application — must also be made available. An EO that applied before July 15, 1987, is excused from this requirement if it had no copy on July 15, 1987. ____

    f. Regional and local offices with at least three employees must have duplicates of the forms available. ____

    g. EOs covered by a group exemption must furnish the group's returns, plus the information listed above. ____

    h. The EO's response to a request must be immediate unless it has no principal place of business. ____

☐ 2. The penalty for noncompliance is $10 for each day inspection is not allowed, up to a maximum of $5,000 for each return. (There is no maximum for failure to supply Form 1024.)

Social Clubs (See Chapter 9.)

☐ 1. Can the organization meet the 35/15 gross revenue tests?

    a. No more than 35 percent of receipts from nonmember sources. ____

    b. No more than 15 percent of total use of club facilities and services by general public. ____

☐ 2. Does the club lose money on its provision of nonmember services?

    a. Do accounting records allow identification of direct and indirect costs? ____

    b. Are fixed club expenses charged against nonmember income? ____

Group Exemptions

☐ 1. If the exempt organization is a chapter or affiliate of a group, will the central organization include it in the group's return?

    a. If so, has financial information been furnished to the parent organization? ____

    b. If not, must the EO file a separate Form 990? ____

☐ 2. If the exempt organization is the parent, is a separate return required?

Checklist 19–2   (*continued*)

ANNUAL TAX COMPLIANCE FOR NON-501(c)(3) ORGANIZATIONS

☐ 3. For parent: At least 90 days before close of fiscal year, file annual report of subsidiary changes.

☐ 4. For subsidiaries: In time to allow the parent to timely file annual group member changes, furnish parent the following:

    a. Changes in name or address. ____

    b. Notice of withdrawal as member of group. ____

    c. Intention to become new member of group (furnish organizational documents for filing with IRS). ____

    d. Description of changes in purpose, method of operations, or other "substantial" changes in activities. ____

Checklist 19-3

SHORT FORM FOR ANNUAL TAX COMPLIANCE FOR TAX-EXEMPT ORGANIZATIONS

Organizational Test

☐ 1. Have all exemptions been applied for in a timely manner?

    a. Federal final determination received.   ____

    b. State franchise, income, sales, or other exemptions.   ____

    c. Local property taxes.   ____

☐ 2. Were there changes in charter, bylaws, or purposes?

Operational Test

☐ 1. Were there any insider transactions causing private inurement?

☐ 2. Are activities in furtherance of exempt purposes?

    a. Started new activities to report to IRS?   ____

    b. Are files maintained to document nature of activities?   ____

    c. If EO lobbies, should Form 5768 be filed?   ____

    d. Any political activity?   ____

    e. Is there excessive unrelated business income?   ____

    f. Is payroll tax withholding required?   ____

☐ 3. Are exempt disbursements sufficient for commensurate test?

☐ 4. Are fund balances excessive?

Filing Requirements

☐ 1. Is Form 990 required? If so, can and should EZ be filed?

☐ 2. Is Form 990-T required? (Complete UBI checklist.)

☐ 3. Are payroll and information returns filed? (Complete checklist.)

☐ 4. Should extension of time to file be requested?

☐ 5. Has change of accounting method occurred? (See Chapter 28.)

☐ 6. Should tax filing year be changed? (See Chapter 28.)

Checklist 19–3 (*continued*)

SHORT FORM FOR ANNUAL TAX COMPLIANCE FOR TAX-EXEMPT ORGANIZATIONS

☐ 7. Is Form 4720 required for excise taxes?

☐ 8. Is Form 8283 or 8282 due for property gifts received?

☐ 9. Do fund solicitations reveal fair market value or nondeductibility of benefits to donors? (See Chapter 24.) For non-(c)(3) is nondeductibility conspicuously disclosed?

☐ 10. Are Forms 990 and 1023 made available for public inspection?

☐ 11. If EO is part of a group, should group exemption be obtained?

☐ 12. Has there been an IRS examination? Changes to consider?

☐ 13. Is there a signed engagement letter in the file?

☐ 14. If EO is a PF, complete private foundation checklist.

☐ 15. If EO is a (c)(7), complete social club checklist.

CHAPTER TWENTY

Private Inurement
or Benefit

Organizations exempt under most categories of IRC §501 must meet two separate tests in order to retain exemption. The first test, called the organizational test, assures that no one owns an exempt organization. No dividends are paid; shareholders exist only in certain membership organizations; and the circumstances under which funds can be returned to the members in the business league, social club, or other category are very limited. When recognizing an organization's exempt status, the IRS applies this test in reviewing the initial charter, bylaws, and other organizational documents.

The second test, though, is an ongoing one. Exempt organizations (EOs) of all categories must continually operate "exclusively" for their particular exempt purposes, whether charitable, agricultural, or pension fund management. The EO must not devote itself to benefiting private individuals. To describe the requirements of tax-exempt status, IRC §501 uses the word "inures" to limit the activities of §501(c)(3), (6), (7), (9), (10), (13), and (19) organizations. These subsections all require that, "no part of the net earnings inure to the benefit of any private shareholder or individual."

The last of the six definitions of "inure" found in Webster's Deluxe Unabridged Dictionary, second edition, is the one applied for federal tax exemption purposes: "to serve to the use or benefit of, as a gift of land inures to the heirs of a grantee or it inures to their benefit."

The IRS 1981 Continuing Professional Education manual for EO agents[1] comments that inurement is "likely to arise where the EO transfers financial resources to an individual solely by virtue of the individual's relationship with the organization, and without regard to accomplishing exempt purpose, or more plainly stated, a private person cannot pocket the organization's funds" Whether private benefit is incidental to overall public benefit or interest turns on the nature and quantum of the activity under consideration and the manner by which the public benefit will be derived. The 1983 manual asserts that "the forms which inurement can take are limited only by the imagination of the insiders involved."[2]

Private inurement potentially occurs whenever a person receives funds from an exempt organization in return for which he or she gives insufficient consideration—in other words, receives something for less than it is worth. An organization that devotes too much of its funds to providing private inurement may not qualify for exemption.

To eliminate the possibility of private inurement in a privately funded charity, Congress in 1969 introduced the concept of self-dealing, which is found in IRC §4941. As a rule, all financial transactions with insiders are absolutely prohibited for private foundations. The fact that the transaction actually benefits the charity (a bargain sale, for example) does not lift the ban. Neither will the facts that the transaction is at arm's length and for fair market value rescue the transaction from self-dealing sanctions (as these facts would for a public charity). A few limited exceptions, involving compensation for personal services, expense reimbursements, no-interest loans, and no-rent leases, are pointed out in the following sections. See Chapter 14 for more details.

20.1 "PRIVATE SHAREHOLDERS OR INDIVIDUALS"

An exempt organization must monitor its financial relations with "private shareholders or individuals," a very broad group. The regulations narrow the group somewhat by saying that it "refers to persons having a personal and private interest in the activities of the organization."[3] While this language does not specifically say so, the "interest" commonly stems from control.

(a) Insiders

Most simply, the rule is usually (but not always) applied to insiders. Insiders include:

- Someone with the ability to decide (e.g., vote) to authorize payments (e.g., a member of the board, trustee, executive committee member, or officer);

---

[1]Exempt Organizations Continuing Professional Education Technical Instruction Program for 1981, p. 92; G.C.M. 38459.
[2]Exempt Organizations Continuing Professional Education Technical Instruction Program for 1983, p. 50.
[3]Reg. §1.501(a)(1)–1(c).

- A member of the family of such a person;

- A substantial contributor able to influence the EO; and

- A business controlled or owned by one of the above types of insider.

(b) Outsiders

Outsiders, i.e., those persons not on the above insider list, can also receive unacceptable advantage or gain, and in their case the prohibited result is called private benefit, not inurement. Persons having a relationship that might produce some private benefit, include employees, consultants, and exempt function beneficiaries (those persons who participate in the EO's activities and are the intended recipients of its services). The IRS does not limit its challenges to members of the board or other persons in direct authority. Although the primary concern is for private inurement, the IRS and the courts have found that private benefit in the following relationships can jeopardize exempt status:

- Doctors and the hospitals that need to attract their services;[4]

- Ministers whose churches pay them lavishly;

- Football coaches of a university;

- Development directors who receive a percentage of funds raised.

For private foundations, IRC §4946 prescribes specific rules to identify "disqualified persons" with whom the PF is constrained from engaging in "self-dealing." Other EOs could also use this definition to define their insiders. See Section 12.4.

20.2 BASIC CRITERIA FOR JUDGING INUREMENT

In most cases, financial transactions involving insiders are not specifically prohibited, but they are constrained and liable to be scrutinized. In each case, the same basic criteria are applied to evaluate the presence of disqualifying inurement to insiders and their family members. IRS agents are instructed to examine contracts for supplies and services, loan and lease agreements, and compensation contracts, and to be alert "to the appearance of insiders' names in a context indicating that the individuals are not acting as representatives or the exempt organization."[5] The answer will be based upon the facts of each case. The burden of proof is on the exempt organization.

Reasonableness. Is the amount paid reasonable?

Documentation. Is the transaction properly documented?

Independent approval. Is the transaction sanctioned by disinterested persons or by an independent appraiser?

State law. Does the deal violate fiduciary responsibility law or state fund solicitation regulations?

---

[4] G.C.M. 39862.
[5] Exempt Organizations Examination Guidelines (IRM 7(10-69), §153.

20.3 MEANING OF NET EARNINGS

For inurement or private benefit to result, the organization's net earnings must be paid in an impermissible fashion to one or more individuals. The meaning of "net earnings" is *not* the customary accounting definition—gross revenues less associated expenses.[6] Instead, the term is very broadly construed to mean all assets of an exempt organization held as permanent capital, restricted funds, current or accumulated surpluses, or net profits. Presumably, the EO has "earned" each penny it has received and still holds.

A prohibited distribution of net earnings or profits is not limited to an arrangement based upon some sharing agreement, incentive, or ownership. It can take many forms, including but not limited to:

- Salaries or directors' fees;

- Rents or royalties;

- Purchase or sale of property;

- Loans or guarantees;

- Services rendered to members; and

- Joint ventures or other risk of EO assets.

20.4 SALARIES AND OTHER COMPENSATION

Reasonable compensation for personal services rendered can be paid to insiders in the form of salaries, directors' fees, or other payment. The IRS position on compensation is expressed in its training literature.

> "The National Office has found that benefit to an exempt organization's employees, so long as it constitutes no more than reasonable compensation for services rendered, is not necessarily incompatible or inconsistent with the accomplishment of the exempt purpose of the employer. Exempt organizations can establish and operate incentive plans that devote a portion of receipts to reasonable compensation of productive employees so long as the benefits derived from the plans generally accrue not only to the employees but also to the charitable employers through, for instance, increased productivity and cost stability, thus aiding rather than detracting from the accomplishment of exempt purpose."[7]

The exempt organization must be able to substantiate that the payments are not excessive for the work performed, because the payment of excessive compensa-

[6]Exempt Organizations Annual Technical Review Institutes for 1983, p. 41.
[7]*Ibid* p. 46, n.2.

tion clearly will jeopardize exempt status.[8] The following questions must be answered:

1. Is the amount of any payment for personal services excessive or unreasonable?[9]

2. Are the payments ordinary and necessary to carry out the exempt purposes of the EO? (Apply the same tests used under IRC §162 to judge the reasonableness of business deductions.)[10]

3. What are the individual's responsibilities and duties? Is there a written job description, a contract for services, or personnel procedures?

4. Is the person qualified for the job through experience, education, or other special expertise?[11] How much time is devoted to the job?

5. To evaluate compensation accurately, count not only salary but all benefits,[12] including:

   - Salary or fees (current and deferred);

   - Fringe benefits;

   - Contribution to pension or profit-sharing plans;

   - Housing or automobile allowances;

   - Directors' and officers' (D&O) liability insurance;

   - Expense reimbursements;

   - Clubs, resort meetings, or other lavish items; and

   - Compensation to family members.

6. Does the method of calculation imply inurement? Paying a percentage of profits from operations or fund-raising efforts may suggest inurement. The IRS has not always won this one, particularly when the overall pay is reasonable.[13] See Section 20.4(c).

7. Are adequate accounting records, such as time sheets or diaries, maintained to document the actual time expended on the job?

8. How does the individual's salary compare to those of other staff members and to the total organization budget?

9. How does the compensation structure compare to those of similar EOs or commercial businesses of similar size?[14] Compare the exempt organi-

---

[8]*Birmingham Business College, Inc. v. Commissioner*, 276 F.2d 476 (5th Cir. 1960).

[9]*The Labrenz Foundation, Inc. v. Commissioner*, 33 T.C.M. 1374 (1974).

[10]*Enterprise Railway Equipment Company v. U.S.*, 161 F. Supp. 590 (Ct.Cl. 1958).

[11]*B.H.W. Anesthesia Foundation, Inc. v. Commissioner*, 72 T.C. 681 (1979).

[12]*John Marshall Law School vs. U.S.*, 81-2 T.C. 9514 (Ct.Cl. 1981); Rev. Rul. 73-126, 1973-1 C.B. 220.

[13]*World Family Corporation v. Commissioner*, 81 T.C. 958 (1983).

[14]Reg. §1.162-7(b)(3).

zation to commercial businesses of similar size, if possible. There is no ruling that says that nonprofit employees or consultants cannot be paid salaries commensurate with businesses', nor that they need to donate their services.

(a) Finding Salary Statistics

Comparative information is critical to evaluating the reasonableness of a salary. The most appropriate comparison is made to similar EOs in the same field of endeavor (for example, health care, academia, music, or college administration). Surveys of compensation in the EO's area of interest can be obtained, and should be retained for IRS scrutiny.

Perhaps the easiest way to obtain compensation information is to look at Forms 990 for relevant organizations. The forms are required to be made available upon request at the organization's office. Any amounts paid to officers and directors for compensation, employee benefit plans, and expense accounts are to be reported, along with their titles and average amounts of time devoted to the position each week. For charitable organizations only, Form 990, Schedule A also reports on the five highest paid employees other than officers, directors, and trustees, and the same information is reported for all persons paid over $30,000 a year. In addition, for the five highest paid persons earning over $30,000 a year for professional services, a description of the type of services and total compensation is reported.

The Council on Foundations publishes a biennial *Foundation Management Report* which contains private foundation compensation levels by size of foundation, position, and area of the country. The Society for Nonprofit Organizations annually publishes *Compensation for Nonprofit Organizations*, a comprehensive survey of salaries and benefits by size of organization, by focus or purpose of the entity (health, education, day care, and so on), and by positions (executive director, controller, clerical assistant, program manager, and so on). In Houston, Texas, the Management Assistance Program of the United Way compiles a similar annual survey of area compensation.

(b) Avoiding Conflict of Interest

When compensation is paid to directors, officers, or other controlling members of an organization, additional proof of the reasonableness of compensation is required. It is critical that local conflict of interest statutes be observed to prove that the payments do not violate fiduciary responsibility concepts.

An organization compensating insiders should adopt conflict of interest policies to evidence its good faith in securing independent and impartial approval for the payments. Such policies should require, at a minimum, that interested parties abstain from approving their own compensation and that there are enough noncompensated members of the board to achieve independent or disinterested approval for the compensation.

In a highly-publicized case, L. Ron Hubbard's payments from the Church of Scientology were found to result in inurement, and revocation of the church's exemption was upheld.[15] The funds paid to Hubbard by the church came in the form of fees, commissions, rental payments, loans, and excessive salaries—taken together, clearly a flagrant abuse. The court commented that "what emerges from these facts is the inference that the Hubbard family was entitled to make ready personal use of the corporation's earnings."

(c) Incentive Compensation

Compensation that is measured by the results of activities—net profits, number of patients served, funds raised, and so on—are subject to enhanced scrutiny. One court has said, that "there is nothing insidious or evil about a commission-based compensation system," and decided that procuring contributions with a six percent commission was reasonable, despite the absence of a ceiling on the total commission that could be paid.[16]

In evaluating a "fixed percentage of income" formula, the IRS dissected a hospital's policies and intentions. A radiologist was hired to run the radiology department for the hospital. His compensation was a fixed percentage of the department's gross revenues less bad debts. The IRS found this incentive compensation method to be acceptable because the physician had no control over compensation decisions, either managerial or governance position. He was simply an employee. It also noted that the negotiations over compensation were conducted at arm's length.[17] According to the IRS training literature, the following factors are used to find reasonableness in incentive compensation. Not all factors need be present:[18]

1. The contingent payments serve a real and discernible business purpose of the organization itself, not the financial need of the employee. The risk of paying the higher salary due to higher revenues is self-insured by its tie to revenue or profit level.

2. Compensation amount is not dependent upon curtailing expenses or skimping on services, but instead is based upon accomplishment of exempt purposes, such as serving more patients, writing more books, or increasing test scores. A plan to pay a percentage of revenues exceeding the budgeted amount has even been sanctioned.[19]

3. Actual operating results show that prices for services are comparable to those at similar organizations, and are not manipulated to increase the compensation.

4. There is a ceiling or maximum amount of compensation, so as to avoid "the possibility of windfall benefit to the employee/professional based

---

[15]*Founding Church of Scientology v. U.S.*, 412 F.2d 1197 (Ct.Cl. 1969).
[16]*National Foundation, Inc. v. U.S.*, 87-2 USTC ¶9602 (Ct.Cl. 1987).
[17]Rev. Rul. 69-383, 1969-2 C.B. 113.
[18]Exempt Organization Annual Technical Review Institutes for 1983, p. 45.
[19]G.C.M. 39674. Also see G.C.M. 32453, 36918, 39498, and 39670.

upon factors bearing no direct relationship to the level of services provided."[20]

20.5 HOUSING AND MEALS

An exempt organization may have a good reason to provide housing or meals, or allowances for these purposes, to its officers, directors, or employees. Using the four basic criteria outlined in Section 20.2, amounts actually incurred for meals and other travel expenses incurred on EO business can be paid. Questions to ask to assure that the four criteria are met include the following:

1. Is the insider a staff member whose presence is required on the premises of the EO at all hours (a school or home for orphans, for example)?

2. Does the housing allowance or provision qualify for IRC §119 income exclusion from insider income because it is furnished for the convenience of the employing EO?

3. Is the location of the project remote or temporary? Is the research conducted on an island or in a city away from the EO's and the employee's permanent residence?

4. Is the housing lavish or unreasonably expensive?[21]

5. Are board meetings held in resort locations?

Documentation is essential to prove both the amount and nature of each expense, as well as its connection to EO affairs. A diary should be kept of meetings, persons entertained, and the project to which discussions relate.

Due to the self-dealing rules, scrutiny can be expected, but a private foundation can reimburse its disqualified persons for "reasonable expenses" incurred in conducting the foundations affairs. Daily expenses in excess of the federal per diem reimbursement rate might require explanation.

20.6 PURCHASE, LEASE, OR SALE OF PROPERTY OR SERVICES

An exempt organization can buy, lease, or sell property to or from an insider in certain circumstances. The appropriateness of any such transaction depends partly on whether the property is devoted to exempt functions, such as administrative offices, or to production of income, i.e., an investment. In any

---

[20] *People of God Community v. Commissioner*, 75 T.C. 127, 132 (1980).
[21] *John Marshall Law School, supra*, n. 12.

case, the following tests must be satisfied:

1. Is no more than the current fair market value being paid for the property or services which the EO is buying? At least full fair market value must be paid if the insider is buying.

   ▪ Is there a readily established market price for the property being purchased or leased?[22]

   ▪ If not, was an appraisal or other independent evidence of its value obtained? Does the appraisal consider a number of different valuation factors, such as income forecast, resale value of underlying property, goodwill, and comparative prices?

   ▪ Was the organization established to promote the insider's business, as was found in cases involving a travel agent,[23] a musical instructor,[24] a doctor who established a hospital,[25] or a minister?[26]

2. Are the terms for payment of the purchase price favorable?

   ▪ Is the rate of interest on a mortgage equal to or less than prevailing rates for similar commercial mortgages (if the EO is buying), or more than these rates (if the insider is buying)?

   ▪ If the property is encumbered, can the income generated by the property carry the note and provide a reasonable return? Or does the amount of the debt exceed the value of the property purchased or given?[27]

3. Does the purchase, lease, or sale make economic sense?

   ▪ Is the proportion of EO capital devoted to the purchase reasonable in relation to the capital needed to carry out exempt purposes?

   ▪ Will the income yield a rate of return commensurate with the EO's overall financial needs?

   ▪ Does the amount of cash paid down deprive the EO of needed working capital?

   ▪ Is the arrangement beneficial for the EO? The rates or rents should be favorable.[28]

4. Does the purchase or sale serve an exempt function?

[22] Priv. Ltr. Rul. 8234084 and 9130002.
[23] *International Postgraduate Medical Foundation v. Commissioner*, 56 T.C.M. 1140 (1989).
[24] *Horace Heidt Foundation v. U.S.*, 170 F. Supp. 634 (Ct.Cl. 1959).
[25] *Kenner v. Commissioner*, 33 T.C.M. 1239 (1974).
[26] *Church by Mail, Inc. v. Commissioner*, 48 T.C.M. 471 (1984).
[27] Rev. Rul. 76-441, 1967-2 C.B. 147.
[28] *Texas Trade School v. Commissioner*, 30 T.C. 642 (1958), aff'd, 272 F.2d 168 (5th Cir. 1959); *Founding Church of Scientology, supra*, n. 15.

Although a private foundation is absolutely prohibited from buying, selling, or leasing anything to or from its disqualified persons for any price—even one dollar—a rent-free lease to the PF is allowed if it serves an exempt purpose. A PF can pay its proportion of occupancy costs, but "sharing arrangements" can present problems. See Section 14.8.

20.7 LOANS AND GUARANTEES

An exempt organization should think very carefully before lending money to or borrowing from an insider. One court has commented that the very fact that an EO was a source of credit for an insider represented inurement.[29] Loans are subject to the same criteria as leases and sales of property, and many of the same questions apply. Additionally, one should ask:

1. Is the EO serving exempt purposes by making the loan?[30]
2. Are the rates and terms favorable to the EO?[31]
3. Is there substantial market risk inherent in the loan?
4. Is there adequate security for the loan?
5. Is it a good investment? Is the rate of return good?[32]
6. Does a low- or no-interest loan to an employee or director serve a permissible compensatory purpose?

A private foundation is prohibited from borrowing money from or lending money to a disqualified person. A gift of indebted property to a PF is prohibited unless the debt was placed on the property 10 years before the gift.[33] Essentially the PF's taking over responsibility for the debt is treated as compensation or a loan to the donor.

20.8 CONVERTING A FOR-PROFIT ENTERPRISE TO NONPROFIT FORM

Contributing a business with purely gratuitous motivation to a newly-created nonprofit organization does not necessarily result in private inurement or benefit to the donor, but such transactions will be closely scrutinized. If such a transfer occurs for tax avoidance purposes, as when the donor retains the right to occupy the property and essentially continues to operate the business for his

[29] *Lowry Hospital Association v. Commissioner*, 66 T.C. 850 (1976).
[30] *Best Lock Corp. v. Commissioner*, 31 T.C. 1217 (1959).
[31] *Hancock Academy of Savannah, Inc. v. Commissioner*, 69 T.C. 488 (1977).
[32] Donald G. and Lillian S. Griswold, 39 T.C. 620 (1962), *acq.*, 1965-1 C.B. 4.
[33] IRC §4941 (d)(2)(A).

or her own purposes, the level of private interest prevents tax-exempt status for the new nonprofit organization.[34]

When the conversion is basically a sale to the newly-created organization, the purchase must be examined for unreasonable price or terms favorable to the seller, as discussed in Section 20.6. In a sale of a proprietary school to a newly-created educational organization, the consideration paid for goodwill was found to be excessive.[35] Payments for intangible earning capacity are not, however, prohibited per se. When an exempt organization intends to operate a facility and will clearly benefit from the goodwill that has been established, the intangible assets will contribute to the new organization's exempt functions and can be paid for. The IRS has ruled that the "capitalization of excess earnings" formula is an acceptable manner by which to value such an intangible asset.[36]

20.9   SERVICES RENDERED FOR INDIVIDUALS

When does the rendering of services to members or insiders result in private benefit and evidence that the organization does not operate to benefit the public? When is service revenue classified as unrelated business income? (See Chapter 21 regarding unrelated business income.) As a general proposition, these questions are of most concern to §501(c)(3) organizations, but all EOs must serve some exempt constituency—be it the poor, the pipefitters, or the social set—in a group sense, not on an individual level. For (c)(3) organizations, the basic question is whether the charitable class is sufficiently broad that the individuals are served as a means of achieving the public purpose. The distinction is best made through examples, although the logic is not necessarily clear. (See also Section 2.2(a).)

(a) Services Providing Public Benefit

Certain types of services provide public benefit even though they are furnished to individuals, because they serve a societal purpose that is also charitable. Examples include:

- Medical services, including hospitals and health maintenance organizations;

- Schools, both private and public;

- Cultural providers, such as art galleries and all types of performing arts; and

- Grants of money, food, housing, or other services to poor people or students.

---

[34]Rev. Rul. 69-266, 1969-1 C.B. 151.
[35]*Hancock Academy of Savannah, Inc. supra* n. 31.
[36]Rev. Rul. 68-609, 1968-2 C.B. 227.

(b) When Private Benefit is Found

Some services produce more than incidental private benefit to individual recipients, and therefore cause the activity to be considered nonexempt. Examples of such services include:

- A bus service for private school students;[37]
- Cooperative art gallery management;[38]
- Preferential housing to employees of one of the exempt organization's directors.[39]
- A genealogical society for a particular common name;[40]
- Financial planning for charitable giving;[41]
- Management consulting for small businesses;[42]
- Real estate multiple listing services.[43]

(c) Membership Perks

Member benefit is an especially confusing aspect of this issue. In the §501(c)(3) and (c)(4) context, a membership composed of contributors can be given preferential treatment in certain circumstances. For example, reduced or free admission, discounts in bookstores, attendance at conferences or receptions, and other benefits directly connected with the EO's exempt function are permitted when their value is small in relation to the charges. On the other hand, services construed to benefit individuals on a personal level unrelated to the exempt activities, such as group insurance plans, are troublesome.

Because (c)(5), (c)(6), and (c)(7) organizations are formed to benefit members, they have wider latitude in providing services. Nevertheless, services still must be directed toward the particular exempt function of the EO.

Labor unions provide a wide range of work-related services, including day care, job training, and placement services germane to their members' gainful employment. A union might incur nonexempt function income and potential UBIT from its sale of housing, food, or medical products. The IRS *Exempt Organizations Handbook* instructs the specialist to refer any inurement questions concerning a labor union to the national office, due to the lack of published precedents.

Business leagues run afoul of the inurement test more often than unions, and a clearer distinction is possible. Such a league must carry out programs that benefit an industry or locality, and while incidental individual benefit can result, the overriding purpose must be to serve the industry. For example, the

---

[37]Rev. Rul. 69-175, 1969-1 C.B. 149.
[38]Rev. Rul. 71-395, 1971-2 C.B. 228.
[39]Rev. Rul. 72-147, 1972-1 C.B. 147.
[40]*The Callaway Family Association, Inc. v. Commissioner*, 71 T.C. 340 (1978).
[41]*Christian Stewardship Assistance, Inc. v. Commissioner*, 70 T.C. 1037 (1978).
[42]*B.S.W. Group, Inc. v. Commissioner*, 70 T.C. 352 (1978).
[43]Rev. Rul. 59-234, 1959-2 C.B. 149.

American Institute of Certified Public Accountants can perform peer reviews and administer qualifying tests which maintain the standards of its profession, but it cannot run an executive search department to secure job placement for individual members. Many examples of individual benefits can be found in Revenue Rulings, such as:

- Group purchases of supplies or inventory;[44]

- A trading stamp program;[45]

- Research made available only to members, not to the industry as a whole.[46]

20.10 JOINT VENTURES

Private inurement occurs when an exempt organization's assets are placed at unreasonable risk of loss in comparison to the assets of private investors joining it in a venture. Of equal importance is whether the EO receives a share of ownership equivalent to the non-EO investors. As usual, there is also the burden of proving that the transaction serves the exempt purposes of the EO.

The IRS has repeatedly refused to allow §501(c)(3) organizations to be general partners in any venture, in order to prevent them from "taking on an obligation to further the private financial interests of their other partners." Only when the venture is buying exempt function property (not investment property), such as a school building or opera production, has the IRS recently allowed an EO to be a general partner. The Plumstead Theatre Society[47] won a decision that yielded the following characteristics of a limited investor venture:

- The venture served an exempt purpose: to produce a play;

- The amount invested by and provided for return to the limited partners was reasonable;

- The transaction was at arm's length;

- Plumstead was not obligated to return the invested capital;

- Investors had no control over Plumstead's operations; and

- Investors were not officers or directors of Plumstead.

The medical community is fraught with controversy about private inurement. In past years, the most troublesome case for the IRS was conversion of a doctor-owned hospital to charitable status. Recently, there have been hundreds of applications for private letter rulings seeking approval of hospital reorganizations involving for-profit subsidiaries and the use of health care properties. For

[44]Rev. Rul. 66-338, 1966-2 C.B. 226.
[45]Rev. Rul. 65-244, 1965-2 C.B. 167.
[46]Rev. Rul. 60-106, 1969-1 C.B. 153.
[47]*Plumstead Theatre Society, Inc. v. Commissioner*, 74 T.C. 1324 (1980).

some time the IRS has refused to approve such structures, but careful study of the most recent rulings is imperative in answering a health care organization question. Private foundations are not only prohibited from entering into joint ownership with their disqualified persons, but also face the possibility that a joint venture could be classified as a jeopardizing investment or an excess business holding. See Chapter 22.

20.11 DIVIDENDS

The question of dividends arises infrequently, because most states prohibit the establishment of a nonprofit corporation, especially a charitable one, as a stockholding company. In the rare instance when shares are issued, dividend payments would indicate private inurement. Certain mutual benefit organizations and pension plans, however, can attribute earnings to individual "shareholders" when it serves their exempt purposes.

Unrelated Business Income

Exempt organizations (EOs) receive two types of income: earned and unearned. Unearned income—income for which the EO gives nothing in return—comes from grants, membership fees, and donations. Think of it as "one-way-street" money. The motivation for giving the money is gratuitous and/or of a non-profit character with no expectation of gain on the part of the giver; there is donative intent.

In contrast, an EO furnishes services/goods or invests its capital in return for earned income: an opera is seen, classes are attended, hospital care is provided, or credit counseling is given, for example. The purchasers of the EO's goods and services do intend to receive something in return; they expect the street to be "two-way." An investment company holding the EO's money expects to have to pay reasonable return to the EO for using the funds. In these examples, the EO receives earned income. The important issue this chapter considers is when earned income becomes unrelated business income subject to income tax.

There are complex rules that govern when an EO's earned income becomes unrelated business income (UBI). The concepts of UBI are vague and contain many exceptions carved out by special interest groups. The House of Representatives Subcommittee on Oversight held hearings and drafted revisions over a four-year period during 1987 to 1990 and still has not proposed tax legislation. (See list of proposals at Section 21.22.)

21.1 IRS SCRUTINY FOCUSED ON UNRELATED BUSINESS INCOME (UBI)

Beginning in 1989 with the addition of a new page 5 to Form 990, the IRS is studying the UBI issue. Until page 5, with its "Analysis of Revenue-Producing Activities," was added to the annual EO reporting requirements, UBI was not identified in any special way on Form 990; the income was simply included with related income of the same character. The Congressional representatives and the IRS agreed that there was insufficient information to propose changes to the existing UBI rules.

Now, EOs filing Internal Revenue Service (IRS) Form 990 (not including Form 990EZ filers whose gross income is less than $100,000) complete the new page 5 to separate income into three categories:

1. Unrelated income (identified with a business code from Form 990T that describes its nature);

2. Unrelated income identified by the specific Internal Revenue Code section by which the income is excluded from UBI; and

3. Related or exempt function income, along with a description of the relationship of the income-producing activity to the accomplishment of exempt purposes.

This statistical information is being gathered to evaluate the consequences of proposed changes to the UBIT rules. Marcus Owens of the IRS National Office announced, in May 1991, the initiation of a compliance program with a public educational effort and emphasis on large case examinations. The exams started in 1992 and the results may be known in 1993.

21.2 HISTORY OF THE UNRELATED BUSINESS INCOME TAX (UBIT)

A historical note helps to understand how the rules have evolved. Before 1950, an EO could conduct any income-producing activity and, in fact, did operate businesses without paying income tax. Using a "destination of income" test, as long as the income earned from the business was totally expended for grants and other exempt activities, any amount of business activity was permissible. One famous tax case involved New York University Law School's operation of a highly successful spaghetti factory.[1] In view of the extensive profits and businesslike manner in which the factory was operated, the IRS tried to impose an income tax on the profits. The courts decided, however, that no tax could be imposed under the then-existing tax code as long as the profits were used to operate the school.

In response to pressure from businesses, Congress established the unrelated business income tax (UBIT) with the intention of eliminating the unfair competition charitable businesses represented, but it did not prohibit its receipt. The Congressional committee thought that the:

> Tax free status of exemption section 501 organizations enables them to use their profits tax free to expand operations, while their competitors can expand only with profits remaining after taxes. The problem...is primarily that of unfair competition.[2]

The key questions in finding UBI are, then, whether the activity that produces earned income competes with commercial businesses and whether the method of operation is distinguishable from that of businesses. Another way to ask the question is, "Does it serve an exempt purpose and therefore is it related?" The distinction between for-profits and nonprofits has narrowed over

---

[1] *C. F. Mueller Co. v. Commissioner*, 190 F.2d 120 (3rd Cir. 1951).
[2] House of Representatives No. 2319, 81st Cong., 2nd Sess. (1950) at 36–37.

the years as organizations have searched for creative ways to pay for program services. Consider what the difference between a museum bookstore and a commercial one is, other than the absence of private ownership. Privately owned for-profit theaters operate alongside nonprofit ones. Magazines owned by nonprofits, such as *National Geographic* and *Harper's*, contain advertising and appear indistinguishable from Condé Nast's *Traveler* or *Life Magazine*. The health care profession is also full of indistinguishable examples.

21.3 CONSEQUENCES OF RECEIVING UNRELATED INCOME

There are potentially several unpleasant consequences of earning unrelated income.

- *Payment of unrelated income tax.* Unrelated net income may be taxed at corporate or trust rates with estimated tax payments required. Social clubs, homeowner associations, and political organizations also pay the UBI tax on their passive investment income in addition to the business income.

- *Exempt status revocation.* Exempt status could be revoked. Separate and apart from the UBI rules, the basic exemption statute under §501 of the Internal Revenue Code[3] requires that an organization be organized and operated *exclusively* for an exempt purpose, although "exclusively" has not been construed to mean 100 percent. Some commentators say any amount of UBI under 50 percent of the EO's gross income is permissible, although many others recommend no more UBI than 15 to 20 percent. The courts have allowed higher amounts; the IRS tends to vote for lower amounts in measuring whether the EO is operating "exclusively" for exempt purposes rather than for business purposes. An organization can run a business as a secondary purpose, but not as a primary purpose.

In evaluating the amount of unrelated business activity that is permissible, not only the amount of gross revenue but other factors may be taken into consideration. Nonrevenue aspects of the activity, such as staff time devoted or value of donated services, are factors in determining whether UBI is substantial.

A complex of nonexempt activity caused the IRS to revoke the exemption of the Orange County Agricultural Society.[4] The unrelated business revenues represented between 29 to 34 percent of the gross revenue; although troublesome, they were not the sole factor in the decision of the Tax Court to uphold

---

[3]References to sections of the Internal Revenue Code are designated by use of the symbol "§," while cross-references to sections of this book use "Section."
[4]*Orange County Agricultural Society*, 90.1 USTC ¶50.076 (2d Cir. 1990), *aff'g* 55 T.C.M. 1602 (1988).

the IRS's revocation. The presence of private inurement in doing business with the Society's board of directors influenced the decision.

- *All income taxed.* Income from all sources will be taxed if exempt status is lost.

- *Private foundation issue.* Private foundations' ownership of unrelated businesses would likely trigger "excess business holdings" tax and cause loss of exemption.

21.4 DEFINITION OF TRADE OR BUSINESS

To have UBI, the EO must first be found to be engaging in a trade or business. *Trade or business* is defined to include any activity carried on for the production of income from the sale of goods or performance of services.[5] This is a very broad, sweeping definition. The language seems pretty straightforward and, as a safe rule of thumb, would literally mean that any activity for which the exempt receives revenues constitutes a business. Unfortunately, this is an area where the tax rules are very gray and the statutory history is difficult to follow. The word "income" does not mean receipts or revenue and also does not necessarily mean net income. IRC §513(c) provides: "Where an activity carried on for profit constitutes an unrelated trade or business, no part of such trade or business shall be excluded from such classification merely because it does not result in profit."

If one delves deeper into the Internal Revenue Code ("the Code") and the Treasury Regulations ("the Regulations"), it becomes more difficult to find what is meant by "trade or business." The Regulations couch the definition in the context of unfair competition with commercial businesses, saying that "when an activity does not possess the characteristics of a trade or business within the meaning of Section 162," the unrelated business income tax (UBIT) will not apply. These Regulations, however, were written before the IRC §513(c) profit motive language was added to the Code, and they are the subject of continuing arguments between taxpayers and the IRS.

(a) Profit Motive Test

The confusion has produced two tests: profit motive and commerciality. Under the profit motive test, an activity conducted simply to produce some revenue but without an expectation of producing a profit (similar to the hobby loss rules) is not a business.[6] This test is used by the IRS in situations when an EO has more than one unrelated business. Losses from the unprofitable activity or hobby cannot be offset against profits from other businesses. Likewise, the excess expenses (losses) generated in fundamentally exempt activity, such as an educational publication undertaken without the intention of making a profit,

---

[5]Reg. §1.513-1(b).
[6]*West Virginia State Medical Association*, 89-2 U.S.T.C. §9491 (4th Cir. 1989); 91 T.C. 651 (1988), *Commissioner v. Groetzinger*, 480 U.S. 23 (1987).

cannot be deducted against the profits from a profit-motivated project. See Section 9.5(e).

(b) Commerciality Test

The commerciality test looks instead to the type of operation: if the activity is carried on in a manner similar to a commercial business, it constitutes a trade or business.[7] This test poses serious problems for the unsuspecting because there are no statutory or regulatory parameters to follow. A broad range of UBI cases where the scope of sales or service activity was beyond that normally found in the exempt setting have been decided by examining the commercial taint of the activity. Checklist 21–1 highlights situations which may jeopardize an organization's exempt status.

[7]*Better Business Bureau v. United States*, 326 US. 279, 283 (1945); *United States National Water Well Association, Inc. v. Commissioner*, 92 T.C. 7 (1989); *Scripture Press Foundation v. United States*, 285 F.2d 800 (Ct.Cl. 1961); *Greater United Navajo Development Enterprises, Inc. v. Commissioner*, 74 T.C. 69 (1980).

Checklist 21–1

COMMERCIALITY TEST

Warning SIGNS. "YES" answers to these questions signals exposure to challenge that the organization operates in a commercial manner and may not be exempt.

☐ COMPETITIVENESS: Does the exempt organization's activity compete with for profit businesses conducting the same activity? Is there a counterpart for the activity in the business sector, particularly a "small" business?

☐ PERSONNEL MOTIVATION: Do managers receive generous compensation? Is the activity run by well paid staff members?

☐ SELLING TECHNIQUES: Advertising and promotional materials are utilized. Retailing methods, such as mail order catalog or display systems, are similar to for profit enterprise.

☐ PRICING: Highest price market will bear is charged for goods and services. There are no scaled or reduced rates available for members of a charitable class.

☐ CUSTOMER PROFILE: The organization's services and goods are for sale to anyone. They are available to the general public on a regular basis, rather than only for persons participating in the organization's other exempt activities.

☐ ORGANIZATION'S FOCUS "GOOD WORKS RATIO": The organization conducts no significant other activity. The income-producing activity is its primary focus rather than exempt ones.

☐ CHARACTER OF ORGANIZATION'S SUPPORT: Very little or none of the organization's support come from voluntary contributions and grants or other unearned sources.

(c) Fragmentation Rule

Further evidence of the overreaching scope of the term "trade or business" is found in the *fragmentation rule*.[8] This rule carves out an activity carried on alongside an exempt one and provides that unrelated business does not lose its identity and taxability when it is earned in a related setting. Take, for example, a museum shop. The shop itself is clearly a trade or business, often established with a profit motive and operated in a commercial manner. Items sold in such

---

[8]IRC §513(c).

shops, however, often include both educational items, such as books and reproductions of art works, and souvenirs. The fragmentation rule requires that all items sold be analyzed to identify the equational, or related, items the profit from which is not taxable and the unrelated souvenir items that do produce taxable income. (See Section 21.19 for more information about museums.)

21.5   WHAT IS UBI?

UBI is defined as the gross income derived from any *unrelated trade or business regularly carried on*, less the *deductions* connected with the carrying on of such trade or business, computed with *modifications* and *exceptions*.[9] These terms are key to identifying UBI. Exhibit 21–1 shows them graphically. All the prongs of the circle surrounding the circle must be considered, to determine what earned income is to be classified as UBI.

Exhibit 21–1
COMPONENTS OF UNRELATED BUSINESS INCOME

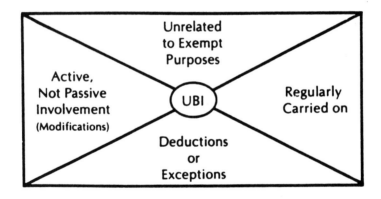

21.6   "REGULARLY CARRIED ON"

A trade or business regularly carried on is considered to compete unfairly with commercial business and is fair game for classification as a taxable business. In determining whether an activity is regularly carried on, the IRS looks at the *frequency and continuity* of an activity when examined by comparison to commercial enterprises. The normal time span of comparable commercial activities

[9] IRC §512(a)(1).

can also be determinative.[10] Compare the following:

Irregular	Regular
Sandwich stand at annual county fair.	Cafe open daily.
Annual golf tournament.	Racetrack operated during racing "season."
Nine-day antique show.	Antique store.
Gala Ball held annually.	Monthly dance.
Program ads for annual fund-raising event.	Advertisements in quarterly magazine.

(a) Meaning of Irregular

Intermittent activities may be deemed "regularly carried on" or commercial unless they are discontinuous or periodic. For example, the revenue from a weekly dance would be more likely to be taxed than the profits from an annual fund-raising event. By the same token, ads sold for a monthly newsletter would more likely be classed as commercial than program ads sold for an annual ball. Where the planning and sales effort of a special event or athletic tournament is conducted over a long span of time, the IRS may argue that the activity itself becomes regularly carried on despite the fact that the event occurs infrequently. (See the NCAA advertising sales discussion following under "Agency theory," Section 21.8(i).)

In a 1981 case, the IRS lost in arguing that the engagement of professionals to stage the show and produce a program guide containing advertising caused a patrolmen's fund-raising event profits to be UBI.[11] The fact that the solicitors worked for 16 weeks in preparing and organizing the event made the activity regular in the IRS eyes; the Tax Court disagreed.

(b) Seasonal Activity

Activities conducted during a period traditionally identified as seasonal, such as Christmas, if conducted during the "season," will be considered regular and the income will not qualify to be excluded from UBIT. Christmas card sales during October or November, or Independence Day balloons sold in June/July, would be "regular."

21.7 "SUBSTANTIALLY RELATED"

"Any business the conduct of which is not substantially related (aside from need to make money) to the performance of an organization's charitable,

---

[10]Reg. §1.513-1(c).

[11]*Suffolk County Patrolmen's Benevolent Association, Inc. v. Commissioner*, 77 T.C. 1314 (1981), acq. 1984-1 C.B. 2.

educational, or other purposes or function constituting the basis of its exemption is defined as unrelated," according to the Regulations.[12]

An activity is substantially related only when it has a causal relationship to the achievement of an EO's exempt purpose (that is, the purpose for which the EO was granted exemption according to its Form 1023 or 1024 or subsequent Form 990 filings). The Regulations suggest that the presence of this requirement necessitates an examination of the relationship between the business activities (of producing or distributing goods or performing services) that generate the particular income in question and the accomplishment of the organization's exempt purposes.[13]

The size and extent of the activity itself and its contribution to exempt purposes are determinative. The "nexus" (association, connection, or linkage) between the activity and accomplishment of exempt purposes is examined to find "relatedness." The best way to illustrate the concept is with examples.

(a) Examples of Related Activity

Related income-producing activities include:

- Admission tickets for performances or lectures;

- Student or member tuition or class fees;

- Symphony society sale of symphonic musical recordings;

- Products made by handicapped workers or trainees;[14]

- Hospital room, drug, and other patient charges;

- Agriculture college sale of produce or student work;

- Sale of educational materials;

- Secretarial and telephone answering service training program for indigent and homeless;[15]

- Operation of diagnostic health devices, such as CAT scans or magnetic imaging machines by a hospital or health care organization;[16]

- Sale of online bibliographic data from EO's central data bases;[17]

- "Public entertainment activities," or agricultural and educational fair or exposition (Section 21.9(d));

- "Qualified conventions and trade shows" (Section 21.9(d));

- Producing tapes of endangered ethnic music.[18]

[12] Reg. §1.513-1(a).
[13] Reg. §1.513-1(d).
[14] Rev. Rul. 73-128, 1973-1, C.B. 222; Prv. Ltr. Rul. 9152039.
[15] Priv. Ltr. Rul. 9009038.
[16] Tech. Adv. Mem. 8932004.
[17] Priv. Ltr. Rul. 9017028.
[18] Priv. Ltr. Rul. 9210026.

21.8 UNRELATED ACTIVITIES

Potentially unrelated categories of UBI are numerous, as the following controversial types of income illustrate. The examples do not always follow a logical pattern because courts and the IRS do not always agree, and the IRS has not always been consistent in its rulings.

(a) Rentals

Rentals of equipment and other personal property (for example, computer or telephone systems) to others are specifically listed in IRC §512(b)(3) for inclusion in UBI. Such rental presumably is undertaken only to earn revenue and cover costs, with no direct connection to the EO's own exempt purposes; it "exploits" the exempt holding of the property. However, the following situations should be noted:

- Renting to (or sharing with) another EO (or, conceivably, an individual or a for-profit business) is related if the rental expressly serves the landlord's exempt purposes, such as a museum's rental of art works—that would otherwise be kept in its storage—to other institutions to ensure maximum public viewing of the work or relieve storage.

- Mailing list rentals produce UBI except for narrow exceptions allowed to §501(c)(3) organizations.[19] For business leagues and other EOs that are not 501(c)(3)s, revenues from the exchange or rental of mailing lists produce UBI. The Disabled American Veterans fought a valiant battle in the tax courts to avoid this tax. Twice—in 1982, and again in July 1991 —it lost in the Tenth Circuit court its attempt to characterize its mailing list sales as royalty income. (Refer to "The Royalty Dilemma" in Section 21.20(e), for more information.)

- Whether rental charges are at, below, or above cost can be determinative in evaluating relatedness. A full fair market value rental arrangement does not evidence exempt purposes (although the taint can be overcome by other reasons for the rental, such as dissemination of specialized educational information).

- Real estate revenues may also be excluded from UBI under the passive exceptions, but only if the property is unencumbered (see later discussion of debt-financed property).[20]

(b) Services

Providing services (such as billing, technical assistance, administrative support) to other EOs does not serve the exempt purposes of the furnishing EO and is unrelated, according to the IRS. The fact that sharing services creates efficiencies that allow all the EOs involved to save money does not necessarily sway

[19] IRC §513(h).
[20] IRC §512(b)(3).

the IRS. Only where the services themselves represent substantive programs better accomplished by selling the services to other EOs has the IRS classified the revenue as related. The services themselves must be exempt in nature. Selling computer time to enable another EO to maintain its accounting records would create UBI, but selling computer time to analyze scientific information might be related. Where an organization is created to serve a consortium of organizations with a common building or pooled investment funds, the IRS has generally allowed its exemption when the new organization itself is partly supported by independent donations.

Training courses furnished by a university to a business was sanctioned in Priv. Ltr. Rul. 9137002. But in Priv. Ltr. Rul. 9232003, the IRS decided that an HMO service provider created to provide management consulting to other exempt HMOs was not itself exempt.

- Certain cooperative service organizations have been specifically exempted by Congress, to avoid the IRS position that such rendering of services was a taxable business activity. IRC §501(e) grants exempt status to cooperative hospital organizations that are formed to provide on a group basis specified services including data processing, purchasing (including the purchase of insurance on a group basis), warehousing, billing and collection, food, clinical, industrial engineering, laboratory, printing, communications, record center, and personnel (including selection, testing, training, and education of personnel services). Note that laundry is not on the list.

- Cooperative services organizations established to "hold, commingle, and collectively invest" stocks and securities of educational institutions are also provided a special exempt category under IRC §501(f).

IRC §513(e) allows a special exclusion from UBI for the income earned by a hospital providing the types of services listed in IRC §501(e) to another hospital that has facilities to serve fewer than 100 patients, provided the price for such services is rendered at cost plus a "reasonable amount of return on the capital goods used" in providing the service.

The IRS recently considered "related services" being rendered by a IRC §501(c)(6) tourist and convention organization for the local government. Their memo discusses a broad range of services provided to businesses planning conventions in the city (which the EO was organized to benefit) and finds them related activity. Commissions received from hotels in return for referring groups and conventions for reservations, however, were deemed unrelated.[21]

(c) Sale of Name

Sale of the organization's name normally is accomplished by a licensing contract permitting use of the EO's intangible property—its name—with the compensation constituting royalty income that is excluded from UBI under concepts discussed later. However, in the IRS's view, such arrangements usually consti-

---

[21] Tech. Adv. Mem. 9032005

tute commercial exploitation of an exempt asset. Since issuing a Revenue Ruling in 1981, the IRS has been trying to tax EOs on the sale of their names in connection with insurance programs, affinity sales, and other commercial marketing schemes.[22]

To add flavor to the problem, in April 1990, the IRS reversed its position that a "royalty arrangement" licensing an EO's name, logo, and mailing list to an insurance agent (to promote life insurance to its membership) did not produce UBI for the exempt organization.[23] Because of the extensive involvement (active, not passive) of the exempt organization in servicing the membership lists, IRC §513(h)(1)(B)'s narrow exemption of mailing lists, and the agency theory (discussed below), the IRS ruled that the supposed "royalty arrangement" produced UBI. The American Bar Association lost a similar battle in 1986, although its case was made more complicated by an arrangement whereby its members made substantial donations of the program profits.[24]

When the sale of the organization's name or logo is accompanied by any additional requirements on the part of the EO, such as servicing the mailing list as discussed above, endorsing a product, performing any other services for the purchaser, the IRS has made it very clear they consider such arrangements to produce unrelated income. Also suspect would be contracts in which the "royalty" amount paid for use of the name is tied to the number of times it is used in solicitations, all of which are mailed to the separately-purchased mailing list of the EO.

Affinity card revenues are in the same category, as far as the IRS is concerned, and do not qualify for the "royalty" exception. When first ruling on affinity cards, the IRS allowed royalty exclusion for a fraternal order's card income.[25] By 1988, it had reversed its initial position.[26] While use of the EO's name and logo alone can produce royalty income, the credit card arrangements often depend on an accompanying sale of the organization's mailing list and, in some cases, endorsements and promotion by the EO in its publications and member/donor correspondence. The IRS therefore again applies an "agency-type" theory to deem that the EO itself, rather than the intermediary organization, performed valuable services that produced unrelated income. Some organizations try to avoid this problem by bifurcating the royalty and mailing list aspects of the contract. The IRS position is to see them as one transaction, in reality, one contract, and apply UBIT.

(d) Advertising

Sale of advertising in an otherwise exempt publication is almost always considered unrelated business income by the IRS. The basic theory is that the advertisements promote the interests of the individual advertiser and cannot

---

[22]Rev. Rul. 81-178, 1981-2 C.B. 135.

[23]Priv. Ltr. Rul. 9029047.

[24]*United States v. American Bar Endowment*, 477 U.S. 105 (1986).

[25]Priv. Ltr. Rul. 8747066.

[26]Priv. Ltr. Rul. 8823109.

therefore be related to the charitable purposes of the organization. The following examples are indicative:

- The American College of Physicians was unsuccessful in arguing with the IRS that the drug company ads in its health journal published for physicians educated the doctors. The College argued that the ads provided the reader with a comprehensive and systematic presentation of goods and services needed in the profession and informed physicians about new drug discoveries, but the court disagreed.[27]

- A college newspaper training program for journalism students enrolled in an advertising course produced related income.[28]

- Institutional or sponsor ads produce UBI if they are presented in a commercial fashion with a business logo, product description, or other sales information. Only when sponsors are listed without typical advertising copy can the money given for the listing be considered a donation. Different sizes for different amounts of money may not cause the ad to be classified as commercial.[29]

- Despite classification of ad revenues as UBI, the formula for calculating the taxable UBI yields surprising results, however, enabling some ad sale programs to escape tax. (A more thorough discussion of advertising and the formula appears in Section 21.20.)

(e) Sponsorships

Corporate sponsorships of a wide variety of events—golf tournaments, fun runs, football bowl games, public television, art exhibitions, and so on—are a favorite form of corporate support for exempt organizations. The appeal of wide public exposure for sponsoring worthy causes and cultural programs has gained extensive popularity. *The Wall Street Journal* ran a series of articles during 1991 discussing the extent of such support and why it made good business sense.

Under examination and now in a heavily-edited Private Letter Ruling 9147007, the IRS said the Cotton Bowl's payments from Mobil Oil Company are taxable, essentially because the Cotton Bowl was rendering services for Mobil. Substantial benefit in the form of advertising was given to Mobil and such revenue was business income, not a contribution. Legislation has been introduced to carve out a special exemption for such revenues, but, until it is passed, caution is advised. Even if such arrangements create UBI, the EO may be able to argue that the event or activity is irregularly carried on, although the IRS may not agree.

The IRS announced in early 1992 that "[t]ax exempt organizations can publicly acknowledge donors for their contributions, but if the organizations conduct advertising for donors, the payments are taxable income, not tax

---

[27]*American College of Physicians v. United States*, 457 U.S. 836 (1986).
[28]Reg. 1.513-1(d)(4)(iv), Example 5.
[29]*Fraternal Order of Police, Illinois State Troopers Lodge No. 41 v. Commissioner*, 833 F.2d 717 (7th Cir. 1987), *aff'g* 87 T.C. 747 (1986); Priv. Ltr. Rul. 8640007.

exempt contributions." The following examination guidelines were proposed and public comments solicited.[30]

- In analyzing corporate sponsored events, the contract or arrangements (either written or oral) are reviewed to determine whether the agreement requires the exempt organization to perform any services.

- Copies of the organization's meetings and correspondence or other written statements between the EO and the sponsor must be reviewed. It was noted that it "may be beneficial to review films, videotapes or photographs of the event over the years to determine the extent the corporate sponsor's name is mentioned or depicted."

- Factors to consider in evaluating the provision of services or other benefits in return for the payment received were enumerated. Factors "tending to indicate an unrelated business" include:

  —Inclusion of the corporate sponsor's name or logo in the official event title;

  —Prominent placement of the sponsor's name or logo throughout the stadium, arena, or other site where the event is held;

  —Printing the sponsor's name or logo on materials related to the event;

  —Placement of the sponsor's name or logo on participant or other support personnel uniforms;

  —Reference to the sponsorship in corporate advertisements during the course of the contract;

  —Making participants available to the sponsor for personal appearances and endorsements;

  —Special seating, accommodations, transportation, and hospitality facilities at the event provided to sponsors;

  —Requirement of media coverage for the event.

The IRS has announced an "audit tolerance" and says it will not apply the guidelines to organizations of a purely local nature, such as Little League baseball and soccer teams (but there is no mention of basketball, football, or any other sport), and local theaters and youth orchestras (presumably, intentionally excluding ballet companies or symphony orchestras).

Providing "mere name recognition" will "normally" continue to be considered "incidental benefit" to the sponsor and not of sufficient value to the contributor to convert the funds to UBI. Specific examples cited in the announcement include naming a university professorship, scholarship, or building after the corporation; acknowledging the underwriting of a public radio or television program or museum exhibition; and listing a contributor's name in a

---

[30] IRS Announcement 92-15, IRB 1992-4.

fund-raising event or performing arts program. The issue is whether quid pro quo services are rendered by the charity to the sponsor. Legislation exempting public sporting and cultural event sponsorship revenues were under consideration in the summer of 1992. Hearing about the IRS audit guidelines raised many questions and were inconclusive. Watch for new developments.

(f) Member Services

Services to members will be scrutinized carefully by IRS. Note especially the following:

- Sale of legal forms by a bar association, billing and credit services for members, and testing fees have all been argued with decisions for and against the organizations. EOs considering this type of income-producing activity should research this question thoroughly.[31]

- Free bus service provided to a particular shopping center versus a downtown area of a city was ruled to produce unrelated income for a chamber of commerce.

The question is whether services rendered to members constitute private inurement or private benefit for the members versus the general public or the profession (for a business league).

(g) Insurance

Group insurance programs have been a subject of active litigation among trade unions, business leagues, and the IRS, with the IRS currently prevailing in classifying revenues produced in an insurance program for members as UBI. The American Bar Endowment lost its battle to classify the dividends assigned to it by members participating in its group insurance plan as donations. Here again, careful planning in view of the most recent rulings and court decisions is in order to avoid UBI.[32]

(h) Real Estate

Real estate development projects can be characterized as related (low-income or elderly housing), as a trade or business (subdivision, debt-financed rental, hotel), as an investment (unindebted rental), or sometimes as a combination of all three.

Any EO anticipating such a program should study Private Letter Ruling 8950072, in which the IRS outlines the UBI consequences of four different methods of developing a piece of raw land owned by an exempt organization. Leasing or selling raw land unquestionably produced no UBI because of the passive income modifications. Completion of the preliminary development work of obtaining permits and approval prior to the property's sale did not

---

[31]*San Antonio Bar Association v. United States*, 80-2 U.S.T.C. §9594 (W.D. Tex. 1980).
[32]*Louisiana Credit Union League v. United States*, 693 F.2d 525 (5th Cir. 1982).

convert the sale into a business transaction. But total development of the property prior to the sale converts the property into a business asset and produces UBI.

Development of an apartment building and parking garage as a part of an urban renewal effort is a related business for an organization whose purpose is to combat community deterioration. The organization operates to assist the city by encouraging revitalization of its downtown area. While the activity would result in UBI if conducted for investment, in this case the activity served the EO's exempt purposes.[33]

(i) Agency Theory

An *agency theory* may be applied to look through certain arrangements. To avoid UBI classification for potentially unrelated activities listed above, an organization might engage an independent party to conduct the activity in return for a royalty or a rental payment. Inherently "passive" activities for which compensation is paid in the form of rent or royalty are not subject to UBIT, even if the activity is deemed unrelated. The question is, however, whether the IRS can look through the transactions and attribute the activity of the independent party back to the organization, as it did in the following example.

The National Collegiate Athletic Association (NCAA) hires an unrelated commercial publishing company to produce its tournament programs. NCAA gives the publisher a free hand in soliciting the advertisements, designing the copy, and distributing the programs, in return for a percentage of the advertising and direct sales revenues. Because it has little or no involvement in the activity, the NCAA treats the income as a passive and irregularly carried on activity not subject to the unrelated business income tax. There is no argument that selling the program itself produces related income; nor is there any question that the advertising income is unrelated. The tournament lasts only three weeks.

The issue considered by the Tax Court[34] was whether the NCAA had sufficiently disengaged itself under the contract. Did it sell the right to use its name or did it engage in the ad activity itself? The Tax Court adopted an agency theory, and held that because the publisher acted as the NCAA's agent, the activity was totally attributable to the NCAA. The Tenth Circuit Court agreed with the Tax Court but reversed the decision (because the activity was irregularly carried on and not in competition with business); the agency theory was not disputed. The IRS disagrees with the appellate decision regarding irregularity.

Another athletic tournament-sponsoring organization also failed the agency test. The independently-hired promoter's efforts during a 15-month ad campaign were attributed to the organization.[35] The agency theory was escaped, however, by an organization which turned over the publication of its

---

[33]Priv. Ltr. Rul. 9208033.

[34]*National Collegiate Athletic Association v. Commissioner*, 90-2 U.S.T.C. §50513 (10th Cir. 1990), *rev'g* 92 T.C. No. 27 (1989). See also Priv. Ltr. Rul. 9137002 and 9211004.

[35]Tech. Adv. Mem. 8932004; Priv. Ltr. Rul. 9150047.

monthly journal to a commercial company, retaining one-third of the net revenues from subscriptions and reprints. All advertising income, two-thirds of the circulation revenues, and all the risk of publication expenses were borne by the company. The IRS decided, under the circumstances, that the company was acting on its own behalf, not as agent for the charity. No advertising revenue was allocated to the charity.[36]

21.9 THE EXCEPTIONS

Despite their literal inclusion in the "unrelated" prong of the UBI rules, certain types of revenue-raising activities are not subject to UBIT, presumably because they are not businesslike and do not compete with commercial businesses.[37] Charitable §501(c)(3) organizations qualify for all of the following exceptions. Certain exceptions do not apply to non-501(c)(3) organizations, as noted under the particular exception.

(a) Volunteers

Any business in which substantially all the work is performed without compensation is excluded from UBI. "Substantially" means at least 80 to 85 percent of the total work performed, measured normally by the total hours worked. A paid manager or executive, administrative personnel, and all sorts of support staff can operate the business if most of the work is performed by volunteers.

In most cases the number of hours worked, rather than relative value of the work, is used to measure the 85 percent test. This means that the value of volunteer time need not necessarily be quantified for comparison to monetary compensation paid. In the case of a group of volunteer singing doctors, the value of the doctors' time was considered. Because the doctors were the stars of the records producing the income, their time was counted by the court at a premium, which offset administrative personnel whose time was paid.[38]

Expense reimbursements, in-kind benefits, and prizes are not necessarily treated as compensation unless they are compensatory in nature. Particularly when the expenses enable the volunteers to work longer hours and serve the convenience of the EO, the payments need not be counted in measuring this exception. However, when food, lodging, and total sustenance were furnished to sustain members of a religious group, the members working for the group's businesses were not treated as volunteers.[39]

(b) Donated Goods

The selling of merchandise, substantially all of which is received as gifts or contributions, is not subject to the UBIT. Thrift and resale shops selling donated

---

[36] Tech. Adv. Mem. 9023003; similar result in Priv. Ltr. Rul. 9137002 and 7926003.
[37] IRC §513(a).
[38] *Greene County Medical Society Foundation v. United States*, 345 F. Supp. 900 (W.D. Mo. 1972).
[39] *Shiloh Youth Revival Centers v. Commissioner*, 88 T.C. 579 (1987).

goods do not report UBI on donated goods they sell. A shop selling goods on consignment as well as donated goods would have to distinguish between the two types of goods. UBI would be earned for the consigned goods, but might escape tax if the shop is run by volunteers.

(c) Bingo Games

Bingo games not conducted in violation of any state or local law are excluded. IRC §513(f) defines bingo as any game of bingo of a type in which usually (1) wagers are placed, (2) winners are determined, and (3) distribution of prizes or other property is made, in the presence of all persons placing wagers in such game.

The Regulations expand the definition:

> A bingo game is a game of chance played with cards that are generally printed with five rows of five squares each. Participants place markers over randomly called numbers on the cards in an attempt to form a preselected pattern such as a horizontal, vertical, or diagonal line, or all four corners. The first participant to form the preselected pattern wins the game. Any other game of chance including but not limited to, keno, dice, cards, and lotteries, is not bingo [and will create UBI].[40]

Pull-tabs and other forms of "instant bingo" are not bingo in the IRS's opinion, and produce unrelated business income despite the fact that such variations of the bingo game are so classified by the state bingo authority. During 1990, the IRS aggressively examined EOs in the Southwest District and assessed tax on any bingo variations not strictly meeting the Code and Regulation definitions.

(d) Public Entertainment Activities

Public entertainment is defined as that traditionally conducted at fairs or expositions promoting agricultural and educational purposes (including but not limited to animals or products and equipment) and does not produce UBI for §501(c)(3), (4), or (5) organizations. IRC §513(d)(2) requires that the event be held in conjunction with an international, national, state, regional, or local fair, or be in accordance with provisions of state law that permit such a fair.

(e) Qualified Conventions and Trade Shows

A convention or trade show is intended to attract persons in an industry generally (without regard to membership in the sponsoring organization), as well as members of the public, to the show for the purpose of displaying industry products, or stimulating interest in and demand for industry products or services, or educating persons engaged in the industry in the development of

---

[40]Reg. §1.513-5.

new products and services or new rules and regulations affecting the industry. A "qualified" show is one conducted by §501(c)(3), (4), (5), or (6) organizations in conjunction with an international, national, state, regional, or local convention, annual meeting, or show. Exhibitors are permitted to sell products or services and the organization can charge for the display space.

21.10 EXCEPTIONS FOR §501(c)(3) ORGANIZATIONS AND VETERAN POSTS

(a) Low-Cost Articles

Gift premiums costing (not fair market value) the organization no more than $6.01 (during 1992—indexed annually for inflation) and distributed with no obligation to purchase in connection with the solicitations of contributions are not treated as a sale of the gift premium. The gift must be part of a fund-raising campaign.

The recipient of the premium must not request or consent to receive the premium. Literature requesting a donation must accompany the premium and a statement that the recipient may keep the low-cost article regardless of whether a charitable donation is made. If the donation is less than $30.09 (during 1992—indexed annually), the fair market value of the premium reduces the deductible portion of the donor's gift.[41]

(b) Mailing Lists

A business involving the exchange or renting of mailing lists between two organizations eligible to receive charitable donations under IRC §170(c)(2) or (3) is excluded from UBI classification. In other words, charitable organizations exempt under IRC §501(c)(3) and veteran organizations qualify for this special treatment added by Congress in 1986.[42] Sale or exchange of mailing lists by all other types of §501(c) organizations now create UBI.

21.11 EXCEPTIONS FOR §501(c)(3) ORGANIZATIONS

(a) Convenience

A cafeteria, bookstore, residence, or similar facility used in the EO's programs and operated for the convenience of patients, visitors, employees, or students is specifically excepted from UBI classification by IRC §513(a)(2) for §501(c)(3) organizations only. Presumably, it benefits hospital patients to have family and friends visiting or staying with them in the hospital, and the cafeteria facilitates the visits. Museum visitors can spend more time viewing art if they can stop to rest their feet and have a cup of coffee. Parking lots for the exclusive use of participants in an exempt organization's activities also produce related income.

[41] Rev. Proc. 90-12 (Feb. 1990), updated in Rev. Proc. 92-58, 1992-2 IRB 10.
[42] IRC §513(h).

When the cafe, shop, dorm, or parking lot is also open to the general public, the revenue produced by public use is unrelated income. Some commentators suggest that the whole facility becomes subject to UBIT, particularly when the facility has an entrance to a public street. At best, the income from a facility used by both qualified visitors and the disinterested public off the street is fragmented. The taxable and nontaxable revenues are identified and tabulated and the net taxable portion is calculated under the dual use rules discussed in Section 21.14.

When the unrelated income is rental income, there is still a possible escape route from application of the UBIT. The technical question becomes whether the lot rentals are excludable UBI under the "passive income modifications."

The IRS admits that it has issued unclear and conflicting positions on the matter. An IRS memo states unequivocally that revenue from direct lot operation never produces rent, and refers to the Regulations.[43] Only when the lot is operated by an independent party under a lease arrangement in which the exempt organization performs no services can the revenue be classified as passive rental income, excludable from UBI.

21.12 PASSIVE INCOME MODIFICATIONS

Income earned from passive investment activities is not included in UBI unless the underlying property is subject to debt. Social clubs, voluntary employee benefit associations, supplemental unemployment plans, and veterans groups are taxed on such income. Types of passive income excluded from UBI under IRC §512(b) include "all dividends, interest, royalties, rents, payments with respect to security loans, and annuities, and all deductions connected with such income." It is important to note from the outset that passive income of a sort not specifically listed is not necessarily modified or excluded from UBI.

(a) Dividends and Interest

Dividends and interest paid on amounts invested in savings accounts, certificates of deposit, money market accounts, bonds, loans, preferred or common stocks, and payments in respect to security loans and annuities, net of any allocable deductions are excluded from UBI.

- In 1978, the general exclusion of interest and dividends was expanded to include the words "payments in respect of security loans." Since then, there has been uncertainty regarding sophisticated techniques such as "strips," interest rate swaps, and currency hedges. After two private letter rulings were issued in 1991, proposed regulations were announced in September 1991, to recognize that such investments were "ordinary and routine" and to make it clear that income earned from such transactions in security portfolios would be considered as investment income for §512 purposes.[44]

[43]G.C.M. 39825.
[44]Prop. Reg. §§1.509(a)-3, 1.512(b)-1 and 53.4940-1.

- Such securities acquired with indebtedness are swept back into UBI by IRC §514, and an EO must be careful to use new money to acquire each element of investment in its portfolio. A recent Tax Court case provides a good example. A pension fund, stuck with five-year certificates of deposit (CDs) in 1979 when interest rates shot up over five points, negotiated a plan to purchase new CDs using its old CDs as collateral, thereby escaping an early withdrawal penalty and receiving a higher rate of interest. The court found that, despite the fact that the transaction was not abusive, it fell squarely within the literal definition of a debt-financed asset purchase. The CD switch was not a "payment in respect of a security loan" within the meaning of §512(b)(1). Such a loan involves allowing a broker to use the EO's securities in return for a fee, not a loan against which the securities are used as collateral. Thus, the fund's original CD produced "modified" or nontaxable income, and the new higher-rate CD acquired with the loan proceeds was held to be taxable as unrelated debt-financed income.[45]

(b) Capital Gains

Gains from sale, exchange, or other disposition of property generally are not UBI.

- Gains on lapse or termination of covered and uncovered operations, if written as a part of investment activity, are not taxable according to §512(b)(5), added to the Code in 1976.
- Sales of stock in trade or other inventory-type property, or of property held for sale to customers in the ordinary course of trade or business, do produce UBI.

(c) Rentals

Rental income is excluded, except:

- Personal property rentals are taxable unless they are rented incidentally (not more than 10 percent of rent) with real property.
- Net profit (versus gross revenue) interests produce UBI.
- When substantial services are rendered, such as the rental of a theater complete with staff, the rental is not considered passive.

(d) Royalties

Royalties, whether measured by production or by the gross or taxable income from the property, are excluded. Oil and gas working interest income would not be excluded.

---

[45] *Kern County Electrical Pension Fund v. Commissioner*, 96 T.C. No. 41 (June 20, 1991).

(e) Subsidiary Payments

Controlled subsidiary payments for interest, rents, royalties, or annuities, however, are includable in UBI. Control exists when one organization owns stock possessing at least 80 percent of the total combined voting power of all classes of stock entitled to vote and at least 80 percent of all other classes of stock of another organization (exempt or nonexempt). A nonstock organization measures control by quantifying its interlocking directors. If at least 80 percent of the directors of one organization are members of the second organization or have the right to appoint or control the board of the second, control exists according to the Regulations.

That portion of a controlled organization's income which would have been taxed as UBI to the parent EO if the income had been earned by it is includable (whether or not regularly carried on). Thus, payments from a subsidiary corporation conducting a related activity would qualify as a modification and would not be UBI.

(f) Research

Research income is not taxable if the research is performed for the United States, its agencies, or a state or political subdivision thereof by any EO. In addition:

- A college, university, or hospital can exclude all research income from private or governmental contractors.

- An EO performing fundamental research, the results of which are freely available to the general public, can also exclude all research income.

21.13 CALCULATING TAXABLE INCOME

Gross unrelated business income, minus expenses and exemptions (listed below), is subject to tax. As long as the percentage of revenues from UBI is modest in relation to the organization's overall revenues, the only problem UBIT presents is the reduction in profit because of the income tax paid. Tax planning of the sort practiced by a good businessperson is in order. Maximizing deductions to calculate the income is important. The income tax sections of the Internal Revenue Code of 1986 govern, and the same concepts apply, including:

- *Tax rates.* The income tax is calculated using the normal tables for all taxpayers, i.e., §1(e) for trusts and §11 for corporations. For controlled groups of exempt organizations (also including 80-percent-owned for-profit subsidiaries), the corporate tax bracket must be calculated on a consolidated basis under the rules of §1561.

- *Alternative minimum tax.* Accelerated depreciation, percentage depletion, and other similar tax benefits are subject to the alternative minimum tax, just as with for-profit taxpayers.

- *"Ordinary and necessary" criteria.* Deductions claimed against the unrelated income must be "ordinary and necessary" to conducting the activity and must meet the other standards of §162 for business deductions. Ordinary means common and accepted for the type of business operated; necessary means helpful and appropriate, not indispensable. The activity for which the expenditure is incurred must also be operated with profit motive.[46]

- *Profit motive.* To be deductible, an expenditure must also be paid for the production of income, or in a business operated for the purpose of making a profit. IRC §183 specifically prohibits the deduction of "hobby losses," or those activities losing money for more than two years out of every five. The IRS will challenge the deduction for UBI purposes of any expenditures not paid for the purposes of producing the profit.[47]

- *Depreciation.* Equipment, buildings, vehicles, furniture, and other properties that have a useful life to the business are deductible, theoretically over their life. As a simple example, one-third of the total cost of a computer that is expected to be obsolete in three years would be deductible during each year the computer is used in the business. Unfortunately, Congress uses these calculation rates and methods as political and economic tools, and the Code prescribes rates and methods that are not so simple. IRC §§167, 168, and 179 apply and must be studied to properly calculate allowable deductions for depreciation.

- *Inventory.* If the EO keeps an inventory of items for sale, such as books, drugs, or merchandise of any sort, it must use the inventory method to deduct the cost of such goods. The concept is one of matching the cost of the item sold with its sales proceeds. If the EO buys ten widgets for sale and, as of the end of a year, only five have been sold, the cost of the five is deductible and the remaining five are capitalized as an asset to be deducted when they are sold. Again, the system is far more complicated than this simple example, and an accountant should be consulted to ensure use of proper reporting and tabulation methods. IRC §§263A and 471–474 also apply.

- *Capital and nondeductibles.* A host of nondeductible items contained in IRC §§261–280H might apply to disallow deductions, either by total disallowance or required capitalization of permanent assets. Again, all the rules applicable to for-profit businesses apply, such as the luxury automobile limits, travel and entertainment substantiation requirements, and 20 percent disallowance for meals.

- *Dividend deduction.* The dividends received deduction provided by IRC §§243–245 for taxable nonexempt corporations is not allowed. As a general rule, a corporation is allowed to exclude 70 percent of the dividends it receives on its investments; exempt organizations are not.

---

[46]Reg. §1.512(a)-1(a).
[47]*Iowa State University of Science and Technology v. United States*, 500 F.2d 508 (Ct. Cl. 1974); *Commissioner v. Groetzinger*, 480 U.S. 23 (1987); Reg. §1.513-1(4)(d)(iii).

This rule only presents a problem for dividends received from investments that are debt-financed. Most dividends received by exempts are excluded from the UBI under the modifications previously discussed.

21.14 SPECIFIC CATEGORIES OF DEDUCTIBLE COSTS

As a general rule, there are two categories of expenses allowed as deductions for purposes of calculating UBIT: direct and dual use expenses. No portion of the organization's basic operating expense theoretically is deductible against UBI because of the exploitation rules discussed below. However, when there is an ongoing plan to produce UBI and such revenue is part of the justification affording a particular exempt activity, allocation of overhead is permitted, although it is technically challenging, as discussed in Section 27.14.

(a) Directly Related

Those expenses attributable solely to the production of unrelated gross income are fully deductible. According to the IRS, a "proximate and primary relationship" between the expense and the activity is the standard for full deduction. Proximate means near, close, or immediate. A "but for" test can be applied by asking the question, "Would the expense be incurred if the unrelated activity was not carried on?"[48]

(b) Dually-Used Facilities or Personnel

A portion of the cost of so-called "dual use," or shared, employees and facilities, is deductible. An allocation between the two types of activities is made on "a reasonable basis." The only example given in the Regulations allocates 10 percent of an EO president's salary to an unrelated business activity to which he or she devotes 10 percent of his or her time. When actual time records are maintained to evidence effort devoted to related versus unrelated activities, deduction of the applicable personal costs is ensured. In the IRS *Manual*, examining agents are instructed that any reasonable method resulting in identifying a relationship of the expenses to revenue produced is acceptable. There is no particular method that must be followed.[49]

Absent time records, an allocation based on relative gross income produced might be used if the exempt activity reaps income. Take, for example, a museum bookstore that sells both related and unrelated items. Sales could be used in this case as the allocation base. When an income-producing activity is carried out alongside one that is not producing revenue, time records must be maintained.

When a portion of the building is devoted totally to unrelated activity, building costs, including utilities, insurance, depreciation of the cost, interest on mortgage, and maintenance, are allocated based on total square footage of the

---

[48] IRC §512(a)(1).

[49] *Exempt Organization Examination Guidelines Handbook*, Internal Revenue Manual 7(10)69 §720(7).

building used for the UBI activity. If UBI space is shared with related space, again, a reasonable method is used. For a publication project, the lineage devoted to advertising could be calculated for its relationship to the total publication.

Taxpayers and the IRS have argued about allocation methods, and there are differences of opinion. An EO with this question should be sure to determine the current situation. For hospitals, the Medicare cost allocations methods "usually fail to accurately reflect UBI," in the IRS's opinion.[50]

(c) Direct vs. Indirect Expenses

A subset of the expense allocation problem is the application of different methods for direct and indirect expenses. Direct expenses in accounting terms are those that increase proportionately with the usage of a facility or the volume of activity; they are also called variable. The number of persons attending an event influences the number of ushers or security guards needed, and represents a direct cost; in other words, the cost is attributable to that specific use that would not have been incurred except for the particular event.

Indirect costs, on the other hand, are incurred without regard to usage or frequency of participation and are usually called the fixed expenses of the organization. Building costs are an example. The presumption is that the organization's underlying building costs, for example, do not vary with usage.

(d) Formula Denominator Question

The denominator of the fraction used to calculate costs allocable to UBI is significant in reducing or increasing allowable deductions. The question must be considered in view of the exploitation rules, and the point is again whether the EO would conduct the related activity without the unrelated revenue stream. Arguably, no fixed costs of an exempt institution should be allocated to UBI, but to date the courts have chosen to allow allocation among both the exempt and nonexempt functions that benefit from building use.

In allocating fixed facility costs, the courts have not agreed on whether the appropriate denominator is the total number of hours a facility is used, or the total number of hours in the year. Each factor yields vastly different results. Watch for new legislation or regulations; more complicated and varied formulas have been proposed.

- In a college football stadium case the Second Circuit Court of Appeals[51] allowed:

$$\frac{\text{number of hours or days used for unrelated purposes}}{\text{total number of hours or days in USE}}$$

---

[50]G.C.M. 39843.

[51]*Rensselaer Polytechnic Institute v. Commissioner*, 732 F.2d 1058 (2nd Cir. 1984), *aff'g* 79 T.C. 967 (1982).

- The IRS argues that fixed costs should be allocated by:

$$\frac{\text{number of hours or days used for unrelated purposes}}{\text{total number of hours or days in YEAR}}$$

(e) Gross-to-Gross Method

The gross-to-gross method of cost allocation is applied when costs bear a relationship to the revenue produced from exempt and nonexempt factors. For example, when students and members are charged one fee and nonmembers and nonstudents are charged another (usually higher) fee, an allocation using the total revenue from each different category would not be reflective of the true cost to produce the revenue. A proration based on the overall number of individuals in each group might be more accurate. This type of formula is often used in calculating allocations for social clubs and publications serving all participants at the same price.

(f) Exploitation

When a fundamentally exempt activity, such as a publication or a bookstore, produces some UBI from advertising or sales of unrelated items, the Regulations provide a limitation on the deduction of underlying exempt activity cost against the UBI. This limitation presents a classic "chicken and egg" or "tail wagging the dog" situation. Is the UBI activity an afterthought? Probably the best question is whether the exempt activity would be carried on regardless of the UBI funds. It is curious that the football stadium case cited above allows allocation of expenses, despite the obvious assumption that a college must have a sports facility, and without regard to its ability to rent it during the down time, a seemingly classic "exploitation." Nonetheless, when an EO chooses to consider UBI as produced in connection with an exploited activity, deduction limitations are based on income.

- Expenses of an exploited activity are allowable as a general rule only to the extent of the gross unrelated income it produces.

- Exempt function expenses related to the activity are first reduced by any related revenues, then the excess expenses are allocated to the unrelated income to the extent of the unrelated income. No loss resulting from an excess of exempt function plus unrelated activity expenses over total revenues can be used to offset other UBI.

See the calculation of deductible expenses on an exploited publication in Section 21.20.

(g) Charitable Deduction

Up to 10 percent of an exempt corporation's UBI and 100 percent of a charitable trust's UBI is deductible for contributions paid to a charitable organization. The deduction is not allowed for internal project expenditures of the organization itself. Excess contributions are eligible for the normal five-year carryover allowed to for-profit taxpayers. Social clubs, voluntary employee business associations, unemployment benefit trusts, and group legal service plans can take a 100 percent deduction for direct charitable gifts and "qualified set asides" for charitable purposes.

(h) Administrative Overhead

A portion of the organization's administrative expenses may be deductible against UBI, which substantially reduces the tax burden from unrelated activity. Adequate proof of the allocation methods and escape of the exploitation rule discussed above is important to support an EO's overhead deduction against UBI.

(i) $1,000 Exemption

An exemption of $1,000 ($5,000 under Congressional Select Committee Proposals) is allowed by IRC §512(b)(12).

21.15 ACCOUNTING METHOD CONSIDERATIONS

(a) In-Kind Gifts

Donated goods and services properly recorded under accounting principles promulgated by the Accounting Principles Board (APB 78-10) should be booked and deducted as discussed in Section 27.14(e).

(b) Documentation

To correctly calculate the EO's expenses that are allocable to UBI, documentation is critical. Time records, expense identification, departmental approval systems, and similar internal control techniques will allow the organization to compute maximum allowable deductions against UBI. Particularly for staff time allocations and administrative expense items such as printing and supplies, capturing the information is simple once documentation methods are installed. See Chapter 27.

(c) Accrual Method

If the EO's gross income from UBI exceeds $5 million annually, the accrual method of accounting must be used. If an inventory of goods and products for sale is maintained and is a "material" income-producing factor, the accrual method must be utilized.

(d) Net Operating Losses

A loss realized in operating an unrelated business in one year may be carried back for three years and forward for 15 years, for offset against another year's operating income. Gains and losses for different types of UBI earned within any single EO are netted against profits from the various business activities of the organization, including acquisition of indebted investment property. Tax years in which no UBI activity is realized are counted in calculating the number of years for permissible carryovers. Conversely, net operating losses are not reduced by related income.

A social club cannot offset losses on serving nonmembers against income from its other investments, according to the Supreme Court, which sided with the IRS.[52] There has been a conflict of decisions among the U.S. Circuit Courts of Appeal for several years, and clubs claiming such losses must now consider filing amended returns to report tax resulting from the loss disallowance.

It is extremely important for an EO to file Form 990T despite the fact that it incurs a loss. Reporting the loss allows for carryback or carryover of the loss to offset past or future income. An election is available to carry losses forward and forgo any carryback in situations where the EO has not previously earned UBI.

21.16   ESTIMATED TAX

Income tax liability for UBI is payable in advance during the year, as the income is earned, similar to for-profit businesses and individuals.

21.17   DEBT-FINANCED INCOME

The modifications exempting passive investment income, such as dividends and interest, from the UBIT do not apply to the extent that the investment is made with borrowed funds. Debt-financed property is defined by IRC §514 as including property held for the production of income that was acquired with borrowed funds and has a balance of acquisition indebtedness attributable to it during the year. The classic examples are a margin account held against the EO's endowment funds or a mortgage financing a rental building purchase.

(a) Properties Excluded from Debt-Financed Rules

Real or other tangible or intangible property used 85 percent or more of the time when it is actually devoted to such purpose, and used directly in the EO's exempt or related activities, is exempt from these rules. If a university borrows money and builds an office tower for its projected staff needs over a 20-year period, and if less than 85 percent of the building is used by its staff and net

---

[52] *Portland Golf Club v. Commissioner*, 90-1 U.S.T.C. §50,332; *Iowa State University of Science and Technology v. United States*, 500 F.2d (Ct.Cl. 1974); *Commissioner v. Groetzinger, supra* n.6. 110 S.Ct. 2780 (1990).

profit is earned, the nonuniversity-use portion of the building income is taxable as UBI.

- Property the income of which is included in UBI for some other reason is specifically excluded by the Code and need not be counted twice for this reason.

- Future-use property acquired and held for use by the organization (within 10 years from the date it is acquired and located in the neighborhood in which the EO carries out a project) is exempt from this provision.

- A life estate does not constitute a debt. When some other individual or organization is entitled to income from the property for life or another period of time, a remainder interest in the property is not considered to be indebted.

- Debt placed on property by a donor will be attributed to the organization when the EO agrees to pay all or part of the debt or makes any payments on the equity. Property that is encumbered and subject to existing debt at the time it is received by bequest or devise is not treated as acquisition indebted-property for 10 years from its acquisition, if there is no assumption or payment on the debt by the EO.

- Gifted property subject to debt is similarly excluded, if the donor placed the mortgage on the property over 5 years prior to gift and had owned the property over 5 years, unless there is an assumption or payment on the mortgage by the EO.

- Property used in unrelated activities of an EO, the income of which is excepted from UBI because it is run by volunteers for the convenience of members, or sale of donated goods, can be indebted and still not be subject to this classification.

- Research property producing income otherwise excluded from the UBIT is not subject to the acquisition indebtedness taint.

(b) "Acquisition Indebtedness"

Acquisition indebtedness is the unpaid amount of any debt incurred to purchase or improve property or any debt "reasonably foreseen" at the time of acquisition which would not have been incurred otherwise.

- Securities purchased on margin are debt-financed; payments for loan of securities already owned are not.

- The formula for calculation of income subject to tax is:

$$\text{income from property} \times \frac{\text{average acquisition indebtedness}}{\text{average adjusted basis}}$$

The average acquisition indebtedness equals the arithmetic average of each month or partial month of the tax year. The average adjusted basis is similarly calculated, and only straight-line depreciation is allowed.

(c) Calculation of Taxable Portion

Only that portion of the net income of debt-financed property attributable to the debt is classified as UBI. Each property subject to debt is calculated separately, with the resulting income or loss netted to arrive at the portion includable in UBI. Expenses directly connected with the property are deducted from gross revenues in the same proportion.

The capital gain or loss formula is different in one respect: the highest amount of indebtedness during the year preceding sales is used as the numerator.

21.18 PLANNING IDEAS

The first rule in reducing UBIT is to keep good records. The accounting system must support the desired allocation of deductions for personnel and facilities with time records, expense usage reports, auto logs, documentation reports, and so on. Aggressive avoidance of the "exploitation rule" must be backed up with proof.

Minutes of meetings of the board of directors or trustees should reflect discussion of relatedness of any project claimed to accomplish an exempt purpose, if it could appear that the activity is unrelated. For example, contracts and other documents concerning activities which the organization wants to prove are related to its exempt purposes should contain appropriate language to reflect the project's exempt purposes.

An organization's original purposes can be expanded and redefined to broaden the scope of activities or to justify some proposed activity as related. Such altered or expanded purpose can be reported to the IRS to justify the relatedness of a new activity.

If dual-use facilities can be partly debt-financed and partly paid for, an EO could purposefully buy the nontaxable exempt function property with debt and buy the unrelated part of the facility with cash available. Or, separate notes could be executed, with the taxable and unrelated property's debt being paid off first.

If loss of exemption is a strong possibility because of the extent and amount of unrelated business activity planned, a separate for-profit organization can be formed to shield the EO from a possible loss of exemption due to excessive business activity.

21.19 MUSEUMS

Museum gift shop sales and related income-producing activities are governed by the "fragmentation" and "exploitation" rules discussed earlier. Since 1973, when it published a ruling concerning greeting cards,[53] the IRS has agreed that items printed with reproductions of images in a museum's collection are educational, related to the exempt purposes, and their sale does not produce UBI. The ruling expressed two different reasons: (1) the cards stimulated and enhanced public awareness, interest in, and appreciation of art; and (2) a self-advertising theory stating that a "broader segment of the public may be encouraged to visit the museum itself to share in its educational functions and programs as a result of seeing the cards."

Another 1973 ruling[54] explored the fragmentation rule and expanded its application to trinkets and actual copies of objects and distinguished items. The IRS felt that educational benefit could be gained from utilitarian items with souvenir value. Since that time, it has been clearly established that a museum shop often contains both related and unrelated items, and the museum must keep exacting records to identify the two.

(a) Identifying Related and Unrelated Objects

After the IRS and museums argued for 10 years about the relatedness of a wide variety of objects sold, four exhaustive private rulings were issued in 1983 and are still followed as of November, 1992.[55] The primary concern for a museum is to identify the "relatedness" of each object sold in its shops, and to segregate any unrelated sales. The connection between the item sold and achievement of the museum's exempt purpose is evidenced by the facts and circumstances of each object and the policy of the curatorial department in identifying, labeling, and categorizing objects on public view.

IRS rulings direct the "facts and circumstances" of each object to be examined, to prove that the objects being sold have educational value, and list the following factors to consider in designating an item:

- "Interpretive material" describing artistic, cultural, or historical relationship to the museum's collection or exhibits;

- Nature, scope, and motivation for the sale activity;

- Are sales solely for production of income or are they an activity to enhance visitor awareness of art?

- Curatorial supervision in choosing related items;

- Reproductions of objects in the particular museum or in other collections, including prints, slides, posters, postcards and greeting cards, are generally exempt;

- Adaptations, including imprinted utilitarian objects such as dishes, ashtrays, and clothing, must be accompanied by interpretive materials and must depict objects or identify an exhibition. Objects printed with

---

[53]Rev. Rul. 73-104, 1973-1 C.B. 263.
[54]Rev. Rul. 73-105, 1973-1 C.B. 265.
[55]Priv. Ltr. Ruls. 8303013, 8326003, 8236008, and 8328009.

logos were deemed unrelated, although in practice, the IRS has been lenient.

- Souvenirs and convenience items are generally unrelated unless imprinted with reproductions or promoting a particular event or exhibition. Souvenirs promoting the town in which the museum is located are not considered related to the museum's purposes; and

- Toys and other teaching items for children are deemed inherently educational and therefore related.

(b) Original Works of Art

Original works of art created by living artists and sold by museums are considered unrelated by the IRS. They think it is inconsistent with the purpose of exhibiting art for public benefit to deprive the public the opportunity of viewing the art by selling it to an individual. This policy can apply as well to deceased artists.

- A cooperative art gallery established to encourage individual "emerging artists" was not allowed to qualify as an exempt organization because, in the IRS's opinion, the interests of the general public were not served by promoting the careers of individual artists. The art sales served no exempt purpose and constituted unrelated business income. Because the organization was supported entirely by unrelated business income from the sales of art of the artists, it was not exempt.[56]

- A community art center located in an isolated area with no commercial galleries obtained exemption, and the Tax Court decided that its sales of original art were related to exempt purposes. The decision was based on the fact that no other cultural center existed in the county, the art sales were not the center's sole source of support, and a complex of other activities were conducted.[57]

- An unrelated gallery managed by volunteers and/or selling donated works of art produces unrelated income, but the income is not taxable because of exceptions. Exempt status depends on whether the gallery is a substantial part of the EO's activities.

(c) Study Tours

Museums and other types of exempt organizations sponsor study tours as promotional, educational, and fund-raising tools. The issue is whether such tours compete with travel agents and commercial tour guides and thus produce UBI. A study tour led by professionals and qualifying for university credit qualifies as related to a museum's educational purposes. Generally, the IRS will scrutinize the bona fide educational methodology of the tour, including the professional status of leaders and the educational content of the program. The

[56]Priv. Ltr. Rul. 8032028.
[57]*Goldsboro Art League, Inc. v. Commissioner*, 75 T.C. 337 (1980).

amount of advance preparation, such as reading lists, can be a factor. The actual amount of time spent in formal classes, mandatory participation in the lectures, or opportunity for university credit are other attributes evidencing the educational nature of a tour.[58] Conversely, a large amount of recreational time allowed to participants, the resort-taint of the places the tour visits, and holiday scheduling suggest predominantly personal pleasure purposes and cause the tour to not qualify as educational.[59]

Not only the profit from the tour itself, but the "additional donation" requested as an organizational gift from all participants in a travel tour program, may be classed as unrelated income if the tour is not considered as educational.[60]

21.20 PUBLISHING

EO publications present two very different exposures to trouble: the unrelated income tax and potential revocation of exemption. As discussed above, the most universal problem is that publication advertising sales create UBIT in most cases. A less common, but more dangerous, situation occurs when the underlying exemption is challenged because the publication itself is a business.

(a) Advertising

Revenue received from the sale of advertising in an otherwise exempt publication is considered business income by the IRS, and is taxed unless:

- The publication schedule or ad sale activity is irregularly carried on;
- The advertising is sold by volunteers;
- The advertising activity is related to one of the organization's underlying exempt purposes, such as ads sold by college students or trainees; and
- The ads do not contain commercial material, appear essentially as a listing without significant distinction among those listed, and represent acknowledgment of contributors or sponsors.

The IRS has continually taken the position that advertising sold using the EO's name is unrelated activity, despite creative contracts attributing the activity to an independent commercial firm. See Section 21.8(i).[61]

(b) Readership vs. Ad Lineage Costs

Even if ad revenue is classified as UBI, the tax consequence is limited by the portion of the readership and editorial costs allowed as deductions against the

---

[58]Rev. Rul. 70-534, 1970-2 C.B. 113.
[59]Rev. Rul. 77-366, 1977-2 C.B. 192.
[60]Tech. Adv. Mem. 9027003.
[61]Rev. Rul. 73-424, 1973-2 C.B. 190; Tech. Adv. Mem. 9222001.

Exhibit 21–2

CALCULATING THE TAXABLE PORTION OF ADVERTISING REVENUE

(a) BASIC FORMULA

$$A - B - (C - D) = \text{Net taxable advertising income or loss}$$

where A = Gross sales of advertising
    B = Direct costs of advertising
    C − D = Readership costs in excess of readership revenue

(b) DEFINITIONS

B = Direct costs of advertising:
    Occupancy, supplies, and other administrative expenses $____
    Commissions or salary costs for ad salespeople   ____
    Clerical or management salary costs directly allocable   ____
    Artwork, photography, color separations, etc.   ____
    Portion of printing, typesetting, mailing, and other direct publication costs allocable in the ratio of total lineage in the publication to ad lineage $____

C = Readership costs:
    Occupancy, supplies, and other administrative expenses   ____
    Editors, writers, and salary for editorial content   ____
    Travel, photographs, and other direct editorial expenses   ____
    Portion of printing, typesetting, mailing, and other direct publication costs allocable in ratio of total lineage in publication to editorial lineage (in general, all direct publication costs not allocable to advertising lineage) $____

D = Readership (or circulation) revenues:
    If publication sold to all for a fixed price, then readership revenue equals total subscription sales.   ____

---

ad revenue. The important question is what portion of the expense of producing and distributing the publication can be allocated against the revenue.[62] It is helpful first to study the *Calculation of Taxable Portion of Advertising Revenue* (Exhibit 21–2), a worksheet reflecting the order in which readership and editorial costs versus advertising costs are allocated.

The formula prorates deductions in arriving at taxable advertising income. Publication costs are first divided into two categories: direct advertising and readership. Because readership costs are exempt function costs, under the

---

[62] Reg. §1.512(a)-1(f)(6).

"exploitation rule" they theoretically should not be deductible at all against the UBI income. In a limited exception, the Regulations allow readership costs, if any, in excess of readership income to be deducted against advertising income. In other words, advertising revenues can be offset with a readership loss.

Arriving at a readership loss, however, means the publication's underlying production costs must be more than its revenues.

(c) Circulation Income

Circulation income is income attributable to the production, distribution or circulation of a periodical (other than advertising revenue), including sale of reprints and back issues.[63] When members receive an EO's publication as a part of their basic membership fee, a portion of the member dues is allocated to circulation income. Other types of member income, such as educational program fees or convention registration, are not allocated.[64] When the publication is given free to members but is sold to nonmembers, a portion of the members' dues is allocated to readership revenue. The IRS formula requires allocation of a hypothetical portion of the dues, as described in the calculation.

1. Free copies given to nonmembers are subject to controversy with IRS, (so check the latest decisions).

2. If the EO has more than one publication, the IRS and the courts disagree on the denominator of the fraction for calculation of allocable exempt function costs.[65]

(d) Commercial Publication Programs

The overall publication program can be considered a commercial venture, despite its educational content. Distinguishing characteristics, according to the IRS, are found by examining the EO's management decisions.

Characteristics deemed commercial by the IRS include:

- *Presence of substantial profits*. Accumulation of profits over a number of years evidences a commercial purpose. The mere presence of profits, by itself, will not bar exemption,[66] but other factors will be considered. For what purpose are profits being accumulated? Do the reserves represent a savings account for future expansion plans?

- *Pricing methods*. The method of pricing books or magazines sold yields significant evidence of commercial taint. Pricing at or below an amount calculated to cover costs shows nonprofit motive. Pricing below comparable commercial publications is not required, but certainly can evi-

---

[63] Reg. §1.512(a)-(f)(3)(iii).
[64] Tech. Adv. Memo. 9204007.
[65] *North Carolina Citizens for Business and Industry v. United States*, 89-2 U.S.T.C. §9507 (Cl. Ct. 1989).
[66] *Scripture Press Foundation v. United States*, 285 F.2d 800 (Ct. Cl. 1961), *cert. denied*, 368 U.S. 985 (1982).

dence an intention to encourage readership and to educate, rather than to produce a profit.

■ *Other factors.* Other factors can show commerciality:

—Aggressive commercial practices resembling those undertaken by commercial publishers;[67]

—Substantial salaries or royalties paid to individuals;

—Distribution by commercial licensers.

■ *Nonprofit publications.* By contrast, nonprofit and noncommercial publications:[68]

—Rely on volunteers and/or modest wages;

—Sell some unprofitable books and magazines;

—Prepare and choose materials according to educational methods, not commercial appeal;

—Donate parts of press runs to other EOs or members; and

—Balance deficit budgets with contributions.

(e) The Royalty Dilemma

It is the IRS's opinion that IRC §512(b)(2), which says that royalty income is not unrelated business income, does not apply to certain types of "royalties," including those received in return for the sale of an organization's mailing list and the EO's name or logo.[69] While agreeing that mailing lists are intangible property the use of which produces royalty income, the IRS argues that royalties are inherently passive. In the IRS view, when the royalty income is produced in an active, commercial manner in competition with tax-paying businesses, it is contrary to the underlying scheme of the UBIT to allow such royalties to escape taxation.

Among the UBIT changes proposed by the House Oversight Committee (discussed in the next Section), royalties received for licensing property created by the EO, or property involving substantial services and costs on the part of the EO, would be subject to UBIT—a rule which the IRS is now applying without statutory authority. After its success in the DAV case (discussed below), the IRS may turn its "active" argument to other types of licensing arrangements as it pursues its UBI Compliance Program. The issue is very unsettled and the details of the history may be useful.

Unfortunately, the term "royalties" is not defined under the Code or Regulations concerning unrelated income. In response to objections by large charities whom the IRS was subjecting to UBIT on their list revenues, IRC §513(h)(1)(B) was added to provide special exception only for organizations

---

[67]*American Institute for Economic Research v. United States*, 302 F.2d 934 (Ct. Cl. 1962).
[68]*Presbyterian and Reformed Publishing Co. v. Commissioner*, 70 T.C. 1070, 1087, 1083 (1982).
[69]G.C.M. 39827; Priv. Ltr. Rul. 9029047.

eligible to receive charitable contributions, primarily 501(c)(3)s, to exclude from UBI any mailing list sales and exchanges with other similar organizations. By reference, mailing list sales by all other categories of tax-exempts would be includable in UBI.

In an interesting case, the Sixth Circuit Court of Appeals in July 1991 reversed the Tax Court and said the Disabled American Veterans (DAV) mailing list revenues were taxable unrelated business income.[70] DAV (a §501(c)(4) organization) was arguing to escape tax deficiencies of over $4 million based on $279 million of revenue. The IRS partly based its position on the active business principle, contending that the level of active business involvement in servicing the list rental activity prevented the revenue from being classified as passive and, thereby, excludable from the UBIT.

The DAV admitted that the revenue was from an unrelated business activity. There was no argument that DAV managed the activity in a businesslike manner. DAV had several personnel working full-time to keep the list current (not a volunteer operation), placed conditions on the name usage, required advance approval of the client copy, had a complicated rate structure printed and widely circulated on rate cards, and belonged to the Direct Mail Marketing Association, a trade association composed of organizations using direct mail in their operations.

The DAV argued that the revenue was a royalty excepted from UBI. The Tax Court had decided that it was up to Congress to cause "active" royalties to be taxed when the Code plainly excludes all royalties. It found nothing in the policy of the statute to offer any basis for characterizing royalties earned by a tax-exempt organization differently than royalties earned by a commercial organization. This issue is of particular interest in the scientific and medical fields, where considerable sums are earned from royalties paid for the use of patented devices and methods.

The DAV case is complicated by the fact that the Court of Claims had already decided in 1981 that DAV's mailing list sale income was taxable. (However, it specifically declined to decide about exchanges.) The Sixth Circuit decided, in overruling the Tax Court, that DAV was collaterally estopped by the 1981 decision from bringing the argument again to court, not that mailing lists sales were necessarily taxable. Thus, although the DAV lost on a technicality, the Tax Court decision still stands as to sales, and no decision has ever been made about list exchanges.

What appears from the facts to be the Interscholastic League failed in its effort to turn advertising revenues into royalties. Under licensing agreements with sporting goods manufacturers and insurance providers, the league was required to perform services and provide free advertising for the commercial concerns.[71]

Look for a new decision on this subject. The Sierra Club is rumored to have filed a suit with the Tax Court in May 1991, but no decision had been published when this book went to press.

---

[70] *Disabled American Veterans v. Commissioner, rev'g* 91-2 U.S.T.C. §50.336 (6th Cir. 1991), 94 T.C. 60 (1990).
[71] Tech. Adv. Memo. 9211004.

Given the present economic climate, with Congress responding to revenue-raising possibilities, it is reasonable to expect future changes to narrow the royalty exception, particularly as it relates to mailing lists and other types of name or logo sales. Proposals for UBI changes have contained several different versions regarding royalties, since first being proposed in 1987.

21.21 HOUSE SUBCOMMITTEE ON OVERSIGHT HEARING PROPOSALS

In June 1987, under the leadership of Representative Jake Pickle of Texas, the House of Representatives Subcommittee on Oversight held hearings on the unrelated business income tax. The hearings were in response to pressure brought by a wide variety of small business owners complaining that exempt organizations are allowed unfair advantage by the existing UBI tax laws.

Actual legislative proposals were not introduced by the subcommittee because of insufficient data. The issues of concern and suggested changes to the existing rules are outlined below:

- One proposal would tax categories of income deemed to unfairly compete with business:

    —Off-premises (e.g., mail order or telephone) sales;

    —Affinity card (credit cards imprinted with an EO's logo) revenue;

    —Food sales (except for members, patients, and students);

    —Hotels, condominiums, and theme and amusement parks;

    —Sales and rentals of medical devices.

- Definitions may be narrowed for the following:

    —Only royalties measured by gross income or expressed as a fixed amount would be excluded;

    —Deductions from advertising revenue would be limited to direct costs;

    —General administrative costs and depreciation would not be deductible against rents from joint-use property.

- Form 990 would be expanded to report details of revenue sources. Special studies to evaluate "unfair competition" may also be mandated.

- The allocation formula for dual-use facilities costs used in both related and unrelated activities would be revised.

- Exemption would be raised to $5,000 from $1,000.

- For-profit subsidiary income would be attributed to the nonprofit parent when ownership is 50 percent or more (now it must be 80 percent).

- The House subcommittee proposed an "aggregation rule" to combine all subsidiary activities with the exempt parent for purposes of measuring ongoing qualification for exemption. The subcommittee wants some method for measuring the extent of the EO's involvement in the subsidiary's actual operations. Under existing rules, there is no cross-attribution between controlled subsidiaries of an exempt organization. Stock owned by one EO subsidiary in another subsidiary is not attributed to the parent EO. The intention is to view a controlled group as an integrated enterprise to ensure that the parent exempt's primary purpose comprises a significant portion of the whole. This proposal was not included in the Treasury Department's report.

As of fall 1992, none of the proposed changes to the unrelated business income tax provisions has been made, and it appears that no changes will be proposed until 1993 or 1994, after the IRS completes its study of the UBI using the new page 5 of Form 990 shown in Appendix 27-2.

CHAPTER TWENTY-TWO

Relationships with Other Organizations and Businesses

22.1 ORGANIZATIONAL SPIN-OFFS

Sometimes an exempt organization, its board, or its staff wish to undertake an activity not appropriate for the organization itself, but suitable for another form of organization. There are two classic types of spin-offs, specific aspects of which are presented in other portions of the book. One is a title-holding company (discussed in Chapter 10) formed to hold assets for the benefit of the organization. The other is an IRC §501(c)(4) organization formed by a §501(c)(3) charity to conduct lobbying activities which would be unallowable for the reasons outlined in Chapter 23.

A new and separate EO might be formed to conduct a program that exposes the organization's assets to unacceptable risk of financial loss. The motivation is similar to the reasons for forming a title-holding company, except that a title-holding company cannot actively operate programs or projects.

A new organization might also be formed because it can qualify for funding not available to the existing organization. A common example of this type of spin-off is an auxiliary formed to allow the individuals involved in fund-raising to control the funds that they raise while not controlling the underlying organization. The creation of a charity to benefit a business league or labor union can attract deductible gifts which will not be available to the benefited organization itself.

The new organization must, of course, meet the requirements for the category of exemption under which it is formed. The application for recognition of exemption must describe in detail the relationship and the reasons why the new organization is being created. While interlocking directorates are not prohibited in either situation, prudence usually dictates that a separate, uncontrolling board be established for the new organization. Criteria for attributing activities back to the creating organization have been developed by the IRS to evaluate for-profit subsidiaries.

As a practical matter, the existing organization's assets are not usually transferred as might be implied by the term "spin-off," except in the formation of a title-holding company. In fact, to retain the distinct tax exemption and legal identity, separate and distinguishable operations are imperative. Nevertheless, the two organizations often operate side by side and share employees and facilities. Recordkeeping may need to be expanded to assure documentation of the new entity's separate existence. See Section 22.4(c).

22.2   CREATION OF A (c)(3) BY A (c)(4), (5), OR (6)

Business leagues, labor unions, civic clubs, and other noncharitable exempt organizations are typically organized and operated to further the interests of their members. Conversely, a (c)(3), often called a charitable organization, is created to raise funds in support of programs benefiting the general public, as described in Chapter 2. The possible motivations for non-(c)(3)s to establish a (c)(3) are many. Often, such organizations already conduct charitable programs and wish to raise grant funds from nonmembers to support them. A (c)(3) organization might also be created as a vehicle to honor respected members upon their deaths or as the recipient of split-interest trust or life insurance gifts during members' lives. A charitable wing might be created to enhance the public image of the profession through the sponsorship of scholarships and educational programs.

(a) Form of Relationship

The relationship between the two organizations can take many forms. Typically the board members will overlap, and it is acceptable for both boards to be identical. If public status as a supporting organization is desired, the link must be tight and the purposes and organizational documents must meet the specific requirements found in Chapter 11.

(b) Category of Public Charity

Public charity status is perhaps the most important question in structuring this type of relationship. The best type of public charity is dictated partly by the anticipated sources of funding. If the majority of the support will be received from the related organization or a small group of members, formation of a supporting organization under IRC §509(a)(3) is appropriate. If donations are expected from a wide segment of the membership and general public, the new organization might also qualify for public status under IRC §509(a)(1) or (2). When the proposed organization can qualify as publicly supported under all three of the categories of IRC §509, a choice must be made. The §509(a)(1) and (2) categories allow the new organization to operate and be controlled more independently than it could as a supporting organization under §509(a)(3). In making a choice between §509(a)(1) and (a)(2), the difference is primarily mathematical and depends upon the sources of revenue. See Chapter 11 for the intricacies of public status.

(c) Donation Collection System

A subset of the public support question arises when the professional society, civic league, or union solicits donations as a part of its annual dues collection process. Typically, the separate charitable foundation donations are optional for society members, who add whatever amount they choose. The society collects the donations and periodically pays them over to the charity. The question is who is making the gift, the individual member or the society? While there is no statutory authority for the policy, IRS specialists in the Austin District accept treatment of the gifts as individual donations. Particularly for optional gifts, there is evidence of donative intention on the member's part, rather than the society's. To so qualify, the donations must be clearly segregated and recorded on the society's books as a liability being held by the society as agent for the foundation.

(d) Grants to and from the (c)(3)

The (c)(3) organization raises the funds to carry out educational, scientific, or other charitable activities on behalf of the organization that creates it. The interesting question is whether the (c)(3) must disburse the funds itself and directly undertake the charitable projects, or whether it can grant funds to the (c)(4), (5), or (6) to enable it to undertake the activities. Both scenarios are permissible. If the funds are paid over to the non-(c)(3) organization, the grant should be restricted under a written agreement specifying the qualifying purposes for which the moneys can be spent and, if possible, annual reports should be made back to the funding charity.

Often the society furnishes the charity with office space, personnel, and other necessary operating overhead items. Reimbursement of expenses incurred by either organization is permissible as outlined in Section 22.4(c). However, the charity has the burden of proving that the expenditures do not benefit the society and its members. When it is financially possible, payment of the expenses by the society without reimbursement eliminates any possible challenge.

In Private Letter Ruling 9017003, the IRS decided that a related foundation of a business or professional association (§501(c)(6)) was not truly engaged in appropriate tax-exempt activities because it operated primarily for the benefit of the association. The foundation's only activity was to provide a no-rent lease to the related membership association. The IRS concluded that leasing is not usually an inherently charitable activity, and that the charity in this case was only operated to further the interest of the parent organization and therefore did not qualify for exemption.

22.3 FORMING A PARTNERSHIP WITH INVESTORS

In the face of declining governmental support for housing and education during the 1970s, EOs began to turn to the private sector for capital funding for buildings and equipment. In the medical field, the cost of new medical technology and the establishment of health care conglomerates compounded capital needs. Accelerated depreciation rates encouraged such arrangements until 1984[1] and again in 1986, with the advent of longer depreciable lives and the passive loss limitations. Despite the reduced tax benefits, joint ventures with private individuals and businesses still proliferate, both to raise capital and to gain their participation and expertise.

(a) Exempt Organization as General Partner

While there are many private letter rulings and some important general counsel memoranda on the subject, there is very little judicial guidance, except for the well-known Plumstead Theater Society case,[2] which means that any decision to form a partnership must be considered carefully. The primary IRS policy on the subject has concerned charitable organizations. Originally, the IRS ruled that an EO was completely prohibited from serving as a general partner with private limited partners. Since the general partner has an obligation to maximize profits for the benefit of the limited partners, the IRS took the position that the general partner role violates the basic private inurement standards and automatically causes loss of exempt status. In other words, the arrangement is "inherently incompatible with being operated exclusively for charitable purposes."[3]

(b) Careful Scrutiny of Facts and Circumstances

By 1980, the IRS relaxed its prohibition and agreed that an EO could serve as a general partner if (but only if) the venture is one that serves the EO's charitable purposes. Each case is to be carefully scrutinized and the facts and circumstances considered in detail to evaluate the purposes served by the venture. First and foremost, the underlying exempt purposes of the EO are considered. Building ventures have been condoned when they attract and keep qualified physicians to a charity hospital.[4] Acquisition of new equipment necessary to

---

[1]IRC §168(j)(9), the so-called "tax-exempt entity leasing rules" lengthened depreciable lives for certain properties.
[2]Plumstead Theatre Society, Inc. v. Commissioner, 675 F.2d 244 (9th Cir. 1982), aff'g 74 T.C. 1324 (1980).
[3]G.C.M. 36293 (May 30, 1975).
[4]Priv. Ltr. Rul. 8940039.

serve the community with home health care, made possible with investor funds, has also been condoned.[5]

Not only must exempt purposes be primarily served, but the EO must not bear unreasonable risk to its financial condition. Insulating the exempt partner's assets from venture liabilities is equally important. Among the facts that provide such insulation are:

1. Contractual limitation of liability;[6]

2. Right of first refusal or option to purchase on dissolution or sale granted to the EO;[7]

3. Limitation or ceiling on returns to limited partners;[8]

4. Presence of other general partners or managers with responsibility to serve the limited partners;[9]

5. Organizational control is exercised by the exempt partner and attention is paid to the charitable mission carried on by the partnership;[10] and

6. Methods for calculating profit sharing, asset purchases, and cost reimbursements can be designed to protect the EO's interests.

The first factor is of primary concern in protecting the EO's assets. The organizational test for continued charitable exemption requires that the assets be dedicated to charitable purposes and that earnings be similarly used. Consequently, liabilities associated with any joint venture must be identifiable and limited, and must not pose a threat to the organization's underlying assets. Such protection can be achieved with insurance coverage, with indemnity agreements specifying the extent of exposure, or by the nature of the activities. For example, a student dormitory building project has less inherent risk than a nuclear fission research laboratory, and may provide lower exposure to an exempt general partner.

The second and third factors assure that the limited partners do not reap unreasonable compensation or gain at the expense of the EO. Conversely, the EO taking the risk of serving as general partner should be appropriately rewarded with the greater share of the return. Another method of protecting the EO's interest is to allow the charity to repurchase the venture asset or to specifically limit the profits. Suitable terms under which a laboratory venture operated can be found in G.C.M. 37852. The discussion regarding management contracts and compensation levels (Section 22.5(b)) has more examples of fair compensation.

The fourth factor mitigates the fiduciary responsibility problem. An important IRS objection to exempt general partners is the conflict between their

---

[5]Priv. Ltr. Rul. 8943063.
[6]G.C.M. 39546 (August 27, 1986).
[7]Priv. Ltr. Rul. 8344099.
[8]Priv. Ltr. Ruls. 8940039, 8417054 and 8344099.
[9]G.C.M. 39005 (June 29, 1983).
[10]Priv. Ltr. Ruls. 9122061, 9122062, 2122070, 9021050.

responsibilities to create gain for the limiteds partners and to serve their exempt constituents. In some cases, the EO requires a dual general partner to actually manage the venture to suitably limit its role.

The last two factors were used by the IRS in approving the reorganization of a resonance imaging center established by an exempt hospital group's for-profit corporate subsidiary, partly with its own funds and partly with funds furnished by limited partner physicians. All financial arrangements between the parties were at fair market value, and profits and losses were to be allocated in relation to the investments made and risks assumed. Mutually binding termination and buy-out agreements were in place to protect the charitable interests from undue risk of loss.

(c) Trouble-Free Relationships

A joint venture with another EO of the same §501 category, to own and operate exempt function assets or to sponsor a charitable program, poses no threat to either EO's status. A trouble-free example might have three museums buying a Georgia O'Keefe painting, each receiving an undivided one-third interest. The costs are shared equally and each museum exhibits the work one-third of each year. This joint ownership is established to reduce the funds expended by each museum and to enable them to reduce their storage requirements, and thus serves an exempt purpose.

What if the venture borrows money from a private individual to buy a painting? Assume that the loan is to be paid back over a four-year period, as fund-raising permits. Interest on the debt is paid at the prevailing prime rate. If the loan is unpaid at the end of four years, the painting can be foreclosed by the lender in return for any principal payments made against the loan, adjusted for any increase in value as determined by an independent outside appraiser. Since purchasing and exhibiting art work advances the educational purposes of the museums, and since their underlying endowments are not used to purchase the painting (i.e., limited liability), and since the museums reap any increase in the value of the art work, this venture involving a private investor should not pose a treat to their exempt status.

Another arrangement is possible when an EO needs to expand. Assume that it needs to acquire a building to provide additional space. After meetings with major donors, it is clear that funds cannot be raised entirely through donations. Some of the donors, however, offer to build the facility and lease it back to the organization. If the building serves exempt purposes and the four factors discussed above are present, the relationship of tenant-landlord is permissible. The private inurement rules discussed in Chapter 20 should be reviewed in connection with such a relationship.

(d) Net Revenue Joint Ventures

In 1983, Medicare changed its cost-based reimbursement system for inpatient hospital services to fixed, per case, prospective payments. Cost recoupment became dependent upon the number of patients served and hospitals began to adopt policies to enhance patient population. Consequently, the emphasis shifted to admissions and physician referrals. To give tangible encouragement to the doctors, hospitals designed incentive profit sharing arrangements based upon patient revenue. As long as the total compensation to the doctor is reasonable, incentive compensation is not necessarily prohibited.

One version of such plans attracted IRS attention. Joint ventures to operate certain departments were set up between the hospitals and physicians. The EO hospital and the doctors both invested funds. The transferability of the doctor partners was restricted. (In one case, there was a mandatory repurchase agreement.) Basically, the patients would still be served in the same manner, and the hospitals retained the equipment, overhead, and so on. The significant factor was that the net revenue stream (discounted to present value) from the department was sold to the venture up front, sometimes with and sometimes without investment by the doctors.

The IRS initially approved such ventures.[11] In December 1991,[12] it reversed its position with a general counsel memorandum. The memo reviewed three net revenue stream purchase ventures and found that the exempt status of the hospital venturers should be revoked. In essence, the IRS found that the physicians had been able to buy a part of or invest in the exempt hospitals, i.e., that the ventures were not compensation plans. Three specific reasons were given for the revocation:

1. The transactions caused the hospital's net earnings to inure to the benefit of private individuals;

2. Such private inurement was not incidental to the public purposes accomplished; and

3. The arrangements might violate the "anti-kickback" rules of the Medicare Anti-Fraud and Abuse Act, because they are essentially forms of referral fee.

Hospitals participating in similar joint ventures were given the opportunity to undo the relationships without losing exempt status. Such entities were given until September 1, 1992 to enter into closing agreements with the IRS.[13] The factors enumerated above were incorporated into the IRS hospital audit guide.[14] It was noted that some joint ventures may be allowed to continue if they are properly restructured. Bringing more business to the hospital and its doctors is no longer an automatic justification for proving the community or public benefit.

(e) Unrelated Business Income Aspect

Formation of a partnership does not shelter an EO from classification of an activity's income as unrelated business income, because the attributes of income

---

[11]Priv. Ltr. Rul. 8820093; revocation discussed in Priv. Ltr. Ruls. 9231047 and 8942099.
[12]G.C.M. 39862.
[13]IRS Announcement 92-70, 1992-19 IRB. This deadline apparently may be extended for organizations voluntarily requesting an agreement, but not for ventures involuntarily discovered during an audit.
[14]*Exempt Organizations Examination Guidelines Handbook*, ¶333 (IRM 7(10)69-38).

pass directly through to the partners, retaining its same character. The partnership itself pays no tax but submits Form 1065 reporting each partner's distributive share of profits or losses. The EO partner then reports its share of profits or losses directly on its own Form 990 or 990T and pays an applicable tax directly.

Other UBI questions are whether the business activities of the partnership (or of a corporate subsidiary) will be attributed to the EO, and, if so, will the exempt status of the organization be jeopardized because of the partnership activity? The primary purpose of the EO cannot be to participate in the venture. The IRS has adopted a "more than incidental" test, which in a private ruling it deemed to be satisfied when an organization projected that no more than 15 percent of its computerized database users would be nonexempt users.[15] (See also Chapter 21.)

22.4 CREATION OF A FOR-PROFIT CORPORATE SUBSIDIARY

A customary motivation for forming a corporation instead of a partnership is to segregate the tax aspects of unrelated business activities, and to avoid the liability problems inherent in the partnership form of organization. Typically, the subsidiary is formed to conduct a business: to commercially develop a medical school's patents, to operate a restaurant and ski loge on investment property being held for future expansion, or to establish a computer facility open to the public. More often, a corporation is formed when outside investors are not involved, so that the more flexible profit/loss sharing ratios available to a partnership are not needed. In such cases, the factors discussed in Section 22.3 regarding relationships with partners should be reconsidered with regard to outside investor shareholders.

(a) Maintaining Separate Corporate Identity

Attribution of the subsidiary's activities back to its exempt parent defeats the purpose for its formation. Thus, it is important to structure the subsidiary to assure its separate corporate identity. If the EO owns less than 100 percent of the stock (for UBI purposes, under 79 percent is desirable), the outside owners provide the separateness. When the EO owns all of the stock, proof of independence includes a separate board of directors or officers, and independent management of daily affairs.[16] Actual evidence of separate operation should be maintained, such as board meetings, operating budgets, and financial reports. The fact that the parent corporation retains control over significant corporate actions, such as dissolution, does not constitute interference with the subsidiary's day-to-day affairs.[17]

The make-up of the board of directors can be evidence of the subsidiary's independent operation. While there is technically no requirement for it, independent and nonemployee members of the board are noted as a positive factor in a number of private letter rulings. The IRS considered a hotel operating

[15] Priv. Ltr. Rul. 8636079.
[16] G.C.M. 39326 (January 17, 1985); G.C.M. 39598 (January 23, 1987).
[17] Priv. Ltr. Rul. 8909029.

corporation established by a historic village foundation. The corporation was ruled to be autonomous and "operated at arms' length" partly because of the outsiders sitting on the board of directors.[18] A for-profit subsidiary in a hospital conglomerate group was also found to be valid because of its independent board.[19]

The subsidiary must be established for a valid business purpose to avoid its being considered merely a "guise" to allow the EO to conduct excess business or other impermissible activity. The IRS is concerned that the subsidiary not be merely an arm, agency, or integral part of the parent.[20]

In a recent letter ruling, the IRS sanctioned the creation of a subsidiary by a business league to "isolate into one single taxable entity" all of its unrelated activities. The league provided that it would not be involved in the business planning or day-to-day operations of the subsidiary, and that all transactions between the two entities would be conducted at arm's length. There was no mention of interlocking control. All insurance plans, including the group health and welfare plans and the IRC §401(k) retirement plans were to be transferred to the subsidiary. The IRS ruled that the rendering of service by the subsidiary and its payment of dividends to the exempt league would not jeopardize the league's exempt status.[21]

(b) Subsidiary Pays Its Own Income Tax

As a separate taxpayer, the subsidiary files its own Form 1120 and pays its own income tax. Dividends are therefore paid to the exempt parent with after-tax profits. To avoid circumvention of this rule, payments to a controlled parent (owning 80 percent or more or the stock) in the form of rent, interest, or royalty are taxed to the parent under IRC §512(b)(13). In other words, tax on unrelated business income cannot be escaped by paying it back to an exempt parent as a deductible expense. Note that the percentage of control is decreased to 50 percent under UBI reform proposals advanced by the Treasury Department. Check the latest version of IRC §512(b)(13).

(c) Sharing Facilities and/or Employees

Combining EOs of more than one category of §501(c), private foundations, and/or nonexempt organizations into sharing arrangements for office space, employees, group insurance, project management, or a variety of other operating necessities may be permissible. There is no absolute prohibition as long as the following conditions are met:

1. The activity (rental of office space, hiring of employees, etc.) serves an exempt purpose of the organization.

2. The organization reaps cost savings by combining with others in securing the shared items or services.

[18] Priv. Ltr. Rul. 8952076.
[19] Priv. Ltr. Rul. 9046045.
[20] G.C.M. 33912 (August 15, 1968).
[21] Priv. Ltr. Rul. 9119060.

3. Documentation is maintained to evidence each organization's allocable portion of each expenditure. This may be done through:

- Time sheets.

- Space utilization.

- Asset cost (e.g., "We buy the copier, you buy the phones.")

- Automobile and travel logs.

4. The arrangement does not allow unfair advantage to any of the parties, unless such advantage inures to the 501(c)(3)s involved.

5. No exempt organization assumes any risk of loss on behalf of the other organization(s).

6. For PFs only, the organization pays its share directly to the outside vendors. See Section 14.8 on self-dealing.

The first condition is of primary importance in evaluating a sharing relationship between one EO and another, or between an EO and a nonexempt organization. The primary motivation for the expenditure of the organization's funds must always be to serve its own exempt purposes, not another's.

The proof is often easy, however. Space in which to operate the EO is necessary. Why not accept the use of space in a major contributor's building? Major equipment, not owned by the organization, may be made available at little or no cost; a lease and/or a deposit may not be required. Often the rent is under market value because it is space not otherwise rentable at the time, although payment of full fair market value is not prohibited.

Another common arrangement is the sharing of employees. If a new charity needs a part time secretary, it may engage the available time of an associated organization's employee. As long as the compensation paid to such workers is fairly allocated among the organizations for whom each person performs services, there again is no reason why staff cannot be shared.[22] Evidence of the time actually devoted to each organization must be maintained as a basis for allocating salary and associated costs.

Combining related organization employees into one group for health insurance has been specifically sanctioned by the IRS.[23] In a hospital conglomerate group, the (c)(3) charitable hospital, its (c)(3) supporting, fund-raising arm, and two for-profit subsidiaries (a health equipment rental company and an administrative services provider) combined their employees into a self-funded, self-insured major medical plan. The inclusion of the subsidiary employees increased the number of plan participants and resulted in decreased cost of insurance, spreading the risk of loss over more participants. The per-participant cost for all entities was the same. The IRS found that providing employee benefits was consistent with the hospital's exempt purposes. It also noted that

[22] Priv. Ltr. Rul. 8944017.
[23] Priv. Ltr. Rul. 9025089. Priv. Ltr. Rul. 9242039 reaches the same result.

the insurance trust was separate from all of the organizations. Presumably this fact was important because the 501(c)(3)s were not assuming any unforeseen risks on behalf of the for-profits.

22.5 ACTIVE BUSINESS RELATIONSHIPS

Partly due to limited access to investment capital and limited ability to compete for qualified permanent personnel, an EO may wish to engage an outside professional, either an individual or a company, to manage a project, facility, or other activity. The issues involved in consideration of such a relationship with a for-profit company are similar to the partnership/subsidiary issues.

(a) Criteria for Approval

The exempt organization must satisfy itself that two important criteria exist before entering into such a relationship. The issues of primary concern are:

1. Are exempt purposes served by the relationship? Can the EO more effectively promote its exempt purpose by engaging the commercial manager to set up and administer the new facility?

2. Is the compensation reasonable? Are terms equal to similar commercial arrangements? Is there other evidence of private inurement in the relationship?

Proof that exempt purposes are served could include a broad range of factors. The ability to secure, on a part time basis, the medical staff, development personnel, and insurance claims staff necessary to operate a proposed health care facility, at an estimated cost savings equal to one-half of the organization's reserves, and allowing the facility to obtain licensing and begin serving the public six months earlier than otherwise, are good examples of factors indicating that an arrangement serves the organization's underlying exempt purpose. In the case of a blood bank's joint venture with a commercial laboratory for a plasma fractionation facility, costs were reduced, plasma was more effectively furnished, and thereby the project served the EO's exempt purposes.[24]

Particularly if the manager is supervised by representatives of the EO, assuring adherence to the EO's standard of care for charitable constituents, there is no constraint against an EO operating efficiently and with a high level of expertise and professionalism. As provided in a recent private letter ruling, "the university lacked the skills to operate a first-rate university press and is concerned about the financial risks inherent in publishing purely academic works." A publishing venture in which the university retained five percent of the adjusted gross revenues and proprietary rights in the publications was permissible.[25] A charitable health care provider can contract with a for-profit

[24]Priv. Ltr. Rul. 7921018.
[25]Priv. Ltr. Rul. 9036025.

medical group to provide its needed radiology services.[26] A day care center can hire a for-profit center operator.[27]

(b) Factors to Evaluate Reasonableness

A number of factors can indicate reasonableness of the compensation. An excessive amount, however, cannot be paid to secure such services. To test for reasonableness, another series of questions can be asked:

1. Are the outside managers or professionals totally independent of the organization? Is the compensation being negotiated at arm's length? Are there interlocking directorates or family relationships? In other words, can the managers influence the decision to hire themselves?

2. Are the terms equivalent to (or more favorable than) similar commercial arrangements? Is the price equal to the fair market value? Were competitive bids or comparable price studies obtained? Were CPAs, economists, appraisers, or others capable of determining the value engaged?

3. Does the relationship prevent earnings from accruing to the benefit of the private individuals, or on the other hand, does it provide economic gain to the manager(s) at the expense of the exempt organization's charitable public interests?

4. How is the compensation calculated: a fixed fee, percentage of gross or net income, or some other basis?

5. Does the contract provide for sufficient funds to the EO to compensate for its allocation of resources, the capital it is investing, and the risks it assumes?

6. Is the contract period too long or too short?

7. Are services rendered for constituents unable to pay? Will the credit policies of the manager recognize the organization's charitable nature and lack of profit motive in conducting the operation?

(c) Net Profit Agreements

A long-standing IRS policy frowns upon net profit agreements. On one hand, maximizing profits assures efficiency and would provide the funds for the EO as well as for the manager, which is usually a desirable result. The quality of services rendered to the exempt constituency, however, must not be compromised by the manager's desire to produce profits. For some time, the IRS policy was to allow net profits-interest contracts if they contained a ceiling, cap, or maximum amount which the for-profit company or individual is to receive. The policy was intended to avoid the possibility of windfall benefit to the managers.[28]

---

[26] Priv. Ltr. Rul. 9215046.
[27] Priv. Ltr. Rul. 9208028.
[28] G.C.M. 38905.

In any arrangement, it is advisable to require by contract that the compensation terms be alterable, if necessary, to retain tax-exempt status, along with self-serving language that the relationship must be conducted in a fashion that serves the exempt constituents of the engaging organization. Regarding pricing, the IRS has in some circumstances required that charitable services must be provided at the least feasible cost.[29] Again, the contract must require the manager to operate the project in a fashion that serves the exempt purposes. See Section 22.3(d) for additional consideration of this subject.

[29] Rev. Rul. 75-198, 1975-1 C.B. 157.

CHAPTER TWENTY-THREE

Political and
Legislative Activity

Part of the price of achieving 501(c) status is a loss of freedom to participate in political campaigns and certain other processes of government. All of the categories of IRC §501 specifically require an exempt organization to devote itself "primarily" to achieving its defined purpose (whether, for example, that is advancement of labor, promoting early childhood education, or maintaining a cemetery). The IRS policy is that political and legislative activities further narrow partisan interests instead of broad public interests, and are therefore not exempt. Thus, as a basic concept, any funds and organizational efforts expended on political campaigns and legislative activity are presumed to be nonexempt activities. However, some EOs can undertake "germane" lobbying. See Section 17.1(a).

The amount or extent of the nonexempt political and legislative activity allowed for any particular type of EO is limited by both the Internal Revenue Code of 1986 and the Federal Election Campaign Act (FECA). Private foundations are strictly prohibited from conducting legislative activity, and penalties for such actions are imposed by IRC §4945. In 1988, IRC §4955 was added to place a similar penalty tax upon all (c)(3)s and their managers for prohibited political activities. A (c)(3) that loses its exempt status due to excessive political or lobbying activities cannot thereafter obtain exemption as a (c)(4).

Before describing the different limitations, it is important to distinguish political from legislative activity. A political action involves the election or appointment of someone to office, or intervention in the electoral process. Legislative action involves influencing persons once they have been elected or appointed.

The definition of political campaign activity found in the Regulations says that an organization has political activity if it "participates or intervenes, directly or indirectly, in any political campaign on behalf of or in opposition to any candidate for public office. The term *candidate for public office* means an individual who offers himself, or is proposed by others, as a contestant for an elective public office, whether such office be national, state, or local.[1]

Which local offices constitute "public office" within the meaning of the Regulations, and whether an appointment is in fact an election must be determined under the applicable local election laws. The answers vary from state to state. Organizations have unexpectedly lost exempt status for involvement in school board, water commission, and other local campaigns.

In a memo on the subject,[2] the IRS provided an example of an organization losing its exempt status due to involvement in political party precinct elections. An analysis of relevant local election laws indicated to the IRS that the precinct committee position possessed the characteristics of public office. The organization's counsel had advised it that the positions were administrative, not political. Alongside the exempt organization's strong and active legislative activities, the organization had classified the expenses as lobbying expense: permissible, but limited.

In another important distinction, the IRS does not consider appointed members of the federal judicial system to be elected public officials. Attempts to influence the U.S. Senate confirmation of a nominee to the Supreme Court does not constitute intervention in a political campaign, but in the IRS's view, it constitutes influencing or attempting to influence legislation.[3] Efforts to influence appointments are "political" activities (but not campaign activity) for purposes of imposing the IRC §527 tax.

The absolute ban against participation by (c)(3) organizations in political campaigns has given way to refinements and distinctions among actual campaign intervention, voter education, and other political activities as discussed below.

---

[1] Reg. §1.501(c)(3)-1(c)(3)(iii).
[2] G.C.M. 39811.
[3] IRS Notice 88-1988-2 C.B. 392.

23.1 PERMITTED CAMPAIGN INVOLVEMENT

A question all EOs must answer each year on Form 990 is:

> Does the EO participate or intervene, directly or indirectly, in any political campaign on behalf of or in opposition to any candidate for public office (direct political campaign activity)?

The answer for each category of exempt organization can be different. The basic guidelines are as follows:

§501(c)(3): An organization qualified as charitable is absolutely prohibited from such participation or intervention.[4]

§501(c)(4): A civic welfare organization must be "exclusively" devoted to social welfare (not, oddly enough, a 100 percent test), and the regulations simply state that political activity does not promote social welfare. There is not a complete ban. The IRS has stated that supporting candidates cannot be a primary purpose of a civic organization, but can be a secondary one.[5]

§501(c)(5): A labor organization will not "be disqualified merely because it engages in some political activity."[6]

§501(c)(6): A business league's permissible political activity is not mentioned in the Code, Regulations, or *Handbook*. Rulings indicate that, like (c)(5)s, business leagues may have political involvement as long as they devote their primary attention and resources to their exempt purposes.[7]

When political involvement is permitted, the percentage of the annual budget expended on the campaign must be quantified to prove that the activity is not a substantial one. Any money above $100 spent on political activity is taxed under IRC §527(f). Form 1120-POL must be filed. To avoid both tax on the EO level and controversy regarding the extent of political activity, a 501(c)(4), (5), or (6) or other EO (but not a (c)(3)) can create a separate political action committee (PAC).

23.2 VOTER EDUCATION VS. CANDIDATE PROMOTION

In addition to direct political campaign involvement such as endorsement of a particular candidate, activities focused on political issues and public policy makers may also be classified as prohibited political activity.

(a) Endorsements

Endorsements of political candidates or other electioneering statements by an EO's officers and directors in their individual capacities should not disturb an

---

[4]Reg. §1.501(c)(3)-1(b)(3) and (c)(3)(iii); *Exempt Organizations Handbook* (IRM 7751) §370.
[5]Rev. Rul. 81-95, 1981-1 C.B. 332.
[6]*Exempt Organizations Handbook* (IRM 7751) §544.
[7]Rev. Rul. 61-177, 1961-2 C.B. 117.

EO's exempt status. However, such endorsements will be imputed to the organization if the EO, directly or indirectly, authorized or ratified their actions.[8] Federal election laws make it unlawful for a corporation to make a contribution or expenditure in a federal election.

(b) Voter Registration

Voter registration drives do not constitute intervention in a political campaign when conducted in a nonpartisan manner. Drives that are targeted at members of a particular party, or that are in support of or against named candidates, will be classified as political activity. Partisan language on materials handed out to potential voter registrants will cause the campaign to be classified as political activity.[9] Private foundations may finance voter registration drives under very specific rules outlined in Section 17.2.

(c) Voter Information

The IRS retroactively revoked an ostensible educational organization's exemption due to a variety of political activity. It found the following language to be incriminating:

> Conservatives in the U.S. Senate and House of Representatives are giving us economic prosperity, reducing government intervention and instilling pride in America and our way of life. All of this will be lost if Conservatives like you and me do not head off the huge voter registration drive by the liberals.

The ruling contains a broad analysis of voter education and campaign workshops, and is mandatory reading for any organization participating in such activities.[10] If an EO publishes materials that discuss and, particularly, criticize governmental policies and officials, it important that the information be nonpartisan. The following questions should be asked in evaluating whether the analysis constitutes participation in a campaign:

- Can the "discussions" be tied to a candidate running for election?

- Are the voting records of government officials reported, compared, or critized?

- Is there an attempt to affect voter acceptance or rejection of a candidate?

- Are materials distributed only to the membership or to the public?

- Do the evaluations relate directly to the EO's exempt purpose?

[8]G.C.M. 33912.
[9]*American Campaign Academy v. Commissioner*, 92 T.C. 1053 (1989).
[10]Priv. Ltr. Rul. 9117001.

- Are the reports based upon scientific studies or research?

- Do the comments include "full and fair exposition" of all facts about the issue, or will they be construed as biased opinion?

The following criteria are used to judge whether publication of Congressional representatives' voting records on selected issues constitutes "political action:"[11]

- Voting records of all incumbents are presented.

- Candidates for re-election are not identified.

- No comment is made on any individual's qualification for public office.

- No candidate is endorsed or rejected.

- No comparison of the candidates is made.

- A statement is included pointing out the inherent limitations of judging a candidate on the basis of selected votes, and stating the need to consider such unrecorded matters as performance on subcommittees and constituent service.

- The EO does not distribute the report widely, but distributes it only to members.

- Publication is not targeted toward particular areas in which elections are occurring, nor timed to concur with elections.

(d) Examples of Permissible Political Education

- Public television and radio stations can provide air time to political candidates as long as it does so equally to candidates.[12] The Federal Communications Commission has developed procedures for neutral debates or forums that allow candidates to explain their views to the public.

- Publishing a newsletter containing voting records and grading the votes according to the EO's ideals, without any expression of endorsement for or opposition to the candidates themselves, is educational. The newsletter's circulation must be directed at constituents and must not be aimed at affecting an election.[13]

- Disseminating information concerning campaign practices, furnishing teaching aids to political science and civic teachers, and publicizing

---

[11]Rev. Rul. 80-282, 1980-2 C.B. 154, *amplifying* Rev. Rul. 78-248, 1978-1 C.B. 154; G.C.M. 38444.
[12]Rev. Rul. 74-574, 1974-2 C.B. 160.
[13]G. C. M. 38444.

proposed codes of fair campaign practices without soliciting the signing or endorsement of the code by candidates, are all qualified political education.[14]

■ As a part of a political science program, a university can require students to participate in political campaigns for candidates of their choice.[15]

■ A student newspaper's coverage of political campaigns and student editorial opinions about such elections are not considered to be university political activity.[16]

■ An EO established for the purpose of collecting and collating campaign speeches, interviews, and other materials of a candidate for a historically important elective office for donation to a university or public library, was engaged in permissible political education.[17]

■ Read Technical Advice Memorandum 8936002 for a surprisingly lenient IRS position regarding peach promotions run during the 1984 Presidential campaign. Advertisements urged the reader to "Think about it when you vote this November," and to "Choose leaders who will lead us away from a nuclear nightmare, not into one." The IRS "reluctantly concluded that the organization probably did not intervene in the campaign," apparently because the ads did not overtly support a candidate (even though everyone knew that the peace candidate was Democratic nominee Walter Mondale).

(e) Impermissible Political Activity

■ Attempting to improve a public school system by campaigning on behalf of candidates for election to the school board is political campaign activity.[18]

■ A bar association that published a rating system for elective judicial candidates was also deemed to be intervening in a political campaign.[19]

■ Assisting a governor-elect was held to be involvement in a political campaign. The organization interviewed and screened applicants for appointive offices and prepared the legislative message to a reflect a party's platform and budget.[20]

[14]Rev. Rul. 76-456, 1976-2 C.B. 151.
[15]Rev. Rul. 72-512, 1972-2 C.B. 246.
[16]Rev. Rul. 72-513, 1972-2 C.B. 246.
[17]Rev. Rul. 79-321, 1970-1 C.B. 129.
[18]Rev. Rul. 67-71, 1967-1 C.B. 125.
[19]*The Bar Association of the City of New York v. Commissioner*, 88-2 USTC ¶9535 (2nd Cir. 1988), *rev'g* 89 T.C. 599, 609-610 (1987).
[20]Rev. Rul. 74-117, 1974-1 C.B. 128.

The *Exempt Organizations Continuing Professional Education Technical Instruction Program for 1985* comments that it is possible for a relationship to exist between a §501(c)(3) EO and a political organization (PO), as long as the PO is not established by, administered by, solicited for, or funded by the EO. The article furthermore states that PO could rent EO space at its fair market value or purchase EO materials, but notes that this could produce unrelated business income.

IRC §4955 imposes an excise tax of at least 10 percent (up to 100 percent) on political campaign expenditures of a 501(c)(3), in addition to a two and a half percent tax on the "manager(s)" involved in the activity. In 1987, Congress decided that in addition to losing its exemption, a 501(c)(3) should pay a penalty for political involvement. The primary targets were ostensibly "educational" 501(c)(3)s established to promote the campaign of particular candidates and/or which were controlled by candidates.

23.3 TAX ON POLITICAL EXPENDITURES

Until 1968, the tax status of political organizations and political expenditures was uncertain, except for the absolute prohibition for 501(c)(3)s. In that year, the IRS announced that the investment income of a political organization was to be taxed by filing a fiduciary income tax return on Form 1041. Political contributions received would continue to be untaxed as gifts, but would not be deductible for the giver.

Effective in 1975, a IRC §527 entitled "Political Organizations" took its place among the Code sections governing nonprofit organizations, and Form 1120-POL was introduced for reporting the taxable income. IRC §527 essentially taxes any investment income expended for political purposes. The tax applies to POs (nonprofits devoted solely to political activity) and to §501(c) EOs that expend their own funds for political purposes. The definitions and constraints are found both in IRC §527 and in the Federal Election Campaign Act.

(a) What is a Political Organization?

The Internal Revenue Code defines a "political organization" as:

> a party, committee, association, fund, or other organization (whether or not incorporated) organized and operated primarily for the purpose of directly or indirectly accepting contributions or making expenditures, or both, for an exempt function.

The "exempt function" for this purpose is:

> the function of influencing or attempting to influence the selection, nomination, election, or appointment of any individual to any federal, state, or local public office or office in a political organization, or

the election of presidential or vice-presidential electors, whether or not such individual or electors are selected, nominated or appointed.[21]

A political organization need not engage exclusively in activities that are exempt functions. However, the distinction between exempt and nonexempt expenses is important. Any funds spent for nonexempt functions lose their tax-free status. Examples include:

- Nonpartisan educational workshops.

- An incumbent's office expenses.

- Appearing before a legislative body, at its written request (as opposed to voluntarily), for the purpose of influencing the appointment or confirmation of an individual to public office is *not* an excempt function.

- Nonpartisan voter registration or "get-out-the-vote" efforts.

Permissible expenditures by political campaign committees may include certain lobbying efforts, according to the IRS. A candidate's committee funded a direct mail piece promoting a nonbinding statewide referendum on fiscal responsibility. The candidate was named and pictured on the flyer, and was identified as the leader of the effort. Even though the candidate had not yet filed to run for governor, the ruling found that the piece was packaged to identify him as a potential candidate for governor, and was therefore an appropriate expense for the campaign committee.[22]

In a pair of private letter rulings, the IRS ruled that temporarily keeping PAC funds in a general interest-bearing checking account provided administrative efficiency, and did not constitute an investment of the funds as prohibited by IRC §527. For ease of collection, a professional association and a labor union issued billings for normal dues and PAC contributions together to its membership. Moneys were collected continually throughout the year. For the organizations' convenience, PAC funds were periodically transferred (in one case twice a month and in the other once a month) to the PAC. The "negligible" amount of interest that was retained by the exempt organizations was permissible.[23]

A political organization must meet an organizational test, but the test is not clearly defined. Formal articles of incorporation, association, or trust are acceptable, but are not required. The regulations provide that "consideration is given to statements of the members as to how they intend to operate the PO primarily to carry on one or more exempt functions."[24] A officeholder's newsletter fund is taxed as a PO, but funds cannot be expended for campaign, personal, or any other purposes. Special distinctions, affecting tax rates and permissible activities, apply to segregated funds and to the principal campaign

---

[21] IRC §527(e)(2)
[22] Priv. Ltr. Rul. 913008.
[23] Priv. Ltr. Ruls. 9105001 and 9105002.
[24] Reg. §1.527-2(a)(2).

committee of any office seeker. The regulations and legislative history should be studied for those types of organizations.

(b) Taxable Income

A §501(c) EO which spends any amount directly for an exempt function (as defined by IRC §527) is taxed on such expenditure or its net investment income (interest, dividends, rents, royalties, and capital gains), whichever is lower. A grant from one EO to another EO to be used specifically for political purposes will be taxed to the granting EO under IRC §527. For EOs with political expenditures and for political organizations, Form 1120-POL is filed, and a tax is imposed basically upon the investment income.

Exempt function revenues are taxed only if they are expended for exempt functions. Such revenues include:

- Contributions of money or other property;

- Membership dues or assessments;

- Proceeds of fund-raising or entertainment events; and

- Sales of political campaign materials (including sales of campaign materials not sold in a commercial manner).[25]

- Proceeds of bingo games are the subject of a proposed regulation.

Taxable income is taxed at the highest corporate tax rate (currently 34 percent) and is defined to include:

- Gross income (not including exempt function);

- Less deductions directly related to production of such income (excluding exempt function expenses but including an allocable part of dual-use facilities or personnel);

- Modified (reduced) by $100 (except for newsletter funds).

- No net operating loss or dividend received deductions are allowed.[26]

(c) Segregated Funds (Political Action Committees)

A segregated fund, usually called a political action committee (PAC), can be created by a §501(c) EO, or by any individual, that plans to engage in political activity and wishes to assure proper identification of the funds subject to tax.[27] A segregated fund is treated as a political organization for tax purposes. Thus, when funds are collected directly from the members or employees of the EO and are paid directly into the segregated fund, the conduit EO can easily prove that it has not made an exempt (political) expenditure. (In fact, Congressional

---

[25] Reg. §1.527-3(a).
[26] IRC §527(b), Reg. §1.527-4.
[27] Reg. §1.527-2(b)(1).

committee reports indicate that an EO can solicit and collect the funds in its own accounts, as long as they are disbursed promptly to the PAC and no interest is earned by the EO on the funds.)

Indirect EO expenses attributable to the creation of and management of the fund pose an unanswerable question, because no regulations have been issued on the subject. To be safe, the PAC should reimburse the EO for expenses of soliciting and paying over the funds.

The Federal Election Campaign Act specifically permits labor unions and business leagues to spend money for internal communications involving support of particular candidates with members and their families, but not with the general public. Also permitted is the establishment, administration, and solicitation of contributions to PACs.

23.4 LOBBYING ACTIVITY OF §501(c)(3) ORGANIZATIONS

All exempt organizations (EOs), except private foundations and title-holding companies, can engage in some lobbying, or attempts to influence legislation. The extent of the allowed involvement differs for each category. For (c)(3) EOs, different rules apply for organizations falling in each of three categories:

1. EOs that elect to lobby and be subject to the expenditure test.

2. EOs that choose not to lobby whose lobbying is limited by a substantial part test.

3. Private foundations that can conduct absolutely no lobbying, as explained in Chapter 17.

(a) Rules for Nonelecting Exempt Organizations

An organization choosing not to make a §501(h) election to govern its lobbying activity is subject to the basic exemption criteria requiring that "no substantial part" of its activities consist of attempting to influence legislation by propaganda or otherwise. A (c)(3) with substantial legislative activity is an "action organization" and does not qualify for exemption. A (c)(3) organization is regarded as attempting to influence legislation if it:

- Contacts or urges the public to contact members of a legislative body for the purpose of proposing, supporting, or opposing legislation; or

- Advocates the adoption or rejection of particular legislation.[28]

"Legislation" is defined to include "actions by the Congress, by any State legislature, by any local council or similar governing body, or by the public in a referendum, initiative, constitutional amendment, or similar procedure.[29] After the Senate hearings on Robert Bork's nomination to the Supreme Court, the IRS

---

[28] Reg. §1.501(c)(3)-1(b)(3).
[29] Reg. §1.501(c)(3)-1(c)(3)(i).

issued notice that the U.S. Senate's action of advising and consenting to a judicial appointment is "legislative activity." (The IRS position stems from the §501(h) rules.) In interpreting the congressional mandate to limit exempt organization lobbying, the IRS has adopted the following clarifying rules:

- The desirability of the legislation (such as protecting the environment, animals, or children, or other issues unquestionably serving the public good) does not legitimize lobbying for it.[30]

- "Legislation" includes proposals for making laws in other countries.[31]

- Acts undertaken by the organization itself, not by its members or constituents as individuals, are constrained.[32]

- A common measure of "substantial" is the actual dollars expended by the organization on lobbying efforts. No specific limit is provided, and as little as five percent of an organization's budget has been questioned.[33] However, the efforts of volunteers, such as research and discussion to formulate a position on a legislative matter, and the whole context in which the activity is conducted may also be considered.[34] It is important to note that only actual dollars are considered under the expenditure test.

"Goodwill advertising or institutional pieces intended to bring the organization's name before the general public by presenting views on economic, financial, social, or other subjects of a general nature is not lobbying if the material does not directly or indirectly propose, support or oppose legislation."[35] See discussion of grassroots lobbying in Section 23.4(g).

(b) The §501(h) Election

Congress has enacted specific perimeters within which (c)(3)s can conduct lobbying efforts. The complex rules are outlined in IRC §501(h). The regulations under IRC §501(h) and §4911 total 57 pages, and were proposed and reproposed three times over a four year period before the final version became effective on August 31, 1990. The rules are surprisingly lenient for public charities, and they allow private foundations to publish nonpartisan analyses and comments which many had thought were not permissible.

The regulations interact with a number of other provisions: Regulations under IRC §501 (conversion of (c)(3) to a (c)(4); §501(h); §504 (revocation of exempt status due to excessive lobbying); §4911 (excise tax on excessive lobbying); §4945 (lobbying by private foundations); and §170, §2055, and §2522

---

[30] Rev. Rul. 67-293, 1967-2 C.B. 185.
[31] Rev. Rul. 73-440, 1973-2 C.B. 177.
[32] Rev. Rul. 72-513, 1972-2 C.B. 246.
[33] *Seasongood v. Commissioner*, 227 F.2d 907, 912 (6th Cir. 1955).
[34] *League of Women voters v. U.S.*, 180 F. Supp. 379 (Ct. Cl. 1960), *cert. den.*, 364 U.S. 822 (1960); *Christian Echoes National Ministry, Inc. v. U.S.*, 470 F.2d 849 (10th Cir. 1972), *cert. den.*, 414 U.S. 864 (1973).
[35] Reg. §1.162-29(a)(2).

(limitations on charitable donations). It is important to note that the rules of IRC §501(h) and §4911, outlined below, apply *only* to charities electing to limit their lobbying expenditures.

The following material only skims the surface. A comprehensive treatment of the subject can be found in *Charity, Advocacy, and the Law*,[36] a "must read" book for any organization conducting more than an insignificant amount of lobbying. Unless the extensive examples in the Regulations are studied and evaluated, an expert should be engaged to monitor the activity.

(c) Definition of Lobbying

Lobbying is defined in IRC §4911 as:

- Any attempt to influence any legislation through an attempt to affect the opinions of the general public or any segments thereof, or

- Any attempt to influence any legislation through communication with any member or employee of a legislative body, or with any government official or employee who may participate in the formulation of the legislation.

The IRS *Handbook* cautions that lobbying is not limited to these definitions, and the Regulations contain eight pages of examples on direct and grassroots lobbying alone. The facts and circumstances of each communication can be questioned.

(d) What is Legislation?

Legislation is defined to include "action with respect to Acts, bills, resolutions, or similar items by the Congress, any State legislature, any local council, or similar governing body, or by the public in a referendum, initiative, constitutional amendment, or similar item."[37] Legislative bodies do not include executive, judicial, or administrative bodies such as school boards, housing authorities, sewer and water districts, and zoning board, whether they are appointive or elective.

A "similar item," according to examples in the Regulations, includes confirmation of a cabinet level appointee and a Supreme Court nominee.[38] A proposed treaty subject to Senate approval is a legislative matter from the time when treaty negotiations start.[39] Referenda and ballot initiatives are legislative actions in which the members of the general public constitute the legislature, so an attempt to influence a referendum vote is direct lobbying.[40]

---

[36] Bruce Hopkins, John Wiley & Sons, 1992.
[37] IRC §4911(2); Reg. §56.4911-2(d).
[38] Reg. §56.4911-2(b)(4)(ii)(B), Example (6).
[39] Reg. §56.4911-2(d)(1)(i).
[40] Reg. §56.4911-2(b)(1)(iii).

(e) What Lobbying is Not

IRC §4911(d) excludes the following activities from the meaning of the term "influencing legislation":

- Dissemination of the results of nonpartisan analysis, study, or research;

- Provision of technical advice or assistance in response to a written request by a governmental body;

- Appearances before, or communications to, any legislative body with respect to a possible decision by that body that might affect the existence of the organization, its powers and duties, its tax-exempt status, or the deduction of contributions to it (self-defense);

- Communications between the organization and its bona fide members with respect to legislation or proposed legislation of direct interest to them, unless the communications directly encourage the members to influence legislation or urge members to contact nonmembers to influence legislation; and

- Routine communications with government officials or employees, including the executive branch and agencies.[41]

(f) Nonpartisan Analysis

An independent and objective exposition on a particular subject that advocates a viewpoint on legislation is not considered lobbying if it qualifies as nonpartisan analysis, study, or research.[42] Sufficiently fair and full exposition of the pertinent facts on the subject, not merely unsupported opinion, must be communicated to the general public to enable the public to form an independent opinion or conclusion.

The information can be communicated in any form, whether visual or auditory: radio, television, public forums, magazines, publications, or newspapers. No direct encouragement to "take action" may be contained in the materials. If the research material is subsequently used for lobbying purposes, the expenses of preparing the research paid within six months of such use is reclassified as a lobbying expense.[43] The regulations contain eleven pages of examples.

(g) Grassroots Lobbying

Contacting the general public (instead of the legislators themselves) is classified as grassroots lobbying.[44] More restrictive limitations apply to this indirect

---

[41] Reg. §56.4911-2(c).
[42] Reg. §56.4911-2(c)(1).
[43] Reg. §56.4911-2(b)(2)(v).
[44] IRC §4911(c)(3); Reg. §56.4911.2(b)(2).

lobbying method, so the distinction between "direct" and "grassroots" is important. Grassroots expenditures cannot comprise more than 25 percent of an electing organization's overall lobbying expenditures. The portion of a member's dues attributable to grassroots lobbying is not deductible under IRC §162.

This issue has been the focal point of much controversy between the IRS and the exempt community. The regulations somewhat narrowly define grassroots lobbying to include only communications that contain the following three elements:

1. It refers to "specific legislation" (including legislation that has already been introduced in a legislative body *and* specific legislative proposals that the EO either supports or proposes);

2. It reflects a view on such legislation; and

3. It encourages the recipient of the communication to take action with respect to the legislation.[45]

Mass media communication may be classified as lobbying even if it does not meet the three-part definition. When a press release or advertisement sponsored by the exempt organization and taking a position on legislation is published within two weeks before the vote is scheduled, such a publication will be considered grassroots lobbying if it either refers to the highly publicized legislation or encourages the public to lobby about the legislation.

A requisite characteristic of a lobbying communication is that it directly urges the public to take action. Taking action is urged directly if any one of the first three elements below is present. The fourth attribute, taken alone, does not constitute a call to action.[46]

1. The communication states that the recipient should contact legislators, their employees, or other governmental representatives who may participate in the formulation of the legislation;

2. The address, telephone number, or similar information facilitating contact is furnished on the notice, letter, or other form of communication;

3. A petition, tear-off postcard, or the like is provided for the recipient to communicate views to the appropriate governmental party; or

4. One or more legislators who will vote on the legislation is specifically identified as opposing it or undecided, is the recipient's representative, or is a member of the committee considering the legislation.

Attempts to influence highly-publicized legislation, such as paid advertisements placed in mass media (television, radio, billboards, and general circulation newspapers and magazines) that do not contain one of the "take action"

---

[45] Reg. §56.4911-2(b)(2)(ii).
[46] Reg. §56.4911-2(b)(2)(iii).

elements may still be grassroots lobbying if:

- The advertisement is placed within two weeks prior to a vote by a legislative body or a committee (but not a subcommittee).

- The advertisement offers a view on the general subject of the legislation, and either refers to the legislation or encourages the public to communicate with legislators on the general subject of the legislation.[47]

The presumption that an advertisement fits these conditions can be rebutted if the organization can show that (1) it regularly publishes such communications without regard to the timing of legislation, or (2) the timing of the particular advertisement is unrelated to the legislative action. In other words, if the organization can prove that it placed the advertisement without any knowledge that the vote would occur within two weeks, it may escape its classification as grassroots lobbying.

Member communications are another area of confusion. The member rules were substantially altered each time the proposed regulations were issued (in 1980, 1986, and again in 1988), becoming more lenient with each new version. Under the following specific conditions, information sent to members is *not* treated as lobbying:

1. The communication is directed only at members;

2. The communication refers to and reflects a view on specific legislation which is of direct interest to the organization and its members;

3. Members are not encouraged to engage in direct lobbying; and

4. Grassroots lobbying is not encouraged.

Direct lobbying occurs when the third requirement is failed; grassroots lobbying occurs when the fourth one is failed.

A "member" is one who pays dues or makes a contribution of more than a nominal amount, makes a contribution of more than a nominal amount of time, or is one of a limited number of "life or honorary" members. Prospective members are not considered members. A member of one of an affiliated group of organizations is treated as a member of each of the EOs in the group.[48]

23.5   PERMISSIBLE AMOUNTS OF LOBBYING

Nonelecting 501(c)(3)s must prove that their lobbying activities do not represent a substantial part of their activities. The portion is measured largely, though not

---

[47]Reg. §56.4911-2(b)(5)(ii).
[48]Reg. §56.4911-5(f).

entirely, by expenditures. Five to 10 percent of the EO's overall budget is generally considered permissible in the field. Note that the elective test is based on a percentage of exempt purpose expenditures, which is normally a lower number than the total budget. The amount of lobbying is measured by considering the actual dollar amounts expended, the amount of time expended by staff and board, and/or the degree of success. For example, the EO may use its prestige to influence legislation, achieving a high degree of success with a minimal expenditure of money.

IRC §4912 places an excise tax on nonelecting 501(c)(3)s and their managers when excessive lobbying causes the EO to lose its exemption.

When lobbying activities are insignificant and an EO wishes to avoid the increased recordkeeping and scrutiny presumed to be caused by a §501(h) election, this "nonelective method" is preferable.

(a) Making the Election

A (c)(3) organization which elects to monitor its lobbying expenditures under IRC §501(h) buys a safe harbor and removes the discretionary factors used in the "substantial part" test. Under this election, the EO agrees to a mathematical limit based upon a percentage of its exempt purpose expenditures (EPE) to prove that legislative efforts are not "substantial." Unless lobbying expenditures exceed 150 percent of the prescribed amounts over a four-year period, exempt status remains intact.[49]

Form 5768 is filed to make the election (See Appendix 23–1). It can be filed with form 1023 or with an annual Form 990. The election is effective until it is revoked. It can be voluntarily revoked at any time, effective for the next tax year. Private foundations, churches, and supporting organizations cannot make the election.

(b) Mechanical Test

Lobbying expenditures cannot exceed the sum of:

20 percent of the first $500,000 of the exempt organization's EPE, plus

15 percent of the next $500,000 of EPE, plus

10 percent of the next $500,000 of EPE, plus

5 percent of the rest up to a maximum total lobbying allowance of $1 million for any one organization.

Grassroots lobbying expenditures (contacting the general public rather than contacting legislators directly) cannot exceed 25 percent of the total lobbing limit above.

---

[49] IRC §501(h)(2)(B).

Exempt purpose expenditures[50] (EPE) include:

- Amounts paid to accomplish one or more charitable purposes, including grants paid for charitable projects, employee compensation, and administrative expenses;

- Lobbying expenditures;

- Amounts paid for nonpartisan analysis, study, or research, and for examination of broad social, economic, and similar problems; and

- Expenses for responding to requests for technical advice, self-defense efforts, and member nonlobbying communications.

EPE does not include expenses of producing unrelated income, nor related trade or business expenditures. Costs of managing an endowment or other investments are also not included in exempt purpose expenditures. Certain fund-raising costs are also excluded.

Affiliated organizations are consolidated for application of the lobbying tests, to prevent the creation of new entities to avoid the spending limits. An EO which is bound under its governing instrument by the decisions of another EO regarding legislative issues is affiliated. Interlocking directorates also create affiliation.[51]

Accounting for lobbying involves identifying expenditures directly connected with specific legislation, as opposed to matters that are subjects of legislation. It is critical to associate research on issues and review of pending legislation until the EO decides to support or oppose the legislation. Mixed-purpose expenditures involving both direct and grassroots lobbying activities are presumed to be grassroots, except to the extent that the EO can demonstrate a reasonable allocation between the two types of lobbying.[52] Likewise, the expense of publications or communications sent to members or to the public must be allocated among the various elements of lobbying, fund-raising, and education. The portion of telephone, fax, computer, staff, and other costs attributable to lobbying efforts must be documented with time sheets and usage records.

A 25 percent tax is imposed under IRC §4911 on direct or grassroots lobbying expenses (whichever is greater) in excess of the above limits for electing 501(c)(3)s.

23.6   PROS AND CONS OF ELECTION

Although the elective lobbying provisions were expected to eliminate confusion about the consequences of lobbying, the three sets of regulations proposed over the past 10 years contain radically different interpretations of the terms. Due

---

[50] Reg. §56.4911-4.
[51] Reg. §56.4911-7.
[52] Reg. §56.4911-3(a)(2).

partly to the resulting confusion, very few organizations have made the election. Accordingly, there is little guidance in the area and the pros and cons must be carefully considered. Among the advantages of electing are these facts:

(a) Advantages of Electing

- Volunteers' time and influence are not counted; only actual expenditures count.

- The revocation of exemption calculation is based on a four-year average, not on an ongoing annual test.

- Mathematical limits are specific.

- The degree of certainty provided by specific tests applied to electing organizations is preferrable to the subjective and untested standards for nonelecting ones. IRC §501(h) allows examining agents to use the definitive rules only for electing organizations, not for nonelecting ones.

- Many practitioners expect the IRS to scrutinize nonelecting organizations.

- The membership communications exclusion does not classify as lobbying the "objective reporting on the contents and status of legislation" to members.

- Recordkeeping requirements may be less because volunteer time need not be recorded.

(b) Advantages of Not electing

The advantages of not making the election under IRC §501(h) include the following:

- Grassroots lobbying limit is not separately limited to five percent of exempt purpose expenditures.

- Recordkeeping requirements may be less if the organization need not distinguish between direct lobbying and grassroots efforts. However, the information furnished on Form 990 may need to be more detailed.

- Drawing attention to the organization by making the election may trigger an audit. (There is disagreement in the field about this issue.)

- Directors and officers can be personally liable for penalties for excess lobbying.

- Affiliated organization's lobbying activities must be consolidated or combined to measure limitations under the election, but are otherwise measured on a per entity basis.

- The maximum amount of expenditures allowed is $1 million for any one organization. For an organization with a $50,000,000 annual budget, for example, the maximum of $1 million equals two percent of the budget, a de minimus amount in relation to the five percent considered permissible by some experts.

- It may be preferrable to avoid the uncertainty caused by the multiple proposed regulations and the controversy surrounding the allocation of indirect expenses.

23.7 LOBBYING LIMITS FOR 501(c)(4), (5), (6), AND OTHER EXEMPT ORGANIZATIONS

There is no specific numerical lobbying limit for most exempt organizations. The facts of each case will determine whether it remains the "primary" purpose of the EO to accomplish its exempt purpose, when lobbying or political activities are carried on alongside more traditional exempt purposes.

A 1961 ruling allowed a business league to spend all of its money on lobbying as long as the legislation was germane to its specific exempt purpose.[53] Member dues deductions are limited under IRC §162. To the extent that dues finance political campaigning, grassroots lobbying, or direct lobbying, they are not deductible. If an association spends a substantial portion of its funds for lobbying, the dues deduction is allowed only for that portion that can be clearly identified as attributable to exempt activities.[54]

Lobbying activities are also restricted by the U.S. Postal Service, which denies second and third class mailing permits to nonprofits whose primary purpose is lobbying. Registration of lobbying activities is also required in many states and by federal election laws.

23.8 ADVOCACY VS. LOBBYING

A number of activities, while not overtly political or legislative, have caused organizations potentially exempt under IRC §501(c)(3) to be denied exempt status by the Internal Revenue Service. Since the underlying reason why organizations are granted charitable tax exemption is that they relieve the burdens of government by performing socially useful activities, it is easy to see why opinions change from one presidential administration to another regarding the types of actions EOs can take. Stopping commercial development in the national forests may or may not be a concern of a particular administration in the White House. A nationwide boycott campaign against Exxon in response to its oil spill may or may not primarily serve to preserve the environment. An IRS agent to whom I addressed the Exxon question said, "No!" But a U.S. District Court allowed the exempt status of the Infant Formula Action Coalition, whose

[53] Rev. Rul. 61-177, 1961-2 C.B. 117.
[54] Reg. §1.162-20(c)(2)(i).

only activity is relieving starving children by boycotting Nestle', a company that manufactures baby formula for sale in underdeveloped countries.[55]

IRS policies may change according to the political whim of the current administration. Although the definitions contained in the Internal Revenue Code and the Regulations offer seemingly absolute rules on actions that will not be classed as exempt activity, the following subjects may present problems with the determination and field representatives of the IRS:

Issues of race:	segregation
	immigration
Issues of sex:	gay or lesbian rights
	abortion
Issues of faith:	abortion
	"sun worship"
	mailorder churches
Economic issues:	tax protesters
	communists/capitalists
Survival issues:	pollution
	nuclear power
Human rights:	legal representation
	refugee centers
	freedom of speech
	age discrimination
Foreign policy:	weapons treaties
	apartheid
	war
	peace

Pursuing one of the above subjects with "action" can jeopardize exempt status. The Regulations describe three different possibilities for classification as an "action" organization:

1. A (c)(3) that has substantial lobbying;

2. A (c)(3) that participates or intervenes in political campaigns; or

3. A (c)(3) whose primary objectives (as distinguished from its incidental or secondary objectives) may be attained only by legislation or a defeat of proposed legislation, and that advocates or campaigns for such objective (as distinguished from engaging in nonpartisan analysis, study, or research and making the results available to the general public).[56]

---

[55]*Infant Formula Action Coalition v. U.S.* (D.D.C. No. 79-0129)
[56]Reg. §1.501(c)(3)-1(c)(3).

The most troublesome provision is the third action category. An exempt organization involved in controversial subjects must be able to pass the following hurdles:

- Prove that its purposes can be accomplished through means other than legislation, such as court intervention to enforce existing laws, publication of educational materials, or direct provision of services not being provided by the government.

- Show that its activity is not illegal or is protected by the rights of free speech and association. Demonstrations, boycotts, strikes, and picketing raise red flags with the IRS.

- Conduct its politically-tainted activity within a larger complex of traditionally exempt activities. (litigation can be the only activity of an environmental concern organization, for example.)

- Meet the "educational" test for information published in its newsletters, publications, or research reports on topics or issues that are potentially the subject of legislation. "Disparaging terms, insinuations, innuendoes, and suggested implications drawn from incomplete facts" are not educational.[57]

23.9 ADVOCACY: CHARITABLE OR EDUCATIONAL?

In clearing the hurdles to obtain exemption, an EO must first decide whether to claim exemption as a charitable or as an educational organization. A stricter standard, with more fully developed criteria, exists for educational organizations. The IRS regulation defining "charitable" organizations says:

> "The fact that an organization, in carrying out its primary purpose, advocates social or civic changes or presents opinion on controversial issues with the intention of molding public opinion or creating public sentiment to an acceptance of its views does not preclude such organization from qualifying under IRC §501(c)(3) so long as it is not an 'action' organization."[58]

The IRS regulation defining "educational" organizations instead provides that "education relates to:"

- the instruction or training of the individual for the purpose of imporving or developing his capabilities;

- The instruction of the public on subjects useful to the individual and beneficial to the community.

---

[57]Rev. Rul. 68-263, 1968-1 C.B. 256.
[58]Reg. §1.501(c)(3)-1(d)(2).

The same regulation goes on to provide that:

> "An organization may be educational even though it advocates a particular position or viewpoint so long as it presents a sufficiently full and fair exposition of the pertinent facts as to permit an individual or the public to form an independent opinion or conclusion. On the other hand, an organization is not educational if its principal function is the mere presentation of unsupported opinion."[59]

This Regulation was held to be unconstitutionally vague by the District Columbia Circuit Court of Appeals in the Big Mama Rag, Inc. case in 1980.[60] The IRS had argued that the newspaper, in celebrating the cause of lesbians, failed to present a "full and fair exposition of the facts" as required by the regulations. The court noted that the regulations do not make it clear what groups are advocacy groups that must meet this test, nor do they provide any objective standard for distinguishing facts from opinions.

Without answering the specific questions posed by the D.C. Circuit, the IRS in November 1986 issued a ruling outlining its "methodology test" for applying the regulation.[61] The presence of any of the following factors indicates that the method used by the organization to advocate its viewpoints or positions is not educational:

1. The presentation of viewpoints or positions unsupported by facts is a significant portion of the organization's communications.

2. The facts that purport to support the viewpoints or positions are distorted.

3. The organization's presentations make substantial use of inflammatory and disparaging terms, and express conclusions more on the basis of strong emotional feelings than of objective evaluations.

4. The approach used in the organization's presentations is not aimed at developing an understanding on the part of the intended audience or readership because it does not consider their background or training in the subject matter.

The ruling states that in applying the regulations, the IRS has attempted to "eliminate or minimize the potential for any public official to impose his or her preconceptions or beliefs in determining whether the particular viewpoint or position is educational." It is the method used by the organization to communicate its viewpoint or position to others, not the viewpoint itself, that will be tested. However, as the IRS admits, the ruling falls short of clarifying the meaning of "advocacy."

[59]Reg. §1.501(c)(3)-1(d)(3).
[60]*Big Mama Rag, Inc. v. U.S.*, 631 F.2d 1030 (D.C. Cir. 1980), *rev'g* 79-1 USTC ¶9362 D.C. 1979).
[61]Rev. Rul. 86-43, 1986-2 C.B. 729.

For examples of nonqualifying and qualifying EOs, compare an EO established to combat alcoholism, one of whose objectives is to outlaw the advertisement of alcoholic beverages, cigarettes, and other harmful substances, to an EO that plans to study and report on the causes of substance abuse. Or compare an EO whose purpose is to help poor people in Central America, by reallocating U.S. funds granted to those countries away from military aid and into humanitarian aid, to an EO whose purpose is to promote peace in Central America through documenting the displacement and other consequences to the people of the civil wars.

23.10 WHEN LITIGATION IS ACTION

Organizations performing legal services must successfully answer a series of questions to prove that their law practice serves charitable purposes. One concern is whether their clients qualify as members of a charitable class, such as the poor, persons who are discriminated against, or persons whose freedom is jeopardized. Another concern is how their business policies are distinguishable from those of commercial law firms.

The expectation of a legal fee or award cannot be a motivating factor in selection of cases, and the organization cannot withdraw from a case if the client later becomes unable to pay. Also, charges may not exceed the actual cost of the litigation. In essence, charges based upon the client's ability to pay, rather than the amount of work involved, support designation as an exempt organization some portion of the organization's financial support must come from donations of cash and services.

A new set of guidelines providing specific sanctions for public interest law firms (PILFs) was issued in 1992 (effective retroactively to taxable years beginning after December 31, 1987). To be exempt, the organization must possess the following characteristics:

- Litigation must not represent a private interest, but must instead be "said to be in representation of a broad public," such as class actions, suits seeking injunctions against actions harmful to the public, or test cases where the private interest is small.

- Litigants are not represented in actions between private persons when the financial interests at stake would warrant private legal representation, except that the PILF can serve as a friend of the court when an issue in litigation affects or will have an impact on a broad public interest

- The EO must achieve its objectives through legal and ethical means with no disruption of the judicial system, illegal activity, or violations of applicable canons of ethics.

- Litigated cases are described in detail annually on Form 990, including a rationale for the determination that they would benefit the public generally. Fees sought and recovered in each case must also be reported.

- Organizational authority, including approval of policies, programs, and compensation arrangements, rests with an independent board of trustees or a committee that is not controlled by employees or litigators.

- There must be no arrangement to accept as "donations" costs to cover from litigants.

- The EO is not operated, through sharing of office space or otherwise, in a manner so as to create identification or confusion with a particular private law firm.

- Fees charged to clients may not exceed the cost of providing the legal services, and, once representation is started, the PILF cannot withdraw because the litigant is unable to pay the contemplated fee.

- Out-of-pocket cost reimbursements may be accepted from clients.

- Total attorney fees, both court-awarded and received from clients, may not exceed 50 percent of the EO's total costs of performing litigation services, calculated on a five year rolling average basis. If an exception to this limit "appears warranted," a ruling request may be submitted.

- Attorneys must be paid on a straight salary basis; compensation levels must be reasonable and not established by reference to any fees received in connection with the cases they have handled; and the fees must be paid to the organization, not to the individual attorneys.[62]

23.11 WHEN RELIEF OF THE POOR IS NOT CHARITABLE

EOs assisting refugees have faced unique questions in obtaining recognition of exemption, because their purposes were considered "contrary to public policy." Efforts to provide food and shelter to aliens clearly relieves the poor, distressed, and underprivileged—an unquestionably charitable activity. However, what if those aliens entered the United States illegally?

Central American refugee projects have been denied exemption in the past on the basis that the presence of refugees is contrary to U.S. policy. On the other hand, legal counsel provided to the same refugees has been considered exempt, based upon published rulings sanctioning defense of human and civil rights secured by law.

The issue is of particular interest because a U.S. charitable organization furnishing food to the same people on the other side of the border would unquestionably be an exempt activity. In a similarly contradictory manner, the IRS did not challenge the existing exempt status of schools that provide education to illegal aliens, or of churches that provide sanctuary to them. EOs providing such assistance to Vietnamese and Cuban refugees during the 1970s were also granted exemption.

---

[62]Rev. Proc. 92-59, 1992-29 I.R.B. 11. For historical background, see Rev. Ruls. 75-47, 75-75, and 75-76, 1975-1 C.B. 152–154.

23.12 SHOULD A 501(c)(4) BE ESTABLISHED?

Even when an exempt organization's purposes can be accomplished only through passage of legislation which the EO plans to advocate for, and even when the questions raised in this chapter make it clear that charitable organization status would be difficult to obtain or maintain, all is not lost. Lobbying and other potentially controversial "actions" can be primary functions of a §501(c)(4) exempt organization, as long as it promotes in some way the common good and general welfare of the people of a community. A new or existing organization that plans lobbying expenditures in excess of the permissible limits has two choices:

1. Become a (c)(4) organization, either from inception as a new organization or by conversion from a (c)(3).

2. Create two sister organizations: a (c)(4) to carry out lobbying activities and a (c)(3) for strictly charitable activities.

Proper timing is important for existing (c)(3) organizations, because conversion is not allowed after an organization loses its exempt status due to excessive lobbying. An existing (c)(3) organization which expects that its future lobbying efforts will cause it to lose its charitable status can, however, apply to convert. A (c)(4) may only have limited, if any, political involvement.

The relationship between a related (c)(3) and (c)(4) will be carefully scrutinized and will be subject to nonstatutory rules about control, funding, and staffing. The IRS can evaluate the subject with a series of questions asked on Form 990.

Interlocking board members reflect common control, and this may be presumed to indicate the subversive operation of the (c)(3) for (c)(4) purposes. The safest relationship is for each organization to have independent control. Funding and staff members can be shared between the organizations but only when their purposes are clearly documented. Staff overlap must be carefully documented with time records and evidence of staff activity. Shared facilities, memberships, funding campaigns, publications, and other overt products of activity deserve careful allocations, as they will be scrutinized by the IRS.

A grant from the (c)(3) to the (c)(4) is allowed, but only if the grant is restricted to charitable purposes (most commonly, research). If allocated to lobbying, the grant should not be for a sum that would violate the (c)(3)'s limitations. Clearly, the (c)(3) organization cannot raise general support funds to be transmitted to the (c)(4), but the reverse could be done.

The last, but not the least important, factor to consider in converting a (c)(3) to a (c)(4) is the loss of deductibility of donations to the resulting organization (c)(4).

FORM 5768

Form **5768** (Rev. January 1990) Department of the Treasury Internal Revenue Service	**Election/Revocation of Election by an Eligible Section 501(c)(3) Organization To Make Expenditures To Influence Legislation** (Under Section 501(h) of the Internal Revenue Code)	For IRS Use Only ►

Name of organization	Employer identification number

Address (number and street)

City or town, state, and ZIP code

1   Election.—As an eligible organization we hereby elect to have the provisions of section 501(h) of the Code, relating to expenditures to influence legislation, apply to our tax year ending _____ and all subsequent tax years until revoked.
(Month, day, and year)

Note: *This election must be signed and postmarked within the first taxable year to which it applies.*

2   Revocation.—As an eligible organization we hereby revoke our election to have the provisions of section 501(h) of the Code, relating to expenditures to influence legislation, apply to our tax year ending _____
(Month, day, and year)

Note: *This revocation must be signed and postmarked before the first day of the tax year to which it applies.*

Under penalties of perjury, I declare that I am authorized to make this (check applicable box) ►   ☐ election/   ☐ revocation on behalf of the above named organization.

_____   _____   _____
(Signature of officer or trustee)   (Title)   (Date)

Instructions

(References are to the Internal Revenue Code.)

Section 501(c)(3) provides that an organization exempt under that section will lose its tax-exempt status and its qualification to receive deductible charitable contributions if a substantial part of its activities are carried on to influence legislation. Section 501(h), however, permits certain eligible 501(c)(3) organizations to elect to make limited expenditures to influence legislation. An organization making the election will, however, be subject to an excise tax under section 4911 if it spends more than the amounts permitted by that section. Furthermore, the organization may lose its exempt status if its lobbying expenditures exceed the permitted amounts by more than 50% over a 4-year period. For any tax year in which an election under section 501(h) is in effect, an electing organization must report the actual and permitted amounts of its lobbying expenditures and grass roots expenditures (as defined in section 4911(c)) on its annual return required under section 6033. See Schedule A (Form 990). Each electing member of an affiliated group must report these amounts for both itself and the affiliated group as a whole.

To make or revoke the election, enter the ending date of the tax year to which the election or revocation applies in item 1 or 2, as applicable, and sign and date the form in the spaces provided.

Eligible Organizations.—A section 501(c)(3) organization is permitted to make the election if it is not a disqualified organization (see below) and is described in:

(a)   section 170(b)(1)(A)(ii) (relating to educational institutions),

(b)   section 170(b)(1)(A)(iii) (relating to hospitals and medical research organizations),

(c)   section 170(b)(1)(A)(iv) (relating to organizations supporting government schools),

(d)   section 170(b)(1)(A)(vi) (relating to organizations publicly supported by charitable contributions),

(e)   section 509(a)(2) (relating to organizations publicly supported by admissions, sales, etc.), or

(f)   section 509(a)(3) (relating to organizations supporting certain types of public charities other than those section 509(a)(3) organizations that support section 501(c)(4), (5), or (6) organizations).

Disqualified Organizations.—The following types of organizations are not permitted to make the election:

(a)   section 170(b)(1)(A)(i) organizations (relating to churches),

(b)   an integrated auxiliary of a church or of a convention or association of churches, or

(c)   a member of an affiliated group of organizations if one or more members of such group is described in (a) or (b) of this paragraph.

Affiliated Organizations.—Organizations are members of an affiliated group of organizations only if: (1) the governing instrument of one such organization requires it to be bound by the decisions of the other organization on legislative issues, or (2) the governing board of one such organization includes persons who (i) are specifically designated representatives of another such organization or are members of the governing board, officers, or paid executive staff members of such other organization, and (ii) by aggregating their votes have sufficient voting power to cause or prevent action on legislative issues by the first such organization.

For more details, see section 4911 and section 501(h).

Note: *A private foundation (including a private operating foundation) is not an eligible organization.*

Where To File.—Mail Form 5768 to the applicable **Internal Revenue Service Center** listed below.

If the principal office of the organization is located in: ▼	Use this address: ▼
Alabama, Arkansas, Florida, Georgia, Louisiana, Mississippi, North Carolina, South Carolina, Tennessee	Atlanta, GA 39901
Arizona, Colorado, Kansas, New Mexico, Oklahoma, Texas, Utah, Wyoming	Austin, TX 73301
Indiana, Kentucky, Michigan, Ohio, West Virginia	Cincinnati, OH 45999
Alaska, California, Hawaii, Idaho, Nevada, Oregon, Washington	Fresno, CA 93888
Connecticut, Delaware, Maine, Massachusetts, New Hampshire, New Jersey, New York, Pennsylvania (ZIP codes beginning with 169–171 and 173–196 only), Rhode Island, Vermont	Holtsville, NY 00501
Illinois, Iowa, Minnesota, Missouri, Montana, Nebraska, North Dakota, South Dakota, Wisconsin	Kansas City, MO 64999
District of Columbia, Maryland, Pennsylvania (ZIP codes beginning with 150–168 and 172 only), Virginia, any U.S. possession, any foreign country	Philadelphia, PA 19255

Form **5768** (Rev. 1-90)

Truth in Fund-Raising

Contributors to nonprofit organizations have grown accustomed to receiving benefits in return for their gifts: dinner, entertainment, and prizes. Often, the proceeds of fund-raising events add directly to an organization's coffers because businesses and patrons donate the items of benefit offered to the attendees. Until 1988, a charity was neither expected nor required to assign value to such benefits, or to inform the givers that the ticket price is not fully deductible.

Misconceptions and indecision plague fund-raisers, because there is no absolute legal requirement underlying the IRS's request that an organization voluntarily furnish donors information in connection with fund-raising events, membership drives, and other revenue programs, when donors are given premiums, discounts, meals, prizes, or other valuable items in return for their donation. Ethical and tactical issues are involved.

The IRS initiated a "special emphasis program" entitled *Exempt Organization Charitable Solicitations Compliance Improvement Study* to enforce the charitable deduction rules by studying and enhancing compliance. In August 1988, *Publication 1391* was sent to all exempt organizations qualified to receive donations (Appendix 24–1). Interestingly, although the IRS claims to have mailed 500,000 copies of this publication, there remains a high level of confusion about the requirements, and there is total ignorance of the issue on the part of many organizations and their advisors.

The publication was instigated by the House Budget Committee, which had found that "some charities fail to make sufficient disclosures in soliciting gifts to allow donors to calcualte the nondeductible portion of donations." In

1987, Congress made it mandatory for non-501(c)(3) organizations to prominently print on all fund-raising materials that payments were not deductible[1] and directed the IRS to measure tax revenues lost due to overstated donations to §501(c)(3) organizations and to investigate any abuses found.

24.1 WHAT IS DEDUCTIBLE?

To understand what is deductible, look first to the Internal Revenue Code's contribution deduction sections which have not changed since 1939. The Revenue Ruling explaining the relevant sections, Code reprinted in *Publication 1391*, was issued in 1967. Charities are not faced with a new law, but need a better understanding of the old law.

In a deceptively simple fashion the Internal Revenue Code states that an income tax deduction is allowed for "a contribution or gift to or for the use of qualified charitable organizations."[2] Neither the Code nor the regulations define "contribution." The commonly understood definition of a contribution is "a voluntary transfer without consideration." In other words, *only a gift for which nothing is received in return is fully deductible*. The intention must be present to make a gift with no expectation of financial benefit. In one court's words, "the gift must proceed from detached and disinterested generosity."[3]

When a donor receives services, goods, or other property of value, a rebuttable presumption arises that there is no gift.[4] Therefore, all the moneys paid in return for membership dues, attendance at dinners, balls, theatrical performances, and other fundraising events are at the outset, presumed to be payments for value received and not deductible. To overcome the presumption, the donor must prove that the fair market value (FMV) of the benefits, entertainment, or other items furnished is less than the amount paid.

For example, a $25 meal provided during a $100 benefit reduces the deduction to $75. A $25 meal, plus $35 performance, plus a $20 chance for the door prize, would reduce the gift to $20. Some professionals suggest that the minimum price charged for an event, which is often in excess of the value of the benefits received, establishes its fair market value. The IRS argues further that the social nature of fund-raising events implies lack of donative intent. Fortunately, intangible recognition, such as having one's name placed on a building or donor listing, is as a general rule considered to be of incidental or tenuous benefit, and does not reduce the value of the gift.[5]

To add to the difficulty, items of tangible personal property give for resale in a charity auction or resale shop are also limited in their deductibility. Such property is only deductible to the extent that it is given "to or for the use of"

---

[1]IRC §6116 (applies to organizations with gross receipts over $100,000).
[2]IRC §170(c).
[3]*Duberstein v. Commissioner*, 363 S. Ct. 278 (1960); *William S. Allen v. U.S.*, 541 F. 2d 786 (9th Cir. 1976); Rev. Rul. 86-63, 1986-1 C.B. 88; Rev. Rul. 76-232, 1976-2 C.B. 62.
[4]Rev. Rul. 67-246, 1967-2 C.B. 104, 105.
[5]Reg. §53.4941 (d)-2(f)(2); Rev. Rul. 66-358, 1966-2 C.B. 216; Rev. Rul. 73-407, 1973-2 C.B. 383.

Exhibit 24–1

SUGGESTED GUIDELINES FOR VALUING GIFTS	
Meals at hotel or other place selling meals to general public.	= Coffee shop or dining room price for same meal, including drinks and tips.
Dancing and entertainment.	= Price charged in club or other public establishment for same musician, singer, or band.
Attendance at private reception.	= Value of food and drink only (intangible value of associating with famous persons not valued).
Cultural performance ticket.	= Normal seat price to public.
Preferred seating.	= Equal to price paid if in excess of normal price (IRC §501(m) has special rule for college stadiums).
Raffle, lottery, or door prize ticket.	= Price of ticket.
Free admission.	= Admission charged nonmembers times average annual attendance.
Discount for books, classes, trips, etc.	= Dollar amount of discount.
Trinkets, bumper stickers, labels, buttons, pens, etc.	= Nothing if item cost $6.01 or less for a gift of at least $25 (see de minimus rule in Section 24.2(a)).

the charity itself.[6] A work of art given to a museum to exhibit on its wall is used by the museum directly in its exempt programs, so the full value of the art is deductible. If instead, the work of art is given to an AIDS hospice for a benefit auction, the deduction is limited to the giver's tax basis.

24.2 HOW ARE BENEFITS VALUED?

The value of a benefit provided to a donor is the fair market value (FMV), or the amount "a willing buyer will pay a willing seller for the same item, object or service purchased individually in the normal marketplace in which the item is sold."[7] The value is not necessarily equal to the organization's cost, particularly when the items are donated or purchased below market prices. Under existing tax law, the burden of proving value of a gift is placed on the taxpayer claiming the deduction. Typical benefits and suggestions for valuing gifts are shown in Exhibit 24–1. Failure to use the tickets or privileges does not entitle the purchaser to a deduction, but written refusal of the ticket or privilege from the

[6] IRC §170(e)(B)(i).
[7] Reg. §1.170A-1(c)(2).

outset enables the donor to evidence a gift. Returning tickets received can also convert such transactions into a pure gift.[8]

The fact that the money paid is used exclusively for charitable purposes does not reduce the fair market value of the benefits,[9] nor does the fact that objects or services are donated at no cost to the charity. An ostensibly charitable performance to which entertainers donate their services has value to those attending. Despite the donation by the performers, the admission price is not deductible unless it exceeds the normal price for similar performances in the same theater.

(a) The de Minimus Rule

Revenue Procedure 90-12[10] was issued by the IRS in response to charities' complaints that the valuation process was too difficult and subjective. Premiums or benefits of insubstantial value given in connection with a qualified fund-raising campaign are de minimus and can be ignored in the following circumstances:

- The fair market value of all benefits received for the payment is not more than two percent of the payment, or $50, whichever is less (e.g., a benefit worth up to $50 can be given to a $2,500 contributor);

- The donation is $30.09 during 1992 ($28.58 in 1991, $27.26 for 1990, $26.03 for 1989, and $25.00 for 1988) or more, adjusted annually for inflation *and* the benefits received are token items (bookmarks, calendars, key chains, mugs, posters, tee shirts, etc.) bearing the organization's name or logo, with a cost (as opposed to FMV) of no more than $6.01 during 1992, ($5.71 in 1991, $5.45 in 1990, $5.21 in 1989 and $5.00 in 1988—the inflation-adjusted number).

- All benefits received during a year are aggregated to calculate the total amount furnished. For example, the combined cost of a $3.00 mug and a $4.00 tee shirt exceed the de minimus amount, and thus reduce the donation by the entire $7.00.

(b) Qualified Campaign

A qualified fund-raising campaign has three elements:

1. It is designed to raise tax deductible donations.

2. The charity uses reasonable methods to value benefits offered in return for donations.

3. Solicitations state how much of the donation is deductible and how much is not. (This statement may be written on tickets, or receipts, broadcast, telephoned, or made in person.)

[8]Rev. Rul. 65-432, 1968-2 C.B. 104.
[9]Rev. Rul. 67-246, 1967-2 C.B. 104.
[10]Rev. Proc. 90-12, IRS News Release IRB 90-20, February 1990; updated by Rev. Proc. 92-58, 1992-2, IRB 10.

(c) Commercial Quality Publications

Publications, such as newsletters or program guides, are assigned value if they are commercial quality publications (CQPs). A CQP has the following characteristics:

- The primary purpose of the publication is *not* to inform members about the organization's activities;

- It is available to the general public;

- It contains paid advertising; and

- It contains articles written for compensation.

Organizations following this procedure are instructed to include this statement in their fund-raising literature:

> "Under IRS guidelines, the estimated value of [benefits received] is not substantial; therefore the full amount of your payment is a deductible contribution."

24.3 BENEFITS THAT NEED NOT BE VALUED

It is sometimes difficult to tell whether a donor is receiving a quid pro quo, (something of value which reduces the contribution), or if the charity instead is simply fulfilling its exempt functions by furnishing services. Furnishing educational benefits in the form of newsletters, lectures, or training, is normally considered an exempt function. Making such benefits available to contributors at no charge is not assigned value, whether they are available to the general public or not. Compare the human service and performing arts organizations, such as hospitals and symphonies, that charge for the services they render. Examples are useful:

- Civil Air Patrol squadron dues entitling members to be trained for rescue missions and to purchase items at a military exchange were deemed to be deductible, because the specific benefits were merely incidental to the charitable purposes of the patrol and to the public services rendered by the members.[11]

- Pew rents, building fund assessments, and periodic dues paid to churches have traditionally been classed as charitable donations.[12] However, religious services for which Church of Scientology members pay specific charges were deemed by the Supreme Court to be valuable personal services, so the disallowance of their deductions were upheld.[13]

[11]*Miller v. Commissioner*, 34 T.C.M. 1207 (1975).
[12]Rev. Rul. 70-47, 1970-1 C.B. 49.
[13]*Hernandez v. Commissioner*, 109 S.Ct. 2137 (1989).

- The rights to attend an annual meeting, vote for officers, attend semiannual social functions, and conduct an annual rummage sale did not make a children's convalescent home member dues nondeductible.[14]

- The distinction is easier to make when the general public also receives the services for a fee. If members receive free admission or other privileges while nonmembers are required to pay for similar services, the privileges are assigned value.[15]

- Member dues represent a pure charitable donation only if members are given no "commensurate rights and privileges" other than the personal satisfaction of being of service to others and furthering the charitable cause in which the members share a common interest.[16]

24.4 IRS EXAMINATION PROGRAM

In early 1990, the IRS expanded its voluntary public information program and announced a "Charitable Solicitations Compliance Improvement Program." To gather statistics to report back to Congress, the IRS used a newly-designed examination checklist to review the fund-raising practices of charities. During the initial examinations, a fairly high degree of noncompliance was found. The checklist is still being used for examinations in late 1992 but it is expected such examinations will not continue.

The examination checklist looks at fund-raising activities in a comprehensive fashion and goes well beyond calculations of the deductible portion of donations to events. Compensation arrangements with professional fund-raisers inspire 12 questions seeking proof that such arrangements do not result in excessive payments. High fees may evidence operation of the charity to benefit the individual fund-raisers, and may constitute prohibited private inurement of the organization's funds. Noncash contributions and Form 8282 and 8283 filings are also reviewed for valuations.

The IRS is also concerned about the amount of net profit generated by fund-raising activities. If too little (under 20 percent) of the gross proceeds of a benefit end up in the charitable coffer, the charity may fail the "commensurate test" required for continued tax exemption. Bingo operations, travel tours, thrift shops, and noncash contributions are looked at in depth. The checklist, Form 9215, follows at the end of the chapter as Appendix 24-2.

24.5 UNRELATED BUSINESS INCOME ASPECTS OF FUND-RAISING

Another costly aspect of the solicitation compliance program has been the payment of unrelated business income tax. Basically, all fund-raising events are business activities conducted in competition with businesses that sell the same

[14] Rev. Rul. 55-70, 1955-1 C.B. 506.
[15] Rev. Rul. 68-432, 1968-2 C.B. 104.
[16] Rev. Rul. 55-70, 1955-1 C.B. 506.

goods and services, and are potentially subject to tax as unrelated business income (UBI). Typically, event profits are not taxable as UBI because the fund-raising events are organized and operated by volunteers[17] and are irregularly carried on,[18] involve the sale of donated merchandise,[19] or are related to the entity's exempt purposes.

The IRS has targeted for examination the types of fund-raisers usually claimed to be excluded from UBI classification because of their relatedness to the organization's exempt purposes. Travel tours were one of the first targets. To be classified as related to an organization's exempt purposes, a tour must include a fairly high level of educational content and professional direction. A recent ruling found that a typical travel tour program was unrelated, so that all of the proceeds, including the "donation element," were subject to the UBI tax.[20]

Bingo games are given a special exclusion from UBI if the operation of bingo by the organization does not violate state law.[21] It is extremely important to note that other games of chance (such as raffles, lotteries, and casino parties) do not qualify for this exclusion. The IRS definition of bingo includes only those games in which (1) wagers are placed, (2) winners are determined, and (3) prizes or other property is distributed, in the presence of all persons placing wagers in such game. The regulations clarify this definition to include games of chance played with cards that are generally printed with five rows of five squares each, during which participants place markers over randomly-called numbers on the cards in an attempt to form a preselected pattern such as a horizontal, vertical, or diagonal line, or all four corners.[22]

Dallas Key District IRS agents conducted a study of charitable bingo operators during 1990 to disqualify "instant bingo" from the IRC §513(f) exception, despite the fact that state law allows it as "legal bingo." The Cypress Creek EMS Association in Texas has filed a petition with the Tax Court to overturn the IRS position. Look for a late 1992 decision.

24.6 STATE AND LOCAL REGULATIONS

Fund-raising materials which do not reflect the actual amount of money devoted to charitable purposes constitute a deceptive trade practice under local law in many states. It clearly is the opinion of the Texas Attorney General's office that charities have a fiduciary responsibility to maximize funds available for programs. All but eight states have charitable solicitation statutes. The focus of local registration is on fund-raising costs, private benefit to professional fund-raisers, and truth in solicitation materials.

[17] IRC §513(a)(1).
[18] IRC §512(a)(1).
[19] IRC §513(a)(3).
[20] IRS Technical Advice Memorandum 9029001 (March 21, 1990).
[21] IRC §513(f).
[22] Reg. §1.513-5(d).

24.7 PRACTICAL CONSIDERATIONS

When the IRS started its examination program, few organizations or their contributors had adequate information with which to place a value on benefit tickets or charitable auction payments. After being made aware of the issue, most organizations made a good faith effort to comply with the voluntary program.

(a) Useful Facts

To handle the task of valuing benefits, it is helpful to know the following practical tips:

- While the cost of rendering a service or benefit to members and/or attendees it not the prescribed measure of the value, the cost may be determinative absent a comparable market. Formal independent appraisals are not necessary. The actual number of persons attending an event, rather than the (often much higher) number of tickets sold, should be used to calculate the per person cost.

- A catalog listing the FMV of items to be sold at a charitable auction establishes the nondeductible portion. Purchasing goods for more than their FMV results in a partial gift, i.e., the amount in excess of the catalog's price.

- The IRS policy is that any good faith, reasonable method to establish FMV will be acceptable. Evidence of the factors used, preferably independent information, is to be maintained by the charity.

- Timing of the disclosure can be a complicated matter. Must the valuation disclosure be placed on the event invitation? Often, a charity cannot calculate the value of an event before its presentation. In such a case, the announcement can contain an estimated value, but a follow-up receipt should be furnished afterward if the actual valuation is significantly different.

- Additional accounting records and analyses may be necessary to properly calculate the value of services to members. There are important unanswered questions: Is a portion of organization staff time allocable to the cost of events? Should a portion of the organization's overhead be so allocated?

- Accounting principles recommend against reporting certain donated goods and volunteer services and this has fostered the charitable community's widespread ignorance of proper reporting.

- The distinction between gift and sale elements is not often reported on financial statements, although Form 990 separates them and asks for details.

- Form 990 now asks: "Did you solicit any contributions or gifts that were not tax deductible? If yes, did you include with every solicitation an express statement that such contributions or gifts were not tax deductible?"

Fund-raising methods can evolve in creative ways. Rather then relying on benefits to contributors, philanthropy can be emphasized as the motivation for making a gift to an organization. Higher profits to the organization may result from reduced costs of premiums, benefits and the other hoopla furnished in connection with fund-raising events.

(b) The Reporting Dilemma

Since an exempt organization is not required to report the deductible portion of its contributor's gifts and since the burden of proving value is placed on the contributor, some charities choose not to comply with the IRS request that benefits be valued and reported voluntarily. Some of these charities take a silent approach and disclose no information; others continue to use the old refrain, "Deductible to the extent allowed by law," which may ironically serve as a red flag to the IRS. In Texas, IRS agents collect invitations and news clippings to assist them in choosing organizations to examine. IRS agents have reminded professional groups that a penalty can be imposed under IRC §6701 on one "who aids or assists in" presentation of tax information which that person knows will result in an understatement of income tax liability of another person. Conceivably, that "one" includes a board member who votes not to furnish FMV information regarding contributions.

It is safe to expect that discovery of any appreciable degree of noncompliance with the IRS's voluntary request will lead the IRS to recommend that Congress require disclosure. In the fall of 1990, Congress placed a percentage floor on itemized deductions, including contributions, evidencing once again its willingness to remove tax benefits from charitable giving. Congress added such a requirement (that gifts over $100 be reported by charities to the IRS) to the 1992 Tax bill that then President Bush vetoed. Charities and their advisors can expect required reporting of donations in the future.

Most individual donors wish to comply with the tax laws and welcome cooperation on the charity's part. On the other hand, reduction of tax benefit is perceived to discourage giving. (This is clearly true in the case of appreciated property gifts of stock, art, and land.) Fortunately, most charities are making the ethical choice to comply and furnish deductibility information. They are happy to report no significant reductions in giving levels as a consequence. Nonetheless, donor goodwill is both enhanced and crippled by voluntarily furnishing FMV information. Some contributors want it, some do not, and therein lies the dilemma.

Appendix 24-1

Department of the Treasury
Internal Revenue Service

Deductibility of Payments Made to Charities Conducting Fund-Raising Events

From the Commissioner

As Commissioner of Internal Revenue, I am sending this message to charities to ask your help in more accurately informing taxpayers as to the deductibility of payments by patrons of your fund-raising events.

I am concerned that sponsors of fund-raising events have often failed to provide written information on the extent to which payments for such affairs are deductible as charitable contributions. There has been widespread misunderstanding of the limitations on the deductibility of such payments. This misunderstanding has led, of course, to erroneous tax reporting of these payments by some patrons.

The Congress also has evidenced some concern in this area. The House Budget Committee, in its Report on the Omnibus Budget Reconciliation Act of 1987, page 1607, states that it "... is concerned that some charitable organizations may not make sufficient disclosure, in soliciting donations, membership dues, payments for admissions or merchandise, or other support, of the extent (if any) to which the payors may be entitled to charitable contributions for such payments." The Report, on page 1608, then states:

"...the committee anticipates that the Internal Revenue Service will monitor the extent to which taxpayers are being furnished accurate and sufficient information by charitable organizations as to the nondeductibility of payments to such organizations where benefits or privileges are received in return, so that taxpayers can correctly compute their Federal income tax liability. The committee also anticipates that groups representing the charitable community will further educate their members as to the applicable tax rules and provide guidance as to how charities can provide appropriate information to their supporters in this regard."

Publication 1391 (Rev. 1-90)

Appendix 24–1 *(continued)*

Because of this expression of Congressional interest, as well as the continued concern of IRS, a Special Emphasis Program was instituted which will focus on the fund-raising practices of charitable organizations, as well as organizations that perform fund-raising functions for charities. Through this Special Emphasis Program, the IRS shall seek to ascertain the extent to which taxpayers are furnished accurate and sufficient information concerning the deductibility of their contributions.

In applying the law, there is a presumption that the total amount paid represents the fair value of substantial benefits received in return—thus eliminating any charitable contribution deduction. Organizations, nevertheless, can use these fund-raising affairs to solicit gifts—and they can help ensure that these gifts will be recognized as deductible—if they follow certain relatively simple soliciting and receipting practices.

Revenue Ruling 67-246, 1967-2 C.B. 104, describes the rules on charitable contributions and gives a number of examples illustrating how the rules apply in common situations. The full text of the ruling follows this message. I hope you will keep this ruling in mind if your organization sponsors or participates in a fund-raising event.

I would particularly like to emphasize that part of the ruling which states the importance of determining, in advance of solicitation, the portion of payment attributable to the purchase of admission or other privilege and the portion solicited as a gift.

The ruling says that in those cases in which a fund-raising activity is designed to solicit payments intended to be in part a gift and in part the purchase price of admission or other participation in an event, separate amounts should be stated in the solicitation and clearly indicated on any ticket or other evidence of payment furnished to the contributor.

By following this rule, the organization engaged in fund-raising events will be helping taxpayers comply with the income tax laws, as well as avoiding possible embarrassment to itself and its patrons.

If you have any questions regarding Revenue Ruling 67-246, or you would like us to explain how the ruling applies to your particular situation, please contact your local Internal Revenue office.

Commissioner of Internal Revenue

Rev. Rul. 67-246

Deductibility, as charitable contributions under section 170 of the Internal Revenue Code of 1954, of payments made by taxpayers in connection with admission to or other participation in fund-raising activities for charity such as charity balls, bazaars, banquets, shows, and athletic events.

Advice has been requested concerning certain fund-raising practices which are frequently employed by or on behalf of charitable organizations and which involve the deductibility, as charitable contributions under section 170 of the Internal Revenue Code of 1954, of payments in connection with admission to or other participation in fund-raising activities for charity such as charity balls, bazaars, banquets, shows, and athletic events.

Affairs of the type in question are commonly employed to raise funds for charity in two ways. One is from profit derived from sale of admissions or other privileges or benefits connected with the event at such prices as their value warrants. Another is through the use of the affair as an occasion for solicitation of gifts in combination with the sale of the admissions or other privileges or benefits involved. In cases of the latter type the sale of the privilege or benefit is combined with solicitation of a gift or donation of some amount in addition to the sale value of the admission or privilege.

The need for guidelines on the subject is indicated by the frequency of misunderstanding of the requirements for deductibility of such payments and increasing incidence of their erroneous treatment for income tax purposes.

In particular, an increasing number of instances are being reported in which the public has been erroneously advised in advertisements or solicitations by sponsors that the entire amounts paid for tickets or other privileges in connection with fund-raising affairs for charity are deductible. Audits of returns are revealing other instances of erroneous advice and misunderstanding as to what, if any, portion of such payments is deductible in various circumstances. There is evidence also of instances in which taxpayers are being misled by questionable solicitation practices which make it appear from the wording of the solicitation that taxpayer's payment is a "contribution," whereas the payment solicited is simply the purchase price of an item offered for sale by the organization.

Section 170 of the Code provides for allowance of deductions for charitable contributions, subject to certain requirements and limitations. To the extent here relevant a charitable contribution is defined by that section as "a contribution or gift to or for the use of" certain specified types of organizations.

To be deductible as a charitable contribution for Federal income tax purposes under section 170 of the Code, a payment to or for the use of a qualified charitable organization must be a gift. To be a gift for such purposes in the present context there must be, among other requirements, a payment of money or transfer of property without adequate consideration.

As a general rule, where a transaction involving a payment is in the form of a purchase of an item of value, the presumption arises that no gift has been made for charitable contribution purposes, the presumption being that the payment in such case is the purchase price.

Appendix 24–1 *(continued)*

Thus, where consideration in the form of admissions or other privileges or benefits is received in connection with payments by patrons of fund-raising affairs of the type in question, the presumption is that the payments are not gifts. In such case, therefore, if a charitable contribution deduction is claimed with respect to the payment, the burden is on the taxpayer to establish that the amount paid is not the purchase price of the privileges or benefits and that part of the payment, in fact, does qualify as a gift.

In showing that a gift has been made, an essential element is proof that the portion of the payment claimed as a gift represents the excess of the total amount paid over the value of the consideration received therefor. This may be established by evidence that the payment exceeds the fair market value of the privileges or other benefits received by the amount claimed to have been paid as a gift.

Another element which is important in establishing that a gift was made in such circumstances, is evidence that the payment in excess of the value received was made with the intention of making a gift. While proof of such intention may not be an essential requirement under all circumstances and may sometimes be inferred from surrounding circumstances, the intention to make a gift is, nevertheless, highly relevant in overcoming doubt in those cases in which there is a question whether an amount was in fact paid as a purchase price or as a gift.

Regardless of the intention of the parties, however, a payment of the type in question can in any event qualify as a deductible gift only to the extent that it is shown to exceed the fair market value of any consideration received in the form of privileges or other benefits.

In those cases in which a fund-raising activity is designed to solicit payments which are intended to be in part a gift and in part the purchase price of admission to or other participation in an event of the type in question, the organization conducting the activity should employ procedures which make clear not only that a gift is being solicited in connection with the sale of the admissions or other privileges related to the fund-raising event, but also, the amount of the gift being solicited. To do this, the amount properly attributable to the purchase of admissions or other privileges and the amount solicited as a gift should be determined in advance of solicitation. The respective amounts should be stated in making the solicitation and clearly indicated on any ticket, receipt, or other evidence issued in connection with the payment.

In making such a determination, the full fair market value of the admission and other benefits or privileges must be taken into account. Where the affair is reasonably comparable to events for which there are established charges for admission, such as theatrical or athletic performances, the established charges should be treated as fixing the fair market value of the admission or privilege. Where the amount paid is the same as the standard admission charge there is, of course, no deductible contribution, regardless of the intention of the parties. Where the event has no such counterpart, only that portion of the payment which exceeds a reasonable estimate of the fair market value of the admission or other privileges may be designated as a charitable contribution.

The fact that the full amount or a portion of the payment made by the taxpayer is used by the organization exclusively for charitable purposes has no bearing upon the determination to be made as to the value of the admission or other privileges and the amount qualifying as a contribution.

Also, the mere fact that tickets or other privileges are not utilized does not entitle the patron to any greater charitable contribution deduction than would otherwise be allowable. The test of deductibility is not whether the right to admission or privileges is exercised but whether the right was accepted or rejected by the taxpayer. If a patron desires to support an affair, but does not intend to use the tickets or exercise the other privileges being offered with the event, he can make an outright gift of the amount he wishes to contribute, in which event he would not accept or keep any ticket or other evidence of any privileges related to the event connected with the solicitation.

The foregoing summary is not intended to be all inclusive of the legal requirements relating to deductibility of payments as charitable contributions for Federal income tax purposes. Neither does it attempt to deal with many of the refinements and distinctions which sometimes arise in connection with questions of whether a gift for such purposes has been made in particular circumstances.

The principles stated are intended instead to summarize with as little complexity as possible, those basic rules which govern deductibility of payments in the majority of the circumstances involved. They have their basis in section 170 of the Code, the regulations thereunder, and in court decisions. The observance of these provisions will provide greater assurance to taxpayer contributors that their claimed deductions in such cases are allowable.

Where it is disclosed that the public or the patrons of a fund-raising affair for charity have been erroneously informed concerning the extent of the deductibility of their payments in connection with the affair, it necessarily follows that all charitable contribution deductions claimed with respect to payments made in connection with the particular event or affair will be subject to special scrutiny and may be questioned in audit of returns.

In the following examples application of the principles discussed above is illustrated in connection with various types of fund-raising activities for charity. Again, the examples are drawn to illustrate the general rules involved without attempting to deal with distinctions that sometimes arise in special situations. In each instance, the charitable organization involved is assumed to be an organization previously determined to be qualified to receive deductible charitable contributions under section 170 of the Code, and the references to deductibility are to deductibility as charitable contributions for Federal income tax purposes.

Example 1:

The *M* Charity sponsors a symphony concert for the purpose of raising funds for *M*'s charitable programs. *M* agrees to pay a fee which is calculated to reimburse the symphony for hall rental, musicians' salaries, advertising costs, and printing of tickets. Under the agreement, *M* is entitled to all receipts from ticket sales. *M* sells tickets to the concert charging $5 for balcony seats and $10 for orchestra circle seats. These prices approximate the established admission charges for concert performances by the symphony orchestra. The tickets to the concert and the advertising material promoting ticket sales emphasize that the concert is sponsored by, and is for the benefit of *M* Charity.

Notwithstanding the fact that taxpayers who acquire tickets to the concert may think they are making a charitable contribution to or for the benefit of *M* Charity, no part of the payments made is deductible as a

Appendix 24-1 (*continued*)

charitable contribution for Federal income tax purposes. Since the payments approximate the established admission charge for similar events, there is no gift. The result would be the same even if the advertising materials promoting ticket sales stated that amounts paid for tickets are "tax deductible" and tickets to the concert were purchased in reliance upon such statements. Acquisition of tickets or other privileges by a taxpayer in reliance upon statements made by a charitable organization that the amounts paid are deductible does not convert an otherwise nondeductible payment into a deductible charitable contribution.

Example 2:

The facts are the same as in *Example 1*, except that the *M* Charity desires to use the concert as an occasion for the solicitation of gifts. It indicates that fact in its advertising material promoting the event, and fixes the payments solicited in connection with each class of admission at $30 for orchestra circle seats and $15 for balcony seats. The advertising and tickets clearly reflect the fact that the established admission charges for comparable performances by the symphony orchestra are $10 for orchestra circle seats and $5 for balcony seats, and that only the excess of the solicited amounts paid in connection with the admission to the concert over the established prices is a contribution to *M*.

Under these circumstances a taxpayer who makes a payment of $60 and receives two orchestra circle seat tickets can show that his payment exceeds the established admission charge for similar tickets to comparable performances of the symphony orchestra by $40. The circumstances also confirm that that amount of the payment was solicited as, and intended to be, a gift to *M* Charity. The $40, therefore, is deductible as a charitable contribution.

Example 3:

A taxpayer pays $5 for a balcony ticket to the concert described in *Example 1*. This taxpayer had no intention of using the ticket when he acquired it and he did not, in fact, attend the concert.

No part of the taxpayer's $5 payment to the *M* Charity is deductible as a charitable contribution. The mere fact that the ticket to the concert was not used does not entitle the taxpayer to any greater right to a deduction than if he did use it. The same result would follow if the taxpayer had made a gift of the ticket to another individual. If the taxpayer desired to support *M*, but did not intend to use the ticket to the concert, he could have made a qualifying charitable contribution by making a $5 payment to *M* and refusing to accept the ticket to the concert.

Example 4:

A receives a brochure soliciting contributions for the support of the *M* Charity. The brochure states: "As a grateful token of appreciation for your help, the *M* Charity will send to you your choice of one of the several articles listed below, depending upon the amount of your donation." The remainder of the brochure is devoted to a catalog-type listing of articles of merchandise with the suggested amount of donation necessary to receive each particular article. There is no evidence of any significant difference between the suggested donation and the fair market value of any such article. The brochure contains the further notation that all donations to *M* Charity are tax deductible.

Payments of the suggested amounts solicited by *M* Charity are not deductible as a charitable contribution. Under the circumstances, the amounts solicited as "donations" are simply the purchase prices of the articles listed in the brochure.

Example 5:

A taxpayer paid $5 for a ticket which entitled him to a chance to win a new automobile. The raffle was conducted to raise funds for the *X* Charity. Although the payment for the ticket was solicited as a "contribution" to the *X* Charity and designated as such on the face of the ticket, no part of the payment is deductible as a charitable contribution. Amounts paid for chances to participate in raffles, lotteries, or similar drawings or to participate in puzzle or other contests for valuable prizes are not gifts in such circumstances, and therefore, do not qualify as deductible charitable contributions.

Example 6:

A women's club, which serves principally as an auxiliary of the *X* Charity, holds monthly membership luncheon meetings. Following the luncheon and any entertainment that may have been arranged, the members transact any membership business which may be required. Attendance of the luncheon meetings is promoted through the advance sale of tickets. Typical of the form of the tickets is the following:

Suburban Women's Club of X County
LUNCHEON—ENTERTAINMENT
Benefit of
The Handicapped Childrens Fund
of
X Charity
Readings by GASTON
Noted Lecturer and Author
THE Z COUNTRY CLUB
Tuesday, October 31, 1967
12:00 Noon $5.50 Donation

While the ticket does not specifically state that the amount is tax deductible, the characterization of the $5.50 price of the ticket as a "donation" is highly misleading in that it is done in a context which suggests that the price of the ticket is a charitable contribution and, therefore, tax deductible. On the facts recited, no part of the payment is deductible, since there is no showing that any part of the price of the ticket is in fact a gift of an amount in excess of the fair market value of the luncheon and entertainment.

Example 7:

In support of its summer festival program of 10 free public concerts, the *M* Symphony, a charitable organization, mails out brochures soliciting contributions from its patrons. The brochure recites the purposes and activities

Appendix 24–1 *(continued)*

of the organization, and as an inducement to contributors states that:

"A contribution of $20 entitles the donor to festival membership for the season and free admission to the premiere showing of the motion picture * * * starring * * * and * * *.

Cocktails—7:00 P.M.   Curtain—8:15 P.M.

This special premiere performance is not open to the public.

* * * * *

"Your contribution will benefit an important community function; it also entitles you to choice reserved seats for all summer festival concerts and events."

The envelope furnished for mailing in payments contains the following:

"Enclosed is my tax-deductible membership contribution to the M Symphony summer concert program in the amount of $_____.

"☐ Send me _____ tickets to the May 1 premiere performance.

"☐ I do not desire to attend the special premiere performance for festival members, but I am enclosing my contribution."

A taxpayer mails in a payment of $20, indicating on the envelope form that he desires a ticket to the premiere showing of the film.

No part of the payment is deductible as a charitable contribution. Payment of the $20 entitles an individual not only to the privilege of attending the cocktail party and the premiere showing of the film, but also the privilege of choice reserved seats for the summer festival concerts. Under the circumstances, no part of the payment qualifies as a gift, since there is no showing that the payment exceeds the fair market value of the privileges involved. Even if a "contributor" indicates he does not desire to attend the cocktail party and premiere showing of the film, it would still be incorrect for the organization to characterize the $20 payment as a deductible charitable contribution, since under these circumstances the fair market value of the privilege of having choice reserved seats for attending the concerts would, in all likelihood, exceed the amount of the payment. However, if the taxpayer wishes to support the M Symphony, and advises the organization that he does not desire the ticket to the premiere and does not want seats reserved for him, the amount contributed to M is deductible as a charitable contribution.

Example 8:

In order to raise funds, W Charity plans a theater party consisting of admission to a premiere showing of a motion picture and an after-theater buffet. The advertising material and tickets to the theater party designate $5 as an admission charge and $10 as a gift to W Charity. The established admission charge for premiere showings of motion pictures in the locality is $5.

Notwithstanding W's representations respecting the amount designated as a gift, the specified $10 does not qualify as a deductible charitable contribution because W's allocation fails to take into account the value of admission to the buffet dinner.

Example 9:

The X Charity sponsors a fund-raising bazaar, the articles offered for sale at the bazaar having been contributed to X by persons desiring to support X's charitable programs.

The prices for the articles sold at the bazaar are set by a committee of X with a view to charging the full fair market value of the articles.

A taxpayer who purchases articles at the bazaar is not entitled to a charitable contribution deduction for any portion of the amount paid to X for such articles. This is true even though the articles sold at the bazaar are acquired and sold without cost to X and the total proceeds of the sale of the articles are used by X exclusively for charitable purposes.

Example 10:

The members of the M Charity undertake a program of selling Christmas cards to raise funds for the organization's activities. The cards are purchased at wholesale prices and are resold at prices comparable to the prices at which similar cards are sold by regular retail outlets. On the receipts furnished to its customers, the difference between the amount received from the customer and the wholesale cost of the cards to the organization is designated by the organization as a tax-deductible charitable contribution.

The organization is in error in designating this difference as a tax-deductible charitable contribution. The amount paid by customers in excess of the wholesale cost of the cards to the organization is not a gift to the organization, but instead is part of the purchase price or the fair market value of the cards at the retail level.

Example 11:

In support of the annual fund-raising drive of the X Charity, a local department store agrees to award a transistor radio to each person who contributes $50 or more to the charity. The retail value of the radio is $15. B receives one of the transistor radios as a result of his contribution of $100 to X. Only $85 of B's payment to X qualifies as a deductible charitable contribution. In determining the portion of the payment to a charitable organization which is deductible as a charitable contribution in these circumstances, the fair market value of any consideration received for the payment from any source must be subtracted from the total payment.

Example 12:

To assist the Y Charity in the promotion of a Halloween Ball to raise funds for Y's activities, several individuals in the community agree to pay the entire costs of the event, including the costs of the orchestra, publicity, rental of the ballroom, refreshments, and any other necessary expenses. Various civic organizations and clubs agree to undertake the sale of tickets for the dance. The publicity and solicitations for the sale of the tickets emphasize the fact that the entire cost of the ball is being borne by anonymous patrons of Y and by the other community groups, and that the entire gross receipts from the sale of the tickets, therefore, will go to Y Charity. The price of the tickets, however, is set at the fair market value of admission to the event.

No part of the amount paid for admission to the dance is a gift. Therefore, no part is deductible as a charitable contribution. The fact that the event is conducted entirely without cost to Y Charity and that the full amount of the admission charge goes directly to Y for its uses has no bearing on the deductibility of the amounts paid for admission, but does have a bearing on the deductibility of the amounts paid by the anonymous patrons of the event. The test is not the cost of the event to Y, but the fair market value of the consideration received by the purchaser of the ticket or other privileges for his payment.

Appendix 24–2

Exempt Organizations Charitable Solicitations Compliance Improvement
Program Study Checksheet – Phase II

I. Entity Data	National Office Hotline Phone for:

1. Name of Organization:

2. Street Address:

3. City, State, ZIP Code:

National Office Hotline Phone for:
- Project and Checksheet Questions – 566–6181
- Technical (fundraising) Questions – 566–4332

4. EIN: |___|___|___| – |___|___|___|___|___|___|___| 5. Type of Return: ☐ Form 990 ☐ Form 990–PF

6. Tax Period: |___|___|___|___|___| 7. Foundation Code: |___|___|___| 8. Classification Code: |___|___|___|___|

9. Activity Codes   Per EO/BMF: _____ _____ _____
Per Exam: _____ _____ _____

10. Income/Asset Codes   Per EO/BMF: ___/___
Per Exam: ___/___

II. Fundraising Activities Present?

11. Did you find the organization was involved in fundraising activities?   ☐ Yes   ☐ No

[Based upon the response to this item, please refer to "Note 2" in Attachment 5 of the Manual Supplement for further instruction for the completion of this checksheet.]

12. What was the nature of the fundraising activities? [Check the applicable activities listed below and give a brief description of the activities in the space below or complete the descriptive "items" mentioned which appear later on this checksheet.]

Auction	☐	Fashion Show	☐
Musical Concert	☐	Theatrical Show	☐
Spectator Sporting Event	☐	Thrift Store [or similar activity (items 56 – 60)]	☐
Luncheon, Dinner, or Banquet	☐	Membership Drive	☐
Carnival, Bazaar, or Fair	☐	Awards Ceremony	☐
Raffle, Lottery, or Sweepstakes	☐	Cultural Exhibition	☐
Las Vegas or Monte Carlo Nights	☐	Annual Solicitation Campaign	☐
Bingo [and any other Games of Chance (items 39–46)]	☐	Other (specify):[ ]	☐
Charity Ball	☐		

[Describe activity here.]

13. Did the organization conduct any fundraising activities designed to solicit payments which were intended to be, in part, a gift and, in part, a payment for admission to the fundraising event, participation in the fundraising event, or for other benefits conferred on the donor?
[If "Yes", please refer to items 63–67].   ☐ Yes   ☐ No   ☐ N/A

14. Did the charity receive any "noncash" contributions with a fair market value greater than $500 from any donor(s)? [If "Yes", please refer to items 70 – 76].   ☐ Yes   ☐ No   ☐ N/A

15. Did the charity sell, exchange, consume or otherwise dispose of any "noncash" contribution(s) within two years of receipt of the "noncash" property? [If "Yes", please refer to items 70–69].   ☐ Yes   ☐ No   ☐ N/A

III. General Information on Fundraising Activities

16. If the charity engaged in fundraising activities, complete items 17–25. Otherwise, enter an "X" in "N/A".   ☐ N/A

17. Did the charity acknowledge receipt of the cash donation in writing?   ☐ Yes   ☐ No   ☐ N/A

18. Did the charity acknowledge receipt of the noncash donation in writing?   ☐ Yes   ☐ No   ☐ N/A

19. Was an outside/professional fundraiser hired to conduct the fundraising program?
[If "Yes", please refer to items 27–37].   ☐ Yes   ☐ No   ☐ N/A

Form 9215 (1-90)   Page –1–   Department of the Treasury – Internal Revenue Service

TRUTH IN FUND-RAISING

Appendix 24–2 *(continued)*

Charitable Solicitations Compliance Improvement Program Study Checksheet – Phase II

III. General Information on Fundraising Activities (Continued)

	Yes	No	N/A
20. Did the charity maintain any record(s) of the names and addresses of the donors?	☐	☐	☐
21. Did the charity maintain sample copies of the solicitation materials, advertisements of the fundraising event(s), tickets, receipts, or other evidence of payment received in connection with the fundraising activity(ies)?	☐	☐	☐
22. Did the charity maintain copies of script, transcripts, or other evidence of on–air solicitations for TV and/or radio fundraising solicitations?	☐	☐	☐
23. Did the charity indicate in membership literature or other written evidence that the "cost" of membership dues was tax deductible?	☐	☐	☐
24. If "Yes" to Item 23, were there any benefits associated with joining the charity as a member?	☐	☐	☐

25. Describe in the space below the benefits that a new member would receive in return for his/her membership contribution:

IV. Outside/Professional Fundraiser

26. If the charity hired an outside/professional fundraiser, complete Items 27–37. Otherwise, enter an "X" in "N/A", and go to Item 38. . . . . ☐ N/A

27. Who was the professional fundraiser? [Check the box at the right that best applies and provide the name and address]:

- For-Profit Entity . . . ☐
- Individual . . . . ☐
- Tax Exempt Entity . . ☐
- Other . . . . ☐
- N/A . . . . ☐

28. Please provide the following information, as it relates to the fundraising activities of the "outside" fundraiser:

28(a). Total number of mailings .... _____

28(b). Total aggregate cost of the mailings .... $_____

28(c). Total number of donor responses to the mailings .... _____

28(d). Total dollar amount of contributions generated from the mailings .... $_____

	Yes	No
29. Was there a written agreement between the charity and the professional fundraiser? If "Yes", attach a copy of the agreement.	☐	☐
30. If "Yes" to Item 29, was the compensation arrangement based upon a flat fee or as a percentage of the income generated by the professional fundraiser? Please describe the arrangement in the space provided:	☐	☐
31. Was the charity created by an owner, officer, director, trustee, or employee of the professional fundraiser? If "Yes", please specify in the space provided:	☐	☐
32. Is any officer, director, trustee, or employee of the charity employed by or connected with the professional fundraiser in any ownership of business, investment venture, or family relationship? If "Yes", please explain in the space below:	☐	☐

Appendix 24–2 *(continued)*

Charitable Solicitations Compliance Improvement Program Study Checksheet – Phase II

IV. Outside/Professional Fundraiser (Continued)

	Yes	No
33. Did the charity have "approval" rights, as client of the professional fundraiser, over any of the fundraising program implemented by the professional fundraiser?	☐	☐
34. Did the professional fundraiser have check "writing" authority?	☐	☐
35. Did the professional fundraiser have check "cashing" authority?	☐	☐
36. Did the charity retain copies of fundraising materials prepared by the professional fundraiser? If "Yes", please attach copies of the fundraising materials.	☐	☐
37. Did the charity meet the "commensurate test" as set forth in Rev. Rul. 64–182?	☐	☐

V. Bingo and Other Games of Chance

	Yes	No	N/A
38. If the charity conducted bingo or other games of chance, complete items 39–48. Otherwise, enter an "X" in "N/A", then go to item 49.			☐ N/A
39. Did the bingo activity meet the tests of IRC 513(f)(2), specifically including the requirements that the activity meet the definition of a "Bingo game"; the conduct of which is not an activity ordinarily carried out on a commercial basis; and the conduct of which does not violate any state or local law?	☐	☐	☐
40. If the tests under IRC 513(f)(2) were not met, did the charity timely file Form 990–T?	☐	☐	☐
41. If "No" to Item 40, did you secure the delinquent Form 990–T?	☐	☐	☐
42. Did the games of chance, other than bingo, take place in North Dakota? If "Yes", go to Item 43. If "No", go to Item 44.	☐	☐	☐
43. If the games of chance, other than bingo, were conducted in North Dakota, and the gross income was not reported on a filed Form 990–T, did the organization meet all the tests set forth in Section 311 of the Deficit Reduction Act of 1984? If "No", go to Item 44. [These tests specifically include the requirements that the games must be conducted by non-profit entities; that there must have been a state law (originally enacted on 4–22–77) in effect on 10–5–83, which permitted the conduct of such games of chance; and the games must not violate state or local law.]	☐	☐	☐
44. Did the charity timely file Form 990–T?	☐	☐	☐
45. If "No" to Item 44, did you secure the delinquent Form 990–T?	☐	☐	☐
46. Was the income from either bingo or any other games of chance subject to any of the UBI exceptions, e.g. volunteer labor, as described in IRC 513(a)? If "Yes", please specify the exception in the space provided.	☐	☐	☐
47. Did the charity timely file the proper information returns (Form 1099–MISC) and withholding returns (Form W2–G) for the winners of bingo and other games of chance?	☐	☐	☐
48. Did the charity hire outside contractors to specifically operate bingo and other games of chance?	☐	☐	☐

Appendix 24–2 (continued)

Charitable Solicitations Compliance Improvement Program Study Checksheet – Phase II

VI. Travel Tours

	Yes	No	N/A
49. If the charity conducted travel tours, complete Items 50–54. Otherwise, enter an "X" in "N/A", then go to Item 55.			☐ N/A
50. Did the promotional travel literature and/or other written documentation indicate that the tours were educational? [Please attach copies of the tour literature or documentation.]	☐ Yes	☐ No	☐ N/A
51. Did the promotional travel literature and/or other written documentation contain discussions of any social/recreational aspects of the tour?	☐ Yes	☐ No	☐ N/A
52. Did the charity have a contract or do business with a for–profit travel agency?	☐ Yes	☐ No	☐ N/A
53. If "Yes" to Item 52, did the charity receive any fee from the travel agency? If "Yes", please explain in the space below:	☐ Yes	☐ No	☐ N/A

54. Please indicate if the charity was related to the for–profit travel agency by means of:

54(a). Sharing the same address or building . . . . ☐
54(b). Sharing the same office space, equipment, or personnel . . . . ☐
54(c). Creator of charity and owner of for–profit entity . . . . ☐
54(d). Officer, director, trustee, or employee of the charity and the travel agency . . . . ☐
54(e). Presence of family ties between the charity and travel agency . . . . ☐
54(f). No Relationship exists between charity and travel agency . . . . ☐
54(g). Other, specify:[ ] . . . . ☐

VII. Thrift Store or Similar Type Activity

	Yes	No	N/A
55. If the charity operated a thrift or "second–hand" store, complete Items 56–60. Otherwise, enter an "X" in "N/A", then go to Item 61.			☐ N/A
56. Did the charity solicit used clothing, furniture, etc. from donors for resale by a for–profit entrepreneur?	☐ Yes	☐ No	☐ N/A
57. Did the charity receive compensation from the for–profit entrepreneur? If "Yes", please describe the terms of the compensation agreement in the space below, i.e. flat fee, percent of revenues, etc.:	☐ Yes	☐ No	☐ N/A
58. Was there a co–venture, partnership, or similar type arrangement between the charity and the thrift store or similar type operation? If "Yes", please describe the arrangement in the space below and provide the name and address of the other entity:	☐ Yes	☐ No	☐ N/A
59. Did the charity receive any new goods from corporate inventories designated as surplus or not saleable by the corporation?	☐ Yes	☐ No	☐ N/A
60. If "Yes" to Item 59, please describe the goods received, including the fair market value and use made of the goods:	☐ Yes	☐ No	☐ N/A

Appendix 24–2 *(continued)*

Charitable Solicitations Compliance Improvement Program Study Checksheet – Phase II

VIII. Goods or Services Received in Exchange for a Charitable Contribution

61. If the charity gives goods or services for charitable donations, complete items 62-67. Otherwise, enter an "X" in "N/A", then go to item 68. . . . . . ☐ N/A

62. What was the nature of the benefits, goods, or services given to the donor? Please indicate those goods or services that apply and give a brief description in the space below:

62(a). Retail merchandise . . . . ☐

62(b). New and donated merchandise received at an auction . . . . ☐

62(c). Tickets for a raffle, lottery, bingo, or other game of chance . . . . ☐

62(d). Tuition at a school or other educational institution . . . . ☐

62(e). Travel or other transportation . . . . ☐

62(f). Tickets to an athletic, cultural, entertainment, or other event . . . . ☐

62(g). Discounts on goods or services . . . . ☐

62(h). Free subscriptions to publications . . . . ☐

62(i). Preferential seating at a college or university athletic event . . . . ☐

62(j). Other, specify:[   ] . . . . ☐
Description:

	Yes	No	N/A
63. Did the charity disclose the deductible amount or make reference to deductibility in its solicitations and/or promotional literature? [Please attach representative copies of the literature.]	☐	☐	☐
64. Did the charity disclose the deductible amount or refer to deductibility in any thank you letter, receipt, ticket, or other written receipt? [Please attach representative copies of receipts.]	☐	☐	☐
65. Did the charity disclose the deductible amount or make reference to deductibility in any other manner, e.g. via oral communication? If "Yes", please select the item that best describes the manner of oral communication: 65(a). Radio . . . . ☐ 65(b). Television . . . . ☐ 65(c). Door-to-door solicitation . . . . ☐ 65(d). Other, specify:[ ] . . . . ☐	☐	☐	☐
66. Was the charity aware of Rev. Rul. 67-246 prior to the examination?	☐	☐	☐
67. Did the charity receive Publication 1391 in the mail in 1988? If "No", please provide a copy of the publication to the charity.	☐	☐	☐

IX. Noncash Contributions

68. If the charity received or disposed of any noncash charitable contributions, complete items 69-80. Otherwise, enter an "X" in "N/A", then go to item 81. ☐ N/A

69. If the charity received any noncash contributions in the year examined, complete items 70-74. Otherwise, enter an "X" in "N/A". . . . . ☐ N/A

70. Please attach a listing (if more than one item) of all noncash charitable contributions, whose fair market value (FMV) exceeded $500, given to the charity during the year examined. The listing should include the following:
70(a). Name and Address of donor:
70(b). Item Name:
70(c). Description of item:
70(d). Date item Received:
70(e). FMV: $

71. Who determined the FMV of the contributed noncash property? Select one below:

71(a). Donor . . . . ☐

71(b). Charity . . . . ☐

71(c). Independent Appraiser . . . . ☐

71(d). Other, specify:[   ] . . . . ☐

Appendix 24–2 (*continued*)

Charitable Solicitations Compliance Improvement Program Study Checksheet – Phase II

IX. Noncash Contributions (Continued)

	Yes	No	N/A
72. For contributed noncash property with a FMV of $5,000 or less, did the charity provide the donor with a receipt containing the following information? 72(a). Donee name, 72(b). Date and location of the contributed property, and 72(c). A description of the property in detail, including its value.	☐	☐	☐
73. Was there any kind of an agreement between the charity and donor concerning the use, sale, or other disposition of the property? If "Yes", please explain below:	☐	☐	☐
74. Did the charity complete Section B, Part I of Form 8283? (If "No", please explain below. If "Yes", complete Items 75 and 76.)	☐	☐	☐
75. Was Form 8283 signed by a properly authorized official of the charity?	☐	☐	☐
76. Did the charity retain a copy of Form 8283?	☐	☐	☐

77. If the charity disposed of any noncash property within two years of its receipt, complete Items 78–80. Otherwise, enter an "X" in "N/A". . . . . ☐ N/A

78. Please attach a listing (if more than one item) of all noncash donated property, valued at $500 or more, that was sold, exchanged, consumed, or otherwise disposed of during the year under examination, which the charity received within two years of the disposal date. The listing should include:

78(a). Description of the donated noncash property disposed of:
78(b). Date the charity received the property:
78(c). Date the property was disposed of:

	Yes	No	N/A
79. Did the charity timely file Form 8282, Noncash Charitable Contributions Donee Information?	☐	☐	☐
80. Did the charity furnish a copy of Form 8282 to the donor of the noncash property?	☐ Yes	☐ No	☐ N/A

X. Penalty Assessments

81. If any penalty was assessed against the charity, complete Item 82. Otherwise, enter an "X" in "N/A", then go to Item 83. . . . . ☐ N/A

82. Select the penalty(ies) which you assessed against the charity and give a brief explanation below:

82(a). § 6651(a)(1) – Failure to file tax return . . . . ☐
82(b). § 6652(a)(2) – Failure to pay tax . . . . ☐
82(c). § 6652(c)(1)(A)(ii) – Failure to file complete or accurate EO information return . . . . ☐
82(d). § 6661 – Substantial understatement of liability . . . . ☐
82(e). § 6700 – Promoting abusive tax shelters . . . . ☐
82(f). § 6701 – Aiding and abetting understatements of tax liability . . . . ☐
82(g). § 6721 – Failure to file certain information returns . . . . ☐
82(h). § 6722 – Failure to file certain payee statements . . . . ☐
82(i). § 6723 – Failure to include correct information on an information return or payee statement . . . . . ☐
82(j). Other, specify(§   ) . . . . ☐

Please explain the reason for the assessment and state the amount of the penalty:

Appendix 24–2 *(continued)*

Charitable Solicitations Compliance Improvement Program Study Checksheet – Phase II

XI. Form 990/990–PF Return Information

REVENUE			Per Return	Per Exam
83. Contributions, gifts, and grants received:			$ ___	$ ___
84. Membership dues and assessments:			$ ___	$ ___
85. Special fundraising events & activities:	Per Return	Per Exam		
85(a). Gross Revenue:	$ ___	$ ___	[ ]	[ ]
85(b). Minus – Direct Expenses:	$ ___	$ ___	[ ]	[ ]
85(c). Net Income:			$ ___	$ ___
86. Total Revenue:			$ ___	$ ___

EXPENSES	Per Return	Per Exam
87. Program services:	$ ___	$ ___
88. Management and General:	$ ___	$ ___
89. Fundraising:		
89(a). Professional fundraising:	$ ___	$ ___
89(b). Total Fundraising:	$ ___	$ ___
90. Total Expenses:	$ ___	$ ___
91. Excess (deficit) for the year:	$ ___	$ ___

XII. Control Data

92. Project Code: |9 |0 |2 | 93. District Name: ___   94. KDO: |_|_|

95. Examiner Name: ___   96. Examiner Grade: |_|_| 97. Date:

98. Time on Case: ___   99. Principal Issue Code: |_|_| 100. Disposal Code: |_|_|

101. Group Manager's Name and Telephone Number: 102. Date:

XIII. REMARKS

103. Remarks [Enter Item Number to which remarks refer and use the space below for general remarks.]:

CHAPTER TWENTY-FIVE

Employment Taxes

Employment taxes and associated payroll costs, such as workers compensation and health insurance, often comprise 10 to 30% of an exempt organization's payroll. These taxes represent a substantial expense to most EOs and there is always a temptation to classify a worker as an independent contractor, in order to avoid such costs.

25.1 CHANGE IN IRS EXAMINATION POLICY

Until 1983, exempt organizations were exempt from Social Security taxes, and their employees were only eligible to be covered if the organization elected to participate in the system. Until 1989, IRS exempt organization examiners had no authority to look at employment taxes. For these reasons, EOs could ignore the complexities of employment taxes, until the IRS announced its intention to emphasize employment tax issues.

Since 1978, the IRS's hands have been tied by a congressionally-mandated "safe harbor" that prevents IRS reclassification of workers for an entity that uses some reasonable basis for its policy and files information returns reporting compensation to nonemployees. An organization is presumed to be correct if it relies upon IRS precedent, long-standing industry practice, or a prior IRS audit. Generally, EOs have operated under this safe harbor. However, the General Accounting Office and the Treasury Department are actively looking for ways to enhance collections of income taxes from independent contractors, so new legislation and IRS pronouncements can be expected.

25.2 DISTINCTIONS BETWEEN EMPLOYEES AND INDEPENDENT CONTRACTORS

Whether a worker is an employee or an independent contractor is a factual question based on common law, which often requires a detailed analysis. The case law and rulings provide some guidance, and the IRS has developed a 20-factor test.[1] IRS Form SS-8, Determination of Employee Work Status for Purposes of Federal Employment Taxes and Income Tax Withholding, reflects the twenty factors Appendix 25–1. The criteria developed by the courts and the IRS are briefly capsulized in Checklist 25–1 Employee vs. Independent Contractor Status. There are a variety of complex factors involved.

(a) Employees

Employees are typically subject to tighter employer controls than independent contractors are: hours of work are regular and specified; the place of work is the employer's; compensation is regular and continuing; and tools, training, and work supplies are normally furnished by the employer, among other benefits and advantages. Employees are given paid vacations and accrue pension and sick pay benefits, and are generally thought to have a more secure position than independent contractors.

The term "contract worker" is often misleading. Typically, workers hired on a part-time or temporary basis are given this title, and are often not treated as employees, partly because they do not possess certain advantages of employees. Nonetheless, the fact that a worker is not hired for a permanent position does *not* determine his or her status as an employee, and most such workers are employees subject to withholding.

(b) Independent Contractors

True independent contractors are often hired by EOs. As the title implies, independent contractors work when they please, use their own tools, have independent professional standing, and bear a risk of loss if the job is not

[1]Reg. §31.3401(c)-1(a) and (d); Rev. Rul. 87-41, 1987-1 C.B. 296; see also *Revival of the Independent Contractor Issue*, American Institute of Certified Public Accountants, September 1991.

Checklist 25–1

EMPLOYEE VS. INDEPENDENT CONTRACTORS STATUS

Revenue Ruling 87-41 lists the primary characteristics distinguishing employees from independent contractors. These characteristics are listed on this checklist. Whichever blank best describes the predominant characteristic of a worker or position is to be checked. There is no specific mathematical test, although more than one-half of the checkmarks on either side is a strong indication. The facts and circumstances of each payee – payor relationship should be analyzed. Classifying a worker as an employee is seldom challenged; finding justification for treating one as independent is more troublesome. The most common reason for making the distinction is to identify persons — the employees — who are subject to federal income tax withholding and unemployment taxes. Independent contractors are abbreviated as "ICs"

Instruction and Training

☐ Employees are required to comply with instructions as to when, where, and how work is performed, and their training is provided either by formal program or work supervision.

☐ ICs are free to perform work according to their own professional standards, use their own methods, and receive no training from purchasers of their services.

Payment Terms

☐ Employees are paid by the hour, week, or month on a regular, indefinite, and continuous basis. Employees' business expenses are paid. Fringe benefits are usually provided.

☐ ICs are often paid by the engagement with a fee often calculated without regard to time spent. ICs are not paid for excess time to perform task nor given paid vacation or sick leave. ICs pay their own expenses.

Engagement Terms

☐ Employer has the right to discharge an employee; control is exercised with threat of dismissal. Employees have the right to quit without incurring liability.

☐ ICs may suffer damages if work is not performed as contracted. Payment is still due if the IC is fired.

Relation to Entity

☐ Employees' services are an integral part of the ongoing success and continuation of the organization. Services are

☐ ICs consult on a per job, limited term, or special project basis. ICs can hire and pay assistants to perform the

Checklist 25–1 (*continued*)

EMPLOYEE VS. INDEPENDENT CONTRACTORS STATUS

☐ rendered personally by employees, who work only for, have loyalty to, and do not compete with the employer. Employees are bonded and provided workers compensation.

☐ work. ICs' services are available to the general public on a regular basis. Some ICs work under a company name.

Work Place and Hours

☐ Employees work on business premises or are physically directed and supervised by employer. Hours of work are established by employer.

☐ ICs may work at their own places of business, and usually set their own time for performing work.

Investment

☐ Employees are dependent upon employer for tools and facilities, and usually make no investment in the job. Employees bear no risk of loss for financial costs of employer.

☐ ICs buy their own tools, hire workers, pay licensing fees, and are responsible for costs of engagement. ICs bear financial risk of losing money.

completed satisfactorily or within the prescribed time. Outside accountants, computer consultants, fundraising advisors, and consulting psychologists are typical examples of independent workers.[2] No vacation or sick pay is provided no taxes are withheld, pension eligibility is not furnished, and the engagement is for a limited time period for a specific task.

Form SS-8 can be completed for each contractor about which there is any question of status. (See Appendix 25-1.) Form SS-8 can be used to show that the organization made a good faith effort to determine a worker's proper classification. The form's length and the variety of criteria developed by the IRS indicate the subjective nature of the distinction and the difficulty that may occur in identifying the proper category for a worker.

The terms of engagement should validate a worker's status as an independent contractor. At the minimum, three important documents evidence the

[2]See Priv. Ltr. Rul. 9231011 regarding a part-time grant proposed writer and Priv. Ltr. Rul. 9227025 about a food bank manager—both deemed employees.

Exhibit 25–1

INDEPENDENT CONTRACTOR AGREEMENT

In consideration of payment by _____ [name of employer] _____

Fixed fee   _____

Hourly rate $ __ per hour times __ hours =   _____

Reimbursible expenses:

_____   _____

_____   _____

Payments will be made monthly, based upon invoices submitted by you, along with receipts and other documentation for reimbursible expenses agreed to.

For consideration, you agree to perform the following work:

_____

_____

_____

In consideration of payment by [name of employer], you agree that you are an independent contractor, not an employee, agent, or representative of the company. You are responsible for all federal and state payroll taxes and insurance. You — on behalf of yourself, your assigns, and your estate — waive and release any and all claims or rights whatsoever you may have against us. This agreement may be terminated by either party at any time, except that you will be paid for any unpaid services properly chargeable to us prior to termination. In acknowledgment of our understandings, we have both signed below.

By: _____   By: _____

Date: _____   Date: _____

---

arrangement and prove that the person is not an employee:

1. A contract or other type of engagement letter with the contractor (see Exhibit 25-1) describing the respective responsibilities and terms of the contract, including three important elements:

   - The engaging company does not essentially control the work product of the independent contractor;

   - The contractor cannot be fired as long as the work is performed to specifications and all obligations are met; and

   - The contractor has the right to hire and fire assistants.

2. A signed Form W-9, Request for Taxpayer Identification Number and Certification (Appendix 25–2) shows that the contractor claims exemption from withholding and that the organization is therefore not responsible for backup withholding. This step also obtains the federal identification number for purposes of preparing Form 1099.

3. An invoice or periodic billing statement evidences the independence of the contractor. The billing should appear professional and support the organization's position that the worker is independent.

25.3 SPECIAL TYPES OF PAYMENTS

The character of payments made by exempt organizations to individuals—whether employees or independent contractors—is basically governed by the same rules as those applied to nonexempt persons and businesses. There are a few exceptions, but the rules for payroll tax deposits, annual reporting, and taxability of pensions paid to retirees are mostly the same.

(a) Employee Fringe Benefits

Payments made on behalf of employees for benefits, expense reimbursements, and deferred compensation are, as a general rule, not taxed to an exempt organization's employees. The rules governing the taxability of such payments are the same as for employees working for nonexempt entities. For example, an EO employee's car allowance is reportable on Form W-2 unless the employee submits an accounting for the mileage.

An EO can adopt a cafeteria plan to provide day care, tuition, and other benefits.[3] Health insurance and medical reimbursement plans can be established for employees.[4] Most types of qualified pension plans, including defined benefit, defined contribution, thrift, and simplified employee plans (SEP) can be provided for EO employees. A "401(k)" plan cannot be adopted by an exempt,[5] but the similar "403(b)" plan can be. Special limitations are placed upon deferred compensation arrangements.[6] A thorough discussion of pension benefits is beyond the scope of this book.

(b) Volunteer Fringe Benefits

An EO may pay certain expenses on behalf of its volunteers, and may reimburse its volunteers for expenses they incur on behalf of the organization in conducting its projects. After some years of question, the IRS has proposed regulations providing that a "bona fide volunteer" who performs services (including services as a director) for an exempt organization or for a federal, state, or local

[3] IRC §125.
[4] IRC §106.
[5] IRC §401(k)(4)(B).
[6] IRC §457.

governmental unit, is deemed to have a profit motive for purposes of IRC §162.[7] This means that such expenses, up to the value of services rendered, are not taxable to the individual volunteer and are not reportable by the EO. Of particular importance to some EOs, the regulation provides the example of officer and director liability insurance. Premiums were previously reportable as compensation to the officers, directors, and volunteers.

(c) Fellowships, Scholarship Grants, and Awards

Although it seems incongruous with the motivation for making grants to individuals, certain individual grants must be reported to the IRS on Form 1099 or Form W-2, and taxes must be withheld as outlined below.

Tuition and fees. A scholarship grant is fragmented into two parts. The portion awarded for payment of tuition and related expenses required for enrollment in an educational institution (such as books, fees, supplies and equipment) is not taxable to the recipient, nor is it reportable to the IRS by the organization. Such payments are called "qualified scholarship" payments and are specifically excluded from gross income of a person that is a candidate for a degree.[8]

Room and board. Payments for room, board, travel, and any other expenses are includible in income after the 1986 Tax Reform Act. For some reason, however, such taxable payments are not reportable to the IRS as income unless they represent compensation.[9] The 1991 instructions to Form 1099 clearly state, "DO NOT use this form to report scholarship or fellowship grants." They go on to say, "Other taxable scholarship or fellowship payments are not required to be reported by you to IRS on any form."[10] In 1987, the IRS said that it intended to promulgate regulations on the matter, but to date, no such regulation has been finalized.

Teaching fellowships. Scholarships or fellowships paid on the condition that recipients teach, perform research, or provide other services for the institution granting the scholarship do produce taxable income.[11] Such income is considered to be wages and is reportable on Form W-2.[12] Income tax withholding is also required, although students are eligible to claim a student exemption. Social Security taxes are likewise due to be withheld, matched, and paid unless the institution is a state or federal agency that does not participate in the Social Security system.

Awards. Prizes or awards paid to recognize someone's accomplishment are taxable to the recipient and reported on Form 1099-MISC. Only if the money is paid over to a charitable organization does the award excape taxation.[13]

Foreign grant recipients. For foreign grant recipients, the portion of a scholarship grant paid for study, training, or research in the U.S. (not including

[7] Prop. Regs. §1.132-5.
[8] IRC §117.
[9] Prop. Reg. 6041-3(q).
[10] IRS Notice 87-31, 1987-1 C.B. 475.
[11] IRC §117(c).
[12] Prog. Reg. 1.117-6(d)(4).
[13] IRC §74.

tuition and fees) is also taxable. Income tax must be withheld at the rate of 14 percent on the taxable portion.[14] Treaties may exempt certain of these payments. However, for most payments, the IRS ruled in 1989 that all payments made by U.S. grantors to persons outside the United States must be treated as U.S.-based income, subject to backup withholding.[15] A broad range of grant-making organizations have lobbied to overturn this ruling, but there has been no success as of November, 1992.

25.4 MINISTERS

Duly ordained ministers of a church hold a special place in employment tax procedures. The clergy of some sects take vows of poverty and, as a matter of religious conscience, take no compensation for their work. The procedures have also evolved to respect the need to maintain separation of church and state. The result is a set of confusing rules.

(a) Who is a Minister?

The term "minister" is defined in the Internal Revenue Code and Regulations by a job description. The Regulations provide that services provided by a minister in the exercise of his (her) ministries include:

1. Ministration of sacerdotal functions (marriage, baptism, funerals, and similar services);

2. Conduct of religious worship;

3. Conduct, control, and maintenance of religious organizations, including religious board, societies, and other integral agencies of such organizations (such as schools); and

4. Performance of teaching and administrative duties at theological seminaries.[16]

A minister need not be "ordained," but may be commissioned, licensed, appointed, or otherwise authorized by a religious organization. The important criterion is that the minister must perform religious duties within the scope and practices of a religious denomination.[17]

In a 1992 private ruling, the IRS considered whether a particular sect's "commissioned ministers" qualified for the housing allowance exclusion discussed below. The sect ordained ministers who officiated in public administration of the sacraments and led public worship. The commissioned ministers "in some circumstances lead the liturgy in prayer, read the scriptures or perform a baptism but more often served as deacon or director of Christian education."

[14] IRC §1441(b)(1).
[15] Rev. Rul. 89-67, I.R.B. 1989-20, 4.
[16] Reg. §1.1402(c)-5(b)(2).
[17] Rev. Rul. 78-301, 1978-2 C.B. 103.

The IRS found that the commissioned ministers performed full-time ministerial duties. The qualifying functions included classroom teaching; evangelizing; counseling individuals; leading Bible study groups, devotion, worship studies for youth, and a congregation's music ministry; giving the children's service at Sunday worship service; addressing the congregation in worship services; coordinating lay church workers; administering or guiding the congregation's youth ministry events; participating in ministries to those with special needs; and caring spiritually for the sick, the imprisoned, and their families.[18]

Qualifying ministers also include a probationary member of the United Methodist Church,[19] cantors of the Jewish faith,[20] and retired ministers.[21]

Not qualifying as ministers are chaplains not employed by a religious organization or its integral auxiliary. "Ministers" do not include chaplains employed to teach at a university,[22] employed at a human service organization[23] or the Veterans Administration,[24] or chaplains in the Armed Services (chaplains are commissioned officers).[25]

(b) How Ministers are Special

Ministers are in many cases classified as employees because the factors discussed in Section 25.2 are present. However, ministers are exempt from income tax and Social Security tax withholding[26] and, consequently, their earnings sometimes go unreported. Compensation for services performed as a minister may not be subject to income and the self-employment tax in situations listed below. However, if the minister is subject to one or both of these taxes, the compensation is considered to be attributable to the carrying on of a trade or business,[27] which permits the deduction of ordinary and necessary expenses in arriving at taxable income for both income (as an itemized deduction for employees) and self-employment purposes.[28]

Income tax. Any amounts paid as compensation to a minister for services are subject to income tax, just as for other individual taxpayers. If the minister is classified as an employee, the income tax liability is paid either through the estimated tax system or through voluntary income tax withholding. An employed minister receives Form W-2, in most cases reflecting only the gross wage amount. If the minister is not an employee, the tax is paid individually through the estimated income tax system, and the church reports the compensation on Form 1099.

---

[18] Priv. Ltr. Rul. 9221025.

[19] *Wingo v. Commissioner*, 89 T.C. 922 (1989).

[20] Rev. Rul. 78-301, 1978-2 C.B. 103; *D. Silverman*, 73-2 USTC ¶9546 (8th Cir. 1973), *aff'g* 57 T.C. 727 (Dec. 31,290).

[21] Rev. Rul. 63-156, 1963-2 C.B. 79.

[22] *L. D. Boyer*, 69 T.C. 521 (Dec. 34,900).

[23] Rev. Rul. 68-68, 1968-1 C.B. 51.

[24] Rev. Rul. 72-462, 1972-2 C.B. 76.

[25] Reg. §1.107-1(a).

[26] Reg. 31.3401(a)(9)-1; IRC Circular E, *Employer's Tax Guide*, For 1992, p. 20.

[27] IRC §1402(c)(2)(D).

[28] Rev. Rul. 80-110, IRB 1980-16, 10.

Housing allowances. Amounts designated by a church as housing allowance for its ministers are not taxable for income tax purposes,[29] but are subject to self-employment tax (unless the minister conscientiously objects and elects out. See Section 25.5.). The allowance must be designated in advance of its payment or provision, as evidenced by an employment contract, church budget, deacons' resolution, or similar official action. The minister must actually expend the amount provided. Any allowance not used or used for nonresidential purposes (such as a farm) is taxed.[30] The taxable amount is equal to the fair rental value of housing (including utilities and other costs). A parsonage may be furnished rent-free, or allowances may be paid to cover the parsonage utilities and other maintenance, or to cover rents, or to cover the minister's costs of individually owning and maintaining a house.

Self-employment tax. A minister's earnings are excepted from "employment" for the purpose of imposing the Social Security tax.[31] A minister is subject to the self-employment tax, unless he or she is one of the following persons:

- Members of a religious order whose members have taken vows of poverty.[32]

- Duly ordained ministers who have not taken a vow of poverty but who make an individual election out of the Social Security system on Form 4361. A statement must be signed indicating that the minister is opposed by conscience or religious principle to the acceptance of any public insurance and is so informing his or her church.

- Clergy members of a church or church-controlled organization which makes the election for its employees to be exempt from Social Security coverage pursuant to IRC §3121(w). This exemption only applies to remuneration of less than $100 per year and generally applies to "vow of poverty" situations.

25.5 CONSCIENTIOUS OBJECTORS

Religious organizations, peace groups, and other exempt organizations employ or engage individuals (other than ministers) who protest payments of federal income taxes for spiritual reasons. These conscientious objectors have traditionally protested money allocated to armaments, and harm to human beings caused by war and abortion. How should an organization respond if it is asked not to levy taxes against such an employee? What is the responsibility of the organization to the IRS? The answer is that the IRS basically holds the exempt organization responsible, but may use some leniency.

The Quakers produced answers to some of these questions when they faced a federal district court in December, 1990. The judges decided that the collection of taxes applied to all citizens equally, and did not specifically

[29] IRC §107.
[30] Reg. §1.107-1(c).
[31] IRC §3121(b)(8)(A) for purposes of the Federal Insurance Contributions Act.
[32] IRC §1402(c); see also Chapter 3.3.

regulate religious practice or beliefs. The church was therefore required to withhold the full amount of taxes from its regular employees' wages. Out of deference to the church's exercise of religious freedom, however, the court imposed no penalties for failure to withhold the taxes in question.[33]

25.6 REPORTING REQUIREMENTS

Whether paid to employees, individual contractors, or individual grant recipients, almost all payments made by exempt organizations to individuals or unincorporated entities are reportable to the IRS. Annual W-2 Form is filed for employees. Form 1099 Miscellaneous (also called an information return) is filed for most other payments to independent contractors and other nonemployees. Checklist 25–2 is used to facilitate annual compliance review.

(a) Heavy Penalties

The penalty for failure to file an information return is $50. However, if the IRS determines that a contractor should have been classified as an employee, the EO will be billed for all employment taxes that would have been payable if the worker had been classed as an employee, plus interest and penalties. Responsible parties, starting with the board members, may be assessed a penalty up to 100 percent of this amount for failure to withhold the taxes.

(b) Tax Withholding Requirements

An exempt organization is subject to the income and Social Security tax withholding system for most of its employees.[34] An individual paid less than $100 is not subject to Social Security tax withholding, but is subject to income tax withholding. Special rules apply to ministers and foreigners, as discussed above and in the special circumstances discussed below.

(c) Unemployment Tax

Only charitable organizations classified as exempt under IRC §501(c)(3) are exempt from the federal unemployment tax; all other exempt organizations are subject to such tax. Exemptions may be available in some states. In Texas, two exemptions are available, but only for charities:

1. Charities with fewer than four employees are not subject to the tax.

2. A charity may elect to be a "reimbursing employer" by agreeing to directly pay any benefits that may come due as employee claims are made.

[33]*U.S. v. Philadelphia Yearly Meeting, Religious Society of Friends*, No. 88-6386 (E.D. Pa), Dec., 19901.
[34]IRS Circular E, *Employer's Tax Guide*.

(d) Backup Withholding

The backup withholding system allows the U.S. Treasury to collect funds up front from independent contractors who potentially will not pay their taxes. Form W-9, Request for Taxpayer Identification Number and Certification (Appendix 25–2) is furnished by organizations to payment recipients. This is the same form used by banks and stockbrokers to ask individuals to verify their federal identification numbers and to claim exemption from backup withholding.

Unless the organization receives correct Social Security numbers from nonemployees receiving payments for services and from individuals receiving taxable grant or fellowship payments, income tax must be withheld from the payments. Absent completion of Form W-9 (the certificate that withholding is not required) or when there is some reason to believe that the Social Security number furnished is incorrect, a flat 20 percent of the amounts paid must be withheld and remitted. The system is designed to cause the organization to collect the tax if the individual is unable or unlikely to do so.

(e) Payroll Depository Requirements

Charities faced with tight cash flows are sometimes tempted to pay the employees the net amount of salary (less taxes) and use the tax money to pay the rent or some other pressing expense. However, the amounts withheld from an employee's salary are held in trust on behalf of the employee, so the money does not belong to the organization. The penalties for failure to pay over such taxes are steep, and the organization's board members are ultimately responsible for payment of the taxes if the organization is unable to do so. The first question which the IRS examiner will ask, and which all board members should ask themselves, is whether the employee's withheld taxes have been matched and deposited in a timely fashion.

Taxes withheld are due to be deposited in as few as three days from the date wages are paid. New depository requirements were put into effect on January 1, 1993.[35] There are now only two depository time periods, as follows:

Monthly. Employers with modest payrolls are to deposit their tax liability, including both the employee withholding and the matched FICA, by the fifteenth day following month end.

Semi-weekly. Employers whose tax liability exceeds $50,000 a year ($4,166.67 per month) deposit within three banking days of the date the tax is withheld.

(f) Other Withholding Requirements

Income taxes are imposed on gambling winnings, including prizes of all sorts won in a raffle, sweepstakes, lottery, or other contest. The rules for exempt organizations are the same as those for nonexempts.[36] A serious trap for the unsuspecting exempt is the 28 percent withholding requirement placed upon

[35] Reg. §31.6302-1(c)(1).
[36] IRC 3402.

an organization (exempt or nonexempt) awarding any prize with a value in excess of $5000 (in 1992). Form W-2G is due to be filed reporting the winnings.

Cash prizes. In the case of a cash prize, the organization must withhold the tax liability from the prize and make a net payment. For example, $200 would be withheld from a $1000 prize, resulting in a cash payment of $800. If the organization pays the winner the full $1000 without withholding the $200 tax, the organization still must pay the tax. Unless the cash is collected up front in such a case, the reported prize is increased by the imputed compensation resulting from the organization's payment of the winner's tax liability. The amount is calculated under an algebraic formula found in the regulations.[37]

Noncash prizes. Cars, trips, paintings, and other tangible merchandise won as prizes are also taxed, and income tax must be withheld if their value exceeds $5000. The value is equal to the amount a willing buyer would pay a willing seller in the normal marketplace in which such goods are sold. A car donated to a charity auction by a car dealer is not valued at the dealer's cost, but at the price at which the dealer normally sells the car.

Before releasing a prize having a value that exceeds $5000, the charity should require the winner to pay the tax. Twenty-eight (20% in 1992) percent of the prize's value should be collected by the awarding organization. The organization is obligated to pay taxes, as described above under cash prizes, whether or not the prize winner furnishes the cash.

Tuition and other bonuses. Free admission, tuition, or other valuable services must also be valued with income taxes paid, as described above. A private school conducting a raffle to award a year of free tuition to a parent is faced with a choice of diluting the gift by requiring the parent to pay the 20 percent tax, or increasing its fund-raising budget by the amount of tax it must pay on behalf of the winner.

[37] Reg. §31.3402(q)-1(d).

Checklist 25–2

EMPLOYER TAX REQUIREMENTS

Nonprofit organization employers are subject to the same rules that govern for-profit employers, including rules administered by the Department of Labor, workers compensation statutes, the Employee Retirement Insurance Security Act (ERISA) rules, and federal and state employment taxes. Since the costs of employee benefits range from 10 to 30 percent of direct payroll costs, these matters deserve close attention. The most severe penalties in the Internal Revenue Code are imposed upon failure to pay over employment taxes.

☐ 1. Does the organization have a policy for distinguishing between employees and independent contractors?

   a. Verify satisfaction of at least four factors in Checklist 25–1, Employee vs. Independent Contractor Status. _____

Checklist 25–2 *(continued)*

EMPLOYER TAX REQUIREMENTS

    b. Review questions on Form SS-8, Information for Use in Determining Whether a Worker Is an Employee for Federal Employment Taxes and Income Tax Withholding.   ____

    c. Does the organization have a contract with independent contractors? (See Exhibit 25–1.)

    d. Have Social Security numbers been secured?   ____

    e. Are invoices obtained from independent contractors to prove their professionalism?   ____

    f. Is a signed Form W-9 on file for each (Appendix 25–2)?   ____

☐ 2. Are meals, cars, tuition, or housing allowances furnished to employees?

    Determine whether they are reportable compensation and whether withholding is required.

☐ 3. Does the pension plan adhere to ERISA rules?

☐ 4. Is Form 5500, 5500C, or 5500R required for the pension plan?

☐ 5. Are the terms of any qualified or nonqualified deferred compensation plan being adhered to?

☐ 6. Do Consolidated Omnibus Budget Reconciliation Act (COBRA) rules entitle former employees to continued medical benefit coverage?

☐ 7. Is workers compensation coverage required?

☐ 8. Verify adherence to federal withholding requirements. Study IRS Circular E, Employer's Tax Guide, for filing requirements and an excellent chart on wages subject to or exempt from taxes. The types of employment taxes are:

    a. Income tax withholding. Most wages are subject to this tax, but certain ministers, members of religious orders, student workers, and fellowship or grant recipients are exempt.   ____

    b. Social Security tax. Review Circular E chart; wages over $100 are taxable.   ____

    c. Federal unemployment tax. §501(c)(3) organizations are exempt from this tax. Several types of compensation subject to income tax are also exempt. See Circular E.   ____

Checklist 25–2 (*continued*)

EMPLOYER TAX REQUIREMENTS

☐ 9. Verify timely filing of the following IRS reports:

    a. Form 940, federal unemployment tax report.
       due January 31 (Form 940 is not filed by §501(c)(3)
       organizations.)   ____

    b. Form 941, employer's quarterly federal tax return.
       due January 31
       due April 30
       due July 31
       due October 31   ____

    c. W-2 Forms for all employees.
       due January 31   ____

    d. W-3 Form to IRS with copies of W-2s.
       due February 28   ____

    e. W-4 placed in each employee's file.   ____

    f. Form 1099-MISC for all independent contractors.   ____

    g. Form W-2G Prizes and Awards   ____

    h. Form W-2P Statement for Recipients of Pensions.   ____

☐ 10. Verify timely deposit of federal employment taxes.

    a. Taxes deposited by fifteenth of next month following wage
       payment;   ____

    b. Tax deposited biweekly for employers whose tax for prior year
       exceeded $50,000.   ____

☐ 11. Is the EO subject to unemployment taxes?

    a. On the federal level, only 501(c)(3)s are exempt.

    b. On the state level, obtain instructions from the employment
       commission of the state where the worker is employed. The
       rules differ by state.

    c. Many states exempt 501(c)(3) EOs with fewer than four
       employees.

    d. A "reimbursing" or self-insured employer status may be avail-
       able. In Texas the procedure is:

    A new organization must first obtain an account number by filing
    a status report. Within 45 days of notification of the number, a
    letter requesting classification as a reimbursing employer is filed.

Checklist 25–2 (*continued*)

EMPLOYER TAX REQUIREMENTS

Employers currently paying the tax can elect to become reimbursing by making a written request by November 15, to be effective for the next year. Employers currently classified as reimbursing can opt out by filing a written request by November 30, to be effective for the next year. The change in status is effective for a two-year period.

☐ 12. Are state employment commission requirements satisfied?

    a. Are quarterly returns filed and tax paid on time?
       due January 31   ____
       due April 30   ____
       due July 31   ____
       due October 31   ____

    b. New organizations must first obtain an account number by filing a status report.   ____

☐ 13. Verify timely payment of federal unemployment tax liability (if applicable).

Under $100 per year: pay or deposit when filing Form 940 (January 31).   ____

Over $100 for quarter: by thirtieth of next month.   ____

Over $100 per year but under $100 per quarter: by thirtieth of month after the quarter (or combination of quarters) in which liability exceeds $100.   ____

Appendix 25–1

FORM SS-8

Form **SS-8** (Rev. October 1990) Department of the Treasury Internal Revenue Service	**Determination of Employee Work Status for Purposes of Federal Employment Taxes and Income Tax Withholding**	OMB No. 1545-0004 Expires 10-31-93

Paperwork Reduction Act Notice.—We ask for the information on this form to carry out the Internal Revenue laws of the United States. You are required to give us this information. We need it to ensure that you are complying with these laws and to allow us to figure and collect the right amount of tax.

The time needed to complete and file this form will vary depending on individual circumstances. The estimated average time is: **recordkeeping,** 34 hrs., 41 min., **learning about the law or the form,** 6 min. and **preparing and sending the form to IRS,** 40 min. If you have comments concerning the accuracy of these time estimates or suggestions for making this form more simple, we would be happy to hear from you. You can write to both the **Internal Revenue Service,** Washington, DC 20024, Attention: IRS Reports Clearance Officer, T:FP, and the **Office of Management and Budget,** Paperwork Reduction Project (1545-0004), Washington, DC 20503. **DO NOT** send the tax form to either of these offices. Instead, see the instructions for information on where to file.

Instructions

This form should be completed carefully. If the firm is completing the form, it should be completed for ONE individual who is representative of the class of workers whose status is in question.

If a written determination is desired for more than one class of workers, a separate Form SS-8 should be completed for one worker from each class whose status is typical of that class. A written determination for any worker will apply to other workers of the same class if the facts are not materially different from those of the worker whose status was ruled upon.

Please return Form SS-8 to the Internal Revenue Service office that provided the form. If the Internal Revenue Service did not ask you to complete this form but you wish a determination on whether a worker is an employee, file Form SS-8 with your District Director.

Caution: Form SS-8 is **not** a claim for refund of social security tax or Federal income tax withholding. Also, a determination that an individual is an employee does not necessarily reduce any current or prior tax liability.

Name of firm (or person) for whom the worker performed services

Name of worker

Address of firm (include street address, apt. or suite no., city, state, and ZIP code)

Address of worker (include street address, apt. or suite no., city, state, and ZIP code)

Trade name

Telephone number

Worker's social security number

Telephone number

Firm's taxpayer identification number

Check type of firm:
☐ **Individual**   ☐ **Partnership**   ☐ **Corporation**   ☐ **Other** (specify) ▶

This form is being completed by: ☐ FIRM   ☐ WORKER

If the form is being completed by the worker, do you object to disclosing your name or the information on this form to the firm? . . . . ☐ Yes ☐ No

(If your answer is "Yes," we cannot furnish you a determination on the basis of this form. You may write to your District Director for further information. **Do not complete the rest of the form, unless the IRS requests it.**)

All items must be answered or marked "Unknown" or "Not Applicable" (NA). **If you need more space, attach another sheet.** This form is designed to cover many work activities, so some of the questions may not pertain to you.

Total number of workers in this class (if more than one, please see item 19) ▶ --

This information is about services performed by the worker from ▶ ----------------------------- to ----------------------
                                                                                 (Month, day, year)   (Month, day, year)

What was the first date on which the worker performed services of any kind for the firm? ▶ -----------------------------
                                                                                                         (Month, day, year)

Is the worker still performing services for the firm? . . . . ☐ Yes ☐ No
If "No," what was the date of termination? ▶ --
In which IRS district are you located? ---------------------------------- (Month, day, year) -----------------------------

1a   Describe the firm's business --
----
b   Describe the work done by the worker --

2a   If the work is done under a written agreement between the firm and the worker, attach a copy.
b   If the agreement is not in writing, describe the terms and conditions of the work arrangement -----------------------
----

Form **SS-8** (Rev. 10-90)

1/14/91

SS-8.1

Appendix 25–1 *(continued)*

FORM SS-8

Form SS-8 (Rev. 10–90)   Page **2**

c If the actual working arrangement differs in any way from the agreement, explain the differences and why they occur ....

....

3a Is the worker given training by the firm? . . . . ☐ Yes ☐ No

If "Yes":

What kind? ....

How often? ....

b Is the worker given instructions in the way the work is to be done? . . . . ☐ Yes ☐ No

If "Yes," give specific examples. ....

c Attach samples of any written instructions or procedures.

d Does the firm have the right to change the methods used by the worker or direct that person on how to do the work? ☐ Yes ☐ No

Explain your answer ....

e Does the operation of the firm's business require that the worker be supervised or controlled in the performance of

the service? . . . . ☐ Yes ☐ No

Explain your answer ....

4a The firm engages the worker:

☐ To perform and complete a particular job only

☐ To work at a job for an indefinite period of time

☐ Other (explain) ....

b Is the worker required to follow a routine or a schedule established by the firm? . . . . ☐ Yes ☐ No

If "Yes," what is the routine or schedule? ....

c Does the worker report to the firm or its representative? . . . . ☐ Yes ☐ No

If "Yes":

How often? ....

For what purpose? ....

In what manner (in person, in writing, by telephone, etc.)? ....

Attach copies of report forms used in reporting to the firm.

d Does the worker furnish a time record to the firm? . . . . ☐ Yes ☐ No

If "Yes," attach copies of time records.

5a State the kind and value of tools and equipment furnished by:

The firm ....

The worker ....

b State the kind and value of supplies and materials furnished by:

The firm ....

The worker ....

c What expenses are incurred by the worker in the performance of services for the firm?

....

d Does the firm reimburse the worker for any expenses? . . . . ☐ Yes ☐ No

If "Yes," specify the reimbursed expenses ....

6a Will the worker perform the services personally? . . . . ☐ Yes ☐ No

b Does the worker have helpers? . . . . ☐ Yes ☐ No

If "Yes": Are the helpers hired by: ☐ Firm ☐ Worker

If hired by the worker, is the firm's approval necessary? . . . . ☐ Yes ☐ No

Who pays the helpers? ☐ Firm ☐ Worker

Are social security taxes and Federal income tax withheld from the helpers' wages? . . . . ☐ Yes ☐ No

If "Yes": Who reports and pays these taxes? ☐ Firm ☐ Worker

Who reports the helpers' incomes to the Internal Revenue Service? ☐ Firm ☐ Worker

If the worker pays the helpers, does the firm repay the worker? . . . . ☐ Yes ☐ No

What services do the helpers perform? ....

SS-8.2   1/14/91

Appendix 25-1 *(continued)*

FORM SS-8

Form SS-8 (Rev. 10-90)   Page **3**

7   At what location are the services performed?   ☐ Firm's   ☐ Worker's   ☐ Other (specify) ....

8a   Type of pay worker receives:
    ☐ Salary   ☐ Commission   ☐ Hourly wage   ☐ Piecework   ☐ Lump sum   ☐ Other (specify).............

  b   Does the firm guarantee a minimum amount of pay to the worker? . . . . ☐ Yes   ☐ No

  c   Does the firm allow the worker a drawing account or advances against pay?. . . . . ☐ Yes   ☐ No
    If "Yes": Is the worker paid such advances on a regular basis? . . . . ☐ Yes   ☐ No

  d   How does the worker repay such advances? ....

9a   Is the worker eligible for a pension, bonuses, paid vacations, sick pay, etc.? . . . . ☐ Yes   ☐ No
    If "Yes," specify.............................

  b   Does the firm carry workmen's compensation insurance on the worker? . . . . ☐ Yes   ☐ No

  c   Does the firm deduct social security tax from amounts paid the worker? . . . . ☐ Yes   ☐ No

  d   Does the firm deduct Federal income taxes from amounts paid the worker? . . . . ☐ Yes   ☐ No

  e   How does the firm report the worker's income to the Internal Revenue Service?
    ☐ Form W-2   ☐ Form 1099   ☐ Does not report   ☐ Other (specify) ....

  f   Does the firm bond the worker?. . . . . ☐ Yes   ☐ No

10a   Approximately how many hours a day does the worker perform services for the firm? ....

  b   Does the worker perform similar services for others? . . . . ☐ Yes   ☐ No   ☐ Unknown
    If "Yes": Are these services performed on a daily basis for other firms? . . . . ☐ Yes   ☐ No   ☐ Unknown
    Percentage of time spent in performing these services for:
    This firm ....% Other firms...........%   ☐ Unknown
    Does the firm have priority on the worker's time? . . . . ☐ Yes   ☐ No
    If "No," explain....................

  c   Is the worker prohibited from competing with the firm either while performing services or during any later period? . . ☐ Yes   ☐ No

11a   Can the firm discharge the worker at any time without incurring a liability? . . . . ☐ Yes   ☐ No
    If "No," explain..................

  b   Can the worker terminate the services at any time without incurring a liability? . . . . ☐ Yes   ☐ No
    If "No," explain..................

12a   Does the worker perform services for the firm under:
    ☐ The firm's business name   ☐ The worker's own business name   ☐ Other (specify) ....

  b   Does the worker advertise or maintain a business listing in the telephone directory, a trade journal, etc.? ☐ Yes   ☐ No   ☐ Unknown
    If "Yes," specify...................

  c   Does the worker represent himself or herself to the public as being in business to perform the
    same or similar services? . . . . ☐ Yes   ☐ No   ☐ Unknown
    If "Yes," how?...................

  d   Does the worker have his or her own shop or office? . . . . ☐ Yes   ☐ No   ☐ Unknown
    If "Yes," where?.....................

  e   Does the firm represent the worker as an employee of the firm to its customers? . . . . ☐ Yes   ☐ No
    If "No," how is the worker represented? ....

  f   How did the firm learn of the worker's services? ....

13   Is a license necessary for the work? . . . . ☐ Yes   ☐ No   ☐ Unknown
    If "Yes," what kind of license is required?..................................
    By whom is it issued? ....
    By whom is the license fee paid?..............................

14   Does the worker have a financial investment in a business related to the services performed? . . . . . ☐ Yes   ☐ No   ☐ Unknown
    If "Yes," specify and give amounts of the investment ....

15   Can the worker incur a loss in the performance of the service for the firm? . . . . ☐ Yes   ☐ No
    If "Yes," how?...................

16a   Has any other government agency ruled on the status of the firm's workers? . . . . ☐ Yes   ☐ No
    If "Yes," attach a copy of the ruling.

  b   Is the same issue being considered by any IRS office in connection with the audit of the worker's tax return or the
    firm's tax return, or has it recently been considered? . . . . ☐ Yes   ☐ No
    If "Yes," for which year(s)?..........................

17   Does the worker assemble or process a product at home or away from the firm's place of business?. . . . . ☐ Yes   ☐ No
    If "Yes":
        Who furnishes materials or goods used by the worker?   ☐ Firm   ☐ Worker
        Is the worker furnished a pattern or given instructions to follow in making the product? . . . . ☐ Yes   ☐ No
        Is the worker required to return the finished product to the firm or to someone designated by the firm? . . . ☐ Yes   ☐ No

1/14/91   SS-8.3

FORM SS-8

Form SS-8 (Rev. 10-90) Page **4**

Answer items 18a through n if the worker is a salesperson or provides a service directly to customers.

18a Are leads to prospective customers furnished by the firm? . . . . ☐ Yes ☐ No ☐ **Does not apply**
 b Is the worker required to pursue or report on leads? . . . . ☐ Yes ☐ No ☐ **Does not apply**
 c Is the worker required to adhere to prices, terms, and conditions of sale established by the firm? . . . . ☐ Yes ☐ No
 d Are orders submitted to and subject to approval by the firm? . . . . ☐ Yes ☐ No
 e Is the worker expected to attend sales meetings? . . . . ☐ Yes ☐ No
   If "Yes": Is the worker subject to any kind of penalty for failing to attend? . . . . ☐ Yes ☐ No
 f Does the firm assign a specific territory to the worker? . . . . ☐ Yes ☐ No ☐ **Does not apply**
 g Who does the customer pay? ☐ Firm ☐ Worker
   If worker, does the worker remit the total amount to the firm?. ☐ Yes ☐ No
 h Does the worker sell a consumer product in a home or establishment other than a permanent retail establishment? . ☐ Yes ☐ No
 i List the products and/or services distributed by the worker, such as meat, vegetables, fruit, bakery products, beverages (other than milk), or laundry or dry cleaning services. If more than one type of product and/or service is distributed, specify the principal one. ....
 j Did the firm or another person assign the route or territory and a list of customers to the worker? . . . . ☐ Yes ☐ No
   If "Yes," please identify the person who made the assignment. ....
 k Did the worker pay the firm or person for the privilege of serving customers on the route or in the territory? . . . . ☐ Yes ☐ No
   If "Yes," how much did the worker pay (not including any amount paid for a truck or racks, etc.)? $ ....
   What factors were considered in determining the value of the route or territory? ....
 l How are new customers obtained by the worker? Explain fully, showing whether the new customers called the firm for service, were solicited by the worker, or both. ....
 m Does the worker sell life insurance? . . . . ☐ Yes ☐ No
   If "Yes":
   Is the selling of life insurance or annuity contracts for the firm the worker's entire business activity? . . . . . ☐ Yes ☐ No
   If "No," state the extent of the worker's other business activities ....
   Does the worker sell other types of insurance for the firm? . . . . ☐ Yes ☐ No
   If "Yes," state the percentage of the worker's total working time spent in selling such other types of insurance .... %
   At the time the contract was entered into between the firm and the worker, was it their intention that the worker sell life insurance for the firm: ☐ on a full-time basis ☐ on a part-time basis
   State the manner in which such intention was expressed. ....
 n Is the worker a traveling salesperson or city salesperson? . . . . ☐ Yes ☐ No
   If "Yes":
   Specify from whom the worker principally solicits orders on behalf of the firm. ....
   If the worker solicits orders from wholesalers, retailers, contractors, or operators of hotels, restaurants, or other similar establishments, specify the percentage of the worker's time spent in such solicitation. ....%
   Is the merchandise purchased by the customers for resale, or is it purchased for use in their business operations? If used by the customers in their business operations, describe the merchandise and state whether it is equipment installed on their premises or a consumable supply. ....

19 Attach the names and addresses of the total number of workers in this class from page 1, or the names and addresses of 10 such workers if there are more than 10.
20 Attach a detailed explanation for any other reason why you believe the worker is an independent contractor or is an employee of the firm.

IMPORTANT INFORMATION NEEDED TO PROCESS YOUR REQUEST
Under section 6110 of the Internal Revenue Code, the text and related background file documents of any ruling, determination letter, or technical advice memorandum will be open to public inspection. This section provides that before the text and background file documents are made public, identifying and certain other information must be deleted.
Are the names, addresses, and taxpayer identifying numbers the only items you want deleted? . . . . ☐ Yes ☐ No
If you checked "No," and believe additional deletions should be made, we cannot process your request unless you submit a copy of this form and copies of all supporting documents indicating, in brackets, those parts you believe should be deleted in accordance with section 6110(c) of the Code. Attach a separate statement indicating which specific exemption provided by section 6110(c) applies to each bracketed part.

Under penalties of perjury, I declare that I have examined this request, including accompanying documents, and to the best of my knowledge and belief, the facts presented are true, correct, and complete.

Signature ▶   Title ▶   Date ▶

If this form is used by the firm in requesting a written determination, the form should be signed by an officer or member of the firm.
If this form is used by the worker in requesting a written determination, the form should be signed by the worker. If the worker wants a written determination with respect to services performed for two or more firms, a separate form should be furnished for each firm.
Additional copies of this form may be obtained from any Internal Revenue Service office.

SS-8.4   1/14/91

Appendix 25-2

FORM W-9

Form **W-9** (Rev. September 1991) Department of the Treasury Internal Revenue Service	**Request for Taxpayer Identification Number and Certification**	Give this form to the requester. Do NOT send to IRS.

Please print or type

Name (If joint names, list first and circle the name of the person or entity whose number you enter in Part I below. **See instructions on page 2 if your name has changed.**)

Business name (Sole proprietors see instructions on page 2.)

Address (number and street) | List account number(s) here (optional)

City, state, and ZIP code

Part I   **Taxpayer Identification Number (TIN)**   **Part II**   **For Payees Exempt From Backup Withholding (See instructions on page 2)**

Enter your TIN in the appropriate box. For individuals, this is your social security number (SSN). For sole proprietors, see the instructions on page 2. For other entities, it is your employer identification number (EIN). If you do not have a number, see **How To Obtain a TIN,** below.

Social security number

OR

Employer identification number

Note: *If the account is in more than one name, see the chart on page 2 for guidelines on whose number to enter.*

Requester's name and address (optional)

Certification.—Under penalties of perjury, I certify that:

(1) The number shown on this form is my correct taxpayer identification number (or I am waiting for a number to be issued to me), **and**

(2) I am not subject to backup withholding because: **(a)** I am exempt from backup withholding, or **(b)** I have not been notified by the Internal Revenue Service (IRS) that I am subject to backup withholding as a result of a failure to report all interest or dividends, or **(c)** the IRS has notified me that I am no longer subject to backup withholding.

Certification Instructions.—You must cross out item (2) above if you have been notified by the IRS that you are currently subject to backup withholding because of underreporting interest or dividends on your tax return. For real estate transactions, item (2) does not apply. For mortgage interest paid, the acquisition or abandonment of secured property, contributions to an individual retirement arrangement (IRA), and generally payments other than interest and dividends, you are not required to sign the Certification, but you must provide your correct TIN. (Also see **Signing the Certification** on page 2.)

Please Sign Here   Signature ▶   Date ▶

(Section references are to the Internal Revenue Code.)

Purpose of Form.—A person who is required to file an information return with the IRS must obtain your correct TIN to report income paid to you, real estate transactions, mortgage interest you paid, the acquisition or abandonment of secured property, or contributions you made to an IRA. Use Form W-9 to furnish your correct TIN to the requester (the person asking you to furnish your TIN) and, when applicable, (1) to certify that the TIN you are furnishing is correct (or that you are waiting for a number to be issued), (2) to certify that you are not subject to backup withholding, and (3) to claim exemption from backup withholding if you are an exempt payee. Furnishing your correct TIN and making the appropriate certifications will prevent certain payments from being subject to backup withholding.

Note: *If a requester gives you a form other than a W-9 to request your TIN, you must use the requester's form.*

How To Obtain a TIN.—If you do not have a TIN, apply for one immediately. To apply, get **Form SS-5,** Application for a Social Security Number Card (for individuals), from your local office of the Social Security Administration, or **Form SS-4,** Application for Employer Identification Number (for businesses and all other entities), from your local IRS office.

To complete Form W-9 if you do not have a TIN, write "Applied for" in the space for the TIN in Part I, sign and date the form, and give it to the requester. Generally, you will then have

60 days to obtain a TIN and furnish it to the requester. If the requester does not receive your TIN within 60 days, backup withholding, if applicable, will begin and continue until you furnish your TIN to the requester. For reportable interest or dividend payments, the payer must exercise one of the following options concerning backup withholding during this 60-day period. Under option (1), a payer must backup withhold on any withdrawals you make from your account after 7 business days after the requester receives this form back from you. Under option (2), the payer must backup withhold on any reportable interest or dividend payments made to your account, regardless of whether you make any withdrawals. The backup withholding under option (2) must begin no later than 7 business days after the requester receives this form back. Under option (2), the payer is required to refund the amounts withheld if your certified TIN is received within the 60-day period and you were not subject to backup withholding during that period.

Note: *Writing "Applied for" on the form means that you have already applied for a TIN OR that you intend to apply for one in the near future.*

As soon as you receive your TIN, complete another Form W-9, include your TIN, sign and date the form, and give it to the requester.

What Is Backup Withholding?—Persons making certain payments to you are required to withhold and pay to the IRS 20% of such payments under certain conditions. This is called "backup withholding." Payments that could be subject to backup withholding include interest, dividends,

broker and barter exchange transactions, rents, royalties, nonemployee compensation, and certain payments from fishing boat operators, but do not include real estate transactions.

If you give the requester your correct TIN, make the appropriate certifications, and report all your taxable interest and dividends on your tax return, your payments will not be subject to backup withholding. Payments you receive will be subject to backup withholding if:

1. You do not furnish your TIN to the requester, or

2. The IRS notifies the requester that you furnished an incorrect TIN, or

3. You are notified by the IRS that you are subject to backup withholding because you failed to report all your interest and dividends on your tax return (for reportable interest and dividends only), or

4. You fail to certify to the requester that you are not subject to backup withholding under (3) above (for reportable interest and dividend accounts opened after 1983 only), or

5. You fail to certify your TIN. This applies only to reportable interest, dividend, broker, or barter exchange accounts opened after 1983, or broker accounts considered inactive in 1983.

Except as explained in (5) above, other reportable payments are subject to backup withholding only if (1) or (2) above applies. Certain payees and payments are exempt from backup withholding and information reporting. See **Payees and Payments Exempt From**

Form **W-9** (Rev. 9-91)

Appendix 25–2 *(continued)*

FORM W-9

Form W-9 (Rev. 9-91)   Page **2**

Backup Withholding, below, and **Exempt Payees and Payments** under **Specific Instructions,** below, if you are an exempt payee.

Payees and Payments Exempt From Backup Withholding.—The following is a list of payees exempt from backup withholding and for which no information reporting is required. For interest and dividends, all listed payees are exempt except item (9). For broker transactions, payees listed in (1) through (13) and a person registered under the Investment Advisers Act of 1940 who regularly acts as a broker are exempt. Payments subject to reporting under sections 6041 and 6041A are generally exempt from backup withholding only if made to payees described in items (1) through (7), except a corporation that provides medical and health care services or bills and collects payments for such services is not exempt from backup withholding or information reporting. Only payees described in items (2) through (6) are exempt from backup withholding for barter exchange transactions, patronage dividends, and payments by certain fishing boat operators.

(1) A corporation. (2) An organization exempt from tax under section 501(a), or an IRA, or a custodial account under section 403(b)(7). (3) The United States or any of its agencies or instrumentalities. (4) A state, the District of Columbia, a possession of the United States, or any of their political subdivisions or instrumentalities. (5) A foreign government or any of its political subdivisions, agencies, or instrumentalities. (6) An international organization or any of its agencies or instrumentalities. (7) A foreign central bank of issue. (8) A dealer in securities or commodities required to register in the United States or a possession of the United States. (9) A futures commission merchant registered with the Commodity Futures Trading Commission. (10) A real estate investment trust. (11) An entity registered at all times during the tax year under the Investment Company Act of 1940. (12) A common trust fund operated by a bank under section 584(a). (13) A financial institution. (14) A middleman known in the investment community as a nominee or listed in the most recent publication of the American Society of Corporate Secretaries, Inc., Nominee List. (15) A trust exempt from tax under section 664 or described in section 4947.

Payments of **dividends** and **patronage dividends** generally not subject to backup withholding include the following:

● Payments to nonresident aliens subject to withholding under section 1441.

● Payments to partnerships not engaged in a trade or business in the United States and that have at least one nonresident partner.

● Payments of patronage dividends not paid in money.

● Payments made by certain foreign organizations.

Payments of **interest** generally not subject to backup withholding include the following:

● Payments of interest on obligations issued by individuals.

Note: *You may be subject to backup withholding if this interest is $600 or more and is paid in the course of the payer's trade or business and you have not provided your correct TIN to the payer.*

● Payments of tax-exempt interest (including exempt-interest dividends under section 852).

● Payments described in section 6049(b)(5) to nonresident aliens.

● Payments on tax-free covenant bonds under section 1451.

● Payments made by certain foreign organizations.

● Mortgage interest paid by you.

Payments that are not subject to information reporting are also not subject to backup withholding. For details, see sections 6041, 6041A(a), 6042, 6044, 6045, 6049, 6050A, and 6050N, and their regulations.

Penalties

Failure To Furnish TIN.—If you fail to furnish your correct TIN to a requester, you are subject to a penalty of $50 for each such failure unless your failure is due to reasonable cause and not to willful neglect.

Civil Penalty for False Information With Respect to Withholding.—If you make a false statement with no reasonable basis that results in no backup withholding, you are subject to a $500 penalty.

Criminal Penalty for Falsifying Information.—Willfully falsifying certifications or affirmations may subject you to criminal penalties including fines and/or imprisonment.

Specific Instructions

Name.—If you are an individual, you must generally provide the name shown on your social security card. However, if you have changed your last name, for instance, due to marriage, without informing the Social Security Administration of the name change, please enter your first name, the last name shown on your social security card, and your new last name.

If you are a sole proprietor, you must furnish your **individual** name and either your SSN or EIN. You may also enter your business name on the business name line. Enter your name(s) as shown on your social security card and/or as it was used to apply for your EIN on Form SS-4.

Signing the Certification.—

(1) Interest, Dividend, and Barter Exchange Accounts Opened Before 1984 and Broker Accounts Considered Active During 1983.— You are required to furnish your correct TIN, but you are not required to sign the certification.

(2) Interest, Dividend, Broker, and Barter Exchange Accounts Opened After 1983 and Broker Accounts Considered Inactive During 1983.—You must sign the certification or backup withholding will apply. If you are subject to backup withholding and you are merely providing your correct TIN to the requester, you must cross out item (2) in the certification before signing the form.

(3) Real Estate Transactions.—You must sign the certification. You may cross out item (2) of the certification.

(4) Other Payments.—You are required to furnish your correct TIN, but you are not required to sign the certification unless you have been notified of an incorrect TIN. Other payments include payments made in the course of the requester's trade or business for rents, royalties, goods (other than bills for merchandise), medical and health care services, payments to a nonemployee for services (including attorney and accounting fees), and payments to certain fishing boat crew members.

(5) Mortgage Interest Paid by You, Acquisition or Abandonment of Secured Property, or IRA Contributions.—You are required to furnish your correct TIN, but you are not required to sign the certification.

(6) Exempt Payees and Payments.—If you are exempt from backup withholding, you should complete this form to avoid possible erroneous backup withholding. Enter your correct TIN in Part I, write "EXEMPT" in the block in Part II, sign and date the form. If you are a nonresident alien or foreign entity not subject to backup withholding, give the requester a completed **Form W-8,** Certificate of Foreign Status.

(7) TIN "Applied for."—Follow the instructions under **How To Obtain a TIN,** on page 1, sign and date this form.

Signature.—For a joint account, only the person whose TIN is shown in Part I should sign the form.

Privacy Act Notice.—Section 6109 requires you to furnish your correct TIN to persons who must file information returns with the IRS to report interest, dividends, and certain other income paid to you, mortgage interest you paid, the acquisition or abandonment of secured property, or contributions you made to an IRA. The IRS uses the numbers for identification purposes and to help verify the accuracy of your tax return. You must provide your TIN whether or not you are required to file a tax return. Payers must generally withhold 20% of taxable interest, dividend, and certain other payments to a payee who does not furnish a TIN to a payer. Certain penalties may also apply.

What Name and Number To Give the Requester

For this type of account:	Give name and SSN of:
1. Individual	The individual
2. Two or more individuals (joint account)	The actual owner of the account or, if combined funds, the first individual on the account [1]
3. Custodian account of a minor (Uniform Gift to Minors Act)	The minor [2]
4. a. The usual revocable savings trust (grantor is also trustee)	The grantor-trustee [1]
b. So-called trust account that is not a legal or valid trust under state law	The actual owner [1]
5. Sole proprietorship	The owner [3]

For this type of account:	Give name and EIN of:
6. Sole proprietorship	The owner [3]
7. A valid trust, estate, or pension trust	Legal entity [4]
8. Corporate	The corporation
9. Association, club, religious, charitable, educational, or other tax-exempt organization	The organization
10. Partnership	The partnership
11. A broker or registered nominee	The broker or nominee
12. Account with the Department of Agriculture in the name of a public entity (such as a state or local government, school district, or prison) that receives agricultural program payments	The public entity

[1] List first and circle the name of the person whose number you furnish.

[2] Circle the minor's name and furnish the minor's social security number.

[3] Show the individual's name. See item 5 or 6. You may also enter your business name.

[4] List first and circle the name of the legal trust, estate, or pension trust. (Do not furnish the identification number of the personal representative or trustee unless the legal entity itself is not designated in the account title.)

Note: *If no name is circled when there is more than one name, the number will be considered to be that of the first name listed.*

W-9.2

12/16/91

CHAPTER TWENTY-SIX

Bankruptcy

Despite the best intentions and dreams of their creators and managers, exempt organizations (EOs) on occasion expend funds in excess of their resources. Some organizations are fortunate enough to have philanthropists or other supporters who are willing and able to cover their operating deficits. Sometimes, however, an EO may become insolvent to the point that it must declare bankruptcy. In such cases, the interests of the (normally) for-profit creditors and the nonprofit constituents of the organization can be in conflict, and a number of issues must be considered.

26.1 BANKRUPTCY CODE

A thorough consideration of the federal Bankruptcy Code is beyond the scope of this book, and any organization facing insolvency and considering bankruptcy should seek an attorney knowledgeable about the field. In most respects, the Bankruptcy Code provides the same rules for nonprofit and for-profit organizations. The intention of the rules is to protect the insolvent organization, to prevent any particular creditor from taking unfair advantage, and to allow an orderly allocation among creditors of the proceeds of the asset liquidation.[1]

The Bankruptcy Code is divided into eight chapters, number 1, 3, 5, 7, 9, 11, 12, and 13 to allow room for future provisions. Bankruptcy cases are referred to by the numbers of the chapters they are brought under. A Chapter 7 bankruptcy allows the organization, under the supervision of a court-appointed trustee, to sell off its assets, allocate the proceeds of such sales among its creditors, dissolve its legal existence, and cease to operate. The other common type of bankruptcy, Chapter 11 allows the organization to reorganize and remain in existence after providing for a payment plan for its indebtedness.

Bankruptcy may be voluntary or involuntary. A voluntary bankruptcy is filed by an insolvent organization to seek the protection from unfriendly

---

[1] 11 U.S.C. §303.

creditors. In contrast, an involuntary bankruptcy is filed by three or more creditors together. However, only a "moneyed, business, or commercial operation" qualifies for an involuntary bankruptcy, a significant matter on which the Bankruptcy Code provides different treatment for nonprofit corporations. "Moneyed" organizations are profit-motivated ones operated to create income for their shareholders or members. Most tax-exempt organizations would not continue to qualify for exemption if they could meet such a definition. Thus, it is generally the case that an organization qualified for tax exemption under one of the subsections of IRC §501(c) cannot be placed in involuntary bankruptcy.

Failure to qualify for the exception from involuntary bankruptcy, on the other hand, can cause the organization to lose its tax-exempt status, because it would show that the assets are not dedicated to exempt purposes, as discussed below.

26.2 HOW FEDERAL TAX STATUS IS AFFECTED BY A BANKRUPTCY

IRC §501 organizations of all categories—(c)(1–25) plus §501(d), (e), and (f)—must be organized and operated for their specifically defined category as discussed in Chapters 2–10. Charities, social welfare organizations, business leagues, social clubs, and all other types of exempt organization must permanently dedicate their assets under organizational documents to their specified purposes, and must then, in fact, operate for such purposes throughout the life of the organization to maintain tax-exempt status.

An insolvent exempt organization considering bankruptcy may face a challenge that it did not operate for exempt purposes. Any revocation of exemption would be based upon the facts and circumstances of the case. There is no rule that automatically revokes exempt status upon the declaration of bankruptcy, and there are no revenue rulings or other statements of IRS policy on the subject. The questions that must be asked in reviewing a particular situation (all versions of the same theme) would include:

- Were the activities in which the debt was incurred exempt activities?

- Why was adequate revenue not provided to pay for the exempt activities? Were revenues diverted to some other nonexempt purposes? Are there unrecorded liabilities attributable to restricted donors whose funds were diverted to other purposes?

- If the debts were incurred in connection with an unrelated business activity, did that business subsume the exempt activities and therefore evidence lack of substantial exempt purposes?

- Were exempt assets diverted to some nonexempt project violating the requirement that assets be dedicated to exempt purposes? Where "jeopardizing investments" purchased? Particularly for a private foundation, this could provide the additional complication of excise taxes discussed in Chapter 16.

- How can assets be allocated to creditors when the organization's charter requires that assets be dedicated permanently to exempt purposes?

■ Were members of the governing body of trustees or directors in any way fiscally irresponsible in allowing the deficits to occur? Should any of the deficiencies be paid by such directors to preserve the organizational assets for the exempt constituents?

26.3 REVOCATION OF EXEMPT STATUS

The Bankruptcy Code automatic stay against collection, assessment, or recovery of a claim against the bankrupt organization does not prevent the IRS from revoking exempt status. In abusive situations, i.e., when the debts were incurred in providing benefits to insiders rather than in serving the exempt public or membership, an attempt to revoke should be expected. The challenge is also bolstered when there are no assets left upon dissolution for distribution for exempt purposes, as is required by any exempt organization's charter.

The revocation has been ruled to be a preliminary step or prerequisite to the collection of tax and not restrained by the filing of bankruptcy.[2] The anti-injunction provision of IRC §7421 prohibits the bankruptcy trustee or others from interfering in the revocation of exempt status when the IRS deems it appropriate. Whether the IRS can be successful in collecting any taxes assessed is another question to be answered by a bankruptcy specialist.

When exempt status is revoked, tax issues resulting from forgiveness is indebtedness, deductions for bad debts, and recapture of tax attributes, among other issues, must be carefully considered. Even if the exempt status is not revoked, such issues would be of consequence in calculating any tax liability for unrelated business income.

(a) No New Organization

After the exempt organization voluntarily files bankruptcy, a new organization does not come into being. Under IRC §1399, the existing entity continues and normal filing requirements continue. As a matter of IRS policy, the exempt status of organization is allowed to remain intact unless factors evident in the bankruptcy indicate that the exempt status of organization should be revoked, as discussed above.

(b) Filing Requirements

The gross annual revenues of the bankrupt organization govern its annual federal filing requirements, as outlined in Section 27.1. As the bankruptcy proceeds, returns are to be filed as usual except in the year of liquidation, dissolution, termination, or substantial contraction. An entity with over $25,000 but less than $100,000 of gross receipts files Form 990EZ, and one with over $100,000 files Form 990. In the contracting or final year, a lower threshold of $5,000 of gross receipts sets the limit for required reporting. In other words, the Form 990 must be filed in almost all cases.

---

[2]*Bob Jones University v. Simon*, 416 U.S. 725 (1974); *Heritage Village Church and Missionary Fellowship, Inc.*, 851 F.2d 104 (4th Cir., 1988).

Prior to the actual year of dissolution or termination, the filing requirements for other purposes—annual information, payroll, and all other types of federal returns—remain the same during the period of bankruptcy. Even though the organization ceases normal operations and receives no contributions, gross revenue for filing purposes includes proceeds from the sale of its assets.

The parties responsible for filing information returns are either the board of directors and the organization's ongoing managers or the bankruptcy trustee appointed to replace the directors or organizational trustees.

Information revealing the bankrupt status should be attached to Form 990 in response to the question on page 4, line 76 and page 2, line 33 of Form 990EZ; or page 4, question 2 of Form 990-PF: "Has the organization engaged in any activities not previously reported to the IRS?" At a minimum, the documents filed with the bankruptcy trustee and a synopsis of the expected outcome should be attached to the return. An explanation of the cause of the bankruptcy and its effects on ongoing operations (under Chapter 11) or on its orderly dissolution (under Chapter 7) should also be attached to the return. It is very important at this point to indicate that the exempt purposes of the organization are not compromised by the bankruptcy, and that the exempt status should not be revoked or jeopardized as a consequence (when it is possible to so argue).

IRC §6043 contains specific requirements for information to be reported in the year of dissolution of an exempt organization, which apply to organizations dissolving due to bankruptcy. Although the answer is full of innuendo from the question of jeopardy to exempt status, this section specifically requires that the following information be reported in Form 990 for the distribution year:

- Fact that the assets are distributed and dates of distribution;
- Names and addresses of persons receiving the terminating distributions;
- Kinds of assets distributed; and
- Each asset's fair market value.

When the asset distribution and settlement with creditors takes place over a series of reporting years, the regulations should be carefully considered for determining when a "substantial contraction" occurs, to allow properly timed reporting.

(c) Related Organizations

What if one member of an affiliated group of exempt organizations becomes insolvent and is considering declaring bankruptcy? Particularly in a statewide or nationwide group whose reputation might be damaged by the bad credit rating of a related entity, there may be consequences for the parent organization or another branch of the group for bailing out the insolvent entity. All of the questions asked above under "consequences to exempt status" must be considered.

Although there will almost certainly be disagreement on the question, as a general rule, the assets of one member of a group should not be used to bail out the creditors of another branch, particularly when each entity is an independent corporate or fiduciary entity. Only if it can be argued that the continued existence of the related entities would be jeopardized, and therefore, that the exempt purposes are better saved by the preservation of the ailing member, could such a bailout serve the purposes of the remaining members of the exempt group.

The systems for monitoring, planning, and controlling related organizations should theoretically prevent such insolvencies. When they occur, these systems should be reviewed and revised to avoid reoccurrence.

CHAPTER TWENTY-SEVEN

Successful Preparation of Forms 990, 990EZ, 990-T and 990-PF

Good accounting is the key to successful preparation of federal information returns for nonprofit organizations. The trick is to allocate and attribute revenues and expenses to the proper lines and columns on Forms 990. How do you determine grant administrative expenses or program services? How can you figure the portion of overhead deductible against the sale of advertising in your journal? Particularly for organizations paying tax on unrelated business income, proper identification of allocable expenses is the goal.

Documentation and cost accounting records must be developed to capture revenues and costs in categories and to report them by function, sometimes called joint cost allocations. When expenses are attributable to more than one function, "organizations are required to develop techniques that will provide verifiable bases upon which expenses may be related to program or supporting service functions. The functional classification of expenses permits an agency to tell the reader of the financial statements not only the nature of its expenses, but also the purpose for which they were made."[1] At a minimum, all exempt organizations (EOs) need to maintain the following:

1. A staff salary allocation system is essential for recording the time employees spend on tasks each day. The possibilities are endless. Each staff member could maintain an individual computer database or fill out a time sheet. The reports should be completed often enough to assure accuracy, preferably weekly. In some cases, as when personnel perform repetitive tasks, preparing one week's report for each month or one month each year might be sufficient. Percentages of time spent on various functions can then be tabulated and used for accounting allocations.

2. Office/program space utilization charts to assign occupancy costs can be prepared. All physical building space rented or owned must be allocated according to its usage. Floor plans must be tabulated to arrive at square footage of the space allocable to each activity center. In some cases, the allocation is made by using staff/time ratios. For dual-use space, records must reflect the number of hours or days space is used for each purpose.

3. Direct program or activity costs should be captured whenever possible. The advantages include reduction of unrelated business income, proof of qualifying distributions for a private foundation, and insurance against an IRS challenge for low program expenditures. A minimal amount of additional time should be required by administrative staff to accumulate costs by programs. A departmental accounting system is imperative. Some long-distance telephone companies will assist in developing a coding system that prints an EO's phone bill with a break-

---

[1]*Standards of Accounting and Financial Reporting for Voluntary Health and Welfare Organizations.*

down by department. The organization can establish separate accounts with vendors for different departments.

4. Joint projects allocations must be made on a reasonable and fair basis recognizing the cause and effect relationship between the cost incurred and where it is allocated.[2] Four possible methods of allocating include:

- activity-based allocations (identifying departmental costs);

- equal sharing of costs (e.g., if three projects, divide by three);

- cost allocated relative to stand-alone cost (e.g., what it would cost if that department had to hire and buy independently); and

- cost allocated in proportion to cost savings.

5. Supporting, administrative, or other management costs should be allocated to departments to which the work is directly related. The EO's size and the scope of administrative staff involvement in actual programs determine the feasibility of such cost attributions. Staff salaries are most often allocable. For example, say the executive director is also the editor of the EO's journal. If a record of time spent is maintained, his or her salary and associated costs could be attributed partly to the publication. Watch for "exploitation of exempt functions" when allocating expenses to unrelated business income. The deductible amount may be limited. (See Section 21.14(f).)

6. A computer-based fund accounting system is preferable, in which department codes are automatically recorded as moneys are expended. A number of good programs are available. The cost of the software is easily recouped in staff time saved, improved planning, and possibly tax savings due to a reduction in UBIT or excise taxes.

The accounting profession has been struggling for several years to revise the GAAP rules for nonprofit organizations. Due to controversy about valuing the art collections of museums, allocation systems for joint costs, and reporting of charitable pledges, revisions are still under discussion in November, 1992. The reader should be alert for new rules and promulgations that might affect cost allocations for Form 990 purposes.

As a start, the following references are indispensable:

AICPA Audit and Accounting Guide, Audits of Certain Nonprofit Organizations, including Statement of Position (SOP) 78-10 (as amended by SOP 87-2), "Accounting for Joint Costs of Informational Materials and Activities of Not-for-Profit Organizations That Include a Fund-Raising Appeal," issued by the Accounting Standards Division of the American Institute of Certified Public Accountants. The AICPA also publishes audit guides for hospitals, colleges, and universities and voluntary health and welfare organizations.

[2] Dennis P. Tishlian "Reasonable Joint Cost Allocations in Nonprofits," *Journal of Accountancy*, November 1992, page 66.

Financial and Accounting Guide for Not-for-Profit Organizations 4th Edition, Malvern J. Gross, Jr., William Warshauer, Jr., and Richard F. Larkin, published by John Wiley and Sons, New York.

Exempt Organizations Handbook Internal Revenue Service, Publication 7751, Chapter 48.

Exempt Organizations Continuing Professional Education Technical Instruction Programs, Internal Revenue Service (published annually and available from the IRS Reading Room in Washington, D.C.).

Accounting and Financial Reporting, *A Guide for United Ways and Not-for-Profit Human-Service Organizations*, 2nd Edition Revised United Way Institute, Alexandria, Virginia.

Standards of Accounting and Financial Reporting for Voluntary Health and Welfare Organizations, 3rd Edition, National Health Council, Inc., National Assembly of National Voluntary Health and Social Welfare Organization, Inc., United Way of America (known as the "Black Book").

27.1 FILING FORMS 990

The annual Forms 990 are sent to the area service bureau, although the IRS is considering creation of a service bureau exclusively for exempt return filing. In past years, notices regarding attachments or unanswered questions have been common, even when the forms were prepared correctly.

The IRS instructions for the various Forms 990 total 80 pages in length and are quite good. They should be read alongside this chapter, which does not repeat the IRS directions, but elaborates on them.

(a) What the IRS is Seeking

The various Forms 990 are designed to accomplish two purposes. First, the basic financial information—the revenues, disbursements, assets, and liabilities—are classified into meaningful categories to allow the IRS to statistically evaluate the scope and type of EO activity. Second, the questions fish for failures to comply with the federal requirements for maintenance of tax exempt status, such as:

- Do the fund-raising costs reported on line 15 of Part I equal too high a percentage of the total expenses so that the organization fails the "commerciality test"? (See Section 21.4(b).)

- Are officers' salaries reported on line 25 of Part II so excessive that private inurement results? (See Section 20.4.)

- Does the EO operate to benefit private individuals as payments in Part II, lines 22, 23, and 24 reflect? (See Section 20.9.)

- Has the EO spent too much money on lobbying efforts reported on Schedule A, Part VI-A or B? (See Section 23.5.)

- Do the EO's sources of support shown on Schedule A, Part IV allow it to continue to be classified under its current category of public charity? (See Section 11.4.)

(b) Form 990 Changes

The forms have evolved over the years through cooperative efforts between the IRS, the nonprofit community, and state charity officials. Congress mandated the addition of page 5, as explained below in Section 27.10. In 1989, a Nonprofit Qualify Reporting Project was initiated by the Nonprofit Management Group at Baruch College of the City University of New York. Weaknesses and reporting problems found during this study will be highlighted below, as specific parts of the form are discussed. The study moved into a second phase in 1992 and the reader should be alert for resulting changes in Forms 990.

(c) Who is Required to File What?

The numerous categories of organizations exempt from income tax are reflected in the different types of returns to be filed. Not all organizations are required to file annual reports with the Internal Revenue Service. Churches and their affiliated organizations, in a manner similar to the Form 1023 rules, do not file Forms 990, except for 990T. Modest-sized organizations may also be excused from filing. The different types of exempt organization annual reports and their basic requirement are as follows:

- **No Form Filed** Organizations with gross annual receipts "normally" under $25,000, churches and certain of their affiliates, and other types of organizations listed below need not file. (But see why to file at Section 27.1(f).)

- **Form 990EZ** All exempt organizations, except for private foundations, whose gross annual receipts equal between $25,000 and $100,000 and whose total assets are less than $250,000 file Form 990EZ.

- **Form 990** All exempt organizations, except private foundations, whose gross annual receipts are over $100,000 or which have assets of over $250,000 must file Form 990.

- **Form 990PF** All private foundations (PFs) file Form 990PF annually, regardless of gross annual receipts (even if the PF has no gross receipts).

- **Form 990T** Any organization exempt under IRC §501(a), including churches, and IRC §401 pension plans (including individual retirement accounts) with $1,000 or more gross income from an unrelated trade or business must file Form 990T.

- **Form 990BL** Black lung trusts (IRC §501(c)(21)) file an annual Information and Initial Excise Tax Return for Black Lung Benefit Trusts and Certain Related Persons.

- **Form 5500** One of several Forms 5500 are filed annually by pension, profit-sharing, and stock bonus plans whose assets exceed $100,000. Form 5500EZ is filed for one-participant pension benefit plans and 5500 C/R is filed for organizations with fewer than 100 participants in their employee plans.

(d) Federal Filing Not Required

Organizations not required to file include:

- Church affiliates including an interchurch organization of local units of a church, a convention or association of churches, an integrated auxiliary of a church (such as a men's or women's society, religious school, mission society, or youth group) or an internally supported, church-controlled organization;

- Schools below college level which are affiliated with a church or operated by a religious order;

- Mission societies sponsored by or affiliated with one or more churches or church denominations, if more than half of the society's activities are conducted in, or directed at persons in, foreign countries;

- Exclusively religious activities of any religious order;

- State institutions whose income is excluded from gross income under IRC §115; and

- IRC §501(c)(1) organizations that are instrumentalities of the United States and organized under an act of Congress.[3]

(e) Other Uses for Forms 990

Forms 990 are used for a wide variety of state and local purposes. In many states, an exempt organization can satisfy its annual filing requirement by furnishing a copy of Form 990 to the appropriate state authority. Many grant-making foundations request a copy of Form 990 in addition to or in lieu of audited financial statements, to verify an organization's fiscal activity.

(f) Why to File Even if Not Required to

Organizations not filing annual Forms 990 are removed from *Publication 78*, the master list of qualifying charitable organizations published by the IRS. This IRS policy came to light recently in connection with a disallowed charitable deduction, as discussed in Section 18.8(b) concerning reliance on determination letters. Prudence dictates that any organization seeking donations should assure that its name is listed in *Publication 78*.

Annual filings are also advisable for organizations whose annual gross receipts hover around the $25,000 mark, to assure that the organization remains on the IRS mailing list to receive the forms for annual filing and other announcements issued by the IRS every year or so. Form 990EZ can be filed with the simple notation, "gross receipts under $25,000," without completing any other information.

Finally, a modest organization seeking grants from private foundations may be asked to furnish Form 990. Some grantors use Form 990 rather than

---

[3]IRC §6033(a)(2) and (3).

financial statements to compare organizations, because the presentation may be more consistent.

(g) Filing Deadline

The due date for Forms 990 give tax practitioners and exempt organizations a reprieve. Forms 990 are due to be filed within four and a half months after the end of the organization's fiscal year, rather than the two and a half months allowed for Form 1120 and the three and a half months for Form 1040. An extension of time can be requested if the organization has not completed its year end accounting soon enough to timely file. For Forms 990T and 990PF, the filing extension does *not* extend the time to pay the tax.

The penalty for late filing is $10 a day, not to exceed the greater of $5,000 or five percent of the annual gross receipts for the year of late filing. The penalty can also be imposed if the form is filed incompletely.

27.2 PUBLIC INSPECTION OF FORMS 990

Effective for reporting years beginning in 1987, a copy of Form 990 must be made available to any individual for inspection at the organization's principal office during regular business hours for three years after it is filed.[4]

The organization's exemption application, Form 1023, together with any IRS letters and inquiries about the application, must also be made available unless the organization was in existence on July 15, 1987 (when the rule became effective) and a copy of its application cannot be located.

The penalty for refusing to furnish Form 990 is payable by the responsible person at a rate of $10 per day for each day of failure up to a maximum of $5,000. For withholding Form 1023, another $10 per day is charged and there is no maximum penalty. If the refusal is a willful act, an additional $1,000 can be assessed.[5]

(a) Method of Inspection

The organization must allow inquirers to inspect the forms in its office and to make notes. Copies of the returns need not be furnished, but the EO can offer to do so for a charge not exceeding the prevailing government rate. An inspector who brings his or her own photocopying equipment must be allowed to use it. If the EO wishes, it can offer to send a copy of the return in lieu of a personal visit by an inspector. An EO may not, however, refuse to allow the person to visit its office.

An organization having more than one administrative office must have a copy available at each office where three or more full-time employees work. Service-providing facilities are not counted for this purpose if management functions are not performed there. A branch organization which does not file its

[4]IRC §6104(e); IRS Notice 88-120, 1988-2 C.B. 454.
[5]IRC §6685.

own Form 990 because it is included in a group return must make the group return available.

A request to see a copy of the return can also be sent to the District Director of the Internal Revenue Service in the area in which the organization is located, or to the National Office of the IRS. Form 4506-A can also be used to request a copy of any return, and a photocopying fee will be imposed.

(b) Disclosure Not Required

The names and addresses of the organization's contributors (except for PFs) are not subject to public inspection and can be omitted from the copy made available to the public. All other parts of the Form, including officer compensation, must be disclosed, Forms 990T and 1120-POL are considered nonpublic returns and need not be made available.

(c) Private Foundations

The annual return of a private foundation, Form 990PF, must be made available under a system dating from 1969 that differs from the other Form 990 rules in several respects. The foundation managers make the form open for inspection by any citizen at the principal office during regular business hours, on request made within 180 days after the date of publication of notice of its availability.[6] A notice of availability is to be placed in a newspaper having general circulation in the county in which the PF's principal office is located. It must be placed in the paper by the due date of the annual return, including extensions.[7] The name and telephone number of the foundation's principal manager must be given. Contributor information must be revealed. Form 1023 must also be made available under the circumstances described above. There are penalties for failure to comply, as described above.

27.3 FORM 990EZ, SHORT FORM RETURN OF ORGANIZATION EXEMPT FROM INCOME TAX

An abbreviated version of Form 990, condensed from five to two pages, can be filed by exempt organizations whose gross receipts are normally more than $25,000 but less than $100,000. The entity's total assets shown on line 25, column B for the current year must be under $250,000 and it may not be a private foundation. (PFs file Form 990PF even if they have no revenue.) Organizations qualified for exemption under IRC §501(c)(3) must also file Schedule A.

(a) Measuring Filing Requirement

The filing requirement is not based solely on the current year's gross revenue but on the amount the organization "normally" receives. Normally receiving under $25,000 of gross receipts occurs in the following circumstances and

---

[6]IRC §6104(d).
[7]Instructions to 1992 Form 990PF, page 5.

relieves the organization from filing Form 990EZ:

- *New organization.* An organization up to one year old that receives, or has donors pledging to give, $37,500 or less during its first year;

- *One to three year old organization.* Between one and three years of age, an organization may average $30,000 or less in gross receipts during its first two years and not have to file;

- *Three or more year old organizations.* All other organizations which receive an average of $25,000 or less in the immediately preceding three tax years, including the year for which the return would be filed, are excused from filing. See Section 27.1(f) for possible reasons to file anyway.

(b) Chart to Form 990 Suggestions

This form was designed by the IRS to simplify reporting requirements for modest organizations and to reduce their auditing burden. Essentially, Form 990EZ is a condensed version of the five page Form 990. The information reported is basically the same, but it is combined and abbreviated. Fortunately, the most difficult and dangerous part of the 990—Part VII, Analysis of Income-Producing Activities, (which pinpoints unrelated business income)—is totally absent.

The suggestions for completing Form 990 can be used to complete Form 990EZ. To assist the reader, a blank copy of 990EZ follows as Appendix 27–1, with notations of where those instructions can be found.

27.4 PART I, STATEMENT OF REVENUE, EXPENSES, AND CHANGES IN NET ASSETS OR FUND BALANCES

Appendix 27–2 is a sample Form 990, filled out for a fictitious organization, the Campaign to Clean up America. Note in the example that all nonapplicable questions are answered with "N/A." It is also useful to enter "none" in the blank for any part's total where no amounts are entered. It is especially important to answer the questions on board and staff compensation.

Sections 27.4 through 27.11 offer practical guidance for completing Form 990, which is divided into parts.

Although the title of Part I is similar to that found in the accountants' financial statement (possibly "Statement of Activity"), its arrangement, and in some cases the amount, is very different. Also, the tremendous difference in the operations and purposes of EOs adds complexity to completing the form. A few concepts must be defined at the outset.

Contributions are called "support" on line 1 of this part. "Support" means gratuitous transfer and is essentially a type of revenue received only by an exempt organization. Support represents money given to the EO for which the donor receives nothing in return. Payments for which the payer expects something specific in return are not support. A labor union or a business league reports its member dues on line 3 instead of reporting them as support on line

1. An IRC §501(c)(3) organization reports its member dues payments either on line 1 or line 3, depending upon the value (if any) assigned to the member privileges and benefits, as described in Section 24.2.

IRS *Publication 1391, Deductibility of Payments Made to Charities Conducting Fund-Raising Events* (Appendix 24-1) asks charities to more accurately inform taxpayers as to the deductibility of payments for fund-raising activities. The Commissioner's accompanying letter notes that there is widespread misunderstanding of the limitations; in other words, taxpayers take deductions they are not entitled to. The old refrain used by charities for many years, "deductible to the extent allowed by law," is no longer acceptable. Chapter 24 discusses this issue in detail and provides guidance for valuing such benefits.

Sales of tangible or intangible objects are particularly troublesome because they can be reported on line 2, 8, 9, or 10. Hospitals and colleges using special accounting procedures are allowed to report in accordance with their prescribed categories.

Unrelated business income (UBI) is reported alongside other income without specific identification. Some experts suggest that lines 10 and 11 are troublesome because they are often the appropriate slot for UBI, although the instructions anticipate that both exempt function and unrelated sales will be included on line 10. It is noteworthy that the statute of limitations for assessment of UBIT runs in three years if sufficient information is submitted with Form 990 to allow the IRS to review the status of each category of revenue, even if Form 990T is not filed.

The primary goal in classifying an exempt organization's revenues depends upon the exemption category. For a charitable EO, donations that enable it to satisfy the public support tests may be of utmost importance. A labor union is more concerned about distinguishing between member payments that are taxable UBI and those that are dues. All income, including UBI, is reported on page 1. This section discusses types of income that often cause classification questions.

(a) Definition of Gross Receipts

Filing requirements are based upon gross receipts as reflected in Part I. The definition of gross receipts is all cash receipts of the organization during a year, not including borrowing, interfund transfers, and expense reimbursements. To determine the annual federal filing requirement for Forms 990, the calculation can be tied to the front page of the form itself. For Form 990, the following lines are added:

- Line 1: Contributions, gifts and grants

- Line 2: Program service revenue

- Line 3: Membership dues and assessments

- Line 4: Interest on savings and investments

- Line 5: Dividends and interest from securities

- Line 6a: Gross rent

- Line 7: Other investment income
- Line 8a: Gross amount from sale of assets other than inventory
- Line 9a: Gross revenue from special fund-raising events and activities
- Line 10a: Gross sales less returns and allowances
- Line 11: Other revenue.

The total can be checked by adding back all the costs deducted on page one on lines 6b, 8b, 9b, and 10b to the total revenue on line 12.

For Form 990EZ, follow the same pattern using the somewhat different designations on fewer lines, adding all gross income before the expense deductions.

(b) Line 1: Contributions, Gifts, Grants, and Other Similar Amounts Received

Most often it is IRC §501(c)(3) and §501(c)(4) organizations that receive voluntary contributions and grants reportable on line 1.

Individual contributions. Volunteer payments motivated by the desire to help finance the EO's exempt activities, or "one-way street receipts," are reported here. Moneys reported on this line include those paid with the intention of making a gift with no expectation of return or consideration other than intangible recognition, such as inclusion of a name on a sponsor list or on a church pew. For a §501(c)(3) organization, amounts that qualify for the IRC §170 charitable deduction would appear on this line. Amounts given in return for privileges or goods are reported on line 2, 8, 9, or 10.

Corporate gifts. Grants from corporations or other businesses are reported as direct public support. Although it seems logical to call it an indirect gift, money raised by a business in a cause-related marketing campaign is reported here. The IRS instructions calls such fund-raising "commercial co-ventures." Typically, a business uses the charity's name in a sales promotion and promises to contribute a stated dollar amount for each item sold or for the occurrence of some action on the public's part. For example, for every person attending a sporting event, a beer company gives a dollar to a local charity.

Grants from other organizations. Grants received from other charitable organizations for support in operating the organization's programs, building its facilities, conducting its research, and the like are reported on line 1a, along with individual and corporate donations. Restricted grants to be used for a specific purpose, such as acquisition of a work of art to be owned and held by the grantee, are reported on line 1. Grants to perform services of benefit to the grantor are reported instead on line 2, as explained below.

Indirect public support. Line 1b includes amounts received through solicitation campaigns of federated fund-raising agencies, such as the United Way or community trust. Support received from a parent or subordinate organization or other group that raises funds on behalf of the organization is also to be reported here, as is money transferred to the charitable arm of a professional society whose members voluntarily add donations to their dues payments.

Government grants. Report on line 1c grants or other payments from a governmental unit that enable the organization to perform services of benefit to the general public or a charitable class. For example, a Health and Human Services (HHS) Department grant to a college to develop a curriculum for its engineering department would be reported here. A grant to develop a national engineering curriculum which the HHS will distribute to its grantees would be reported on line 2 or 11.

Non-cash donations. Gifts of marketable securities, real estate, and other non-cash property are included on line 1a at their fair market value on the date of gift.[8] For such gifts exceeding $500, the donor must attach Form 8283 to his or her individual return to claim a deduction. The charity receiving such a gift must file Form 8282 if it disposes of the property within two years from the date of gift, unless it is distributed for exempt purposes.

In-kind contributions. Donations of time, services, or the use of property are *not* reported as support on page 1 or in Schedule A. They are not reported even if the services are recorded for financial reporting purposes in accordance with generally accepted accounting principles (GAAP). If they are so recorded, they can be reported for 990T purposes as discussed in Section 27.14(e).

Contributor names. A schedule of contributors who gave the organization money or other property worth $5,000 or more during the year is to be attached. Addresses, the date received, and a description of the property must be reported (not open to public inspection). The name of an employer withholding gifts from paychecks that are turned over to the charity, is to be reported, but the individual employee names are not. An IRC §509(a)(1) organization whose past year gross receipts exceed $250,000 need only report those gifts exceeding its two percent public donor floor. See Section 11.2(f) for this calculation.

(c) Line 2: Program Service Revenue

Line 2 calls for revenues produced from exempt function services rendered, such as student tuition, testing fees, golf course green fees, trade show admission, ticket sales for cultural events, interest on student or credit union loans, low-cost housing rent, or convention registrations. Fees for services generated in an exempt activity but taxed as unrelated business income are included, such as advertising revenues in an exempt publication. See the instructions for Part VII, in which this type of income is detailed.

Grants that represent payments for services rendered on behalf of the donor are reported here, for example, a grant received by a scientific laboratory testing for automobile emissions for a state government. See more discussion of such grants at Section 11.4(b). Sales of "inventory," such as books, posters, reproductions, or other items sold in a bookstore, crafts produced by the handicapped, or tennis balls sold in the country club shop, even though they are related to exempt function activities, are not reported here, but on line 10 instead.

Hospitals and colleges whose accounting systems do not allow them to readily extract the cost of goods sold attributable solely to inventory are permitted to report inventory sales on line 2.

---

[8]The estate tax rules at Reg. §20.2031 prescribe valuation methods.

(d) Line 3: Membership Dues and Assessments

For all exempt organizations, the first question is: What do members receive in return for their dues payments? The value attributable to services received by members is reported as membership dues and assessments. For most EOs, the total amount of member dues used as general support by the organization is reported on line 3. Separate charges for specific activities, such as an educational seminar conducted by a business league, are reported on line 2.

For a charitable EO, the excess amount of dues over fair market value of services received by the donor is separately reported as a donation on line 1, as explained above. According to the IRS, if the rights and privileges of membership are incidental to making the organization function, and if the benefit of membership is the personal satisfaction of being of service to others and furthering the exempt purposes, the membership is a gift.[9] This distinction may be important for public support purposes. An organization that wishes to maintain its status as a IRC §509(a)(1) organization prefers contributions, because membership dues are not counted as public support. Conversely, membership dues are fully counted as support for IRC §509(a)(2) purposes.

One example of the distinction between dues and donations is that Civil Air Patrol (CAP) members make contributions when their dues entitle them to receive training to perform services for the CAP for the benefit of the public, not for the member.[10] The IRS has ruled that an educational newsletter is incidental to the exempt purposes and is thus not an individual benefit unless it is a "commercial quality" publication.[11]

By contrast, preferential seating, attendance at receptions, discounts at a bookstore, free parking, and other privileges are considered to be valuable services rendered to the member. This negates the gift element and causes classification as dues, not donations.[12] See Section 24.2 for instructions on measuring such benefits.

(e) Line 4: Interest on Savings and Temporary Cash Investments

This line is mostly self-explanatory. Interest earned on a program-related investment, however, goes on line 2 instead. Whether or not an employee loan is program-related is unclear. Money market interest also presents a question. Clearly, the interest on a bank money market checking or savings account is to be reported on line 4, but the Dreyfus Temporary Cash fund is reportable as a dividend on line 5.

Interest on a privately placed loan to an individual or a corporation, not representing a security interest (meaning it is not regulated by state or federal securities law), is reported on line 11. If the loan is an investment, the interest is reported on line 7. Interest on a note receivable from the sale of an exempt function asset is also reported as other income on line 11. A labor union loaning

---

[9]Reg. §1.509(a)-3(h). Also see Section 11.4(c).
[10]*Miller v. Commissioner*, 34 T.C.M. 1207 (1975).
[11]Rev. Proc. 90-12, 1990-1, C.B. 471. See Section 24.2(c) for definition of the terms.
[12]See Section 24.1 and 24.2.

funds to a faltering company to protect the jobs of its worker members would report the interest on line 2.

(f) Line 5: Dividends and Interest from Securities

Income payment from investments in stocks, bonds, and security loans are reported on line 5. Mutual fund shares capital gain dividends, however, are reportable on line 8. Dividends from a subsidiary operated as a program related investment would be reported on line 2.

(g) Line 6: Gross Rents

Rents from investment real or personal property are reported on line 6. Rents produced through exempt programs, such as low-income housing, are included on line 2. Rental of office space to other unaffiliated exempt organizations are usually reportable as rents on this line. Such rents are only reported on line 2 as exempt function income if the rental rate is well below the fair rental value of the property, and if the rental itself serves the lesser EO's exempt purposes.

Expenses directly connected with the rental income are deducted on line 6b, but need not be itemized. Maintenance, interest on mortgages, depreciation, and other direct costs are placed here and are not included on page 2.

(h) Line 7: Other Investment Income

Income produced by "investments-other" on line 56 of the balance sheet is reported on line 7. Mineral royalties are a good example. Such income is expected to be explained and the information can be tied to the balance sheet, where an explanation is also requested. The instructions specifically provide that the unrealized gains or losses on investments carried at market value are to be reported, not on this line, but on line 20 as an "other change in fund balance."

(i) Line 8: Capital Gains and Losses

Gains or losses from sales of all types of capital assets, including those held for investment, those held for exempt purposes, and those that produce UBI, are reported on line 8. A detailed schedule similar to that included in a normal income tax return is prepared—date acquired and sold, gross sales price and selling expenses, cost basis, and any depreciation. Multiple sales of publicly traded securities can be aggregated and reported as one number.

Capital gains distributed from partnerships or trusts are includible here. Unrealized gains reported for financial statement purposes should be reported on line 20.

(j) Line 9: Fund-Raising Events

Amounts paid as admission to events in excess of the value of services or goods received are classified as donations on line 1 and noted in parentheses on line

9a. The amount attributable to the goods or services sold is reported under this event category.

Fund-raising campaign gifts for which donors receive nothing in return for their gifts are totally reported on line 1. The instructions direct §501(c)(3) organizations to keep both their solicitations and the receipts they furnish to participants in events, as well as proof of the method used to determine the noncontribution portion of the proceeds. Services or goods received are to be valued at their fair market value, which is often difficult to determine. The cost of the event is not necessarily determinative. What is the comparable value of a costume ball at the museum? See discussion at Section 27.4(b) and in Chapter 24.

A detailed description of the three largest events sponsored during the year must be furnished. The direct costs attributable to the event are deducted on line 9b to arrive at the net income. The allocable portion of administrative or fund-raising departments is not reported on this line but on the applicable line of Part II.

(k) Line 10: Gross Sales Minus Returns and Allowances

Sales of inventory property made or purchased for resale, but not sales of capital assets, are reported here. An educational center's bookstore, a retirement home's pharmaceuticals, a thrift shop's used clothing, or other objects purchased or produced for resale constitute inventory items. Hospitals and colleges can report inventory items on line 3.

(l) Line 11: Other Revenues

Interest earned on loans not made as investments, such as an employee advance or officer loan, are cited by the IRS instructions as reportable on this line. Royalties paid for use of the EO's name are also reported here.

(m) Lines 13–15: Expense Totals

IRC §501(c)(3) and (4) organizations and IRC §4947(a)(1) charitable trusts must complete these lines. All other Form 990 filers leave these lines blank. Totals from Part II on page 2, where expenses are divided into functional categories, are reported here. The organization should note that the ratio between these lines is an evaluation tool used by some readers. For example, assume:

Line 13 Program services	$600,000	67%
Line 14 Management and general	200,000	22%
Line 15 Fund-raising	100,000	11%
Line 17 Total expenses	$900,000	100%

Some advisors in the nonprofit community have opinions about the proper level of program spending as compared to general and administrative and fund-raising expenses. The Better Business Bureau thinks that program services equaling at least 80 percent of the total expense is preferred. Spending 67 percent as shown above may be questionable.

(n) Line 16: Affiliate Payments

Required payments to a national, state, or other closely related EO under a predetermined formula for sharing support or dues are deducted here. The IRS instructions to the form comprise half a page and provide clear guidance for this line.

(o) Lines 18–21: Fund Balances

The information reported for Form 990 purposes is reconciled to the financial records on these lines. The balance sheet in Part IV is reported according to the EO's financial statements. Differences in reporting treatment might stem from a change in accounting method or from an adjustment of a prior year's mistake in reporting. The EO must decide if a change is significant enough to require amendment of the previously-filed Form 990. If not, the difference would be reported on line 20. The IRS may question such a correction if it reflects an overall accounting method change for which permission was not secured in advance, and if the amount is material. Particularly if the change affects unrelated business income tax, an amended return may be proper. See Section 28.6.

Other possible explanations for differences here include unrealized gain or loss reported for financial statement purposes not includible on lines 1–17, and in-kind contributions reported on financial statements but not reportable on lines 1–11.

27.5 PART II, STATEMENT OF FUNCTIONAL EXPENSES

In this part, the organization's total operating expenses are reported in Column A by object classification, such as salaries, occupancy, and so on. This column must be completed by all exempt organizations filing this form. An EO's total expenses are to be reported, including those paid to produce unrelated business income (UBI). While it might seem wrong to include UBI expenses with related expenses of program services rendered, the form's design requires it. Deductible UBI expenses may appear on any line (but not in Column D). For example, grants reported on line 22 may qualify as a charitable deduction in calculating the UBI tax. Section 21.14 discusses UBI deductions and defines direct and indirect costs—an accounting concept which applies in preparing this part.

Completing columns B, C, and D to break down an organization's total expenses according to its departments for program services, management and general expenses, and fund-raising is optional for:

1. Voluntary employee benefits associations and other EOs substituting Department of Labor forms;

2. All EOs except §501(c)(3) and §501(c)(4) organizations; and

3. Organizations whose receipts are normally under $25,000 annually.

Program services are those activities performed to accomplish the purposes for which the EO is exempt (its "exempt function"). Direct expenses specifically incurred in association with a project are included, along with an allocable part of indirect costs, such as salaries of employees directly involved in the project, occupancy cost for space utilized, and the cost of printing the reports. Colleges and hospitals whose internal accounting systems allocate indirect costs into cost centers have options for reporting such costs, and should read the instructions carefully.

Management and general expenses include overhead and administration—those expenses that are not allocable to programs or fund-raising. The executive director or controller and her or his staff and expenses, personnel and accounting departments, auditors, and lawyers are reported in column C. The cost of organizational meetings, such as the annual membership meeting, monthly board, staff, and committee meetings, and other meetings unrelated to a specific program or fund-raising are reported in column C. The investment or cash management function, budgeting, personnel, and staff cafeteria operations typify the costs reported here. Organizational and officer and director liability coverage is a management expense.

Fund-raising includes expenses incurred in soliciting donations, memberships, and grants voluntarily given to the exempt organization.

Fund-raising expenses include:

- Annual giving campaign costs of printing, publicity, mailing, staffing, and the like;
- Professional fees to plan and execute the campaign or to draw documents for planned giving;
- Development or grant-writing department;
- Costs of collecting fund campaign pledges;
- Portion of event costs not reported on line 8b; and
- Advertisements soliciting support.

Fund-raising expenses do *not* include:

- Unrelated business expenses (these go in Column B or C, or possibly only on page 1 if directly related to revenue);
- Fund-raising event, rental, or inventory direct expenses deducted directly from the gross receipts on page one (lines 6b, 8b, 9b, or 10b); and
- Costs associated with collecting exempt income, such as student tuition or seminar registration fees. Report these in Column B.

(a) Line 22: Grants and Allocations

Grants to other exempt organizations and to individuals are reported on line 22. Attach details summarizing the following information:

1. Recipient's name and address and amount given;
2. Class or type of grant, such as scholarship, educational research, or building construction; and

3. Relationships, if any, between the grantor and its directors or trustees and an individual grantee. (This information allows the IRS to identify private inurement, discussed in Chapter 20.)

Voluntary payments to affiliated organizations are reported on this line, rather than on line 16. Scholarship, fellowship, and research grants to individuals are reported on line 22, even though it is surprising, given the title of line 23. Only the grant award amounts are reported. The cost of administering the grant program, such as selection of recipients and monitoring compliance, is included on lines 25 through 43. If the grant is made in property rather than cash, more details are required. A description of the property, its book value, how the fair market value was determined, and the date of the gift are to be listed. Any gain or loss on the transaction is reported on line 11 in Part I.

(b) Line 23: Specific Assistance to Individuals

Medical care, food, clothing, or cash to indigents or other members of a charitable class are reported on line 23, with a summary by type of assistance attached. The individual names are not reported. A (c)(3) organization must be alert to defining its charitable class and avoiding challenges, as outlined in Section 2.2(a).

A grant to a homeless shelter for its operating expenses is reported on line 22, as is payment to the shelter for a particular individual's room and board.

(c) Line 24: Benefits Paid to or for Members

Payment of member benefits is usually antithetical to the purposes of an IRC §501(c)(3) organization, which, as a rule, would avoid such payment. Consult Section 20.9 for the problems involved with member benefits.

Labor unions, fraternal benefit societies, voluntary employee beneficiary associations, unemployment benefit trusts, and other nonprofit associations are formed to benefit their members in a nonprofit mode, and set aside moneys for such payments as a part of their underlying exempt function. A schedule reflecting the amount and type of benefits paid for sickness, death, unemployment, and the like should be attached and the total reported on line 23. Such payments and the insurance premiums associated with such protection paid on behalf of employees are reported on lines 27 and 28.

(d) Line 25: Compensation of Officers, Directors, etc.

Line 25 calls for total officer compensation and should equal the totals reported in columns C, D, and E of Part V. The instructions to this line give no explanation of the terms, and the 1992 instructions to Part V, column E contain contradictory instructions. The first sentence says that only amounts reportable on the recipients' tax returns are included. The last sentence says that both taxable and nontaxable fringe benefits are to be reported. The author has discussed this problem with the IRS and it is their intention that all forms of compensation, taxable and nontaxable, paid to persons governing an EO should be reported in total on this part and on line 25.

Salaries, fees, commissions, and other types of compensation, including pension plan contributions, deferred compensation accruals (even if unfunded), health insurance, and other employee benefits (taxable and nontaxable) are included. Amounts earned by directors in their capacity as directors and/or as staff or management are reported. An officer may be an employee or an independent contractor.

The total gross wages or fees reported as paid to an individual should be corroborated with Forms 941, W-2, and 1099 separately filed with the Internal Revenue Service to report the individual compensation and tax withholding. The IRS began to emphasize this subject in its large case examinations during 1992. See Chapter 25 for details of those reporting rules and discussion of taxable compensation for various types of payments made to individuals.

(e) Lines 26, 27, 28, and 29: Salaries, Wages, Pension Contributions, Employee Benefits, and Payroll Taxes

Total payments to all salaried individuals, other than officers reported on line 25, are reported on line 26. Again, other reporting requirements are signaled to the IRS by the numbers on these lines. In addition to payroll taxes mentioned above, state unemployment taxes may be due, and Form 5500 may be due for pension plans.

(f) Lines 30, 31, and 32: Professional Fund-raising, Accounting, and Legal Fees

These lines report compensation paid to independent advisors for fund-raising, accounting, auditing, financial consulting, and legal services. Note that the combination of lines 25–32 represents the direct amounts paid by the organization to individuals for services rendered. If this total number is high in relation to the overall expenses of the organization shown on line 44, an alarm may be sounded in someone's mind—the IRS, the inspecting member of the general public (see Section 27.2), a news reporter, or potential contributor. The IRS will ask the questions raised in Chapter 20 concerning private inurement.

Some states require charitable registration, and amounts reported on line 32 may signal the need for additional compliance. Consult another book in the Wiley Nonprofit Series, *The Law of Fund-Raising* by Bruce R. Hopkins for a useful guide to such requirements.

(g) Lines 33–43: Supplies, Telephone, Postage, Occupancy, etc.

These lines are largely explained by their titles. Some comments follow:

Travel. An organization reporting travel should use a system of documentation designed to prove the travel's exempt purpose. Expense vouchers reflecting the nature of the expenditures and indicating any personal elements are appropriate. Staff members using an EO's vehicles must maintain a log of their mileage to prove what use is devoted to EO affairs, as well as any personal use. The personal portion, if any, is part of compensation and reportable on line 25, 26, or 28. Vehicle expense is reported as a part of travel or shipping.

Interest. Amounts paid for interest on rental property is not reported here but on line 6b of Part I, and, for property occupied by the EO for its own operations, on line 36. Otherwise, interest expense is reported on line 41. The total interest reported on the three lines mentioned must be coordinated with the answer to indebtedness in Part IV, Balance Sheets.

Depreciation. A detailed schedule of depreciation showing the current expense, reserves, asset costs, additions and deletions, and dates is to be prepared and attached in answer to line 42, possibly line 6b, line 7 (for depletion on mineral properties), or line 11, and for the Balance Sheet of Part IV at lines 55a and b and 57a and b.

(h) Functional Expense Allocations

The challenge in this part is dividing the expenses into functional categories of program service, management and general, and fund-raising. The columns allow the IRS and others to evaluate the proportion of costs devoted to exempt activities—optimally, a high proportion. Conversely, fund-raising costs should be low; some states limit them to 20 or 25 percent of total expenses. The administrative expense level depends upon the nature of the organization.

Joint costs. To allocate costs that are of benefit to more than one function of the EO's operations, the IRS instructions suggest, "Use an appropriate basis for each kind of cost."[13] Some expenses, such as salaries, are allocated based on time expended. Occupancy can be based on space assigned or people using it, (and may be partly based on their time allocation).

The accounting profession provides some guidance for allocating materials that serve both an educational and informational purpose.[14] See the accounting references listed at the beginning of this chapter.

Private foundations. At the behest of Congress, the IRS decided that the portion of administrative expense a private foundation can count as a qualifying distribution should be limited to 13 percent of its minimum distribution requirement during the years 1985–1989. The limit was not extended because the IRS found that most foundation administrative costs were lower than the upper limit, and the reporting methods were not consistent.

Unrelated business expenses. A portion of program and administrative expenses may be attributable to unrelated business activity. Any expenses so allocated reduce UBIT payable, so they deserve particular attention. Expenses related to UBI are reported in many places, though. Direct costs of rental property and assets and inventory sold are deducted against the revenue on page 1 (lines 6b, 9b, 10b, and 11). An educational magazine's publication costs allocable to advertising revenue would be deducted on line 38 as program service. The treatment on Form 990T should not be influenced by the presentation on Form 990, but an examining agent will certainly draw inferences from it. See Sections 21.13 and 27.14(c) for more information.

[13]IRS Instructions to 1992 Form 990, Part II, In General, at page 11.
[14]American Institute of Certified Public Accountants, Statement of Position 87-2, *Accounting for Joint Costs of Informational Materials and Activities of Not-for-Profit Organizations that Include a Fund-Raising Appeal.*

27.6 PART III, STATEMENT OF PROGRAM SERVICE ACCOMPLISHMENTS

Form 990 asks the EO to describe what was achieved in carrying out its exempt purposes. IRC §501(c)(3) and (4) organizations and wholly charitable trusts must also present the cost of each program activity, including the amount of grants and allocations paid to others individuals and organizations. For other categories of Form 990 filers, submission of total expenses by program service category is not required.

In other words, the EO must take the expenses reported in Column B of Part II and further identify them by particular projects, reporting the total for its four major programs. Functional accounting records maintained by program are clearly a must for completing this part.

To describe the EO's accomplishments, the services provided are summarized along with numerical data. How many members are served, classes taught, meals served, patients healed, sites restored, books published, products certified, or similar data evidencing public benefit provided is to be reported for the EO's four major projects.

A private elementary school with 400 students can easily answer this question A 400 bed hospital would report the number of patients served and quantify the amount of charity care, if any. Reasonable estimates can be furnished if the exact number of recipients is not known. If numerical results are not pertinent or available, the project objectives for the return period and the long range plans can be described. An EO conducting research on heart disease and testing a controlled group of 100 women over a five year period would state this. Similarly, assume that an EO commissions a study of an area's history and expects the project to take ten years. Four scholars are hired to annually deliver a minimum of 100 pages each, with citations and appropriate photographic documentation or other archival materials. How the documents will be eventually published is not known, so the number of copies and eventual public benefit cannot be measured. However, the research modality can be described to evidence the work's educational nature.

Brochures, publication lists, and rate sheets can also be attached to convey a picture of the EO's activities.

27.7 PART IV, BALANCE SHEET

An exempt organization's beginning and ending assets, liabilities, and fund balances or net assets are reported in Part IV, using the same method which the EO uses for maintaining its normal accounting books and records. Fair market value of the assets is *not* reported, except when gain and loss on investments is recognized annually to carry investments at their current value. The amounts are most often reported at original cost, or "book value." If detailed schedules are requested, they need only be furnished for the year end numbers. The instructions for this part are quite good and need not be repeated here.

Loans. Certain lines in this part alert the IRS to problem issues, and in those cases detailed schedules are requested. For most loans receivable by or payable by the organization, ten detailed items of information are required:

borrower's name and title, original amount, balance due, date of note, maturity date, repayment terms, interest rate, security provided by borrower, purpose of the loan, and description and fair market value of consideration furnished by the lender. Loans to and from officers, directors, trustees, and key employees are presented as a separate total on line 50. The issues discussed in Sections 20.6 and 20.7 may need attention if the EO has such loans. A modest $5,000 loan for college education to the vice-president may not cause additional scrutiny, but a $100,000 loan to refinance his credit cards might.

Coordinated schedules. Schedules for depreciable assets should be prepared to coordinate with the information required to be attached for Part I and II. Likewise, receivable and payable information can be tied to interest expense.

Incomplete information. In its instructions, the IRS cautions the preparer that penalties are imposed for failure to complete this part. The IRS thoughtfully reminds the organization that the reports are open to public inspection, and recommends that an effort be made to correctly complete the report. Labor unions filing Form LM-2 or LM-3 with the U.S. Department of Labor and certain employee benefit plans may substitute those forms for his part.[15]

27.8 PART V, LIST OF OFFICERS, DIRECTORS, AND TRUSTEES

Part V calls for the names, addresses, titles, and times devoted to the positions for all members of the EO's governing body or "those persons having responsibilities or powers similar to those of officers, directors, or trustees,"[16] whether or not they are compensated. All such persons are to be listed, even if there are 50 board members. If an attachment is prepared, consider entering totals across the bottom of the form or noting "none" in each column where applicable.

Total compensation paid to persons serving on the governing board, for all services rendered, is to be reported, whether they are employees or independent contractors. For persons serving in more than one position—e.g., both as a director and officer or staff member—the compensation for each respective position should be separately presented. Three distinct types of pay are reported in one of three columns.

Column C: Salary, fees, vacation pay, sick leave, severance pay, deferred compensation (whether or not reported in column D in a prior year), and any other amounts paid for personal services rendered, are reported here.

Column D. All forms of deferred compensation—whether funded or unfunded, whether pursuant to a qualified or an unqualified plan—are reported in this column. Qualified pension plans include defined contribution, defined benefit, and money purchase plans under IRC §401(a), so-called "employee annuity plans" under IRC §403(b), and IRA/SEP plans under IRC §408. Unqualified and unfunded "rabbi" trust benefits accrued would also be reported. In a duplicative manner, the current year amount set aside is reported in this column as it accrues, while the actual payment made in a later year is reported in column C.

[15] IRS Instructions to 1992 Form 990, General Item F, at page 4.
[16] IRS Instructions to 1992 Form 990, Part V, at page 16.

Column E. "Expense account and other allowances" are included in this column. As noted in Section 27.4, the instructions for this column contain contradictory instructions for 1992 and prior years. The first sentence says to include amounts reportable on the recipient's tax return; the last sentence says to include taxable and nontaxable fringe benefits. Hopefully, the titles to this part and the instructions will be changed in the near future.

If the purpose of this part is to quantify an amount to evaluate the presence of private inurement to the EO's insiders, all type of payments providing funds or assets to insiders for their personal use and benefit should be reported. It is the author's understanding that the IRS intends a wide range of benefits to be included in this column, such as medical, life, disability, and other private insurance premiums, automobile usage for personal driving (but not the exempt activity portion), tuition payments, day care, housing, meal, or other personal allowances, and any other amounts paid pursuant to a "cafeteria" plan.

27.9 PART VI, OTHER INFORMATION

The other information desired by the IRS to evaluate an organization's qualification for ongoing tax exemption is solicited by seventeen questions on page 4 of Form 990. Certain answers can cause serious problems for the organization, as outlined below.

Line 76 alerts the IRS to review organizational changes by asking if the EO "engaged in any activities not previously reported to the IRS." The question is sometimes hard to answer when the EO's activity has evolved or expanded, but has not necessarily changed in its focus or overall purpose. The real question is whether the EO wants IRS approval for its evolving or admittedly new activity. Simply answering this question "yes" and attaching a detailed description of a change does not result in an IRS response, in most cases. When the EO should report a change or expansion in its operations or activities to the Key District Director, instead of simply answering this question "Yes" is discussed in Section 28.2. If the board or contributors need the security of written IRS approval for the new projects or change in purpose, a formal ruling request should be filed with the Key District.

Line 77 serves a function similar to line 76 by asking if "changes were made in the organizing or governing documents, but not reported to the IRS?" Conformed copies (see Section 18.3(a) at line 10 for meaning) should be attached if the answer is "Yes." Again, it is not customary to get an IRS response to any information submitted. Consult Chapter 2, 6, 7, 8, or 9 to ascertain whether a change violates the standards for the type of EO involved. See Chapter 28 to decide if the Key District should be informed directly.

Line 78 tells the IRS that the EO has unrelated business income in excess of $1,000 and that Form 990T is due to be filed. Woe to the EO that checks this question "yes" and fails to do so!

Line 79 reveals whether a liquidation, termination, or substantial contraction has occurred. Section 28.9 defines these terms and describes the consequences and constraints placed on such an organization. The instructions provide specific information to be attached if the answer is "Yes," and direct the preparer to read the regulations for special rules and exceptions.[17]

Line 80 asks "Are you related to any other exempt or nonexempt organization?" If so, the entity is to be named. Such relationships are permitted and do not necessarily expose the EO to loss of its exemption. Chapter 22 discusses the consequence of such relationships and the constraints within which they are permitted. Part IX of Form 990 (see Section 27.13) and Part VII of Schedule A (see Section 27.12(f)) also request similar information.

Line 81. The amount of political expenditures are entered on this line. "None" *must* be the answer for (c)(2) and (c)(3) EOs. Political activity is aimed at influencing the election of persons who make local, state, or national laws (not to be confused with lobbying, which is influencing the elected persons once they are in office). An excise tax is imposed on any (c)(3) involved in politics[18] and its exemption may be revoked.

Such activity is not absolutely prohibited for many types of EOs. See Section 23.1 for permissible amounts of political activity. EOs must file Form 1120-POL if their investment income and political expenditures exceed $100.

Line 82 allows an EO to voluntarily report any donated services or facilities it receives during the year and to indicate their value. Such donations are not included on page 1 or Schedule A because they are not deductible to the donor and are difficult to value. Because returns are open to public inspection, this question permits an EO to reveal such support.[19]

Line 83. The EO must inform the IRS whether anyone has requested to see either its annual return or exemption application and, if so, whether the organization complied. Failure to comply leads to imposition of penalties as outlined in Section 28.2. Over 58 percent of randomly selected EOs in Washington, D.C. failed to make their reports available to staff investigators of Congressman Richard Schulze during 1989 and 1990. This failure, among other reasons, has led some to suggest that public charities and other exempt organizations be subject to sanctions similar to those applied to private foundations.

Line 84. "Did you solicit any contributions or gifts that were not tax deductible?" EOs which are not eligible to receive deductible donations,[20] and which have over $100,000 annual gross receipts, must expressly say that they are not eligible. The notice must appear in a conspicuous and easily recognizable format on fund solicitation materials distributed in printed form, by television or radio, or by telephone.

Organizations eligible to receive deductible gifts answer this question "N/A," in accordance with the instructions. The 1992 tax bill vetoed by then-president Bush contained a requirement that charitable organizations furnish deductibility information. Watch for a change in these rules and see Chapter 24 for more details on this issue.

Lines 85 through 88 ask questions pertaining to the particular types of organizations listed below. Consult the referenced chapters before answering the questions.

---

[17] Reg. §1.6043-3.
[18] IRC §4955.
[19] IRS Instructions to 1992 Form 990, Part VI, at page 17.
[20] IRC §170(c).

- IRC §§501(c)(5) and (6). See Chapters 7 and 8. This alerts the IRS that a labor organization or business league potentially has grassroots lobbying expenses not deductible by its members.

- IRC §(c)(7). See Chapter 9. The requested information furnishes statistics to calculate the social club's continuing qualification, based upon the proportionate amount of nonmember receipts and investment income. Discrimination based upon race, color, or religion is prohibited, so the answer to question 86(c) should be "No."

- IRC §501(c)(12). Benevolent life insurance associations of a purely local character, mutual ditch or irrigation companies, mutual or cooperative telephone companies, and like organizations must receive 85 percent or more of their income from members. Compliance with the test is measured by the question.

- Public interest law firms. Section 23.10 describes the requirements for exemption. A detailed report of cases handled must be attached, describing how they accomplish exempt purposes.

Line 91 asks for the name and number of the person who is in care of the books. This person will receive the call if the IRS wishes to examine the organization's records.

27.10   PART VII, ANALYSIS OF INCOME-PRODUCING ACTIVITY

Part VII was added to Form 990 in 1989 and contains a host of pitfalls and traps for the unwary. At the behest of Congress, the IRS designed this form as an audit trail to find unrelated business income (UBI). Selection of the appropriate code to identify income is difficult in some cases and can have adverse consequences. Some choices are not absolute, and discretion can be important. For example, code 40 highlights activities conducted for nonexempt purposes and operated at a loss—potentially representing use of EO funds for private purposes and the possibility that the IRS should revoke the EO's exemption. Such losses, in the IRS's opinion, are also not available to offset against profit-motivated UBI. (See the *Portland Golf Club* decision discussed in Section 9.5(e) regarding limitations on a social club's activities not entered into to produce a profit.)

A thorough review of the unrelated business income provisions discussed in Chapter 21 will be very useful before completing this part.[21] An understanding of the terms "regularly carried on," "member convenience," "related and unrelated," and "fragmented" is absolutely necessary for correct completion of this page. The form forces the organization to report items of income appearing on page 1, lines 2 through 11 (except for contributions) in one of three categories by columns.

---

[21]See also IRS Publication 598, *Tax on Unrelated Business Income of Exempt Organizations*.

(a) What the Columns Include

Columns (a) and (b) Unrelated Business Income. Income from unrelated business activities is reported in column (b). Any amounts included here must be reported on Form 990T and are subject to income tax if a profit is generated from the activity. Column (a) codes are used in Form 990T (Exhibit 27–1) to identify the type of business conducted—mining, construction, manufacturing, services, and so on. The codes are very similar to those used in Forms 1120 and 1065 for corporate and partnership income tax returns.

Columns (c) and (d): Revenues excluded or modified from tax. Income from investments, fund-raising events, and business activities statutorily excluded from tax are included in these columns. The reason for exclusion of the income from tax is claimed by inserting one of forty code numbers (explained below under line numbers and shown at Exhibit 27–2) in column (c). If more than one exclusion code applies, the lowest applicable code number is used according to the instructions. Certain codes, such as bingo (9), membership lists (13), and royalties (15), which are the subjects of current IRS vs. taxpayer battles as described in Chapter 21 may be troublesome, as the IRS uses this page to choose the EOs it will examine.

Column (e): Related or exempt function income. Income generated through charges for services rendered or items sold in connection with the EO's underlying exempt (or program) activities are entered in column (e). Student tuition and fees, hospital charges, admissions, publication sales, handicraft or other byproduct sales, seminar registrations, and all other revenues received in return for providing exempt functions[22] are included. This column is a safe harbor because it contains income not potentially subject to the UBI tax: that income which is generated by "substantially related" activities (those with a causal relationship, contributing importantly to the EO's programs). An explanation of the related aspect of each number in this column must be entered in Part VIII, as described below.

Some exempt function income is also described by specific exclusion codes. Rentals from low income housing fits into code 16 and therefore could also properly be placed in columns (c) and (d). It is preferable to place such an item in column (e) because the taint of UBI character is removed. Interest income earned under a student loan program or by a credit union and royalties from scientific research patents are other examples of potential dual classifications.

(b) Line-by-Line Description

First, note that for certain lines gross income before any deductions is reported, and for others (lines 97, 98, 100, and 101) net income is reported.

Line 93: Program service revenue. Revenues produced from activities forming the basis for exemption, described above under column (e), are considered program service revenues. As a general rule, all revenues on this line would be reportable in column (e). One important exception is fees for social club services

---

[22] IRC §512(a)(3)(B); see Section 27.3(c).

Exhibit 27–1

Codes for Unrelated Business Activity

(If engaged in more than one unrelated business activity, select up to three codes for the principal activities. List first the largest in terms of unrelated income, then the next largest, etc.)

AGRICULTURE, FORESTRY, AND FISHING

Code
0400 Agricultural production
0600 Agricultural services (except veterinarians), forestry, fishing, hunting and trapping
0740 Veterinary services

MINING

Code
1330 Crude petroleum, natural gas and natural gas liquids
1399 All other mining

CONSTRUCTION

Code
1510 General building contractors
1798 All other construction

MANUFACTURING

Code
2000 Food and kindred products
2100 Tobacco manufacturers
2200 Textile mill products
2300 Apparel and other textile products
2400 Lumber and wood products, except furniture
2500 Furniture and fixtures
2600 Paper and allied products

Printing, publishing and allied industries
2710 Newspapers
2720 Periodicals
2730 Books
2750 Commercial printing (except advertising)
2770 Greeting cards
2799 All other printing and printing trade services
2800 Chemicals and allied products
2900 Petroleum refining and related industries (including those integrated with extraction)
3000 Rubber and miscellaneous plastics products
3100 Leather and leather products
3200 Stone, clay, glass and concrete products
3300 Primary metal industries
3400 Fabricated metal products, except machinery and transportation equipment
3500 Industrial and commercial machinery and computer equipment
3600 Electronic and other electrical equipment and components, except computer equipment
3700 Transportation equipment

Measuring, analyzing, and controlling instruments; photographic, medical and optical goods; watches and clocks
3841 Surgical and medical instruments and apparatus
3842 Orthopedic, prosthetic, and surgical appliances and supplies
3899 Other instruments; photographic and optical goods; watches and clocks
3900 Miscellaneous manufacturing industries

TRANSPORTATION, COMMUNICATIONS, ELECTRIC, GAS AND SANITARY SERVICES

Code

Transportation
4117 Sightseeing buses
4118 Ambulance service (local)
4140 Bus charter service
4199 Other local and suburban transit and interurban highway passenger transportation
4724 Travel agencies
4725 Tour operators
4799 All other transportation

Communication
4830 Radio and television broadcasting
4898 Other communication services
4900 Electric, gas and sanitary services

WHOLESALE TRADE

Code
5000 Durable goods
5100 Nondurable goods

RETAIL TRADE

Code
5200 Building materials, hardware, garden supply and mobile home dealers
5300 General merchandise stores

Food stores
5410 Grocery stores
5460 Bakeries
5495 Health food stores
5498 Other food stores
5500 Automotive dealers and gasoline service stations
5600 Apparel and accessory stores

Home furniture, furnishings, and equipment stores
5734 Computer and computer software stores
5799 Home furniture, furnishings, and other equipment stores

Eating and drinking places
5811 Caterers
5812 Other eating places
5813 Drinking places (alcoholic beverages)

Miscellaneous retail
5910 Drugstores and proprietary stores
5930 Used merchandise stores
5941 Sporting goods stores and bicycle shops
5942 Book stores
5947 Gift, novelty, and souvenir shops
5961 Catalog and mail order houses
5992 Florists
5994 News dealers and newsstands
5995 Optical goods
5996 Hearing aids
5997 Orthopedic and artificial limbs stores
5998 Miscellaneous retail stores

FINANCE, INSURANCE AND REAL ESTATE

Code

Depository institutions
6020 Commercial banks, including bank holding companies
6030 Savings institutions
6060 Credit unions
6098 Other depository institutions

Nondepository credit institutions
6140 Personal credit institutions, including mutual benefit associations
6199 Other nondepository credit institutions
6200 Security, commodity brokers, dealers, exchanges and services

Insurance
6310 Life insurance
6321 Accident and health insurance
6324 Hospital and medical service plans
6330 Fire, marine and casualty insurance
6370 Pension, health and welfare funds
6398 All other insurance carriers
6410 Insurance agents, brokers and services

Real estate
6512 Operators of nonresidential buildings
6513 Operators of apartment buildings
6515 Operators of residential mobile home sites
6518 All other real estate operators (except developers) and lessors
6530 Real estate agents and managers
6550 Land subdividers and developers
6599 Other real estate

Holding and other investment companies, except bank holding companies
6730 Trusts
6797 Investment clubs
6798 Miscellaneous holding and investment offices

SERVICES

Code

Hotels, rooming houses, camps, and other lodging places
7010 Hotels and motels
7020 Rooming and boarding houses
7030 Camps and recreational vehicle parks
7040 Organization hotels and lodging houses, on membership basis

Personal services
7210 Laundry, cleaning and garment services
7298 Miscellaneous personal services

Business services
7310 Advertising (including printing)
7331 Direct mail advertising services
7334 Photocopying and duplicating services
7345 Building cleaning and maintenance services
7352 Medical equipment rental and leasing
7360 Personnel supply services
7371 Computer programming services
7374 Computer processing and data preparation, and processing services
7377 Computer rental and leasing
7378 Computer maintenance and repair
7388 Other business services
7500 Automotive repair, services, and parking
7600 Miscellaneous repair services
7800 Motion pictures

Amusement and recreation services
7910 Dance studios, schools, and halls
7920 Theatrical producers (except motion pictures), bands, orchestras, and entertainers
7933 Bowling centers
7940 Commercial sports
7991 Physical fitness facilities
7992 Public golf courses
7996 Amusement parks
7997 Membership sports and recreation clubs
7998 Amusement and recreation services, not elsewhere classified

Health services
8010 Offices and clinics of doctors
8020 Offices and clinics of dentists
8045 Offices and clinics of other health practitioners
8050 Nursing and personal care facilities
8060 Hospitals
8071 Medical laboratories
8072 Dental laboratories
8080 Home health care services
8094 Specialty outpatient facilities
8095 Blood banks
8096 Invitro fertilization
8097 Family planning clinics
8098 Health and allied services, not elsewhere classified
8100 Legal services

Educational services
8210 Elementary and secondary schools
8220 Colleges, universities, and professional schools
8240 Vocational schools
8298 Schools and educational services, not elsewhere classified

Social services
8320 Individual and family social services
8330 Job training and vocational rehabilitation services
8351 Child day care services
8361 Residential care
8399 Social services, not elsewhere classified
8400 Museums, art galleries and botanical and zoological gardens

Engineering, accounting, research, management, and related services
8712 Architectural services
8715 Engineering and surveying services
8720 Accounting, auditing and bookkeeping services
8734 Testing laboratories
8735 Research and development
8745 Management and management consulting services
8980 Miscellaneous services

OTHER

Code
9000 Unrelated debt-financed activities other than rental of real estate
9100 Investment activities by section 501(c)(7), (9), (17), or (20) organizations
9200 Rental of personal property
9300 Passive income activities with controlled organizations
9400 Exploited exempt activities

Exhibit 27–2

Exclusion Codes

General Exceptions

01— Income from an activity that is not regularly carried on (section 512(a)(1))

02— Income from an activity in which labor is a material income-producing factor and substantially all (at least 85%) of the work is performed with unpaid labor (section 513(a)(1))

03— Section 501(c)(3) organization— Income from an activity carried on primarily for the convenience of the organization's members, students, patients, visitors, officers, or employees (hospital parking lot or museum cafeteria, for example) (section 513(a)(2))

04— Section 501(c)(4) local association of employees organized before 5/27/69— Income from the sale of work-related clothes or equipment and items normally sold through vending machines; food dispensing facilities; or snack bars for the convenience of association members at their usual places of employment (section 513(a)(2))

05— Income from the sale of merchandise, substantially all of which (at least 85%) was donated to the organization (section 513(a)(3))

Specific Exceptions

06— Section 501(c)(3), (4), or (5) organization conducting an agricultural or educational fair or exposition—Qualified public entertainment activity income (section 513(d)(2))

07— Section 501(c)(3), (4), (5), or (6) organization—Qualified convention and trade show activity income (section 513(d)(3))

08— Income from hospital services described in section 513(e)

09— Income from noncommercial bingo games that do not violate state or local law (section 513(f))

10— Income from games of chance conducted by an organization in North Dakota (section 311 of the Deficit Reduction Act of 1984, as amended)

11— Section 501(c)(12) organization— Qualified pole rental income (section 513(g))

12— Income from the distribution of low-cost articles in connection with the solicitation of charitable contributions (section 513(h))

13— Income from the exchange or rental of membership or donor list with an organization eligible to receive charitable contributions by a section 501(c)(3) organization; by a war veterans' organization; or an auxiliary unit or society of, or trust or foundation for, a war veterans' post or organization (section 513(h))

Modifications and Exclusions

14— Dividends, interest, or payments with respect to securities loans, and annuities excluded by section 512(b)(1)

15— Royalty income excluded by section 512(b)(2)

16— Real property rental income that does not depend on the income or profits derived by the person leasing the property and is excluded by section 512 (b)(3)

17— Rent from personal property leased with real property and incidental (10% or less) in relation to the combined income from the real and personal property (section 512(b)(3))

18— Proceeds from the sale of investments and other non-inventory property (capital gains excluded by section 512(b)(5))

19— Income (gains) from the lapse or termination of options to buy or sell securities (section 512(b)(5))

20— Income from research for the United States; its agencies or instrumentalities; or any state or political subdivision (section 512(b)(7))

21— Income from research conducted by a college, university, or hospital (section 512(b)(8))

22— Income from research conducted by an organization whose primary activity is conducting fundamental research, the results of which are freely available to the general public (section 512(b)(9))

23— Income from services provided under license issued by a Federal regulatory agency and conducted by a religious order or school operated by a religious order, but only if the trade or business has been carried on by the organization since before May 27, 1959 (section 512 (b)(15))

Foreign Organizations

24— Foreign organizations only—Income from a trade or business NOT conducted in the United States and NOT derived from United States sources (patrons) (section 512(a)(2))

Social Clubs and VEBAs

25— Section 501(c)(7), (9), (17), or (20) organization—Non-exempt function income set aside for a charitable, etc., purpose specified in section 170(c)(4) (section 512(a)(3)(B)(i))

26— Section 501(c)(7), (9), (17), or (20) organization—Proceeds from the sale of exempt function property that was or will be timely reinvested in similar property (section 512(a)(3)(D))

27— Section 501(c)(9), (17), or (20) organization—Non-exempt function income set aside for the payment of life, sick, accident, or other benefits (section 512(a)(3)(B)(ii))

Veterans' Organizations

28— Section 501(c)(19) organization— Payments for life, sick, accident, or health insurance for members or their dependents that are set aside for the payment of such insurance benefits or for a charitable, etc., purpose specified in section 170(c)(4) (section 512(a)(4))

29— Section 501(c)(19) organization— Income from an insurance set-aside (see code 28 above) that is set aside for payment of insurance benefits or for a charitable, etc., purpose specified in section 170(c)(4) (Regs. 1.512(a)-4(b)(2))

Debt-financed Income

30— Income exempt from debt-financed (section 514) provisions because at least 85% of the use of the property is for the organization's exempt purposes **(Note:** *This code is only for income from the 15% or less non-exempt purpose use.) (section 514(b)(1)(A))*

31— Gross income from mortgaged property used in research activities described in section 512(b)(7), (8), or (9) (section 514(b)(1)(C))

32— Gross income from mortgaged property used in any activity described in section 513(a)(1), (2), or (3) (section 514(b)(1)(D))

33— Income from mortgaged property (neighborhood land) acquired for exempt purpose use within ten years (section 514(b)(3))

34— Income from mortgaged property acquired by bequest or devise (applies to income received within ten years from the date of acquisition) (section 514(c)(2)(B))

35— Income from mortgaged property acquired by gift where the mortgage was placed on the property more than five years previously and the property was held by the donor for more than five years (applies to income received within ten years from the date of gift (section 514(c)(2)(B))

36— Income from property received in return for the obligation to pay an annuity described in section 514(c)(5)

37— Income from mortgaged property that provides housing to low and moderate income persons, to the extent the mortgage is insured by the Federal Housing Administration (section 514(c)(6)) **(Note:** *In many cases, this would be exempt function income reportable in column (e). It would not be so in the case of a section 501(c)(5) or (6) organization, for example, that acquired the housing as an investment or as a charitable activity.)*

38— Income from mortgaged real property owned by: a school described in section 170(b)(1)(A)(ii); a section 509(a)(3) affiliated support organization of such a school; a section 501(c)(25) organization, or by a partnership in which any of the above organizations owns an interest if the requirements of section 514(c)(9)(B)(vi) are met (section 514(c)(9))

Special Rules

39— Section 501(c)(5) organization— Farm income used to finance the operation and maintenance of a retirement home, hospital, or similar facility operated by the organization for its members on property adjacent to the farm land (section 1951(b)(8)(B) of Public Law 94-455))

Trade or Business

40— Gross income from an unrelated activity that is regularly carried on but, in light of continuous losses sustained over a number of tax periods, cannot be regarded as being conducted with the motive to make a profit (not a trade or business)

charged to nonmembers, which must be reported in column (b) and labeled with UBI code 7997 or 7998.

A short description of the type of income—student tuition, admission fees, and so on—is entered under line 93 (a–f). Program service revenue in the form of interest, dividend, rent, or royalty is entered on this line. Sales of goods or "inventory items," such as student books, blood bank sales, or museum gift shop items are not entered here but on line 102, except for hospitals and colleges. According to the instructions to page 1, they may include inventory sales items as program services revenue when it is consistent with their overall reporting system under GAAP.

Governmental grants for services rendered, not entered as contributions on line 1(c) of page 1, are entered on line 93(g). Contractual services, such as research, student testing, medical and food services, child welfare program fees, and similar services performed on a fee basis for governmental agencies are to be included here.

Line 94: Membership dues and assessments. As the title connotes, dues and other charges for services rendered to members are included on this line. When a member pays dues primarily to support the organization's activities, rather than to derive benefits of more than nominal monetary benefit, that dues payment represents a contribution. To the extent that a (c)(3) EO's membership dues are treated as a contribution because they have no monetary value, they are not included here. See Section 24.2 for a description of member items to be included, such as "commercial quality publications," discounts on admission or store purchases, free admission, educational classes, referral services, and other items of value given to members in return for their dues.

A business league, labor union, social club, veterans group, or similar organization would report its members' dues, not including any portion allocable to inventory items sold or program services, such as decals or group insurance. Varying levels of membership with different amounts of dues, such as associate or junior members, raise a question. As long as the privileges given to a different class of member do not provide special benefit to any individuals, all types of dues can be aggregated.[23]

Dues would be most commonly placed in column (e). To the extent that member services (such as group insurance or job placement services) are considered UBI, they would be included in column (b) and labeled with a UBI code (6310-6330 for insurance and 7338 for placement services).

Line 95: Interest on savings and temporary cash investment. Payments from savings and loan, bank, and credit union cash deposits are entered on this line. Typically, this income is entered in column (d) and identified with code 14. Interest income on student, low income housing, and other program-related loans are reported on line 93. Interest on a loan to an officer or employee would be reported as other revenue, line 103, in column (d), unless the loan is in the nature of compensation (e.g., a temporary loan to buy a new home), in which case it could be reported in column (e).

Line 96: Dividends and interest from securities. Dividends earned on common or preferred stock, money market accounts, mutual fund shares, U.S. or local government and corporate bonds, and any other securities are usually reported

[23]Priv. Ltr. Rul. 8515061.

on line 96 in column (d) and are also labeled with code 14. Dividends received from an 80 percent-owned for-profit subsidiary would also be reported in column (d). However, interest, rent, or other payments deductible to the subsidiary go in column (b). Capital gains distributed by a mutual fund are reported on line 100.

Securities purchased with borrowed funds, either through a margin account or other debt (called "acquisition indebtedness"), produce UBI. Income from such indebted securities is reported in column (b); in the case of partial indebtedness, only the portion calculated in the ratio of the cost to the debt would be reported in column (b) (UBI code 9000), with the balance reported in column (d).

Line 97: Net rental income (loss) from real estate. The net income, calculated after deduction of expenses such as depreciation, interest on debt, and other direct costs of maintaining real property, is reported on line 97 (code 16). This line does not come directly from page 1. On page 5, real estate and personal property rentals are separated. Also, this is the first line on page 5where the net income, instead of gross, is entered in column (b), (d), or (e).

Real estate rentals can be classified under one of ten codes, and careful study of IRC §§512—514 may be necessary to assure correct property classification under particular facts and circumstances. The majority of real property rentals are received on unindebted property held for investment, the income from which is reported in column (d) and identified with code 16. Lease rentals dependent upon the tenants' profits are classed as UBI and must be reported in column (b). Rents on program-related real estate properties are placed in column (e) on line 93.

Codes 30—38 apply specifically to debt-financed income reportable in column (d) but excludable from UBI classification due to a statutory exception. The portion of income attributable to acquisition indebtdness which is not excluded (see Section 21.17) is reported in column (b), line 97a (UBI code 6512—6599).

Rents paid by an 80 percent or more owned subsidiary are reported in column (b) as taxable UBI and identified with UBI code 9300. If services are rendered to benefit the individual occupant, such as in a hotel, boarding house, parking lot, or storage facility, the rental is also classed as UBI (codes 7010, 7020, 7500, 7388). Services customarily provided for all tenants, such as utilities, security, cleaning of public entrances, elevators, and other common areas do not constitute services rendered to individual tenants.

Line 98: Net rental income (loss) from personal property. Rentals from personal property earned for purely investment purposes create UBI (whether indebted or not) and are reported in column (b) and identified with the appropriate business code, such as 7353, 7377, or 9200. Such rentals could be program-4-related, in which case they are reported on line 93 in column (e) with no code.

If more than 50 percent of a combined real and personal property lease revenue is attributable to personal property, the rental is reported on line 98, column (b), and is subject to UBI. A manufacturing or printing plant, a scientific research facility, and an exhibition hall with booths are examples of the types of rentals which might fall into this category. A Form 990T code again applies and this income, net of directly allocable expenses, is entered in column (b) (UBI code 6512).

Line 99: Other investment income. Royalty income from mineral or intellectual property interests are entered on this line. In most cases such income is entered in column (d) and identified with modification code 15. Royalties from educational publications or research patents might be classed as program service revenue on line 93 and entered in column (e) instead. (See line 103 for certain royalties.)

Unrealized gain or loss on an investment portfolio is not considered as current income on page 1 or page 5, but is entered as a surplus adjustment on line 20 of page. 1.

Line 100: Gain (loss) from sales of assets other than inventory. Capital gains and losses reported on line 8 of page 1 from the disposition of all EO assets, other than inventory, are reported on this line (code 18). Gains and losses from the sale of investment portfolio assets, real estate, office equipment, program-related assets, partnership interest, and all sorts of property are included.

Most gains or losses are reportable in column (d), except for debt-financed property that must be shown in column (b). EOs with sophisticated UBI activity may realize gain from sale of assets used in that business which would also be reportable in column (b). Gain (loss) from the sale of program-related assets is reported in column (e).

Gain or loss on purchase, sale, or lapse of security options can be reported on this line (code 19). It has been suggested that revenue attributable to lapsed options, as distinguished from options sold or "covered" before maturity, should be reportable on line 99. However, the IRS instructions are silent and for convenience all option activity can be combined.

Line 101: Net income from special fund-raising events. Fund-raising event net income, excluding any portion allocated to donations (not reported in this part), is technically UBI. The typical charitable event is excepted from UBI under the irregular (code 01) or volunteer (code 02) exception, and the net profit is reported in column (d). When the primary purpose of the event is educational or otherwise exempt, such as a cultural festival, it is conceivable that the profits could be reported as related income in column (e). Any other fund-raising profits must be reported as UBI in column (b) (code 7998). (See Section 24.2 for more information about fund-raising event revenue calculations.)

Line 102: Gross profit (loss) from sales of inventory. Gross revenues from the sale of inventory, less returns and allowances and cost of goods sold (line 10c on page 1), is entered here. Inventory includes objects purchased or made for resale, rather than to hold as an investment. In contrast to the instruction for rents and interest produced from program-related investments, exempt function inventory sales are to be reported on this line, rather than on line 93.

Line 103: Other revenue. Revenues not suitable for inclusion on lines 93—102 are entered here. Two particular types of revenue that fit on this line are the subject of constant battles between the IRS and EOs. Advertising revenues not classified as program-related can be entered in either column (b) or (d). Ads produce unrelated income (column (b), code 7310) unless the irregular or the volunteer exception applies. Likewise, royalties from use of the EO's name, logo, or mailing list could be entered in either column. If the EO disagrees with the IRS's current position that such income is unrelated, such revenue would be entered in column (d) with modification code 15. See code 13 for the narrow exception available to (c)(3)s and certain veterans organizations for exchanges or rentals of lists between similar types of organizations.

Some have speculated that use of code 15 is an invitation to be examined, because the IRS will scrutinize EOs claiming modification of royalties, despite the fact that some royalties are clearly passive income.

Recoveries of prior year expenditures, interest on loans not made for investment or program purposes (e.g., to employees or managers), and any other items of revenue not properly reported elsewhere would also be entered on line 103.

For further information on specific lines on this page, consult Section 27.4 and the instructions for the page 1 lines that provide the best IRS guidance.

(c) Rationale for Column (e) Amounts

Part VII, Relationship of Activities to the Accomplishment of Exempt Purposes asks the EO to explain how each activity for which income is reported in column (e) contributes importantly to the accomplishment of its exempt purposes (other than by providing funds for such purposes). Although it seems contradictory, dues payments providing funds to support the organization's exempt activities are included in column (e). Not much room is provided and the debate is how much to submit. There are two possible answers to this question, depending upon the nature of the income.

For clearly and unquestionably related types of revenue, such as student tuition, hospital room fees, symphony performance admission tickets, and member dues, the answer can simply be such a description. For revenues received in activities which might arguably produce UBI, such as charges for computer services, sale of standard forms, advertising, or logo sales, a more convincing description is recommended.

The IRS sample contained in the instructions suggests sentences like: "Fee from county for finding foster homes for 2 children—this furthers our exempt purpose of ensuring quality care for foster children," and "Members are social services workers who receive information and advice on problem cases from our staff as part of our counseling, adoption, and foster care programs."

The explanation here need not repeat the same information, but can refer back to Part III, Statement of Program Service Accomplishments, where a very similar question is asked.

Also, consider combinations of similar types of revenue, such as student fees and tuition, rather than reporting tuition on a separate line from student fees. A social club reporting only members fees and services in column (e) (with nonmember fees reported in column (b)), must clearly indicate this dichotomy.

(d) The Codes

Each numerical entry on page 5 is individually explained either with a code or literal description.

Column (b) is described by column (a) codes (Exhibit 27–1) which mimic those used for the unrelated business income tax return, Form 990T. These codes describe the type of business and are easy to assign because they are so literal—dance studio, or physical fitness facility, for example. Each major category has a miscellaneous number. There is little harm from a choosing the wrong code, because the EO is already admitting that the income is UBI.

Column (d) is described by "exclusion" codes, and the correct choice of these is very important. These codes explain that, while the EO is admitting it has unrelated business income, it claims that the UBI is not taxable for one of forty different reasons. A review of Sections 21.9 through 21.12 is extremely useful in making the choices.

27.11 PART IX, INFORMATION REGARDING TAXABLE SUBSIDIARIES

The purpose of Part IX is to gather information to report back to Congress. In this case, the IRS will quantify EO ownership of taxable subsidiaries. This part is to be completed if the EO owns a 50 percent or more interest in a taxable corporation or partnership, as asked in Question 78c on page 4. Total assets and income of the subsidiary are reported.

27.12 SCHEDULE A: FOR §501(c)(3) ORGANIZATIONS ONLY

With Schedule A, IRC §501(c)(3) organizations and nonexempt IRC §4947(a)(1) wholly charitable trusts furnish information to let the IRS review their continued satisfaction of several tests. See Appendix 27–3.

(a) Parts I and II, Compensation

Both of these parts look for private benefit to highly paid personnel and consultants. Although technically private benefit is not as damaging to the organization's exempt status as private inurement (as explained in Chapter 20), the IRS considers excess compensation to persons *not* controlling an exempt to be almost as bad as such payments made to insiders. See Section 27.8 for the meaning of the columns in these parts.

(b) Part III, Statements about Activities

Part III canvasses for a host of sins. The sections of this book which apply to each question are listed below:

Question 1, lobbying. See Chapter 23.

Question 2, self-dealing. See Chapter 20. Transactions with the persons who control an exempt organization are not strictly prohibited, except for private foundations, as explained in Chapter 14. They are, however, subject to scrutiny to prove that the nonexempts do not unfairly benefit at the expense of the exempt. Is too high a price paid for property sold to the executive director? Does the organization need to maintain a New York apartment for its treasurer to monitor the investments? If such a transaction occurred, the organization must explain in this part how its exempt purposes were served.

Questions 3 and 4, individual grants. See the questions asked in Schedule H of Form 1023 at Section 18.3(e) of this book to get a flavor of the appropriate and expected answers to these questions.

(c) Part IV, Reason for Non-Private Foundation Status

The "reason for non-private foundation status" rests upon the organization's ability to qualify as a public charity and to fit into one of the ten boxes (presented as items 5 through 13) on page 2. For organizations checking boxes 10, 11, or 12, public status is based upon sources of revenue and lines 15 through 27 are completed. Each of the box categories is discussed in Chapter 11. This part repeats the information originally furnished with Form 1023, and the materials at Section 18.3(c) at line (9) can be reviewed for suggestions.

It is somewhat disconcerting that this part does not clearly indicate whether the EO has maintained its public status, since the information is furnished to allow the IRS to make the determination. Among the questions raised by this part are the following:

Q: When and how can an exempt organization change its status from a §509(a)(1) to a §509(a)(2) organization, or vice versa?
A: Apparently, an EO can change annually, depending on the category into which it fits. The only serious danger of a change would be loss of public status. Usually the consequence is minimal, except that IRC §509(c)(2) organizations are not qualified recipients for a PF terminating distribution.

Q: For what period after selling its major assets and ceasing operation can a hospital or school maintain its public status? When would it convert to a private foundation?
A: The usual "facts and circumstances" in each case determine the EO's status. Are there plans for new facilities? Will assets be distributed to another public charity after termination? If so, public status could probably be maintained. If the EO makes permanent investments with the funds and begins to make grants to other organizations, it will become a PF. (In other words, conversion occurs when its intention to convert becomes clear from its actions and resolutions of its board, and the active conduct of its school or hospital ceases.)

Q: If the EO fails the test mechanically, are there any exceptions or alternatives to becoming classified as a private foundation?
A: An EO receiving as little as 10 percent of its support from public sources can be permitted to qualify as a public charity under a "facts and circumstances test." Section 11.2(f) outlines the requirements for achieving this status.

Timing can be extremely important for an organization which inadvertently loses its public status. The organization can make an application to terminate PF status under a so-called "60-month termination." However, as explained in Section 12.6(d), such a conversion must be filed prior to the period for which it is effective. An inattentive EO may not realize its need to file until after the end of the year in which the failure occurs.

(d) Part V, Private School Questionnaire

Part V requests information on the nondiscrimination policies of private schools. Action taken to publicize such policies to the community served by the school must be reported at item 31. Form 5578 (Appendix 27–4) can be used to furnish the information, but is not specifically required. The questions in this part reflect the school discrimination policy adopted by the IRS in 1975.[24] It is imperative that all private schools correctly answer them to assure continued qualification for exemption.

Questions 29 through 32 need a "Yes" answer. All parts of question 33 must be answered "No."

(e) Part VI-A, Lobbying Expenditures by Electing Public Charities and Part VI-B, Lobbying Activity by Nonelecting Public Charities

Part VI is completed to allow the IRS to evaluate the levels of an EO's lobbying efforts. Those charities that elect the mathematical lobbying limitations of IRC §501(h) complete part VI-A, which reflects the specific numerical test that is applied. Successful completion of this part depends on good accounting and an ability to identify direct expenses and to allocate indirect ones. The terms are defined in Sections 23.4 and 23.5. Appendix 23–1 is Form 5768, which is to be used for making or revoking the election during the reporting period.

Capital expenses are not included in the calculation of lobbying expense limitations. Only straight-line depreciation on assets directly used in connection with lobbying efforts are included as lobbying expenses.

Part VI-B asks nine questions of organizations which do not elect to conduct limited lobbying. Such organizations face a subjective and qualitative measure to ascertain if the lobbying comprises a "substantial part" of their activities, as discussed in Section 23.4(a). There are two and a half pages of instructions to this part of Schedule A, and they should be read in detail if the answer to any of the items (a) through (h) is "Yes."

(f) Part VII, Information Regarding Transfers, Transactions, and Relationships with Other Organizations

Part VII was added in 1988 in response to a congressional mandate to the IRS to search for connections between private foundations and non-501(c)(3) organizations. Particularly in regard to organizations that lobby or enter the political arena, the IRS is scouting for relationships that allow benefits to the noncharitable organization.

This part looks for use of EO assets to benefit non-(c)(3) organizations and asks the EO to report any financial transactions, such as sales, transfers, or rentals of assets to or from another EO. The reportable transactions are those with affiliated or related organizations. Again, the instructions are very specific and should be consulted if transactions are to be reported. To answer, consider

[24]Rev. Proc. 75-50, 1975-2 C.B. 587.

that the following factors must be present to have a related organization:

1. A historic and continuing relationship between two organizations evidenced by sharing of facilities, staff, joint effort, or other work in concert towards accomplishing a common goal.

2. Common control whereby one or more of the officers, directors, or trustees (managers) of one organization is elected or appointed by those of the other. Similarly, control is found when 25 percent or more of the managers are interlocking.

The few transactions that need *not* be reported include:

1. Any transaction totaling $500 or less annually; and

2. Specific transactions totaling less than one percent of the EO's annual gross receipts involving subscriptions, conferences, seminars, or other functionally related services or goods.

This part indicates yet another type of special records required to be kept by an EO. To answer this part correctly, an EO having the described relationship will want to establish subcodes or new departments in its chart of accounts to tabulate the answers. See Chapter 22 for more discussion of such relationships.

27.13   SPECIAL CONSIDERATIONS FOR FORM 990-PF

In addition to reporting financial activity for the year, the 12-page Form 990-PF enables the IRS to evaluate a private foundation's compliance with the IRC §4940 and §4945 sanctions and limitations on activities. Form 990-PF is reproduced as Appendix 27–5. The Form 990-PF instructions are 26 pages long and exemplify the complexity of reporting and compliance requirements for a private foundation.[25] The technical aspects of the sanctions applied to PFs, presented in Chapters 12 through 17, should be studied along with the following suggestions for completion of the form. The applicable sections of this book will be referred to throughout this discussion.

Each private foundation, including a §4947(a)(1) trust, must file a Form 990-PF, regardless of gross revenues received during the year. Even a PF with a non-interest-bearing checking account making no disbursements is theoretically required to file Form 990-PF, publicize its availability to the general public, and submit the form to the state attorney general. A PF converting its status to public under IRC §507 (see Section 12.6) also must file Form 990-PF rather than Form 990.

Form 990-PF has evolved over 20 years as the law of private foundations has developed, retaining original concepts and adding new ones. Certain interdependent calculations do not follow in logical order. The most efficient

---

[25] The instructions for the 1990 form contained 22 pages—proof that this form is not getting simpler.

order in which to prepare the form is the following:

1. Parts I, II, III, and IV.	5. Part V.
2. Skip to Parts VII, VIII, IX-A and B, XV, XVI-A and B, XVII, and XVIII.	6. Part VI.
	7. Part XI.
3. Part X.	8. Part XIII or XIV.
4. Part XII.	

Proper allocation of expenses among administrative, investment, and program costs is a significant aspect of the form, so the accounting practices discussed at the beginning of this chapter are recommended. A PF has only two types of expenses—investment-related and disbursements for charitable purposes or exempt function expenses. (See Section 27.5.) Similar to the issue of maximizing UBI deductions (Section 27.14(c)), investment expenses reduce the PF excise tax on investment income. Ordinary and necessary expenses of producing investment income are deductible to arrive at net investment income. Basically, the rules are the same as the individual and business expense provisions of IRC §162 and §212 pertaining to deductible expenses. What portion of the director's salary or bank trustee, legal, or accounting fees are allocable to investment management, oversight, or consultations? A reasonable portion, usually one-fourth to one-half of such fees, is customarily allotted to investment income. Upon examination, the IRS will request substantiation of this allocation.

From 1985 through 1990, Congress placed a limit on a PF's administrative expenses. General and administrative (G&A) expense over the limit (.65% of assets) essentially fell through the cracks—it did not reduce tax nor count toward the distribution requirements. Based upon a study, the IRS found the limits ineffective. They were designed to curb abusive situations often found in larger organizations, such as excessive compensation, but the formula missed that mark. It was the smaller PFs who had high G&A, but had correspondingly high qualifying distributions. Finally, the IRS admitted that the calculations were complicated and burdensome to PFs, and did not recommend their continuance.

(a) Part I, Analysis of Revenue and Expenses

Each of the columns in Part I serves a different purpose in the IRS regulatory scheme for private foundations. Deciding what goes where and why is not a logical process. Different accounting methods are used for reporting information in different columns, and some items are included in more than one column, while others are not.

Column (a), revenue and expenses "per books." This column agrees with financial reports prepared for the board or for public dissemination by the organization. The cash or accrual method of accounting is permitted, again in keeping with the system regularly used to prepare financial statements for other purposes.

In-kind contributions of services or use of property, even though properly booked for financial statement purposes, are excluded. Capital gains are calculated using "book basis" rather than "tax basis," which is reported in column (b), line 7 or 8.

Column (b), net investment income. This column reports the income less associated deductions used to arrive at income subject to the excise tax. Only investment income is reported (see Sections 13.3 and 13.4). It does not include:

- UBI separately reported on Form 990-T;

- Program service revenue;

- Gain from sale of exempt function assets; or

- Profits from fund-raising events.

Column (c), adjusted net income. This column became obsolete for most PFs in 1976, although it is still important for two types of PFs:

1. Private operating foundations (Section 15.5) must spend 85 percent of their adjusted net income[26] on charitable projects they conduct directly. This column essentially includes investment income plus short-term capital gains and unrelated business income, less long-term capital gains.

2. PFs receiving program service income use the column to isolate the income from program services. Expenses of such a program are reported in column (c). Only the excess expenses over the revenues are reported in column (d).

Column (d), disbursements for charitable purposes. The cash method must be used for this column. Amounts reported in this column are significant because they count toward calculation of the required charitable expenditures (Section 15.4). As a general rule, any expenses claimed as allocable to investment income would not also be reportable in this column. Column (d) includes direct charitable expenditures, grants, and administrative and fund-raising costs not allocable to investment income.

Line 1. The total amount of gifts, grants, and other voluntary donations are reported on this line (Section 27.4(b)). Details are reported for gifts of $5,000 or more. Distributions from split interest trusts are included here for column (a) purposes.

Line 2. Split interest trust distributions for amounts placed in trust after October 26, 1969 are taxed (Section 13.2(f)). Amounts earned on trust assets owned prior to that date, when the PF tax was introduced in Congress, are not subject to the excise tax.

Lines 3 and 4. See Section 13.2(b). Interest from tax-exempt government obligations is excluded from column (b) and associated expenses are excluded.

Line 5. Gross rent is reported. Associated expenses are reported in lines 13–23.

Line 6. The PF's capital gains or losses per the books are entered on this line and entered only in column (a).

---

[26] Reg. §53.4942-2(d).

Line 7. Note that this line carries only to column (b). Gains (short- and long-term) from the sale of property that ordinarily produces interest, dividends, royalties, or rents are taxed even if the property never produced any income. The gain on a growth stock producing no dividends is also taxed. Program-related investments are not taxed because they are not held for investment. Special exceptions apply for certain gains listed in Section 13.3(c).

It is very important to note that property received by the foundation as a donation retains the donor's basis.[27] Since the wealth of PF creators often comes from business interests that are highly appreciated, the PF ends up paying tax on its contributor's gains, albeit at a much lower rate. There had been disagreement for years about the taxability of property sold immediately after its receipt and which never produced income, but the debate is now settled. See Section 13.3(b).

Capital losses are deductible only to the extent of gains, and there is no carryover. PFs need careful year end tax planning for this purpose.

Line 8. The short-term capital gains are separately reported for column (c) purposes only, with the amount carrying from Part IV, line 3.

Line 9. Income modifications also pertain only to column (c), and include repayments of amounts previously treated as qualifying distributions (Section 15.3) that must be added back to the distributable amount in the current year.

Line 10. This line is rarely used. A foundation conducting a self-initiated project might generate sales, such as an educational store selling books or similar items of inventory. A program-related business operation, such as a handicapped worker factory, might have such sales. The instructions suggest reporting fund-raising events (Section 27.4(j)) on this line. This income is not subject to the excise tax, but might be subject to the UBIT.

Line 11. All other types of income, including royalties (Section 13.2(e)) and interest not reported on line 3 or 4, income from a partnership, and any other investment income not reported on lines 2 through 7, are reported here.

Line 13. Officer, trustee, and director salaries must not result in excessive compensation or self dealing (Section 14.4) may occur. The concerns facing public charities about insider compensation and the reporting questions (Sections 27.5(d) and 27.8) can be reviewed to assure proper reporting here.

Lines 14—17, 20—23. See the suggestions at Section 27.5(e)—(g). Also, note that a POF reports its direct expenditures in column (d) on these lines by expense type, not on line 25.

Line 18. Taxes of all sorts are reported in column (a), including excise taxes on investment income, property taxes on real estate, and any unrelated business income tax. Only taxes paid on investment property are reported in column (b). POFs include both excise taxes and investment property taxes in column (c). Only taxes paid on exempt function property is reported in column (d). For non-operating PFs, the excise tax is taken into account in Part XI, line 2a.

Line 19. Depreciation is reported in column (a) using the PF's book method. Column (b) depreciation must be calculated using the straight-line

---

[27] Reg. §53.4940-1(f)(2)(i)(B), which refers to IRC §1015.

method and only cost depletion is allowed for mineral properties, not percent-age depletion. The basis of property for this purpose is the same as that for calculating gain without a December 31, 1969 step-up to value.[28]

Column (c) depreciation for POFs would usually be the same as column (d). Note that column (d) has no depreciation because asset acquisitions (Section 15.4(b)) are treated as qualifying distributions. Thus, asset cost is essentially written off as a charitable distribution in the year the asset is purchased.

Line 21. Only 80 percent of the cost of meals is deductible in column (b). This limitation parallels the individual income tax rules for deductible meals.

Line 25. Grants paid to other charitable organizations are reported on this line (Section 15.4). Nonqualifying grants are not included, such as those paid to a controlled organization and certain pass-through grants (Section 15.4). Such grants would be reported in Part III, line 5. The following omissions are also made:

Returned grant funds are not entered here but in Part X.

No set-asides are entered; see Part XIII.

Line 26. The total of disbursements for charitable purposes in column (d) is transferred to Part XII, line 1 to measure compliance with the minimum distributions requirement test (Chapter 15).

(b) Part II, Balance Sheets

Both the book value of the foundation assets and liabilities and the ending fair market value are presented in Part II. The total in column (c), line 16, must agree with item I on page one, top left side. Column (c) need not be completed for a PF with under $5,000. A considerable amount of detail is requested. The instructions should be read carefully for the following lines on the balance sheet.

Line 6.   Insider receivables.

Line 10.   Investments—securities.

Line 11.   Investments—land, buildings, and equipment.

Line 13.   Investments—other.

Line 14.   Land, buildings, and equipment.

Line 15.   Other assets.

Line 19.   Support and revenue designated for future periods.

Line 20.   Insider payables.

Line 21.   Mortgages and other notes payable.

---

[28] IRC §4940(c)(3)(B).

(c) Part III, Analysis of Changes in Net Worth or Fund Balances

This schedule reconciles the fund balances. Examples of matters that might be reflected here include:

- A prior-period accounting adjustment not corrected on an amended return.

- Adjustment to unrealized gain or loss on investment assets recorded for book purposes but not reported in column (a) on page 1.

- Nonqualifying grants not reported on page 1.

See Chapter 28 for issues involved in amended returns and reporting back to the IRS.

(d) Part IV, Capital Gains and Losses for Tax on Investment Income

This schedule reports only investment property. Note that the totals from this schedule carry only to columns (b) and (c) of Part I. Transactions involving exempt function assets or program-related investments (Section 15.1(a)) are not included.

Basis for property received by the foundation as a gift is reported in column (g) and equals the donor's basis. This schedule accommodates the so-called "carryover basis" rules for calculating gains and losses for excise tax purposes. Property received through a bequest is valued as of the date of death or the alternate valuation date for the decedent.[29] Purchased property is reported at its actual cost.[30]

Short-term gains are significant only for POFs and carry to column (c), Part I.

(e) Part V, Qualification for Reduced Tax on Net Investment Income

A private foundation can cut its tax in half (from two percent to one percent of net investment income) by essentially giving the tax to charity (Section 13.1).[31] If the PF's current-year qualifying distributions (Part XII) exceed its past five-year average payout plus one percent tax for the current year, the tax is reduced to one percent. Achieving this reduction is complicated because not all of the factors are known until the last day of the taxable year, such as line 4 (the average month end value of investment assets). Except for the most generous foundations, reducing the excise tax requires very careful planning.

(f) Part VI, Excise Tax on Investment Income

Except for exempt private operating foundations, PFs pay a tax of two percent, or possibly one percent, on their net investment income reported in Part I,

---

[29] Id. note 26.
[30] The income tax rules contained in IRC §§1011, 1012, 1014, 1015, and 1016 apply in completing this part.
[31] IRC §4940(e).

column (b), line 27b. Foreign PFs that receive more than 15 percent of their investment income from U.S. sources pay a 4 percent tax on such income.

If the annual tax is under $500, it is paid with a check accompanying the return as it is filed. If the tax is over $500, it is paid in advance through the estimated tax system, using depository receipts. Form 990-W is used to compute the tax. PFs with over $1 million of income must make quarterly payments based on actual income earned during the second, third, and fourth quarters, similar to the "large corporation" rules.

Penalties are due for failure to pay a sufficient amount by the quarterly due dates.[32] Form 2220 is attached to Form 990–PF to calculate the penalty. Penalties are also imposed for failure to deposit taxes with a federal tax deposit coupon (Form 8109) at a qualified bank or federal reserve bank.

(g) Part VII, Statements Regarding Activities

Line 1. Answering this question "Yes" is tantamount to admitting that the exempt status should be questioned.

Lines 2—5. See answers to lines 76—79 at Section 27.9.

Line 6. The private foundation must answer this question "Yes" and would not have been recognized as exempt is it had not.

Line 8a. Even if a private foundation is not registered to do business in a particular state, filing may be required if it has donations from certain states, such as New York.

Line 9. See Section 15.5. Part XIV must be completed by private operating foundations.

Lines 10—14. These questions probe for violations of the excise tax sanctions and all "No" answers reduce reporting requirements. Any "Yes" answers require details. Certain "Yes" answers reveal the need to file Form 4720 (Appendix 27–6) to report transactions subject to excise tax. Consult the following chapters for guidance:

Line 10: Chapter 14, Self-Dealing.

Line 11: Chapter 15, Minimum Distribution Requirements.

Line 12: Chapter 16, Excess Business Holdings.

Line 13: Chapter 16, Jeopardizing Investments.

Line 14: Chapter 17, Taxable Expenditures.

(h) Part VIII, Information About Officers, Directors, Trustees, Foundation Managers, Highly Paid Employees, and Contractors

To assist the IRS in detecting self-dealing and private inurement, details of compensation are to be reported. This part must be completed even if officers

[32] IRC §6655.

and directors receive no compensation or benefits. All persons in each category, even if they number fifty or more, must be listed. Make an entry in each column, even if the answer is "None." If an attachment is required, submit totals for each column again at the bottom of page 5. See Section 27.8 for the meaning of the column titles and conflicting IRS instructions.

(i) Part IX-A and B, Summary of Direct Charitable Activities and Program-Related Investments

The foundation's four largest direct charitable projects (see Section 15.5) are to be reported, including "relevant statistical information such as the number of organizations and other beneficiaries serviced, conferences convened, research papers produced, etc." This part is a welcome addition to permit PFs, particularly POFs, conducting projects to describe their activities. This part parallels the Form 990 exempt function activity report and the same suggestions apply (Section 27.6).

Program-related investments made during the year are reported in Part IX-B. (See Section 15.1(c).) For a foundation with ongoing investments, this report can be coordinated with the balance sheet reporting and expenditure responsibility reporting requirements.

(j) Part X, Minimum Investment Return

Refer to Chapter 15 for definitions and parameters before completing this part. Line 6 represents the PF's required amount of annual charitable giving. The number is entered in Part XI, line 1. The amount on Part X, line 5 is entered in Part V, line 4.

(k) Part XI, Distributable Amount

POFs do not complete this part; they answer "N/A—private operating foundation." See Sections 15.3 and 15.4 for discussion of the terms.

(l) Part XII, Qualifying Distributions

Again, see Chapter 15 for definition of the terms. Section 15.4(c) discusses set-asides that are reported on line 3. The number on line 4 carries to Part V, line 8; Part XIII, line 4; and Part XIV, line 2c.

(m) Part XIII, Undistributed Income

This part surveys five years of grant-making history to determine if the PF has expended sufficient funds on charitable giving to meet the IRC §4942 tests. If this schedule reflects a balance remaining on line 2(b), 6(d), or 6(e), Form 4720 (Appendix 27–6) should be filed to calculate the penalty on under-distributions.

The order in which distributions are applied is important. See Section 15.6 for examples of payment application.

Qualifying distributions entered on line 4 should be the same as on line 4 of Part XII, but the trick is knowing how to apply the total among the four columns and when a distribution is charged to corpus. As the form's design indicates, current-year distributions are first applied to column (c), the remaining undistributed income from the immediately preceding year. This can create a cash flow problem when a PF (or the IRS) finds that deficient distributions from the past must be corrected. The current-year required payments must be paid before the correction can be made. Next, corrections of prior-year deficiencies are applied to line 4(b) (not required).

A PF might elect to apply current-year grants to corpus on line 4c, column (a) under certain circumstances. For example, the corpus election is appropriate for a PF redistributing a donation for which the contributor desires the maximum deduction.[33] Some commentators suggest that this adjustment be made to Part XI, line 6. The point is that the PF cannot count a gift attributable to a pass-through contribution as part of its qualifying distributions. Other instances when a corpus election is appropriate involve grants paid to a controlled public charity and pass-through grants to another PF. The instructions should be read carefully before making this choice.[34]

To make the corpus election, a PF manager signs a statement declaring that the PF is making an election and designating whether it is out of a specific year's prior income or corpus.

It is useful to know that the source of line 5 distributions is always from line 3f.

(n) Part XIV, Private Operating Foundations

POFs submit information to calculate their ongoing qualification based on a four year average of their qualifying distributions, income, and assets. See Section 15.5 for definition of the terms.

(o) Part XV, Supplementary Information

This part is completed for foundations with assets of $5,000 or more. It lists the names of substantial contributors (Section 12.4(b)) and foundation managers with potential excess business holdings (Section 16.1). Grant application details, including the name and address, application form requirements, deadlines, and grant restrictions and limitations are also reported.

Grant seekers use the information submitted in this part to select the PFs to whom they will make applications for funding. The Foundation Center and other organizations publish books containing this information. Public libraries

[33] IRC §170(b)(1)(E).
[34] IRS Instructions to 1992 Form 990-PF at page 22.

in many cities cooperate in making Forms 990-PF available for public inspection. Most often, inspectors look at this and the following part to find out what kind of grants a PF makes.

Foundations that make grants only to preselected charities and do not accept unsolicited requests for funds can check the blank on line 2. Because the paper load for some PFs is immense, there is a temptation in some cases to check the box although it does not necessarily apply. There are on-going philosophical discussions about the pros and cons of the box: Should a PF with unrestricted funds close the door to grant applicants by checking the blank?

(p) Grants and Contributions Paid During the Year or Approved for Future Payment

This part lists grants paid during the year and approved for future payment. The total under 3a should agree with the amount reported on line 25, column (d). The line 3b total of future grant commitments is provided for public inspection purposes only, and does not carry to any other part of the form.

Grant recipients' relationships to the foundation must be entered to alert the IRS to possible disqualifying grants to controlled organizations (Section 15.4(a)).

(q) Part XVI-A and B, Analysis of Income-Producing Activities and Relation of Activities to the Accomplishment of Exempt Purposes

Since 1989 when these parts were added, private foundations must characterize their income according to its relatedness to their exempt purposes, to allow the IRS to find unrelated business income which is not identified in Part I. The columns, lines, and codes are thoroughly described at Section 27.10. The typical PF will only submit information in column (d). Part XVI-B explains how the income-producing activity reported in column (e) furthers the organization's exempt purposes.

(r) Part XVII, Information Regarding Transfers, Transactions and Relationships with Noncharitable Exempt Organizations

This part was designed for Form 990, and does not apply to most private foundations. See Section 27.12(f) for the meaning and import of the requested information.

(s) Part XVIII, Public Inspection

Form 990-PF must be made available to the general public for inspection for 180 days after a notice of its availability is published in a newspaper of general circulation in the area where the PF operates.[35] As an alternative, the founda-

---

[35] IRC §6104(b) and (d).

tion can offer to mail a copy of its return to anyone requesting it by mail. The notice is to be filed just before Form 990-PF is filed with the Internal Revenue Service Center. The penalty for failure to make proper notice is $10 a day until the notice is filed, with a $5,000 maximum for each return.[36]

Interestingly, this inspection system is less onerous than the system imposed on public charities, which, since 1987, must make Form 990 available for three years (Section 27.2). Form 1023 must continually be made available for inspection, along with any letters or other documents issued by the IRS in response to the application.[37]

27.14   FORM 990-T: EXEMPT ORGANIZATION BUSINESS INCOME TAX RETURN

All domestic and foreign exempt organizations, including churches, state colleges and universities, trusts, IRA accounts, and others not required to file Forms 990, must file Form 990-T, Exempt Organization Business Income Tax Return, (Appendix 27–7) to report gross income from unrelated business income over $1,000.[38] An "unrelated business" means:

> "Any trade or business the conduct of which is not substantially related (aside from the need of such organization for income or funds or the use it makes of the profits derived) to the exercise or performance by such organization of its charitable, educational, or other purpose or function constituting the basis for its exemption."[39]

Not included in the term "unrelated business" is any trade or business that:

- Is 85 percent operated by a volunteer workforce (Section 21.9(a));

- Sells donated merchandise (Section 21.9(b));

- Conducts public fairs and conventions (Sections 21.9(d) and (e));

- Sponsors certain bingo games (Section 21.9(c));

- Is operated for the convenience of members, student, patients, and others participating in the activities of IRC §501(c)(3) organizations (Section 21.11(a));

---

[36] IRC §6652(c).
[37] IRC §6104(a).
[38] Reg. §1.6012-2(e). Gross income for this purpose means gross receipts less cost of goods sold as provided in Reg. §1.61-3. Instrumentalities of the United States exempt under IRC §501(c)(1) are also exempt from this tax.
[39] IRC §513(a).

- Produces passive income in the form of interest, dividends, capital gains, rentals, royalties, and certain research income (Section 21.12); or

- Distributes low-cost articles and certain mailing lists (Section 21.10).

"Trade or business" is any activity carried on for the production of income from selling goods or performing services. An activity does not lose its identity as a trade or business merely because it is carried on within a larger group of similar activities which may or may not be related to the exempt purposes of the organization (Section 21.4).[40]

"Taxable unrelated business income" is defined as:

"Gross income derived by any organization from any unrelated trade or business (as defined in §513) regularly carried on by it, less the deductions allowed by this chapter which are directly connected with the carrying on of such trade or business. ..."[41]

The bottom line question is whether the income producing activity contributes importantly to, aids in accomplishing, or has a nexus to the EO's exempt purposes. Chapter 21 discusses this subject in detail. Following are suggestions for preparing the form are provided there, along with references to Chapter 21.

The IRS estimates the time needed to complete and file Form 990-T, which it admits will vary depending on individual circumstances, totals an average time of:

Recordkeeping	60 hours	59 minutes
Learning the law	20	20
Preparing the form	32	28
Total estimated time	113 hours	47 minutes

Hopefully, the following suggestions will help alleviate this burden.

(a) Filing Dates, Tax Rates, and Accounting Matters

Due date. Most Forms 990-T are due to be filed on the same day as the other Forms 990—the 15th day of the fifth month following the close of the

---

[40] Reg. §1.513-1(b). The term is defined in reference to IRC §162.
[41] IRC §512(a)(1).

EO's fiscal year. (It used to be the third month). Trusts and IRAs file by the fourth month. Corporations may obtain an automatic six-month extension of this time to file by submitting Form 7004, Application for Extension of Time to File Certain Excise, Income, Information, and Other Returns. Trusts use Form 2758, Application for Extension of Time to File, to obtain a two to three month extension.

Payment of tax. The tax liability is paid in advance through the quarterly estimated tax system if the annual tax is in excess of $500. Taxpayers with taxable income of $1 million or more must use the "actual" method and pay tax quarterly based on income earned for the quarter, rather than basing the payment on the prior year. The rates of tax are:

Tax Rate Schedule for Corporations (Section 11 of the Internal Revenue Code)		
If the amount on line 5, page 1 is:		Enter on line 7, page 1:
Over —	but not over —	
$0	$50,000	15% of the amount over $0
50,000	75,000	$7,500 plus 25% of the amount over $50,000
75,000	100,000	$13,750 plus 34% of the amount over $75,000
100,000	335,000	$22,250 plus 39% of the amount over $100,000
335,000	—	34% of the amount on line 5

Tax Rate Schedule for Trusts (Section 1(e) of the Internal Revenue Code)	
If the amount on line 5, page 1 is:	Enter on line 8, page 1:
not over $3,450	15% of the amount on line 5 page 1
Over $3,450 but not over $10,350	$517.50, plus 28% of the amount over $3,450
Over $10,350	$2449.50, plus 31% of the amount over $10,350

Affiliated exempt organizations that are commonly controlled must combine their incomes. The 15 percent bracket applies only to the first $50,000 of their combined income; the 25 percent applies to the next $25,000, and so on. The EOs can apportion the tax brackets among themselves as they please, or they can share the lower brackets equally.[42] An apportionment plan must be signed by all members and attached to their Forms 990-T.

Credits and alternative minimum tax. An EO earning unrelated income is taxed just like all other business corporations and trusts. The general business and foreign tax credits and alternative minimum taxes apply.[43] A discussion of these tax rules is beyond the scope of this book. The author recommends an EO seek the help of competent consultants if these matters apply.

---

[42] Reg. §1.1561-3(b).
[43] IRC §§27, 28, 29, 38–44, 51, 55–59, and 59A.

Interest and Penalties. Several different charges are imposed when a return is filed late. The worst is the failure to file penalty of five percent (of the tax due) per month the return is late, up to 25 percent maximum,[44] unless the EO can show reasonable cause for the delay. In the author's experience, the IRS is lenient on first time filers who voluntarily submit Forms 990-T and pay tax. The failure must not be willful neglect; ordinary business care and prudence must be used to ascertain the requirement,[45] particularly if the EO regularly engages independent accountants who failed to advise it of the obligation to do so. An explanation can be attached to the return requesting relief and explaining why the return was filed late.

Next, a penalty may be assessed for failure to pay of 1/2 percent of the unpaid tax (i.e., an annual rate of 6 percent up to a maximum of 25 percent of the amount due. Additionally, a penalty may be due for failure to pay the tax in advance as described above. Form 2220 is used to calculate this penalty, which is assessed on a daily basis at the prevailing federal rate.

Accounting methods and periods. Taxable income is calculated using the method of accounting regularly used in keeping the EO's books and records.[46] EOs with over $5 million of annual gross receipts must use the accrual method.[47] Also, an EO selling merchandise or goods that is accounted for piece by piece must maintain inventory records and use the accrual method.[48]

When a change in accounting method occurs, income and deductions are accelerated or deferred. This so-called "Section 481 adjustment" is reflected in income over a period of four years. Form 3115 must be filed to request an accounting method change, and Form 1128 is used to change the fiscal year, as discussed in Section 28.4.

Accounting for costs attributable to more than one activity, also called joint costs, is a significant part of preparing this form. Maximizing deductions is desirable. An EO must keep its records in a manner that will support the claimed business deductions. "Overhead can be applied, but the organization must be able to justify both the method of allocation and the reasonableness of the resulting amount."[49] See the opening remarks in this chapter for guidance on cost allocation and recordkeeping systems, and see Section 27.14(c).

A detailed discussion of accounting theories is beyond the scope of this book, and the author recommends the use of independent CPAs for such matters.

(b) Part I, The Line Game

Part I, in which gross income is reported, has evolved over the years to accommodate court decisions and IRS regulations. Some of the line titles are

---

[44] IRC §6651. When the return is delinquent over 60 days, the minimum tax for failure to file is the smaller of the actual tax or $100.

[45] Reg. §301.6651-1(c) explains the acceptable excuses.

[46] IRC §446(a).

[47] IRC §448(c).

[48] IRC §§263A and 471.

[49] *Financial and Accounting Guide for Not-For-Profit Organizations*, Fourth Edition, Malvern J. Gross, Jr., William Warshauer, Jr., and Richard F. Larkin, page 507.

Exhibit 27–3
TABLE OF INCOME SOURCES

Type of Income	Form 990-T Line Number	Book Section Reference
Advertising	11	21.20(a)
Affinity cards	1 or 10	21.10(b) and (c)
Bingo games	1	21.9(c)
Capital gains	4	21.12(b)
Bookkeeping services or credit counseling for small businesses	1 or 10	21.8(b)
Computer time charges	1 or 10	21.8(b)
Dividends from wholly-owned subsidiaries	8	21.12(e)
Exploited exempt functions	9	21.14(f)
Gift shop sales	1 or 10	21.19(a)
Insurance	1 or 10	21.8(g)
Mailing list sales	1 or 10	21.10(b)
Member services	10	21.8(f)
Merchandise sales	1 or 10	21.8
Partnership distributions	5	21.5
Rent from real and personal property (unindebted)	6	21.12(c)
Rental debt-financed property	7	21.17
Social club charges for meals, golf, or other club activities	1	Chapter 9
Social club investment income	9	Chapter 9
Sponsorships	1 or 11	21.8(e)
Study tours	1	21.19(c)

unique to the UBIT and the sequence of lines is different from other tax forms. The suggestions for this part will therefore be presented according to the various types of UBI, rather than line by line.

Line 13. Modest organizations whose gross unrelated income does not exceed $10,000 need not play the line game; the total UBI is entered on line 13. For Form 990 and 900-PF filers, line 13 should equal the total on line 15, column (b).

Columns (b) and (c). This part was revised for 1992 by adding a column to present the direct expenses alongside gross income for which supporting schedules are completed. Previously, only the net income was carried to this part. This redesign reflects the IRS intention to evaluate deductible expenses. However, for line 1 income, the direct expenses other than cost of goods sold are deducted in Part II and may cause some confusion, particularly in relation to lines 26 and 27 (see Section 27.14(c)). Use Exhibit 27–3 as a guide for placement of different type of income on the lines of Part I and to find the sections of this book that discuss each type of income.

(c) Part II, Deductions Not Taken Elsewhere

On Form 990-T, expenses are deducted either in Part I or Part II, not due to the nature of particular types of expenses, but strictly according to the form's design, as the title admits.

Income tax provisions apply. Conceptually, one must keep in mind that the entire Internal Revenue Code as it applies to the income tax governs and determines deductible expenses for UBIT purposes. Thus, the cardinal rule applies that the "ordinary and necessary" expenses of doing business offset business income.[50] For a totally isolated income-producing activity, calculating direct expenses solely attributable to the activity involves following the income tax rules. Discussion of those rules is beyond the scope of this book, and the reader must either understand them or seek assistance in applying them to the preparation of this form. The IRS instructions for lines 14–25 of this part refer to the applicable rules in some cases and should be consulted during preparation.

Cost allocations. The complexity of Form 990-T goes beyond the task of understanding the income tax system. Exempt organizations, in their efforts to raise funds, have devised creative methods to make money utilizing their tangible and intangible assets and their staffs. In the words of the regulations, such money-making schemes "exploit" the exempt functions. (See Section 21.14(f)). People and things are mingled and used for both exempt and income-producing purposes.

Three types of expense. Whatever method is used to arrive at deductible expenses, including overhead or general and administrative costs, the method must not permit the amalgamation of for-profit and nonprofit activities.[51] The regulations provide three types of expenses:

1. *Expenses Attributable Solely to Unrelated Business Activities.* Expense that is directly connected with producing unrelated business income is deductible in arriving at taxable UBI. Such expense must have a "proximate and primary relationship" to the business activity. Examples include persons employed full-time to work exclusively on the business, and a building devoted solely to the business.[52] The requisite "direct" expense for deduction against the income is not always easy to ascertain and good recordkeeping is required. Some of the rules that have evolved are explained in Sections 21.14 and 21.15.

2. *Dual-use Facilities and Personnel.* When people and offices are used both to carry on exempt activities and to conduct unrelated trade or business activities, a reasonable allocation of expenses is made. If the president devotes 10 percent of her time to the business activity, 10 percent of her salary and associated costs are deductible for UBIT purposes.[53]

---

[50] IRC §162; Reg. §1.512(a)-1(b).
[51] *Iowa State University of Science and Technology v. U.S.,* 500 F.2d 508 (Ct.Cl. 1974).
[52] IRC §512(a)(1); Reg. §1.512(a)-1(b).
[53] Reg. §1.512(a)-1(c).

3. *Exploited Activity.* When an activity is incident to and necessary to accomplish the organization's exempt purpose, peripheral income-producing activity is considered to exploit the exempt purpose. Underlying costs in such a case are deductible only to the extent of income and cannot produce a loss.[54] A good example is sale of the organization's membership mailing list. The EO cannot function without its list. As another example, EOs commonly sell advertisements in their educational publications. In both examples, the activity is conducted without regard to the revenue. The permissible deduction from an exploited activity equals its cost less any exempt income, but not more than the unrelated income, as the schedules below reflect.[55]

AICPA Position. The AICPA rules for allocating expenses are discussed at the beginning of this chapter. If followed consistently from year to year, an EO can use its financial statement numbers as a reasonable basis for claiming UBI deductions. The UBI sections of the Code "do not specifically address how expenses are to be allocated when exempt organizations are computing their UBI."[56]

New Emphasis. The first reference to cost allocations in the index covering 15 years of IRS EO professional training was in 1991. The 1992 book includes cost allocations as a specific section under three major categories: sponsorships, hospitals, and mailing lists and travel tours. Now that the gross revenue from unrelated activity is pinpointed on page 5 of Form 990, the IRS is turning its attention to the properly claimed deductions against such income.

(d) Cost Allocation Schedules

Some years ago, the IRS designed systems of presenting the allocation of costs, as shown on Schedules I and J on page 4. The deductible expense is calculated through a series of steps designed to limit the deduction of exempt function expenses to the income from the mingled activity. The form will not allow a loss from an exploited activity to be deducted. An activity entered into without profit motive is not deductible.[57]

The number reflected in column 7 of Schedules I and J is carried to the front page as a deduction, after it is limited to the amount of unrelated income. This amount should not exceed the income shown on line 10. Prior to 1992, the amounts on new lines 26 and 27 were netted against what is now line 10, bringing only one number to the front page. With the addition of a new line, the IRS can quantify the amount of exploited activity deductions. Exhibit 27–4 illustrates the concepts:

[54]Reg. S1.512(a)-1(d)(1).
[55]Reg. §1.512(a)-1(d)(2).
[56]1991 Exempt Organizations Continuing Professional Education Technical Instruction Program, at page 20.
[57]*Portland Golf Club v. Commissioner*, 110 U.S. 2780 (Sup. Ct. 1990); See also Sections 9.5(e) and 21.4(a).

Exhibit 27-4

SCHEDULE J—ADVERTISING INCOME AND ADVERTISING LOSS (see instructions for line 11 on page 9)

Part I   Income From Periodicals Reported on a Separate Basis

1. Name of periodical	2. Gross advertising income (Enter the total of this column on line 11, col. A, Part I, page 1)	3. Direct advertising costs (Enter the total of this column on line 11, col. B, Part I, page 1)	4. Advertising gain or loss (col. 2 minus col. 3). If a gain, compute cols. 5 through 7.	5. Circulation income	6. Readership costs	7. Excess readership costs (column 6 minus column 5, but not more than column 4). Enter the total of this column on line 27, Part II, page 1.
Example News					Exempt Function	
(1)	100,000	20,000	80,000	20,000	100,000	80,000
(2)	100,000	40,000	60,000	20,000	100,000	60,000
(3)	100,000	90,000	10,000	0	40,000	10,000
(4)	100,000	100,000	0	0	40,000	0

The other schedules are very helpful in reporting special types of income for which the expenses are limited. The titles are complete and leave very little to chance in following the general concepts. Briefly, the schedules serve the following function:

- *Schedule C* calculates the portion of personal property rentals that are taxable, described at Section 21.12(d).

- *Schedule E* calculates the taxable portion of revenues attributable to debt-financed income (Section 21.17).

- *Schedule F* calculates the taxable portion of revenues from controlled subsidiaries (Section 21.12(e)).

- *Schedule G* calculates the taxable income of social clubs setting aside part of their income for charitable purposes (Section 9.5(g)).

- *Schedule K* reports officer, director, and trustee compensation attributable to unrelated business income. This amount should be calculated using the accounting allocation principles discussed at the beginning of this chapter.

(e) In-Kind Donations

Three different types of in-kind donations may be received by an exempt nonprofit organization: services, facility use, and material goods. Such donations received by an exempt organization are not reported for Form 990 purposes (Section 27.9, line 82) for three reasons:

1. Gifts of services and facilities are not deductible to the contributor, although material goods may be deductible;[58]

2. Accounting theory is misunderstood; and

3. A business operated primarily by volunteers[59] and a business selling donated goods[60] are not subject to the unrelated business income tax.

In-kind donations can and should, however, be booked for purposes of Form 990-T, in the author's opinion.[61] Statement of Position 78-10 contains very specific and clear guidelines for recording such donations and is reprinted in Exhibit 27–5.[62] Note under item 67(d) that in-kind services are not recorded if

---

[58] IRC §170(e).
[59] IRC §513(1).
[60] IRC §513(3).
[61] There is no published precedent for this position. An IRS EO specialist's informal opinion was that there could be no deduction because no cash changed hands. There are several precedents in the tax code for imputed income. Under IRC §482, income can be allocated between related companies, essentially on paper. Interest income is imputed to certain below-market rate loans under IRC §7872.
[62] Issued by the Accounting Standards Division of the American Institute of Certified Public Accountants, effective December 31, 1989, also referred to as SOP 78-10.

Exhibit 27–5

EXCERPT FROM ALCPA STATEMENT OF POSITION 78-10: ACCOUNTING PRINCIPLES AND REPORTING PRACTICES OF CERTAIN NONPROFIT ORGANIZATIONS

Donated and Contributed Services

67. The nature and extent of donated or contributed services received by organizations vary and range from the limited participation of many individuals in fund-raising activities to active participation in the organization's service program. Because it is difficult to place a monetary value on such services, their values are usually not recorded. The accounting standards division believes that those services should not be recorded as an expense, with an equivalent amount recorded as contributions or support, unless all of the following circumstances exist:

    a. The services performed are significant and form an integral part of the efforts of the organization as it is presently constituted; the services would be performed by salaried personnel if donated or contributed services were not available for the organization to accomplish its purpose; and the organization would continue this program or activity.

    b. The organization controls the employment and duties of the service donors. The organization is able to influence their activities in a way comparable to the control it would exercise over employees with similar responsibilities. This includes control over time, location, nature, and performance of donated or contributed services.

    c. The organization has a clearly measurable basis for the amount to be recorded.

    d. The services of the reporting organization are not principally intended for the benefit of its members. Accordingly, donated and contributed services would not normally be recorded by organizations such as religious communities, professional and trade associations, labor unions, political parties, fraternal organizations, and social and country clubs.

68. Participation of volunteers in philanthropic activities generally does not meet the foregoing criteria because there is no effective employer-employee relationship. (See criterion *b,* above.)

69. Services that generally are not recorded as contributions, even though the services may constitute a significant factor in the operation of the organization, include the following:

    a. Supplementary efforts of volunteer workers that are provided directly to beneficiaries of the organization. Such activities usually involve auxiliary activities or other services that would not otherwise be provided by the organization as a part of its operating program.

    b. Periodic services of volunteers in concentrated fund-raising drives. The activities of volunteer solicitors are not usually subject to a degree of operating supervision and control by the organization sufficient to provide a basis for measuring and recording the value of time devoted. However, if individuals perform administrative functions

---

Exhibit 27–5 (*continued*)

**EXCERPT FROM ALCPA STATEMENT OF POSITION 78-10:
ACCOUNTING PRINCIPLES AND REPORTING PRACTICES OF
CERTAIN NONPROFIT ORGANIZATIONS**

in positions that would otherwise be held by salaried personnel, consideration should be given to recording the value of those services.

70. Notes to the financial statements should disclose the methods used by the organization in valuing, recording, and reporting donated or contributed services and should distinguish between donated or contributed services for which values have and have not been recorded.

Donated Materials and Facilities

71. Donated materials and facilities, if significant in amount, should be recorded at their fair value, provided the organization has a clearly measurable and objective basis for determining the value. If the materials are such that values cannot reasonably be determined, such as clothing, furniture, and so forth, which vary greatly in value depending on condition and style, they should not be recorded as contributions. If donated materials pass through the organization to its charitable beneficiaries, and the organization serves only as an agent for the donors, the donation should not be recorded as a contribution. The recorded value of the use of contributed facilities should be included as revenue and expense during the period of use.

SOURCE: Statement of Position 78-10: [Accounting Principles and Reporting Practices of Certain Nonprofit Organizations]. Copyright © 1989 by American Institute of Certified Public Accountants, Inc. Reprinted with permission.

the services are intended for the benefit of the organization's members, so that non-(c)(3) organizations would not normally book donated services. Donated office space and donated goods can be booked.

This tax planning opportunity can be significant. Booking the in-kind donations does not produce taxable gross income because voluntary contributions are gifts and not subject to income tax.[63] Presumably, they are not received in connection with a trade or business. The corresponding expense, to the extent that it is directly associated with or is partly allocable to an unrelated business activity, can result in a saving of UBIT.

[63] IRC §102.

SUCCESSFUL PREPARATION OF FORMS 990, 990EZ, 990-T AND 990-PF

Appendix 27–1

FORM 990EZ

<table>
<tr><td colspan="2" rowspan="2">Form **990EZ**

Department of the Treasury
Internal Revenue Service</td><td colspan="2">**Short Form**
Return of Organization Exempt From Income Tax
Under section 501(c) of the Internal Revenue Code (except black lung benefit trust or
private foundation) or section 4947(a)(1) charitable trust
▶ For organizations with gross receipts less than $100,000 and total assets less
than $250,000 at the end of the year.
The organization may have to use a copy of this return to satisfy state reporting requirements.</td><td>OMB No. 1545-1150</td></tr>
<tr><td colspan="2"></td><td>**1992**
This Form is
Open to Public
Inspection</td></tr>
</table>

A For the calendar year 1992, or fiscal year beginning _____ , 1992, and ending _____ , 19 ____

<table>
<tr><td rowspan="4">Please
use IRS
label or
print or
type.
See
Specific
Instruc-
tions.</td><td>**B** Name of organization
DISPOSABLE BOTTLE ACTION COMMITTEE</td><td>**C** Employer Identification number
42 : 2222222</td></tr>
<tr><td>Number and street (or P.O. box no., if mail is not delivered to street address) | Room/suite
1111 ANY STREET</td><td>**D** State registration number
none</td></tr>
<tr><td>City, town, or post office, state, and ZIP code
HOMETOWN, STATE 44444</td><td>**E** Enter four-digit group exemption
number (GEN)</td></tr>
</table>

F Check type of organization—Exempt under section ▶ ☒ 501(c) (3) (insert number), OR ▶ ☐ section 4947(a)(1) charitable trust

G Check ▶ ☐ if exemption application pending. | **H** Check ▶ ☐ if address changed.

I Accounting method: ☒ Cash ☐ Accrual ☐ Other (specify) ▶

J Check ▶ ☐ if the organization's gross receipts are normally not more than $25,000. The organization need not file a return with the IRS; but if the organization received a Form 990 Package in the mail, the organization should file a return without financial data. **Some states require a complete return.**

K Enter the organization's 1992 gross receipts (add back lines 5b, 6b, and 7b, to line 9) . . . . . ▶ $ _____ | SECTION 27.4(a)

If $100,000 or more, the organization must file Form 990 instead of Form 990EZ.

Part I Statement of Revenue, Expenses, and Changes in Net Assets or Fund Balances

1	Contributions, gifts, grants, and similar amounts received (attach schedule—see instructions) . . .	**1**	27.4(b)
2	Program service revenue	**2**	27.4(c)
3	Membership dues and assessments (see instructions)	**3**	27.4(d)
4	Investment income	**4**	27.4(e),(f),(g)&(h)
5a	Gross amount from sale of assets other than inventory	5a		
b	Less: cost or other basis and sales expenses	5b		
c	Gain or (loss) (line 5a less line 5b) (attach schedule)	**5c**	27.4(i)
6	Special events and activities (attach schedule—see instructions):			
a	Gross revenue (not including $ _____ of contributions reported on line 1)	6a		
b	Less: direct expenses	6b		
c	Net income or (loss) (line 6a less line 6b)	**6c**	27.4(j)
7a	Gross sales less returns and allowances	7a		
b	Less: cost of goods sold	7b		
c	Gross profit or (loss) (line 7a less line 7b)	**7c**	27.4(k)
8	Other revenue (describe ▶ _____)	**8**	27.4(l)
9	**Total revenue** (add lines 1, 2, 3, 4, 5c, 6c, 7c, and 8) . . . . ▶	**9**	
10	Grants and similar amounts paid (attach schedule)	**10**	27.5(a)&(b)
11	Benefits paid to or for members	**11**	27.5(c)
12	Salaries, other compensation, and employee benefits	**12**	27.5(d)&(e)
13	Professional fees and other payments to independent contractors	**13**	27.5(f)
14	Occupancy, rent, utilities, and maintenance	**14**	27.5(g)
15	Printing, publications, postage, and shipping	**15**	27.5(g)
16	Other expenses (describe ▶ _____)	**16**	27.5(g)
17	**Total expenses** (add lines 10 through 16) . . . . ▶	**17**	
18	Excess or (deficit) for the year (line 9 less line 17)	**18**	
19	Net assets or fund balances at beginning of year (from line 27, column (A)) (must agree with end-of-year figure reported on prior year's return)	**19**	
20	Other changes in net assets or fund balances (attach explanation)	**20**	27.4(o)
21	Net assets or fund balances at end of year (combine lines 18 through 20) (must agree with line 27, column (B)) . . . . ▶	**21**	

Part II Balance Sheets—If Total assets on line 25, column (B) are $250,000 or more, Form 990 must be filed instead of Form 990EZ.

			(A) Beginning of year	(B) End of year
22	Cash, savings, and investments	**22**		
23	Land and buildings	**23**		
24	Other assets (describe ▶ _____)	**24**		
25	**Total assets**	**25**		
26	**Total liabilities** (describe ▶ _____)	**26**		
27	**Net assets or fund balances** (column (B) must agree with line 21)	**27**		

For Paperwork Reduction Act Notice, see page 1 of the separate instructions. Cat. No. 10642I Form **990EZ** (1992)

FORM 990EZ (*continued*)

Form 990EZ (1992)	DISPOSABLE BOTTLE ACTION COMMITTEE	EIN# 42-2222222	Page **2**

Part III **Statement of Program Service Accomplishments**—(see instructions)

Expenses
(Required for 501(c)(3) and (4) organizations and 4947(a)(1) trusts; optional for others.)

Describe what was achieved in carrying out the organization's exempt purposes. Fully describe the services provided, the number of persons benefited, or other relevant information for each program title.

28 ....
.... SECTION 27.5(d) ....
.... (Grants $ ....)

29 ....
....
.... (Grants $ ....)

30 ....
....
.... (Grants $ ....)

31 Other program services (attach schedule) . . . . (Grants $ ....)

32 Total program service expenses (add lines 28 through 31) . . . . ▶

Part IV **List of Officers, Directors, Trustees, and Key Employees** (List each one even if not compensated. See instructions.)

(A) Name and address	(B) Title and average hours per week devoted to position	(C) Compensation (If not paid, enter -0-.)	(D) Contributions to employee benefit plans	(E) Expense account and other allowances
....				
.... SECTION 27.5(d)&(e)				
....				
....				

Part V **Other Information**—Section 501(c)(3) organizations and section 4947(a)(1) charitable trusts must also complete and **attach Schedule A (Form 990)**. (See General Instruction D1.) Section 27.9

		Yes	No

33 Did the organization engage in any activity not previously reported to the Internal Revenue Service? line 76 . .
 If "Yes," attach a detailed description of each activity.

34 Were any changes made to the organizing or governing documents but not reported to the IRS? . line 77 . .
 If "Yes," attach a conformed copy of the changes.

35 *If the organization had income from business activities, such as those reported on lines 2, 6, and 7 (among others), but NOT reported on Form 990-T, attach a statement explaining your reason for not reporting the income on Form 990-T* line 78

 a Did the organization have unrelated business gross income of $1,000 or more during the year covered by this return? . .

 b If "Yes," has it filed a tax return on Form 990-T, Exempt Organization Business Income Tax Return, for this year? .

36 Was there a liquidation, dissolution, termination, or substantial contraction during the year? (See instructions.) line 79
 If "Yes," attach a statement as described in the instructions.

37a Enter amount of political expenditures, direct or indirect, as described in the instructions. ▶ | 37a | line 81 |

 b Did the organization file Form 1120-POL, U.S. Income Tax Return for Certain Political Organizations, for this year? .

38a Did the organization borrow from, or make any loans to, any officer, director, trustee, or key employee, OR were any such loans made in a prior year and still unpaid at the start of the period covered by this return? no comparison

 b If "Yes," attach the schedule specified in the instructions and enter the amount involved . . | 38b |

39 *Section 501(c)(7) organizations.*—Enter:

 a Initiation fees and capital contributions included on line 9 . . . . | 39a | line 86 |

 b Gross receipts, included on line 9, for public use of club facilities (see instructions) . . | 39b |

 c Does the club's governing instrument or any written policy statement provide for discrimination against any person because of race, color, or religion? (If "Yes," attach statement; see instructions.). . . . .

40 List the states with which a copy of this return is filed. ▶ ....

41 The books are in care of ▶ .... Telephone no. ▶ (.......) line 91
 Located at ▶ .... ZIP code ▶ ....

42 Section 4947(a)(1) charitable trusts filing Form 990EZ in lieu of Form 1041, U.S. Fiduciary Income Tax Return.—Check here ▶ ☐
 and enter the amount of tax-exempt interest received or accrued during the tax year . . . ▶ | 42 |

Please Sign Here

Under penalties of perjury, I declare that I have examined this return, including accompanying schedules and statements, and to the best of my knowledge and belief, it is true, correct, and complete. Declaration of preparer (other than officer) is based on all information of which preparer has any knowledge.

▶ Signature of officer | Date | ▶ Title

Paid Preparer's Use Only

| Preparer's signature ▶ | | Date | Check if self-employed ▶ ☐ |
| Firm's name (or yours if self-employed) and address ▶ | BLAZEK, ROGERS & VETTERLING 3101 RICHMOND AVE., STE 220 HOUSTON, TX | ZIP code 77098 | |

FORM 990

Form **990**	**Return of Organization Exempt From Income Tax**	OMB No. 1545-0047
	Under section 501(c) of the Internal Revenue Code (except black lung benefit trust or private foundation) or section 4947(a)(1) charitable trust	**1992**
Department of the Treasury Internal Revenue Service	Note: *The organization may have to use a copy of this return to satisfy state reporting requirements.*	This Form is Open to Public Inspection

A For the calendar year 1992, or fiscal year beginning July 1 , 1992 and ending June 30 , 19XX

B Name of organization CAMPAIGN TO CLEAN UP AMERICA		**C** Employer Identification number 44 : 4444444
Please use IRS label or print or type. See Specific Instructions.	Number and street (or P.O. box if mail is not delivered to street address)	Room/suite
	1111 ANY STREET	
	City, town, or post office, state, and ZIP code	
	HOMETOWN, TEXAS 77777	

D State registration number NONE

E If address changed, check box. . . ▶ ☐

F Check type of organization—Exempt under section ▶ ☒ 501(c)(3) (insert number),
OR ▶ ☐ section 4947(a)(1) charitable trust

G If exemption application pending, check box . ▶ ☒

H(a) Is this a group return filed for affiliates? . . . . ☐ Yes ☒ No
(b) If "Yes," enter the number of affiliates for which this return is filed: . ▶ _____
(c) Is this a separate return filed by an organization covered by a group ruling? ☐ Yes ☒ No

I If either box in H is checked "Yes," enter four-digit group exemption number (GEN) ▶

J Accounting method: ☐ Cash ☒ Accrual ☐ Other (specify) ▶

K Check here ▶ ☐ if the organization's gross receipts are normally not more than $25,000. The organization need not file a return with the IRS; but if it received a Form 990 Package in the mail, it should file a return without financial data. Some states require a complete return.

Note: *Form 990EZ may be used by organizations with gross receipts less than $100,000 and total assets less than $250,000 at end of year.*

Part I Statement of Revenue, Expenses, and Changes in Net Assets or Fund Balances

1	Contributions, gifts, grants, and similar amounts received:			
a	Direct public support	1a	974,700	
b	Indirect public support	1b		
c	Government grants	1c		
d	Total (add lines 1a through 1c) (attach schedule—see instructions) Schedule 1 . .	1d		974,700
2	Program service revenue (from Part VII, line 93)	2		37,700
3	Membership dues and assessments (see instructions)	3		
4	Interest on savings and temporary cash investments	4		5,000
5	Dividends and interest from securities	5		4,000
6a	Gross rents	6a	2,000	
b	Less: rental expenses	6b		
c	Net rental income or (loss)	6c		2,000
7	Other investment income (describe ▶)	7		
8a	Gross amount from sale of assets other than inventory	(A) Securities 8a	(B) Other	
b	Less: cost or other basis and sales expenses	8b		
c	Gain or (loss) (attach schedule) . . .	8c		
d	Net gain or (loss) (combine line 8c, columns (A) and (B))	8d		
9	Special fundraising events and activities (attach schedule—see instructions):			
a	Gross revenue (not including $_____ of contributions reported on line 1a)	9a		
b	Less: direct expenses	9b		
c	Net income	9c		
10a	Gross sales less returns and allowances	10a	40,000	
b	Less: cost of goods sold . . . . (see instructions) .	10b	10,000	
c	Gross profit or (loss) (attach schedule)	10c		30,000
11	Other revenue (from Part VII, line 103)	11		
12	Total revenue (add lines 1d, 2, 3, 4, 5, 6c, 7, 8d, 9c, 10c, and 11)	12		1,053,400
13	Program services (from line 44, column (B)) (see instructions)	13		476,700
14	Management and general (from line 44, column (C)) (see instructions)	14		130,800
15	Fundraising (from line 44, column (D)) (see instructions)	15		103,500
16	Payments to affiliates (attach schedule—see instructions)	16		
17	Total expenses (add lines 16 and 44, column (A))	17		711,000
18	Excess or (deficit) for the year (subtract line 17 from line 12)	18		342,400
19	Net assets or fund balances at beginning of year (from line 74, column (A)) . . .	19		43,800
20	Other changes in net assets or fund balances (attach explanation)	20		
21	Net assets or fund balances at end of year (combine lines 18, 19, and 20)	21		386,200

For Paperwork Reduction Act Notice, see page 1 of the separate Instructions.   Cat. No. 11282Y   Form **990** (1992)

Appendix 27-2

FORM 990 *(continued)*

Form 990 (1992)   CAMPAIGN TO CLEAN UP AMERICA   EIN# 44-4444444   Page 2

Part II Statement of Functional Expenses

All organizations must complete column (A). Columns (B), (C), and (D) are required for section 501(c)(3) and (4) organizations and 4947(a)(1) charitable trusts but optional for others. (See instructions.)

	Do not include amounts reported on line 6b, 8b, 9b, 10b, or 16 of Part I.		(A) Total	(B) Program services	(C) Management and general	(D) Fundraising
22	Grants and allocations (attach schedule)	22				
23	Specific assistance to individuals (attach schedule)	23				
24	Benefits paid to or for members (attach schedule)	24				
25	Compensation of officers, directors, etc.	25				
26	Other salaries and wages	26	300,000	215,000	65,000	20,000
27	Pension plan contributions	27				
28	Other employee benefits	28	25,000	18,000	5,000	2,000
29	Payroll taxes	29	25,000	17,000	5,000	3,000
30	Professional fundraising fees	30	40,000			40,000
31	Accounting fees	31	10,000		10,000	
32	Legal fees	32	10,000		10,000	
33	Supplies	33	15,000	12,000	2,000	1,000
34	Telephone	34	18,000	12,000	4,000	2,000
35	Postage and shipping	35				
36	Occupancy	36	60,000	43,000	14,000	3,000
37	Equipment rental and maintenance	37	10,000	10,000		
38	Printing and publications	38	62,000	52,000	2,000	8,000
39	Travel	39	25,000	16,000	3,000	6,000
40	Conferences, conventions, and meetings	40	7,000	6,000	1,000	
41	Interest	41				
42	Depreciation, depletion, etc. (attach schedule)	42	26,000	24,700	800	500
43	Other expenses (itemize): a	43a				
b	Advertising	43b	50,000	29,000	3,000	18,000
c	Dues/library	43c	5,000	2,000	3,000	
d	Outside consultants	43d	18,000	16,000	2,000	
e	Miscellaneous	43e	5,000	4,000	1,000	
f		43f				
44	Total functional expenses (add lines 22 through 43) Organizations completing columns (B)-(D), carry these totals to lines 13-15	44	711,000	476,700	130,800	103,500

Reporting of Joint Costs.—Did you report in column (B) (Program services) any joint costs from a combined educational campaign and fundraising solicitation? . . . . ▶ ☐ Yes ☐ No
If "Yes," enter (i) the aggregate amount of these joint costs $ 31,500 ; (ii) the amount allocated to program services $ 20,500 ;
(iii) the amount allocated to management and general $ 0 ; and (iv) the amount allocated to fundraising $ 11,000 .

Part III Statement of Program Service Accomplishments (See instructions.)

Describe what was achieved in carrying out the organization's exempt purposes. Fully describe the services provided; the number of persons benefited; or other relevant information for each program title. Section 501(c)(3) and (4) organizations and section 4947(a)(1) charitable trusts must also enter the amount of grants and allocations to others.

	Expenses (Required for 501(c)(3) and (4) organizations and 4947(a)(1) trusts; optional for others.)
a VOLUNTEER TEAMS: To prevent litter and organize pick-up teams, the Campaign holds community meetings to recruit volunteers. Teams are provided equipment, including rakes, shovels, gloves, trash bags, and safety signs with which to clean up their communities. (Grants and allocations $)	261,900
b PUBLIC EDUCATION: Literature describing Campaign purposes to rid America of litter and clean up our cities, towns and country sides is prepared and distributed. Mailings, newspaper and magazine advertisements and pamphlet packages are used. (Grants and allocations $)	146,600
c PROGRAMS AND SEMINARS: The Campaign sponsors educational meetings to bring together government officials, businesses and citizens to discuss new methods of trash collections, recycling and litter reduction. (Grants and allocations $)	58,200
d LEGISLATIVE ALERTS: The Campaign promotes the passage of legislation to reduce litter, including a recent bottle ordinance to require production of returnable bottles. (Grants and allocations $)	10,000
e Other program services (attach schedule) . . . (Grants and allocations $)	0
f Total (add lines a through e) (should equal line 44, column (B)) . . . . ▶	476,700

Appendix 27–2

FORM 990 (*continued*)

Form 990 (1992)   CAMPAIGN TO CLEAN UP AMERICA   EIN# 44-4444444   Page **3**

Part IV   Balance Sheets

Note: *Where required, attached schedules and amounts within the description column should be for end-of-year amounts only.*

			(A) Beginning of year		(B) End of year
Assets					
45	Cash—non-interest-bearing			45	
46	Savings and temporary cash investments		12,000	46	29,000
47a	Accounts receivable Interest	47a			
b	Less: allowance for doubtful accounts	47b		47c	2,000
48a	Pledges receivable	48a			
b	Less: allowance for doubtful accounts	48b		48c	
49	Grants receivable			49	12,000
50	Receivables due from officers, directors, trustees, and key employees (attach schedule)			50	
51a	Other notes and loans receivable (attach schedule)	51a			
b	Less: allowance for doubtful accounts	51b		51c	
52	Inventories for sale or use			52	
53	Prepaid expenses and deferred charges			53	
54	Investments—securities (attach schedule) Schedule 3		19,000	54	250,200
55a	Investments—land, buildings, and equipment: basis	55a			
b	Less: accumulated depreciation (attach schedule)	55b		55c	
56	Investments—other (attach schedule)			56	
57a	Land, buildings, and equipment: basis	57a	152,000		
b	Less: accumulated depreciation (attach schedule)	57b	27,000	57c	125,000
58	Other assets (describe ▶)		18,000	58	
59	**Total assets** (add lines 45 through 58) (must equal line 75)		49,000	59	418,200
Liabilities					
60	Accounts payable and accrued expenses		5,200	60	14,000
61	Grants payable			61	
62	Support and revenue designated for future periods (attach schedule)			62	18,000
63	Loans from officers, directors, trustees, and key employees (attach schedule)			63	
64	Mortgages and other notes payable (attach schedule)			64	
65	Other liabilities (describe ▶)			65	
66	**Total liabilities** (add lines 60 through 65)		5,200	66	32,000
Fund Balances or Net Assets					
Organizations that use fund accounting, check here ▶ [X] and complete lines 67 through 70 and lines 74 and 75 (see instructions).					
67a	Current unrestricted fund		25,800	67a	256,000
b	Current restricted fund			67b	
68	Land, buildings, and equipment fund		18,000	68	130,200
69	Endowment fund			69	
70	Other funds (describe ▶)			70	
Organizations that do not use fund accounting, check here ▶ ☐ and complete lines 71 through 75 (see instructions).					
71	Capital stock or trust principal			71	
72	Paid-in or capital surplus			72	
73	Retained earnings or accumulated income			73	
74	Total fund balances or net assets (add lines 67a through 70 OR lines 71 through 73: column (A) must equal line 19 and column (B) must equal line 21)		43,800	74	386,200
75	Total liabilities and fund balances/net assets (add lines 66 and 74)		49,000	75	418,200

Form 990 is available for public inspection and, for some people, serves as the primary or sole source of information about a particular organization. How the public perceives an organization in such cases may be determined by the information presented on its return. Therefore, please make sure the return is complete and accurate and fully describes the organization's programs and accomplishments.

Appendix 27–2

FORM 990 (*continued*)

Form 990 (1992) CAMPAIGN TO CLEAN UP AMERICA   EIN# 44-4444444   Page **4**

Part V List of Officers, Directors, Trustees, and Key Employees (List each one even if not compensated. See instructions.)

(A) Name and address	(B) Title and average hours per week devoted to position	(C) Compensation (If not paid, enter -0-)	(D) Contributions to employee benefit plans	(E) Expense account and other allowances
John J. Environmentalist 333 First Street, Hometown, TX 77777	President Part	None	None	0
Jane D. Environmentalist 333 First Street, Hometown, TX 77777	Secretary/Treas. Part	None	None	0
James F. Friend 444 Second Street, Hometown, TX 77777	Vice President Part	None	None	0
Samantha Engineer 222 MIT Dr., Boston, MA 01234	Board Member Part	None	None	2,000

Did any officer, director, trustee, or key employee receive aggregate compensation of more than $100,000 from your organization and all related organizations, of which more than $10,000 was provided by the related organizations? ▶ ☐ Yes ☒ No
If "Yes," attach schedule (see instructions).

Part VI Other Information

Note: *Section 501(c)(3) organizations and section 4947(a)(1) trusts must also complete and attach Schedule A (Form 990).*

			Yes	No
76	Did the organization engage in any activity not previously reported to the Internal Revenue Service? . . If "Yes," attach a detailed description of each activity.	76		X
77	Were any changes made in the organizing or governing documents, but not reported to the IRS? . . . . If "Yes," attach a conformed copy of the changes.	77		X
78a	Did the organization have unrelated business gross income of $1,000 or more during the year covered by this return?	78a	X	
b	If "Yes," has it filed a tax return on **Form 990-T**, Exempt Organization Business Income Tax Return, for this year?	78b	X	
c	At any time during the year, did the organization own a 50% or greater interest in a taxable corporation or partnership? If "Yes," complete Part IX.	78c		X
79	Was there a liquidation, dissolution, termination, or substantial contraction during the year? (See instructions.) If "Yes," attach a statement as described in the instructions.	79		X
80a	Is the organization related (other than by association with a statewide or nationwide organization) through common membership, governing bodies, trustees, officers, etc., to any other exempt or non-exempt organization? (See instructions.)	80a		X
b	If "Yes," enter the name of the organization ▶ .... and check whether it is ☐ exempt **OR** ☐ nonexempt.			
81a	Enter amount of political expenditures, direct or indirect, as described in the instructions . .	81a	None	
b	Did the organization file **Form 1120-POL**, U.S. Income Tax Return for Certain Political Organizations, for this year?	81b	N/A	
82a	Did the organization receive donated services or the use of materials, equipment, or facilities at no charge or at substantially less than fair rental value?	82a	X	
b	If "Yes," you may indicate the value of these items here. Do not include this amount as revenue in Part I or as an expense in Part II. See instructions for reporting in Part III .	82b		
83a	Did anyone request to see either the organization's annual return or exemption application (or both)? . .	83a	X	
b	If "Yes," did the organization comply as described in the instructions? (See General Instruction L.) . . .	83b	X	
84a	Did the organization solicit any contributions or gifts that were not tax deductible?	84a		X
b	If "Yes," did the organization include with every solicitation an express statement that such contributions or gifts were not tax deductible? (See General Instruction M.)	84b	N/A	
85a	*Section 501(c)(5) or (6) organizations.*—Did the organization spend any amounts in attempts to influence public opinion about legislative matters or referendums? (See instructions and Regulations section 1.162-20(c).) . .	85a		
b	If "Yes," enter the total amount spent for this purpose	85b		
86	*Section 501(c)(7) organizations.*—Enter:			
a	Initiation fees and capital contributions included on line 12	86a		
b	Gross receipts, included on line 12, for public use of club facilities (see instructions)	86b		
c	Does the club's governing instrument or any written policy statement provide for discrimination against any person because of race, color, or religion? (If "Yes," attach statement. See instructions.)	86c		
87	*Section 501(c)(12) organizations.*—Enter amount of:			
a	Gross income received from members or shareholders	87a		
b	Gross income received from other sources. (Do not net amounts due or paid to other sources against amounts due or received from them.)	87b		
88	*Public interest law firms.*—Attach information described in the instructions.			
89	List the states with which a copy of this return is filed ▶ Texas, Michigan, New York, CA			
90	During this tax year did the organization maintain any part of its accounting / tax records on a computerized system?	90	X	
91	The books are in care of ▶ Joan Controller ....Telephone no. ▶ (404) 444-4444			
	Located at ▶ 1111 ANY STREET, HOMETOWN, TEXAS .... ZIP code ▶ 77777			
92	*Section 4947(a)(1) charitable trusts filing Form 990 in lieu of Form 1041*, U.S. Fiduciary Income Tax Return, should check here ▶ ☐ and enter the amount of tax-exempt interest received or accrued during the tax year . . . ▶	92		

Appendix 27–2

FORM 990 *(continued)*

Form 990 (1992)   Campaign to Clean Up America   EIN # 44-4444444   Page **5**

Part VII   Analysis of Income-Producing Activities

Enter gross amounts unless otherwise indicated.

	Unrelated business income		Excluded by section 512, 513, or 514		(e) Related or exempt function income (See instructions.)
	(a) Business code	(b) Amount	(c) Exclusion code	(d) Amount	
93 Program service revenue:					
(a) Seminars					12,000
(b) Publication sales					13,700
(c) _____					
(d) _____					
(e) _____					
(f) _____					
(g) Fees from government agencies					
94 Membership dues and assessments					
95 Interest on savings and temporary cash investments .			14	5,000	
96 Dividends and interest from securities . . .			14	4,000	
97 Net rental income or (loss) from real estate:					
(a) debt-financed property					
(b) not debt-financed property					
98 Net rental income or (loss) from personal property .	9200	2,000			
99 Other investment income					
100 Gain or (loss) from sales of assets other than inventory					
101 Net income from special fundraising events . .					12,000
102 Gross profit or (loss) from sales of inventory .					
103 Other revenue: (a)_____					
(b) Advertising	7310	30,000			
(c) _____					
(d) _____					
(e) _____					
104 Subtotal (add columns (b), (d), and (e)) . . .		32,000		9,000	37,700
105 TOTAL (add line 104, columns (b), (d), and (e)) . . . . ▶					78,700

Note: *(Line 105 plus line 1d, Part I, should equal the amount on line 12, Part I.)*

Part VIII   Relationship of Activities to the Accomplishment of Exempt Purposes

Line No. ▼	Explain how each activity for which income is reported in column (e) of Part VII contributed importantly to the accomplishment of the organization's exempt purposes (other than by providing funds for such purposes). (See instructions.)
93a	Community meetings were held in Hometown, Dallas, Houston, Lubbock, and Laredo, Texas. An average of 80 people attended a one-day meeting where educational information was presented.
93b	Pamphlets on recycling, litter campaign organizational procedures and volunteer recruitment skills are sold for $5.00 each.
102	The Campaign sells garbage bags bearing its logo and slogan "CLEAN UP AMERICA." Bags are sold in 50 count boxes for $5.00 each.

Part IX   Information Regarding Taxable Subsidiaries (Complete this Part if the "Yes" box on 78c is checked.)

Name, address, and employer identification number of corporation or partnership	Percentage of ownership interest	Nature of business activities	Total income	End-of-year assets
Not applicable				

Please Sign Here — Under penalties of perjury, I declare that I have examined this return, including accompanying schedules and statements, and to the best of my knowledge and belief, it is true, correct, and complete. Declaration of preparer (other than officer) is based on all information of which preparer has any knowledge.

▶ Signature of officer   Date   ▶ Title

Paid Preparer's Use Only

Preparer's signature ▶	Date 5-10-xx	Check if self-employed ▶ ☐
Firm's name (or yours if self-employed) and address ▶ BLAZEK, ROGERS & VETTERLING 3101 Richmond, Houston Tx	ZIP code 77098	

Appendix 27–2

FORM 990 (*continued*)

CAMPAIGN TO CLEAN UP AMERICA   EIN#44-4444444

Attachment 1 to Form 990

Fiscal Year ending June 30, 19X0

Part 1, line 1

Contributions and Grants Received:

			1992	1991
John & Jane Environmentalist 333 First Street Hometown, TX 77777	Cash	12-1-X0	$20,000	$50,000
Friendly Corporation 101 Business Tower Hometown, TX 77777	Cash	1-1-X0	10,000	10,000
Environmentalist Fund 111 Any Street Hometown, TX 77777	Cash	12-30-XI	160,000	110,000
Waste Disposal Company 290 Allied Tower Chicago, IL 60555	Cash	4-4-X0	100,000	0
All others, under $5,000 each.			390,000	90,000
Total contributions and grants			$974,700	260,000
Amounts treated as public gifts				-106,200
Contributions considered private (Sch.A)				$153,800

Part 1, line 10B

Costs of goods sold:

Garbage bag direct cost:		
Beginning inventory	$ None	
Purchases	20,000	
Ending Inventory	-10,000	
Total cost of goods sold		$10,000

Schedule 1

FORM 990 (*continued*)

CAMPAIGN TO CLEAN UP AMERICA—DEPRECIATION

EIN #44-4444444

Attachment 2 to Form 990

Fiscal year ending June 30, 19XI

	SL Method Years	Asset Account			Reserve Account		
		7-1-X0	Additions	6-30-XI	7-1-X0	Additions	6-30-XI
Office furnishings	8	$ 8,000	$ 4,000	$ 12,000	$ 400	$ 800	$ 1,200
Computers	8	8,000	4,000	12,000	400	800	1,200
Printers	8	3,000	3,000	6,000	200	500	700
Vans	5		30,000	30,000		6,000	6,000
Lawn equipment	5		30,000	30,000		6,000	6,000
Tools	4		62,000	62,000		11,900	11,900
		$19,000	$133,000	$152,000	$1,000	$26,000	$27,000

Schedule 2

Appendix 27–2

FORM 990   (*continued*)

CAMPAIGN TO CLEAN UP AMERICA   EIN #44-4444444

Attachment 3 to Form 990

Part V, line 54

Investments

Face Value	Description	Beginning Cost	Ending Cost
Short Term:			
24M	U.S. Treasury bills due 4-4-XX	$19,000	$23,000
50M	U.S. Treasury bills due 7-1-XX		46,000
100M	U.S. Treasury notes due 9-1-XX		91,000
	Total Short-Term Securities		$160,000
Marketable Securities:			
Number of Shares			
500	High return stock		$50,000
100	Good quality common		10,000
250	Best yield preferred		25,000
52	Highly diversified corporation		5,200
	Total Investments	$19,000	$250,000

Part VI-B, lines b & g

The Campaign's program director, Andrew Organized, contacted Texas legislators several times during the year to request their support for proposed legislation. Organized maintained a diary of time spent and phone costs incurred. The allocable portion of his salary for the year based upon time expended was $2,700; long distance charges totalled $300.

Schedule 3

Appendix 27–3

SCHEDULE A

SCHEDULE A (Form 990) Department of the Treasury Internal Revenue Service	**Organization Exempt Under Section 501(c)(3)** (Except Private Foundation), 501(e), 501(f), 501(k), or Section 4947(a)(1) Charitable Trust Supplementary Information ► Attach to Form 990 (or Form 990EZ).	OMB No. 1545-0047 **1992**

Name	Employer Identification number
CAMPAIGN TO CLEAN UP AMERICA	44 : 4444444

Part I Compensation of the Five Highest Paid Employees Other Than Officers, Directors, and Trustees
(See specific instructions.) (List each one. If there are none, enter "None.")

(a) Name and address of employees paid more than $30,000	(b) Title and average hours per week devoted to position	(c) Compensation	(d) Contributions to employee benefit plans	(e) Expense account and other allowances

Total number of other employees paid over $30,000 . . . . ►	None	

Part II Compensation of the Five Highest Paid Persons for Professional Services
(See specific instructions.) (List each one. If there are none, enter "None.")

(a) Name and address of persons paid more than $30,000	(b) Type of service	(c) Compensation

Total number of others receiving over $30,000 for professional services . . . . ►	None	

Part III Statements About Activities

		Yes	No
1	During the year, has the organization attempted to influence national, state, or local legislation, including any attempt to influence public opinion on a legislative matter or referendum? **1**		X
	If "Yes," enter the total expenses paid or incurred in connection with the lobbying activities. $ 2,000		
	Organizations that made an election under section 501(h) by filing Form 5768 must complete Part VI-A. Other organizations checking "Yes," must complete Part VI-B AND attach a statement giving a detailed description of the lobbying activities.		
2	During the year, has the organization, either directly or indirectly, engaged in any of the following acts with any of its trustees, directors, principal officers, or creators, or with any taxable organization or corporation with which any such person is affiliated as an officer, director, trustee, majority owner, or principal beneficiary:		
a	Sale, exchange, or leasing of property? **2a**		X
b	Lending of money or other extension of credit? **2b**		X
c	Furnishing of goods, services, or facilities? **2c**		X
d	Payment of compensation (or payment or reimbursement of expenses if more than $1,000)? **2d**		X
e	Transfer of any part of its income or assets? **2e**		X
	If the answer to any question is "Yes," attach a detailed statement explaining the transactions.		
3	Does the organization make grants for scholarships, fellowships, student loans, etc.? **3**		X
4	Attach a statement explaining how the organization determines that individuals or organizations receiving grants or loans from it in furtherance of its charitable programs qualify to receive payments. (See specific instructions.)		

For Paperwork Reduction Act Notice, see page 1 of the Instructions to Form 990 (or Form 990EZ).   Cat. No. 11285F   Schedule A (Form 990) 1992

Appendix 27–3

SCHEDULE A (*continued*)

Schedule A (Form 990) 1992   CAMPAIGN TO CLEAN UP AMERICA   EIN# 44-4444444   Page **2**

Part IV	**Reason for Non-Private Foundation Status** (See instructions for definitions.)

The organization is not a private foundation because it is (please check only **ONE** applicable box):

5 ☐ A church, convention of churches, or association of churches. Section 170(b)(1)(A)(i).

6 ☐ A school. Section 170(b)(1)(A)(ii). (Also complete Part V, page 3.)

7 ☐ A hospital or a cooperative hospital service organization. Section 170(b)(1)(A)(iii).

8 ☐ A Federal, state, or local government or governmental unit. Section 170(b)(1)(A)(v).

9 ☐ A medical research organization operated in conjunction with a hospital. Section 170(b)(1)(A)(iii). **Enter name, city, and state of hospital ▶** ....

10 ☐ An organization operated for the benefit of a college or university owned or operated by a governmental unit. Section 170(b)(1)(A)(iv). (Also complete Support Schedule.)

11a ☒ An organization that normally receives a substantial part of its support from a governmental unit or from the general public. Section 170(b)(1)(A)(vi). (Also complete Support Schedule.)

11b ☐ A community trust. Section 170(b)(1)(A)(vi). (Also complete Support Schedule.)

12 ☐ An organization that normally receives: **(a)** no more than ⅓ of its support from gross investment income and unrelated business taxable income (less section 511 tax) from businesses acquired by the organization after June 30, 1975, and **(b)** more than ⅓ of its support from contributions, membership fees, and gross receipts from activities related to its charitable, etc., functions—subject to certain exceptions. See section 509(a)(2). (Also complete Support Schedule.)

13 ☐ An organization that is not controlled by any disqualified persons (other than foundation managers) and supports organizations described in: **(1)** boxes 5 through 12 above; or **(2)** section 501(c)(4), (5), or (6), if they meet the test of section 509(a)(2). (See section 509(a)(3).)

Provide the following information about the supported organizations. (See instructions for Part IV, box 13.)

(a) Name(s) of supported organization(s)	**(b)** Box number from above

14 ☐ An organization organized and operated to test for public safety. Section 509(a)(4). (See specific instructions.)

Support Schedule (Complete only if you checked box 10, 11, or 12 above.) *Use cash method of accounting.*

Calendar year (or fiscal year beginning in) ▶	(a) 1991	(b) 1990	(c) 1989	(d) 1988	(e) Total
15 Gifts, grants, and contributions received. (Do not include unusual grants. See line 28.). .	260,000				260,000
16 Membership fees received					
17 Gross receipts from admissions, merchandise sold or services performed, or furnishing of facilities in any activity that is not a business unrelated to the organization's charitable, etc., purpose					
18 Gross income from interest, dividends, amounts received from payments on securities loans (section 512(a)(5)), rents, royalties, and unrelated business taxable income (less section 511 taxes) from businesses acquired by the organization after June 30, 1975. . . .	10,000				10,000
19 Net income from unrelated business activities not included in line 18					
20 Tax revenues levied for the organization's benefit and either paid to it or expended on its behalf .					
21 The value of services or facilities furnished to the organization by a governmental unit without charge. Do not include the value of services or facilities generally furnished to the public without charge . .					
22 Other income. Attach schedule. Do not include gain or (loss) from sale of capital assets . .					
23 Total of lines 15 through 22.	270,000				270,000
24 Line 23 minus line 17.	270,000				270,000
25 Enter 1% of line 23	2,700				//////////
26 Organizations described in box 10 or 11:					
a Enter 2% of amount in column (e), line 24					5,400
b Attach a list (not open to public inspection) showing the name of and amount contributed by each person (other than a governmental unit or publicly supported organization) whose total gifts for 1988 through 1991 exceeded the amount shown in line 26a. Enter the sum of all excess amounts here . . . . ▶					154,400

(Continued on page 3)

Appendix 27–3

SCHEDULE A (*continued*)

Schedule A (Form 990) 1992 CAMPAIGN TO CLEAN UP AMERICA   EIN# 44-4444444   Page **3**

Part IV   Support Schedule (continued) (Complete only if you checked box 10, 11, or 12 on page 2.) Not Applicable

27 Organizations described in box 12, page 2:

   a Attach a list for amounts shown on lines 15, 16, and 17, showing the name of, and total amounts received in each year from, each "disqualified person," and enter the sum of such amounts for each year:

   (1991) .... (1990) .... (1989) .... (1988) ....

   b Attach a list showing, for 1988 through 1991, the name of, and amount included in line 17 for, each person (other than a "disqualified person") from whom the organization received more during that year than the larger of: **(1)** the amount on line 25 for the year; or **(2)** $5,000. Include organizations described in boxes 5 through 11 as well as individuals. Enter the sum of these excess amounts for each year:

   (1991) .... (1990) .... (1989) .... (1988) ....

28 For an organization described in box 10, 11, or 12, page 2, that received any unusual grants during 1988 through 1991, attach a list (not open to public inspection) for each year showing the name of the contributor, the date and amount of the grant, and a brief description of the nature of the grant. Do not include these grants in line 15. (See specific instructions.)

Part V   **Private School Questionnaire**   Not Applicable
(To be completed ONLY by schools that checked box 6 in Part IV)

		Yes	No
29	Does the organization have a racially nondiscriminatory policy toward students by statement in its charter, bylaws, other governing instrument, or in a resolution of its governing body?	29		
30	Does the organization include a statement of its racially nondiscriminatory policy toward students in all its brochures, catalogues, and other written communications with the public dealing with student admissions, programs, and scholarships?	30		
31	Has the organization publicized its racially nondiscriminatory policy through newspaper or broadcast media during the period of solicitation for students, or during the registration period if it has no solicitation program, in a way that makes the policy known to all parts of the general community it serves?.	31		

   If "Yes," please describe; if "No," please explain. (If you need more space, attach a separate statement.)

   ....
   ....
   ....

32	Does the organization maintain the following:			
a	Records indicating the racial composition of the student body, faculty, and administrative staff?	32a		
b	Records documenting that scholarships and other financial assistance are awarded on a racially nondiscriminatory basis?	32b		
c	Copies of all catalogues, brochures, announcements, and other written communications to the public dealing with student admissions, programs, and scholarships?	32c		
d	Copies of all material used by the organization or on its behalf to solicit contributions?	32d		

   If you answered "No" to any of the above, please explain. (If you need more space, attach a separate statement.)

   ....
   ....

33	Does the organization discriminate by race in any way with respect to:			
a	Students' rights or privileges?.	33a		
b	Admissions policies?	33b		
c	Employment of faculty or administrative staff?	33c		
d	Scholarships or other financial assistance? (See instructions.).	33d		
e	Educational policies?	33e		
f	Use of facilities?	33f		
g	Athletic programs?	33g		
h	Other extracurricular activities?	33h		

   If you answered "Yes" to any of the above, please explain. (If you need more space, attach a separate statement.)

   ....
   ....

34a	Does the organization receive any financial aid or assistance from a governmental agency?	34a		
b	Has the organization's right to such aid ever been revoked or suspended?	34b		

   If you answered "Yes" to either 34a or b, please explain using an attached statement.

35	Does the organization certify that it has complied with the applicable requirements of sections 4.01 through 4.05 of Rev. Proc. 75-50, 1975-2 C.B. 587, covering racial nondiscrimination? If "No," attach an explanation. (See instructions for Part V.)	35		

Appendix 27–3

SCHEDULE A (*continued*)

Schedule A (Form 990) 1992   CAMPAIGN TO CLEAN UP AMERICA   EIN# 44-4444444   Page **4**

Part VI-A **Lobbying Expenditures by Electing Public Charities** (see instructions)
(To be completed **ONLY** by an eligible organization that filed Form 5768)   NOT APPLICABLE

Check here ▶ **a** ☐ If the organization belongs to an affiliated group (see instructions).
Check here ▶ **b** ☐ If you checked **a** and "limited control" provisions apply (see instructions).

Limits on Lobbying Expenditures ("Expenditures" means amounts paid or incurred)		(a) Affiliated group totals	(b) To be completed for ALL electing organizations
36	Total lobbying expenditures to influence public opinion (grassroots lobbying) **36**		
37	Total lobbying expenditures to influence a legislative body (direct lobbying) **37**		
38	Total lobbying expenditures (add lines 36 and 37) **38**		
39	Other exempt purpose expenditures (see Part VI-A instructions) **39**		
40	Total exempt purpose expenditures (add lines 38 and 39) (see instructions) **40**		
41	Lobbying nontaxable amount. Enter the amount from the following table—		

If the amount on line 40 is—   The lobbying nontaxable amount is—

Not over $500,000 . . . . 20% of the amount on line 40 . . . . . ⎫
Over $500,000 but not over $1,000,000 . . $100,000 plus 15% of the excess over $500,000 ⎪
Over $1,000,000 but not over $1,500,000 . $175,000 plus 10% of the excess over $1,000,000 ⎬ **41**
Over $1,500,000 but not over $17,000,000 . $225,000 plus 5% of the excess over $1,500,000 ⎪
Over $17,000,000 . . . . $1,000,000. . . . . ⎭

42	Grassroots nontaxable amount (enter 25% of line 41) **42**		
43	Subtract line 42 from line 36. Enter -0- if line 42 is more than line 36 . . . . **43**		
44	Subtract line 41 from line 38. Enter -0- if line 41 is more than line 38 . . . . **44**		

Caution: *File Form 4720 if there is an amount on either line 43 or line 44.*

4-Year Averaging Period Under Section 501(h)
(Some organizations that made a section 501(h) election do not have to complete all of the five columns below.
See the instructions for lines 45–50 for details.)

		Lobbying Expenditures During 4-Year Averaging Period				
	Calendar year (or fiscal year beginning in) ▶	(a) 1992	(b) 1991	(c) 1990	(d) 1989	(e) Total
45	Lobbying nontaxable amount (see instructions)					
46	Lobbying ceiling amount (150% of line 45(e))					
47	Total lobbying expenditures (see instructions)					
48	Grassroots nontaxable amount (see instructions)					
49	Grassroots ceiling amount (150% of line 48(e))					
50	Grassroots lobbying expenditures (see instructions)					

Part VI-B **Lobbying Activity by Nonelecting Public Charities**
(For reporting by organizations that did not complete Part VI-A.)

During the year, did the organization attempt to influence national, state or local legislation, including any attempt to influence public opinion on a legislative matter or referendum, through the use of:		Yes	No	Amount
a	Volunteers		X	
b	Paid staff or management (include compensation in expenses reported on lines c through h) . . .		X	
c	Media advertisements		X	
d	Mailings to members, legislators, or the public		X	
e	Publications or published or broadcast statements		X	
f	Grants to other organizations for lobbying purposes		X	
g	Direct contact with legislators, their staffs, government officials, or a legislative body	X		2,000
h	Rallies, demonstrations, seminars, conventions, speeches, lectures, or any other means			
I	Total lobbying expenditures (add lines c through h)			2,000

If "Yes" to any of the above, also attach a statement giving a detailed description of the lobbying activities.

Appendix 27–3

SCHEDULE A (*continued*)

Schedule A (Form 990) 1992 CAMPAIGN TO CLEAN UP AMERICA   EIN# 44–4444444   Page **5**

Part VII	Information Regarding Transfers To and Transactions and Relationships With Noncharitable Exempt Organizations

51 Did the reporting organization directly or indirectly engage in any of the following with any other organization described in section 501(c) of the Code (other than section 501(c)(3) organizations) or in section 527, relating to political organizations?

		Yes	No
a Transfers from the reporting organization to a noncharitable exempt organization of:			
(i) Cash	51a(i)		X
(ii) Other assets	a(ii)		X
b Other Transactions:			
(i) Sales of assets to a noncharitable exempt organization	b(i)		X
(ii) Purchases of assets from a noncharitable exempt organization	b(ii)		X
(iii) Rental of facilities or equipment	b(iii)		X
(iv) Reimbursement arrangements	b(iv)		X
(v) Loans or loan guarantees	b(v)		X
(vi) Performance of services or membership or fundraising solicitations	b(vi)		X
c Sharing of facilities, equipment, mailing lists or other assets, or paid employees	c		X

d If the answer to any of the above is "Yes," complete the following schedule. The "Amount involved" column below should always indicate the fair market value of the goods, other assets, or services given by the reporting organization. If the organization received less than fair market value in any transaction or sharing arrangement, indicate in column (d) the value of the goods, other assets, or services received.

(a) Line no.	(b) Amount involved	(c) Name of noncharitable exempt organization	(d) Description of transfers, transactions, and sharing arrangements

52a Is the organization directly or indirectly affiliated with, or related to, one or more tax-exempt organizations described in section 501(c) of the Code (other than section 501(c)(3)) or in section 527?. . . . . ☐ Yes ☒ No

b If "Yes," complete the following schedule.

(a) Name of organization	(b) Type of organization	(c) Description of relationship

Appendix 27–4

FORM 5578

Form **5578** (Rev. March 1990) Department of the Treasury Internal Revenue Service	**Annual Certification of Racial Nondiscrimination for a Private School Exempt from Federal Income Tax** (For Use by Organizations That Do Not File Form 990 or 990EZ)	OMB No. 1545-0213 Expires 03-31-93 **For IRS use ONLY** ▶

For the period beginning _____ , 19 ____ , and ending _____ 19 ____

1a Name of organization which operates, supervises, and/or controls school(s)	1b Employer identification number
Address (number and street)	
City or town, state, and ZIP code	

2a Name of central organization holding group exemption letter covering the school(s). (If same as 1a above, write "Same" and complete 2c.) If the organization in 1a above holds an individual exemption letter, write "Not Applicable."	2b Employer identification number
Address (number and street)	2c Group exemption number (see instructions under **Definitions**)
City or town, state, and ZIP code	

3a Name of school (if more than one school, write "See Attached," and attach list of the names, addresses, ZIP codes, and employer identification numbers of the schools). If same as 1a above, write "Same."	3b Employer identification number, if any
Address (number and street)	
City or town, state, and ZIP code	

Under penalties of perjury, I hereby certify that I am authorized to take official action on behalf of the above school(s) and that to the best of my knowledge and belief the school(s) has (have) satisfied the applicable requirements of section 4.01 through 4.05 of Revenue Procedure 75-50 for the period covered by this certification.

_____ (Signature)   _____ (Title or authority of signer)   _____ (Date)

Instructions

This form is open to public inspection.

Paperwork Reduction Act Notice.—We ask for this information to carry out the Internal Revenue laws of the United States. We need it to ensure that taxpayers are complying with these laws. You are required to give us this information.

The time needed to complete and file this form will vary depending on individual circumstances. The estimated average time is 4 hours and 45 minutes. If you have comments concerning the accuracy of this time estimate or suggestions for making this form more simple, we would be happy to hear from you. You can write to the **Internal Revenue Service,** Washington, DC 20224, Attention: IRS Reports Clearance Officer, T:FP; or the **Office of Management and Budget,** Paperwork Reduction Project (1545-0213), Washington, DC 20503.

Purpose of Form

Form 5578 may be used by organizations that operate tax-exempt private schools to provide the Internal Revenue Service with the annual certification of racial nondiscrimination required by Rev. Proc. 75-50, 1975-2 C.B. 587.

Who Must File

Every organization that claims exemption from Federal income tax under section 501(c)(3) of the Internal Revenue Code and that operates, supervises, or controls a private school or schools must file a certification of racial nondiscrimination. If an organization is required to file **Form 990,** Return of Organization Exempt From Income Tax, or **Form 990EZ,** Short Form Return of Organization Exempt From Income Tax, either as a separate return or as part of a group return, the certification must be made on Schedule A (Form 990) rather than on this form.

An authorized official of a central organization may file one form to certify for the school activities

of subordinates, that would otherwise be required to file on an individual basis, but only if the central organization has enough control over the schools listed on the form to ensure that the schools maintain a racially nondiscriminatory policy as to students.

Definitions

A **"racially nondiscriminatory policy as to students"** means that the school admits the students of any race to all the rights, privileges, programs, and activities generally accorded or made available to students at that school and that the school does not discriminate on the basis of race in the administration of its educational policies, admissions policies, scholarship and loan programs, and other school-administered programs.

The IRS considers discrimination on the basis of race to include discrimination on the basis of color and national or ethnic origin.

A **school** is an educational organization which normally maintains a regular faculty and curriculum and normally has a regularly enrolled body of pupils or students in attendance at the place where its educational activities are regularly carried on. The term includes primary, secondary, preparatory, or high schools, and colleges and universities, whether operated as a separate legal entity or as an activity of a church or other organization described in Code section 501(c)(3). The term also includes pre-schools and any other organization that is a school as defined in Code section 170(b)(1)(A)(ii).

A **central organization** is an organization which has one or more subordinates under its general supervision or control. A subordinate is a chapter, local, post, or other unit of a central organization. A central organization may also be a subordinate, as in the case of a state organization which has subordinate units and is itself affiliated with a national organization.

The **group exemption number (GEN)** is a four-digit number issued to a central organization by the IRS. It identifies a central organization that has received a ruling from the IRS recognizing on a group basis the exemption from Federal income tax of the central organization and its covered subordinates.

When To File

Under Rev. Proc. 75-50, a certification of racial nondiscrimination must be filed annually by the 15th day of the 5th month following the end of the organization's calendar year or fiscal period.

Where To File

If the principal office of the organization is located in ▼	Use the following Internal Revenue Service Center address ▼
Alabama, Arkansas, Florida, Georgia, Louisiana, Mississippi, North Carolina, South Carolina, Tennessee	Atlanta, GA 39901
Arizona, Colorado, Kansas, New Mexico, Oklahoma, Texas, Utah, Wyoming	Austin, TX 73301
Indiana, Kentucky, Michigan, Ohio, West Virginia	Cincinnati, OH 45999
Alaska, California, Hawaii, Idaho, Nevada, Oregon, Washington	Fresno, CA 93888
Connecticut, Delaware, Maine, Massachusetts, New Hampshire, New Jersey, New York, Pennsylvania (ZIP codes beginning with 169–171 and 173–196 only), Rhode Island, Vermont	Holtsville, NY 00501
Illinois, Iowa, Minnesota, Missouri, Montana, Nebraska, North Dakota, South Dakota, Wisconsin	Kansas City, MO 64999
District of Columbia, Maryland, Pennsylvania (ZIP codes beginning with 150–168 and 172 only), Virginia, any U.S. possession, any foreign country	Philadelphia, PA 19255

Form **5578** (Rev. 3-90)

FORM 5578 (*continued*)

Certification Requirement

Section 4.06 of Rev. Proc. 75-50 requires an individual authorized to take official action on behalf of a school that claims to be racially nondiscriminatory as to students to certify annually, under penalties of perjury, that to the best of his or her knowledge and belief the school has satisfied the applicable requirements of sections 4.01 through 4.05 of the Revenue Procedure, reproduced below:

Rev. Proc. 75-50

4.01 Organizational requirements. A school must include a statement in its charter, bylaws, or other governing instrument, or in a resolution of its governing body, that it has a racially nondiscriminatory policy as to students and therefore does not discriminate against applicants and students on the basis of race, color, and national or ethnic origin.

4.02 Statement of Policy. Every school must include a statement of its racially nondiscriminatory policy as to students in all its brochures and catalogues dealing with student admissions, programs, and scholarships. A statement substantially similar to the Notice described in subsection (a) of section 4.03, *infra,* will be acceptable for this purpose. Further, every school must include a reference to its racially nondiscriminatory policy in other written advertising that it uses as a means of informing prospective students of its programs. The following references will be acceptable:

The (name) school admits students of any race, color, and national or ethnic origin.

4.03 Publicity. The school must make its racially nondiscriminatory policy known to all segments of the general community served by the school.

1. The school must use one of the following two methods to satisfy this requirement:

(a) The school may publish a notice of its racially nondiscriminatory policy in a newspaper of general circulation that serves all racial segments of the community. This publication must be repeated at least once annually during the period of the school's solicitation for students or, in the absence of a solicitation program, during the school's registration period. Where more than one community is served by a school, the school may publish its notice in those newspapers that are reasonably likely to be read by all racial segments of the communities that it serves. The notice must appear in a section of the newspaper likely to be read by prospective students and their families and it must occupy at least three column inches. It must be captioned in at least 12 point bold face type as a notice of nondiscrimination policy as to students, and its text must be printed in at least 8 point type. The following notice will be acceptable:

NOTICE OF NONDISCRIMINATORY POLICY AS TO STUDENTS

The (name) school admits students of any race, color, national and ethnic origin to all the rights, privileges, programs, and activities generally accorded or made available to students at the school. It does not discriminate on the basis of race, color, national and ethnic origin in administration of its educational policies, admissions policies, scholarship and loan programs, and athletic and other school-administered programs.

(b) The school may use the broadcast media to publicize its racially nondiscriminatory policy if this use makes such nondiscriminatory policy known to all segments of the general community the school serves. If this method is chosen, the school must provide documentation that the means by which this policy was communicated to all segments of the general community was reasonably expected to be effective. In this case, appropriate documentation would include copies of the tapes or script used and records showing that there was an adequate number of announcements, that they were made during hours when the announcements were likely to be communicated to all segments of the general community, that they were of sufficient duration to convey the message clearly, and that they were broadcast on radio or television stations likely to be listened to by substantial numbers of members of all racial segments of the general community. Announcements must be made during the period of the school's solicitation for students or, in the absence of a solicitation program, during the school's registration period.

Communication of a racially nondiscriminatory policy as to students by a school to leaders of racial groups as the sole means of publicity generally will not be considered effective to make the policy known to all segments of the community.

2. The requirements of subsection 1 of this section will not apply when one of the following paragraphs applies:

(a) If for the preceding three years the enrollment of a parochial or other church-related school consists of students at least 75 percent of whom are members of the sponsoring religious denomination or unit, the school may make known its racially nondiscriminatory policy in whatever newspapers or circulars the religious denomination or unit utilizes in the communities from which the students are drawn. These newspapers and circulars may be those distributed by a particular religious denomination or unit or by an association that represents a number of religious organizations of the same denomination. If, however, the school advertises in newspapers of general circulation in the community or communities from which its students are drawn and paragraphs (b) and (c) of this subsection are not applicable to it, then it must comply with paragraph (a) of subsection 1 of this section.

(b) If a school customarily draws a substantial percentage of its students nationwide or world-wide or from a large geographic section or sections of the United States and follows a racially nondiscriminatory policy as to students, the publicity requirement may be satisfied by complying with section 4.02, *supra.* Such a school may demonstrate that it follows a racially nondiscriminatory policy within the meaning of the preceding sentence either by showing that it currently enrolls students of racial minority groups in meaningful numbers or, when minority students are not enrolled in meaningful numbers, that its promotional activities and recruiting efforts in each geographic area were reasonably designed to inform students of all racial segments in the general communities within the area of the availability of the school. The question whether a school satisfies the preceding sentence will be determined on the basis of the facts and circumstances of each case.

(c) If a school customarily draws its students from local communities and follows a racially nondiscriminatory policy as to students, the publicity requirement may be satisfied by complying with section 4.02, *supra.* Such a school may demonstrate that it follows a racially nondiscriminatory policy within the meaning of the preceding sentence by showing that it currently enrolls students of racial minority groups in meaningful numbers. The question whether a school satisfies the preceding sentence will be determined on the basis of the facts and circumstances of each case. One of the facts and circumstances that the Service will consider is whether the school's promotional activities and recruiting efforts in each area were reasonably designed to inform students of all racial segments in the general communities within the area of the availability of the school. The Service recognizes that the failure by a school drawing its students from local communities to enroll racial minority group students may not necessarily indicate the absence of a racially nondiscriminatory policy as to students when there are relatively few or no such students in these communities. Actual enrollment is, however, a meaningful indication of a racially nondiscriminatory policy in a community in which a public school or schools became subject to a desegregation order of a federal court or otherwise expressly became obligated to implement a desegregation plan under the terms of any written contract or other commitment to which any Federal agency was a party.

The Service encourages schools to satisfy the publicity requirement by the methods described in subsection 1 of this section, regardless of whether a school considers itself within subsection 2, because it believes these methods to be the most effective to make known a school's racially nondiscriminatory policy. In this regard it is each school's responsibility to determine whether paragraph (a), (b), or (c) of subsection 2 applies to it. On audit, a school must be prepared to demonstrate that the failure to publish its racially nondiscriminatory policy in accordance with subsection 1 of this section was justified by the application to it of paragraph (a), (b), or (c) of subsection 2. Further, a school must be prepared to demonstrate that it has publicly disavowed or repudiated any statements purported to have been made on its behalf (after November 6, 1975) that are contrary to its publicity of a racially nondiscriminatory policy as to students, to the extent that the school or its principal official were aware of such statements.

4.04 Facilities and Programs. A school must be able to show that all of its programs and facilities are operated in a racially nondiscriminatory manner.

4.05 Scholarship and loan programs. As a general rule, all scholarship or other comparable benefits procurable for use at any given school must be offered on a racially nondiscriminatory basis. Their availability on this basis must be known throughout the general community being served by the school and should be referred to in the publicity required by this section in order for that school to be considered racially nondiscriminatory as to students. . . . [S]cholarships and loans that are made pursuant to financial assistance programs favoring members of one or more racial minority groups that are designed to promote a school's racially nondiscriminatory policy will not adversely affect the school's exempt status. Financial assistance programs favoring members of one or more racial groups that do not significantly derogate from the school's racially nondiscriminatory policy similarly will not adversely affect the school's exempt status.

5578.2

Published by Tax Management Inc., a Subsidiary of The Bureau of National Affairs, Inc.

4/23/90

58

■ **632** ■

FORM 990-PF

Form **990-PF**	**Return of Private Foundation** or Section 4947(a)(1) Charitable Trust Treated as a Private Foundation (See separate instructions.)	OMB No. 1545-0052 **1992**
Department of the Treasury Internal Revenue Service	Note: You may be able to use a copy of this return to satisfy state reporting requirements.	

For calendar year 1992, or fiscal year beginning _____ , 1992, and ending _____ , 19 __

	Name of organization		A Employer identification number
Please type, print, or attach label. See Specific Instructions.	ENVIRONMENTALIST FUND		43 .3333333
	Number, street, and room (or P.O. box number) 1st NAT'L BANK TRUST 456 MAIN STREET		B State registration number (see instruction F) none
	City or town, state, and ZIP code HOMETOWN, TX 77777		C If application pending, check here . . ▶ ☐

D ☐ Foreign organizations, check here . . ▶ ☐

E ☐ Organizations meeting the 85% test, check here and attach computation . ▶ ☐

H Check type of organization: ☒ Exempt private foundation

☐ 4947(a)(1) trust (see instruction C)   ☐ Other taxable private foundation

E If your private foundation status terminated under section 507(b)(1)(A), check here . ☐

I Fair market value of all assets at end of year (from Part II, col. (c), line 16) $ 2,220,000

J Accounting method: ☐ Cash ☒ Accrual ☐ Other (specify) _____ (Part I column (d) must be on cash basis.)

F If the foundation is in a 60-month termination under section 507(b)(1)(B), check here . ▶ ☐

G If address changed, check here. . . ▶ ☐

Part I — Analysis of Revenue and Expenses (The total of amounts in columns (b), (c), and (d) may not necessarily equal the amounts in column (a) (see instructions).)

		(a) Revenue and expenses per books	(b) Net investment income	(c) Adjusted net income	(d) Disbursements for charitable purposes (cash basis only)
1	Contributions, gifts, grants, etc., received (attach schedule)				
2	Contributions from split-interest trusts . . .				
3	Interest on savings and temporary cash investments	4,000	4,000		
4	Dividends and interest from securities	160,000	160,000		
5a	Gross rents				
b	(Net rental income or (loss) _____)				
6	Net gain or (loss) from sale of assets not on line 10	30,000			
7	Capital gain net income (from Part IV, line 2) . .		50,000		
8	Net short-term capital gain				
9	Income modifications				
10a	Gross sales minus returns and allowances				
b	Minus: Cost of goods sold . .				
c	Gross profit or (loss) (attach schedule). . . .			not	
11	Other income (attach schedule)			applicable	
12	Total (add lines 1 through 11).	194,000	214,000		
13	Compensation of officers, directors, trustees, etc.				
14	Other employee salaries and wages . . .				
15	Pension plans, employee benefits				
16a	Legal fees (attach schedule) sch. 1	5,000	2,500		2,500
b	Accounting fees (attach schedule) sch. 1	5,000	2,500		2,500
c	Other professional fees (attach schedule) sch. 1	6,000	3,000		3,000
17	Interest				
18	Taxes (attach schedule) (see instructions). . .	4,000			
19	Depreciation (attach schedule) and depletion .				
20	Occupancy.				
21	Travel, conferences, and meetings	2,000			2,000
22	Printing and publications	2,800			2,800
23	Other expenses (attach schedule)				
24	Total operating and administrative expenses (add lines 13 through 23)	24,800	8,000		12,800
25	Contributions, gifts, grants paid	160,000			160,000
26	Total expenses and disbursements (add lines 24 and 25)	184,800	8,000		172,800
27a	Excess of revenue over expenses and disbursements (line 12 minus line 26)	9,200			
b	Net investment income (if negative, enter "-0-")		206,000		
c	Adjusted net income (if negative, enter "-0-") .			n/a	

For Paperwork Reduction Act Notice, see page 1 of the instructions.   Cat. No. 11289X   Form **990-PF** (1992)

FORM 990-PF (*continued*)

Form 990-PF (1992) ENVIRONMENTALIST FUND	EIN # 43-3333333		Page 2

Part II Balance Sheets — Attached schedules and amounts in the description column should be for end-of-year amounts only. (See instructions.)

		Beginning of year (a) Book Value	End of year (b) Book Value	End of year (c) Fair Market Value
Assets	1 Cash—non-interest-bearing			
	2 Savings and temporary cash investments	20,800	50,000	50,000
	3 Accounts receivable ▶			
	minus: allowance for doubtful accounts ▶			
	4 Pledges receivable ▶			
	minus: allowance for doubtful accounts ▶			
	5 Grants receivable			
	6 Receivables due from officers, directors, trustees, and other disqualified persons (attach schedule) (see instructions)			
	7 Other notes and loans receivable (attach schedule) ▶			
	minus: allowance for doubtful accounts ▶			
	8 Inventories for sale or use			
	9 Prepaid expenses and deferred charges			
	10a Investments—U.S. and state government obligations (attach schedule)			
	b Investments—corporate stock (attach schedule) sch.1	535,555	515,555	2,170,000
	c Investments—corporate bonds (attach schedule)			
	11 Investments—land, buildings, and equipment: basis ▶			
	minus: accumulated depreciation (attach schedule) ▶			
	12 Investments—mortgage loans			
	13 Investments—other (attach schedule)			
	14 Land, buildings, and equipment: basis ▶			
	minus: accumulated depreciation (attach schedule) ▶			
	15 Other assets (describe ▶)			
	16 Total assets (completed by all filers—see instructions)	556,355	565,555	2,220,000
Liabilities	17 Accounts payable and accrued expenses			
	18 Grants payable			
	19 Support and revenue designated for future periods (attach schedule)			
	20 Loans from officers, directors, trustees, and other disqualified persons			
	21 Mortgages and other notes payable (attach schedule)			
	22 Other liabilities (describe ▶)			
	23 Total liabilities (add lines 17 through 22)			
Fund Balances or Net Assets	Organizations that use fund accounting, check here ▶ ☒ and complete lines 24 through 27 and lines 31 and 32.			
	24a Current unrestricted fund	556,355	565,555	
	b Current restricted fund			
	25 Land, buildings, and equipment fund			
	26 Endowment fund			
	27 Other funds (describe ▶)			
	Organizations not using fund accounting, check here ▶ ☐ and complete lines 28 through 32.			
	28 Capital stock or trust principal			
	29 Paid-in capital or capital surplus			
	30 Retained earnings or accumulated income			
	31 Total fund balances or net assets (see instructions)	556,355	565,555	
	32 Total liabilities and fund balances/net assets (see instructions)	556,355	565,555	

Part III Analysis of Changes in Net Assets or Fund Balances

1 Total net assets or fund balances at beginning of year—Part II, column (a), line 31. (must agree with end-of-year figure reported on prior year's return)	1	556,355
2 Enter amount from Part I, line 27a	2	9,200
3 Other increases not included in line 2 (itemize) ▶	3	
4 Add lines 1, 2, and 3	4	565,555
5 Decreases not included in line 2 (itemize) ▶	5	
6 Total net assets or fund balances at end of year (line 4 minus line 5)—Part II, column (b), line 31.	6	565,555

Appendix 27–5

FORM 990-PF   (*continued*)

Form 990-PF (1992)   ENVIRONMENTALIST FUND   EIN # 43-3333333   Page 3

Part IV   Capital Gains and Losses for Tax on Investment Income

(a) List and describe the kind(s) of property sold, e.g., real estate, 2-story brick warehouse; or common stock, 200 shs. MLC Co.	(b) How acquired P—Purchase D—Donation	(c) Date acquired (mo., day, yr.)	(d) Date sold (mo., day, yr.)
1 100 shares of Environmentals, Inc.	D	1-1-xx	6-1-xx

(e) Gross sales price minus expense of sale	(f) Depreciation allowed (or allowable)	(g) Cost or other basis	(h) Gain or (loss) (e) plus (f) minus (g)
50,000		none	50,000

Complete only for assets showing gain in column (h) and owned by the foundation on 12/31/69

(i) F.M.V. as of 12/31/69	(j) Adjusted basis as of 12/31/69	(k) Excess of col. (i) over col. (j), if any	(l) Losses (from col. (h)) Gains (excess of col. (h) gain over col. (k), but not less than "-0-")

2 Capital gain net income or (net capital loss). { If gain, also enter in Part I, line 7
{ If (loss), enter "-0-" in Part I, line 7 } .... | 2 | 50,000

3 Net short-term capital gain or (loss) as defined in sections 1222(5) and (6):
If gain, also enter in Part I, line 8, column (c) (see instructions) If (loss), enter "-0-" in Part I, line 8 .... } | 3

Part V   Qualification Under Section 4940(e) for Reduced Tax on Net Investment Income

(For optional use by domestic private foundations subject to the section 4940(a) tax on net investment income.)

If section 4940(d)(2) applies, leave Part V blank.

Were you liable for the section 4942 tax on the distributable amount of any year in the base period? . ☐ Yes ☐ No
If "Yes," you do not qualify under section 4940(e). Do not complete this part.

1   Enter the appropriate amount in each column for each year; see instructions before making any entries.

(a) Base period years Calendar year (or fiscal year beginning in)	(b) Adjusted qualifying distributions	(c) Net value of noncharitable-use assets	(d) Distribution ratio (col. (b) divided by col. (c))
1991	178,200	1,800,000	.0990
1990	112,800	1,600,000	.0705
1989	121,800	1,400,000	.0870
1988	109,200	1,200,000	.0910
1987	90,000	1,000,000	.0900

2 Total of line 1, column (d) . . . . | 2 | .4375

3 Average distribution ratio for the 5-year base period—divide the total on line 2 by 5, or by the number of years the foundation has been in existence if less than 5 years . . . . . | 3 | .0875

4 Enter the net value of noncharitable-use assets for 1992 from Part X, line 5 . . . . . . | 4 | 2,019,250

5 Multiply line 4 by line 3 . . . . | 5 | 176,684

6 Enter 1% of net investment income (1% of Part I, line 27b) . . . . | 6 | 2,060

7 Add lines 5 and 6 . . . . | 7 | 178,744

8 Enter qualifying distributions from Part XII, line 4 . . . . | 8 | 172,800

If line 8 is equal to or greater than line 7, check the box in Part VI, line 1b, and complete that part using a 1% tax rate. See the Part VI instructions.

Appendix 27–5

FORM 990-PF (*continued*)

Form 990-PF (1992)   ENVIRONMENTALIST FUND   EIN # 43-3333333   Page 4

Part VI   Excise Tax on Investment Income (Section 4940(a), 4940(b), 4940(e), or 4948—see instructions)

1a Exempt operating foundations described in section 4940(d)(2), check here ☐ and enter "N/A" on line 1. Give date of ruling letter .... (attach copy of ruling letter if necessary—see instructions)		
b Domestic organizations that meet the section 4940(e) requirements in Part V, check here ☐ and enter 1% of Part I, line 27b.	1	4,120
c All other domestic organizations enter 2% of line 27b. Exempt foreign organizations enter 4% of line 27b		
2 Tax under section 511 (domestic section 4947(a)(1) trusts and taxable foundations only. Others enter "-0-")	2	
3 Add lines 1 and 2	3	4,120
4 Tax under subtitle A (domestic section 4947(a)(1) trusts and taxable foundations only. Others enter "-0-")	4	
5 Tax on investment income (line 3 minus line 4 (but not less than "-0-")).	5	4,120
6 Credits/Payments:		
a 1992 estimated tax payments and 1991 overpayment credited to 1992.	6a	4,000
b Exempt foreign organizations—tax withheld at source	6b	
c Tax paid with application for extension of time to file (Form 2758) .	6c	
d Backup withholding erroneously withheld	6d	
7 Total credits and payments (add lines 6a through d).	7	4,000
8 Enter any PENALTY for underpayment of estimated tax. Check here ☐ if Form 2220 is attached .	8	
9 TAX DUE. If the total of lines 5 and 8 is more than line 7, enter AMOUNT OWED . . . ▶	9	120
10 OVERPAYMENT. If line 7 is more than the total of lines 5 and 8, enter the AMOUNT OVERPAID . . . ▶	10	
11 Enter the amount of line 10 you want: Credited to 1993 estimated tax ▶	Refunded ▶	11

Part VII   Statements Regarding Activities

File Form 4720 if you answer "No" to question 10b, 11b, or 14b or "Yes" to question 10c, 12b, 13a, 13b, or 14a(2), unless an exception applies.

	Yes	No
1a During the tax year, did you attempt to influence any national, state, or local legislation or did you participate or intervene in any political campaign? . . . . [1a]		x
b Did you spend more than $100 during the year (either directly or indirectly) for political purposes (see instructions for definition)? [1b]		x
If you answered "Yes" to 1a or 1b, attach a detailed description of the activities and copies of any materials published or distributed by the organization in connection with the activities.		
c Did you file Form 1120-POL, U.S. Income Tax Return for Certain Political Organizations, for this year? [1c]		x
2 Have you engaged in any activities that have not previously been reported to the Internal Revenue Service? If "Yes," attach a detailed description of the activities. [2]		x
3 Have you made any changes, not previously reported to the IRS, in your governing instrument, articles of incorporation, or bylaws, or other similar instruments? If "Yes," attach a conformed copy of the changes [3]		x
4a Did you have unrelated business gross income of $1,000 or more during the year? [4a]		x
b If "Yes," have you filed a tax return on Form 990-T, Exempt Organization Business Income Tax Return, for this year? [4b]	n/a	
5 Was there a liquidation, termination, dissolution, or substantial contraction during the year? . . . . . [5]		x
If "Yes," attach the schedule required by General Instruction T.		
6 Are the requirements of section 508(e) (relating to sections 4941 through 4945) satisfied either:		
● By language written into the governing instrument, or		
● By state legislation that effectively amends the governing instrument so that no mandatory directions that conflict with the state law remain in the governing instrument?. . . . . [6]	x	
7 Did you have at least $5,000 in assets at any time during the year? . . . . [7]	x	
If "Yes," complete Part II, column (c), and Part XV.		
8a Enter the states to which the foundation reports or with which it is registered (see instructions) ▶ ....Texas.		
b If you answered "Yes" to line 7, have you furnished a copy of Form 990-PF to the Attorney General (or his or her designate) of each state as required by General Instruction G? If "No," attach explanation . [8b]	x	-
9 Are you claiming status as a private operating foundation within the meaning of section 4942(j)(3) or 4942(j)(5) for calendar year 1992 or fiscal year beginning in 1992 (see instructions for Part XIV)? If "Yes," complete Part XIV. [9]		x
10 Self-dealing (section 4941):		
a During the year did you (either directly or indirectly):		
(1) Engage in the sale or exchange, or leasing of property with a disqualified person? . . . . . . [10a(1)]		x
(2) Borrow money from, lend money to, or otherwise extend credit to (or accept it from) a disqualified person?. [10a(2)]		x
(3) Furnish goods, services, or facilities to (or accept them from) a disqualified person? . . . . . [10a(3)]		x
(4) Pay compensation to or pay or reimburse the expenses of a disqualified person? . . . . [10a(4)]		x
(5) Transfer any of your income or assets to a disqualified person (or make any of either available for the benefit or use of a disqualified person)? . . . . [10a(5)]		x
(6) Agree to pay money or property to a government official? (Exception: Check "No" if you agreed to make a grant to or to employ the official for a period after he or she terminates government service, if he or she is terminating within 90 days.). . . . . [10a(6)]		x

Appendix 27–5

FORM 990-PF (*continued*)

| Form 990-PF (1992) | ENVIRONMENTALIST FUND | EIN # 43-3333333 | Page 5 |

Part VII Statements Regarding Activities (continued)

		Yes	No
10b	If you answered "Yes" to any of questions 10a(1) through (6), were the acts you engaged in excepted acts as described in Regulations sections 53.4941(d)-3 and 4?.	10b	n/a
c	Did you engage in a prior year in any of the acts described in 10a, other than excepted acts, that were acts of self-dealing not corrected by the first day of your tax year beginning in 1992?	10c	x
11	Taxes on failure to distribute income (section 4942) (does not apply for years you were a private operating foundation as defined in section 4942(j)(3) or 4942(j)(5)):		
a	Did you at the end of tax year 1992 have any undistributed income (lines 6d and 6e, Part XIII) for tax year(s) beginning before 1992? If "Yes," list the years ▶ ...., ..., ..., ...	11a	x
b	If 11a is "Yes," are you applying the provisions of section 4942(a)(2) (relating to incorrect valuation of assets) to the undistributed income for ALL such years? (If "Yes," attach statement—see instructions.)	11b	n/a
c	If the provisions of section 4942(a)(2) are being applied to ANY of the years listed in 11a, list the years here. ▶ ...., ..., ..., ...		
12	Taxes on excess business holdings (section 4943):		
a	Did you hold more than a 2% direct or indirect interest in any business enterprise at any time during the year?	12a	x
b	If "Yes," did you have excess business holdings in 1992 as a result of (1) any purchase by you or disqualified persons after May 26, 1969; (2) the lapse of the 5-year period (or longer period approved by the Commissioner under section 4943(c)(7)) to dispose of holdings acquired by gift or bequest; or (3) the lapse of the 10-, 15-, or 20-year first phase holding period? (Use Schedule C, Form 4720, to determine if you had excess business holdings in 1992.)	12b	n/a
13	Taxes on investments that jeopardize charitable purpose (section 4944):		
a	Did you invest during the year any amount in a manner that would jeopardize your charitable purposes?	13a	x
b	Did you make any investment in a prior year (but after December 31, 1969) that could jeopardize your charitable purpose that you had not removed from jeopardy on the first day of your tax year beginning in 1992? . . .	13b	x
14	Taxes on taxable expenditures (section 4945) and political expenditures (section 4955):		
a	During the year did you pay or incur any amount to:		
(1)	Carry on propaganda, or otherwise attempt to influence legislation (section 4945(e))?	14a(1)	x
(2)	Influence the outcome of any specific public election (see section 4955); or to carry on, directly or indirectly, any voter registration drive?.	14a(2)	x
(3)	Provide a grant to an individual for travel, study, or other similar purposes?	14a(3)	x
(4)	Provide a grant to an organization, other than a charitable, etc., organization described in section 509(a)(1), (2), or (3), or section 4940(d)(2)?	14a(4)	x
(5)	Provide for any purpose other than religious, charitable, scientific, literary, or educational purposes, or for the prevention of cruelty to children or animals?	14a(5)	x
b	If you answered "Yes" to any of questions 14a(1) through (5), were all such transactions excepted transactions as described in Regulations section 53.4945?	14b	n/a
c	If you answered "Yes" to question 14a(4), do you claim exemption from the tax because you maintained expenditure responsibility for the grant?	14c	n/a
	If "Yes," attach the statement required by Regulations section 53.4945-5(d).		
15	Did any persons become substantial contributors during the tax year?	15	x
	If "Yes," attach a schedule listing their names and addresses.		
16	During this tax year, did you maintain any part of your accounting/tax records on a computerized system?	16	x
17a	Did anyone request to see either your annual return or exemption application (or both)?	17a	x
b	If "Yes," did you comply pursuant to the instructions? (See General Instruction Q.)	17b	n/a
18	The books are in care of ▶ ..1st.National.Bank.Trust.Dept..... Telephone no. ▶..707-777-7777
	Located at ▶ ....456 Main Street, Hometown, Tx 77777.................
19	Section 4947(a)(1) charitable trusts filing Form 990-PF in lieu of Form 1041, U.S. Fiduciary Income Tax Return.—Check here ▶ ☐ and enter the amount of tax-exempt interest received or accrued during the year. . . . . ▶	19	

Part VIII Information About Officers, Directors, Trustees, Foundation Managers, Highly Paid Employees, and Contractors

1 List all officers, directors, trustees, foundation managers and their compensation (see instructions):

(a) Name and address	(b) Title, and average hours per week devoted to position	(c) Contributions to employee benefit plans	(d) Expense account, other allowances	(e) Compensation (if not paid, enter -0-)
Jane D. Environmentalist 333 First St., Hometown Tx 77777	President Part	none	none	-0-
John J. Environmentalist 333 First St., Hometown Tx 77777	Secretary Part	none	none	-0-
Bryon B. Banker 456 Main St., Hometown Tx 77777	Treasurer Part	none	none	-0-

Appendix 27–5

FORM 990-PF (*continued*)

Form 990-PF (1992)   ENVIRONMENTALIST FUND   EIN # 43-3333333   Page 6

Part VIII Information About Officers, Directors, Trustees, etc. (continued)

2 Compensation of five highest paid employees (other than those included on line 1—see instructions). If none, enter "NONE."

(a) Name and address of employee paid more than $30,000	(b) Title and time devoted to position	(c) Contributions to employee benefit plans	(d) Expense account, other allowances	(e) Compensation
Not applicable				none

Total number of other employees paid over $30,000 . . . . ▶

3 Five highest paid persons for professional services—(see instructions). If none, enter "NONE."

(a) Name and address of persons paid more than $30,000	(b) Type of service	(c) Compensation
Not applicable		none

Total number of others receiving over $30,000 for professional services . . . . ▶ | 0

Part IX-A Summary of Direct Charitable Activities

List the foundation's four largest direct charitable activities during the tax year. Include relevant statistical information such as the number of organizations and other beneficiaries served, conferences convened, research papers produced, etc.   **Expenses**

1 ......Not applicable......

   ....   none

2 ....

3 ....

4 ....

Part IX-B Summary of Program-Related Investments

Describe any program-related investments made by the foundation during the tax year.   **Amount**

1 ....Not applicable........

   ....   none

2 ....

3 ....

Appendix 27–5

FORM 990-PF (continued)

Form 990-PF (1992)	ENVIRONMENTALIST FUND	EIN # 43-3333333		Page 7

Part X — Minimum Investment Return (All organizations must complete this part.)

1	Fair market value of assets not used (or held for use) directly in carrying out charitable, etc., purposes:		
a	Average monthly fair market value of securities	1a	1,995,000
b	Average of monthly cash balances	1b	55,000
c	Fair market value of all other assets (see instructions)	1c	
d	Total (add lines 1a, b, and c)	1d	2,050,00
e	Reduction claimed for blockage or other factors (attach detailed explanation) ▶	1e	
2	Acquisition indebtedness applicable to line 1 assets	2	
3	Line 1d minus line 2	3	2,050,000
4	Cash deemed held for charitable activities—Enter 1½% of line 3 (for greater amount, see instructions)	4	30,750
5	Net value of noncharitable-use assets—Line 3 minus line 4 (Enter in Part V, line 4.)	5	2,019,250
6	Minimum investment return (Enter 5% of line 5.)	6	100,962

Part XI — Distributable Amount (see instructions) (Section 4942(j)(3) and (j)(5) private operating foundations check here ▶☐ and do not complete this part.)

1	Minimum investment return from Part X, line 6	1	100,962
2a	Tax on investment income for 1992 from Part VI, line 5 ... 2a 4,120		
b	Income tax under subtitle A, for 1992 ... 2b		
c	Line 2a plus line 2b	2c	4,120
3	Distributable amount before adjustments (line 1 minus line 2c)	3	96,842
4a	Recoveries of amounts treated as qualifying distributions ... 4a		
b	Income distributions from section 4947(a)(2) trusts ... 4b		
c	Line 4a plus line 4b	4c	
5	Line 3 plus line 4c	5	96,842
6	Deduction from distributable amount (see instructions)	6	
7	Distributable amount as adjusted (line 5 minus line 6) (Also enter in Part XIII, line 1.)	7	96,842

and certain foreign organizations

Part XII — Qualifying Distributions (see instructions)

1	Amounts paid (including administrative expenses) to accomplish charitable, etc., purposes:		
a	Expenses, contributions, gifts, etc.—total from Part I, column (d), line 26	1a	172,800
b	Program-related investments—total of lines 1-3 of Part IX-B	1b	
2	Amounts paid to acquire assets used (or held for use) directly in carrying out charitable, etc., purposes	2	
3	Amounts set aside for specific charitable projects that satisfy the:		
a	Suitability test (prior IRS approval required)	3a	
b	Cash distribution test (attach the required schedule)	3b	
4	Qualifying distributions (add lines 1a through 3b). (Enter in Part V, line 8 and Part XIII, line 4.)	4	172,800
5	Organizations that qualify under section 4940(e) for the reduced rate of tax on net investment income—enter 1% of Part I, line 27b (see instructions)	5	
6	Adjusted qualifying distributions (line 4 minus line 5)	6	172,800

Note: The amount on line 6 will be used in Part V, column (b), when calculating the section 4940(e) reduction of tax in subsequent years.

Appendix 27–5

FORM 990-PF (*continued*)

Form 990-PF (1992)   ENVIRONMENTALIST FUND   EIN # 43-3333333   p. 8

Part XIII   Undistributed Income (see instructions)

		(a) Corpus	(b) Years prior to 1991	(c) 1991	(d) 1992
1	Distributable amount for 1992 from Part XI, line 7				96,842
2	Undistributed Income, if any, as of the end of 1991:				
a	Enter amount for 1991 only			0	
b	Total for prior years: 19___,19___,19___		0		
3	Excess distributions carryover, if any, to 1992:				
a	From 1987 10,000				
b	From 1988 20,000				
c	From 1989 30,000				
d	From 1990 40,000				
e	From 1991 50,000				
f	Total of lines 3a through e	150,000			
4	Qualifying distributions for 1992 from Part XII, line 4: $ 172,800				
a	Applied to 1991, but not more than line 2a .			0	
b	Applied to undistributed income of prior years (Election required—see instructions) .		0		
c	Treated as distributions out of corpus (Election required—see instructions) . . .	0			
d	Applied to 1992 distributable amount . .				96,842
e	Remaining amount distributed out of corpus	75,958			
5	Excess distributions carryover applied to 1992. (If an amount appears in column (d), the same amount must be shown in column (a).)	0			0
6	Enter the net total of each column as indicated below:				
a	Corpus. Add lines 3f, 4c, and 4e. Subtract line 5 .	225,958			
b	Prior years' undistributed income (line 2b minus line 4b)				
c	Enter the amount of prior years' undistributed income for which a notice of deficiency has been issued, or on which the section 4942(a) tax has been previously assessed				
d	Subtract line 6c from line 6b. Taxable amount—see instructions				
e	Undistributed income for 1991 (line 2a minus line 4a). Taxable amount—see instructions .				
1/ f	Undistributed income for 1992 (line 1 minus lines 4d and 5). This amount must be distributed in 1993				
7	Amounts treated as distributions out of corpus to satisfy requirements imposed by section 170(b)(1)(E) or 4942(g)(3) (see instructions) . .	0			
8	Excess distributions carryover from 1987 not applied on line 5 or line 7 (see instructions) .	10,000			
9	Excess distributions carryover to 1993 (line 6a minus lines 7 and 8)	215,958			
10	Analysis of line 9:				
a	Excess from 1988 . . . 20,000				
b	Excess from 1989 . . . 30,000				
c	Excess from 1990 . . . 40,000				
d	Excess from 1991 . . . 50,000				
e	Excess from 1992 . . . 75,958				

Appendix 27–5

FORM 990-PF (*continued*)

Form 990-PF (1992)   ENVIRONMENTALIST FUND   EIN # 43-3333333   p. 9

Part XIV Private Operating Foundations (see instructions and Part VII, question 9)

1a If the foundation has received a ruling or determination letter that it is a private operating foundation, and the ruling is effective for 1992, enter the date of the ruling . . . . . ▶   n/a

b Check box to indicate whether you are a private operating foundation described in section ☐ 4942(j)(3) or ☐ 4942(j)(5).

	Tax year	Prior 3 years			
2a Enter the lesser of the adjusted net income from Part I or the minimum investment return from Part X (for 1991 and 1992; previously Part IX)	(a) 1992	(b) 1991	(c) 1990	(d) 1989	(e) Total
b 85% of line 2a.	Not applicable				
c Qualifying distributions from Part XII, line 4 (for 1991 and 1992; previously Part XIII, line 4)					
d Amounts included in line 2c not used directly for active conduct of exempt activities . .					
e Qualifying distributions made directly for active conduct of exempt activities (line 2c minus line 2d)					
3 Complete 3a, b, or c for the alternative test on which you rely:					
a "Assets" alternative test—enter:					
(1) Value of all assets					
(2) Value of assets qualifying under section 4942(j)(3)(B)(i) .					
b "Endowment" alternative test— Enter ⅔ of minimum investment return shown in Part X, line 6, (for 1991 and 1992; previously Part IX, line 6) . .					
c "Support" alternative test—enter:					
(1) Total support other than gross investment income (interest, dividends, rents, payments on securities loans (section 512(a)(5)), or royalties) . . .					
(2) Support from general public and 5 or more exempt organizations as provided in section 4942(j)(3)(B)(iii) . . .					
(3) Largest amount of support from an exempt organization.					
(4) Gross investment income. .					

Part XV Supplementary Information (Complete this part only if you had $5,000 or more in assets at any time during the year—see instructions.)

1 Information Regarding Foundation Managers:

a List any managers of the foundation who have contributed more than 2% of the total contributions received by the foundation before the close of any tax year (but only if they have contributed more than $5,000). (See section 507(d)(2).)

Jane D & John D Environmentalist

b List any managers of the foundation who own 10% or more of the stock of a corporation (or an equally large portion of the ownership of a partnership or other entity) of which the foundation has a 10% or greater interest.

2 Information Regarding Contribution, Grant, Gift, Loan, Scholarship, etc., Programs:

Check here ▶ ☒ if you only make contributions to preselected charitable organizations and do not accept unsolicited requests for funds. If you make gifts, grants, etc., (see instructions) to individuals or organizations under other conditions, complete items 2a, b, c, and d.

a The name, address, and telephone number of the person to whom applications should be addressed:

b The form in which applications should be submitted and information and materials they should include:

c Any submission deadlines:

d Any restrictions or limitations on awards, such as by geographical areas, charitable fields, kinds of institutions, or other factors:

Appendix 27–5

FORM 990-PF (*continued*)

ENVIRONMENTALIST FUND   EIN # 43-3333333   page 11

Form 990-PF (1992)

Part XV Supplementary Information (continued)

3 Grants and Contributions Paid During the Year or Approved for Future Payment

Recipient Name and address (home or business)	If recipient is an individual, show any relationship to any foundation manager or substantial contributor	Foundation status of recipient	Purpose of grant or contribution	Amount
a Paid during the year				
Campaign to Clean Up America 1111 Any Street Hometown Tx 77777		509(a)(1)	General support	160,000
c Total . . . . ▶ **3a**				160,000
b Approved for future payment				
Total . . . . ▶ **3b**				

Appendix 27-5

FORM 990-PF (*continued*)

Form 990-PF (1992)   ENVIRONMENTALIST FUND   EIN # 43-3333333   p. 11

Part XVI-A Analysis of Income-Producing Activities

Enter gross amounts unless otherwise indicated.	Unrelated business income		Excluded by section 512, 513, or 514		(e) Related or exempt function income (See instructions.)
	(a) Business code	(b) Amount	(c) Exclusion code	(d) Amount	
1 Program service revenue:					
(a) _____					
(b) _____					
(c) _____					
(d) _____					
(e) _____					
(f) _____					
(g) Fees from government agencies .					
2 Membership dues and assessments					
3 Interest on savings and temporary cash investments			14	4,000	
4 Dividends and interest from securities			14	160,000	
5 Net rental income or (loss) from real estate:					
(a) debt-financed property					
(b) not debt-financed property.					
6 Net rental income or (loss) from personal property					
7 Other investment income					
8 Gain or (loss) from sales of assets other than inventory			18	50,000	
9 Net income from special fundraising events . .					
10 Gross profit or (loss) from sales of inventory . .					
11 Other revenue: (a) _____					
(b) _____					
(c) _____					
(d) _____					
(e) _____					
12 Subtotal (add columns (b), (d), and (e))				214,000	
13 TOTAL (add line 12, columns (b), (d), and (e)). . . . . ▶					214,000

(See worksheet for line 13 instructions to verify calculations.)

Part XVI-B Relationship of Activities to the Accomplishment of Exempt Purposes

Line No. ▼	Explain below how each activity for which income is reported in column (e) of Part XVI-A contributed importantly to the accomplishment of your exempt purposes (other than by providing funds for such purposes). (See instructions.)

FORM 990-PF (*continued*)

Form 990-PF (1992)   ENVIRONMENTALIST FUND   EIN # 43-3333333   Page 14

Part XVII Information Regarding Transfers To and Transactions and Relationships With Noncharitable Exempt Organizations

1 Did the organization directly or indirectly engage in any of the following with any other organization described in section 501(c) of the Code (other than section 501(c)(3) organizations) or in section 527, relating to political organizations?

		Yes	No
a	Transfers from the reporting organization to a noncharitable exempt organization of:		
	(i) Cash	1a(i)	X
	(ii) Other assets	a(ii)	X
b	Other Transactions:		
	(i) Sales of assets to a noncharitable exempt organization	b(i)	X
	(ii) Purchases of assets from a noncharitable exempt organization	b(ii)	X
	(iii) Rental of facilities or equipment	b(iii)	X
	(iv) Reimbursement arrangements	b(iv)	X
	(v) Loans or loan guarantees	b(v)	X
	(vi) Performance of services or membership or fundraising solicitations	b(vi)	X
c	Sharing of facilities, equipment, mailing lists or other assets, or paid employees	c	X

d If the answer to any of the above is "Yes," complete the following schedule. The "Amount Involved" column below should always indicate the fair market value of the goods, other assets, or services given by the reporting organization. If the organization received less than fair market value in any transaction or sharing arrangement, indicate in column (d) the value of the goods, other assets, or services received.

(a) Line no.	(b) Amount Involved	(c) Name of noncharitable exempt organization	(d) Description of transfers, transactions, and sharing arrangements

2a Is the organization directly or indirectly affiliated with, or related to, one or more tax-exempt organizations described in section 501(c) of the Code (other than section 501(c)(3)) or in section 527? ☐ Yes ☒ No
b If "Yes," complete the following schedule.

(a) Name of organization	(b) Type of organization	(c) Description of relationship

Part XVIII Public Inspection

1 Enter the date the notice of availability of the annual return appeared in a newspaper ▶ 5-1-XX
2 Enter the name of the newspaper ▶ Hometown Daily News
3 Check here ▶ ☒ If you have attached a copy of the newspaper notice as required by the instructions. (If the notice is not attached, the return will be considered incomplete.)

Under penalties of perjury, I declare that I have examined this return, including accompanying schedules and statements, and to the best of my knowledge and belief, it is true, correct, and complete. Declaration of preparer (other than taxpayer or fiduciary) is based on all information of which preparer has any knowledge.

Signature of officer or trustee: Jane Environmental   Social security no. 444-xx-4444   Date 5-1-XX   Title President

Preparer's signature ▶   Date 5-1-XX   Check if self-employed ▶ ☐   Preparer's social security no. XXX XX XXXX
Firm's name Blazek, Rogers & Vetterling   E.I. No. ▶ 77-7777777
3101 Richmond, Houston, Tx   ZIP code ▶ 77098

Appendix 27–5

FORM 990-PF (*continued*)

ENVIRONMENTALIST FUND

EIN #43-3333333

Attachment 1 to Form 990-PF

Part I, line 16a, b

Legal fees paid to: Bruce Hopkins, Washington, D.C.	Nature of services: General corporate counseling.	Fees: $5,000
Accounting fees paid to: Blazek, Rogers & Vetterling Houston, Texas	Preparation of Form 990-PF; tax and financial planning.	$5,000
Other professional fees: First National Bank Hometown, Texas	Trustees' fee.	$6,000

Part II, Balance Sheets, line 10

INVESTMENTS - SECURITIES

Number of Shares	Name of Company	Book Value	Market Value
4,344	Environmentals, Inc.	$555,555	$2,170,000

Schedule 1

Appendix 27–6

FORM 4720

Form 4720

Department of the Treasury
Internal Revenue Service

Return of Certain Excise Taxes on Charities and Other Persons Under Chapters 41 and 42 of the Internal Revenue Code

(Sections 4911, 4912, 4941, 4942, 4943, 4944, 4945, and 4955)

OMB No 1545-0052

1988

For the calendar year 1988 or other tax year beginning _____ , 1988, and ending _____ , 19 ____

Name of foundation or public charity	Employer identification number
Number and street	Check box for type of annual return ☐ Form 990
City or town, state, and ZIP code	☐ Form 990-PF ☐ Form 5227

	Yes	No

A Is the organization a foreign private foundation within the meaning of section 4948(b)? . . . .

B Has corrective action been taken with respect to any transaction that resulted in Chapter 42 taxes being reported on this form? . . . .

If "Yes," attach a detailed documentation and description of the corrective action taken and, if applicable, enter the fair market value of any property recovered as a result of the correction ▶ $ _____   For any uncorrected acts, attach explanation (see instructions).

Part I   Taxes on Private Foundation or Public Charity (Sections 4911(a), 4912(a), 4942(a), 4943(a), 4944(a)(1), 4945(a)(1), and 4955(a)(1))

1	Tax on undistributed income—Schedule B, line 4	**1**
2	Tax on excess business holdings—Schedule C, line 7	**2**
3	Tax on investments that jeopardize charitable purpose—Schedule D, Part I, column (e)	**3**
4	Tax on taxable expenditures—Schedule E, Part I, column (g)	**4**
5	Tax on political expenditures—Schedule F, Part I, column (e)	**5**
6	Tax on excess lobbying expenditures—Schedule G, line 4	**6**
7	Tax on disqualifying lobbying expenditures—Schedule H, Part I, column (e)	**7**
8	**Total** (add lines 1–7)	**8**

Part II-A   Taxes on Self-dealers, Foundation Managers, and Organization Managers (Sections 4912(b), 4941(a), 4944(a)(2), 4945(a)(2), and 4955(a)(2))

	(a) Name and address of person subject to tax	(b) Taxpayer identifying number
a		
b		
c		
d		

	(c) Tax on self-dealing—Schedule A, Part II, col. (d), and Part III, col. (d)	(d) Tax on investments that jeopardize charitable purpose—Schedule D, Part II, col. (d)	(e) Tax on taxable expenditures—Schedule E, Part II, col. (d)	(f) Tax on political expenditures—Schedule F, Part II, col. (d)
a				
b				
c				
d				
Total				

	(g) Tax on disqualifying lobbying expenditures— Schedule H, Part II, col. (d)	(h) Total—Add cols. (c), (d), (e), (f), and (g)
a		
b		
c		
d		
Total		

Part II-B   Summary of Taxes (See General Instructions on Tax Payments)

1	Enter the total taxes listed in Part II-A, column (h), that apply to foundation managers, self-dealers and organization managers who sign this form. If all sign, enter the total amount from Part II-A, column (h).	**1**
2	**Total Tax**—add Part I, line 8, and Part II-B, line 1. (Make check or money order payable to Internal Revenue Service.)	**2**

For Paperwork Reduction Act Notice, see page 1 of the Instructions.   Form **4720** (1988)

Appendix 27–6

FORM 4720 (continued)

SCHEDULE A.—Initial Taxes on Self-dealing (Section 4941)

Part I Acts of Self-dealing and Tax Computation

(a) Act no.	(b) Date of act	(c) Description of act
1		
2		
3		
4		
5		

(d) Question no. from Form 990-PF, Part VII, or Form 5227, Part VI, applicable to the act	(e) Amount involved in act	(f) Initial tax on self-dealing (5% of col. (e))	(g) Tax on foundation managers (if applicable) (lesser of $10,000 or 2½% of col. (e))

Part II Summary of Tax Liability of Self-dealers and Proration of Payments

(a) Names of self-dealers liable for tax	(b) Act no. from Part I, col. (a)	(c) Tax from Part I, col. (f), or prorated amount	(d) Self-dealer's total tax liability (add amounts in col. (c)) (see instructions)

Part III Summary of Tax Liability of Foundation Managers and Proration of Payments

(a) Names of foundation managers liable for tax	(b) Act no. from Part I, col. (a)	(c) Tax from Part I, col. (g), or prorated amount	(d) Manager's total tax liability (add amounts in col. (c)) (see instructions)

SCHEDULE B.—Initial Tax on Undistributed Income (Section 4942)

1	Undistributed income for years before 1987, from Part XIV, line 6d, Form 990-PF for 1988.	
a	Enter year	1a
b	Enter year	1b
c	Enter year	1c
2	Undistributed income for 1987, from Part XIV, line 6e, Form 990-PF for 1988	2
3	Total undistributed income at end of current tax year beginning in 1988 and subject to tax under section 4942 (add lines 1a, b, c, and 2)	3
4	Tax under section 4942—Enter 15% of line 3 here and in Part I, line 1, page 1	4

Appendix 27–6

FORM 4720 (*continued*)

Form 4720 (1988)   Page **3**

SCHEDULE C.—Initial Tax on Excess Business Holdings (Section 4943)

Business Holdings and Computation of Tax

If you have taxable excess holdings in more than one business enterprise, attach a separate schedule for each enterprise. Refer to the instructions for each line item before making any entries.

Name and address of business enterprise

Employer identification number . . . . ▶

Form of enterprise (corporation, partnership, trust, joint venture, sole proprietorship, etc.) ▶

		Voting stock (profits interest, or beneficial interest)	Value	Nonvoting stock (capital interest)
		(a)	(b)	(c)
1	Foundation holdings in business enterprise	1	%	%	
2	Permitted holdings in business enterprise	2	%	%	
3	Value of excess holdings in business enterprise . . .	3			
4	Value of excess holdings disposed of within 90 days; or, other value of excess holdings not subject to section 4943 tax (attach explanation)	4			
5	Taxable excess holdings in business enterprise—line 3 minus line 4	5			
6	Tax—5% of line 5	6			
7	Total tax—Add amounts on line 6, columns (a), (b), and (c); enter total here and in Part I, line 2, page 1	7			

SCHEDULE D.—Initial Taxes on Investments That Jeopardize Charitable Purpose (Section 4944)

Part I Investments and Tax Computation

(a) Investment number	(b) Date of investment	(c) Description of investment	(d) Amount of investment	(e) Initial tax on foundation (5% of col. (d))	(f) Initial tax on foundation managers (if applicable)— (lesser of $5,000 or 5% of col. (d))
1					
2					
3					
4					
5					

Total—column (e). Carry this amount to page 1, Part I, line 3 . . . .

Total—column (f). Carry this amount or prorated amount to Part II, column (c), below . . . .

Part II Summary of Tax Liability of Foundation Managers and Proration of Payments

(a) Names of foundation managers liable for tax	(b) Investment no. from Part I, col. (a)	(c) Tax from Part I, col. (f), or prorated amount	(d) Manager's total tax liability (add amounts in col. (c)) (see instructions)

■ 648 ■

Appendix 27-6

FORM 4720 (*continued*)

SCHEDULE E.—Initial Taxes on Taxable Expenditures (Section 4945)

Part I — **Expenditures and Computation of Tax**

(a) Item number	(b) Amount	(c) Date paid or incurred	(d) Name and address of recipient	(e) Description of expenditure and purposes for which made
1				
2				
3				
4				
5				

(f) Question number from Form 990-PF, Part VII, or Form 5227, Part VI, applicable to the expenditure	(g) Initial tax imposed on foundation (10% of col. (b))	(h) Initial tax imposed on foundation managers (if applicable)— (lesser of $5,000 or 2½% of col. (b))
Total—column (g). Carry this amount to page 1, Part I, line 4.		

Total—column (h). Carry this amount or prorated amount to Part II, column (c), below. . .

Part II — **Summary of Tax Liability of Foundation Managers and Proration of Payments**

(a) Names of foundation managers liable for tax	(b) Item no. from Part I, col. (a)	(c) Tax from Part I, col. (h), or prorated amount	(d) Manager's total tax liability (add amounts in col. (c)) (see instructions)

SCHEDULE F.—Initial Taxes on Political Expenditures (Section 4955)

Part I — **Expenditures and Computation of Tax**

(a) Item number	(b) Amount	(c) Date paid or incurred	(d) Description of political expenditure	(e) Initial tax imposed on organization or foundation (10% of col. (b))	(f) Initial tax imposed on managers (if applicable) (lesser of $5,000 or 2½% of col. (b))
1					
2					
3					
4					
5					
Total—column (e). Carry this amount to page 1, Part I, line 5.				

Total—column (f). Carry this amount or prorated amount to Part II, column (c), below. . . . .

Part II — **Summary of Tax Liability of Organization or Foundation Managers and Proration of Payments**

(a) Names of organization or foundation managers liable for tax	(b) Item no. from Part I, col. (a)	(c) Tax from Part I, col. (f), or prorated amount	(d) Manager's total tax liability (add amounts in col. (c)) (see instructions)

Appendix 27–6

FORM 4720 (*continued*)

Form 4720 (1988)   Page **5**

SCHEDULE G.—Tax on Excess Lobbying Expenditures (Section 4911)

1 Excess of grass roots expenditures over grass roots nontaxable amount, from Schedule A (Form 990), Part VI, column (b), line 43 (see instructions before making entry)	**1**
2 Excess of lobbying expenditures over lobbying nontaxable amount, from Schedule A (Form 990), Part VI, column (b), line 44 (see instructions before making entry)	**2**
3 Taxable lobbying expenditures—enter the larger of line 1 or line 2	**3**
4 Lobbying expenditures tax—enter 25% of line 3. (Carry this amount to page 1, Part I, line 6.)	**4**

SCHEDULE H.—Taxes on Disqualifying Lobbying Expenditures (Section 4912)

Part I   **Expenditures and Computation of Tax**

(a) Item number	(b) Amount	(c) Date paid or incurred	(d) Description of lobbying expenditures	(e) Tax imposed on organization (5% of col. (b))	(f) Tax imposed on organization managers (if applicable)— (5% of col. (b))
1					
2					
3					
4					
5					

Total—column (e). Carry this amount to page 1, Part I, line 7 . . . .

Total—column (f). Carry this amount or prorated amount to Part II, column (c), below . . . .

Part II   **Summary of Tax Liability of Organization Managers and Proration of Payments**

(a) Names of organization managers liable for tax	(b) Item no. from Part I, col. (a)	(c) Tax from Part I, col. (f), or prorated amount	(d) Manager's total tax liability (add amounts in col. (c)) (see instructions)

Under penalties of perjury I declare that I have examined this return, including accompanying schedules and statements, and to the best of my knowledge and belief it is true, correct, and complete. Declaration of preparer (other than taxpayer) is based on all information of which preparer has any knowledge.

Signature of officer or trustee	Title	Date

Signature (and organization name if applicable) of self-dealer, foundation manager, or organization manager	Date

Signature (and organization name if applicable) of self-dealer, foundation manager, or organization manager	Date

Signature (and organization name if applicable) of self-dealer, foundation manager, or organization manager	Date

Signature of individual or firm preparing the return	Address of preparer	Date

Appendix 27-7

FORM 990-T

Form **990-T**	**Exempt Organization Business Income Tax Return**	OMB No. 1545-0687
Department of the Treasury Internal Revenue Service	For calendar year 1992 or other tax year beginning .... , 1992, and ending .... , 19 .... Instructions are separate. See page 1 for Paperwork Reductions Act Notice.	**1992**

A ☐ Check box if address changed	Please Print or Type	Name of organization CAMPAIGN TO CLEAN UP AMERICA	C Employer Identification number (Employees' trust, see instructions for Block C) 44 : 4444444
B Exempt under section ☒ 501(c)(3) or ☐ 408(e)		Number, street, and room or suite no. (If a P.O. box, see page 3 of instructions.) 1111 ANY STREET City or town, state, and ZIP code HOMETOWN, TEXAS 77777	D Unrelated business activity codes (See instructions for Block D) 9200 : 7310 :

E Check type of organization. . . . . . . ▶ ☒ Corporation ☐ Trust ☐ Section 401(a) trust ☐ Section 408(a) trust

F Group exemption number (see instructions for Block F) ▶

G Describe the organization's primary unrelated business activity. (see instructions for Block G)
   Advertising sales on garbage bags

H During the tax year, was the corporation a subsidiary in an affiliated group or a parent-subsidiary controlled group? . . ▶ ☐ Yes ☒ No
   If "Yes," enter the name and identifying number of the parent corporation. (see instructions for Block H) ▶

Part I   Unrelated Trade or Business Income

			(A) Income	(B) Expenses	(C) Net
1a	Gross receipts or sales _____				
b	Less returns and allowances _____ c Balance ▶	1c			
2	Cost of goods sold (Schedule A, line 7)	2			
3	Gross profit (subtract line 2 from line 1c)	3			
4a	Capital gain net income (attach Schedule D)	4a			
b	Net gain (loss) (Form 4797, Part II, line 20) (attach Form 4797)	4b			
c	Capital loss deduction for trusts	4c			
5	Income (loss) from partnerships (attach statement) . . .	5			
6	Rent income (Schedule C)	6			
7	Unrelated debt-financed income (Schedule E).	7			
8	Interest, annuities, royalties, and rents from controlled organizations (Schedule F)	8			
9	Investment income of a section 501(c)(7), (9), (17), or (20) organization (Schedule G)	9			
10	Exploited exempt activity income (Schedule I)	10			
11	Advertising income (Schedule J)	11	42,000	10,100	31,900
12	Other income (see instructions for line 12—attach schedule) .	12			
13	TOTAL (add lines 3 through 12)	13	42,000	10,100	31,900

Part II   Deductions Not Taken Elsewhere (See instructions for limitations on deductions.)
(Except for contributions, deductions must be directly connected with the unrelated business income.)

14	Compensation of officers, directors, and trustees (Schedule K)	14		
15	Salaries and wages	15		
16	Repairs.	16		
17	Bad debts.	17		
18	Interest (attach schedule).	18		
19	Taxes	19		
20	Charitable contributions (see instructions for limitation rules)	20		
21	Depreciation (attach Form 4562)	21		
22	Less depreciation claimed on Schedule A and elsewhere on return	22a	22b	
23	Depletion	23		
24	Contributions to deferred compensation plans	24		
25	Employee benefit programs	25		
26	Excess exempt expenses (Schedule I)	26	0	
27	Excess readership costs (Schedule J)	27		
28	Other deductions (attach schedule)	28		
29	TOTAL DEDUCTIONS (add lines 14 through 28)	29	NONE	
30	Unrelated business taxable income before net operating loss deduction (subtract line 29 from line 13).	30	31,900	
31	Net operating loss deduction	31		
32	Unrelated business taxable income before specific deduction (subtract line 31 from line 30) . .	32	31,900	
33	Specific deduction	33	1,000	
34	Unrelated business taxable income (subtract line 33 from line 32). If line 33 is greater than line 32, enter the smaller of zero or line 32	34	30,900	

Cat. No. 11291J   Form **990-T** (1992)

FORM 990-T (continued)

Form 990-T (1992) CAMPAIGN TO CLEAN UP AMERICA EIN# 44-4444444 Page **2**

Part III Tax Computation

35	Amount from line 34 (unrelated business taxable income)	**35**	30,900
36	**Organizations Taxable as Corporations** (see instructions for tax computation) Controlled group members (sections 1561 and 1563)—Check here ☐ and:		
a	Enter your share of the $50,000 and $25,000 taxable income bracket amounts (in that order): *(i)* |$_____ *(ii)* |$_____		
b	Enter your share of the additional 5% tax (not to exceed $11,750) |$_____		
c	Income tax on the amount on line 35	**36c**	4,635
37	**Trusts Taxable at Trust Rates** (see instructions for tax computation) Income tax on the amount on line 35 from: ☐ Tax rate schedule or ☐ Schedule D (Form 1041)	**37**	

Part IV Tax and Payments

38a	Foreign tax credit (corporations attach Form 1118; trusts attach Form 1116) .	**38a**		
b	Other credits (see instructions).	**38b**		
c	General business credit—Check if from: ☐ Form 3800 or ☐ Form (specify) ▶..................................	**38c**		
d	Credit for prior year minimum tax (attach Form 8801 or 8827) . . .	**38d**		
39	Total (add lines 38a through 38d)		**39**	0
40	Subtract line 39 from line 36c or line 37.		**40**	4,635
41	Recapture taxes. Check if from: ☐ Form 4255 ☐ Form 8611		**41**	0
42a	Alternative minimum tax .... b Environmental tax		**42c**	0
43	**Total tax** (add lines 40, 41, and 42c).		**43**	4,635
44	Payments: a 1991 overpayment credited to 1992	**44a**	0	
b	1992 estimated tax payments	**44b**	4,600	
c	Tax deposited with Form 7004 or Form 2758	**44c**		
d	Foreign organizations—Tax paid or withheld at source (see instructions) . .	**44d**		
e	Other credits and payments (see instructions).	**44e**		
45	Total credits and payments (add lines 44a through 44e)		**45**	4,600
46	Estimated tax penalty (see the instructions on page 2). Check ▶ ☐ if Form 2220 is attached .		**46**	
47	**Tax due**—If line 45 is less than the total of lines 43 and 46, enter amount owed . . . . . ▶		**47**	35
48	**Overpayment**—If line 45 is larger than the total of lines 43 and 46, enter amount overpaid . . ▶		**48**	
49	Enter the amount of line 48 you want: **Credited to 1993 estimated tax** ▶	Refunded ▶	**49**	

Part V Statements Regarding Certain Activities and Other Information (See instructions on page 8.)

		Yes	No
1	At any time during the 1992 calendar year, did the organization have an interest in or a signature or other authority over a financial account in a foreign country (such as a bank account, securities account, or other financial account)? If "Yes," the organization may have to file Form TD F 90-22.1. If "Yes," enter the name of the foreign country here ▶		X
2	Was the organization the grantor of, or transferor to, a foreign trust that existed during the current tax year, whether or not the organization had any beneficial interest in it? . . . . If " Yes," the organization may have to file Forms 3520, 3520-A, or 926.		X
3	Enter the amount of tax-exempt interest received or accrued during the tax year ▶ $		

SCHEDULE A—COST OF GOODS SOLD (See instructions on page 8.)

Method of inventory valuation (specify) ▶

1	Inventory at beginning of year	**1**		6 Inventory at end of year. . . .	**6**	
2	Purchases.	**2**		7 Cost of goods sold. Subtract line 6 from line 5. (Enter here and on line 2, Part I.)	**7**	
3	Cost of labor	**3**				
4a	Additional section 263A costs (attach schedule)	**4a**		8 Do the rules of section 263A (with respect to property produced or acquired for resale) apply to the organization?	Yes	No
b	Other costs (attach schedule)	**4b**				
5	TOTAL—Add lines 1 through 4b	**5**				

The books are in care of ▶   Telephone number ▶ ( )

Please Sign Here	Under penalties of perjury, I declare that I have examined this return, including accompanying schedules and statements, and to the best of my knowledge and belief, it is true, correct, and complete. Declaration of preparer (other than taxpayer) is based on all information of which preparer has any knowledge.	
	▶ Signature of officer or fiduciary Date	▶ Title

Paid Preparer's Use Only	Preparer's signature ▶	Date	Check if self-employed ▶ ☐	Preparer's social security number
	Firm's name (or yours, if self-employed) and address	BLAZEK, ROGERS & VETTERLING 3101 RICHMOND AVE., SUITE 220 HOUSTON, TEXAS	E.I. No. ▶ 74-4444444 ZIP code ▶ 77098	

Appendix 27-7

FORM 990-T (continued)

Form 990-T (1992) CAMPAIGN TO CLEAN UP AMERICA   EIN# 44-4444444   Page 3

SCHEDULE C—RENT INCOME (FROM REAL PROPERTY AND PERSONAL PROPERTY LEASED WITH REAL PROPERTY)
(See instructions on page 8.)   N/A

1 Description of property

(1) _____

(2) _____

(3) _____

(4) _____

	2 Rent received or accrued		3 Deductions directly connected with the income in columns 2a and 2b (attach schedule)
	a From personal property (if the percentage of rent for personal property is more than 10% but not more than 50%)	b From real and personal property (if the percentage of rent for personal property exceeds 50% or if the rent is based on profit or income)	
(1)			
(2)			
(3)			
(4)			
Total		Total	

Total Income (Add totals of columns 2a and 2b. Enter here and on line 6, column (A), Part I, page 1.) ▶

Total deductions. Enter here and on line 6, column (B), Part I, page 1. ▶

SCHEDULE E—UNRELATED DEBT-FINANCED INCOME (See instructions on page 9.)   N/A

1 Description of debt-financed property	2 Gross income from or allocable to debt-financed property	3 Deductions directly connected with or allocable to debt-financed property	
		(a) Straight line depreciation (attach schedule)	(b) Other deductions (attach schedule)
(1)			
(2)			
(3)			
(4)			

4 Amount of average acquisition debt on or allocable to debt-financed property (attach schedule)	5 Average adjusted basis of or allocable to debt-financed property (attach schedule)	6 Column 4 divided by column 5	7 Gross income reportable (column 2 × column 6)	8 Allocable deductions (column 6 × total of columns 3(a) and 3(b))
(1)		%		
(2)		%		
(3)		%		
(4)		%		
			Enter here and on line 7, column (A), Part I, page 1.	Enter here and on line 7, column (B), Part I, page 1.

Totals . . . . ▶

Total dividends-received deductions included in column 8 . . . . ▶

SCHEDULE F—INTEREST, ANNUITIES, ROYALTIES, AND RENTS FROM CONTROLLED ORGANIZATIONS
(See instructions on page 9.)   N/A

1 Name and address of controlled organization(s)	2 Gross income from controlled organization(s)	3 Deductions of controlling organization directly connected with column 2 income (attach schedule)	4 Exempt controlled organizations		
			(a) Unrelated business taxable income	(b) Taxable income computed as though not exempt under sec. 501(a), or the amount in col. (a), whichever is larger	(c) column (a) divided by column (b)
(1)					%
(2)					%
(3)					%
(4)					%

5 Nonexempt controlled organizations			6 Gross income reportable (column 2 × column 4(c) or column 5(c))	7 Allowable deductions (column 3 × column 4(c) or column 5(c))
(a) Excess taxable income	(b) Taxable income, or amount in column (a), whichever is larger	(c) Column (a) divided by Column (b)		
(1)		%		
(2)		%		
(3)		%		
(4)		%		
			Enter here and on line 8, column (A), Part I, page 1.	Enter here and on line 8, column (B), Part I, page 1.

Totals. . . . . ▶

FORM 990-T (continued)

Form 990-T (1992) CAMPAIGN TO CLEAN UP AMERICA   EIN# 44-4444444   Page **4**

SCHEDULE G—INVESTMENT INCOME OF A SECTION 501(c)(7), (9), (17), OR (20) ORGANIZATION
(See instructions on page 10.)

1 Description of income	2 Amount of income	3 Deductions directly connected (attach schedule)	4 Set-asides (attach schedule)	5 Total deductions and set-asides (col. 3 plus col. 4)
(1)				
(2)				
(3)				
(4)				
Totals ▶	Enter here and on line 9, column (A), Part I, page 1.			Enter here and on line 9, column (B), Part I, page 1.

SCHEDULE I—EXPLOITED EXEMPT ACTIVITY INCOME, OTHER THAN ADVERTISING INCOME
(See instructions on page 10.)

1 Description of exploited activity	2 Gross unrelated business income from trade or business	3 Expenses directly connected with production of unrelated business income	4 Net income (loss) from unrelated trade or business (column 2 minus column 3). If a gain, compute cols. 5 through 7.	5 Gross income from activity that is not unrelated business income	6 Expenses attributable to column 5	7 Excess exempt expenses (column 6 minus column 5, but not more than column 4).
(1) Mailing list rental	2,000	100	1,900	0	0	0
(2) Advertising sales	40,000	10,000	30,000	12,000	5,000	0
(3)						
(4)						
Column totals ▶	Enter here and on line 10, col. (A), Part I, page 1.	Enter here and on line 10, col. (B), Part I, page 1.				Enter here and on line 26, Part II, page 1. 0

SCHEDULE J—ADVERTISING INCOME (See instructions on page 10.)   N/A

Part I Income From Periodicals Reported on a Separate Basis (For each periodical listed in Part I, be sure to fill in columns 2 through 7 on a line-by-line basis.)

1 Name of periodical	2 Gross advertising income (Enter the total of this column on line 11, col. (A), Part I, page 1)	3 Direct advertising costs (Enter the total of this column on line 11, col. (B), Part I, page 1)	4 Advertising gain or (loss) (col. 2 minus col. 3). If a gain, compute cols. 5 through 7.	5 Circulation income	6 Readership costs	7 Excess readership costs (column 6 minus column 5, but not more than column 4). Enter the total of this column on line 27, Part II, page 1.
(1)						
(2)						
(3)						
(4)						

Part II Income From Periodicals Reported on a Consolidated Basis (If you listed periodicals in Part I above, use a separate Schedule J to report income from periodicals on a consolidated basis in Part II and see the instructions.)

(1)						
(2)						
(3)						
(4)						
Column totals ▶	Enter here and on line 11, col. (A), Part I, page 1.	Enter here and on line 11, col. (B), Part I, page 1.				Enter here and on line 27, Part II, page 1.

SCHEDULE K—COMPENSATION OF OFFICERS, DIRECTORS, AND TRUSTEES (See instructions on page 10.)

1 Name	2 Title	3 Percent of time devoted to business	4 Compensation attributable to unrelated business
John J. Environmentalist	President	0 %	None
Jane D. Environmentalist	Secretary	0 %	None
James F. Friend	Vice-President	0 %	None
Samantha Engineer	Board Member	0 %	None
Total (enter here and on line 14, Part II, page 1) ▶			None

* U.S. GPO:1992-315-145

CHAPTER TWENTY-EIGHT

Communicating with the Internal Revenue Service

The IRS is an important player throughout the life of an exempt organization (EO) so it is very useful to understand how to handle both the routine and the not-so-normal filings an EO might need to submit.

28.1 DIVISIONS OF THE INTERNAL REVENUE SERVICE

Two different divisions of the IRS serve exempt organizations.

(a) Key Districts

The IRS has a special branch devoted exclusively to exempt organizations. This branch operates from nine Key District Offices throughout the country, under the supervision of the Exempt Organizations National Office located in Washington, D.C. Each Key District has a Technical Review staff that approves handles appeals. Examinations are initiated by the Planning and Special Programs unit, which receives and reviews the annual Forms 990 from the IRS Service Center. In addition, each district has branches that handle determinations, administration, and "posts of duty" (field offices in four or five major cities in the district).

Applications for recognition of exemption, Forms 1023 and 1024, are filed with the Key District office. Formal ruling requests are also filed with the Key District, as are any other submissions regarding tax-exempt status, such as to seek a copy of a missing determination letter or to report omission from Publication 78. Certain matters can be considered either by this office or the Service Center, as discussed below.

(b) Service Centers

Annual information returns (Forms 990, 990PF, 990EZ, and 990T) are filed with the Service Center designated for the state in which the principal office of the EO is located. This Service Center processes income tax returns, payroll reports, and annual information returns for all other taxpayers. Regretably, the Service Center representatives are not specially trained in EO matters and are sometimes unable to properly handle troublesome matters. A centralized processing center for EO returns will hopefully be established in the future, similar to the one created in 1991 for pension plan filings.

(c) Exempt Organization Specialists

It is reassuring, and sometimes significant, to know that the IRS personnel in the Key District Offices of the Exempt Organizations Branch are well trained, cooperative, and knowledgeable. The author is not aware of any policy requiring it, but their attitude is supportive and helpful. The staff assumes that most EOs operate in good faith as they are supposed to, to benefit the public. Their customary approach is to be helpful and to explain; the publications and handbooks are well written; and they offer good telephone assistance, as a rule.

28.2 WHEN TO REPORT BACK TO KEY DISTRICT

As an exempt organization grows and changes over the years, it may face the question of when it must report back to the EO Key District in its area. Annually on Form 990, the organization is asked whether substantial changes have occurred. The possibilities are endless and the requirements are vague. Changes that affect an exempt organization's current status need to be reported, but a new Form 1023 or 1024 is not necessarily required to be filed.

The dilemma faced by the EO, however, is that written approval is received only in response to changes sent to the Key District Office. The Planning and Special Programs division visually inspects each Form 990, but it issues no response to submissions accompanying Form 990, unless the return is chosen to be audited (which is rare, in the author's experience). Thus, the

Exhibit 28–1
ACTIONS THAT CAUSE SUBSTANTIAL CHANGE IN STATUS

REPORT	KEY DISTRICT DIRECTOR New Form 1023	Letter	IRS SERVICE CENTER Attachment to Form 990 or 990PF
Conversion from:			
Trust to corporation.	X		
PF to public support.		X	
PF to private operating foundation.		X or	X
School to educational organization		X	
Change from 509(a)(1) or (2)		X or	X
Amendment to:			
Corporate charter.		X or	X
Trust instrument.		X or	X
Bylaws.			X
Creation of an endowment.			X
Symphony starting record publishing business.		X or	X
Shift in major source of donations from individuals to United Way funding.			X

decision on where to report is to some extent based upon the EO's or major contributor's desire for written approval of the change.

Exhibit 28–1 lists actions that would suggest a "substantial change in purpose, support or operation" that must be reported to the IRS. Each X indicates the manner and place in which particular changes must be reported.

28.3 WHEN SHOULD A RULING BE REQUESTED?

The procedures described in Section 27.2 concern reporting changes to the IRS after such changes have already occurred. In terms of IRS procedures, it is important to distinguish between gaining approval in advance of a change, rather than risk a sanction for a *fait accompli*.

Once a change has occurred in the form of organization or a major new activity is undertaken, the organization should choose the best method to inform the IRS, based upon the preceding discussion. Such action is taken when the relevant tax laws are clear and established precedents exist, and there is little or no doubt that the change is acceptable.

However, there may be proposed changes for which the organization wishes advance approval because there is a lack of published rulings or other authoritative opinions on the subject. The procedure for obtaining sanction for prospective changes is to request a ruling from the Assistant Commissioner for Employee Plans and Exempt Organizations in the IRS National Office. When significant funds are involved or if disapproval of the change would mean that the organization could lose its exemption, filing of a ruling request may be warranted.

A decision to request a ruling must be made in view of the cost and time involved in the process. Since March 31, 1990, the user fee is $1,250 ($500 for organizations whose gross receipts are under $150,000). The guidelines for seeking a ruling or technical advice are updated early each spring.[1]

28.4 CHANGES IN TAX METHODS

An exempt organization may wish (or may be forced) to make a change in its tax filing methods. Certain procedures must be followed for changing an EO's fiscal year and changing its accounting method.

(a) Fiscal or Accounting Year

One common change that may occur during the life of an EO is a change in its tax accounting year. Although commercial, tax-paying businesses must secure advance IRS approval under IRC §446(e) to change their tax year, a streamlined system is available for EOs. The EO simply files a "timely filed short period" Form 990 (or 990EZ, 990PF, or 990T).

For example, assume that a calendar year EO wishes to change it tax year to a fiscal year spanning July 1 to June 30. A return is filed, reporting financial transactions for the short period year (the six months ending June 30 of the year of change). The June 30 return would be due to be filed by November 15, the normal due date for a full year return ending June 30 (the fifteenth day of the fifth month following the year end).

If the organization has not changed its year within the past ten years (counting backward to include the prior short period return as a full year), the change is indicated on the return. The words "Change of Accounting Period" are simply written across the top of the front page. If a prior change has occurred within the preceding ten years, Form 1128 is attached to the return and a copy is separately filed with the Service Center where the return is filed, along with a user fee of $150 (as of January 1, 1992).

Late applications, which are due when an organization wants to change its year after the short period return filing due date has passed, can also be filed on Form 1128. A user fee of $300 must accompany the Service Center copy, along with a request for Section 9100 relief. See Rev. Proc. 85-37 for more details.[2]

---

[1]Rev. Proc. 92-3, 1992-1 C.B. 55; Rev. Proc. 92-4, 1992-1. C.B. 66; Rev. Proc. 92-5, 1992-1, C.B. 90.
[2]Rev. Proc. 85-37, 1985-2 C.B. 438.

Affiliated organizations holding a group exemption must follow Rev. Proc. 79-3 to effect a change.[3]

(b) Accounting Method Change

Generally accepted accounting principles (GAAP) recommend that the accrual method of accounting be used for financial statement reporting; thus, a certified public accountant (CPA) cannot issue a "clean" or "unqualified" opinion on financial statements prepared on a cash receipts and disbursements basis. Because it is simpler, many EOs in their early years use the cash method, which is perfectly acceptable for filing Form 990 and (possibly) for reporting to boards and contributors. Maturing EOs commonly face the need to change to the accrual method, in order to secure an audited statement or to satisfy granting entities' requirements.

To compound the question, many EOs actually employ a hybrid method of accounting. For example, they may use the cash method for reporting charitable donations and use the accrual method for disbursements. Pledges of donations are not legally enforceable in some states, and many EOs choose not to record pledges because "all events have not occurred" to make recording them as assets a prudent reflection of income. In these circumstances, a change is difficult to discern.

Advance permission from the IRS is required by IRC §446 if a formal change in accounting method occurs. The rules are basically designed for taxpayers whose tax liability may be distorted by such a change. Cases clearly indicating a change of accounting method include:

- An overall switch from cash to accrual basis;

- A decision to delay (defer) the reporting of grant funds as revenues until the project is actually completed (instead of as the grant funds are received); and

- Reappraisal by a museum of its art collection, recording the value of gifts of art as received (versus a previous policy of not recording gifts because of difficulty of ascertaining their true value).

Although there are usually no tax consequences, an EO is well advised to formally seek approval for a change in accounting method. The period of limitation for examining Form 990 might remain open, if the change is significant. Particularly if unrelated business income tax (UBIT) is involved, the time for payment of any tax involved in the change might be accelerated, if approval has not been secured.

(c) Filing Procedures

To change from the cash to accrual method of accounting, Form 3115 must be timely filed. For exempt organizations, an expeditious consent for the change is

[3]Rev. Proc. 79-3, 1979-1 C.B. 483.

obtained under the "simplified procedures" outlined below:

- Form 3115 is filed within 270 days after the start of the year in which the change is effective. The change is automatic and no response or approval for the change is returned to the EO.

- Form 3115 is submitted to the Assistant Commissioner for Employee Plans and Exempt Organizations in Washington, DC (check form for current address). The current instructions (effective until June 30, 1994) provide for filing with:

Attention EO, Box 120, Ben Franklin Station,
Washington, DC 20044.

- No user fee is due.

- A copy of Form 3115 must be included with the return filed for the year of accounting method change.[4]

Late applications can be filed, but will only be considered upon a showing of "good cause" and if it can be shown to the satisfaction of the Commissioner that granting the extension will not jeopardize the government's interests. The guidelines for showing good cause are found in IRC §6110. Since EOs typically do not pay tax, the possibilities for such approval are good. A user fee of $300 must accompany late forms.

(d) IRC §481 Adjustments

A change of accounting method necessitates reporting deferred or accelerated income or expenses that would have been reportable should in the past if the new method had been used. For such prior years, IRC §481 provides that items "necessary to prevent amounts from being duplicated or omitted be taken into account" over a period of years, to mitigate the burden to a taxpaying entity. In most cases, the change has no tax consequence for an EO filing its Form 990 or 990PF, so, as a practical matter, the income or expense adjustments can be made instead in one year. There is no published guidance on this point, but IRS representatives agree with this suggestion, absent tax distortion.

An EO whose unrelated business income is affected by an accounting method change should, however, reflect the adjustments in accordance with the regulations under IRC §481. Careful study is appropriate for any EO making such a change.[5]

---

[4]*Id.*
[5]Reg. §1.481-5.

28.5 CHANGE IN IRC §509(a) CLASS

(a) IRC §509(a)(1) to (a)(2) or Vice Versa

Publicly supported organizations classified under IRC §509(a)(1) or (a)(2) can often qualify for both categories, and sometimes changes in sources of support and exempt function revenues cause an organization to change from one Code subsection to another. The distinctions between qualification for one category or another are described in detail in Section 11.4. The qualification is based upon percentage levels of public support. The calculation is based upon a four year moving average of financial support received annually, and is furnished to the IRS by filing Form 990, Schedule A.

For purposes of this discussion, the issue is what the organization must do if it experiences such a change. In order to be classified as a publicly supported organization and not as a private foundation, passage of either tests suffices. In one narrow circumstance, it is preferable to be classified as a §509(a)(1) organization: Only (a)(1)s qualify to receive terminating distributions from private foundations.[6]

The organization must decide whether to report back to the EO Key District Office (in addition to the Service Center, which is informed on the annual return), as discussed in Section 28.2. Sometimes it is a simple question of the board's tolerance for a bit of uncertainty. When is written verification needed of the particular category of public charity for which the organization qualifies? Is a new determination letter desirable? The factors to consider include the following:

- The IRS does not issue amended or new determination letters when Form 990, Schedule A, indicates that a change has occurred.

- Private foundations need not exercise expenditure responsibility (see Section 17.5) in making a grant to either category, so a new determination letter is not critical.

- IRS Publication 78 makes no distinction in its labeling of public charities, so the information is not entered into that IRS record.

- As of November 1992, the Key District Office does not charge a user fee for submission of the information.

(b) Ceasing to Qualify as a §509(a)(3) Organization

Failure to maintain qualification under IRC §509(a)(3) as a supporting organization could occur for either of two reasons:

1. The organizational documents are altered in a manner that removes the requisite relationship with one or more public charities and the organization becomes a private foundation supporting grantees of its choice.

---

[6] IRC §507(b)(1)(A).

2. A sufficient level of public support is obtained to allow the organization to convert to a §509(a)(1) or (2) organization.

In the first case, conversion to a private foundation (PF) requires no IRS approval. As of the date of conversion to a PF, a final Form 990 would be filed. A short period Form 990PF would then be filed beginning with the date of the change. Required minimum distributions and other PF sanctions would apply as if the organization were newly-created upon the date of conversion. Full disclosure of the changes would be furnished to the IRS by filing both returns. This process also applies to failure to continue to qualify under IRC §509(a)(1) and (2), with resulting reclassification as a PF.

The EO's prior determination letter would become obsolete. If the EO anticipates receiving significant donations, it might also consider submission of the information to the Key District Office for issuance of a new determination letter.

For the second case, the EO should analyze its need to furnish evidence of its new status to potential supporters. This situation is rather unusual, and prudence would dictate reporting back to the Key District Office to assure approval of the new category of public status. For more details on the different public status categories, see Chapter 11.

28.6 AMENDED RETURNS

If a mistake is discovered after Form 990 has been filed, the question arises whether an amended return should be filed or whether the change can simply be reflected in the next year's fund balance section as a prior-period adjustment. This decision can be difficult to make. There is usually no tax involved, so in accountants' language, the change is not "material." (Our clients tend to ask, "So what?")

Amendment is appropriate when correction would cause a change in public charity status, when UBIT would increase or decrease, and when more than about 10 percent of gross receipts has been omitted. As a rule, for an insignificant correction with no effect on retention of exempt status, complete disclosure on the following year's return is sufficient.

28.7 WEATHERING AN IRS EXAMINATION

After securing tax exemption from the IRS Key District office and filing Forms 990 annually with the Internal Revenue Service Center, a call may be received from the Key District branch office for the EO's area. Ongoing qualification as an exempt organization may be questioned by the specialist who wants to look at the organization's financial books and records. The knock on the EO's door comes in the form of a phone call from the IRS agent assigned to the case to the person identified as the contact person on Form 990. The agent will request to arrange an appointment to examine a particular year's return. Many EOs will refer such a call to their professional advisors, usually the accountant who prepared Form 990.

The manner in which the IRS chooses EOs to examine changes from year to year, and is always a matter of great speculation. In some years, the IRS looks at business leagues, some years at unrelated business activity, and in other years it may examine hospitals, related clinics, and doctors. In 1990 and 1991, the IRS conducted a program to examine over-claimed deductions for fund-raising events, with companion examinations of the income tax returns of EO supporters of such events. In Texas, the EO agents collected invitations to such functions and perused the society pages for clues in choosing the organizations to examine.

(a) How the IRS Chooses Returns to Examine

The examination procedures are outlined in the IRS *Exempt Organizations Guidelines Handbook*.[7] Before making contact with the EO to be examined, IRS agents are directed to perform the following steps:

Pre-examination. Review the returns to identify any large, unusual, or questionable items that should be examined for determining the correct tax liability and exempt status. The balance sheet and revenue sources are to be scrutinized for unidentified unrelated business activity. The return is checked for completeness and to identify any times to be secured in the field.

Administrative file. The EO's administrative file is checked for possible caveats in an exemption letter, and to familiarize the agent with the reasons for which the EO was originally exempt. Prior examinations, technical advice, and correspondence with the EO are reviewed. If a prior examination recommended some changes in operations, the agent is to be alert during the current examination to assure that corrective action was taken.

Examination guidelines. Agents are responsible for developing issues raised in the examination. They are to study the relevant portions of the *Exempt Organizations Handbook* concerning the particular type of EO they are examining, and are to gather facts to apply the statutes.

Preliminary work. The examination is to be conducted at the EO's place of business with an authorized representative. Before the books and records are reviewed, the agent conducts an interview with the principal officer or authorized representative. The agent looks into programs and activities, sources of income, purchases of assets, receipts and payments of loans, noncash transactions, internal controls, and any large or unusual items.

On-site tours. The agent may request a tour of the facilities. During this time, other employees who may be able to provide a more detailed description of operations can be interviewed.

(b) Who Handles the Examination?

The first question to ask in connection with the examination is its location. If a professional advisor is involved, the examination might take place in his or her office, depending upon the sophistication of the EO's accounting staff and the volume of records to be examined. If the information cannot be readily moved in a few boxes, the examination should take place in the EO's fiscal offices. In

---

[7] IRM 7(10)69.

either case, the examiner will want to visit the physical location in which the EO's programs are conducted.

(c) What IRS Agents Look At

Routine Examination. After the appointment is made, the examiner will send a letter specifically listing the items to be reviewed. A sample letter for a routine examination follows as Exhibit 28–2. The basic list is standardized, but is sometimes supplemented with additional items.

The records will be sampled by the auditor. All of the board of director meeting minutes are usually read, but not all of the canceled checks are scanned. The breadth of the materials reviewed depends on some extent upon the quality of the accounting workpapers and ledgers, and on the nature of the EO's operations. When accounting records and original source documents can easily be traced to the numbers reported on the Form 990 being examined, the amount of detailed work will be limited and the examination will flow smoothly.

CEPs. The IRS initiated a Coordinated Examination Program (CEP) in early 1992, to bring together a pool of experts to work on complicated cases involving significant charitable institutions. As a part of a "large case initiative," conglomerate EOs with subsidiaries and for-profit and nonprofit related entities, particularly colleges and hospitals, were targeted. Lawyers, accountants, IRS income tax agents, and other specialists join the EO representatives in conducting such examinations.

TCMP. A Taxpayer Compliance Measurement Program audit is not an overview, but instead is a detailed look at all elements of the financial records. In such a case, all bank statements will be reviewed, all deposits will be traced to the cash ledgers, and so on, in great detail. Such audits, while rare, are conducted on a random basis.

Rollover Audits. Sometimes the motivation for the audit is another IRS audit, such as a review of a substantial contributor's or a related organization's return. For example, the IRS examined Pittsburgh doctors in connection with its CEP examination program for hospitals. In such a case, the organization must ask to be informed about all of the facts and circumstances, and should do everything possible to cooperate with the other taxpayers involved. The questions designed for use in the congressionally-mandated Exempt Organizations Charitable Solicitations Compliance Improvement Program Study during 1991 and 1992 have now been incorporated into the regular audit program. See Chapter 24.

(d) How to Prepare for the Audit

Good judgment is called for in culling through an organization's records to prepare for the auditor's appointment. For example, the auditor will ask to see correspondence files. In the case of a United Way agency in a major city, this cannot possibly mean every single correspondence file. Perhaps the correspondence of the chief financial officer or the executive director would be furnished, with an offer to furnish more correspondence if desired.

Too often, some of the requested records are not in appropriate condition to be examined. The most troublesome records are often the board minutes. It is

Exhibit 28–2

Internal Revenue Service
District Director

Department of the Treasury

Date: July 2, 1992

Form:
990
Tax Year Ended:
December 31, 1990
Date of Appointment:
July 21, 1992
Time:
9:00 AM
Place of Appointment:
3130 Richmond
My Telephone Number:
773-7969

Blazek & Rogers
3101 Richmond Ste 220
Houston, Texas 77098

Attn: Ms Blazek

Re: Phi Beta Kappa Alumni of Greater Houston

I am writing to confirm our appointment, as shown above, for the examination of the form indicated.

To help make the examination as brief as possible, please have the following records available for the year to be covered by this examination:

● Governing instruments (articles of incorporation, bylaws, etc.)

● Minutes of meetings

● All books and records of your assets, liabilities, receipts and disbursements

● Check register, cancelled checks, and bank statements

● Auditor's report

● Copies of prior and subsequent year returns

● Copies of any other Federal tax returns filed

● Pamphlets, brochures, and other literature printed

● Correspondence files

● Other: Determination letter and POA

We realize some organizations may be concerned about an examination of their returns. We hope we can relieve any concerns you may have by briefly explaining why we examine exempt organization returns and what your appeal rights are if you do not agree with the results.

(over)

1100 Commerce St., Dallas, Texas 75242

Letter 1126(DO) (Rev. 9–84)

Exhibit 28–2 *(continued)*

We examine returns to verify the correctness of income or gross receipts, deductions, and credits and to determine that the organization is operating in the manner stated and for the purpose set forth in its application for recognition of exemption. An examination of a return does not suggest a suspicion of any wrongdoing. In many cases, the return is closed without change.

At the completion of the examination, an explanation will be made of any proposed recommendation and how it affects your exempt status or tax liability, such as excise taxes or unrelated business income tax. You should understand fully any recommended change, so please do not hesitate to ask questions about anything not clear to you.

If changes are recommended involving your tax liability and you agree with them, you will be asked to sign an agreement form. By signing, you will indicate your agreement to the amount shown on the form as a refund due you or additional tax you owe, and this will simplify closing your case.

You do not have to agree with the recommendations made. You may ask for a conference at a higher level, as explained in the copy of appeal procedures which you will receive.

It will not be necessary for someone to be present throughout the examination, unless that is your wish. I would, however, appreciate your having an officer or your representative available at the beginning of the examination to give me a brief orientation of the operations of the organization and again at the end for a discussion of the results of the examination.

If the examination is conducted with your representative, a power of attorney or tax information authorization must be filed before your representative can receive or inspect confidential information. Form 2848, Power of Attorney and Declaration of Representative, or Form 2848-D, Tax Information Authorization and Declaration of Representative, as appropriate (or any other properly written power of attorney or authorization), may be used for this purpose. Copies of these forms may be obtained from any Internal Revenue Service office.

If you have any questions or need to reschedule our appointment, please contact me at the telephone number shown in the heading of this letter.

Thank you for your cooperation.

Sincerely yours,

Internal Revenue Agent

cc: Tom Lord

Letter 1126(DO) (Rev. 9—84)

important to carefully prepare minutes of the board of directors' meetings. Optimally, such minutes reflect the exempt nature of the organization's overall concerns. If, for example, a commercial-type operation is undertaken because it helps to accomplish exempt purposes, the minutes should reflect that relationship. Why did the organization enter into a joint venture with a theatrical show producer? Was it because the business put up all the working capital so that the organization experienced no financial risk for producing an avant garde opera production? Proving the relatedness of the venture for purposes of avoiding the unrelated business income tax may be easier with carefully documented minutes.

Pamphlets, brochures, and other literature is also an open-ended category. In some cases, the volume of such literature is staggering, so choosing those examples which portray the organization in the best light is acceptable. Obviously, the examiner cannot and will not look at every shred of paper produced by the organization in a three-year period. Someone knowledgeable about the issues involved in ongoing qualification for exempt status should review the materials and choose those most suitable to be furnished to the auditor. Or, such a person should develop guidelines for persons gathering the information, to assure that the best possible case is presented to the IRS.

The physical space in which the examination is conducted is important. In most cases, a private office should be provided as the examiner's workspace, rather than a nook near the coffee bar or copy machine. Affording some privacy will prevent organization staff from involving themselves in the examination, and minimize any distractions that would waste the examiner's time. Particularly when a paid professional is assisting in the examination, it is useful to limit the scope of the work and make the review as efficient as possible, to save professional fees.

(e) Achieving Positive Results

There are three rules for achieving positive results in an IRS examination:

The less said the better.   Answer only the specific question asked. Do not provide more information than is requested. One person in the organization should be identified as the lead contact through whom all answers are to be funneled. If an outside professional is conducting the examination, he or she would be the contact.

The examiner should be given specific answers to specific questions. He or she should not be allowed to go through the organization's file cabinets.

Do not answer a question if you are unsure of its import.   Problem issues should be identified ahead of time, and the materials to be furnished to the IRS should be organized for presentation in the most favorable light. New materials, reports, or summaries of information found lacking can be prepared to better reflect the organization's purposes and accomplishments.

If you are unsure of the answer to any question, say that you are not sure and that you will find out. Make a list for further consideration, consult a professional, or simply get better prepared to present the best picture for the organization.

Expect the best from the EO examiner. The IRS agents who examine exempt organizations are knowledgeable, experienced, cooperative (usually), and sympathetic with the spirit of the nonprofit community. They perceive their purpose as different from that of income tax examiners. Their examination can often be a positive experience for an organization. It can validate the EO's qualification, and can sometimes help the organization staff to understand why in fact organization is exempt. Another very useful aspect is the reminder it serves of the need to document and preserve a clear record of accomplishments, both from a financial and philosophical standpoint.

(f) The Desired Result: A "No Change"

The desired end product of an examination is a "no change" letter stating that the organization will continue to qualify for exempt status. If the examiner find no reason to challenge the status of the organization, he or she will normally convey this conclusion to the organization's representative in the field. The examiner then returns to the office to "write up the case." The report is reviewed by the examiner's superiors and, some months later, the organization should receive a letter similar to Exhibit 28–3.

(g) Changes Suggested

In the unlikely event that the IRS examiner finds the organization is not operating in an entirely exempt fashion, several consequences may follow:

Changes with no consequences to the basic exempt status could be suggested. A change from §509(a)(2) to 509(a)(1) could result from an analysis of the sources of revenue, but this change often has no adverse consequence. More seriously, the agent could discover failure of the support test for public charity status and could reclassify the EO as a private foundation. Even so, the basic exempt status as a §501(c)(3) organization is not revoked.

If the agent finds unreported or underreported unrelated business income (UBI), the consequences depend upon the amount of the UBI in relation to the EO's total revenues. If the UBI is not considered excessive, the organization's exempt status is not challenged. However, excessive UBI may trigger an exemption challenge. If Form 990T has not previously been filed, its preparation will be requested and any delinquent income taxes, penalties, and interest will be assessed. Deductions claimed for UBI are also reviewed.

The agent often comments on documentation policies. Are invoices available to evidence all disbursements? What about expense reimbursements reports, particularly for travel and entertainment? Payments for personal services paid to individuals are closely scrutinized to evaluate employee versus independent contractor classifications. See Chapter 25 concerning employment taxes for details on this issue.

Private schools must prove that they do not operate in a racially discriminatory manner, by presenting proof of publishing notice of the nondiscrimination policy in a widely circulated publication in the community. Additionally, the agent will seek statistical information about the student and teacher population and scholarship grants that might evidence lack of racial balance. Failure to publish the proper notice by a school that does not in fact discriminate will

Exhibit 28–3

Internal Revenue Service District Director	Department of the Treasury

Date: November 1, 19XX

Form:
 990
Tax Year Ended:
 12-31-86
Exemption under Section
 501(c)(3) of the Internal
 Revenue Code

SAMPLE ORGANIZATION

Person to Contact:
 EO Technical Assistor
Contact Telephone
Number:
 (214) 767-3526

Sir/Madam:

Our recent examination of the above information return disclosed that your organization continues to qualify for exemption from Federal income tax. Accordingly, the return is accepted as filed.

However, the following marked item(s) were noted:

☐ Our review of your return, Form 990, and related records indicate that you did not file Forms 1099. Under section 6041 of the Internal Revenue Code, you are required to issue Forms 1099 to recipients of prizes, awards, or fees of $600 or more during a calendar year. Even though we have now obtained these returns, your organization may be responsible for filing similar forms in future years.

☐ During the examination, it was determined you did not file when due Forms 940, Employer's Annual Federal Unemployment Tax Return, or 941, Employer's Quarterly Federal Tax Return, for wages paid to employees. Under section 6011 of the Internal Revenue Code, you are required to file Forms 940 and 941 when wages are paid for services rendered.

☐ Our examination of your organization indicates that you did not file Form 990 (or Form 990-PF) by the due date. Section 6652(d) of the Internal Revenue Code provides for a penalty of $10 for each day the return is late (not to exceed $5,000), unless there is reasonable cause for the late filing.

☐ You established that you had reasonable cause for filing this return late; therefore, the $10 a day penalty will not be

Exhibit 28–3 (*continued*)

charged. However, there may be a penalty if your return is not filed when due for the same reason in a future year.

☐ You were previously billed for this penalty by the service center and there will be no additional penalties. Please be sure to file your return when due to avoid a penalty in the future.

☐ You did not establish reasonable cause for filing late. Therefore, you will receive a bill from the service center for the late filing penalty.

☐ Although no adjustment was made at this time, for future year expenses must be properly allocated between exempt activities and investment activities.

☐ During the examination of your Form 990, we noted that you combined income from different sources instead of reporting the separate amounts as required. When filing future returns, please show each source of income and amount on the appropriate line on your return.

☐ Your current records do not appear to comply with Revenue Procedure 80-53, 1980-2 C.B. 848, which requires you to include fringe benefits in gross income reported on Forms W-2 even if these benefits are not subject to income tax withholding. To avoid a penalty in the future, full compliance is required.

☐ During the examination of your Form 990, we noted that some amounts shown on the balance sheet did not reflect those recorded in your books of account. For future years, you should provide accurate figures on your return to avoid a possible penalty under section 6652(d)(1) of the Internal Revenue Code.

☐ During the review of your Form 990, we determined that your organization did not identify its special fundraising activities. When future returns are filed, you should complete part 1, line 9, of Form 990 and prepare the required schedule for fundraising activities, including the amounts of receipts and expenses. Omitting material information on your Form 990 may subject you to a penalty under section 6652(d)(1) of the Internal Revenue Code.

☒ Please refer to attached Form 886-A for additional information.

We will appreciate your compliance with the above requirements.

Sincerely yours,

Exhibit 28–3 (*continued*)

FORM 886-A (REV APRIL 1968)	EXPLANATION OF ITEMS	Attachment to Letter 1656 (DO)
NAME OF TAXPAYER		YEAR/PERIOD ENDED 12-31-86

During the examination of your Form 990 we noted that cost of goods sold was reported in Part II of the return as an expense. The instructions for Form 990 indicate all cost of goods sold, whether from exempt functions or unrelated business income, should be shown in Part I, line 10.

We also noted that bad credit card sales and bad checks were netted against sales. Since this type expense more closely resembles bad debts (an expense) than sales returns or allowances, it should be shown in Part II as an expense.

Although this examination resulted in all sales being accepted as being related to your exempt function, your continuing expansion in volume of goods being handled and the dynamics of change within your organization provide increasing possibilities that future sales may include some that should be classified as unrelated business income. So that your records will reflect any such sales, you should incorporate a set of criteria into your operations in the field so that acquisition of goods (and their subsequent sale) that do not meet the test of being exempt function related will be treated as unrelated business income. When applicable, Forms 990-T should be filed in the future.

While sales that are not exempt will not automatically jeopardize your exemption, should such unrelated business become your primary activity, your exemption could be jeopardized.

DEPARTMENT OF THE TREASURY - INTERNAL REVENUE SERVICE   FORM 886-A (Rev. 4-68)

Page _____

probably be forgiven. However, such a failure in a school whose students are all one race may cause the agent to recommend revocation of status.

The most serious challenge, of course, is a revocation of exemption. The reasons for revocation could include violations of any of the restraints and sanctions discussed in this book. The organization has the right to appeal the examiner's report. Specific procedures must be followed, and some policy decisions will affect the outcome. For example, appeals can be filed either with the Key District or with the National Office in Washington. Resisting a proposed revocation of exempt status demands the assistance of a trained professional, and is beyond the scope of this book.

28.8 WHAT IF THE ORGANIZATION LOSES ITS TAX-EXEMPT STATUS?

The National Office of the IRS issued General Counsel Memorandum 39,813 in April, 1990, which extensively describes the consequences and tax filing requirements when a public charity's exempt status is retroactively revoked. Such revocation occurs after the IRS has found that an organization has operated to benefit a limited group of insiders, received excessive unrelated business income, engaged in excess lobbying or political activity, or has otherwise failed to serve its charitable or public constituents. The memorandum was reportedly issued to explain the IRS's response to the Tax Court's opinion in *The Synanon Church v. Commissioner.*[8]

(a) Classification of the Organization

For federal income tax purposes, an organization losing its exempt status is treated as a corporation effective on the date of revocation (except for charitable trusts, which will be taxed as trusts). Some relief is provided for innocent failures. Contributions received by a former EO reclassified as a taxable corporation are to be treated as nontaxable gifts under IRC §102, during the years the organization considered itself exempt (or, arguably, under IRC §118 or 362(c) as capital received from nonshareholders).

Gifts received under false pretenses are taxable. If an organization misrepresented itself in its solicitations by stating that it was tax exempt and was devoting the gifts to exempt purposes when the facts indicate otherwise, the gifts can be deemed taxable income. The tax basis for calculating gain or loss or donated goods and property is carried over from the donors.

Regarding deductions that can be claimed against the retroactively taxed income, the memorandum fortunately provides for the deduction of expenses related to the production of business or investment income. To the extent that income is excluded as gifts or contributions to capital, the allocable expenses would not be deductible. Expenditures not otherwise allowable under the normal income tax rules, such as political expenditures or expenses of an activity not entered into for profit motives (such as a hobby), would also not be deductible.

---

[8]*The Synanon Church v. Commissioner* 57 T.C.M. 602 (1989).

Excise taxes could be due and payable by the organization and its officers and directors, if the revocation is due to excess lobbying expenses or political campaign activities.

(b) Consequences to Individual Contributors

One major concern when an EO loses its status may be who is liable for the tax on the unfairly sheltered income. Should the individual contributors lose their tax deductions? Should the organization pay the tax due on the funds? The memorandum makes it clear that the official who diverts funds to his or her own use (resulting in individual financial gain) realizes personal ordinary income to the extent of the economic benefit so derived. Innocent and unknowledgeable contributors do not lose their deductions until notice of revocation is published in the IRS Revenue Bulletin.

28.9 REPORTING TERMINATION

An organization exempt under IRC §501(a) must report its liquidation, dissolution, termination, or substantial contraction to the IRS when it files Form 990 or Form 990PF.[9] The following information must be attached to the return:

- Statement reporting assets distributed and the date.

- Certified copy of any resolution or plan of liquidation or termination with all amendments or supplements not already filed.

- Schedule listing the names and addresses of all organizations and persons receiving assets distributed in liquidation or termination, the kind of assets distributed to each and the asset FMV.[10]

(a) No Reports Filed

Certain types of organizations do not have to provide reports of their dissolution, liquidation, termination, or contraction as follows:

- Any organization not required to file Form 990, including all churches, including their integrated auxiliaries, or conventions or associations of churches and an[11] organization, not a private foundation, normally receiving not more than $5,000 a year of gross receipts.

- A private foundation terminated its status by converting to a public charity. (See Chapter 12 for filing requirements.)

- Subordinate member covered by a group exemption where the central organization files Form 990 for the group.

[9] IRC §6043(b).
[10] IRC Form 990 instructions to Part VI.
[11] Reg. §1.6043-3(b).

- Instrumentality of the US created by an Act of Congress and their title-holding companies.

- Certain pension plans and credit unions.

(b) Substantial Contraction

A partial liquidation or other major disposition of assets is a substantial contraction that must also be reported on Form 990 or Form 990PF. Such a disposition occurs in two situations:

1. At least 25% of the FMV of the organization's net assets at the beginning or the year are given to another organization.

2. Current year grants, when added to related dispositions begun in an earlier year or years, equal at least 25% of the net assets the organization had when the distributions series began.

A sale or transfer for full consideration and an income distribution is not counted as a contraction for this purpose regardless of size.

Appendix 28–1

Revised Hospital Audit Guidelines

The Service has issued stringent new guidelines governing audits of tax-exempt hospitals. The guidelines are included in Manual Transmittal 7(10)69-38, issued March 27, 1992, reproduced below.

333 (3-27-92) 7(10)69 HOSPITALS

333.1 The Community Benefit Standard

(1) A hospital must meet the community benefit standard to be exempt as an organization described in section 501(c)(3). To determine whether a hospital meets the standard, the following factors found in Rev. Rul. 69-545, 1969-2 C.B. 117, should be considered.

(a) Does the hospital have a governing board composed of prominent civic leaders rather than hospital administrators, physicians, etc.? This information should be evident from the Form 990 and the minutes should indicate how active the individual members are.

(b) If the organization is part of a multi-entity hospital system, do the minutes reflect corporate separateness? Do they show that the board members understand the purposes and activities of the various entities?

(c) Is admission to the medical staff open to all qualified physicians in the area, consistent with the size and nature of the facilities?

(d) Does it operate a full-time emergency room open to everyone, regardless of their ability to pay?

(e) Does it provide non-emergency care to everyone in the community who is able to pay either privately or through third parties including Medicare and Medicaid?

(2) Most hospitals today are seeking to attract qualified doctors. However, if you suspect that an "open staff policy" with privileges available to all qualified doctors consistent with the size and nature of the facilities may not be in effect:

(a) Identify qualification requirements for admission to staff by referring to the medical staff bylaws.

(b) Review application procedures and methods of staff selection.

(c) Review minutes of medical staff meetings.

(d) Determine whether staff admission fees are charged on a preferential basis.

(e) Ascertain if new doctors in the geographic area are admitted to the staff. Absence of new members could indicate a closed staff.

(f) Consider the number of doctors in each membership category (i.e., active, associate, courtesy).

(g) Interview knowledgeable officials to determine if doctors have been denied admission to the staff for other than reasonable cause.

(h) Review the minutes of the credentials committee.

(i) Review the hospital's Daily Census Report to determine the percentage of use of hospital facilities by various doctors. Names of patients and doctors providing services for these patients are listed in the report.

(3) To determine if use of the emergency room is restricted:

(a) Review manual of operations, brochures, posted signs, etc.

(b) Interview ambulance drivers to determine whether they are instructed to take indigent patients to another hospital.

(c) Interview emergency room staff to determine admission procedures.

(d) Interview social workers in the community familiar with delivery of emergency health care services to determine whether such services are known to be available at the hospital.

(e) Ascertain when and how determinations of financial responsibility are made and whether a deposit is required of any patient before care is rendered.

(4) Although operation of an emergency room is generally one of the primary determination factors for exemption, Rev. Rul. 83-157, 1983-2 C.B. 94, states that exemption would not be precluded if a hospital did not operate an emergency room where the state health planning agency independently determined that an emergency room would be unnecessary and duplicative. In addition, specialized facilities such as eye or cancer hospitals treat conditions unlikely to need emergency care and do not, as a practical matter, operate emergency rooms. In these cases, where there is no full-time emergency room providing services to everyone regardless of ability to pay, careful consideration must be given to other services and activities such as provision of charity care and the other factors listed in Rev. Rul. 83-157, to determine whether the hospital operates exclusively to benefit the community.

(5) The Consolidated Omnibus Budget Reconciliation Act of 1985 (COBRA) requires hospitals that participate in Medicare and have emergency departments to treat any patient in an emergency condition, regardless of their ability to pay. This applies to *all* patients whether or not the patient is covered by Medicare or Medicaid. Almost all hospitals participate in Medicare. Hospitals that knowingly "dump" indigent emergency patients on other hospitals are subject to fines and possible loss of exemption. The Department of Health & Human Services, Office of Inspector General (HHS/OIG) monitors this requirement. Review the hospital's records on transfers (they are required to keep them for 5 years). Check with HHS to see if the hospital has any violations. Determine

Appendix 28–1 (*continued*)

if the hospital has a sign conspicuously posted in its emergency department which specifies the rights of individuals to emergency treatment and indicating whether it participates in Medicaid.

(6) To determine whether non-emergency services are available to everyone in the community with the ability to pay:

(a) Review the hospital admission policy.

(b) Determine if the hospital admits and treats Medicare and Medicaid patients in a nondiscriminatory manner.

(c) Review files on denied admissions to ascertain the reasons for denial.

(d) Determine whether members of the professional staff also serve in administrative capacities and restrict admissions to only patients of staff members.

(e) Review the CPA report for years ending after 6/30/90 for a statement of the hospital's charity care policy and expenditures.

(f) Compare the proportion of services provided to Medicaid patients to the proportion of Medicaid beneficiaries living in the hospital's service area. The organization may be able to provide the statistics on beneficiaries. Or, if it is suspected the Medicaid patients are not being served in a nondiscriminatory manner, contact the State Medicaid agency personally to secure the statistics.

(7) Ask for copies of any private letter rulings the hospital has received from IRS.

(8) Determine whether the hospital is involved in projects and programs which improve the health of the community. Review newsletters, press releases and calendars of events.

333.2 Private Inurement and Private Benefit (In General)

(1) Inurement and private benefit may occur in many different forms, including, for example, excessive compensation (discussed below); payment of excessive rent (*Texas Trade School v. Commissioner*, 30 T.C. 642 (1958), *aff'd*. 272 F.2d 168 (5th Cir. 1959)); receipt of less than fair market value in sales or exchanges of property (*Sonora Community Hospital v. Commissioner*, 46 T.C. 519 (1966)); inadequately secured loans (*Lowery Hospital Association v. Commissioner*, 66 T.C. 850 (1976)); or other questionable loans, etc. (*Founding Church of Scientology v. United States*, 412 F.2d 1197 (Ct. Cl. 1969), *cert. den.*, 397 U.S. 1009 (1970)). Note that the payment of personal expenses of an insider that the organization did not characterize as compensation at the time of payment may constitute inurement even when, if added to compensation, the total amount of compensation would be reasonable. (*Id.; John Marshal Law School and John Marshall University v. United States*, 81-2 USTC 9514 (Ct. Cl. 1981)).

(2) Although the requirements for finding inurement or private benefit are similar, inurement and private benefit differ in two key respects. The first is that even a minimal amount of inurement resulted in disqualification for exempt status, whereas private benefit must be more than quantitatively or qualitatively incidental in order to jeopardize tax-exempt status. The second is that inurement only applies to "insiders" (individuals whose relationship with an organization offers them an opportunity to make use of the organization's income or assets for personal gain), whereas private benefit may accrue to anyone. Physicians are considered insiders and in their dealings with the hospital are subject to the inurement prohibition. All contracts with insiders should be reviewed to determine if they were negotiated at arm's- length. If a doctor is also a department head or board member, the contracts will require closer scrutiny.

(3) Some private benefit is always present in hospital-physician relationships since physicians use hospital facilities to treat paying patients. All private benefit must be incidental to accomplishment of the public benefits involved. This prohibition on excessive private benefit is not restricted to insiders.

(4) Identify the board of trustees or directors, and key staff members of the administrative and medical staff. Examine any business relationships or dealings with the hospital. Note any pertinent transactions where supplies or services are provided at prices exceeding competitive market or at preferred terms. Be alert for any loan agreement at less than prevailing interest rates. Scrutinize any business arrangements under which hospitals finance the construction of medical buildings owned by staff doctors on favorable financial terms that may result in inurement or more than incidental private benefit.

(5) Review contracts and leases to determine whether there is any inurement. Scrutinize any contracts under which the hospital requires doctors to conduct private practices on hospital premises.

(6) Review the minutes of the board of directors executive committee and the finance committee for indications of transactions with physicians, administrators, or board members.

(7) Review the articles of incorporation, bylaws, minutes, shareholder lists, filings with regulatory authorities, correspondence, brochures, newspaper articles, etc. to determine the existence of related parties.

(8) Determine whether the hospital is engaged in commercial or industrial research or testing benefiting private individuals or firms rather than scientific or medical research benefiting the general public.

(9) Review third party reports (such as C.P.A. Audit Reports, management letters, and annual reports) to determine whether the hospital's activities further an exempt purpose or serve private interests.

(10) To determine if medical staff or board members have an economic interest in, or significant dealings with the hospital, ask to see any conflict of interest statements that have been filed.

333.3 Unreasonable Compensation and Other Inurement Issues

(1) Unreasonable compensation issues are often found in a hospital's dealings with its doctors or senior executives. Areas of concern include recruiting incentives, incentive com-

Appendix 28–1 *(continued)*

pensation, below market loans, below market leases, and hospital purchase of a physician's practice.

(2) Specialists should be alert for compensation arrangements such as open-ended employment contracts or compensation based on a percentage of a hospital's profits.

(3) Look for recruitment/retention arrangements similar to the following:

(a) physicians being charged no rent or below market rent for space in hospital-owned office buildings or being charged less than fair market value for practice management services;

(b) hospitals providing physicians with private practice income guarantees;

(c) hospitals providing financial assistance to physicians for home purchases and/or the purchase of office equipment;

(d) outright cash payments by hospitals to physicians for home purchases to secure or retain their services; or

(e) the hospital purchases the practice of a physician and subsequently employs the physician (in many instances to operate the same practice). All of these arrangements must be closely scrutinized including the valuation of the practice and the reasonableness of the compensation paid to the physician.

(4) In order to establish that any loans, income guarantees or other subsidies used as recruiting incentives further charitable purposes and are reasonable, the specialist must be able to determine that there is a need for the physician in the community served by the hospital. Absent evidence of a compelling community need or a significant other benefit to the community, the recruitment contract should require full repayment (at prevailing interest rates). Evidence of need may include the previous absence of practitioners in a given specialty, governmental studies of health manpower, patient travel patterns, etc.

(5) In order to determine that a recruiting incentive is reasonable, it should be linked to the physician's value to the hospital (e.g., a new service or enhanced productivity) or community (e.g., a needed specialty) and all incentives considered must not exceed a reasonable amount. In addition, the type of practice, the physician's experience, and comparative incomes must be considered. For further information, see GCM 39498.

(6) The following is a list of common compensation arrangements between physicians and hospitals.

(a) Fixed Compensation — This arrangement may be associated with either employee or independent contractor status for the physician. A salary arrangement tends to be associated with employee status and gives the hospital maximum control over the physician's compensation. Fixed compensation is the most predictable and least complicated arrangement and it allows the hospital the greatest control over patient charges and physician compensation. In contrast, an income guarantee arrangement associated with independent contractor status that guarantees private practice income in the form of loans or subsidies for a specified period must be closely scrutinized

for inurement because it typically is not related to services provided to or on behalf of the hospital.

(b) Fee-for-Service — Under this arrangement, the physician is compensated based upon his or her charges or on a fee schedule establishing the fee per unit of professional service rendered. The arrangement may provide for either separate billing by the physician, in which case he or she may not receive any compensation at all from the hospital, or billing by the hospital with separately identified physician charges to be collected and remitted to the physician. When the physician is an employee, the fees billed to patients are generally considered income of the hospital. When the physician is an independent contractor, the fees are generally considered income of the physician. A fee-for-service arrangement generally gives the hospital little control over the physician's compensation. In certain circumstances, an independent contractor may also receive fixed compensation (e.g., for part-time administrative duties) along with the fee-for-service income.

(c) Percentage of Gross or Adjusted Gross Departmental Revenue — Physician compensation is based upon a predetermined percentage of gross departmental revenue derived from combined charges for facility use and professional services. (Adjusted gross revenue is defined as total charges less bad debt, contractual allowances, and other charge adjustments. Or, it is the collections or money actually received by the billing office as payment for services rendered.) This used to be common for determining compensation for hospital-based specialists such as radiologists, but is less common today due to third party payer restrictions. This type of arrangement must be closely scrutinized for potential inurement. See Rev. Rul. 69-383, 1969-2 C.B. 113.

(d) Be alert for arrangements, other than permissible incentive compensation plans, that involve physicians sharing net revenues of the hospital or any portion thereof.

(7) The following additional items are sometimes found in employee or contractor compensation packages.

(a) Guarantee of Private Practice Income — Under certain circumstances this may be acceptable for a one or two-year period as part of a physician recruiting arrangement where the physician is relocating his or her practice to the hospital's service area; there is sufficient evidence of need for the physician in the community; the level of income guaranteed is reasonable; there is a reasonable and explicit ceiling on total outlays by the hospital; and there is an unconditional obligation to repay any amounts advanced by the hospital. Any forgiveness arrangement must be demonstrably related to community benefit and treated as compensation.

(b) Rent Subsidies — The hospital may provide office space in the hospital for use in providing services to the hospital. Office space in the hospital/medical office building for use in the physician's private practice generally must be provided at a reasonable rental rate gauged by market data and by actual rental charges to other tenants in the same facility. If the physician splits activities between duties for the hospital and private practice, it is acceptable to use the same office for both activities. However, time/use of office must be apportioned between hospital activities and private

Appendix 28–1 *(continued)*

practice activities and a reasonable rent must be charged for the private practice activities.

(c) Support Staff — The hospital may provide support staff for use in providing services to the facility. Support staff for use in the physician's private practice generally must be provided at a reasonable rate for the services of support staff gauged by market data and by actual staffing costs for similar physician offices. If the physician splits activities between duties for the hospital and private practice, it is acceptable to use the same support staff for both activities. However, time/use of support staff must be apportioned between hospital activities and private practice activities and there must be a reasonable charge for use attributable to private practice activities.

(8) Unfunded deferred compensation arrangements. For 1987 and subsequent years, tax-exempt organizations may use unfunded deferred compensation arrangements subject to section 457. Arrangements that meet the requirements of section 457 are proper for tax-exempt organizations and need not be questioned. However, many tax-exempt organizations use unfunded deferred arrangements subject to the general rules of section 83. If those arrangements are properly structured they create a deferral of income for the employee that may far exceed the rather low limits of section 457 (usually a maximum of $7500 per year). Thus, such arrangements should be examined to determine if they might contribute to a determination of unreasonable compensation. Further, you should be alert for such arrangements because they are normally provided only to the more highly compensated employees, and do not necessarily show up in financial statements. Since they are unfunded and must be subject to a substantial risk of forfeiture, the only evidence of their existence may be a contract between the parties or a board resolution authorizing them. While exempt organizations have used plans subject to the general rules of section 83, creation of such a plan by an exempt organization after 1/1/87 may be improper and should be brought to the attention of the National Office. You should also be alert to the possible use of these arrangements by a controlled subsidiary.

(9) Because of the different and complex compensation arrangements that may be involved in hospital cases, the determination of what constitutes unreasonable compensation is a facts and circumstances test. Specialists who encounter unusual compensation arrangements and/or are uncertain whether an excess compensation issue exists should request technical advice.

(10) The following factors should be considered to determine whether any loans made to a physician, employee, or other insider are reasonable.

(a) Generally, the agreement should specify a reasonable rate of interest (prime plus 1 or 2 percent) and include adequate security.

(b) The decision should be reviewed by the board and should include consideration of the history of payment on prior loans by the physician or employee.

(c) Even if determined reasonable, any variance in the terms of the loan form what the borrower could obtain from a typical lending institution must be treated as compensation, and reported at the appropriate time on Form W-2 or 1099.

(11) Determine whether any part of the hospital's property (facilities, space, equipment) or services are used by or rented to doctors or others. Examples of services, facilities, *etc.* are x-ray and laboratory services or facilities (including lab work for non patients), pharmacy departments, outpatient treatment facilities, office space, land and buildings. If so, obtain copies of pertinent leases and contracts to determine whether exempt purposes or private interests are being served or whether liability for unrelated business income tax exists. In determining whether private interests are being served in lease transactions, ascertain whether the lease payment represents fair rental value.

(12) Hospitals or medical practices originally owned by private interests may require additional scrutiny.

(a) In these cases, review the transfer agreement with the hospital to determine whether the transfer served private interests more than incidentally.

(b) Determine whether the agreement involved an employment contract between the hospital and the transferor.

(13) Review the actual copy of the Form 990 the hospital makes available to the public. Determine whether accurate and complete compensation information is disclosed and whether the hospitals has fully complied with its disclosure obligations under IRC 6104(e)(1). Consider applicability of penalties under IRC 6652(c)(1).

333.4 Joint Ventures

(1) A joint venture may take a variety of forms: it may be a contractual agreement between two or more parties to cooperate in providing services, or it may involve the creation of a new legal entity by the parties, such as a limited partnership or closely held corporation, to undertake an activity or provide services. Some examples of the items or services provided in these arrangements are clinical diagnostic laboratory services, medical equipment leasing, durable medical equipment, and other outpatient medical or diagnostic services.

(2) Joint ventures between taxable and exempt parties must be carefully examined for inurement and private benefit. The facts must be reviewed to determine whether the partnership serves a charitable purpose, whether and how participation by the exempt entity furthers its exempt purposes, and whether the arrangement permits the exempt entity to act exclusively in furtherance of its exempt purposes. Where the facts suggest possible inurement or private benefit, specialists should request technical advice.

(3) Examples of private inurement issues are: participation imposes obligations on the exempt organization that conflict with its exempt purposes; there is a disproportionate allocation of profits and losses to the non-exempt partners, e.g., physicians; the exempt partner makes loans to the joint venture that are commercially unreasonable (inadequate security or

Appendix 28–1 *(continued)*

low interest rate); the exempt partner provides property or services to the joint venture at less than fair market value; or non-exempt partner receives more than reasonable compensation for the sale of property or services to the joint venture.

(4) The HHS Office of Inspector General has a program to reduce fraud in the Medicare and Medicaid programs. They administer an anti- kickback statute that penalizes anyone who solicits, receives, offers or pays anything of value to induce or in return for

(a) referring an individual to any person for the furnishing or arranging for the furnishing of any item or service payable under Medicare or Medicaid, or

(b) purchasing, leasing or ordering, or arranging for or recommending purchasing, leasing or ordering any good, facility, service, or item payable under Medicare or Medicaid. Be aware that certain joint ventures and other hospital-physician arrangements could include hidden or disguised payment for referrals. See 42 USC 1320a-7b(b).

(5) The Department of HHS has published a Special Fraud Alert containing the following list of questionable features which, separately or together, could indicate that a joint venture is suspect under the anti-kickback Statute.

(a) Investors are chosen because they are in a position to make referrals.

(b) Physicians who are expected to make a large number of referrals are offered a greater investment opportunity in the joint venture than those anticipated to make fewer referrals.

(c) Physician-investors are actively encouraged to make referrals to the joint venture, or are encouraged to divest their ownership interest if they fail to sustain an "acceptable" level of referrals.

(d) The joint venture tracks its sources of referrals, and distributes this information to the investors.

(e) Investors are required to divest their ownership interest if they cease to practice in the service areas, for example, if they move, become disabled, or retire.

(f) Investment interests are nontransferable.

(g) The amount of capital invested by the physician is disproportionately small and the returns on investment are disproportionately large when compared to a typical investment in a new business enterprise.

(h) Physician-investors invest only a nominal amount, such as $500 to $1500.

(i) Physician-investors are permitted to "borrow" the amount of the "investment" from the entity, and pay it back through deductions from profit distributions, thus eliminating even the need to contribute cash to the partnership.

(j) Investors are paid extraordinary returns on the investment in comparison with the risk involved, often well over 50 to 100 percent per year.

(k) The structure of some joint ventures is particularly suspect. For example, one of the parties may be an ongoing entity already providing a particular service. That party may act as, e.g., the reference laboratory or durable medical equipment supplier for the joint venture. In some of these cases, the joint venture can be best characterized as a "shell" that merely allows referring physicians to share in the income derived from their referrals.

(6) For a discussion of the proper analysis of a joint venture with physicians, including the potential for inurement and private benefit and the possible effect of a violation of the anti-kickback law, see GCM 39862.

(7) Be alert for joint ventures involving the sale by a hospital of the gross or net revenue stream from an existing hospital service for a defined period of time to private interests. For further information, see GCM 39862.

(8) Even absent a true joint venture, hospitals may be pressured to pay other providers for a stream of referrals. Be alert for arrangements with physician group practices or clinics where the hospital transfers something of value in return for an agreement to refer patients to the hospital for inpatient, surgical, or diagnostic services. Such arrangements may involve inurement or serve private purposes more than incidentally. If in doubt, seek technical advice.

333.5 Financial Analysis

(1) Review income and expenditures of all affiliated entities to determine if nonexempt purposes, inurement, serving of private interests, or unrelated business income may be present. Also look for lobbying or political activities or expenditures and determine whether an IRC 501(h) election has been made.

(2) Reconcile the books to the Form 990. Reconcile the working trial balance to the general ledger, CPA report, and the return.

(3) Determine if the hospital has complied with IRC 6033(b) in regard to netting of income and expense. Note any unusual accounts that should be analyzed.

(4) Review the CPA report and management letter for indications of UBI. The management letter also provides information in regard to internal control problems that could result in expansion of the audit.

(5) Review Medicare cost reports for indications of insider (related party) transactions. Such transactions could result in UBI and/or private benefit. The Medicare cost report also identifies non-patient revenue which could indicate UBI. Be alert for misuse of Medicare costs in calculating net UBI. For further information, see GCM 39843.

(6) If other reports, such as the Blue Cross audit report are available, review for indications of UBI and private benefit.

(7) Determine whether the hospital reports grants of $5000 or more on the Form 990. This should be reported on a cash basis as required by IRC 6033(b)(5). The accounting practice of hospitals is usually to charge the gift to a balance sheet account and transfer it into income as the grant or gift is consumed or used for its intended purpose.

Appendix 28–1 (*continued*)

(8) Review the correspondence files on the large gifts and grants. Look for unusual transactions that may prohibit the donor from receiving a charitable deduction and prepare a referral if appropriate.

(9) Check the value shown on the books for donated property against any appraisals in the file. If any property was sold, note the difference between the book value and the selling price. Prepare an information report, Form 5346, as needed.

(10) Review noncash contributions received (other than publicly traded securities). Determine what use the hospital is making of the donated assets, whether any have been disposed of by sale or otherwise (a subsequent arm's-length sale might indicate donor's estimate of fair market value was substantially overstated), whether donors still have use of the property, or other factors affecting the amount or deductibility of the contribution.

(11) If the hospital has an adjacent medical office building (MOB), check the financing arrangement to determine if the hospital made low interest loans to private developers. Determine whether any partnerships or joint ventures are involved. Determine whether the lease agreements were negotiated at arm's-length. If the MOB is not located near the hospital, determine the justification for such a facility.

(12) To verify bad debt expense, review contracts with collection agencies and note the compensation arrangement. If the agency retains its fee from the collected bad debt, consider whether Form 1099 is still required. Be alert for arrangements whereby the comptroller releases delinquent patient accounts prematurely to a collection agency and then receives a kickback.

(13) Review the travel ledger accounts of the administrative department and the board of directors. Be alert for personal items such as spouse's travel and ensure that there has been proper accounting.

(14) Review the legal fees ledger account and secure source documents that identify what the fees relate to. Check for Forms 1099 to individuals and partnerships. Check for possible political activity and political contributions being funneled through the law firm or any other professional service provider.

(15) Where private individuals or outside entities operate the hospital cafeteria, gift shop, pharmacy, parking lot, etc., determine whether the agreement with these individuals or firms provide for reasonable payments to the hospital.

(16) Reconcile expenses on Form 990-T to the CPA's workpapers. If specific cost centers are maintained, review cost centers for possible account analysis. If specific cost centers are not maintained, request a copy of the allocation method used and determine if it is reasonable in accordance with IRC 512.

333.6 Balance Sheet Analysis

(1) Review the general ledger control account for receivables from officers, trustees, and members of the medical staff, and analyze for private benefit and additional compen-

sation. Review the loan or other agreements underlying these transactions.

(2) Check notes receivable for interest-free loans to insiders (e.g., a mortgage loan to an administrator given as an inducement to accept or continue employment at the hospital). These arrangements must be scrutinized for inurement, proper reporting, etc.

(3) Review property records to determine whether any assets are being used for personal purposes that should be taxable income to the user (e.g., vehicles, residential property held for future expansion, etc.)

(4) Review trust funds to see if the trusts should be filing separate returns.

(5) Review investment portfolios and check for any controlled entities. See IRC 512(b)(13).

(6) Review the ledger accounts and check for notes and mortgages payable that could lead to IRC 514 issues.

(7) Analyze any self-insurance trust or fund set up by the hospital to provide liability insurance.

(8) Refer to IRM 7(10)7(11) guidelines when there is evidence that the hospital has purchased or sold health care facilities utilizing tax-exempt bonds.

333.7 Package Audit

(1) The package audit procedures in IRM 7(10)44.5 should be followed and, as appropriate, the employment tax procedures in IRM 7(10)(16)0. The following items that are uniquely related to hospitals should also be considered.

(2) Specialists should be alert to any arrangements under which the hospital pays certain personal or business expenses of affiliated doctors and the taxable compensation is not properly reflected as wages in Forms 990, employment tax returns, or Forms W-2 or 1099. For example, college and university medical school faculty physicians often have employment contracts with medical schools that limit their compensation to low levels compared to compensation obtainable in private practice. Such physicians may enter into employment contracts as consultant/practitioners with several hospitals or clinics unrelated to the medical schools for which they teach. The written employment contract with such hospitals or clinics may be supplemented by a verbal agreement that provides for the hospital or a third party to pay associated business or personal expenses (e.g., lease of luxury cars, house improvements, country club memberships, etc.) as part of the total annual employment contract amount. The Forms W-2 issued may reflect the cash amount paid by the hospital or clinic directly to the physician but exclude amounts paid to other parties on the physician's behalf. In such cases, appropriate referrals should be made.

(3) Review agreements with specialists. Certain hospital-based specialists such as anesthesiologists, radiologists, and pathologists may be employees for federal employment tax purposes, including income tax withholding. Interview the anesthesiologist, pathologist, radiologist, and other physicians

Appendix 28-1 (*continued*)

with unusual contracts or arrangements when necessary to clarify and verify contract items.

(4) Professional service contracts usually specify who will carry the malpractice insurance. If the hospital pays for it, the doctor may be an employee, not an independent contractor or there may be private inurement. Be alert to efforts to be treated as an employee for some benefits, such as the 403(b) tax-sheltered annuity, but as an independent contractor for compensation.

(5) If the following factors are present, the physician is most likely an employee even if the contract describes the position as an independent contractor.

(a) The physician does not have a private practice.

(b) Hospital pays straight wage to physician.

(c) Hospital provides supplies and professional support staff.

(d) Hospital bills for physician services.

(e) Percentage division of physician fees with the hospital or vice versa.

(f) Hospital regulation of, or right to control physician.

(g) Physician on-duty at hospital during specified hours.

(h) Physician's uniform bearing hospital name or insignia.

(i) There are, of course, other factors that may indicate an employment relationship. For a list of the 20 common law factors, see Rev. Rul. 87-41, 1987-1 C.B. 296, in any questionable situation; determine whether a Form SS-8 has been filed by the hospital or the employee. Be aware that under section 530 of the Revenue Act of 1978, an employer may have safe harbor protection if you fail to raise an employment tax misclassification issue on audit. See Rev. Proc. 85- 18, 1985-1 C.B. 518.

(6) Review fellowships, stipends, or other payments to interns, residents, medical students, and nursing students. These may represent taxable income subject to withholding and FICA if paid in connection with services rendered. With regard to student nurses, see Rev. Rul. 85-74, 1985-1 C.B. 331.

(7) Determine how private duty nurses are compensated and determine if the hospital has a Form 1099 filing responsibility.

(8) Determine if the hospital contracts to purchase services not described in IRC 501(e)(1)(A) from cooperative hospital service organizations recognized under IRC 501(e) or unrelated exempt organizations recognized under IRC 501(c)(3). Determine whether the nature and extent of the services purchased indicate the exempt organization providing the services should be considered for examination.

(9) Review employment contracts of medical personnel that have annuities under IRC 403(b) to insure that only common law employees are receiving the benefits of such annuities. If other than common law employees are involved, make appropriate referrals. Test check to determine if reduc-

tion agreements are on file and whether exclusion allowances are within the limits of IRC 403(b) and 415. (See Publication 571)

(10) Determine what types of retirement plans, insurance plans and non-qualified deferred compensation arrangements are in place. Inspect brochures given to employees to get background information. Interview hospital officials in regard to transactions between the hospital and the plan. Identify deferred compensation arrangements and determine the correct tax consequences. If the hospital has a profit sharing plan, determine the effect on exempt status. Determine whether an examination of the plan is necessary.

(11) Excess indemnification (patient refunds) received under medical insurance policies that is attributable to an employer's contribution is includable in the gross income of the patient. An information report should be prepared on significant amounts.

(12) Determine if the hospital has filed or is liable for the following:

(a) Form 5578, Annual Certification of Private School

(b) Form 5768, Lobbying Election

(c) Form 720, Quarterly Federal Excise Tax Return

(d) Form 2290, Highway Use Tax

(e) Form 1120, Corporation Income Tax Return (subsidiary)

(f) Form 8282, Donee Information Return

(g) Form 8300, Report of Cash Payments Over $10,000 Received in a Trade or Business

(h) Forms 990 of related entities such as the hospital foundation or auxiliary

(i) Prior and subsequent years Forms 990 and 990-T.

(j) Form 1120 POL, U.S. Income Tax Return for Certain Political Organizations.

333.8 Unrelated Business Income Tax

(1) During interviews, while touring facilities, and while reviewing books and records, the specialist should be identifying activities that are unrelated to exempt purposes and sources of revenue that may be subject to UBIT. The UBIT examination guidelines in text 160 of this handbook should be followed. Specific examples common in health care field are provided below.

(2) Laboratory Testing

(a) Laboratory services provided to hospital patients are related to a hospital's exempt purpose.

(b) To determine whether there is lab income from nonhospital patients, such as lab specimens from patients of private doctors, nursing homes, other hospitals, and commercial labs, you may need to interview the lab director. Ask if the lab maintains a secondary record showing patient vs non-

Appendix 28–1 (*continued*)

patient revenue. Determine if blood from the hospital blood bank is being sold to commercial labs.

(c) Agents should determine whether salesmen are calling on physicians to solicit business, whether a pick-up service is provided to carry specimens, whether the hospital advertises its lab services on television or in the telephone yellow pages, etc.

(d) Determine whether any of the exceptions shown below apply.

1. The casual sales exception under Regs. 1.513-(1)(2)(ii).

2. The tests are available only at the hospital.

3. The hospital lab is the only lab within a reasonable distance for outsiders to send specimens.

4. The specimens are necessary for the teaching of lab students.

5. The hospital sends its own personnel to an outside facility to secure the specimens for lab testing.

6. The tests are performed at cost for a hospital that has 100 or less beds.

(e) The following rulings apply to laboratory testing:

1. Rev. Rul. 68-376, 1968-2 C.B. 246;

2. Rev. Rul. 85-109, 1985-2 C.B. 165;

3. Rev. Rul. 85-110, 1985-2, C.B. 166.

(3) Pharmacy Sales

(a) Determine the locations of the pharmacies. Are there satellite locations in the medical office building? Pharmacies that are located away from the hospital are more likely to engage in non-patient sales.

(b) Be alert for newspaper and telephone yellow page ads for the pharmacy.

(c) determine hospital policies regarding sales to non-patients, other hospitals, nursing homes, non-employee doctors, etc. If they allow sales to outsiders, determine the amount. Consider the casual sales exception under Regs. 1.513-(1)(c)(2)(ii).

(d) Check pharmacy department records including sales registers and prescription logs and compare to patient records. Interview pharmacy personnel.

(e) Determine if the pharmacy sells items other than drugs.

(f) The following references involve hospital pharmacies:

1. Rev. Rul. 68-374, 1968-1 C.B. 242

2. Rev. Rul. 68-375, 1968-2 C.B. 245

3. Rev. Rul. 68-376, 1968-2 C.B. 246

4. Rev. Rul. 85-110, 1985-2 C.B. 166

5. Carle Foundation, 611-F2d 1192 (7th Cir. 1979)

6. Hi-Plains Hospital, 670 F2d 528 (5th Cir. 1982).

(4) Cafeterias, Coffee Shops and Gift Shops — Generally, cafeterias, coffee shops and gift shops are deemed to be for the convenience of employees, patient and visitors. See Rev. Ruls. 69-268 and 69-267, 1969-1 C.B. 160. However, the specialist should check for facilities in adjacent medical office buildings that primarily serve the private patient of doctors in the building.

(5) Parking Facility — The provision of parking facilities is generally considered to be for the convenience of employees and patients. However, if the parking facility is primarily serving private patients of doctors in an adjacent office building, there may be UBI. See Rev. Rul. 69-269, 1969-1 C.B. 160.

(6) Medical Research

(a) Review contracts to determine whether the hospital is engaged in testing drugs for drug companies.

(b) Review grants awarded to physicians/professors to determine the nature of sponsored research and the arrangement between the parties.

(c) Determine if clinical testing of drugs principally serves the private interest of the manufacturer rather than the public interest.

(d) Determine whether the hospital is doing any other type of research and review any agreements.

(e) Determine if the research activities are of a type ordinarily carried on as an incident to commercial or industrial operations. See Regs. 1.512(b)-(f).

(f) Determine if results of research are freely available to the public.

(g) The following references apply to hospital research activity.

1. Rev. Rul. 54-73, 1954-1 C.B. 160

2. Rev. Rul. 68-373, 1968-2 C.B. 206

3. Rev. Rul. 76-296, 1976-2 C.B. 141.

(7) Laundry Services — Determine if the hospital performs services for outsiders such as nursing homes and other unrelated hospitals with more than 100 beds. See Rev. Rul. 69-633, 1969-2 C.B. 121 and IRC 513(e).

(8) Leasing of Medical Buildings

(a) Review leases to determine whether commercial businesses are renting space. Consider the debt financing rules under IRC 514.

(b) The following references apply to construction and leasing of medical office buildings:

1. Rev. Rul. 69-463, 1969-2 C.B. 131

2. Rev. Rul. 69-464, 1969-2 C.B. 132

3. Rev. Rul. 65-269, 1965-2 C.B. 159.

Appendix 28–1 *(continued)*

(9) Supply Department — Determine if the hospital sells medical supplies to outsiders such as nursing homes, private doctors, other hospitals, and commercial labs.

(10) Robinson-Patman Act "Own Use" Rule — Non-Profit institution often are able to obtain supplies and medicines at substantial discounts and are statutorily exempt from the Robinson-Patman Price Discrimination Act for purchases of supplies for their own use. The Supreme Court set the limits of the term "own use" for consumable supplies in *Abbott Laboratories v. Portland Retail Druggists,* 425 U.S. 1 (1976) when it distinguished several categories of sales and dispensations of pharmaceutical products by hospitals.

(a) Resale of items can be made, but only to six classes of resale customers:

1. hospital inpatients;

2. hospital emergency room patients;

3. hospital outpatients for use on hospital premises;

4. patients being discharge from the hospital for immediate take home use;

5. hospital employees and medical staff for their personal use; and

6. member of non-profit HMO's.

(b) Exemption is expressly refused for:

1. prescription refills;

2. hospital medical staff members for use in private practice;

3. resale to walk-in customers who are not being treated at the hospital; and

4. resale to walk-in customers who are not members of the non- profit HMO.

(11) 501(e) Services — If the hospital is providing any of the services specified in IRC 501(e)(1)(a) to another hospital, determine whether the recipient hospital has 100 or less inpatient beds; whether the service constitutes an activity substantially related to furthering the recipient hospital's exempt purpose; and whether the service is provided at cost. If all questions are answered in the affirmative, the activity is not an unrelated trade or business. See IRC 513(e).

(12) Be alert for income and expense allocations set up for Medicare purposes that may not be directly connected with an unrelated trade or business or may not clearly reflect income for federal income tax purposes. For further information see GMC 39843.

Bibliography

American Institute of Certified Public Accountants. 1981. *Audits of Certain Nonprofit Organizations, Including Statement of Position Issued by the Accounting Standards Board*. New York: Author.

The Chronicle of Philanthropy, 1255 Twenty-Third Street, N.W., Washington, D.C.; weekly journal.

Desiderio, R. J., and Taylor, S. A. 1988. *Planning Tax-Exempt Organizations*. New York: Shepard's/McGraw-Hill.

Foundation News, Council on Foundations, Washington, D.C., 20077.

Gross, M. J., Jr., Warshauer, W., Jr., and Larkin, R. F. 1991. *Financial and Accounting Guide for Not-for-Profit Organizations* (4th ed.). New York: John Wiley & Sons.

Hopkins, Bruce R. 1992. *The Law of Tax-Exempt Organizations* (6th ed.). New York: John Wiley & Sons.

_____. 1989. *Starting and Managing a Nonprofit Organization—A Legal Guide*. New York: John Wiley & Sons.

_____. 1992. *Charity, Advocacy, and the Law*. New York: John Wiley & Sons.

_____. 1991. *The Law of Fund-Raising*. New York: John Wiley & Sons.

_____. *The Nonprofit Counsel*. John Wiley & Sons. New York, NY. Monthly newsletter.

New York University Conferences on Tax Planning for 501(c)(3) Organizations. Annual. New York: Matthew Bender. Published Annually.

National Health Council, Inc., National Assembly of Voluntary Health and Social Welfare Organizations, United Way of America, *Standards of Accounting and Financial Reporting for Voluntary Health and Welfare Organizations*, Revised 1988.

Oleck, Howard L. 1992. *Nonprofit Corporations, Organizations, and Associations* (5th ed.). Englewood Cliffs, NJ: Prentice-Hall.

Arnold J. Olenick and Philip P. Olenick, *A Nonprofit Organization Operating Manual, Planning for Survival & Growth*, New York, The Foundation Center, 1991.

Tax-Exempt Organizations. Englewood Cliffs, NJ: Prentice-Hall (loose leaf service).

U.S. Department of the Treasury, Internal Revenue Service. *Exempt Organizations Continuing Professional Education Technical Instruction Programs*. Washington, DC: Author. (Available from IRS Reading Room, Washington, DC.)

_____. *Exempt Organizations Handbook*. 1992. IR Manual 7751. Washington, DC: Author.

The Exempt Organization Tax Review, Tax Analysts. Arlington, VA. Monthly journal.

The Journal of Taxation of Exempt Organizations. Faulkner & Gray, Inc. New York, NY. Quarterly journal.

_____. *Private Foundations Handbook*. 1992. IR Manual 7752. Washington, DC: Author.

United Way of America. 1989. *Accounting and Financial Reporting, A Guide for United Ways and Not-for-Profit Organizations* (2d ed. rev.). Alexandria, VA: United Way Institute.

Table of Cases

TABLE OF CASES

TABLE OF CASES

Table of IRS Revenue Rulings and Procedures

Revenue Rulings	Pages	Revenue Rulings	Pages	Revenue Rulings	Pages
54-394, 1954-2 C.B.131	76	66-147, 1966-1 C.B. 137	64, 65, 66	68-563, 1968-2 C.B. 212	37
55-70, 1955-1 C.B. 506	512			68-609, 1968-2 C.B. 227	423
55-230, 1955-1 C.B. 71	86	66-150, 1966-1 C.B. 147	105, 119	68-639, 1968-2 C.B. 220	106
55-311, 1955-1 C.B. 72	75			68-655, 1968-2 C.B. 613	48
55-406, 1955-1 C.B. 73	47	66-178, 1966-1 C.B. 138	63	69-68, 1969-1 C.B. 153	105
56-84, 1956-1 C.B. 201	94	66-179, 1966-1 C.B. 139	75, 76, 93, 104	69-106, 1969-1 C.B. 153	93
56-138, 1956-1 C.B. 202	48			69-174, 1969-1 C.B. 149	47
56-185, 1956-1 C.B. 202	52			69-175, 1969-1 C.B. 149	424
56-245, 1956-1 C.B. 204	86	66-223, 1966-2 C.B. 224	94	69-256, 1969-1 C.B. 151	28, 31
56-305, 1956-2 C.B. 307	105	66-295, 1966-2 C.B. 207	120	69-257, 1969-1 C.B. 151	51
56-403, 1956-2 C.B. 307	30, 51	66-338, 1966-2 C.B. 226	425	69-266, 1969-1 C.B. 151	423
57-574, 1957-2 C.B. 161	43	66-354, 1966-2 C.B. 207	83	69-279, 1969-1 C.B. 152	28, 31
58-224, 1958-1 C.B. 242	95	66-358, 1966-2 C.B. 216	508	69-383, 1969-2 C.B. 113	55, 419
58-293, 1958-1 C.B. 146	100	66-359, 1966-2 C.B. 219	68	69-384, 1969-2 C.B. 112	75
58-294, 1958-1 C.B. 244	92	67-4, 1967-1 C.B. 121	52, 63	69-386, 1969-2 C.B. 123	83
58-455, 1958-2 C.B. 261	118	67-6, 1967-1 C.B. 135	77	69-441, 1969-2 C.B. 115	47
58-501, 1958-2 C.B. 262	106, 107	67-7, 1967-1 C.B. 137	82, 83	69-526, 1969-2 C.B. 115	66
		67-8, 1967-1 C.B. 142	30, 104	69-527, 1969-2 C.B. 125	105
58-588, 1958-2 C.B. 265	108	67-71, 1967-1 C.B. 125	486	69-528, 1969-2 C.B. 127	120
58-589, 1958-2 C.B. 266	104, 107	67-77, 1967-1 C.B. 138	92	69-545, 1969-2 C.B. 117	52
59-6, 1959-1 C.B. 121	82	67-138, 1967-1 C.B. 129	48	69-635, 1969-2 C.B. 126	104, 106
59-234, 1959-2 C.B. 149	95, 424	67-139, 1967-1 C.B. 129	104		
60-106, 1969-1 C.B. 153	425	67-148, 1967-1 C.B. 132	62	70-31, 1970-1 C.B. 130	97
61-87, 1961-1 C.B. 191	51	67-150, 1967-1 C.B. 133	47	70-32, 1970-1 C.B. 140	105
61-170, 1961-2 C.B. 112	95	67-151, 1967-1 C.B. 134	68	70-47, 1970-1 C.B. 49	511
61-177, 1961-2 C.B. 117	94, 99, 483, 499	67-176, 1967-1 C.B. 140	94	70-48, 1970-1 C.B. 133	107
		67-217, 1967-2 C.B. 181	51	70-81, 1970-1 C.B. 131	98
		67-246, 1967-2 C.B. 104	510	70-95, 1970-1 C.B. 137	94
62-17, 1962-1 C.B. 87	82	67-246, 1967-2 C.B. 104, 105	508	70-129, 1970-1 C.B. 128	66
62-23, 1962-1 C.B. 200	127			70-186, 1970-1 C.B. 128	49
62-167, 1962-2 C.B.142	76	67-248, 1967-2 C.B. 204	108	70-187, 1970-1 C.B. 131	93
62-191, 1962-2 C.B. 146	82	67-250, 1967-2 C.B. 182	48	70-372, 1970-2 C.B. 118	87
63-156, 1963-2 C.B. 79	537	67-251, 1967-2 C.B. 196	87, 98	70-533, 1970-2 C.B. 112	47, 60
63-190, 1963-2 C.B. 212	106, 107	67-252, 1967-2 C.B. 195	87	70-534, 1970-2 C.B. 113	460
		67-292, 1967-2 C.B. 184	48, 63	70-583, 1970-2 C.B. 114	47
63-220, 1963-2 C.B. 208	51	67-293, 1967-2 C.B. 185	491	70-585, 1970-2 C.B. 115	47
63-235, 1963-2 C.B. 210	52	67-294, 1967-2 C.B. 193	75	70-591, 1970-2 C.B. 118	95
64-118, 1964-1 (Part 1) C.B. 182	105	67-295, 1967-2 C.B. 197	95	70-641, 1970-2 C.B. 119	91, 99
64-174, 1964-1 (Part 1) C.B. 183	62	67-392, 1967-2 C.B. 191	62, 63	71-17, 1971-1 C.B. 683	109, 110
64-175, 1964-1 (Part 1) C.B. 185	62	68-14, 1968-1 C.B. 243	76		
64-182, 1964-1 C.B. 186	32	68-15, 1968-1 C.B. 244	48	71-29, 1971-1 C.B. 150	49
64-187, 1964-1 (Part 1) C.B. 354	75	68-68, 1968-1 C.B. 51	537	71-97, 1971-1 C.B. 150	51
		68-70, 1968-1 C.B. 248	48	71-99, 1971-1 C.B. 151	49
		68-72, 1968-1 C.B. 250	37	71-155, 1971-1 C.B. 152	96
65-1, 1965-1 C.B. 226	66	68-118, 1968-1 C.B. 261	75	71-395, 1971-2 C.B. 228	63, 424
65-14, 1965-1 C.B. 236	94	68-165, 1968-1 C.B. 253	62	71-421, 1971-2 C.B. 229	104
65-61, 1965-1 C.B. 234	67	68-168, 1968-1 C.B. 269	105, 107	71-504, 1971-2 C.B. 231, 232	90
65-64, 1965-1 C.B. 241	107				
65-195, 1965-2 C.B. 164	75	68-182, 1968-1 C.B. 263	92	71-544, 1971-2 C.B. 227	119
65-244, 1965-2 C.B. 167	425	68-222, 1968-1 C.B. 243	119	71-545, 1971-2 C.B. 235	63
65-270, 1965-2 C.B. 160	62	68-224, 1968-1 C.B. 222	76	72-101, 1972-1 C.B. 149	77
65-271, 1965-2 C.B. 161	62	68-263, 1968-1 C.B. 256	501	72-124, 1972-1 C.B. 145	55
65-298, 1965-2 C.B. 163	52, 62, 66	68-265, 1968-1 C.B. 265	95	72-147, 1972-1 C.B. 147	424
		68-306, 1968-1 C.B. 257	36	72-228, 1972-1 C.B. 148	48
65-299, 1965-2 C.B. 165	75	68-307, 1968-1 C.B. 258	64	72-391, 1972-2 C.B. 249	87
65-432, 1968-2 C.B. 104	510	68-371, 1968-2 C.B. 204	121	72-430, 1972-2 C.B. 105	127
66-79, 1966-1 C.B. 48	100	68-372, 1968-2 C.B. 205	63	72-462, 1972-2 C.B. 76	537
66-102, 1966-1 C.B. 133	120	68-373, 1968-2 C.B. 206	66, 67	72-512, 1972-2 C.B. 246	486
66-103, 1866-1 C.B. 134	51	68-432, 1968-2 C.B. 104	512	72-513, 1972-2 C.B. 246	486, 491
66-105, 1966-1 C.B. 145	87	68-438, 1968-2 C.B. 609	48		
		68-504, 1968-2 C.B. 211	62	73-104, 1973-1 C.B. 263	458
		68-534, 1968-2 C.B. 217	83	73-105, 1973-1 C.B. 265	458
		68-535, 1968-2 C.B. 219	107	73-126, 1973-1 C.B. 220	417

TABLE OF IRS REVENUE RULINGS AND PROCEDURES

TABLE OF IRS REVENUE RULINGS AND PROCEDURES

Revenue Rulings	Pages	Revenue Procedures	Pages	Revenue Procedures	Pages
83-157, 1983-2 C.B. 94	52	72-5, 1972-1 C.B. 709	43	89-23, 1989-1 C.B. 844	247,
83-164, 1983-2 C.B. 95	92	75-50, 1975-2 C.B. 587	594		308
83-170, 1983-2 C.B. 97	105	77-32, 1977-2 C.B. 541	238	90-12	510
85-1, 1985-1 C.B. 177	49	79-3, 1979-1 C.B. 483	659	90-12, 1990-1, C.B. 471	572
85-2, 1985-1 C.B. 178	50	79-63, 1979-3 C.B. 578	267	90-12 (Feb. 1990)	446
85-175, 1985-2 C.B. 276	237	80-31, 1980-1 C.B. 646	267	90-17, 1990-1 C.B. 479	241
86-43, 1986-2 C.B. 729	502	80-37, 1980-1 C.B. 677	272	91-44, 1991-31 I.R.B. 35	292
86-49, 1986-1 C.B. 243	48	80-39, 1980-2 C.B. 772	238	92-3, 1992-1 C.B. 55	658
86-63, 1986-1 C.B. 88	508	81-65, 1981-2 C.B. 690	238	92-4, 1992-1 C.B. 66	658
86-98, 1986-2 C.B. 74	76	82-2, 1982-1 C.B. 367	26	92-5, 1992-1 C.B. 90	658
87-41, 1987-1 C.B. 296	530,	82-39, 1982-17 I.R.B. 18	308	92-58, 1992-2, I.R.B. 10	510
	531	84-46, 1984-1 C.B. 541	268	92-58, 1992-2 I.R.B. 10	446
88-56, 1988-2 C.B. 126	78	84-47, 1984-1 C.B. 545	268	92-59, 1992-29 I.R.B. 11	504
89-67, I.R.B. 1989-20, 4	536	85-37, 1985-2 C.B. 438	658	92-94, 1992-46 I.R.B. 34	248
90-100, 1990-2 C.B. 156	304	85-51, 1985-2 C.B. 717	238		

Index

INDEX